Technology Transfer

Third edition

Dedicated to Sara
with my love

Technology Transfer

Third edition

General Editor

Mark Anderson, Solicitor
Principal, Anderson & Company

Bloomsbury Professional

Bloomsbury Professional Ltd, Maxwelton House, 41–43 Boltro Road, Haywards Heath, West Sussex, RH16 1BJ

A CIP Catalogue record for this book is available from the British Library.

ISBN 978 1 84766 479 2

Typeset by Phoenix Photosetting, Chatham, Kent
Printed in Great Britain by CPI Antony Rowe, Chippenham, Wiltshire

CONTRIBUTORS

Principal Contributor and Coordinating Editor

Victor Warner, Solicitor
Associate, Anderson & Company

Contributor, Tax chapter

Lionel Jermy, Barrister
Consultant, Anderson & Company

Contributors

Paul Maclennan, Solicitor
Associate, Anderson & Company

Lisa Allebone PhD, Solicitor
Associate, Anderson & Company

Brendan Biggs DPhil
Paralegal, Anderson & Company

PREFACE

Back in the 1990s, when we were deciding the title for the first edition of this book, the publishers felt that the term *technology transfer* was unfamiliar. In effect, they vetoed this term as a title for the book. Instead, we came up with a clumsy compromise: *Technology – The Law of Exploitation and Transfer.* In 2002, when the second edition was published, the title of the book became *Technology Transfer – Law, Practice and Precedents*, the publisher having become comfortable with the term. In 2010, the term is considered by some as old-fashioned, and instead the more general term, *knowledge transfer*, is preferred. Fortunately, being old-fashioned is rarely a problem in the legal world.

Although the terminology may change, the subject of this book has not: it is a book about laws in the context of commercial transactions. Specifically, it concerns transactions that involve the development, use or commercialisation of technology and associated intellectual property rights. Among the many types of transaction that can fall within this category, research and development contracts and intellectual property licences are perhaps the most important, and are the focus of this book.

As with previous editions, this third edition describes different areas of law that affect technology transfer agreements. Intellectual property law (IP) is an important area, and is covered in some detail in the book. However, it is by no means the only, or even the most important, area. My view is that other individual areas of commercial law, including contract, competition and tax, affect technology transfer agreements just as much as IP laws. I am particularly keen on the section of the book that discusses how the English courts have interpreted IP-related agreements. Since the first edition of this book was published, the number of reported cases on the interpretation of IP agreements has dramatically increased (from a very small base).

The changes to English law since the second edition are too numerous to mention in any detail. Some highlights include: new EU competition laws (including a new technology transfer agreements regulation, which is likely to change again at the end of 2010) and greater control over activities involving human and animal tissue and clinical trials. Similarly, IP and tax law seem to be in a constant state of evolution.

For this edition, a different approach to the precedents (template agreements), relevant legislation and other background materials is taken. This material is no longer included with the book but is available online via the website accompanying the book (access details can be found on the card enclosed with your copy).

A number of people have mentioned to me that they have the 'red book' on their bookshelves. Whether intended or not, this name is rather flattering. It has echoes of other colour-themed publications that have a more prestigious pedigree. Readers who are English lawyers will be familiar with the White, Green and Yellow Books and, particularly for those involved with intellectual property law, the Black Book (the CIPA Guide to the Patents Act 1977), to name but a few.

As with previous editions, I am grateful to the friends and colleagues who have assisted with updating or commenting on the text. Any errors that remain are my sole responsibility.

This book attempts to be up-to-date in its discussion of English law as at February 2010.

Mark Anderson
Oxford, March 2010
www.andlaw.eu

CONTENTS

xi

SELECTED BIBLIOGRAPHY

One purpose of this book is to draw together strands of law and practical information that are relevant to technology transfer. It is possible to find these strands in various 'traditional' legal subjects. Some of these are reflected in the chapter headings including intellectual property, tax, contract, competition and regulation of high-tech activities. The following texts provide more detailed treatment of these legal subjects, and are recommended for further reading.

Further books and other sources of information will appear on the website which accompanies the book.

Drafting issues

Introductory

Anderson and Warner, *Drafting and Negotiating Commercial Agreements*, 2nd edn, Tottel Publishing, 2008

Anderson and Warner, *A–Z of Boilerplate and Commercial Clauses*, 2nd edn, Tottel Publishing, 2008

Specialist

Anderson, *Drafting Agreements in the Pharmaceutical and Biotechnology Industries*, Oxford University Press, 2009 (looseleaf, updates)

Byrne & McBratney, *Licensing Technology: Negotiating and Drafting Technology Transfer Agreements*, 3rd edn, Jordans, 2005

Cooke and Horton, *Practical Intellectual Property Precedents*, Sweet & Maxwell, looseleaf

Unico Practical Guides Commercialisation Agreements, available from PraxisUnico, 2006. 9 guides on: 1. Confidentiality agreements; 2. Material transfer agreements; 3. Options; 4. Consultancy agreements; 5. Students and IP; 6. Licence agreements; 7. Spin-out transactions; 8. Key issues in technology transfer agreements; and 9. General legal issues.

Melville: *Forms and Agreements on Intellectual Property and International Licensing*, 3rd edition, Sweet and Maxwell, looseleaf

Regulatory – Data Protection

Introductory

Carey (editor), *Data Protection Handbook*, The Law Society, 2008

Specialist

Carey, *Data Protection: A Practical Guide to UK and EU Law* 3rd edn, Oxford University Press, 2009

Jay, *Data Protection: Law and Practice*, 3rd edn, Sweet & Maxwell, 2007

Jay, Boardman and Grant, *Encyclopaedia of Data Protection and Privacy*, Sweet & Maxwell, Looseleaf Annual Subscription

Singleton, *Tolley's Data Protection Handbook*, 2nd edn, LexisNexis Tolley, 2006

Regulatory – Freedom of Information

Introductory

Carey and Tutle (editors), *Freedom of Information Handbook*, the Law Society, 2006

Specialist

MacDonald, Crail and Jones, *The Law of Freedom of Information*, 2nd edn, Oxford University Press, 2009

Regulatory – Internet

Specialist

Todd, *Gringras: the Laws of the Internet*, 3rd edn, Tottel Publishing, 2008

Smith et al, *Internet Law and Regulation*, 4th edn, Sweet & Maxwell, 2007

Regulatory – Pharmaceuticals, biotechnology etc

Specialist

Cooke, *Pharmaceuticals, Biotechnology and the Law*, 2nd edn, Butterworths, 2009

Feldschreiber (editor), *The Law and Regulation of Medicines*, Oxford University Press, 2008

Competition laws

Introductory

Whish, Richard, *Competition Law*, Oxford University Press, 6th edn, 2009.

Jones and Sufrin, *EC Competition Law*, 3rd edn, Oxford University Press, 2008

Specialist

Bellamy & Child, *European Community Law of Competition,* 6th edn, Oxford University Press, 2010.

Tritton, *Intellectual Property in Europe,* 3rd edn, Sweet & Maxwell, 2007

Green N, *Commercial Agreements and Competition Law,* Kluwer Law International, 2nd edn, 1997.

Korah and O'Sullivan, *Vertical Agreements: Distribution under the EC Competition Rules,* Hart Publishing, 2002.

Mehigan and Kamerling, *A, Restraint of Trade and Business Secrets,* Sweet & Maxwell, 4th edn, 2002.

Personal property laws

Specialist

Bell, *Modern Law of Personal Property in England and Wales*, Butterworths, 1989.

Palmer on Bailment, 3rd edn, Sweet & Maxwell, 2009

Intellectual property – General

Introductory

Brazell (editor), *Intellectual Property Law Handbook,* the Law Society, 2008

Cornish & Llewelyn, *Intellectual Property: Patents, Copyright, Trade Marks and Allied Rights*, 7th edn, Sweet & Maxwell, 2010.

Aplin and Davis, *Intellectual Property Law*: Text, Cases and Materials, Oxford University Press, 2009

Specialist

Cook, *EU Intellectual Property Law*, Oxford University Press, 2010

Tritton, *Intellectual Property in Europe,* 3rd edn, Sweet & Maxwell, 2007

Turner, *Intellectual Property and EU Competition Law,*

Encyclopaedia of Information Technology Law, Sweet & Maxwell, looseleaf

Patents

Introductory

Reid, *A Practical Guide to Patent Law,* 3rd edn, Sweet & Maxwell, 1998

See also books mentioned under Intellectual Property/General above

Specialist

CIPA Guide to the Patents Acts, 6th edn, Sweet & Maxwell, 2009

Terrell on the Law of Patents, 15th edn, Sweet & Maxwell, 2000.

UK Intellectual Property Office, *Manual of Patent Practice in the UK Patent Office*, regularly updated, available from http://www.ipo.gov.uk/pro-types/pro-patent/p-law/p-manual/p-manual-practice.htm

Copyright

Introductory

Flint, Fitzpatrick & Thorne, *User's Guide to Copyright*, 6th edn, Tottel Publishing, 2006

See also books mentioned under Intellectual Property/General above

Specialist

Copinger and Skone *James on Copyright*, 15th edn, Sweet & Maxwell, 2005

Laddie, Prescott and Vitoria, *Modern Law of Copyright and Designs*, 4th edn, Butterworths, 2007

Sterling, *World Copyright Law*, 3rd edn, Sweet & Maxwell, 2008

Databases

Introductory

See also books mentioned under Intellectual Property/General above

Specialist

Davis, *Legal Protection of Databases,* Cambridge University Press, 2008

Design

Introductory

Briffa and Gage, *Design Law: Protecting and Exploiting Rights*, The Law Society, 2004

See also books mentioned under Intellectual Property/General above

Specialist

Fellner, *Industrial Design Law,* Sweet & Maxwell, 1995.

Russell-Clarke and Howe on Industrial Designs, 7th edn, Sweet & Maxwell, 2005

See also Specialist volumes mentioned under Copyright

Trade marks

Introductory

See also books mentioned under Intellectual Property/General above

Specialist

Kitchen, et al, *Kerly's Law of Trademarks and Trade Names*, 15th edn, Sweet & Maxwell, 2010

Confidential information

Introductory

Anderson & Keevey-Kothari, *Drafting Confidentiality Agreements*, 2nd edition, The Law Society, 2004

Specialist

Gurry on Breach of Confidence: The Protection of Confidential Information, 2nd edn, Oxford University Press, 2010

Toulson and Phipps, *Confidentiality*, 2nd edn, Sweet and Maxwell, 2006

Brearley & Bloch, *Employment Covenants and Confidential Information: Law, Practice and Technique*, 3rd edn, Tottel Publishing, 2009.

Mehigan and Kamerling, *Restraint of Trade and Business Secrets*, 4th edn, Sweet & Maxwell, 2002.

Contract

Introductory

Koffman & MacDonald, *Law of Contract,* 7th edn, Oxford University Press, 2010

Chesire, Fifoot & Furmston's Law of Contract, 15th edn, Oxford University Press, 2006.

Peel, *Treitel: The Law of Contract,* 7th edn, Sweet & Maxwell, 2007

Specialist

Chitty on Contracts, 30th edn, Sweet & Maxwell, 2009

Lewison, *The Interpretation of Contracts,* 4th edn, Sweet & Maxwell, 2004 + 2009 supplement.

MacDonald, *Exemption Clauses and Unfair Terms*, 2nd edn, Tottel Publishing, 2006

Melville: Forms and Agreements on Intellectual Property and International Licensing, 3rd edition, Sweet and Maxwell, looseleaf

Tax law

There are textbooks on the subject of taxation of intellectual property which provide more detail than Chapter 17 of this book, and cover taxation of arts-related intellectual property transactions, eg contracts by authors and musicians. However, no current textbook provides an up-to-date and comprehensive treatment of all intellectual property transactions. Reference to standard practitioner texts on tax, *eg Sergeant & Sims on Stamp Duty,* may, therefore, be desirable when considering intellectual property tax issues.

Specialist

Eastaway, Gallafent, Dauppe and Kimber, *Intellectual Property Law and Taxation*, 7th edn, Sweet and Maxwell, 2008

Simon's Taxes, LexisNexis Butterworths, looseleaf plus annual handbooks

De Voil Indirect Tax Service, LexisNexis Butterworths, looseleaf

Sergeant & Sims on Stamp Duty, LexisNexis Butterworths, looseleaf.

Table of Statutes

References are to page numbers

Table of Statutory Instruments etc

References are to page numbers

Table of EC and International Materials

References are to page numbers

xlvii

Table of Cases

S

CHAPTER 1

Overview

INTRODUCTION

This chapter provides an overview of technology transfer in the UK and overseas: the definition of 'technology transfer'; who is involved in it; how it is funded; who benefits from it; and the role of lawyers in these activities.

Later chapters of this book will consider legal and commercial topics that affect the drafting, negotiation and interpretation of technology transfer agreements. The remainder of this first Part will consider other commercial-practice subjects, including how technology transfer agreements are structured, and the main commercial issues that are addressed in technology transfer agreements. Relevant areas of law, and their practical application to technology transfer agreements, are considered in detail in Part B, whilst Part C considers regulatory and competition law controls on technology transfer. Part D addresses how intellectual property is valued and taxed.

WHAT IS 'TECHNOLOGY TRANSFER'?

The term 'technology transfer' is understood as having specific or wider meanings, depending on the context. The specific meanings include:

- For the purposes of the EC Technology Transfer Agreements Block Exemption Regulation,[1] technology transfer effectively means patent, software protected by copyright (but not other forms of copyright) and know-how licensing.[2]

- The term is sometimes used to refer to the transfer of up-to-date technology and products from advanced, industrial nations to poorer countries, sometimes on preferential financial terms, and with a view to enabling the poorer countries to take advantage of modern techniques for producing goods and services.

In this book, the term is used in a broader sense, to include any activity where technology is created and/or made available by one organisation to another. This can best be illustrated by explaining how the term 'technology transfer agreement' will be used. This book discusses a wide range of agreements that are concerned with the creation, transfer or exploitation of technology and related intellectual property rights. Research and development (R&D) agreements, and intellectual property licences and assignments, are two of the main subjects covered. At appropriate points the discussion will extend to related types of agreements, including employment contracts (particularly intellectual property and confidentiality terms), sub-contracting agreements, manufacturing agreements, trials and testing agreements, material transfer agreements, and confidentiality agreements. Occasionally, the term 'technology-related agreements' will be used, particularly in the chapter on EC competition laws, where 'technology transfer agreement' might be confusing, in view of the narrower meaning of that term that is found in the Technology Transfer Agreements Block Exemption Regulation.

In some areas, it is not easy to find a clear dividing line between the law relating to technology transfer and the law relating to other activities such as production, distribution or sales. Two examples, both in the context of EC competition law, come to mind:

- Where a distributor sells software that has been supplied to it by another company (the supplier), it may either do so by simply re-selling copies of the software that have been made and packaged by the supplier, or it may be given a master copy of the software and be licensed to make copies, package them (perhaps with a licence to include the supplier's trademarks on the packaging) and sell them on to purchasers. The former method falls outside the category of technology transfer, the latter method may sometimes fall within that category. For EC competition law purposes, the former method may qualify for block exemption under the Vertical Agreements Regulation whilst the latter method may be regarded as technology transfer. Another example in the software

---

1   Commission Regulation (EC) 772/2004 ([2004] OJ L123/11) on the application of Article 81(3) of the Treaty to categories of technology transfer agreements.
2   See Ch 13 under 'Types of intellectual property covered by the TTR'.

field that is likely to be within the category of technology transfer is where a software author produces a set of tools or a program which needs to be turned into a developed, finished product whether alone or with other programs and the licence to carry out the development also provides the right to sell the finished product incorporating the licensed program or tools, etc.

- Where the parties to a research collaboration project conduct it via a joint venture company, and if that joint venture is a *full-function* joint venture with a *Community dimension*, it will be treated as a corporate merger for competition law purposes and fall to be assessed under the EC Merger Regulation.[3]

Thus, a comprehensive treatment of technology transfer agreements might require a consideration of the law relating to distribution agreements and the law relating to corporate mergers. Another example arises in the university context, where technology transfer departments are increasingly using 'spin-out' companies as a vehicle for technology transfer rather than licensing the technology to an independent, usually large, company. Company law, including company formation, shareholder agreements and investment agreements, is outside the main subject area of this book.[4]

The authors must make a judgement, perhaps arbitrary, as to when a legal subject strays too far from the main theme of the book. At various points the reader will be referred to other sources of information on legal topics that are treated briefly, or not at all, in the text.

ORGANISATIONS INVOLVED IN TECHNOLOGY TRANSFER, INCLUDING RESEARCH AND DEVELOPMENT

Research and development (R&D), and associated technology transfer activities, are conducted by a range of different types of organisation, including:

Large manufacturing companies that typically spend a small percentage of their turnover on R&D, and where R&D may be viewed as ancillary to the main purpose of the business, ie to manufacture and sell products. Traditionally, such R&D activities have often been conducted in-house, making technology transfer agreements unnecessary. In recent years, in-licensing of technology has become more popular, particularly in an area such as pharmaceuticals

---

3   See Ch 12 under 'If the agreement is horizontal, is it a full-function joint venture with a Community dimension to which the Merger Regulation applies, or is it subject to the Article 81 regime?'.

4   For a discussion of legal and practice issues in venture capital, joint ventures and shareholders agreements, see the *Encyclopaedia of Forms and Precedents*, particularly vols 4, 19 and 9 respectively.

where there is a constant pressure to find new sources of drugs. Sometimes, large companies may 'drop' a technology, eg because it doesn't fit their strategic objectives, and be prepared to license it out.

Technology-based companies, many of them small-to-medium-sized companies, that spend a large part of their turnover on R&D, and where the in-licensing and/or out-licensing of technology is a central part of their commercial activities.

Universities and other research-based charities, which have always been involved in research activities and increasingly are becoming involved in commercially-focused R&D work and in the licensing of their inventions to commercial companies.

These categories are clearly generalisations, but they help to clarify the following discussion. In recent years, technology transfer agreements have become of increasing commercial significance, and growinging numbers of lawyers are specialising in this field. This may be partly as a result of an increased willingness on the part of traditional manufacturing companies to contemplate licensing-in technologies – in other words, a move away from the traditional hostility on the part of large companies to technology that was 'not invented here'. It may be partly as a result of universities becoming more actively involved in commercial activities, including technology transfer. Some of the leading UK universities now have sophisticated technology transfer operations that are generating significant revenues for these universities. Perhaps the most significant factor is the increased scale and activity of technology-based companies and the number of organisations promoting and supporting such activity, including the Russell Group, PraxisUnico and Auril.[5]

The newer, technology-based industries are becoming increasingly important to the UK economy, as evidenced by the number of biotech and e-commerce companies that have joined (and, in some cases, quickly left) the FTSE-100 index in recent years, replacing companies in traditional industries. Many of these high-tech companies do not make or sell products, or if they do their stock market value is not based on a multiple of annual product sales. Instead, their value is based on intangibles such as intellectual property and goodwill. In the case of a biotech company, these intangibles might be patents protecting their drugs in development. In the case of an internet bookseller, they might be a customer base that is predicted to generate future revenues. In both of these examples, the company may not have made a profit since formation, and may not be expected to do so for many years to come.

Put another way, many of these companies are valued on the basis that they possess valuable information and a means of protecting that information,

---

5   See 'Representative bodies' below.

and that they are conducting activities to realise value from that information. For example, a biotech company may possess information about its drug in development, may protect that information through patents, regulatory exclusivity and confidentiality agreements, and may intend to realise the value of that information by bringing the drug to the market or by licensing another company to do so. The internet bookseller may not yet have made a profit, but may have generated goodwill and customer loyalty from users of its website (ie information possessed by customers and others about the company); it may possess a valuable database on its customers, and may realise value from that information in a number of ways, eg by using its website to sell products other than books, and to provide advertising space to third parties.

Thus, many technology-based companies are in the business of generating, using and deriving value from information. One of the more important ways in which they do this is by entering into agreements with third parties to create, transfer and commercially exploit the information – in other words, technology transfer agreements.

DIFFERENT PRIORITIES IN TECHNOLOGY TRANSFER

Universities and research institutions

Universities approach R&D agreements, and other forms of technology transfer agreement, with different priorities and objectives to those of most commercial companies. Other types of charitable research institution, eg a cancer research charity that employs research scientists, will often have similar issues and concerns to a university.

Many UK universities, particularly those engaged in prestigious scientific research, are incorporated by Royal Charter and have charitable status. Their charitable status means that most if not all of the income that they receive is exempt from corporation tax. Tax issues are considered later in this book.[6] Some types of R&D agreement with commercial companies are consistent with a university's charitable and tax-exempt status, other types are not. An important test of charitable R&D work is whether the results are made available to the public, usually by means of academic publications. If the R&D is conducted under an agreement that includes restrictions on publications, these may cause the research to be regarded as non-charitable and cause any payments received under the agreement to be subject to corporation tax. HMRC and the Charity Commissioners take the view that a delay in publication of up to six months to allow patents to be filed does not prejudice charitable status, but lenghthier or wider restrictions may do so.

---

6   See ch 17.

Even if the payment is subject to the corporation tax regime, there may not be a tax liability. It is understood that many UK universities fail to charge companies the full costs of commissioned research projects. The university may be able to show that the costs incurred in undertaking the work exceed the payments received, ie there is no 'profit' on which tax would be assessed.

A related issue is that academic scientists and their institutions are judged[7] by the quantity and quality of academic research that they undertake. Some research conducted under agreements with commercial companies qualifies as academic research for these purposes; other commercial research activities do not. Again, a key test is whether the results of the research are published or allowed to be published. A delay in publication of up to a year is generally permitted for this purpose.

These issues may mean that a university is not willing to accept certain restrictions on publications, or if it does it will classify the research as commercial and increase the price for that research work accordingly. In some cases a university may be unwilling to conduct research that is too focused on one company's products or technology.

A related issue that affects the terms of R&D agreements is who is to own and who may use any of the intellectual property that may be generated in the research programme, and on what terms. Some historical background may help to set the scene here.

Traditionally, UK universities have obtained much of their funding from the various UK Research Councils (eg the Medical Research Council (MRC)), and until 1985 there were restrictions on how they could exploit the intellectual property created.[8] Many UK universities now have technology transfer departments or subsidiary companies which are responsible for the commercialisation of inventions made at the university (whether or not funded by a Research Council). In many cases these departments did not exist prior to 1985. Some of them have grown large in recent years and now run a sophisticated operation; others are still at a relatively early stage of development. As well as simply licensing their intellectual property to commercial companies, there is an increasing tendency for universities to form 'spin-out' companies, transfer items of intellectual property into the

---

7   Eg by the Higher Education Funding Council (HEFCE).
8   The work of the Research Councils is described later in this chapter. Until 1985, if any commercially valuable technology resulted from research that was conducted at a UK university and funded by a Research Council, the university was expected to commercialise the technology through the National Research and Development Corporation (NRDC). In 1985 the Government announced that universities were no longer to be restricted to using the NRDC. If they wished, they could pursue other routes to commercialisation. They were, however, required to report what steps they were taking to ensure the proper commercialisation of such technologies. At around the same time, the NRDC was renamed the British Technology Group (BTG), and a few years later the BTG was privatised (and renamed again to 3i).

company and obtain venture capital investment to finance the company's activities.

It should also be mentioned that universities are highly political organisations, with powerful vested interests, particularly amongst the senior academic staff and heads of department. It is predictable that a university's level of interest in pursuing an R&D project will not always be related to whether commercially valuable results are likely to flow from the project. Academic priorities may override purely commercial objectives. What is less easy to predict is whether issues other than the scientific merit of an R&D project will influence the university's approach. To put it bluntly, considerations such as 'keeping Professor X happy', or avoiding controversy or bad public relations, may be important factors. University research contracts offices do not always have much influence in these internal debates; it is sometimes easier to ignore the commercial arguments than the political arguments, particularly when any commercial returns from a technology are likely to be several years ahead, and in an institution whose primary purpose is academic rather than commercial. This can be a source of frustration for research contracts staff, who are not always given clear guidance from the university authorities as to what their objectives (for example, when negotiating an R&D agreement) should be.

There is also the issue of academic freedom, which does not arise in a commercial company. University scientists expect and receive considerable freedom as to the direction that their research takes and they are not usually obliged (unless they agree to be obliged) to co-operate in the university's relationships with commercial companies. Some academics wish to avoid contact with commercial companies; others are happy to work with them.

In the medical and biotech fields, public concern about scientific research activities may also influence the university's approach. Such concerns include the use of animals in medical research, genetic engineering, the use and exploitation of materials found in so-called 'third world' countries (whether for reward or not) and whether academics in UK universities should be working with scientists and academics in certain countries. These are all matters that influence the type of work and the participation of academics in universities. In recent years some of these issues have also affected commercial companies.[9]

---

9 To take one example, in the last decade the issue of use of animals in medical research and testing has become very sensitive, with strong views expressed and high profile campaigns by animal rights campaigners against such testing and research. A case in point is the use of, and building of new, animal research facilities at Cambridge University. Internet searches on this topic (such as YouTube videos and news articles (eg http://news.bbc.co.uk/1/hi/uk/4177200. stm) indicate the need to carefully consider these factors, whether to carry them out at all (a consideration for universities) and whether to invest in or participate in such work (a consideration for commercial concerns).

Revenue sharing within universities

Often, technology transfer agreements involve the payment of royalties or other sums for use of intellectual property. Most UK universities have a policy (or even a contractual obligation; this is not always made clear in the university regulations) to pay a share of such payments to the inventor and his department within the university. A typical apportionment of revenue (they do vary from university to university) might be as follows:

Amount received by the university	Percentage paid to inventor(s)	Percentage paid to inventor's department	Percentage retained by university
First £50,000	75%	12.5%	12.5%
Next £200,000	50%	25%	25%
Over £250,000	25%	37.5%	37.5%

At least one UK university pays its technology transfer company a commission on licence revenues received through the technology transfer company's efforts, and this commission (30 per cent) is deducted before the above apportionment is made.

University patents often name more than one inventor; a practical issue for university technology transfer staff in such situations is how any revenues should be apportioned between individual inventors. Sometimes, disputes arise over who should be named as an inventor. It is sometimes difficult to persuade would-be inventors that their contribution, though valuable, is not inventive in legal terms, and that just because you are named as a joint author of an academic paper reporting on a programme of research, this does not entitle you to be named as an inventor of a patented invention made in the course of that research.

The inventor's share may be subject to deduction of income tax and national insurance contributions, although this may partly depend on whether the inventor is an employee of the university and whether the invention is owned by the university as employer or has genuinely been sold by the inventor to the university in return for the revenue-sharing arrangement. (If the latter, then the university may be able to make the payment without deducting tax and NI, but the inventor may find himself/herself liable to charge the university VAT on the amount of the inventor's share, if the annual amounts exceed the VAT threshold.) It is understood that university practice may vary on whether income tax and NI contributions are deducted before the payment is made to the inventor, and on whether the NI deduction is taken from the inventor's percentage share. In at least one case, the university and the inventor share the 10.4 per cent NI contribution equally. (In relation to tax issues generally, see the section on tax in Chapter 17).

It should be noted that these revenue-sharing policies generally apply to inventions, and are most frequently encountered in relation to patents. They may also apply to know-how and some copyright (eg in relation to computer programs). However, there is often a quite separate policy in relation to copyright in books and other materials. Many universities allow their staff to write books and retain any royalty income generated, although some have a different attitude to copyright in course materials as such.

It is now common for universities to set up 'spin-out' companies as a vehicle for technology transfer, and to obtain outside investment in the spin-out company. Sometimes, the university will receive shares in the company in return for assigning relevant intellectual property to it. In such situations, the university may agree with the academic inventor that he or she will receive shares in the company instead of an entitlement to revenues generated by the university.

Technology transfer within high-tech companies

There is usually a greater commercial focus in biotech and other high-tech companies than in universities; but the people who are employed to carry out research in such companies may not be very different to their colleagues in academia: indeed, many R&D staff in smaller technology-based companies have experience of working in universities. Senior R&D staff in high-tech companies will generally have greater exposure to commercial issues than their counterparts in universities.

This greater commercial focus affects both the terms sought in R&D agreements and the way in which the activities under an R&D agreement are pursued. For instance, freedom to publish will not generally be a concern of the industrial researcher, or at least not as great a concern as for the academic scientist.

Revenue-sharing policies are rarely encountered in commercial companies: scientists who work for companies are paid a salary and are expected to make inventions for the good of the company. There may be a bonus scheme or other special rewards, but it will not generally be directly related to income received from the invention, and will not usually be anything like as generous as the university revenue-sharing policy. Instead, share options in the employing company may provide the more frequently-encountered (but equally unpredictable) route to financial wealth. Patents Act 1977, ss 39–43 provide for inventors to be compensated by their employer in certain circumstances, but in practice it is rare that an employee will qualify for compensation under the statutory provisions.[10]

One of the theories behind setting up small technology-based companies is that the scientists who work in them are more motivated, work harder and

---

10   See further Ch 4 under 'Employee inventions'.

achieve better results than their counterparts in large corporations. They may also have greater freedom in the way in which they pursue their research activities: there is likely to be less corporate bureaucracy than in a large company. This flexible approach is sometimes reflected in the terms of the technology transfer agreements that such companies negotiate; precedents as to deal structure, etc may be less rigidly followed than in some large, established companies. Where precedents or business models are followed, as often as not they tend to be precedents from overseas, particularly from the United States, where biotech and other high-tech companies are longer-established, and in some cases much larger (eg by market capitalisation) than in the UK.

A point that should not be overlooked in discussion of small, high-tech companies is the extent to which their business approach is linked to the personality and opinions of the key member (or members) of the management team. These companies are sometimes founded by entrepreneurs who have a very strong personality and distinctive approach to business life: the 'philosophy' of the person in charge may be a significant factor in the company's technology transfer agreements. For example, some high-tech companies wish to have a reputation in the scientific community as being 'fair' in relation to the terms of their agreements, eg agreements with the academic community. Others take a more buccaneering approach.

Technology transfer in industry generally

Some large UK companies, including household names in areas such as pharmaceuticals, computers, telecommunications, engineering and defence, have many years' (or decades') experience of funding R&D or collaborating in R&D with other organisations. Generally, these companies have an in-house legal department and well-established views on the terms that are appropriate for R&D agreements and other technology transfer agreements. For example, it is understood that GlaxoSmithKline has traditionally taken the view that in R&D agreements with UK universities it should own any intellectual property arising from the R&D project.[11] Some other companies have been willing to take merely a licence to the results. Universities tend to prefer to grant sponsoring companies a licence to resulting intellectual property (IP), or an option to acquire a licence. Much will depend on the nature of the R&D and the relative bargaining strength of the parties, but many companies do accept a licence rather than an assignment of resulting IP.

In large companies, the way in which a technology transfer agreement is negotiated may depend in part on whether the agreement has an influential

---

11   It is understood that this policy may have changed in recent years.

'champion' within the company. In the author's experience, it can greatly assist the smooth negotiation of an agreement, particularly one whose terms vary from the norm within a large company, if it is championed by an influential senior scientist or commercial manager. The champion's influence is seen in a number of ways, from causing the agreement to be approved in principle, to giving direction to the company's legal department on the detailed terms, and speeding up the negotiation and signature process. Without such direction, the technology transfer agreement may receive a lower priority with busy people than other matters. It can be very important to start the relationship on the right footing, with the appropriate contractual structure and the most suitable people involved in any joint R&D project. The champion can greatly assist this process.

International transactions

Many technology transfer agreements are between organisations based in different countries, or have other international aspects (for example, if they concern intellectual property that is registered in several countries). Where lawyers are involved in drafting and negotiating the agreement, they may find that the person they are negotiating with has a different culture and legal framework for drafting and negotiation to the one they are used to. This is probably no different in principle for technology transfer agreements than it is for other types of international commercial transaction. Particular issues (or generalisations) in the context of technology transfer agreements include:

- if any intellectual property is to be jointly owned by the parties, be aware that national laws on the rights of joint owners of patents vary from country to country. In particular, it seems that US patent law allows a joint owner to grant a non-exclusive licence under the patent without the consent of the other joint owner, whereas under UK patent law (and, it seems, the patent laws of most other countries) the consent of the other joint owner is required for any licensing (whether exclusive or non-exclusive). Generally, parties may wish to provide in detail for what happens to jointly-owned property, and this is particularly important in international contracts;

- the US business culture tends to value know-how as a commercial asset to a much greater extent than, say, the Japanese. This is reflected, for example, in the commercial terms sought in intellectual property licence agreements;

- government regulations and other national laws and practices can affect international technology transfer agreements in unexpected ways. For example, if research is funded by the US government, or performed by certain US national research bodies (eg the National Institutes of Health), the US government may have 'walk-in rights', ie certain automatic rights under intellectual property arising under the contract.

12

Another example is that some countries have standard arrangements for compensating patients who are injured in clinical trials of new drugs. However the arrangements differ from country to country, eg as to the minimum levels of insurance that a pharmaceutical or biotech company conducting clinical trials may be required to maintain. This may also affect the terms (eg indemnity terms) that should be included in clinical trials agreements, eg between a pharmaceutical company and a hospital or individual clinician;

- academic scientists often enter into consultancy arrangements with commercial companies; typical financial terms might include an annual fee of £10–£20,000. The standard consultancy provisions of some US corporations are very one-sided, at least in relation to intellectual property issues. Sometimes the provisions of these agreements purport to transfer to the company intellectual property rights far beyond those specifically arising under the consultancy, and such provisions generally need to be scrutinised carefully.

FUNDING OF R&D

The following sections outline the various funding opportunities available to public and private science-based researchers in the UK. There are three main sources of funding:

- the UK government or one of its agencies;

- the European Union; and

- non-commercial (mainly charitable) organisations.

The types of funding opportunities described are largely confined to the scientific field, where most R&D is carried out.

UK Government funding

Foresight programme

The Government provides many funding opportunities to companies, universities and research centres for the advancement of scientific R&D. The Foresight Programme, which forms part of the Government Office for Science within the Department for Business, Innovation and Skills, and is managed by the Foresight Directorate,aims to promote investment in the science base, focusing on long-term competitiveness carried out through exploration of, and investment in, sectors of economic importance. The Programme aims to locate and build upon technologies with the greatest potential economic and social benefits. Funding for the foresight target areas, and grants for basic research, are largely administered through the Research Councils.

Research Councils

Research Councils receive funding through the Government's science budget. Although the Department for Business, Innovation and Skills exercises statutory control over the Councils, they remain autonomous and are non-departmental public funding bodies. The following Research Councils are discussed below:

- Biotechnology and Biological Sciences Research Council;

- Engineering and Physical Sciences Research Council;

- Economic and Social Research Council;

- Medical Research Council;

- Natural Environment Research Council; and

- Science and Technology Facilities Council.

There are in total seven Research Councils (the six listed above together with the Arts and Humanities Research Council). The seven Research Councils invest together almost £3 billion per year on research relating to biological and medical sciences, physics, astronomy, engineering, social sciences, economics, and the arts and humanities. Details about how to apply for funding from the Research Councils can be found on their websites, and details about their websites can be found under the heading 'Contact Information' at the end of this chapter.

Biotechnology and Biological Sciences Research Council

The Biotechnology and Biological Sciences Research Council (BBSRC)[12] promotes and supports research and training in biotechnology and biological sciences in research institutes, centres and higher education institutes. Research is funded through various mechanisms, primarily through research grants for specified projects. Applicants to the BBRC must be residents of the UK and hold positions within eligible institutions.

Engineering and Physical Sciences Research Council

The Engineering and Physical Sciences Research Council (EPSRC) supports research and postgraduate training within engineering and the physical

---

12   The Council incorporates the former Agricultural and Food Research Council and the former Science and Engineering Research Council's biotechnology and biological sciences programmes.

14

sciences.[13] The EPSRC currently invests more than £800 million a year on research grants, collaborative programmes and postgraduate training. Research grant eligibility criteria stipulate that applicants must be employed by a UK university or a similar institution, although exceptions are made for holders of EPSRC fellowships.

Economic and Social Research Council

The Economic and Social Research Council (ESRC) funds research and postgraduate training in the social and economic disciplines.[14] Higher education institutes and ESRC-approved independent institutes are eligible for funding schemes, termed 'responsive mode schemes'. These include research grants, research seminars, research programmes, and fellowships. Certain research establishments and not-for-profit organisations may be eligible for other funding programmes.

Medical Research Council

The core of the Medical Research Council's (MRC) mission relates to improving human health. To meet this aim, the MRC funds research in all of the medical sciences through grants, studentships and fellowships. Higher education institutions are eligible for MRC funding, as are NHS Trusts and 'academic analogues' (non-university academic-based organisations) approved by the Council. The MRC also participates in collaborative and special funding programmes with industry. Such programmes include Framework Programme 7, the Partnership Grants, and Discipline Hopping Awards.

Natural Environment Research Council

The Natural Environment Research Council (NERC) sponsors and manages research, training and knowledge exchange in the environmental sciences. Research is sponsored within its own research centres and at universities.

---

13   The EPSRC supports seven research programme 'landscapes': (1) cross-disciplinary interfaces; (2) information and communication technology; (3) infrastructure; (4) materials, mechanical and medical engineering; (5) mathematical sciences; (6) physical sciences; and (7) process, environment and sustainability. The EPSRC also supports four mission programme 'landscapes': (1) digital economy; (2) energy; (3) nanoscience through engineering to application; and (4) towards next-generation healthcare. In addition, EPSRC contributes to three cross-council programmes: (1) ageing – lifelong health and wellbeing; (2) global uncertainties – security for all in a changing world; and (3) living with environmental change.
14   The ESRC supports research in the following areas: Economic Performance and Development; Environmental and Human Behaviour; Governance and Citizenship; Lifecourse, Lifestyles and Health; Social Stability and Exclusion; Work and Organisation; and Capacity Building Clusters.

The NERC awards research grants and fellowships, and also supports postgraduate training.

Science and Technology Facilities Council

The Science and Technology Facilities Council (STFC) funds researchers based at universities working in the fields of astronomy, particle physics, space science and nuclear physics. In addition, the STFC also supports various facilities such as ISIS and the Central Laser Facility, and is a major stakeholder in the Diamond Light Source.

Funding schemes

Many government and government-associated initiatives exist to encourage collaboration between academia and industry and to promote scientific innovation. It is not possible to provide a comprehensive list of all such funding schemes – this section outlines the major sponsorship programmes.

Co-operative Awards in Science and Engineering

All Research Councils discussed above fund Co-operative Awards in Science or Engineering, or 'CASE', awards which are often called 'CASE studentships'. These studentships are awarded to PhD and postgraduate students who wish to pursue projects that are of academic and industrial interest. The students' higher education institutes collaborate with industry to offer students the opportunity to gain experience in industry. There are two mechanisms for doing this: CASE, and CASE Plus studentships.

Joint Grants Scheme

The Joint Grants Scheme (JGS) funds research with defence applications. It is supported by the Ministry of Defence (MoD). Applicants to the JGS must meet requirements set out by the Research Council peer review, and must propose a research project that is related to the MoD's research objectives.

Other government funding

As well as the funding from the Ministry of Defence mentioned above, there are also various grants available from other government departments such as the Department of Health (which is a major supporter of health-related research), the Department of Environment, Food and Rural Affairs (DEFRA), the Department of Transport and the Defence, Science and Technology Laboratory, which is an agency of the Ministry of Defence.

In addition to direct sources of funding, the Government also grants some corporations Research and Development Relief for Corporation Tax. As the name of the scheme suggests, certain companies and other types of corporations may be entitled to a corporation tax relief that is linked to the size of the organisation's actual expenditure on allowable research and development costs. More details about this type of tax relief can be found on HM Revenue & Customs' website.

University Challenge Seed Fund; Science Enterprise Challenge

The University Challenge Seed Fund (UCSF) and the Science Enterprise Challenge were two government initiatives introduced to specifically address entrepreneurial culture.

The UCSF was a funding initiative launched in 1998 by the DTI in partnership with the Wellcome Trust and the Gatsby Charitable Foundation which provides universities with capital for developing their technologies into new commercial opportunities. In 1999, 15 university-based consortia won a total of £45 million from the UCSF to set up seed funds for developing early-stage research into commercial products and processes. A further £15 million was awarded in October 2001 under this initiative, taking the number of institutions that have access to University Challenge Seed Funding to 57.

In 1998 the Science Enterprise Challenge was announced in which the Government detailed the launch of a new £25 million competition set up to establish enterprise centres. Twelve centres were set up in the UK following the first round of the competition in 1999/2000. The centres support the teaching and practice of entrepreneurship and promote links between universities and businesses. A second round of the competition was set up to establish another centre and to help expand the 12 existing enterprise centres.

Both the activities of the University Challenge Seed Fund and the Science Enterprise Challenge have now been incorporated into the Higher Education Innovation Fund ('HEIF') programme.

EU funding Framework Programmes

Introduction

The value of adopting a common strategy for research and technological development in the EU had been recognised for some time. However, it was not until the early 1980s that these ideas were given formal recognition with the creation of the first of the EU's Framework Programmes. These are multi-national, multi-annual and multi-sectoral programmes for funding scientific and technological R&D.[15] Throughout, the main emphasis has remained on ensuring tangible, exploitable results to benefit European industry.

The current Framework Programme, Framework Programme 7[16] (FP7) runs from 2007–2013 and has as objectives:

- 'to strengthen the scientific and technological base of European industry'; and

- 'to encourage its international competitiveness, while promoting research that supports EU policies';[17]

With an emphasis on collaborative research. The current budget is approximately €52 billion and the majority of that sum will be spent on grants for research.[18]

Framework Programme 7 (FP7)

FP7 has four Specific Programmes:[19]

The Co-operation Programme

This programme is the most important programme in terms of the proportion of the total budget allocated to it: €32.4 billion (out of €52 billion) and its aim is to 'foster ... collaborative research across Europe and other partner countries through projects by transnational consortia of industry and academia'.[20] The research can be carried out in ten 'thematic' areas:[21]

---

15   These programmes have become increasingly ambitious. The budgets for FP2–FP7 are:

Programme	Programme period	Budget (€) (billion)
FP2	1987–91	5.40
FP3	1990–94	7.70
FP4	1994–98	12.30
FP5	1998–2002	14.69
FP6	2002–2006	17.50
FP7	2007–2013	53.00

16   Decision (EC) 1982/2006 of the European Parliament and of the Council of 18 December 2006 concerning the Seventh Framework Programme of the European Community for research, technological development and demonstration activities (2007–2013); Regulation (EC) 1906/2006 of the European Parliament and of the Council of 18 December 2006 laying down the rules for the participation of undertakings, research centres and universities in actions under the Seventh Framework Programme and for the dissemination of research results.

17   See *FP7 in Brief: How to Get Involved in the EU 7th Framework Programme for Research*, p 9. European Commission, see http://ec.europa.eu/research/fp7/index_en.cfm

18   See *FP7 in Brief: How to Get Involved in the EU 7th Framework Programme for Research*, p 6. European Commission, see http://ec.europa.eu/research/fp7/index_en.cfm

19   The material in this section ignores the programme concerning the nuclear industry.

20   See *FP7 in Brief: How to Get Involved in the EU 7th Framework Programme for Research*, p 14. European Commission, see http://ec.europa.eu/research/fp7/index_en.cfm

21   Decision (EC) 1982/2006, Annex 1.

(i) Health;

(ii) Food, agriculture and fisheries, and biotechnology;

(iii) Information and communication technologies;

(iv) Nanosciences, nanotechnologies, materials and new production technologies;

(v) Energy;

(vi) Environment (including climate change);

(vii) Transport (including aeronautics);

(viii) Socio-economic sciences and the humanities;

(ix) Space; and

(x) Security.

Grants are awarded on the basis that in addition to the funds provided by the EC for the costs of the research, applicants would need to provide matching funding.[22]

A condition of the grant is that there must be at least three legal entities involved in the research project, with no two of them being established in the same country (and the legal entities must be independent of each other).[23]

The Ideas Programme

This programme concerns pure investigative research at the frontiers of any area of science or technology (but such research does not have to involve participants from more than one country).

The People Programme

This programme provides support to individual researchers, which includes university/academic and industry partnerships.

The Capacities Programme

The aim of this programme is to provide funds for research infrastructure including research which is for the benefit of small and medium-sized enterprises.

---

22 Regulation (EC) 1996/2006, Art 33. However the EC will provide up to 75 per cent of the costs where a public-sector body is involved, and up to 100 per cent of the costs for consortium management, networking, training, co-ordination and dissemination activities.

23 Regulation (EC) 1906/2006, Arts 5, 6.

Method of awarding grants

The concrete plans for implementing the Specific Programmes are announced by the EC in annual Work Programmes which include what types of proposals will be considered in particular research areas (named 'Call for Proposals'). These are announced in the EC's Official Journal and on the internet.[24] After the closing date, the proposals are considered, and for those which are accepted the EC then enters into financial and scientific/technical discussions with the applications.[25] The end result is that a grant agreement is drawn up.

The grant agreement is entered into between the leading applicant (co-ordinator) and the EC. The grant agreement sets out:

- the names of the co-ordinator and the other applicants for the grant;

- the duration of the research project;

- when reports must be delivered (identified by the description of the research work to be carried out in Annex I to the grant agreement);

- the maximum financial contribution of the EC;

- any pre-financing; and

- provisions dealing with notices and the law which applies.[26]

The grant agreement is only signed between the EC and the co-ordinator; the other applicants each sign a separate document acceding to the grant agreement.[27] The more detailed terms and conditions are found in Annex II of the grant agreement, which is in three parts:

- *Part A*: which deals with the implementation of the programme, how the applicants will be organised, reporting requirements and details concerning payments, how the project will be implemented and details of confidentiality obligations;

- *Part B*: which sets out details of the financial provisions; and

- *Part C*: which sets out the provisions relating to intellectual property rights, use and dissemination.

---

24   Regulation (EC) 1906/2006, Art 13, and see *FP7 in Brief: How to Get Involved in the EU 7th Framework Programme for Research*, p 24. European Commission, see http://ec.europa.eu/research/fp7/index_en.cfm (see www.cordis/europa.eu/fp7/).

25   Further information can be found in the 'Guide for Applicants': see www.cordis/europa.eu/fp7/.

26   The various types of grant agreement can be found at http://cordis.europa.eu/fp7//home_en.html under 'Find a document'. The model grant agreement itself is at http://cordis.europa.eu/fp7/calls-grant-agreement_en.html#standard_ga.

27   The separate document is set out in Annex IV to the grant agreement, and must be signed within 45 days of the grant agreement coming into force.

Intellectual property provisions[28]

Part C of the Annex II to the grant agreement is divided into two sections:

- foreground intellectual property; and
- access rights.

Foreground intellectual property

The grant agreement provides for the following with regard to intellectual property (IP) generated under a project:

- foreground IP belongs to the applicant who generated it,[29] although the applicants are expected to enter into an agreement to deal with who owns the foreground where more than one applicant is to own it; where they do not then they jointly own it if more than one applicant has generated it;

- in a provision which is new in FP7, if there is no joint ownership agreement, each of the joint owners shall be entitled to grant non-exclusive licences to third parties, without any right to sub-licence, subject to two conditions: (i) that at least 45 days' prior notice be given to the other joint owner(s); and (ii) fair and reasonable compensation be provided to the other joint owner(s) ;[30]

- an applicant who wishes to assign ownership of foreground has also (i) to transfer obligations regarding the foreground to the assignee, and (ii) to impose a condition that any subsequent assignee will also have to receive those obligations;[31]

- except where obligations of confidentiality prevent the following, an applicant on a transfer of foreground has to give 45 days' prior notice where it is required to pass on its obligation to provide access rights[32] to the other applicants, including details of the transfer and the name of the new owner, to give time to the other applicants to exercise their access

---

28 A detailed guide to the provisions relating to the generation and use of intellectual property can be found in *Guide to Intellectual Property Rules for FP7 projects*, available from ftp://ftp.cordis.europa.eu/pub/fp7/docs/ipr_en.pdf.

29 Art 26.1, Annex II. 'Foreground' is defined as 'the results, including information, whether or not they can be protected, which are generated under the project. Such results include rights related to copyright; design rights; patent rights; plant variety rights; or similar forms of protection' (Art 1.7, Annex II).

30 Art 26.2, Annex II. 'Fair and reasonable conditions' means 'appropriate conditions including possible financial terms taking into account the specific circumstances of the request for access, for example the actual or potential value of the foreground or background to which access is requested and/or the scope, duration or other characteristics of the use envisaged' (Art 1.6, Annex II).

31 Art 27.1, Annex II.

32 'Access rights' means 'licences and user rights to foreground or background' (Art 1.1, Annex II).

rights.[33] A different period of time can be agreed by a prior written agreement or waived altogether in the case of transfers of ownership from one applicant to a specifically identified third party.[34] The other applicants have 30 days to object and if they can demonstrate that their access rights would be adversely affected, the intended transfer shall not take place until agreement has been reached between the applicants concerned.[35] The EC also has the right to object where an applicant wishes to transfer ownership of foreground to a third party established in a third country not associated with FP7 if such a transfer is not in accordance with the interests of developing the competitiveness of the European economy or is inconsistent with ethical principles or security considerations;[36]

- if foreground is capable of industrial or commercial application, the owner of it shall provide for its effective and adequate protection (subject to taking account of the legitimate interests – particularly the commercial interests – of the other applicants);[37]

- patent applications relating to the foreground need to include a statement that the foreground was generated with support from the EC under FP7; they also need to be reported to the EC in a plan for the use and dissemination of the foreground.[38] Where there is no intention to protect foreground (or transfer it to another applicant or certain third parties), it cannot be disseminated without notifying the EC (on no less than 45 days' notice).[39] The EC can assume ownership of the foreground, with the consent of the applicant concerned, and that applicant can refuse consent only if 'it can demonstrate that its legitimate interests would suffer disproportionately great harm';[40]

- applicants are required to use[41] the foreground[42] as well as disseminate[43] it as soon as possible (if not disseminated sufficiently quickly, then the EC has the power to do so) .[44] Where dissemination is envisaged, the applicant who wishes to carry it out must give 45 days' notice to the other applicants (and another applicant may object where it 'considers

---

33 Art 27.2, Annex II.
34 See n 33.
35 Art 27.3, Annex II.
36 Art 27.4, Annex II.
37 Art 28.1, Annex II.
38 Art 28.2, Annex II.
39 Art 28.3, Annex II.
40 See n 39.
41 'Use' means 'the direct or indirect utilisation of foreground in further research activities other than those covered by the project, or for developing, creating and marketing a product or process, or for creating and providing a service' (Art 1.8, Annex II).
42 Art 29.1, Annex II.
43 'Dissemination' means 'the disclosure of foreground by any appropriate means other than that resulting from the formalities for protecting it, and including the publication of foreground in any medium' (Art 1.5, Annex II).
44 Art 30.1, Annex II.

that its legitimate interest in relation to its foreground or background[45] could suffer disproportionately great harm'[46]) within 30 days (or such period as agreed in writing).[47] Publications or other dissemination of the foreground have to include a statement that the foreground was generated with the support of the EC under FP7 and any dissemination activity needs to be reported to the EC in a plan for the use and dissemination of the foreground.[48]

Access rights[49]

The grant agreement contains the following main provisions in relation to access rights:

- parties can define, in writing, what background is needed for, or is excluded from, a project;[50]

- requests for access rights are to be in writing[51] and can be made subject to conditions so that they are only used for an intended purpose (including the imposition of confidentiality obligations) ;[52]

- an applicant has to inform other applicants if there are to be any restrictions on the grant of access rights to background or any other restriction which might substantially affect the granting of access rights;[53]

- termination of the participation of an applicant will not affect the obligation of that applicant to grant access rights to the remaining applicants;[54]

- the grant of access rights will by default not include the right to grant sub-licences, unless agreed otherwise;[55]

- any agreement to grant access rights to foreground or background to other applicants (or third parties) must also ensure that access rights to potential applicants are maintained;[56]

---

45 'Background' means 'information which is held by beneficiaries prior to their accession to this agreement, as well as copyrights or other intellectual property rights pertaining to such information, the application for which has been filed before their accession to this agreement, and which is needed for carrying out the project or for using foreground' (Art 1.4, Annex II).
46 Art 30.2, 3, Annex II.
47 Art 30.3, Annex II.
48 Art 30.4, Annex II.
49 For the meaning of 'access rights' see n 32.
50 Art 31.1, Annex II.
51 Art 32.1, Annex II.
52 Art 32.2, Annex II.
53 Art 32.3, Annex II.
54 Art 32.4, Annex II.
55 Art 32.5, Annex II.
56 Art 32.6, Annex II. However an exclusive licence for specific foreground or background can be granted if all the applicants waive their access rights and the waiver(s) are in writing. (Art 32.7, Annex II).

- the EC can object and prevent an applicant granting an exclusive licence to specific foreground to a third party who is established in a county not associated with FP7;[57]

- an applicant has the right to be granted access rights to another applicant's foreground (on a royalty-free basis) in order to carry out its own work under a project.[58] The same applies to background, but with the proviso that the applicant who is to grant the access rights to the background is free to do so;[59]

- applicants are to have access rights to foreground in order to use their own foreground either on fair and reasonable conditions[60] or royalty free, unless all the other applicants agree otherwise.[61] The same applies to background (the use of background of one applicant so another can use its foreground), but with the proviso that the applicant who is to grant the access rights to the background is free to do so;[62]

- unless the applicants agree otherwise, access rights for the reasons set out in the previous bullet point can be made up to one year after the end of the project or termination of the participation by the owner of the background or foreground concerned.[63]

Some important differences between FP6 and FP7

The provisions of the grant agreement provide some changes to those in FP6, including:

- the term used for intellectual property generated under a project is known under FP7 as 'foreground' rather than 'knowledge';

- the term used for information and rights held prior to the contract/project is changed from 'pre-existing know-how' under FP6 to 'background' under FP7. Also, the definition of background is different in that it carries a limitation as to what is *needed* for carrying the project or using the foreground;[64]

- under FP7 a default regime is introduced where there is no joint-ownership agreement in place regarding jointly owned foreground with respect to what each joint owner can do with the foreground (ie

---

57   Art 32.7, Annex II.
58   Art 33.1, Annex II.
59   Art 33.2, Annex II. All the applicants can agree that background will not be granted on a royalty-free basis if they make such an arrangement before they accede to the grant agreement.
60   For the meaning of 'fair and reasonable conditions' see n 30.
61   Art 34.1, Annex II.
62   Art 34.2, Annex II.
63   Art 34.4, Annex II.
64   See n 45.

grant licences to third parties without the right to sub-licence subject to conditions) ;[65]

- under FP7 an applicant need not notify a transfer of ownership of its foreground if there is a prior agreement between the applicants waiving their right to notice where the transfer is to be to a specified party;

- under FP6 if an applicant did not protect or has waived protection of its foreground then the EC could step in and protect the foreground. Under FP7 the same condition applies but with one addition: the applicant can transfer the ownership of the foreground to another applicant or certain third parties before the EC has the option of protecting the foreground;

- under FP6 access rights to foreground had to be on a royalty-free basis or as agreed by the applicants. Under FP7, access rights to foreground are now either royalty free or on fair and reasonable conditions[66] with no time limit for reaching an agreement of terms. There is also a change in regard to background, where under FP6 it had to be granted under 'fair and non-discriminatory terms', while under FP7 any grant has to be made consistent with foreground, ie either royalty free or on fair and reasonable conditions;

- the role of the co-ordinator is stronger, requiring responsibility to monitor the applicant's compliance with the grant agreement (including allocating and administering payments to the applicants, and record-keeping);[67]

- the reporting requirements are different between FP6 and FP7 in that instead of providing separate activity and management reports, one combined report needs to be produced. Such reports only need to be provided 60 days from the end of each period (instead of once every 45 days under FP6); but there are now more detailed provisions for certifying financial statements and in regard to EC approval of such reports;[68]

- the period for confidentiality undertakings under FP7 is now five years;[69]

- the list of EC maximum rates of financial contribution to a project is simplified;[70]

- the provisions under FP7 regarding financial audits and reviews by the EC, financial penalties and a guarantee fund are new.[71]

---

65 See second bullet point under 'Foreground intellectual property' above.
66 See n 60.
67 Art 3.2, Annex II. These duties cannot be sub-contracted.
68 Art 4, Annex II.
69 Art 9.1, Annex II.
70 Art 16, Annex II.
71 See Arts 20, 23 and 25, Annex II.

Non-commercial funding bodies

Charitable research

Charities provide most of the funding for R&D by other non-commercial funding bodies. The funding of research is a major function of charities, whatever their size. Most charitable activities can be advanced by research, such as helping the physically, mentally or socially disadvantaged, providing financial aid, and advancing religion and education.

The Charity Commission publishes literature about charitable aims and objectives with regard to research activities. A charity can fund research if it meets its aims and objectives and if the research is for the benefit of the public. The Charity Commission sets out requirements that the proposed research must meet in order to receive charitable funding.[72] The subject matter of the proposed research must be appropriate; it must be intended that knowledge acquired as a result will be disseminated to others; and the research must be conducted for the benefit of the public or a section of the public.[73]

Below are examples of some charities and other non-commercial funding bodies that sponsor scientific research; many belong to the Association of Medical Research Charities (AMRC). The AMRC is one of the largest associations of charities, with 117 registered members. Membership is open to charities that concentrate on medical research and use peer review when evaluating research proposals.[74]

Arthritis Research Campaign

The Arthritis Research Campaign (ARC),[75] a registered charity, supports the investigation of rheumatic diseases through medical research, education and training, and provides information to the public about these diseases. It is the only major charity to support all of the arthritic diseases. The ARC supports grants, fellowships, studentships and clinical trials for the study of arthritis-related diseases. The ARC also provides core funding for two major research institutes; the Kennedy Institute of Rheumatology, which is a part of Imperial College London, and the Epidemiology Unit at the University of Manchester.

---

72 See the Charity Commission's guidance *Research by Higher Education Institutions* (2009). As to charitable research generally, see 'University research and charitable status' below.

73 See the Charity Commission's general guidance on public benefit *Charities and Public Benefit.*

74 The combined total expenditure of these member charities on medical research in the United Kingdom was £935 million according to AMRC subscription data collected in 2008/2009. For contact details see 'Contact information' at the end of this chapter.

75 For contact details see 'Contact information' at the end of this chapter.

Breast Cancer Campaign

The Breast Cancer Campaign[76] is a registered charity whose mission is to 'beat breast cancer by funding innovative world-class research to understand how breast cancer develops, leading to improved diagnosis, treatment, prevention and care'. The Breast Cancer Campaign supports small pilot grants, PhD studentships, project grants and scientific fellowships in universities, medical schools, hospitals and research institutes in the UK and Ireland.

British Academy

The British Academy[77], established by Royal Charter, is the UK's national academy for the humanities and social sciences. It supports research and scholarship in these areas by way of research grants, international programmes, appointments, publications and other mechanisms. The British Academy derives most of its income from the Government, although this is supplemented with voluntary donations, legacies and grants from research foundations. In 1998, the British Academy (along with several other organisations) helped create the Arts and Humanities Research Board.

British Heart Foundation

The British Heart Foundation,[78] a registered charity, supports research into heart disease. Research funding is available to scientists and researchers through programme and project grants, fellowships and studentships.

Cancer Research UK

Cancer Research UK was formed by the merger of two leading cancer charities: The Cancer Research Campaign and Imperial Cancer Research Fund.[79] It is a registered charity which supports the investigation of cancer by sponsoring research in universities, research institutes and clinical centres.

Gatsby Charitable Foundation

The Gatsby Charitable Foundation,[80] one of the Sainsbury Family Charitable Trusts, is an endowed grant-making trust that awards grants for research made in many fields, from cognitive neuroscience to social development.

---

76 For contact details see 'Contact information' at the end of this chapter.
77 For contact details see 'Contact information' at the end of this chapter.
78 For contact details see 'Contact information' at the end of this chapter.
79 For contact details see 'Contact information' at the end of this chapter.
80 For contact details see 'Contact information' at the end of this chapter.

Leverhulme Trust

The Leverhulme Trust[81] makes financial awards that support original research and education, typically making awards that total around £40 million each year.

National Endowment for Science, Technology and The Arts

The National Endowment for Science, Technology and the Arts (NESTA)[82] was established in 1998 after receiving £200 million from the National Lottery to fund innovative projects having commercial and/or social potential within science and the arts. NESTA is involved in testing and demonstrating solutions to social and economic challenges through a variety of practical programmes, research and investment in early-stage companies. NESTA is currently one of the largest seed-stage investors in the UK, providing both capital and non-financial support to early-stage and high-growth-potential companies based in the UK. At the time of writing, NESTA has invested in 48 companies in the information technology, engineering, clean technology, life sciences and healthcare fields.

Nuffield Foundation

The Nuffield Foundation[83] is a registered charity which supports projects with educational or social aims through project grants or other smaller award schemes. Project grants are grants of £5,000 to £150,000 that fund research, and practical development and innovation projects. These projects may address issues relating to child protection; family law and justice; education; access to justice; mental health; older people and their families and other areas concerned with education and welfare. The Foundation's award schemes support academic research in science, social science, and education for women and the elderly. In addition, the Foundation has set up various projects of its own, including the Nuffield Council on Bioethics (which it established with the Wellcome Trust and the Medical Research Council) and the Nuffield Curriculum Centre.

Royal Society

The Royal Society[84], established by a number of Royal Charters and a registered charity, is the national academy of science and supports science and technology through a variety of mechanisms, including fellowships, innovation schemes, research capacity and infrastructure schemes and mobility grant schemes. At the time of writing, the Society offers 19 different

---

81   For contact details see 'Contact information' at the end of this chapter.
82   For contact details see 'Contact information' at the end of this chapter.
83   For contact details see 'Contact information' at the end of this chapter.
84   For contact details see 'Contact information' at the end of this chapter.

funding schemes which fall under the headings listed above. The various funding schemes are all aimed at enhancing the UK science base and fostering collaboration between scientists based in the UK and those based abroad. The Royal Society supports the life and physical sciences, including engineering but excluding clinical medicine.

Wellcome Trust

The Wellcome Trust,[85] the world's largest medical research charity, provides funding for research and activities which have as their aim the protection and improvement of human and animal health. The Trust supports researchers based in the UK and abroad, and offers many types of fellowships and other funding sources in the fields of biomedical science and medical humanities. Funding is also available for technology transfer and public engagement projects, as well as capital funding which Trust offers for large-scale construction and refurbishment projects in the UK that support science.

UNIVERSITY RESEARCH AND CHARITABLE STATUS

Introduction

Universities in the UK have charitable status, since their activities are generally directed towards the advancement of education, one of the four main heads of charity traditionally recognised by English law.[86] Charitable status brings both advantages (for example, universities do not pay corporation tax) and responsibilities. The Charity Commission oversees the fulfilment of those responsibilities.[87]

The current definition of what is deemed to be 'charitable' is found in the Charities Act 2006,[88] although previous case law continues to be relevant.[89] Under the 2006 Act, it is necessary to be able to show that university research meets the criteria for being charitable: there is no longer an automatic presumption that such research is charitable.[90] It is particularly important to consider whether university research is charitable when that research is carried out in collaboration with a commercial sponsor.

---

85 For contact details see 'Contact information' at the end of this chapter.
86 The others being the relief of poverty, the advancement of religion, and other purposes beneficial to the community (*Income Tax Special Purpose Commissioners v Pemsel* [1891] AC 531).
87 See http://www.charitycommission.gov.uk.
88 Charities Act 2006, s 2; and para B2 of the guidance cited below.
89 *Analysis of the Law Underpinning Charities and Public Benefit* (Charity Commission, 2008), p ii: see www.charitycommission.gov.uk/library/publicbenefit/default.asp.
90 Charities Act 2006, s 3(2).

In 2009, the Charity Commission published guidance to help universities with such matters.[91] In this section we summarise that guidance as it relates to (i) university research projects; (ii) the role of university trustees; and (iii) university technology transfer companies.

University research projects

For university research to be considered charitable, it must be carried out (a) for a charitable purpose, such as the advancement of education, and (b) for the public benefit.[92] A university must also ensure that its activities are in furtherance of its charitable objects and in accordance with its constitutional and legal powers. The following is a summary of the Charity Commission's guidance on how universities should approach these issues.

A charitable purpose

First, the proposed research should be calculated to promote the university's charitable aims.[93] These may be set out formally in an objects clause in the university's charter or inferred from its practice over the years. A suitable charitable aim for a university would be the promotion of education and the advancement of knowledge and understanding for the public benefit. A university may act only in pursuance of its charitable aims: if a collaborative project is wider in scope than those aims, then, as far as that project is concerned, the university's resources should be used only on research that falls within those aims.[94] In order to advance knowledge or understanding, the research should be in an appropriate subject or directed towards an outcome that is of value, though it does not have to be of immediate practical application.[95]

The public benefit

Secondly, in order to be charitable, the proposed research must be carried out for the public benefit, that is, for the benefit of the public or a section of the public, and not solely or mainly for self-interest or for private or commercial consumption.[96] It should be possible to identify the public benefit that flows from the research, which should be related to the university's educational aims and not incidental to them. Any private benefits should be incidental.[97]

---

91 *Research by Higher Education Institutions* (Charity Commission, 2009), issued pursuant to Charities Act 2006, s 4: see www.charitycommission.gov.uk/supportingcharities/higherres. asp.
92 Charities Act 2006, s 2.
93 *Research by Higher Education Institutions* (Charity Commission, 2009), para C1.
94 *Research by Higher Education Institutions* (Charity Commission, 2009), para C3.
95 *Research by Higher Education Institutions* (Charity Commission, 2009), para C2.
96 See n 95.
97 *Research by Higher Education Institutions* (Charity Commission, 2009), para D1.

Generally, a university will meet the public benefit requirement by disseminating the knowledge gained, for example by publishing books or papers based on the research, or through teaching.[98] If the university needs to restrict access to the results to those who have sufficient reason to study them, the material should at least be catalogued and its existence made publicly known. Any charge for access should be reasonable and necessary (for example, to cover the costs of publication): a charge so high as to restrict the benefits of the research to those who can afford fees might call the charitable status of the research into question. Research that generates a significant profit should be handled through a non-charitable trading subsidiary.[99]

The results of research should be publicly disseminated within a reasonable time (normally six months) of being completed. The university should be able to show that any pre-publication access given exclusively to a sponsor is necessary, reasonable and in the interests of the university in the circumstances. If the research is intended to produce intellectual property that can be protected by registration, then registration itself may amount to adequate and appropriate dissemination.[100]

If the results of the research are not to be disseminated publicly, they should be applied or exploited practically for the public benefit, for example by licensing them so that they can be applied for public benefit and a financial return for the university. Where the university grants an exclusive licence which precludes publication or further dissemination of the results by the university, however, any non-charitable benefits must be legitimately incidental to the university's charitable aims.[101] Sponsored or contract research may count as charitable, even if not disseminated, if the university already undertakes related charitable research which the sponsored research might benefit. There should be appropriate arrangements to protect any intellectual property rights to be owned by the university, and adequate financial benefit.[102]

Any private benefits accruing to individuals or non-charitable or commercial entities should be legitimately incidental to the achievement of the university's charitable aims for the public benefit.[103] As already noted, the overall purpose of a research agreement between a university and a company may be wider than this, provided that the purpose and scope of the university's participation in the agreement is appropriate. The private benefits of the university's activity should be subsidiary and incidental to its charitable aims; they should be necessary (in furthering the aims by pursuing the research in question),

---

98 *Research by Higher Education Institutions* (Charity Commission, 2009), para C5.
99 See n 98.
100 See n 98.
101 See n 98.
102 See n 98.
103 *Research by Higher Education Institutions* (Charity Commission, 2009), para D2.

reasonable (in relative amounts), and in the interests of the university in the circumstances.[104]

This does not mean that the private benefit must always be small in absolute terms: in a multi-million-pound contract, it may be appropriate for some individuals and businesses to make a significant return in order to achieve the intended result for the public benefit. If, however, the private benefit is not a necessary and reasonable consequence of action taken for the furtherance of the university's charitable aims, then it is a non-charitable aim in its own right.[105] If non-charitable research is undertaken with the aim of raising funds to apply to the university's charitable aims, it may constitute a trade and should normally be channelled through a separate non-charitable trading company (see below at p 34).[106]

Any research undertaken for the Government or a political party should not champion the Government or that party or discredit another party, although the university may express support for particular policies which will facilitate its charitable purposes.[107]

The role of university trustees

This sectionsummarises the Charity Commission's guidelines as they relate to the way in which university trustees should carry out their duties.

University trustees should act in accordance with charity law and their constitutional powers. In deciding whether a university should undertake an activity, they should be able to make a connection between carrying out the university's aims within their own powers on the one hand and the anticipated outcomes of the activity on the other. In the case of research, such a connection must fall within the aims of the university, be for the public benefit, and be within their powers as trustees (see 'University research projects' above).[108]

In carrying out their responsibilities, university trustees should exercise reasonable diligence and care and act in good faith. They should ensure that any decision taken is legally sound and can be justified if challenged. They should make sure that they have adequately informed themselves in order to make the decision, taking all relevant factors into account and disregarding any irrelevant, improper or irrational factors. Any decision

---

104 See n 103.
105 See n 103.
106 *Research by Higher Education Institutions* (Charity Commission, 2009), para E6.
107 *Research by Higher Education Institutions* (Charity Commission, 2009), para C4.
108 *Research by Higher Education Institutions* (Charity Commission, 2009), para D3.

should be within the range of decisions that a reasonable body of trustees could have made.[109]

The trustees should take steps to manage any conflicts of interest that may arise, for example where a trustee's personal interests, or interests owed to another body, may influence his or her decision-making, or appear to do so.[110]

Of course, in practice the trustees will usually delegate decisions about research contracts to staff. Nevertheless, the trustees themselves remain responsible for ensuring that the correct decisions are made.[111] Hence it is important to have in place a proper procedure for delegating the authorisation of contracts: delegates, appointed by the trustees using powers available to them, should examine proposed contracts in detail and take professional advice about them as required. The procedure should ensure that contracts are authorised only if:

(a) the research is in an area which furthers the aims of the university;

(b) the research is for the public benefit (with any private benefit being incidental);

(c) the terms agreed by the university are reasonable in relation to the circumstances that could reasonably be known to the university at the time; and

(d) the university's interests are protected.

See 'University research projects' above for more detail on these points.[112]

Proper records should be kept of the decision-making process, especially of any exceptions made to the university's normal pricing policy or terms and conditions. Staff responsible for authorising contracts should be properly trained and supervised.[113]

After a contract is signed, its performance should be monitored, in order to demonstrate that the research conducted effectively furthers the university's aims. Research proposals and results should be evaluated so as to ensure quality, and there should be a process for ensuring that the research is carried out in a way that is well managed and cost-effective.[114]

The trustees have a duty to secure the protection of inventions capable of protection as intellectual property (IP), through patent or other appropriate means. The contract-approval process should ensure that the university's interests (whether in pre-existing or resulting IP) are protected, so that any

109 *Research by Higher Education Institutions* (Charity Commission, 2009), paras B3, D3, D4.
110 *Research by Higher Education Institutions* (Charity Commission, 2009), para D3.
111 See n 110.
112 *Research by Higher Education Institutions* (Charity Commission, 2009), paras D3–D5.
113 *Research by Higher Education Institutions* (Charity Commission, 2009), para D5.
114 *Research by Higher Education Institutions* (Charity Commission, 2009), para D3.

IP can be used to further the university's aims or to maximise the revenue that the university will receive.[115] If the university is carrying out charitable research on behalf of a commercial body, it should share in any return on the exploitation of the resulting IP even if it does not own it. Any IP owned by the university that is not required for its own research should, where possible, be exploited for the university's benefit, for example by licensing or selling it.[116]

There should be procedures in place to ensure that any non-charitable research is carried out in accordance with the rules and guidelines on non-charitable trading.[117] This would normally be through a non-charitable trading subsidiary of the university:[118] any resulting IP to be used by the sponsor (whether by transfer or licence) should be made available in return for a proper market consideration.[119] However, where the use of IP by a non-charitable company furthers the aims of the university for the public benefit, and such use is enforceable under an agreement between the parties, the university is not required to charge full, or any, value. However the use of the IP to further charitable purposes must fall within the aims and powers of the university and any private benefit should be incidental.[120]

University technology transfer companies

This section summarises the Charity Commission's guidance on the relationship between a university and a subsidiary technology transfer company or spin-out.

In setting up a technology transfer company, the university should first check that it has power to incorporate a non-charitable company and to invest in it.[121] Secondly, in order to be able to use its charitable resources to support a spin-out in conducting research that is non-charitable, the university should ensure that the proposal fulfils one of the following criteria:

- *either* there should be a reasonable prospect of the venture leading to wider public benefit and so furthering the university's charitable work;

- or the use of the university's resources for the company should be justifiable as a prudent investment in the university's interests: the university should have a good reason to undertake the venture as a fundraising activity.[122]

---

115 *Research by Higher Education Institutions* (Charity Commission, 2009), paras C7, D3.
116 *Research by Higher Education Institutions* (Charity Commission, 2009), para C7.
117 *Research by Higher Education Institutions* (Charity Commission, 2009), para B1.
118 *Research by Higher Education Institutions* (Charity Commission, 2009), para C1.
119 *Research by Higher Education Institutions* (Charity Commission, 2009), para C7.
120 See n 119.
121 *Research by Higher Education Institutions* (Charity Commission, 2009), para E1.
122 *Research by Higher Education Institutions* (Charity Commission, 2009), para C6.

The trustees must make a fully informed decision with the university's best interests as their sole consideration.[123]

Any private benefit to the participators should be incidental to the university's aims, the university's interests (for example, in any resulting intellectual property) should be properly secured, and any facilities made available to the company should be at proper market value under a formal arm's-length arrangement. Finally, the trustees should be persuaded that making research resources available to the spin-out would not adversely affect the university's continuing work in pursuit of its charitable aims.[124]

REPRESENTATIVE BODIES

The growth of the technology transfer sector has also led to organisations being formed to represent the interests of those organisations that create the relevant technology in the UK. The following is an outline of the key organisations.

The Russell Group[125]

The Russell Group represents the 20 universities[126] that carry out the most research in the UK. The Group is primarily a lobbying group aimed at ensuring that the research activities of UK universities are recognised and properly funded. The Russell Group has grown from an informal group to one that has its own legal structure and a small staff involved in policy and publicity work.

PraxisUnico

PraxisUnico[127] is a membership organisation for those involved in technology transfer at UK universities and other research organisations. Its primary

---

123 *Research by Higher Education Institutions* (Charity Commission, 2009), para E1.
124 See n 123.
125 Named after the London hotel where the representatives of the university first met.
126 The members of the Russell Group are the University of Birmingham, the University of Bristol, the University of Cambridge, Cardiff University, the University of Edinburgh, the University of Glasgow, Imperial College London, King's College London, the University of Leeds, the University of Liverpool, the London School of Economics and Political Science, the University of Manchester, Newcastle University, the University of Nottingham, the University of Oxford, Queen's University Belfast, the University of Sheffield, the University of Southampton, University College London and the University of Warwick.
127 PraxisUnico was formed in 2009 on the merger of Praxis and UNICO; Praxis was involved mainly in providing technology transfer-type training courses; UNICO stood for Universities Companies Association.

purpose is to provide information[128] and training on aspects of the legal, technical and practical processes involved in commercially exploiting intellectual property within the research organisation. It also carries out some representational and policy work.

Its membership includes all the members of the Russell Group, most other UK universities ,[129] many research councils[130] and relevant governmental/regulatory organisations, plus some overseas organisations.

According to its own figures, more than 97 per cent of UK university research funding is spent in PraxisUnico member institutions.

AURIL

The Association for University Research and Industry Links (AURIL)[131] is a membership organisation whose members are not only universities and research organisations but individuals who work in such organisations, and like PraxisUnico is a forum for exchange of information and provision of training. AURIL work is more directed towards those involved in the creation and development of technology and intellectual property rather than the mechanics of commercialisation. It has a membership of 1,600, drawn from universities, NHS Trusts and public-sector research establishments.

AURIL was instrumental in the creation of the Institute of Knowledge Transfer, which will serve to further enhance the professional recognition of the sector and of those working within it. The Institute has now been incorporated.

Overseas organisations

There are many non-UK organisations involved in the technology transfer sector. Two of the most notable are:

---

128   The information includes guides on various types of deals and agreements, with specific guidance relevant to those involved in technology transfer at universities and research organisations, written by Mark Anderson and members of Anderson & Company.

129   In this category membership is sometimes for the university's company(ies) involved in technology transfer rather than the university itself.

130   For example, Biotechnology & Biological Sciences Research Council, Economic & Social Research Council, Engineering & Physical Sciences Research Council, Natural Environment Research Council, Roslin Institute, Moredun Research Institute, Institute for Animal Health and Science & Technology Facilities Council.

131   AURIL standards for the Association of University Research & Industry Links.

The Association of European Science & Technology Trade Professionals (ASTP)[132] – the primary pan-European organisation; it has more than 600 members in 38 countries, with most of the members working in universities and other research organisations.

The Association of University Technology Managers (AUTM)[133] – the predominant US organisation; it can best be understood as the US equivalent of PraxisUnico, although on a much larger scale, with over 3,500 members.

THE ROLE OF LAWYERS IN TECHNOLOGY TRANSFER AGREEMENTS AND ACTIVITIES

General

Drafting, negotiating and advising on technology transfer agreements has been a niche area for lawyers. The mainstream of commercial transactions has been in higher-profile areas such as mergers and acquisitions, private equity or commercial property.

The same may be said of published precedent material and legal texts. There have been (until recently) fewer published precedents for technology transfer agreements than for many other types of commercial agreement. There are fewer books for lawyers on the law in this area than in many other areas of law. Reported cases on the interpretation of contracts are very rarely concerned with technology transfer agreements compared with, say, shipping or insurance contracts.

The obvious reason is an economic one: until recently very few technology transfer agreements were as economically significant as eg a contract for the charter of a ship, the leasing of a fleet of aircraft or portfolio of commercial property. Nowadays, the pecking order may be changing, but it may take the law some years to catch up. In the meantime, the number of lawyers who are advising on technology transfer agreements is rapidly increasing.

Factors influencing when to use a lawyer

There is a real problem in deciding *when* to use lawyers in the negotiation of a technology transfer agreement. Take the example of an agreement to provide research services. With most types of commercial contract, the price to be paid under the contract may provide a rough measure of whether and when to involve lawyers in the negotiation process. It is relatively easy to decide that the sale of a business for, say, £10 million must involve the extensive use of corporate lawyers in drafting, negotiating and advising on the agreement.

---

132   The Association of European Science & Technology Transfer Professionals.
133   The Association of University Technology Managers

It is less easy to make this judgement with many technology transfer agreements. First, there may not be a direct correlation between the price to be paid under the contract (particularly any up-front payments) and the potential future value of the contract. For example, many R&D agreements, although considered important, involve a relatively modest 'price', eg in the range £50,000 to £200,000, and may not be thought able to support significant legal fees. A typical example of this might be an agreement with a university to conduct a £120,000 research programme over three years. This might, inter alia, fund a post-doctoral research worker to work full time on the research programme. The payment structure will not generally provide a large profit to the university.

Other R&D agreements involve much larger sums. An example of this might be an agreement to conduct large-scale, multi-centre, clinical trials of a pharmaceutical drug, involving payments of tens of millions of pounds over several years.

There may be a reluctance to involve lawyers, or to involve them fully, in a £10 million R&D agreement, which would not be encountered in a £10 million business-sale agreement. There may be any number of reasons for this: perhaps R&D agreements are considered to be more 'co-operative' and straightforward than some types of agreement and therefore less reliant on legal advice. The negotiation of the R&D agreement may be the responsibility of a research director rather than (with some other types of agreement) a commercial director or finance director, and this may account for a rather different (and sometimes more constructive) attitude to the negotiation process. In some instances the project budget will not have been drawn up to include realistic amounts for legal advice. Perhaps more significant is the fact that so many R&D agreements (and technology transfer agreements generally) are concerned with potential value, rather than real, present value. If the R&D programme is successful, it may result in the generation of commercial products. If this happens, with hindsight the parties may wish to have in place a detailed, carefully worded agreement that has received the full input of specialist lawyers. However, at the time the R&D agreement is negotiated, it may be difficult to predict whether it will result in commercially valuable products, processes or intellectual property. The price to be charged for the R&D services may not provide a useful guide to how 'important' the agreement is: a significant breakthrough could come from a relatively small contract.

Some universities, research charities and companies enter into large numbers of research contracts, and feel they cannot justify spending large amounts of time and money in negotiating every one of those contracts. After all, only some of the contracts are likely to result in the marketing of successful, new products. Other research will 'fall by the wayside'.

Many of the above points can also be made about technology that a university or company has developed which is to be licensed.

A further complicating factor, less prominent at the time the previous edition was prepared, has been the work done to create widely available, professionally drafted precedents. Perhaps the most notable examples are the Lambert agreements, which include a range of R&D and consortium agreements with detailed commentary and guidance.[134] Also, for those primarily involved in technology transfer in universities and research organisations, there are guides and precedents available from the organisation set up to represent them, PraxisUnico. These can also influence the decision on whether, and the extent to which, an organisation will want to use a legal adviser (particularly on deals deemed to be of smaller scale or more speculative as to their potential value).[135]

In light of these factors, what level of involvement should the legal adviser propose to his client? One approach is to decide that this is a commercial decision for the client, and that it is not for his lawyer to second-guess that commercial decision. The client will seek advice when he or she is ready to do so.

For some experienced clients, this approach may work, but in many cases it is not the most helpful approach to take. Technology transfer agreements can involve some complex issues, particularly in relation to the management and commercialisation of intellectual property. There is a danger of the client involving his lawyer too early or too late. Too early, and legal bills may become disproportionate. Too late, and the opportunity to help shape the deal to take account of intellectual property and other legal issues may be reduced or lost.

The following approach is suggested, based on past experience of negotiating many types of technology transfer agreement, both small and large:

- At least some involvement should be proposed right from the outset, in order to assist the client to focus on issues that are likely

---

134 http://www.innovation.gov.uk/lambertagreements/index.asp. There are also patent and know-how licences, confidentiality agreements etc; see http://www.innovation.gov.uk/lambertagreements/index.asp?lvl1=2&lvl2=0&lvl3=0&lvl4=0.

135 The danger of using 'standard' precedents is that they are used unthinkingly or without understanding fully or properly their meaning and implications. The use of computer technology permits easy assembly of agreements drawn from different sources. The dangers of such an approach has been shown in a number of cases, and most strikingly perhaps in a case which was reported at the time material for this edition was completed, *Oxonica Energy Limited v Neuftec Limited* [2009] EWCA Civ 668 (see 'On what are royalties payable?' in Ch 10. In this case, the result of not thinking through the meaning of defined terms meant that a spin-out company of Oxford University was liable to pay more royalties then it envisaged.

to arise, eg in relation to intellectual property.[136] If a Heads of Agreement, Letter of Intent, Term Sheet or similar is to be signed, recommend being involved in the drafting of that document.

- Advise the client on any draft agreements that are received from the other side in the negotiations. If your client is to prepare the draft agreement, make sure they are using an appropriate precedent[137] or, if it is an important transaction, draft the agreement yourself.

- You may or may not be involved directly at all stages in the negotiation of the draft agreement. 'Behind the scenes' drafting work may be all that is required or can be justified financially.

- Try to make sure that you are asked to advise on the entire document, not just particular clauses (sometimes easier said than done).[138]

- Be flexible about allowing the client to propose wording or keep a copy of the draft agreement on their computer. The review and compare functions on modern word-processing programmes allow the changes others (including the client) have made to be viewed. Do not do what some organisations do, and refuse to send out draft agreements by email or provide them only as pdf files (ie files that cannot be altered).

Whilst it is not normally necessary for the lawyer advising on such an agreement to understand the detailed science, it is necessary for him or her to understand, in outline, what work is to be done and what is the likely outcome if the work is successful. Ideally, of course, one would use a lawyer who had a perfect understanding of the science, all relevant areas of law, and experience of the type of transaction under consideration. In practice, it is probably more important to use a lawyer who has a good understanding of commercial and IP law and some limited understanding of the science, rather than the other way around. Unlike in

---

136 A modern approach is for the lawyer to prepare a detailed list of issues which is provided to the client, so that the client can be aware of and go through all the relevant issues which arise commonly in certain types of transaction or in particular types of document. Such a document can also be drafted to include the default position of the client on a number of topics, so that when a client looks at a document or an issue is raised the client can know what the default response is. Further refinements include suggested alternatives, which are in line with the client's default position, but are responses to a point or negotiating strategy put forward by the other side.

137 Where the lawyer has prepared the precedent, a modern approach is to provide a detailed commentary to help the client understand not only the wording used but also the context in which it is used and how the specific wording relates to the rest of the precedent.

138 Or at least see the whole agreement to make sure that any advice given on a particular clause is relevant to the agreement.

the case of IP litigation, understanding the detailed science is not usually so critical for the lawyer advising on a technology transfer agreement.[139]

It is, however, desirable that the lawyer should have some experience of advising on technology transfer agreements. Such experience should also extend to the industry sector covered by the agreement. Some of the most prestigious firms of commercial law solicitors in the UK have relatively little experience of such agreements. Or, where they do have relevant experience, are used to dealing with more complex types of agreements, where complicated corporate and financial structures are involved. That is, they cannot 'think small'.

Many technology transfer agreements are factually complex. Often, the agreement will need to be tailored to meet the actual circumstances, with the result that the final document may be significantly different to the precedent on which it is based. This is not to say that precedents are not useful, but they will often need to be adapted. Lawyers in this field probably spend longer getting to grips with the factual background than in some other areas of commercial law.

Drafting the agreement

There is no convention as to which party should draft a technology transfer agreement. Generally, there is much to be said for the party with the greater experience of technology transfer agreements preparing the first draft. Many universities have technology transfer or research contracts offices that are experienced in the preparation of such agreements. Some companies are highly experienced in drafting such agreements and may have in-house lawyers specialising in this area.

There is a wide variation in the quality of the agreements that are encountered. Moreover, as many technology transfer agreements are between parties based in different countries, there is also wide variation in agreement styles. As with many types of commercial agreement, the North American agreements tend to be the most detailed and wordy, whilst Continental European agreements are sometimes very brief. In some areas, more uniform types of document are emerging. Thus, simple confidentiality agreements (or CDAs) to enable scientific disclosures are often similar to one another, at least in the issues

---

139 Often it can be helpful to have a discussion with a scientist or academic who is an expert on the technical subject matter of the agreement. He or she will have the most up-to-date information not only about the technical subject matter, but usually will also know all the steps involved in getting to the point where the technical subject matter is ready for protection, licensing or assignment. Getting information direct from the scientist/academic can sometimes lead to a greater understanding than going through the lawyer's contact at the client, who might be the contract negotiator or drafter, and may not have a detailed knowledge of the subject matter (ie a filter is removed).

that they tend to address. Even here, though, it is surprising how often the documents that one encounters miss some key element (such as a restriction on use, as distinct from disclosure, of the information) or fail to define clearly the purpose for which the information may be used by the recipient.

Negotiating the agreement

The negotiating teams for technology transfer agreements vary, but should generally include at least one person with understanding of the science involved, a commercial representative (who may be the same person) and a lawyer. Some routine agreements are negotiated without legal advice. Where lawyers are involved, they sometimes front all aspects of the negotiations, but it is equally common to find that the commercial representative takes the lead, particularly in the early stages of negotiations, with support from their lawyer. The areas where legal advice is most often sought are on intellectual property issues and liability issues,[140] and the lawyer is often asked to lead the negotiations on these technically complex areas.

As has already been mentioned, a co-operative negotiating approach will often be thought more appropriate for technology transfer agreements than a more 'hard-nosed' style. In the author's experience, the negotiations sometimes run more smoothly where senior scientists from each party take an active role and interest in the negotiations, rather than leaving it all to their commercial and legal colleagues. At the time the negotiations are taking place, the scientists will generally be enthusiastic about the proposed technology transfer and working with the other party, and this enthusiasm and spirit of co-operation may help to carry the negotiations forward. Of course, this will depend partly on the personalities of the scientists involved: some scientists prefer to stay out of commercial negotiations.

Legal costs

It is usual for each party to bear its own legal costs in relation to the drafting and negotiating of technology transfer agreements. Some occasional exceptions to this include:

(a)   where a company or institution enters into an agreement with an individual, wants that individual to take legal advice, and agrees to pay for that advice; and

(b)   where the technology transfer agreement forms part of a financing deal (eg investment in a high-tech company by a venture capitalist), and the party providing the finance has the bargaining strength to insist on its legal costs being covered by the party receiving the finance.

However, these exceptions are not frequently encountered.

---

140   Such as warranties, exclusion from and restrictions on liability and indemnities.

Other costs that might be viewed as 'legal costs' arising in connection with a technology transfer agreement include:

(a) patent prosecution, renewal and infringement costs (and the agreement may specify who is responsible for these costs); and

(b) taxes on payments made under the agreement. The main tax issues that may need to be addressed include:

  (i) whether there will be any withholding of corporation tax on payments under the 'withholding tax' rules;

  (ii) whether payments are inclusive or exclusive of VAT; and

  (iii) whether stamp duty is payable and, if so, who should pay it. Stamp duty is less of an issue in the UK, with its abolition in relation to intellectual property assignments.[141]

CONTACT INFORMATION

Association of Medical Research Charities
61 Gray's Inn Road
London WC1X 8TL
Tel: 020 7269 8820
Fax: 020 7269 8821
www.amrc.org.uk

Cancer Research UK
PO Box 123
Lincoln's Inn Fields
London WC2A 3PX
Tel: 020 7242 0200
Fax: 020 7121 6700
www.cancerresearchuk.org

Gatsby Charitable Foundation
Allington House (1st Floor)
150 Victoria Street
London SW1E 5AE
Tel: 020 7410 0330
www.gatsby.org.uk

National Endowment for Science,
Technology and the Arts (NESTA)
1 Plough Place
London EC4A 1DE
Tel: 0207 438 2500
Fax: 0207 438 2501
www.nesta.org.uk

The Wellcome Trust
Gibbs Building
215 Euston Road
London NW1 2BE, UK
Tel: 020 7611 8888
Fax: 020 7611 8545
www.wellcome.ac.uk

The British Academy
10 Carlton House Terrace
London SW1Y 5AH
Tel: 020 7969 5200
Fax: 020 7969 5300
www.britac.ac.uk

The Leverhulme Trust
1 Pemberton Row
London EC4A 3BG
Tel: 020 7042 9873 (for enquiries about outline applications)
www.leverhulme.org.uk

The Nuffield Foundation
28 Bedford Square
London WC1B 3EG
Tel: 020 7631 0566
Fax: 020 7323 4577
www.nuffieldfoundation.org

141 See further Ch 17.

The Royal Society
6-9 Carlton House Terrace
London
SW1Y 5AG
Tel: 020 7451 2500
www.royalsociety.org

BBSRC
Polaris House
North Star Avenue
Swindon
Wiltshire SN2 1UH
Tel: 01793 413 200
Fax: 01793 414 201
www.bbsrc.ac.uk

ESRC
Polaris House
North Star Avenue
Swindon
Wiltshire SN2 1UJ
Tel: 01793 413 000
Fax: 01793 413 001
www.esrcsocietytoday.ac.uk

NERC
Polaris House
North Star Avenue
Swindon SN2 1EU
Tel: 01793 411 500
Fax: 01793 411 501
www.nerc.ac.uk

The Russell Group
1 Northumberland Avenue
Trafalgar Square
London WC2N 5BW
Tel: 020 7872 5802
www.russellgroup.ac.uk

AURIL
3rd Floor
10 Fleet Place
Limeburner Lane
London, EC4M 7
Tel: 028 9097 2589
Fax: 028 9097 2570
www.auril.org.uk

AUTM
UTM Headquarters
111 Deer Lake Road, Suite 100
Deerfield, IL 60015
Tel: 847.559.0846
Fax: 847.480.9282
www.autm.net

The British Heart Foundation
Greater London House
180 Hampstead Road
London NW1 7AW
Tel: 020 7554 0000
www.bhf.org.uk

EPSRC
Polaris House
North Star Avenue
Swindon
Wiltshire SN2 1ET
Tel: 01793 444 000
Fax: 01793 444 010
www.epsrc.ac.uk

MRC
20 Park Crescent
London W1B 1AL
Tel: 020 7636 5422
Fax: 02074366179
www.mrc.ac.uk

STFC
Polaris House
North Star Avenue
Swindon
Wiltshire SN2 1SZ
Tel: 01793 442000
www.scitech.ac.uk

UNICO
St John's Innovation Centre
Cowley Road
Cambridge CB4 0WS
Tel: 01223–422098
Fax: 01223–420844
www.unico.org.uk

ASTP
Koninginnegracht 22C
2514 AB The Hague
The Netherlands
Tel: +31 (0)70 3926374
Fax: +31 (0)70 3926375
www.astp.net

CHAPTER 2

Drafting Technology Transfer Agreements

THE LEGAL FRAMEWORK

This chapter discusses some practical issues that arise when drafting technology transfer and related agreements – including legal, practice and commercial points.

For this purpose, 'technology transfer agreements' include agreements relating to licensing or assigning intellectual property, or the carrying out of research and development. Specific types of technology transfer agreement are discussed under 'Types of agreement' below.

Drafting technology transfer agreements, and taking them through the negotiation process to final signature by the parties, requires a range of skills and experience, including:

- **Commercial** – knowing what commercial terms to put into the agreement and what commercial risks the organisation is willing to accept.

- **Legal** – understanding the relevant principles and provisions of law to make the agreement legally binding, ensuring appropriate legal obligations on the parties (based on instructions on deal terms and risk from a commercial colleague), knowing the legal meaning of particular expressions and wording used, and (seeking to) achieve the right interpretation by the court or arbitrator.

- **Drafting** – knowing how to write the provisions of the contract so that they are clear, usable and say what the parties intend.[1]

- **Negotiating** – having the right blend of interpersonal skills and experience to interact with colleagues and representatives of the other party, advance the negotiations, and achieve a mutually acceptable signed agreement.

Technology transfer agreements are drafted and negotiated by people with different professional backgrounds, including lawyers, patent agents, accountants, scientists, commercial executives and general managers. There is a wide variety in the level of formal training that such people have in the skills mentioned above. Some people are happy to 'learn on the job', which some may regard as acceptable for commercial and negotiating skills, but is certainly not appropriate for a legal adviser nor, it is suggested, for the contract drafter. Some technology transfer managers, particularly in universities and

---

1   The case of *Oxonica Energy Limited v Neuftec Limited* [2009] EWCA Civ 668 which was reported just as material for this book was written is a good recent illustration of a contract which did not express the intentions that the parties intended.

research organisations, are expected to combine all of the above skills and more, often without formal legal or drafting training.[2]

This chapter provides a checklist of matters that are frequently encountered in the drafting, negotiation and execution of technology transfer agreements. The list is not intended to be comprehensive as to topics or in the level of discussion.[3] Negotiating and general contract-drafting techniques are outside the scope of this book. For more detailed discussion of some of the points mentioned in this chapter and general consideration of drafting and negotiating commercial contracts, readers should consult books dealing with these subjects.[4]

The main part of this book comprises a summary and discussion of legal issues that are relevant to technology transfer. The following sections provide a high-level overview of some legal points that often need to be considered when drafting a technology transfer agreement, and on which legal advice may need to be sought. Most of these points are covered in more detail in other chapters.

Intellectual property and other property laws

Intellectual property issues are at the heart of many technology transfer agreements; some of those issues are discussed in later sections of this chapter. In order to draft and negotiate intellectual property provisions that address those issues, it is important to be familiar with the legal framework of intellectual property laws, including laws that are directly relevant to commercial transactions. Examples include:

- how intellectual property can be licensed and assigned;

- the rights of licensees and assignees;

- the law on co-ownership of intellectual property;

- employee rights to intellectual property;

---

2   The position is changing with regard to persons working in university and research organisations, with extensive training on offer, including negotiating, drafting and interpreting technology transfer agreements, from PraxisUnico and Auril (see Ch 1 under 'Representative bodies').

3   Valuation techniques and taxation are dealt with in Chs 16 and 17 respectively.

4   For example: Anderson and Warner, *Drafting and Negotiating Commercial Contracts* (2nd edn, Tottel Publishing, 2007); Anderson and Warner, *A–Z Guide to Boilerplate and Commercial Clauses* (2nd edn, Tottel Publishing (now Bloomsbury Professional), 2006); Anderson (ed), *Drafting Agreements in the Biotechnology and Pharmaceutical Industries* (looseleaf, Oxford University Press); Anderson and Keevey-Kothari, *Drafting Confidentiality Agreements* (2nd edn, Law Society Publishing, 2004); and Anderson and Warner, *Execution of Documents* (2nd edn, Law Society Publishing, 2008).

- who is the first owner of intellectual property, particularly where intellectual property is commissioned.

It is also important for the technology transfer lawyer to be familiar with certain aspects of general property law which underpin specific provisions of intellectual property laws, eg how more than one person owns property (eg as 'joint tenants' or 'tenants in common') and what implied binding promises a seller of intellectual property makes (eg 'full title guarantee') unless agreed otherwise. Separately, it may be necessary to consider personal property laws in relation to the provision of materials, eg under a material transfer agreement (where one person has possession of the materials supplied by another person, but the other person retains ownership – the law of bailment).

Despite (international) efforts at standardising intellectual property laws,[5] they vary from country to country, and it is useful to have at least a general awareness of some of the differences in those laws between countries when drafting or negotiating a technology transfer agreement. For example, in the case of intellectual property generated by a German inventor, it may be necessary to undertake due diligence on whether the inventor or his employer is the owner of the intellectual property. Whilst this may be an important exercise in most countries, it is particularly important in Germany in view of the distinctive arrangements for employee ownership of inventions under German law.

Contract and commercial laws

Technology transfer agreements are examples of contracts. Contract law is of fundamental importance when determining the legal effect of a contractual document, including whether it is legally binding and how its provisions will be interpreted by a court. To take a couple of common examples:

- will the contract's limitation of liability clause be upheld by the court, in light of the Unfair Contract Terms Act 1977; and

- is there 'consideration' in the agreement, to make it a legally binding contract?

To draft legally effective contracts it is important to have a solid grounding in contract law. This book assumes that the reader is already familiar with basic contract law.

Other areas of commercial law (ie other than contract law) may also be relevant. For example, when drafting an entire agreement clause it is important to be familiar with the law on misrepresentation, which is part of the law of tort.

If the agreement is with a consumer, consumer protection laws will need to be considered; these laws may significantly affect the terms that should be

---

5   Eg, see Ch 3 under 'National and international intellectual property laws: current laws and proposals'.

included in the agreement. A large number of consumer protection laws have been introduced in the UK in recent years, most of them originating in EU Regulations or Directives. However, most technology transfer agreements are not with consumers.

This book does not attempt to cover all areas of commercial law that could be relevant in a dispute over a contract, and instead focuses on features of the law that are specific to technology transfer agreements or have distinctive features when the agreement under consideration involves technology transfer. One of the most useful (and unique) parts of this book, in the authors' opinion, is the discussion of English case law on the interpretation of intellectual property licence agreements, which appears in Chapter 10.

Competition law

Care needs to be taken to ensure that the technology transfer agreement does not contain any terms that are likely to be in breach of Article 81 of the EC Treaty (renumbered as Article 101 by the Lisbon Treaty) and equivalent domestic UK law. In international transactions, it may also be necessary to consider other countries' competition laws (eg US antitrust law).

Competition law is one of the subjects that a technology transfer lawyer will always have in the back of the mind whenever an agreement is prepared. Some small-scale agreements that do not include any so-called 'hardcore' (ie particularly restrictive) anti-competitive terms may need only a cursory competition law review. Other agreements, including intellectual property licence agreements, may require more detailed analysis. Often, the most efficient way to tackle EU competition law issues is to analyse whether the terms of the agreement fit within the scope of a 'block exemption Regulation'. Agreements that fit within a block exemption Regulation are automatically exempted from Article 81 (101) of the EC Treaty.

It will generally not be possible to 'contract out' of a country's competition laws, by specifying a different law of the contract. For example, in the case of a licence agreement where the licensed territory includes the UK, the fact that the licence agreement is made between US parties and made under US law will not avoid the operation of UK competition law.[6]

Regulatory issues

There are many kinds of regulatory issue, including the following:

- For UK universities, does the agreement (and the activities to be performed and payments to be made under the agreement) form part

6   *Chiron v Organon* [1993] FSR 567.

of the university's charitable activities?[7] If not, might the agreement prejudice the university's charitable and tax-exempt status? For US universities, do the terms of the agreement comply with the Bayh-Dole Act, and with relevant state laws (particularly in the case of state universities)?

- For pharmaceutical companies, are the activities under the agreement to be performed in accordance with relevant regulatory requirements, eg for the development of new medicines or medical devices?

- Across many industries, is the agreement consistent with regulations concerning health and safety, the use of human and animal materials and tissue, the use of personal data, and is export of particular technologies or equipment permitted?

- If a company is seeking investment (eg by way of subscription for shares) as part of a technology transfer activity, regulations on the conduct of investment activities may need to be followed, eg in relation to any proposal documents that are circulated.

- If one or more parties to the agreement are listed on a Stock Exchange, it may be necessary to comply with the regulations of that Stock Exchange or listing authority. For example, if a party is listed in the US, it will be required to provide a copy of all 'material contracts' to the Securities and Exchange Commission, which will place them on a public file that can be searched via the internet.

Many technology transfer agreements concern activities in regulated industries. The drafting and negotiating team will often include someone who is familiar with the relevant regulations, and can advise on whether and how they should be reflected in the terms of the agreement. Even where the agreement concerns an activity which is regulated, it may be necessary to register the agreement, the parties or some other element of the deal or relationship between the parties if the agreement is carried out in another country.

Taxation and currency issues[8]

The UK government has favoured technology transfer activities with various tax incentives and concessions in recent years, including:

- R&D tax credits;

- income tax treatment of shares held by academic inventors in spin-out companies;

---

7   See Ch 1 under 'University research and charitable status'.
8   Taxation issues are discussed in detail in Ch 17.

- reduced corporation tax rate for patent income (announced in the 2009 Pre-Budget Report).

Less favourable to taxpayers has been the year-on-year general tightening of tax rules, to the point where many traditional tax saving schemes are no longer effective.

Other areas of tax that may need to be considered when structuring technology transfer agreements include:

- in contracts with universities and other charities, whether the subject matter of the agreement is charitable and therefore tax-exempt;

- whether VAT is chargeable on payments;

- whether income/corporation tax on the payment must be withheld by the payer, under withholding tax rules (usually applicable mainly to licence payments);

- particularly in intra-group agreements, the effect of transfer pricing rules.

In international technology transfer agreements, if the payer is based in a country with exchange controls, this may affect the ability of the payer to transfer contractual payments to the other party. Licence agreements often include a provision dealing with this issue.

BOILERPLATE AND COMMERCIAL CLAUSES

Parties

Care should be taken to identify the parties correctly, with their full name, country or State of incorporation, and address.

There is a risk management question as to whether the other party has the necessary financial resources to meet its obligations and any associated liabilities, and therefore whether it is appropriate to enter into a contract with that party. It is usually the commercial representative's responsibility to determine this question, although sometimes the finance department takes responsibility for financial due diligence checks.

Where the other party is a member of a group of companies, and is not the parent company, another issue is whether to insist on the parent company being the contracting party, or being an additional party to give a 'parent company guarantee'. This assumes that the parent company is considered to have sufficient assets to meet its contractual liabilities, but the subsidiary does not.

Stating the name and status of a party in detail may 'flag up' any issues that may arise in relation to their capacity to enter into contracts and which may need to be investigated further;[9] for example if a party is an unincorporated trust, whether it has the legal capacity to enter into a contract of the type contemplated. To avoid uncertainty, the company's registration number is sometimes stated as, unlike a company's name, this will not change.[10] The status of each party should be stated if not obvious from its full name; for example, whether:

- it is a company (in the UK, limited, plc or limited by guarantee);

- it is a partnership (a limited liability partnership, or an 'old' type of unincorporated partnership, and in this latter case it is conventional to describe it as 'a firm' in the contract); or

- it is incorporated by Royal Charter (as is the case for many UK universities).

Academics: in the case of academic inventors or academics who carry out consultancy work, it is not always clear whether the academic is permitted to enter into contracts personally, or whether someone from the university's central administration or section (or company) which deals with consultancy work should sign. Sometimes academics purport to sign agreements on behalf of the institution when they do not have authority to do so. It may be desirable to check the institution's policy on these matters.

In some types of agreement, such as a clinical trials agreement or a materials transfer agreement with a hospital or university, the hospital or university and at least the lead academic/researcher/doctor may be named as parties. For example, individual researchers may be named as a party in order to give some express warranty that they will comply with some requirements or undertake some confidentiality obligations. Sometimes they are joined to the agreement simply to ensure that the individual researcher who is to receive materials is made aware of the obligations to keep the materials separately from others or to maintain confidentiality. The reasons for joining someone as a party should be clearly stated in the document. Where an individual is a party, their home address, rather than their office address, should usually be stated.

Academic departments: the name of a large organisation, whether commercial or academic, may not identify the relevant department or section. For example, a university may have a policy that only the main address of the university is used, but notices or communications sent to the central address may not reach the person or department who is actually performing the agreement (or may only reach the right person too late). It may therefore be appropriate

---

9   And there is sometimes the practical issue that the person negotiating an agreement from one party may not be aware of who in the group of companies actually enters into an agreement.

10   This is certainly the position in the UK, but may not be true in all countries where companies have numbers.

to include the name and address of the department or section in the parties' clause, as in the following example:

> **University of Shillingford**, incorporated in the United Kingdom by Royal Charter, acting through its Department of Physics, whose address is 76 Wallingford Road, Shillingford, Oxon OX10 7EU ('UOS').

Group companies: with many large organisations it may not be easy to identify the contracting party. For example, a pharmaceutical or biotech company may be organised into a large number of group and subsidiary companies with very similar names, or during negotiations, representatives of organisations may not indicate which subsidiary they represent. As the names of subsidiaries may change frequently, it is advisable to include the company's registration number in the parties' clause.

Divisions of companies: large companies sometimes trade under the name of a division of the company that has no separate legal status. For example, the division may refer to itself as Mega Pharmaceuticals, and may employ thousands of people in several countries; nevertheless it is part of Mega Corporation and has no separate legal status. Although the contract should refer to Mega Corporation as the contracting party, it may be politic to refer to it in the parties clause as 'Mega Corporation acting through its Mega Pharmaceuticals division'.

Parties outside the UK

When dealing with foreign parties, it may be useful to identify their status and how they correspond (if at all) to UK company and other structures; for example, the German 'GmbH' or French 'S.A.R.L' is equivalent to a private limited company.

With respect to the US, as each state has its own law as regards the incorporation of a company, it is important to indicate the state in which a US corporation is incorporated. This may be a different state to the company's headquarters. Many US corporations are incorporated in Delaware but have headquarters or their principal place of business elsewhere. If a US corporation does not indicate in which state it is located, and a dispute occurs, then the UK party may have difficulty locating the state in which it is registered. In some US states (for example Delaware), corporations can be incorporated as limited liability companies or limited liability partnerships; the correct terminology should be used in each case.

Recitals

Recitals, also known as 'whereas' clauses, 'background' clauses or 'preamble', are not essential in English law agreements (and are usually not binding on the parties to the agreement). They are mostly used to provide a short summary of the transaction. Care should be taken not to include any substantive obligations in the Recitals, or any wording that may conflict with the wording of the main agreement (eg when describing a licence that is to be granted under the agreement).[11] Therefore, Recitals should generally be short and bland.

In some countries, eg in civil code countries in Europe, Recitals tend to be more detailed than they are in agreements drafted by English lawyers. Part of the function of Recitals in such jurisdictions may be to explain the nature of the agreement so that it can be placed in a recognised category under the civil code. Once so categorised, terms may be implied into the agreement under the civil code.

Definitions

Technology transfer agreements often have extensive definitions clauses. Provisions such as Intellectual Property (Background and Foreground), Licensed Patents, Products, Field, Net Sales Value and Territory are often defined. The drafting of technical definitions may require a collaboration between the lawyer/drafter and the relevant scientist to ensure that they are both technically accurate and clearly drafted.[12] Similar considerations apply to the drafting of technical specifications and descriptions of technical work that are included in contracts. It is recommended that they are reviewed (and, if necessary, revised) by the contract drafter, as the scientist may not be skilled in contract drafting or be familiar with the principles of contractual interpretation.

Operative provisions generally

For a discussion of general drafting principles, see books dealing with the negotiating and drafting of contracts.[13] Among other drafting principles, it is recommended that:

---

11 Although some Recitals contain a history of the relationship between the parties, or state how the particular agreement relates to other agreements between the parties. For example, if the parties have entered into a series of patent licences, one replacing another, then sometimes these details are included, so that a person reading the latest patent licence some time after the licence is entered into can have an idea of the history of the relationship and the contractual and other obligations entered into.

12 The case of *Oxonica Energy Limited v Neuftec Limited* [2009] EWCA Civ 668 can be usefully mentioned here again, as this is a clear example where a poorly drafted definition led to one party paying considerably more royalties then would otherwise have been the case. The case is discussed in Ch 10 under 'On what are royalties payable?'.

13 For an introduction to contract drafting, see Anderson and Warner, *Drafting and Negotiating Commercial Contracts* (2nd edn, Tottel Publishing (now Bloomsbury Professional), 2007).

- the main commercial terms of the agreement should appear early in the agreement (eg clauses 2 and 3, assuming clause 1 contains the definitions);

- obligations should be organised by theme (eg work, insurance, termination, etc) rather than as a series of obligations on one party followed by a series of obligations on the other party;

- clauses should be organised in short sentences and in short paragraphs, with plenty of headings, numbering, indentation, spacing between paragraphs, etc to assist readability;

- Latin, legalese and old-fashioned language should be avoided;[14]

- boilerplate clauses should be placed at the end of the agreement, as sub-clauses under a main clause headed 'General' or 'Miscellaneous'.

Work obligations

If work is to be performed (eg R&D services), the work should be clearly defined and it should be clear who is obliged to perform which items of work (ie avoid general wording such as 'the Parties shall perform the Project'). Also be clear on whether the outcome of the work is guaranteed; generally this will not be the case with early-stage research. Usually, except for the simplest project, the details of the project are set out in detail in a schedule or appendix to the agreement.

Payment obligations

The contract should clearly state whether the basis of payment is a fixed price or a rate for time spent and services performed. How rates are calculated and other payment formulae should be included and should be carefully checked to ensure that they are robust in different situations, and where appropriate examples should be given to illustrate the operation of the formula (eg where royalties are based on net sales). Also included should be statements about whether payments are to have VAT or similar taxes added, when payments need to be made and what is to happen if a payment is not made by a specified date.

Intellectual property issues

Much of the commercial value of technology transfer activities is based on strong intellectual property protection (particularly the protection provided by

---

14 There has been a lot of work in many areas of law to move towards the use of plain English (such an approach is now required for contracts with consumers). Although the use of plain English is good common sense, with commercial contracts it is still an ideal in particular areas. There are certain words or phrases that have particular legal meanings which sometimes do not accord with the common understandings (eg indemnity).

patents). Many technology transfer agreements address intellectual property issues, including which party owns, controls and can use intellectual property, who is to pay to maintain the (patent) protection, who is to decide what to do if there is patent infringement by a third party (and who is responsible to conduct any action). Sometimes the agreement has different provisions for pre-existing intellectual property and intellectual property arising from the performance of the agreement, respectively.

The intellectual property provisions will often require careful thought; the contract drafter may need to involve patenting, scientific and commercial colleagues in the drafting of intellectual property terms. Someone in the negotiating team should have a clear understanding of underlying intellectual property laws, particularly those relevant to commercial transactions.

Warranties, liability and indemnities

Warranties can be viewed as a method of allocating commercial risk. Technology transfer agreements have widely varying warranty terms, depending in part on how risk averse one or both parties to the agreement may be. Conventional practice varies between types of agreement and industry sector. For example, in commercial software licences the licensor often gives a warranty or indemnity in respect of infringement of third-party intellectual property. Such a provision would very rarely be encountered in a patent licence in respect of a biopharmaceutical compound that is at an early stage of development.

In general, the more money that is being paid, and the closer to market that a technology is, the more likely it is that the agreement will contain detailed warranties.[15]

Various standard practices have grown up for drafting and negotiating warranties. In outline, these include:

- giving warranties that are limited to matters within the warrantor's knowledge;

- making exceptions to warranties for matters disclosed by the warrantor in a separate document, eg in a schedule or 'disclosure letter';

- limiting liability and remedies for breach of warranty, eg by financial amount or duration, or limiting liability to financial damages and excluding the right to rescind the contract.

---

15   Although where the drafting is being carried out by a lawyer who is not a specialist in intellectual property transactions, but comes from a mergers and acquisitions or joint-venture background, then there may be very extensive 'standard' warranties included.

Case law has clarified the extent of a party's obligations under warranties, eg in some cases a warranty given to the best of the warrantor's knowledge may cover matters that the warrantor could have discovered by some reasonable checking of its records. The drafting of warranties has developed to take account of this case law.

The law in this area, as well as commercial practice, varies from country to country. For example (and to take one point of detail), it is understood that in the US it is common to state that a disclosure is only effective against a specific warranty, whereas in England and Wales the agreement will often provide that a disclosure is made against all relevant warranties.

Therefore, the drafting and negotiation of warranties requires specialist legal knowledge and experience. Similarly, the drafting of clauses that limit or exclude liability, and indemnity clauses, requires an understanding of the relevant contract law. For example, if an exclusion clause is to be effective under English law it may be important to clarify that the clause does not seek to exclude liability for death or personal injury caused by negligence.[16] In certain countries, it may be important to clarify that the clause does not seek to exclude liability for gross negligence or fraud (wilful misconduct).

Some technology transfer agreements are negotiated without the close involvement of lawyers, usually on grounds of cost. Whatever the merits of this approach, it becomes highly risky when negotiating warranty, liability and indemnity clauses, for which an understanding of the underlying law is particularly important.

Termination and its consequences

The agreement should include appropriate termination provisions. These may include:

- an expiry date, particularly in the case of long-term agreements; this may be coupled with provisions enabling the agreement to be renewed for additional periods;

- a right to terminate the agreement on the grounds of the other party's breach of contract or insolvency;

- a right for one or both parties to terminate on notice (ie where there has been no breach or insolvency);

---

16 Also, the way such clauses are presented in a document may be important. There have been cases in the courts where an exclusion clause contained several issues and one part of the clause has been held to be unreasonable by a court, and the whole clause has been judged ineffective (the clear implication being that if the one clause had been broken into several separate clauses, only the 'offending' clause would have been deemed ineffective).

- other termination rights, eg if a party is acquired by someone else (known as change of control), or if a *force majeure* situation continues for a defined period of time.

In most cases, it is important to specify in detail what the consequences of termination are, eg by a 'consequences of termination' clause that should appear after the termination clause. This clause might typically cover the following points:

- actions to be taken on termination, eg provision of a final report;

- return of materials and information, or arrangement for long-term storage of such items to comply with regulatory requirements;

- cancellation and termination of rights, eg licences come to an end and any registrations of the licences with national patent offices must be cancelled;

- some provisions may survive for a limited period of time, eg confidentiality obligations, obligations to pay royalties and other sums due;

- some provisions may survive without limit of time, eg indemnities. It is recommended that the relevant provisions be listed in full, rather than the use of some general (and lazy) formula such as 'clauses that are meant to survive will survive' or similar wording.

Law and jurisdiction

In agreements between parties based in different countries, typically each party wishes their own country's law and courts (jurisdiction) to govern the agreement. Often, a compromise is reached on this subject. Some points to consider in coming to a compromise include the following:

- Law and jurisdiction are not points that should be conceded lightly. In negotiations, commercial parties sometimes trade these points too readily, failing to realise how much the choice of law may affect the interpretation of the agreement or even the terms that will be included in the agreement (eg implied terms).

- Law and jurisdiction are separate issues. Specifying English law does not guarantee that the English courts will have jurisdiction to hear the case. The clause should address both law and jurisdiction.

- A fundamental question is whether disputes should be heard by a court or by one or more arbitrators. Commercial parties are sometimes under the impression that arbitration is more user friendly, quick, cheap or less 'legal' than litigation. In fact, arbitration can be more bureaucratic, expensive, time consuming and user unfriendly than using, say, the English courts. There are some potential advantages to arbitration, including the confidentiality of the proceedings, the arbitrator can be someone who has technical/scientific expertise of the subject matter of the agreement or dispute and the fact that international treaties covering arbitration awards mean that they are more often recognised by national courts than overseas court judgments. However, if an authoritative decision is required on a point of law, it may be better to go to court. These and other factors need to be weighed up, on a case-by-case basis, before deciding whether to choose arbitration or litigation.

- If arbitration is chosen, it is usually appropriate to agree to follow the arbitration procedures of a well-known arbitration body, eg the London Court of International Arbitration (LCIA) or World Intellectual Property Organisation (WIPO). If the arbitration is in Sweden, the Stockholm Chamber of Commerce arbitration rules are often used.

- Commercial parties sometimes express a preference for mediation 'rather than' arbitration. Whilst mediation (ie a structured negotiation involving an outside facilitator) may be considered a good way of avoiding arbitration or litigation, if the mediation fails it will still be necessary to choose between litigation or arbitration.

- If litigation in the courts is chosen as the final dispute-resolution mechanism, it is highly desirable that the court should decide the case on the basis of a contract law with which it is familiar. For example, the English courts should decide cases under English law; French courts should decide cases under French law, etc. In the authors' view, a compromise such as English law and the French courts (although entirely possible) would not be sensible.

- The authors' preferences, if English law and jurisdiction cannot be agreed, might include the following, depending on the circumstances:

  — within Europe, a 'north-European' legal system of a reasonably large size, eg the Netherlands or Sweden;

  — within the US, New York or possibly Massachusetts;

  — in the Far East, Australia, New Zealand, Hong Kong or Singapore.

Other boilerplate clauses

Boilerplate clauses are the clauses that are often included at the end of the agreement, covering issues such as assignment, entire agreement,[17] force majeure, waiver etc. Which boilerplate clauses are needed will depend on the agreement.

Clauses dealing with assignment and change of control[18] are sometimes regarded as important, particularly in the case of smaller, technology-based companies that have outside investors. The main assets of such companies sometimes comprise their intellectual property portfolio and their trading relationships, including their technology transfer agreements. These companies sometimes need to raise money, enter into joint ventures or trade sales, or otherwise engage in corporate activity. If the company's technology transfer agreements do not allow for assignment to a purchaser of the company's business, or include clauses allowing for termination of the agreement in the event of a change of ownership or control of the company, these provisions may significantly reduce the value of the company to a prospective purchaser. However if an assignment clause does not contain any restrictions then the intellectual property may end up with a (unsuitable) competitor.

Signing and dating the agreement

The appropriate signature blocks will depend on the law of the contract and, in the case of English law, whether the agreement is simply signed (executed 'under hand') or executed as a deed.[19]

The question of who has authority to sign an agreement on behalf of an organisation is discussed earlier in this chapter. Assuming that the right person is signing, it should also be checked that they have signed in the right place and inserted their job title and other details in the signature block.

There is not any general convention in England and Wales that agreements should be initialled by both parties on every page, although some organisations

---

17   Although entire agreement clauses are considered (and almost always placed) with boilerplate provisions, this type of clause has been the subject of considerable judicial scrutiny in recent years and needs particular attention. The aim of an entire agreement clause is to state that only the provisions of an agreement are those which are contained in the agreement, and that any other document or statement is not binding and does not form part of the agreement between the parties. Entire agreement clauses are considered (with recent case law) in Anderson & Warner, *Drafting and Negotiating Commercial Contracts* (2nd edn, Tottel Publishing (now Bloomsbury Professional), 2007), and Anderson & Warner, *A–Z Guide to Boilerplate and Commercial Clauses* (2nd edn, Tottel Publishing (now Bloomsbury Professional), 2006).

18   A clause dealing with what is to happen if the ownership of one of the parties changes. For example, if two parties enter into a patent licence, neither of whom are competitors; but if one of the parties is taken over by a competitor of the other party, this can have important implications.

19   For examples of signature blocks that can be used with various types of legal entity, see Anderson and Warner, *Execution of Documents* (2nd edn, Law Society Publishing, 2008).

prefer to do this. Practice in other countries varies. Essentially this is an anti-fraud device and to ensure that both parties are agreeing identical terms. If, however, any manuscript revisions have been made to the typed text of the agreement, these revisions should be initialled by both parties (usually in the margin next to the change).

The convention among English solicitors is to write in the date of the agreement once all parties have signed. But the practice does not need to be restricted to solicitors. When the last party has signed the agreement, their solicitors or the persons handling the signing can communicate and agree to insert the date and the date that should be inserted. It is not recommended to type in the date before the parties sign, as it often happens that the agreement is not signed on the stated date (particularly when there are several parties).

It is bad practice to misdate agreements, and in the worst case it could amount to a criminal offence under the Forgery and Counterfeiting Act 1981, s 9.

It is usually acceptable to have an effective date or commencement date that is different to the actual date of signature. Usually this would be done by including a definition of Effective Date or Commencement Date in the definitions clause, and have a separate clause stating that the agreement comes into effect on that date.[20] If the parties are insistent upon putting an effective date at the top of the first page of the agreement, this should be clearly labelled as an effective date, so as to avoid any doubt that it might be purporting to be the date of execution of the agreement.

Schedules and attachments

The traditional English practice was to put schedules before the signature blocks of the agreement. In recent years, the US practice of putting the schedules after the signatures seems to be more prevalent. Whichever method is adopted, it is important to state in the agreement, if this is the intention, that the schedules form part of the agreement.

Schedules are sometimes given a variety of other names, including appendices, annexes, annexures and attachments. The name is less important than clarifying whether the document forms part of the agreement. Sometimes an agreement will have two classes of attachment, eg annexes and attachments. Sometimes a different name is given to distinguish between documents that form part of the agreement and documents that are merely provided for information. Making this distinction may also make it easier to avoid disclosing certain information to regulatory authorities, eg where the terms of a material contract have to be disclosed to a national Stock Exchange.

---

20   For example, it is entirely possible to have the Commencement Date being a date sometime before the date the parties sign the written agreement.

TYPES OF AGREEMENT

Heads of agreement and term sheets

In the early stages of commercial negotiations in respect of technology transfer agreements, parties sometimes prepare a document that records the main principles of their proposed agreement. These documents have a variety of names, including:

- heads of agreement;

- heads of terms;

- term sheet;

- letter of intent;

- memorandum of understanding.

The terminology is less important than ensuring that the status of the document is clear:

- whether it is intended to be legally binding; and

- what will happen if the parties fail to reach agreement on the terms of the full agreement.

To some extent these points can be addressed in the wording of the document. For convenience, these documents will be referred to collectively below as 'term sheets'.

Sometimes, the term sheet states that it is not legally binding, except for clauses (x), (y) and (z), which will be legally binding. Typically, the latter category includes confidentiality provisions and provisions that give an exclusive period of negotiations. It is generally desirable to state a time-frame for the operation of the term sheet.

Particular care should be taken where one of the parties is based overseas, eg in a civil law jurisdiction. It is understood that in some countries, the signing of a term sheet may have legal consequences, eg a party may be liable to the other party if it withdraws from the negotiations without good reason, or fails to act in good faith in the negotiations. Local legal advice should be obtained on any such consequences and on whether they can be avoided by use of appropriate wording in the term sheet.

Assuming that one's client wishes to avoid such legal obligations, and subject to any specific local advice that may be obtained, it may at least do no harm to include in the letter of intent some wording along the following lines:

'This letter of intent is not intended to be legally binding. Any negotiations between the parties are being conducted on a non-exclusive basis. Either party may withdraw from their negotiations at any time [prior to signature of a definitive agreement] without liability. To the extent that any legal issue arises in connection with this letter of intent, this letter shall be interpreted in accordance with English law and shall be subject to the exclusive jurisdiction of the English courts'.

Two distinct approaches to using term sheets can be seen:

- The term sheet is short and concise, perhaps no longer than two pages. The wording of the term sheet is carefully negotiated, then it is signed by senior representatives of the parties. In subsequent negotiations (perhaps conducted by more junior people than the individuals who signed the term sheet), if a party proposes terms that deviate from the term sheet, the other party may object and refer back to what was agreed in the term sheet. This approach is encountered, for example, in the US.

- The term sheet focuses on the main commercial terms that the parties wish to negotiate, and over time, in successive drafts, expands to deal with other issues that come up in the commercial negotiations. Often, with this approach, the term sheet is never actually signed; instead, it either grows into a full agreement draft, or is replaced at some point by an agreement draft that has been prepared by a lawyer.

Sometimes, the parties include in the term sheet a list of preconditions to proceeding with the transaction. These may include:

- obtaining senior management approval;
- obtaining Board and/or shareholder approval;
- being satisfied as to the results of a 'due diligence' exercise;
- reaching agreement on detailed terms;
- raising finance for the transaction;
- satisfactory results coming out of an ongoing study or R&D project.

If the term sheet is stated not to be legally binding, these preconditions may not have any legal effect, but are sometimes thought to be useful as a 'road map' to the process for reaching a binding agreement.

Confidentiality agreements

This section considers some practical and drafting issues relating to confidentiality agreements (sometimes known as CDAs or NDAs – non-disclosure agreements).

Parties

CDAs are sometimes drafted to include references to other group companies, affiliates etc. For example, a confidentiality agreement with a UK subsidiary of a multinational company may include a provision that information passed under the agreement can be passed on to the company's affiliates anywhere in the world. This may lead to one of two problems:

- The information could be provided to an affiliate in a country which gives little or no legal protection to confidential information. If the information is misused, then it might be expensive, difficult and time consuming to stop its use in a foreign jurisdiction.[21]

- It is not always clear that the person signing the agreement has authority to sign on behalf of all the group companies. If group companies (or their authorised agents) do not sign the agreement, then prima facie they are not bound by its terms, under the doctrine of privity of contract.[22] It is clearly important in the case of confidentiality agreements to know who is permitted to receive the confidential information and who is bound by the terms of the agreement, and on what basis.

In some cases, there may be a risk that group companies, other than the company signing the agreement, will claim not to be bound by its terms. At a practical level, this risk may be thought to be lower where the party signing the CDA is the ultimate parent company of a group of companies, and undertakes to ensure that its group companies comply with the provisions of the agreement. By contrast, where a subsidiary company in an international group signs the CDA and purports to make such a commitment on behalf of its parent and sister companies, it may be more doubtful whether it has the necessary authority to make such a commitment. If the subsidiary does not have the necessary authority, it can perhaps be sued for breach of contract if it discloses the information to a company that is not bound by the confidentiality obligations. However, once the information is publicly disclosed, it may lose

---

21   There is also a risk of disclosing information to people who are not bound by the confidentiality agreement that has been signed. For example the contracting party to a draft confidentiality agreement may be based in an offshore jurisdiction, such as Bermuda. There may be some plausible reasons for this, eg that the intellectual property is held by this company for tax reasons. However, if information is being disclosed to individuals who are not employees of that company but of an affiliated company incorporated elsewhere, there is a risk of disclosing information to people who are not bound by the confidentiality agreement.

22   Although this doctrine has been partly replaced by provisions of the Contracts (Rights of Third Parties) Act 1999 in relation to the rights of third parties, it remains unaltered in relation to contracts that seek to impose obligations on a person who is not a party to the contract. Also of importance is that a confidentiality agreement may not be classed as a contract and the party who claims there has to be unauthorised use of their confidential information would have to rely, at least in England, on the case-based principles governing the law of confidence. See Ch 8, and also under 'Consideration' below.

its competitive value.[23] Moreover, when calculating damages from breach of contract, the value of the information may be difficult to establish, particularly with early-stage technology. It may be far more important to ensure that the confidentiality obligations are complied with, rather than have a right to claim damages. Therefore it is important that care is taken about which group company signs the agreement. The only clear way to 'impose' obligations on other members of a group of companies remains to make those members parties to the confidentiality agreement and for sufficient due diligence to be carried out so that the person signing on behalf of those members in fact has the authority to do so.

It is important that caution is exercised in the area of pre-contract negotiations, where the parties often exchange confidential information without any formal protection. The surrounding circumstances may in any event be such as to give rise to an obligation of confidentiality, however it is still better to formalise the situation with properly laid out confidentiality obligations.

Consideration

Another issue that is sometimes overlooked is consideration. Generally, for an agreement to be legally binding, consideration must be given or the agreement must be executed as a deed. Thus in the example of a confidentiality agreement, the disclosing party may 'give' something in return for the recipient's undertaking to keep the information confidential; one example of this arises in the case of a two-way confidentiality agreement where each party undertakes to keep confidential information disclosed to it by the other party.

In practice, even in 'one-way' confidentiality agreements, consideration is often found from the circumstances in which the information is disclosed. However, the rules on consideration[24] should be considered carefully before concluding that this is the case. Sometimes, a disclosing party may wish to include nominal financial consideration in the agreement, eg agreeing to pay the recipient £1 in return for the recipient undertaking the obligations of confidentiality set out in the agreement. In other cases, the agreement may be executed as a deed, thus avoiding the rules on consideration.

Even where there is no consideration, the obligations of confidence may still be binding under the law of equity.[25] However, parties would generally be advised not to rely on the uncertain scope of equitable (discretionary) remedies, but instead to ensure that their agreement is binding under the law of contract.

---

23 And in the case of information regarding an invention, once publicly disclosed the invention may no longer be patentable at all.

24 Eg the rule that 'past consideration is no consideration'.

25 Essentially a set of court-made rules, intended to provide justice, with the key point here being that they are discretionary. As to the scope of the law of confidence, see Ch 8.

Where the express terms of the contract cut down on the protection which might otherwise be granted by equity, then it seems clear from the authorities that to this extent the equitable principles are displaced. For instance, an obligation not to disclose confidential information for a fixed period of time will free the recipient from any obligation not to disclose once that period has expired, even if, in the absence of a contract, equity might have restrained him or her for longer.[26]

Commencement

The date of commencement of the agreement may also need to be considered carefully. In practice, information may have been disclosed prior to signature of the agreement, however ill-advised this may be. It is permissible for English law agreements to take effect retrospectively, ie having a commencement date prior to the date of execution of the agreement. However, this should be done by referring in the agreement to a separate commencement date, and not by misstating the date of execution.[27]

Subject matter of the agreement

Sometimes parties wish to identify in general terms the area of technology in which disclosures will be made under the confidentiality agreement. Clearly a potential danger in this is that if information is disclosed which relates to a topic that is outside the defined area, that information will not be subject to the provisions of the confidentiality agreement. Parties sometimes prefer not to have the agreement limited in this way. On the other hand, a general description of the area of the parties' confidential discussions can be useful, particularly where a company enters into many CDAs each year and wishes to identify briefly the subject matter of the agreement.

At the other extreme, parties sometimes wish to be very secretive, extending the confidentiality obligations to cover the fact that an agreement has been made and even that the parties are in discussions with one another. Sometimes there will be specific provisions governing press releases and other public statements.

Another issue that sometimes arises is whether materials, as well as information, are to be subject to the provisions of the agreement. This issue frequently arises in relation to biological materials which are provided to enable the recipient to evaluate them. Generally, it is desirable to deal with materials separately, either by separate clauses in the agreement or by use of a distinct material transfer agreement. Where the definition of confidential information is simply broadened to cover physical materials, the confidentiality obligations do not always make much sense when applied to

---

26   See *Potters-Ballotini v Weston-Baker and Others* [1977] RPC 202, CA.
27   See comments on signing and dating agreements under 'Signing and dating the agreement'.

materials, rather than information. This is generally not such a problem if the materials are no more than the medium on which information is recorded, as in the case of paper or computer discs. It may, though, be desirable for the agreement to include a specific provision to state that ownership of such materials remains with the providing party (see further below under 'Materials transfer agreements').

Circumstances in which information is covered by the agreement

As well as, or instead of, being limited by general subject matter, the agreement may be limited as to the type of information that will be covered; for example:

- Must the information be in writing and marked confidential in order for it to be subject to the provisions of the agreement? Or:

- Will all information disclosed by one party to the other be subject to the agreement, whether it is disclosed in oral, written, machine-readable or other form?

It will generally be desirable for the agreement to be clear on this point. Attitudes vary as to whether a CDA should include a requirement for information to be in writing. Scientists, for example, often prefer not to include a requirement that information must be reduced to writing in order to be caught by the terms of the agreement, as it is often viewed as an unrealistic and bureaucratic requirement which inhibits discussion. Others, including some business people, prefer the certainty associated with written records of disclosed material in the event of an allegation of breach of confidentiality obligations. There is no 'right' answer to this dilemma. In the event of litigation for breach of confidence, it may be preferable to have written records of what has been disclosed.

Under the general law of confidence, a 'package' or combination of information may be held to be confidential even though the elements of that package are publicly known, particularly if the disclosing party has expended effort putting the package together and the package itself is not public knowledge. In detailed confidentiality agreements, parties sometimes include a provision to clarify that the agreement covers packages of confidential information.

Disclosing and receiving parties

Another issue that sometimes arises is, who must the information be disclosed by, in order to be covered by the agreement? From a disclosing party's point of view, good practice may suggest that all information disclosed *directly or indirectly* by the disclosing party, eg by its employees, agents, contractors, group companies etc should be covered as well as information disclosed by it directly. A further subtlety is to whom must an item of information be disclosed in order for the other party to be bound to keep it confidential?

Would it be sufficient, for example, to disclose it to a consultant engaged by the other party? These issues are more likely to arise in the case of large organisations or where several parties are co-operating on a project. In suitable cases, it may be appropriate to have broad definitions of terms such as 'disclosing party' and 'receiving party'.

Exceptions to confidentiality obligations

Anyone who has experience of confidentiality agreements will be familiar with so-called 'standard' exceptions that are found in many confidentiality agreements; these may include both:

- categories of information that are not subject to the agreement at all; and

- circumstances in which information that is caught by the agreement may be disclosed.

Often, parties will not wish to engage in detailed negotiation of these provisions, regarding them as standard, and not worth debating. However, where the information is particularly sensitive, the terms of any such exceptions should be considered carefully, and in some cases omitted altogether. Two of the more common issues that arise are the following:

- Should an exception be made for information which the recipient claims to have already developed or subsequently develops in a separate part of the organisation, without access to the information disclosed under the confidentiality agreement? In some situations the disclosing party may take the view that it is not prepared to allow such exceptions, perhaps because it does not believe that the information could be developed independently or because he or she does not trust the other party.

- Should the receiving party have the onus of proving that information falls within an exception, and if so what standard of proof should be applied? For example, should he or she be required to produce written records that establish that he or she developed the information prior to its disclosure by the other party? Sometimes confidentiality agreements are specific on these matters.

The main areas where exceptions are sometimes made to the obligations arising under a confidentiality agreement are the following:

- The information is in the public domain. The authors understand the terms 'in the public domain' to mean that the information is both publicly known and freely available for use by the public; for example it is not patented, or if the information is protected by copyright, the owner of the copyright material allows it to be used without restriction or without restricting its disclosure in the way envisaged. An alternative form of words that is sometimes seen in confidentiality agreements is that the information is 'publicly known'.

- The information enters the public domain during the period of the confidentiality agreement, other than through breach by the recipient of his or her obligations under the agreement.

- The information is known to the recipient prior to disclosure by the disclosing party and the recipient was free to disclose the information previously.

- Representatives of the recipient develop the information independently, without access to the disclosing party's information.

- The recipient receives the same information from a third party who is entitled to disclose it to the recipient without imposing confidentiality restrictions upon the recipient.

- The information is required to be disclosed by court order or to comply with regulatory requirements, eg the requirements of a Stock Exchange where the recipient's shares are listed, or other regulatory body. This exception is sometimes made subject to a condition that the recipient will attempt to ensure confidential treatment by the court or other body and/or the recipient will inform the disclosing party so it can make such attempts. Sometimes, this exception is dealt with in a separate clause, as arguably it is not a general exception to confidentiality but merely a situation where some limited disclosure may be permitted.

Sometimes the agreement allows even wider exceptions, generally when the confidentiality agreement is part of a larger transaction. For example:

- The information is disclosed in an academic publication (after giving the disclosing party a right to review the proposed publication and edit out confidential information or apply for patents).

- The information is included in a patent application (generally, if made with the agreement of the parties).

- The information is reasonably required to be disclosed in connection with the development, manufacture, promotion or sale of products.

Restrictions: permitted use, copying, non-disclosure (and disclosure to employees)

These restrictions are generally at the heart of the confidentiality agreement. An obligation not to disclose confidential information will generally be included.

Use

Also common is an obligation not to *use* the confidential information, except for certain defined purposes, eg to enable the recipient to evaluate whether it wishes to enter into a further agreement with the disclosing party, eg a licence agreement.

Parties sometimes forget to include a restriction on use, but this may be just as important as a restriction on disclosure. Without a restriction on use, the recipient will be entitled to use the information internally, eg to make rival products, unless a term restricting use can be implied into the agreement. Although the courts are sometimes prepared to imply such a restriction, in other cases they are not,[28] and a disclosing party would be well advised to include an express term in the agreement.

Copying

The agreement may also prohibit copying of materials containing confidential information. Where the information consists of or includes a computer program, the agreement may permit back-up copies to be made.[29]

Disclosure to employees and representatives

The issue of disclosure to the recipient's employees and representatives is often addressed. In practical terms (leaving aside legal analysis for the moment) it is not possible to disclose information to a company; a company is a legal entity which does not possess the faculties needed to perceive information. Arguably, a company can only receive, perceive and disclose information via its human representatives, eg its owners (the shareholders), those responsible for running the company (the board of directors), its employees or other nominated representative(s).

Equally, if a company is under a legal duty not to disclose certain information but is permitted to use the information for limited purposes, how can it use the information except through the medium of its human representatives? Common sense would seem to suggest that some disclosure within the recipient company may be necessary.

In the absence of express provisions in a confidentiality agreement, it would ultimately be a matter for a court to determine whether disclosure of information within a company amounted to a breach of a confidentiality undertaking by that

---

28 See *Marshall (Thomas) (Exporters) Limited v Guinle* [1979] 1 Ch 227 where it was held that a clause restricting disclosure did not also prohibit use, although the plaintiff was entitled to an injunction preventing use on the grounds that in the circumstances of that case the defendant owed the plaintiff a duty of good faith which was breached by use of the information. This case was referred to in *Triomed (Proprietary) Ltd v Beecham Group plc* [2001] FSR 583, and *American Home Products Corporation v Novartis Pharmaceuticals UK Ltd (No 2)* [2001] FSR 784.

29 Compare the provisions of the EC Software Directive (Council Directive 91/250/EEC, [1991] OJ L122/42) (COM/2000/0199), implemented by Copyright, Designs and Patents Act 1988, s 50A, which requires a licensor of software to allow back-up copies to be made in certain circumstances (see Ch 5 under 'Back up copies').

company. The court would probably attempt to interpret the provisions of the confidentiality undertaking; depending on the circumstances it might imply a term that permitted limited disclosure where necessary for the purposes of the agreement. Rather than have such uncertainties, it will generally be preferable to include specific provision in the agreement to allow disclosure to some or all employees or other representatives. Often, confidentiality agreements include a provision permitting disclosure to employees who need to know the information in connection with the purposes of the agreement, and who have undertaken to comply with the terms of the confidentiality agreement in question. Sometimes parties are prepared to allow disclosure to employees who are under general confidentiality obligations towards their employer, in respect of information learnt in the course of their employment. It should be noted that different countries or states have different laws on the subject of an employee's general duties to keep such information confidential; at the very least, it is desirable to restrict disclosure by the recipient to employees who have *written* confidentiality obligations to their employer.

In some cases it may be appropriate to restrict disclosure to named individuals and have them sign individual confidentiality agreements. In extreme cases, parties have decided that disclosure will only be to an external representative, eg the recipient's lawyer or technical consultant.[30]

Duties: security measures, return of information, reporting results obtained

Duties

Confidentiality agreements sometimes include positive duties upon the recipient of the confidential information, as well as restrictions on disclosure, use or copying.

Security

A common obligation is to take security measures to protect the confidential information, eg by keeping the information in a locked filing cabinet or safe, or specifying a location. A more general obligation is to require the recipient to take the same security measures as he or she takes to protect his or her own confidential information. At the risk of stating the obvious, the suitability of such an obligation will depend on how well the recipient looks after his or her own information.

---

30   In some cases the named individual may only be permitted to see the confidential information in a particular location; eg the information is stored on paper or a computer (without internet access and all its interfaces and ports disabled), in a locked room which requires prior authorisation to access. This is likely to be the situation only in the most extreme cases, but is sometimes seen implemented by large companies (or rather their lawyers) involved in high-value merger and acquisition activities.

Return of information

It is relatively common to include an obligation on the recipient to return any materials containing the information on termination of the agreement, or on demand. Such an obligation can be extended to include the return or destruction of any copies, and a requirement to make no further use of the information as well as obliging a specific person to certify these things.

Reporting results obtained

Less common, but potentially useful for the disclosing party, is an obligation on the recipient to provide the disclosing party with a report on any results obtained by the recipient when evaluating the information, eg the results of any scientific experiments.

Duration: duration of agreement and duration of obligations

Duration

Confidentiality agreements are sometimes unclear on the subject of duration. In the absence of specific duration provisions, it would ultimately be for a court to determine the duration of the obligations.[31] It is likely that the following terms would be implied into many confidentiality agreements:

- *The agreement may be terminated on reasonable notice:*[32] if the agreement contains obligations only on the recipient (so, for example, there are no obligations on the disclosing party to provide information on a continuing basis) then the required notice period may be very short, eg a few weeks or less. If there are continuing obligations on the disclosing party, and the recipient would be disadvantaged by termination, then the notice period might be longer.

- *Any information disclosed after the date of termination would not be subject to the provisions of the agreement:* information disclosed prior to termination might or might not continue to be subject to the restrictions contained in the agreement, depending on the circumstances. In many cases such restrictions would continue. In some cases such restrictions would continue without limit of time, or until the information entered the public domain, or until a reasonable period after the information entered

31   Presumably a court would have to interpret the agreement and imply a term as to the duration of the obligations. On a slightly different point, in a case where confidential information was given under an agreement, and certain uses of the information were permitted under the agreement, it was held that there is no general proposition of law that when the agreement comes to an end, the right to use the confidential information also comes to an end. See *Regina Glass Fibre Ltd v Werner Schuller* [1972] RPC 229, CA.

32   By analogy with cases on termination of licences, distribution agreements etc; eg see *British Leyland Motor Corporation Ltd and another v Armstrong Patents Co Ltd and another*, at Ch 9 under 'Non-derogation from grant'.

the public domain (so that the recipient did not get a head start over his or her competitors through earlier knowledge of the information).[33]

Duration of the agreement

Rather than have such uncertainties, it is generally desirable for the agreement to state both the duration of the agreement (or at least how it may be terminated) and the duration of any obligations after termination. For example, some large corporations have a policy of providing for a one-year agreement (or until either party gives notice of termination to the other), with obligations continuing for a period of five years after termination.

Duration of obligations

Although this five-year period is commonly encountered, the logic behind it is not always apparent. Some companies have a policy that they will not accept obligations unlimited in time; arguments are sometimes made along the lines of 'we need to know when we can finally close the files'. In the authors' experience, such companies can sometimes be persuaded to accept a much longer period, eg 20 years.

The most appropriate time limit will depend on the circumstances. For example, some software will be out of date within less than five years; other technology continues to be valuable more than 30 years after it was developed.[34] Sometimes a company will license a package of intellectual property including patents and know-how. If the patents continue for 20 years or longer (eg through the additional protection of improvement patents), why should know-how be treated as losing its value in a shorter period, at least if it has not entered the public domain during that period?

In summary, parties should consider on a case-by-case basis whether any limit should be placed on the duration of confidentiality obligations, particularly in agreements where there are detailed exceptions to those obligations, eg where the information enters the public domain.

---

33 Applying the so-called springboard doctrine first formulated in *Terrapin v Builders Supply Co (Hayes)* [1967] RPC 375 at 391 (referred to in *Cadbury Schweppes Inc v FBI Foods Ltd* [2000] FSR 491, and also in *Sun Valley Foods Ltd v John Philip Vincent* [2000] FSR 825).

34 To give a now fairly old example concerning the arbitration and litigation in the UK and US between Pilkington and PPG, this concerned the alleged use of Pilkington's float-glass technology by PPG. The dispute lasted 12 years and was finally settled in 1995. According to a report in The Times of 5 April 1995, the parties' combined legal costs approached £70 million, and the dispute was settled on the basis that neither party was guilty of anything. Pilkington's float-glass technology was first developed over 30 years ago, and the dispute related in part to a confidentiality agreement made in the early 1960s. As this example shows, confidential information is sometimes considered valuable and worth protecting more than five years after it is developed.

Obligations on the disclosing party: provision of information, confidentiality

Obligations on the disclosing party

In a typical, simple confidentiality agreement, all the obligations are on the recipient of the information. However, there may be circumstances in which it is appropriate to include obligations on the disclosing party.

Provision of information

It may for example be appropriate to *require* the disclosing party to disclose certain information, particularly if the recipient is giving something in return. It may also be appropriate to require the disclosing party to update the information.

In some situations, it may be appropriate to require the disclosing party not to disclose the information to third parties, ie so that both parties are bound not to disclose the disclosing party's information. For example this might be appropriate if the recipient is considering taking an exclusive licence to know-how; it might also be appropriate in any situation where discussions between the parties are to take place on an exclusive basis. The potential application of competition laws to such restrictions should not be overlooked. Other restrictions on competition are considered below.

Confidentiality

If both parties to the agreement are to disclose information in confidence to the other, a 'two-way' confidentiality agreement may be required.

Implied terms: no licence or other agreement

It is relatively common to include in a detailed confidentiality agreement a statement that a licence to use the confidential information is not to be implied into the agreement; sometimes an exception is made for rights expressly set out in the agreement, eg a right to use the information for evaluation purposes. More general disclaimers of implied terms, representations, etc are sometimes included, eg in some cases even a disclaimer as to the accuracy of any information provided under the agreement.

Law and jurisdiction; notices

Many technology-related agreements, including confidentiality agreements, are between companies based in different countries or jurisdictions. In such cases it is generally desirable to state the law which governs the agreement, and also to state which courts are to have jurisdiction. In the case of CDAs,[35] urgent court action may be needed to obtain an interim injunction to prevent breach of the agreement – ie disclosure of the confidential information. Generally, it is best to bring interim proceedings in a jurisdiction in which the defendant is located.[36] For this reason it may be desirable either to give the courts of the recipient's home territory sole jurisdiction, or at least to allow actions to be brought in such jurisdiction.[37]

Sometimes agreements include a provision to the effect that the disclosing party will be entitled to an injunction if the receiving party discloses the information. If the agreement is subject to the jurisdiction of the English courts, it is doubtful whether such a provision serves a useful purpose. Such a clause might backfire if an English court took offence at what it might perceive as an attempt by the parties to tell it that it had to grant an injunction, as injunctions are a discretionary remedy, not a right. On the other hand such a provision might prevent the defendant from opposing an application for an injunction. So far as the authors are aware, the point has not been decided in any reported English court decision.

Confidentiality agreements are often relatively short agreements, and it may be considered inappropriate to include extensive 'boilerplate' clauses, clarifying how the agreement is to be interpreted etc. It will, though, often be worth including a notices clause.[38]

Competition restrictions

A person learning of some confidential information may find it difficult or impossible to remove it entirely from his or her mind. Even an honest person, who makes no direct use of the information, is likely to find that the information may be used unintentionally or indirectly, as part of his or her background store of knowledge which can affect his or her judgement.

For example, knowledge of a new scientific technique disclosed to a scientist under a CDA might change the scientist's thinking about an area of science, and lead the scientist to make other discoveries which are not directly related to the one which was disclosed. This may give a commercial advantage to the party learning of the information, or a disadvantage to the disclosing party. Yet it might be very difficult to prove that the subsequent discovery was made through use of the confidential information.

---

35 And other types of agreement, but the issue is particularly relevant to confidentiality agreements.
36 Although it may be possible to bring proceedings in the plaintiff's jurisdiction and have the judgment enforced by the courts of the defendant's jurisdiction, this will often be a less practical option.
37 It may also be important, where there are different versions of the agreement in different languages, to state that one version is the definitive version. This not only avoids debate over bad translations, but also may help determine which courts have jurisdiction.
38 As to certain terms that may be implied if an express clause is not included, see Ch 9 under 'Notices'.

This type of reasoning is sometimes given as a justification for contractual restrictions which go beyond restrictions as to the use or disclosure of the confidential information. However, from the public-policy viewpoint, there is a need to balance the public interest requirement that confidences be respected against the public interest requirement that business affairs should be carried on without unjustifiable restraint of trade. Where confidentiality obligations merge into areas of non-competition clauses, then there is a possibility of an infringement of the Competition Act 1998 (or if there is a European dimension to a CDA then European competition laws), if the arrangement is not of minor significance (de minimis).

Examples of what amount to restrictions on competition include the following:

- Where confidential information is disclosed by a company to a potential purchaser of the company, the confidentiality agreement might include a provision along the following lines:

  'For one year from the date of this Agreement the Offeror shall not, without the prior written consent of the Company, directly or indirectly acquire, offer to acquire or announce an intention to acquire an interest in any ordinary shares of the Company or act in concert with any person who acquires, offers to acquire or announces an intention to acquire such an interest'.

- Where information is disclosed in order for parties to bid jointly for a construction project, a provision along the following lines:

  'In consideration of the Partners disclosing the Confidential Information to the Company, the Company agrees that it shall not directly or indirectly, without the consent in writing of the Partners, in any way participate in the Project or any version or part of it unless one or both of the Partners is a participant'.

Competition laws may have a significant impact on provisions of this kind. As well as the possibility of fines, unenforceable provisions, and actions by third parties, there is also the possibility in some situations that a party who seeks to impose such obligations as the examples indicated above could find that its patents or other intellectual property may be unenforceable or void, particularly under foreign patent laws. Before including restrictions on competition in a confidentiality agreement, specialist competition law advice should always be sought.

Materials transfer agreements

Materials transfer agreements (MTAs) set out the terms on which one party provides a sample of biological or chemical material to another party. They are usually fairly short documents. Typically, the purpose of providing the materials is to enable the recipient to perform some research on the materials, or use the materials in research. A few examples may illustrate some different situations in which MTAs may be needed:

- An academic researcher wishes to use some monoclonal antibodies, which were generated by another academic researcher at a different institution, for the purposes of non-commercial research that is unrelated to the research that generated the monoclonal antibodies.

- A company that has a drug in development wishes to provide it to another company that has developed some 'drug-delivery' technology. The drug-delivery technology is used to improve the 'uptake' of a drug in the part of the body where it is needed. The purpose of the materials transfer is to perform some initial experiments to see whether the drug-delivery technology may be suitable for use with the drug.

- A company possesses samples of DNA obtained from patients with a particular disease, which an academic researcher wishes to test as part of a wider investigation into the genetic causes of the disease.

Intellectual property issues

In the above examples, it may be important to the parties to establish who will own, and who may use the results of, the research and on what terms.

In the first example above, the provider of the materials may not have any expectation of a commercial interest in the results. If any patents are filed on inventions made during the research, he or she may not expect to be named as an inventor, although expectations differ and may depend partly on how 'routine' the materials are. Sometimes the provider of materials is named as a joint inventor of any patented inventions made by the recipient using the materials, even though it may be questionable whether the provider is an inventor under patent law.

As academic institutions become more aware of their commercial interests, there is an increasing tendency for academic providers of materials to ask for at least an 'equitable share' of any royalties or other income that is derived from any patents filed by the recipient. Whilst the legal effect of such a provision may be unclear, it is sometimes regarded as sufficient for practical purposes, particularly where two UK academic institutions are involved.

In the second example above, the provider of the drug sample may be very concerned to ensure that it owns all intellectual property that may be generated in respect of its drug. Equally, the owner of the drug-delivery technology will be concerned to ensure that it owns all intellectual property relating to its technology. Sometimes there is a difficulty in negotiating terms in relation to inventions that relate to both parties' technologies – such inventions are not an unlikely outcome.

79

Sometimes the parties are able to agree a solution, eg that neither party will commercialise these inventions without coming to a further agreement, or that one party will have an option to commercialise resulting inventions in a particular field. Sometimes, the parties' positions prove to be too far apart and the proposed research does not take place.

In the third example above, similar intellectual property issues may arise as in the second example. Sometimes, the recipient institution will be willing to grant an option to the providing company to negotiate commercial terms for a licence to any resulting inventions. On other occasions, the providing company's terms may be too unattractive for the academic institution and the materials must be declined. This probably happens only rarely; not least because the technology transfer offices in UK academic institutions are not always asked for their advice on the provisions of MTAs.

Liability, disclaimers and indemnities

Often materials are provided free of charge and for research that does not involve use in human patients.[39] Providers of materials tend to be reluctant to offer any warranties as to the condition or toxicity of the materials, or indeed any warranties at all. Instead they seek indemnities from the recipient against any liability arising from the recipient's use of the materials and warranties that the recipient will comply with applicable laws and regulations.[40] Usually, recipients accept such terms, although problems sometimes arise with organisations that claim to have a policy of never giving indemnities.[41] Much will depend on the background to the material transfer, but where the materials are provided as a 'favour' to the recipient, or in a spirit of academic collegiality, it seems not unreasonable that the recipient should take the risk of problems arising through use of the materials.

Other terms in MTAs

Usually, the other terms in MTAs (ie, other than intellectual property and liability issues) do not require much input from lawyers, particularly if a standard MTA is being used. Points that come up from time to time include the following:

- whether any payment is required for supply of the materials;

- who is responsible for arranging, and paying for, packing, carriage and insurance of the materials (ie when transported from the provider's to the recipient's premises);

---

39   Other than packaging, carriage, insurance and like costs of transporting the materials.

40   For example, if the materials are derived from or come from humans then the provider and recipient will have to comply with the obligations imposed by the Human Tissue Act 2004 and other laws. See Ch 11 for discussion on these issues.

41   For example, some US universities apparently have arranged for state laws to be passed, preventing them from accepting certain terms in contracts.

- who is liable for any loss of the materials in transit (occasionally the parties get involved in discussion of which Incoterms[42] are to apply, but usually the cost of production of the sample is small, so if it is lost in transit another sample can easily be supplied);[43]

- compliance with regulations on the transportation of human, animal and biological materials (eg if genetically modified organisms or human tissue are involved);

- obligations on the provider to provide any safety information known to it concerning the materials;

- limitations on the use that may be made of the materials, eg not using them in humans (sometimes the MTA allows only a defined programme of research using the materials);

- restrictions on the supply of the materials to third parties;

- obligations on the part of the recipient not to reproduce living materials and to destroy all materials or return them to the provider on completion of the research;

- obligations on the recipient to provide data and results obtained from using the materials;

- confidentiality obligations;

- choice of law and jurisdiction, particularly if the parties are based in different jurisdictions.

Option agreements

Terminology

Options are:

- either provisions are contained in an agreement whose main subject involves some other matter such as a research and development or licence agreement; or

- a stand-alone option agreement.

The same issues arise in each case. References to 'option clauses' below should be understood as applying equally to 'option agreements'.

---

42   Incoterms are a set of terms and conditions implied into contracts (where the parties wish to be implied) which govern such matters as who is responsible/liable for the delivery and transportation of goods. They are published by the International Chamber of Commerce, see http://www.iccwbo.org/incoterms/id3045/index.html.

43   Where human and animal tissue is involved, there may be regulatory requirements as to how such tissue is transported as well as notification requirements, at least in England.

Different terms are used, such as:

- option;
- right of first opportunity; or
- right of first refusal.

Sometimes, these terms are used loosely to refer to a number of different arrangements; there is no official definition of what an option is. The authors understand the terms to refer to the following types of arrangement.

Option

Example: the owner of a patent grants a commercial company the right (usually, the exclusive right) to acquire a licence to that patent (which has resulted from a research project that has been funded by the commercial company).[44] Typically:

- during the period of the option, the owner of the patent cannot grant a license under the patent to anyone else;
- the option is exercised by the company, when it notifies the owner of the patent that it wishes to acquire a licence (or when a certain event occurs or at a particular time);
- the option clause requires the parties to negotiate the terms of the licence;
- if the parties cannot agree on the terms, the option lapses (ie the commercial company no longer has the right to acquire a licence under the patent and the owner can grant licences under the patent to third parties); there is, or should be, a time limit on the option (both the time for exercise of the option and the time for negotiation of the terms, if the option is exercised).

Under patent owner's standard wording, the option clause does not ensure that the commercial company will get a licence under the patent; it merely stops a third party obtaining it for period, and allows the commercial company the right to negotiate the terms of the licence for a defined period of time. Variants on this approach that are sometimes encountered include the following terms:

- if the terms cannot be agreed, they are referred to an independent third party to be settled;
- all the licence terms are agreed at the outset, and attached to the option agreement; all that has to be done when the option is exercised is for the parties to sign the licence agreement;
- some key terms are agreed at the outset, eg royalty rates.

---

44   Usually the option will become operational at a specific time or when a certain event occurs (which is called 'exercising' the option).

Right of first refusal

Rights of first refusal (in the sense described below) are less commonly encountered than options. A typical right of first refusal might say:

- the owner of a patent is free to negotiate licence terms (eg in relation to a named patent) with anyone (third party); but

- before signing a licence agreement with anyone other than the commercial company that has the right of first refusal (sponsor), the owner of the patent must offer the sponsor the same terms that have been agreed with the third party; and

- if the sponsor agrees to match the third-party terms, the owner of the patent must license the sponsor rather than the third party.

This type of arrangement might work well in other areas of business, eg on the sale of a building, where personal considerations may be less important. But it is problematic in the area of technology transfer. In the above example, the owner of the patent would either have to tell the third party at the outset of negotiations, that even if terms are agreed, the owner of the patent may have to license elsewhere (ie to the sponsor). This might discourage the third party from entering into licence negotiations, or it might enter into the negotiations but it might only be prepared to pay a lower price than the patent is worth. Or if the right of first refusal is not disclosed to the third party until the sponsor exercises the right, at which point the third party may be very unhappy and think it has been 'strung along'.

Right of first opportunity

This is a rather general expression, but would include the following arrangement:

- the owner of the patent is obliged to tell the sponsor if the owner of the patent decides actively to seek licensees for the patent;

- if the sponsor expresses interest in acquiring a licence, the owner of the patent must give the sponsor an 'opportunity' to propose terms for such a licence;

- usually, this opportunity would be on a non-exclusive basis, ie the sponsor gets 'a seat at the table' and is treated no worse than any other bidder.

Combinations of the above

Sometimes sponsors request a combination of two or more of the above arrangements, eg:

- the owner of the patent must tell the sponsor if it intends to license the patents;

- the sponsor can then demand that it has the exclusive right to negotiate the provisions of a licence for a specified period of time;

- if the parties cannot agree on terms, the owner of the patent is free to license elsewhere, but cannot grant a licence on terms that are more favourable to any licensee than the best terms offered by the sponsor (or before granting such a third-party licence must offer the same terms to the sponsor).

The owner of the patent will usually wish to limit any clause to a simple option to negotiate a licence for a limited period of time.

Some other points to note

- An option clause should always indicate how long it will run for, eg for the period of a research programme. If not, then the sponsor could argue that the option could run beyond the termination of any research agreement and seek to exercise the option at some point convenient to it. This may be some time after the termination of the research agreement and the owner of the patent may have licensed or assigned the patent to a third party.

- An option clause should always indicate how long the period for negotiation should last for. If it is not specified, then the sponsor could argue that the negotiation period could be unlimited which could stop the owner of the patent exploiting it (or responding to opportunities to do so).

- Care should be taken over the wording of any obligation to negotiate. Whilst some wording (eg an obligation to negotiate in good faith) may not be legally enforceable unless bad faith is proved,[45] other wording may be (more) enforceable against an owner of a patent. It is usually best to spell out exactly what the procedure is, including the time limit for the negotiations, in the option clause.

Intellectual property licences and assignments

Intellectual property licence agreements, and licence terms, are central to any discussion of technology transfer. Issues to consider include:

- Which intellectual property is the subject of the licence.

- What acts are being licensed; including any field, territory or other restrictions.

---

45   While an obligation to negotiate in good faith is generally unenforceable under English law, this may not be the position in other countries, particularly those which have a civil law system, eg many European countries and in Latin America.

- which products or services are being licensed.

- Whether it is possible to enter into a sub-licence and the conditions on which it can be granted and operated.

- Who should, and whether to, register a licence with the appropriate patent offices.

- Provisions dealing with improvements and other technologies owned by either party.

- Payment provisions, including timing of payments, how payments are to be calculated (if relevant), record-keeping, auditing and reports.

- Diligence obligations, including consequences of failure to commercialise the licensed products or services.

- Confidentiality obligations.

- Warranties, eg as to the state of the intellectual property being licensed.

- Provisions dealing with protection of the licensed intellectual property,[46] suing infringers, and defending actions by third parties; royalty reduction provisions if the licensee must take a licence from a third party.

- Termination and its consequences.

- Boilerplate provisions, including law and jurisdiction, rights of assignment, entire agreement and notices clauses.

Points that arise in practice include the following:

- Particular care needs to be taken over the drafting of the definitions, eg as to licensed products,[47] field, net sales value, and the drafting of the grant clause.

- A common complaint of licensors, particularly in the case of academic licensors and technologies licensed at an early stage in their development, is that the licensee loses interest in developing licensed products but does not quickly agree to terminate the licence. The reasons for this are varied, but may include: (a) that the technology is under review within the licensee company, and it may take a year or more for that review to be complete; (b) the technology is no longer a priority for the licensee and is being developed but at a very slow rate; or (c) the licensee is developing a competing technology and prefers to keep the licence rather than allow it to go to a competitor. Clear and effective diligence obligations that enable the licensor to recover the licensed intellectual property in these situations, are important.

---

46   Including where there are patents, who is to pay the fees to the relevant patent office to maintain the patents in force.

47   The case of *Oxonica Energy Limited v Neuftec Limited* [2009] EWCA Civ 668 can usefully be mentioned again here, particularly because of the poor drafting of a definition, that of 'Licensed Products'. See Ch 10 under 'On what are royalties payable?'.

- Licensors of early-stage technology will generally wish to be indemnified by the licensee against product liability claims.

- Parties will often try to keep within the terms of the EC Technology Transfer Agreements Block Exemption Regulation,[48] so as to avoid any potential breach of Article 81 (101) of the EU Treaty or Chapter I of the Competition Act 1998.[49]

- The tax treatment of up-front and milestone payments may depend in part on how they are described. This may be an issue particularly in international transactions and where the double tax treaty between the countries of the licensor and licensee does not allow for complete relief from double taxation. Advice should be sought from the parties' tax advisers where appropriate.[50]

The following paragraphs will provide a review of royalty clauses and warranties in licence agreements.

Royalties

- The term 'royalty' is commonly used to refer to payments made under a licence agreement for use of intellectual property, particularly (but not exclusively) payments that are based on the number of licensed products that are sold, supplied or used, or the amount of income received from sales etc of licensed products. The most frequently encountered types of royalty are:

  — royalties that are calculated as a percentage of the price at which the licensee sells licensed products or provides licensed services (for example 5 per cent of the net sales price of licensed products);

  — royalties of a fixed amount on each licensed product sold by the licensee (for example a royalty of 10 cents on each widget sold);

  — royalties calculated as a percentage of income received by the licensee from its sub-licensees (for example a royalty of 25 per cent of the licensee's net receipts from sub-licensees.

The term 'royalty' is also used in other contexts, for example licence fees paid for working a mine. The term is occasionally considered controversial in some countries that have ceased to have a monarchy, for example the Republic of Ireland, even though, when used in intellectual property agreements it now has no connection with royalty, in the sense of hereditary rulers. One could just refer to a 'periodic payment' and avoid 'royalty' altogether.

---

48   See Ch 13.
49   See further Ch 15.
50   See further the discussion of this point in Ch 17.

Drafting royalty clauses

Matters which need consideration when drafting a clause dealing with royalty issues, include:

- *Amount or rate.*

- *Application to types of intellectual property:* whether the same level of royalty is payable for all the intellectual property licensed under the agreement, or should each type of intellectual property have a different royalty rate, for example one for products covered by the licensed patents, and another (generally lower) for products that are (only) covered by the licensed know-how?

- *Application of royalty: w*hat should the royalty be applied to? For example, the price of the product. Should the licensee be allowed to deduct some costs, for example delivery charges, from the price of each licensed product before the royalty is applied?

- *Who should pay the royalty?* Should the royalty be applied only to sales by the licensee or also to sales made by a sub-licensee?

- *Calculation:* if the licensed product is incorporated in another product, and the combined product has a single price, ie there is no separate price for the licensed product element, are royalties calculated on the price of the combined product or a proportion of this, and if a proportion, how is this proportion calculated?

- *Due date:* at what point will the royalty become due from the licensee? For example, in the case of royalties on the sale of products, is the royalty due when the price is invoiced or when it is actually paid or when the product is installed or delivered to a third party?

  When will such royalties actually be payable to the licensor? For example within 30 days of the end of each successive quarterly period, such as 1 October, 1 January, 1 April and 1 July?

- *VAT:* is the royalty payment VAT (or other similar tax) exclusive or inclusive?

- *Tax:* confirmation that withholding tax, if applicable, will be deducted from payments to persons whose usual place of abode is not within the UK or, where a double taxation agreement is applicable, the payer will obtain authority from the Inland Revenue not to deduct tax.

- *Interest:* is interest payable for any late payment, and if so at what rate and on what basis (for example on a daily basis)?

Warranties in licensing agreements

Generally, very few warranties will be implied into a licence agreement (if made under English law).

87

Licence agreements often include express warranties or disclaimers that address the following subjects, among others:

- whether the licensor is the proprietor of, or has title to, the intellectual property or the right to grant a licence;

- whether the intellectual property to be licensed is free of, or subject to, any encumbrance;

- the freedom, right or authority of the licensor to enter into the licensing agreement;

- whether or not any rights or licences granted by the licensor to third parties conflict with the rights and licences granted in the present licensing agreement;

- whether any materials, products or information provided under the licence by the licensor to the licensee comply with a set specification;

- whether the intellectual property to be licensed is valid.

Warranties – points for consideration

The following are some of the main points that should be considered when warranties are to be included:

- *Title:* the licensee should consult the relevant patent office registers (in the UK, the UK Intellectual Property Office) concerning the licensor's title or right to licence the intellectual property in question and as warranted (if so warranted).

- *Multiple owners of the intellectual property and title:* where there are joint owners, a potential licensee should ensure that all the owners of a patent have given their consent to the licensing of the patent to the licensee (unless the owners have agreed otherwise).

- *Freedom from encumbrances:* the licensee may require, in addition to a warranty that the intellectual property to be licensed is free from encumbrances,[51] covenants[52] that:

    — the licensor will not act inconsistently with the licensee's enjoyment of the licence;

    — the licensor will not assign the intellectual property (especially if the licensee requires technical assistance or improvements from the licensor);

---

51 A type of restriction or obligation.

52 A type of binding promise or obligation. For example, where intellectual property is sold (assigned), unless the parties agree otherwise, certain 'covenants' are implied into the assignment. See Ch 9 under 'Implied covenants of title, freedom from encumbrances etc'.

— any proposed assignment, transfer or encumbrance must be notified to the licensee;

— the licensor will obtain the prior written consent of the licensee before so doing.

- *Validity:* it is unlikely that the licensor will wish to warrant that the intellectual property as expressed through a patent is valid or what the scope of the patent is, as it is always open to third parties to challenge the validity of the patent. If an unrestricted warranty is given concerning its validity, and the licensee later finds that the patent is not valid, then the licensor may be liable in damages. If the licensee insists on a warranty of validity, the licensor may be prepared to warrant that:

    — it has not done anything; or

    — as far as it is aware (but without searches or investigations) there is nothing which would invalidate the intellectual property.

- *Validity warranties for confidential information/trade secrets:* unlike, for example, patents, which once published are a matter of public record, confidential information developed by the licensor cannot be independently assessed or quantified until provided. If the licensee is to carry out manufacturing or other such activities with the licensed intellectual property, then it may require access to such (technical) information throughout the lifetime of the licence to assist in the manufacturing process. The licensor might be asked to warrant, for example:

    — that the disclosure of such confidential information to the licensee will not breach a duty of confidence that the licensor has to a third party;

    — that the confidential information has not entered into the public domain at the date of the agreement; or

    — that the confidential information has in the past proved of use in the manufacture of products based on or using the intellectual property that is to be licensed.

Assignments

Assignments (in the sense this term is being used here) are formal transfers of title to intellectual property. They generally have to be in writing, and those involving patents have to be registered with the UK Intellectual Property Office.[53]

A practice point arises where parties agree to assign intellectual property. It may be important to distinguish between the agreement to assign and the

---

53   See further Ch 3 under 'Formalities for the transfer of rights'.

formal assignment. Wording such as 'agrees to assign' can be used where an immediate assignment is not intended; 'hereby assigns' works better where an immediate assignment is intended.

Spin-out company transactions

Universities are increasingly involved in setting up 'spin-out' companies. These usually involve the university assigning or licensing a package of intellectual property (and sometimes know-how) to the company in return for shares in the company. Some of these arrangements also include provisions, for example, that the university will have the right to put its nominated representatives on the board of directors and allow the academics involved in the creation of the intellectual property to own shares in the spin-out. Investors then subscribe for shares in the company for cash, which is used to fund the company's operations and further development of the technology. The corporate aspects of such transactions are outside the scope of this book.[54]

Spin-out transactions may involve a number of technology transfer agreements, including some or all of the following:

- An assignment or licence of intellectual property into the spin-out company.

- An option agreement or 'pipeline agreement' to enable the spin-out company to obtain rights to future intellectual property generated in the relevant department or group of the university.

- A research agreement under which the spin-out company sponsors further research by the university.

- Funding by the spin-out company for research studentships or other activities by the university.

- Personal consultancy agreements between the key academics and the spin-out company.

- Provision for when the spin-out company needs to raise further finance at particular stages (for example when the R&D reaches a defined stage, and when a product or service has been developed to a certain stage), and also deal with such issues as how the finance is to be raised, who from, and whether existing shareholdings will be diluted.

(See the separate discussion of most of these types of agreement elsewhere in this chapter.)

---

54 For further information, see the authors' UNICO Guides to University Commercialisation Agreements, and in particular the *Guide to Spin-out Transactions*, published by PraxisUnico.

Spin-out transactions raise a number of specific legal and policy issues for the university and other participants, including:

- How the university's revenue sharing policy will operate in relation to income generated from shares owned by the university which were acquired in return for an assignment or licence of intellectual property. Does the academic inventor get a share of that revenue, or does the academic get a return through shares in the spin-out company? Has this been agreed in writing with the academic?

- Whether there are any conflicts of interest arising from the spin-out transaction, eg if an academic retains his or her academic post yet becomes a director of the company. Many universities now have policies and procedures in relation to conflicts of interest, eg the academic is required to notify potential conflicts to the university, and in certain cases the university may wish to prevent the academic from participating in activities (eg private consultancies) if they are perceived as conflicting with the academic's duties to the university.

- Whether the university is required to treat the issue of shares to the academic as a benefit of employment for which an immediate income tax liability arises (deductible via the PAYE system), even though the academic has not realised any financial benefit from the shareholding. There are various methods of avoiding such an income tax liability, either by statutory exemption or by HM Revenue & Customs concession, but the issue generally needs to be looked at carefully.

Research and development agreements

Introduction

R&D agreements are concerned with the generation and use of scientific information and, particularly where they include intellectual property provisions, the creation of commercial value from that information.

Many R&D agreements are primarily agreements for the provision of services. The detailed nature of R&D services is sometimes very different to other types of service, but certain core elements are the same as for other professional services. Typically, work will be done for a price. There may be provisions dealing with the preparation of reports, the exchange of information, and, in some cases, the operation of a project review committee. There may also be issues over the level of warranties to be given and over limitations and exclusions of liability. Unlike some other services agreements, R&D agreements often also focus on intellectual property issues, confidentiality obligations and whether the parties can publish the results of the research.

Unsurprisingly, some of the terms of R&D agreements depend on the subject matter of the R&D. For example, in the area of R&D agreements which include trials and testing (such as clinical trials agreements), the provisions are very different from the provisions of agreements for the beta-testing of software.

R&D agreements are an example of commercial agreements that concern an ongoing relationship between parties. They are therefore closer in spirit to, say, a joint-venture agreement than to an agreement for the sale of a business, where the parties may not have any ongoing relationship once the sale is completed.

Common provisions of R&D agreements

At its simplest, one of the most common types of R&D agreement is a two-party agreement under which one party, the researching party, carries out a defined R&D project and the other, the funding party, pays certain agreed costs of that R&D project. The funding party receives a report from the researching party when the project is completed. These agreements often include provisions for:

- participation of the funding party in the conduct of the R&D project, or in a project committee which reviews the progress of the R&D project;

- periodic reports by the research party to the funding party;

- change in content or direction of the R&D project;

- renewal of the agreement, eg annually;

- confidentiality obligations;

- a procedure for the prior review of intended publications;

- ownership, protection, use and commercialisation of intellectual property arising from the project (and, in some cases, intellectual property brought to the project).

They may also include warranty, liability and indemnity, exclusivity and non-compete provisions. In practice, the intellectual property provisions, and for academic clients the publications and liability clauses, often require the most attention from lawyers.

Intellectual property issues

Intellectual property issues are dealt with in many different ways in R&D agreements, including the following:

- *Funding party owns and controls intellectual property:* intellectual property resulting from the R&D project may be owned by the funding party, with the research party retaining no interest or right to receive royalties from its use, and having no say in how it is protected. This type of arrangement is most commonly found in consultancy agreements between a company and an academic scientist, for example where the scientist is being paid to assist the company to solve a particular technical problem related to the company's technology. It is less common in contracts to fund a programme of R&D, where the research party will generally wish to retain some interests in the intellectual property resulting from the project.

• *Funding party receives licence to intellectual property:* the research party may own the intellectual property resulting from the R&D project, but the funding party receives an automatic licence to use and commercialise it. This licence might be non-exclusive but with an option to convert it into an exclusive licence, or exclusive in a particular field or territory. The funding party may be required to pay royalties or other payments to the research party for use or exploitation of the intellectual property. In some cases (for example in R&D agreements between two biotech companies) it may be agreed that both parties will have commercialisation rights, with territories or fields of applications being divided between them.

• *Funding party receives option on licence:* often, the preferred solution for a research party is to retain ownership of the intellectual property generated by the project and grant an option to the funding party to acquire a licence on commercial terms. Depending on the subject matter of the R&D project, the licence may be exclusive or non-exclusive. If the R&D project involves the use of the research party's pre-existing technology, and that technology can be applied to a wide range of applications, the licence may be non-exclusive or limited to areas that are of direct interest to the funding party, leaving the research party free to license other applications to other parties.

Collaborative R&D

Some R&D agreements do not involve a funding party paying for R&D to be conducted by a research party. Instead, two or more parties collaborate on an R&D project and each funds its own R&D activities. A variation on this theme is where each party obtains some or all of its funding from an external source. For example, funding may be obtained from the European Commission under its 'Framework' research programmes or one of the sources of funding available from the UK government.[55] In the case of EC-funded research projects, it is also necessary for the consortium agreement to comply with the detailed (and rather complex) requirements of the European Commission's standard contract terms. The complex intellectual property provisions deal with each party's rights to use and commercialise intellectual property arising from a project.

---

55   See further Ch 1 under 'Funding of R&D'.

Parties

As with other types of agreement, the parties to an R&D agreement should be clearly identified in the parties' clause. With many research-type organisations, the party's name, legal status, and place of incorporation are sometimes not clear from their stationery or other papers. For example, multinational drug companies are often based in several countries in the world. Whilst negotiations may be conducted with a subsidiary in one country, the contract may be, according to the drug company, with its parent company in another country.

R&D Project

Each R&D agreement should include a clause defining the R&D project: it outlines or specifies the work that needs to be done under or in the course of the agreement. The detailed specification of the services and/or research to be carried out under the agreement is usually, but not always, contained in a separate schedule to the agreement. Usually set out in the main body of the agreement are general details about when the work is to start, the amount of effort or resources to be used, and who is to carry out the work (and sometimes their qualifications and experience). Other topics that are often addressed include when the work is to be completed and the role of project managers/directors or a project committee. This section outlines the key matters which should be addressed in drafting clauses relating to the work to be carried out under the agreement.

Checklist of matters to be addressed in a research agreement

Parties responsible for the work

Which party or parties are to carry out the work? For example, the agreement might state:

(a) party A is to carry out the research programme; or

(b) each party shall perform their respective duties in the research programme.

Starting the work

When is the work to start?

(a) On a commencement date?

(b) On the date of the agreement?

(c) Promptly or immediately after a certain date?

Location

Where is the work to be carried out?

94

(a) At a particular location for the party carrying out the work, eg at the (specific) laboratories of a university?

(b) In a particular department or section, for example department of medicine?

The importance of choosing a particular location and/or department can be reflected in other parts of the agreement, for example in confidentiality provisions. If information provided under the agreement is later found outside that department and/or location, then it can be easier to establish that there has been a breach of the agreement.

Amendment of research programme

(a) Can the parties amend the research programme?

   (i)   By mutual agreement between the parties?

   (ii) By one party specifying the change?

For longer-term projects, or where the research is more experimental or involves untried and little-known materials, it is often advisable to include a provision which allows the parties to amend the research project to take account of changing circumstances.

(b) If amendment is allowed:

   (i)   Who shall agree it? For example project leaders or the project committee or someone more senior? Or do different types of changes require persons at different levels of seniority to approve the amendment?

   (ii) In what circumstances will it be allowed? For example when deemed necessary, or because of a specific result being achieved or not achieved.

   (iii) How shall it be recorded? For example by written amendments to an agreement incorporated in a schedule.

   (iv) If changes can be agreed or recommended by the project leaders, can the parties withhold approval of those changes?

   (v)   Can the price be altered and by whom? Do changes in price need to be agreed before the revised work programme is implemented?

Warranties

Do the parties, or one party, warrant or undertake that the research programme will achieve a particular result, be completed by a certain date or will be successful?

The usual provision found in most R&D agreements is that such provisions are expressly excluded and no such warranty etc is provided.

95

Facilities

(a) Is the party carrying out the work required to provide facilities?

    (i) If so, to what standard? For example adequate facilities.

    (ii) And to use what effort? For example to use reasonable endeavours to provide them.

(b) What specific facilities are to be provided by the party carrying out the work?

    (i) Who is to provide (specific) materials?

    (ii) What (specific) equipment will be used and who will provide it (and, in appropriate cases, on what terms)?

    (iii) Who are the (named) personnel who will be carrying out and be responsible for the research project?

Effort in carrying out work

What effort is to be used by the party carrying out the work?

(a) Reasonable endeavours (or variations such as 'all reasonable endeavours' or 'reasonable commercial efforts')?

(b) Best endeavours?

(c) According to the terms and conditions of the agreement (ie specific results are set and the party carrying out the work is expected to them)?

Provision of equipment

If equipment is to be provided to the party performing the work:

(a) Is it to be loaned to them by the other party?

(b) What are the provisions for use of the loaned equipment? (Usually specified, if at all, in a separate loan document attached to the agreement, for example governing issues like insurance and risk and use of the equipment for other purposes.)

(c) Are they to buy the equipment but using funds of the other party?

(d) Will they own the equipment they buy or which is provided to them (or will the other party own it)?

(e) What is to happen to the equipment at the end of the research project (does it get returned if loaned to them, do they get an option to buy the equipment or if they purchased the equipment with the funds of the other party must they give it to the other party, keep it or sell it)?

Provision of materials

(a) If materials are to be provided to the party carrying out the work:

  (i) What are they?

  (ii) When will they be provided (for example within a certain number of days of the agreement or commencement date)?

  (iii) Are they to be provided in sufficient quantities to allow the party to carry out the work? A further issue that sometimes arises is who should be responsible (and at whose cost) for providing additional quantities of materials if the first batch is wasted, for example because the experiments did not work.

(b) Can the party who is to work on the materials:

  (i) Only use them for the purposes of the research programme?

  (ii) Use them only as expressly permitted by the provisions of the agreement?

  (iii) Perform any tests other than those specified in the research programme?

  (iv) Modify the materials?

  (v) Make derivatives of the materials?

(c) Is property in the materials provided to remain with the party providing them?

(d) Are any materials not used to be returned to the party providing them (on request?) or destroyed?

Project leaders

What is their precise role?

(a) Is the work to be carried out under their personal direction?

(b) Do they have the responsibility and authority to manage and direct the work?

(c) Can they agree further direction, goals and timelines of the research programme?

(d) Can they agree changes in the research programme or the work to be carried out?

(e) What is their role on any project committee (for example to chair it)?

Project committee

What is the composition and role of the project committee? For example:

(a) How many members will there be and how many of them for each party?

(b) What is the role of the project leaders on the project committee?

(c) What is the method of selection (for example nominated by each party from time to time)?

(d) Who are to be the members at the date of the agreement or commencement date?

(e) What will be the frequency of meetings (for example meet periodically and confer by telephone)?

(f) What is the role of the project committee? For example:

   (i)   To review and discuss the progress and direction of the research programme?

   (ii) To agree the further direction, goal and timelines for the research programme?

   (iii) To maintain informal dialogue throughout the course of the research programme in addition to (i)?

   (iv) To freely and fully exchange information obtained and/or used in the research programme?

   (v)   To make recommendations to the contracting parties to amend the research programme, but not have authority as the project committee to make such changes (or, sometimes, not have such authority if it would alter the contract price or timescale)?

(g) Will the (reasonable) costs of attending project committee meetings incurred by one party be paid by the other?

Recruitment of staff

(a) Are specific staff to be seconded or recruited?

(b) what will be their specific role?

(c) who is to be responsible for the selection of the specific staff (for example the party carrying out the work)?

(d) Who is to be responsible for the (reasonable) costs of recruiting?

(e) Is the party carrying out the work to report when staff are recruited and provide other details as requested by the other party (such as qualifications, experience etc)?

(f) Are the terms of appointment of staff to include provision that:

   (i)   If the main agreement is terminated early then the staff appointment will also terminate early (or alternatively will continue for the remainder of a fixed term)? And/or:

   (ii) Will the staff be assigned other duties by the party carrying out the work?

Exclusivity, non-competition

Where one organisation commissions another to carry out R&D work, it may wish to influence and/or control some of the following elements relating to the research being undertaken:

- access rights (licence or user rights) to, or outright ownership of, the results and any intellectual property in those results (sometimes called foreground intellectual property); or

- access rights to other intellectual property owned by the other party and needed to exploit the results (sometimes called background intellectual property).

The party commissioning the R&D may also wish to restrict or control other work that the contractor may wish to undertake, for example:

- *activities:* restricting the contractor's ability to conduct R&D activities in the same field with other parties or on its own;

- *use by contractor of its own intellectual property:* whether the contractor can use or license the same research methodologies and techniques (for example background or foreground intellectual property) outside the scope of the contract with the commissioner;

- *restrictions on use of commissioner's intellectual property:* for example, whether the contractor can carry out experimental work (outside the scope of its contract with the commissioner) relating to the subject matter of a patented invention owned by the commissioner, because ownership of such patents may not give the commissioner any right to prevent such work, especially under the exemption provided by Patents Act 1977, s 36.

In principle, such restrictions might be stated to apply:

- during the term of the research programme; or

- during the term of the agreement under which that research was conducted (which may be a longer period than the research programme);

- during and after the agreement has come to an end.

However, the last two restrictions are much more likely to be contentious and to raise competition law issues than the first. The more restrictive the clause is, the more likely it is to be subject to EC Treaty, Article 81 (101) or the Competition Act 1998.

Payment terms

Most agreements concerning R&D activities relate to the provision of some form of service or combination of goods and service by one organisation or person to another organisation or person. Such agreements often do not demand especially difficult or complex provisions for payment. The more involved provisions are usually encountered where an R&D agreement includes provisions concerning the commercialisation of the results of the R&D, for example licence fees and royalties.

Fixing the amount to be paid

It is unlikely that parties will enter into an agreement without at least agreeing a price or determining some method of arriving at a price. However, if the parties do fail, for example where a researcher at a university agrees verbally to carry out some research or testing, then statute law can provide some help. Both the Sale of Goods Act 1979 and the Supply of Goods and Services Act 1982 provide that if:

- a price is not fixed by the parties to the agreement; or

- there is no method of calculation provided for in the agreement; or

- the price cannot be determined from previous dealings between the parties;

then there is an implied term that the party is to pay the supplier of the services or goods a 'reasonable charge', which is a question of fact.[56]

However, if the other provisions are not certain, the agreement may be invalid. The fundamental problem is that if the price is not fixed, or an adequately certain method of calculation is not provided, then the parties to the agreement may argue over what is a 'reasonable charge'. If the agreement provides that the parties will agree charges at a future date, and does not include a mechanism for resolving any failure to agree, this will be an 'agreement to agree' and probably not enforceable. In this situation it will probably not be possible to fall back on the implied term of a 'reasonable charge' because the parties' 'agreement to agree' may be held to override and replace the implied term.

Types of payments

The main types of payments include:

- *Single or split payments:* fixed-price contracts can consist of either:
  - one payment; or
  - several payments split in a number of ways, such as a payment on signature of the agreement, various staged payments at identifiable points in the contract, or at the end of the contract.

---

56 Although who is to decide that fact will be open to interpretation and if the question of what can be charged cannot be agreed, then it will be for a judge to decide. Also many universities and other organisations carrying out research have set rates for the amount they charge or the costs they need to recover.

- *Combination of fixed-price and price-adjustment mechanism:* this combination may be used to allow for:

  — increases in salary costs: the agreement may provide that the organisation carrying out the research will employ a researcher at a fixed price but allow for increases in salary costs based on an agreed formula; for example, if the agreement is with a university and the university is employing the researcher, then it is common to include a clause requiring the sponsor to pay any increases in salary in line with increases in national pay scales for academics;

  — increases in other costs, for example the costs of materials if they are used in the agreement, for example if the research organisation needs to use disposable laboratory or medical equipment such as test tubes; the parties may either use increases in the Retail Prices Index (RPI) as the basis for price increases or use an index that is more closely linked to the industry or products in question, for example the Producer Prices Index.

  — increases in price where the work to be performed under the agreement is changed during the lifetime of the agreement.

- *Price by reference to a rate;* for example:

  — if an agreement provides for testing of compounds, a price per compound; or

  — for the time spent by personnel working on the subject matter of the agreement; or

  — by reference to a separate current pricelist provided by the supplier of the goods or service.

- *Royalties:* based on a percentage of sales revenue as with a patent royalty.

- *Option payment:* a payment may be due if a party to an agreement wishes to exercise an option; for example, R&D agreements often include an option for the party funding the research to acquire an exclusive licence to foreground intellectual property, subject to payment of an option fee.

- *Royalties:* royalties are discussed in the section on intellectual property licences, below.

Factors to be considered in payment clauses

The following issues should be considered when drafting a payment clause:

- *Timing:* when are payments to be made? If payments are made periodically, how frequently should the payment period be? (For example, payment may be made within 30 days of a specified event or date, such as the delivery of goods or the issue of an invoice).

- *Method of calculation:* if payment is calculated by reference to a rate (for example a rate per task, or for time spent or as a percentage of sales revenue – as with patent royalties), the method of calculation of the rate should be clearly specified, for example using a suitable definition of net sales value.

- *VAT:* does the price stated include VAT? Usually prices are stated to be exclusive of VAT which will be charged in addition. If this is not stated, it may be implied that the price includes VAT.

  If the agreement involves a non-UK party, then VAT may not be payable or may need to be calculated at a different rate. The VAT issues may be different depending on whether one or both parties are (a) based in the UK, (b) based in another EU country, or (c) based outside the EU.

- *Payment method:* how are the payments to be made (by cheque, direct bank transfer, letter of credit, or even by accessing the site of the provider of the research and using their online payment method through the use of credit and debit cards, etc)?

- *Late payment:* is interest payable on late payments?[57] Is time of payment 'of the essence', ie can the contract be terminated if any payment is made late?

- *Currency:* the currency in which payments are to be made (in contracts with an international element), any currency conversion method, and who bears any exchange risk.

- *Deductions, set-offs:* whether deductions or set-offs are allowed.

- *Refundable payments:* whether any payments are refundable or to be treated as an advance against future payments, for example initial licence payments or option payments are sometimes creditable against future royalties.

- *Ancillary costs:* who bears any ancillary costs (for example packing, carriage, insurance)?

- *Supporting documents:* whether any statements, receipts or other documents are required to be provided in support of payment claims.

- *Records:* whether any, and what type of, records need to be maintained, for example for the number of products sold, if a royalty statement has to be calculated, and whether it is available for inspection by the agent of the other party.

---

57 The provisions of the Late Payment of Commercial Debts (Interest) Act 1998 should be considered (see Ch 10 under 'Late Payment of Commercial Debts (Interest) Act 1998').

Intellectual property

The aim of many R&D agreements is the creation of intellectual property (patents, copyright, design rights, know-how and confidential information), whether:

- the creation of something; or

- testing of previously created intellectual property which is now to be the subject matter of further R&D.

In addition, the parties will often bring to the R&D agreement a previous R&D track record and will therefore have inventions, information, technical know-how, methods of working, documentation and software programs, for example. These may be of use in carrying out the R&D agreement or may be the basis on which further R&D work is to be carried out.

There is often a need to distinguish between the intellectual property created:

- before the start of the R&D agreement;

- during the R&D agreement by one or more of the parties arising from the research project; and

- during the period of time when the R&D agreement is in force by one or more of the parties, *but not* arising from the research project.

The main purpose of distinguishing between the three circumstances is to indicate which of the parties (singularly or jointly) is to own the intellectual property and in what circumstances.

The party commissioning the R&D will normally wish to own the intellectual property that arises from the research project as well as retaining ownership of intellectual property it brings to the R&D agreement. The party carrying out the R&D will normally wish to retain ownership of any intellectual property it brings to the R&D agreement and any intellectual property that arises from the research project.

Use of the terms 'background' and 'foreground' intellectual property

The terms 'background' and 'foreground' intellectual property are sometimes found in R&D agreements. These are convenient labels to distinguish between different types of intellectual property. These terms are used in the standard contract terms for the EC's Framework 7 research funding programme.[58]

Definition of background intellectual property

The definition of background intellectual property ('background') often comprises the following:

- *background information:* consisting of confidential information, technical know-how and other information known and owned by a party or over which a party has rights to at the date or commencement of the agreement; and

- *background intellectual property:* consisting of patents, copyrights and other similar rights including applications etc owned by or over which a party has rights at the date or commencement of the agreement.

These defined terms are sometimes expanded to include information or intellectual property that is generated after the commencement of the agreement but which is not part of foreground information and foreground intellectual property, for example because it is developed outside the scope of the R&D agreement.

In many commercial agreements, the information and intellectual property definitions are combined in a single definition (usually a definition of 'intellectual property'). However, some research agreements used in universities split the two definitions.

Definition of foreground intellectual property

The definition of foreground intellectual property ('foreground') often comprises:

- *foreground information:* consisting of confidential information, technical know-how and information which is generated by a party in working on or performing the defined research programme; and

- *foreground intellectual property:* consisting of patents, copyrights and other similar rights including applications etc which are generated (or conceived, first reduced to practice or writing or developed, in whole or in part) by a party in working on, or performing the defined research programme.

---

58 See Ch 1 under 'EU funding Framework Programmes'. Under Framework 6 programme, the terminology was different: intellectual property created under a project was known as 'knowledge' and that created prior to the project was known as 'Pre-existing know-how'.

Applying the definitions

The two most basic applications of the definitions of foreground intellectual property ('foreground') and background intellectual property ('background') are that:

- 'background' belongs to the party who introduces it; and

- 'foreground' belongs to the party commissioning the research.

The first bullet point is in essence no more than a statement of what is normally the default position, which is included usually for the sake of avoiding doubt. The second bullet point is of key importance, as it determines ownership of the intellectual property generated by the research programme. Without such a clause, under English intellectual property laws ownership of intellectual property would normally be with the creator, instead of the commissioner (except in the case of design right in commissioned designs). Not all R&D agreements specify that the commissioner should be the owner of foreground. In some instances, ownership of the foreground arising from the research programme remains with the creator. For example, universities often require or request ownership. The (commercial) commissioners of the research may resist this type of provision (particularly those who are not used to dealing with universities and other non-commercial research organisations). If the university will not give up ownership, then the commissioner may need to obtain:

- a licence in respect of the foreground, sometimes (particularly in the case of non-exclusive licences) on a royalty-free basis so that the commissioner can pursue its commercial activities making use of the research that it has funded; or

- an option to obtain such a licence (particularly but not always an exclusive licence) on to-be-determined financial and other terms.

Another common variation is that ownership is retained by the creator of the foreground, but the creator will assign the foreground if it decides not to file or prosecute a patent application with the creator retaining or obtaining a licence to use the foreground. This licence, depending on the creator and the commissioner, may:

- be limited to research only;

- be limited to research only within a certain field; or

- exclude research which would lead to commercial exploitation.

Administering the intellectual property

Ownership of intellectual property requires that it should be properly administered, so that its value is not lost (for example through missing filing dates for patent applications, or failure to pay renewal fees for granted patents). As indicated above, universities often require that they retain ownership of the intellectual property created during an R&D agreement, and the agreement may specify that they are responsible for patent filings and prosecution, with the costs being paid by the commissioner of the foreground. A commissioner who has obtained a licence will require that it is managed and maintained properly. The administrative and cost burden of maintaining a portfolio of patents and other intellectual property can be high, even if some of the costs are reimbursed at some stage.

Patent applications require fees to be paid at certain stages, there are dates to be met in order to prosecute the application, and once granted, and the patent must be maintained via the payment of fees. With copyright, the position is different, but can be just as onerous. Although there are no formal requirements for registration, it is still a requirement that proper documentation is kept of when a copyright comes about and what it is. Proper record-keeping to support an action for breach of copyright can be onerous.

Publication

Requirement to publish

Agreements with academic research organisations, whether universities, research-based charities (such as medical charities), or national or international funding organisations, often require that the results of any R&D be published. The requirement may arise because:

- the organisation carrying out the R&D has charitable status, and charity law requires publication;[59] or

- the funding organisation requires that the results of a project are made available (such as agreements made under EU Framework programmes); or

- the organisation carrying out the R&D, such as a university, has a policy of publishing the results of the research (as well as having charitable status); or

- the ability of academic researchers to progress in their careers is measured primarily through their publications.

These requirements to publish have to be offset against the risks of publication. If publication is not controlled, the patenting of such new discovery may be prevented or it may prejudice the protection of the development as a commercial secret, under confidentiality laws. If some form of publication is required, the contractual document should provide a method for allowing

---

59   See Ch 1 under 'University research and charitable status'.

publication, subject to certain controls and restrictions. That is, allow the organisation carrying out the research to publish the results of the research, but also allow the organisation commissioning or paying for the research the ability to protect any intellectual property developed.

Publication clauses

Publication clauses, particularly in an agreement with a university, will usually include some or all of the following:

- an acknowledgement by the commissioner/payer of the research recognises that the results of the project should be publishable, subject to safeguards;

- a description of who should be able to publish, for example the project director and other researchers involved in the project;

- a description of who should not be able to publish, such as undergraduate students;

- a list of the media in which results can be published, for example seminars, symposia, national or regional professional meetings, journals, theses or dissertations;

- a description of the material that can be published, for example results only or research methods;

- a control or restriction placed by the commissioner of the research on the organisation carrying out the research, usually a notice requirement, for example:

  — that a copy of any publication or presentation is sent to the commissioner a defined period before the publication or presentation is submitted to a third party for publication;

  — that the commissioner has a defined period from the receipt of these copies to object to the publication or presentation;

  — that if the commissioner objects to publication or presentation, the researcher shall not publish or present for a defined period (for example up to six months);

- the grounds on which the commissioner may object to publication or presentation, for example to file patent applications; what universities find more contentious is a clause that allows publications to be vetoed altogether, or gives the commissioner a right to delete from proposed publications material that it wishes to keep confidential.

Charitable research

If research undertaken by a charity is to be considered to be charitable, it must be both within the objects and powers of the charity and carried out for the public benefit.

The Charity Commission has published guidance for universities on when research is charitable in nature and the points that should be considered by university representatives before agreeing to proceed with a research agreement.[60]

Warranties in R&D agreements

Introduction

The usual desire of the party carrying out work under an R&D agreement is to exclude to the fullest extent permissible all warranties relating to the results of the research. This contrasts with the position found in agreements relating to the sale of a business or the setting up of a joint venture, where warranties are normally required and found; for example that the seller is the owner of the intellectual property used in the business being sold (subject to any explicit exclusions stated in a separate document, often called a 'disclosure letter'). Warranty statements made or excluded concerning R&D usually concern issues relating to:

- the materials or the subject matter of the research;

- the use of the resulting intellectual property, services or materials;

- the ownership of any intellectual property brought to or created by an R&D project;

- the validity of any intellectual property.

Disclaimers

The creation of intellectual property or the further development of intellectual property is usually at the heart of an R&D agreement. Most of the warranties that are found or disclaimed in such agreements relate to intellectual property, or in some cases physical property such as biological materials. For convenience, the following are framed as disclaimers, but they could be turned round to be positive warranties:

- that the agreement provides for the carrying out of experimental research, and accordingly specific results cannot be guaranteed;

- that experimental materials shall be used, whose safety or known properties are not established;

- that any materials, information (including advice) or intellectual property provided by the party carrying out the R&D under the agreement are provided 'as is', and accordingly no warranty is given that:

    — they do not infringe third party rights;

60   See n 59.

— they are of merchantable or satisfactory quality (the expression 'merchantable quality' is still used in other jurisdictions, including the US);

— they are fit for any purpose;

— they conform with any sample or description;

— they are viable, safe, uncontaminated or non-toxic;

— they should be relied on;

— they are accurate; or

— any registrable intellectual property will be valid.

Reasons for disclaimers

A party carrying out an R&D project under an agreement would wish to make some or all of the above disclaimers because such research can involve using:

● experimental, untried or not fully tried methods and techniques;

● experimental or fully or partially unknown materials or substances, whose properties or safety is not fully known;[61]

● pre-existing intellectual property (background intellectual property) whose provenance is not fully known (for example, the background intellectual property may be subject to a patent application which is being examined by the Patent Office; it could therefore be challenged, or someone else may also have made the same discovery and has already filed a patent application and/or been granted a patent).

An R&D project can result in the creation of intellectual property where new inventions or discoveries are made, but the creator will not wish to warrant that it will lead to a valid patent application or that it will not infringe third-party rights etc, as to make such a statement may require extensive, costly and lengthy investigation. Universities and other research organisations may not have sufficient resources to carry out such investigations on all the intellectual property generated by their researchers. The value or safety of the intellectual property may be unknown or difficult and costly to determine. It is possible that the true value etc can be determined only by further R&D or by the intellectual property being licensed or combined with other intellectual property.

---

61 With some technologies or materials, particularly those at a very early stage, it is simply not possible for anyone to know their properties or the likely consequences of their use (whether alone or in combination with other things). A related issue can be that an insurer to a party may not be prepared to cover that party for the safety or otherwise of some materials and technologies.

109

Development agreements distinguished from research agreements

The term 'development' is sometimes distinguished from 'research'. Usually, development refers to bringing a specific product or service to market, whereas research refers to an earlier stage – for example, it may involve identifying potential products that are suitable for development. The dividing line between research and development is sometimes hazy.

The terms of research agreements and development agreements respectively tend to have many features in common. Issues such as ownership, protection and use of intellectual property may be addressed in similar ways in each type of agreement. As development implies bringing a product or service closer to market, so the terms of development agreements will often include provisions dealing with issues that arise when a product is brought to market. Examples may include: registration of trade marks; appointment of manufacturing subcontractors; co-promotion and co-marketing rights; beta testing of software; and diligence obligations that are specific to a product in development, eg appointment of a sales director prior to product launch and investment in a marketing infrastructure.

EC-funded research collaborations

The European Commission makes available funding for collaborative research projects under various funding schemes, including its Framework Programmes.[62]

In the case of Framework funding, successful applications for EC research funding will typically involve parties from different EU member states and will involve at least one commercial organisation.

It is common to find EC research collaborations involving, say, six to twelve participants. Each party is required to accede to a contract known at present as a grant agreement. Currently the grant agreement is signed by the European Commission and one of the participants, and then the remaining participants sign a document in a specified form to agree to the grant agreement. However the grant agreement does not establish any contractual relationship between the collaborating parties.

Attached to the grant agreement is Annex II, which includes some standard contract terms dealing with issues such as communications with the European Commission, the preparation of reports on the collaborative research, and perhaps most importantly the ownership of results and the access rights that each participant has to results generated by the other collaborators.

---

62   See Ch 1 under 'EU funding Framework Programmes'.

The provisions of Annex II that deal with ownership of intellectual property generated and access rights need to be considered fully to understand what the default position is, and what the participants agree to regarding varying the default position.

Annex II anticipates that the collaborating parties will enter into a further agreement, known as a consortium agreement, to supplement the provisions of Annex II. Sometimes, where the participants are mostly academic parties and there is one commercial party, the commercial party will prepare what is described as a consortium agreement. Sometimes, this so-called consortium agreement covers only one issue – that the commercial party is to be granted all commercial rights to the results of the collaboration.

Subject to the need to be consistent with the terms of the grant agreement, the issues to be addressed in an EC research consortium agreement are the same as those arising in any research contract, as discussed above.

Subcontracting agreements – generally

Subcontractors are often engaged in the course of an R&D programme. Often the term 'contractor' would be just as accurate as 'subcontractor' – the latter expression is sometimes used where specific services are being provided as part of a larger project. Examples of services and products that might be provided by a subcontractor to the provider of the services to the customer include:

- performing technical tests on materials;
- providing quality assurance services;
- writing software;
- designing a website;
- performing research on a specific aspect of a larger R&D programme;
- manufacturing drug for clinical trials;
- putting drug into vials for the purposes of clinical trials; and
- conducting or managing clinical trials.

Subcontracting agreements often address the following issues:

- what products or services the subcontractor will provide;
- that the subcontractor keeps confidential any results, and any information provided to it, either by the other party to the contract or the ultimate customer;
- intellectual property in the results belongs to the customer and/or to the provider of the services to the customer;

111

- intellectual property relating to the sub-contactor's underlying technology (if any) belongs to the subcontractor, perhaps with a licence to the customer and/or the provider of the services to the customer to enable either or both of them to use the results;

- what if any limitations of liability the subcontractor can include;

- indemnities to be given by the customer to the subcontractor in respect of liability arising from use of the results, unless caused by some default by the subcontractor;

- termination provisions, including whether the customer can terminate early the contract between the customer and the provider of the services to the customer and therefore the contract between the subcontractor and the provider of the services to the customer also terminates;

- consequences of termination, particularly whether the subcontractor is paid for work done prior to termination;

- whether the subcontractor is paid if the provider of the services to the customer is not paid.

Where the subcontracting agreement is sufficiently largescale for Article 81 (101) of the EC Treaty to have potential application, the provisions of the Notice on Sub-Contracting Agreements[63] should be considered. Nor should UK competition law be overlooked.[64]

Small-scale manufacturing agreements (eg for R&D materials)

Small-scale manufacturing agreements are an example of subcontracting agreements, discussed above. Depending on the product being manufactured, the agreement may need to address regulatory issues, eg that the manufacturer should comply with GMP (Good Manufacturing Practices) and other regulatory requirements.[65]

Trials and testing agreements

There are many different types of trial and testing agreement, in different industries, including the following examples:

- beta testing of software;

- agreements to conduct clinical trials;

- testing the qualities of materials, eg strength and durability.

---

63   See Ch 12 under 'Commission notice on subcontracting agreements'.
64   See Ch 14.
65   See Ch 11 under 'The biotechnology and pharmaceutical industries'.

Trial and testing services are often provided by subcontractors; subcontracting agreements are discussed generally, above.

Whilst there is a wide variation in the terms encountered, some agreements include provisions dealing with the following:

- technical standards that must be met in the course of the testing;

- liability and insurance issues, particularly in the case of trials on humans.[66]

Sponsored clinical trials agreements

Introduction

A formal agreement should normally be signed by the sponsor,[67] the principal investigator and the NHS Trust/hospital. Brevity is important wherever practical, but precision and clarity is essential to avoid misunderstanding as non-compliance with the protocol or agreed standards is likely to affect payments and may affect patient safety. (Extra information can be included as a schedule to the agreement, for example synopses of EU guidelines and clinical trial protocol information.)

Contents of agreement

The agreement should refer to the following matters (which may also be covered in detail in the protocol or a separate agreement):

- *Description of the clinical trial:* for example title of the protocol. Any company identifying number for the study and the Medicines Control Agency approval number may be added as appropriate.

- *Standards of conduct:* the standards to which the clinical trial will be performed by the investigator and the consequences if these standards are not met. This should contain as a minimum:

  — agreement to adhere to the protocol, procedures for changes to the protocol, notification of serious adverse events associated with treatment, withdrawal of subjects from the trial and co-operation in verification of source data;

  — agreement that the trial will not commence without the approval of an appropriate ethics committee constituted and operating in accordance with prevailing UK law (ie approval by an ethics

---

66   See n 65.
67   Which may be the pharmaceutical company or a contract trials organisation co-ordinating the trial on behalf of the pharmaceutical company.

      committee[68]) and the responsibilities of the investigator for provision of information concerning approval to the sponsor and for updating information to the ethics committee;

— specification that the clinical trial will be conducted according to the EU guidelines for Good Clinical Practice or such guidelines as are subsequently developed by the International Conference on Harmonisation.

● *Payment terms:* where appropriate, for carrying out the defined clinical trial to the agreed standards. These should specify the circumstances under which payment will or will not be made bearing in mind that the protocol specifies the eligibility of patients or non-patient subjects for the trial and the criteria by which treatment outcome will be judged. Guidance on payment for subject withdrawal and the consequences of termination of the trial may be appropriate. The name and number of the account into which money should be paid and a payment schedule should be included.

● *Term of agreement:* a statement outlining the period of time over which the agreement is to run.

● *Subject recruitment rate:* the expected rate.

● *Confidentiality*: A statement relating to:

— confidentiality;

— retention of records: EU Regulations stipulate that records should be kept for a period of 15 years;

— ownership of study materials and records and return to sponsor on completion of termination of the study;

— the respective obligations of the parties in relation to the disclosure of potentially price-sensitive information and the publication of results;

— the intellectual property rights attaching to any documentation provided by the sponsor and any study findings; normally foreground intellectual property is vested in the sponsor (as it is the sponsor's product that is being tested), and a royalty-free licence to utilise foreground information for research purposes.

● *Equipment:* where equipment is provided for the purposes of the study, the terms of such provision should be included.

● *Termination:* the grounds, as appropriate, for termination of the study prior to completion, for example regulatory action or recruitment difficulties, and the consequences of such termination.

---

68   See Ch 11 under 'Clinical trials'.

- *ABPI guidelines:* agreement of the sponsor to abide by the ABPI guidelines governing compensation for injury to research subjects, and to provide an indemnity to the investigator in the form agreed with the Department of Health.

Costs of clinical research

Proper costing of clinical research is an essential adjunct to the ethical conduct of such trials.

Costs of clinical trials include:

- attendance at and travel to specified investigators' meetings;

- medical, nursing or researchers' time spent interviewing, examining and investigating the patient/non-patient volunteers;

- time spent recording the data in the Case Report Form;

- costs of tests, investigations and pharmacy services specific to the protocol which should not differ in cost from those performed identically on the NHS;

- costs of subjects attending purely for the purpose of the clinical trial, including travel expenses, documented loss of earnings, and where there is no therapeutic benefit or required attendances involving material inconvenience, reasonable participation fees;

- administrative costs arising out of the clinical trial and borne by the institution conducting the trial; and

- overheads charged by the institution or service provider as a reasonable profit upon the provision of services (this item should not be added to items where profit is already included, for example investigators' fees, patient costs, clinical investigations where the overhead is already added into the charge).

Employment and consultancy contracts

Consultancy contracts

Consultancy is an imprecise term. Some consultancy agreements are very close to employment contracts. Others are more like subcontracting agreements or contracts to provide research services.

Within universities, academic (research) staff are often permitted to conduct private consultancy work, as long as the time commitment does not exceed a defined level, eg 40 days per year. In some universities the academic has a choice: either enter into the consultancy arrangement privately with the client, or do it through the university's research or consultancy office. In the latter case, the academic is given support in contract negotiations and the consultancy work may be covered by the university's professional liability insurance policy.

Whilst consultancies vary, one model stands out: the annual contract with an academic scientist, providing for a payment of perhaps £10,000 to £20,000 in return for general advice and assistance in a defined area. Usually the client company will ask the academic to sign its standard consultancy agreement.

From the point of view of the academic and his or her university, the agreement may need to be looked at carefully, particularly on the following issues:

- sometimes the intellectual property provisions are very one-sided in favour of the company, and purport to transfer to the company all intellectual property used by the academic in performing the consultancy services;[69] the academic may not be in a position to assign such intellectual property;

- the consultancy should be limited to a defined field or set of tasks; a consultancy covering all of the academic's areas of interest may be dangerous both in terms of leakage of intellectual property and because the agreement may be used as a cheap way of having the academic perform research services;

- the agreement may provide for the academic to be liable (or may fail to limit liability) in respect of negligence or breach of contract; however, the academic may not be properly insured against such liabilities.

The term 'consultancy agreement' also covers other types of agreement, not involving academic scientists. For example a company that is involved in technology transfer may engage a business development consultant to find potential licensees. Sometimes the client agrees to pay the consultant a commission on any income generated from agreements negotiated by the consultant. The provisions of commission arrangements require careful drafting.

Where the consultancy is very close to being an employment contract, except that the consultant is self-employed, provisions similar to those found in executive service agreements may be more appropriate.

An issue that sometimes arises in consultancy agreements is conflicts of interest. Where the consultant is advising more than one company in the same field, eg a field of technology, it may be appropriate to include terms addressing that possibility, eg a right for the client to terminate the agreement and an

---

69 Ie the agreement prepared by the company may claim ownership of all intellectual property used by the academic, including all of the intellectual property of the academic's employing institution.

obligation on the consultant to inform the client about other consultancies. Similar issues arise with part-time employees.

Employment contracts

For many technology-based companies and organisations, the most valuable intellectual property they have is contained in the brains of their employees. It can therefore be very important to have in place appropriate terms of employment. Provisions dealing with issues such as inventions, creation of copyright and designs, confidentiality and non-competition, may be particularly important. In the case of employment contracts between a university and its academic research staff, it may be unclear what duties the employee has, indeed whether he or she has any formal duties.[70] This makes it difficult to apply the tests in Patents Act 1977, s 39.[71] In practice, where the academic institution licenses or assigns such inventions, it will first obtain a written assignment from the inventor.

Practice points to watch out for include the following:

- A provision that states that the employer owns all inventions made by the employee may not be enforceable under Patents Act 1977, ss 39–43.[72] This is only an issue in relation to inventions and patents; there is no equivalent limitation on the provisions that can be included in an employment contract in relation to copyright, designs or database rights. Obligations in relation to inventions should be suitably qualified.

- Post-termination obligations in relation to confidentiality and non-competition are notoriously difficult to draft and enforce. If in doubt, keep the obligations focussed on what the employer really needs and can justify as needing to protect its interests.

- Contracts with employees working overseas should take into account local employment laws, which may affect provisions dealing with intellectual property etc.

Agreements with students

Students sometimes work on research projects at universities. Sometimes they make, or contribute to, inventions that are made in the course of those projects. Usually, the student is not an employee of the university, and therefore is not bound by any employment contract that gives ownership of his or her inventions to the employer.

---

70 And in particular whether they have any duty or responsibilities to create intellectual property.
71 See further Ch 4 under 'Ownership of employee inventions'.
72 See n 71.

Universities are gradually becoming aware of this issue and some are addressing it, for example by:

- including intellectual property ownership provisions in the student regulations, and making the student agree in writing to comply with those regulations as a condition of admission to the course of study;

- making it a condition of admission to a research project that they agree in writing to assign any intellectual property generated in the project.

A practice point to consider is whether the student is a minor (in which case any contract may not be enforceable against him or her). Even if he or she is an adult, there may be a risk that the university would be regarded as having special responsibilities towards its students, such that normal rules of freedom of contract might not apply. An analogy might be drawn with the line of cases on unfair terms in contracts between record companies and young pop musicians.[73] In any case, a student is likely to be treated as a consumer for the purposes of English law of education services. Accordingly, the provisions of the contract between the student and the academic institution are likely to be interpreted accordingly. Perhaps the university would be expected to take extra care not to act in an unfair way to its students. In the absence of higher court authority on the point, these comments must be speculative.

BEST PRACTICE

The following paragraphs discuss some small, but important, practice points that are not always observed but which are recommended as 'best practice'.

Who should draft the agreement?

There is no general convention as to who should draft a technology transfer agreement. By contrast, contracts for the sale of land or companies are usually drafted by the buyer, and financing agreements are usually drafted by the lender.

In many situations, it may be preferable for the more experienced party to undertake the drafting of a technology transfer agreement. If a party is constrained by policy considerations (eg a US university under the Bayh-Dole Act), it may be sensible for that party to prepare a draft that reflects such considerations.

---

73   Eg see *Panayiotous v Sony Music Entertainment (UK) Ltd* [1994] EMLR 299 and Ch 15 under 'Common law rules on restraint of trade'.

However, a counter argument to the above point is the view that the party who puts forward their draft of an agreement as the one to be negotiated controls the agenda of the matters to be discussed. For example, a proposed deal between a large pharmaceutical company and a university based on the company's 'standard' agreement may contain many provisions (perhaps very detailed and very one-sided) not suitable for the deal but ideal for the company's protection and commercial interest. The university negotiators will be faced with the task of negotiating many points and catching all those points which need to be removed or amended. In such a situation, suggesting that much of the agreement needs to be removed or drafted in a completely different way may not be seen as a negotiating strategy likely to foster harmonious relations.

Who should bear the costs of drafting the agreement?

Usually, each party bears its own (legal and other) costs in drafting and negotiating a technology transfer agreement; there is no general convention that one party or the other will bear both parties's costs. Sometimes, it is explicitly stated in the agreement that each party will bear its own costs, although such provisions are more often seen in situations where there may be a commercial convention (or at least a preference, supported by bargaining power) that one party will bear the other's costs. For example, a party providing finance may require the borrower to bear the lender's legal costs. Or in spin-out or joint-venture types of agreement the party which is to provide finance etc will expect its legal, accountancy and other costs to be paid through an increased royalty, set charges at specific times or may wish to implement other creative strategies for recovering those costs.

Dealing with parties who are, or are not, legally represented

If one party is legally represented, and the other party is not, the represented party and its lawyer should be careful not to suggest, by words or actions, that it is recommending that the other party execute an agreement or is advising the other party to do so. Best practice is to state in a letter to the unrepresented party that they should consider seeking their own legal advice.[74] In some situations (eg in agreements to settle disputes with ex-employees) the represented party may wish to offer to pay some or all of the other party's legal costs in obtaining such advice.

---

74   This is perhaps less necessary where negotiations are taking place between two commercial organisations or an academic institution and a commercial party as it is likely each will have easy access to either in-house or external lawyers, or the parties' representatives will be experienced in negotiating contracts and will know when to take advice. However, it is best practice where the other party is an individual (such as an inventor or academic acting on his or her own).

However, where a party is represented by a solicitor, and that solicitor knows that the other party is legally represented, English solicitors' protocol requires that the first solicitor should communicate with his or her opposite number, and not with the client directly, unless otherwise agreed.[75] This point is reinforced by the Solicitor's Code of Conduct at rule 10.04: 'Contacting other party to a matter. You must not communicate with any other party who to your knowledge has retained a lawyer, or a business carrying on the practice of lawyers, to act in a matter, except: (a) to request the name and address of the other party's lawyer; (b) where it would be reasonable to conclude that the other party's lawyer has refused or failed for no adequate reason either to pass on messages to their client or to reply to correspondence, and has been warned of your intention to contact their client direct; (c) with that lawyer's consent; or (d) in exceptional circumstances.'

In the authors' view this issue is one to be aware of so as to avoid falling into obvious traps, but is probably not one to get too exercised about when dealing with sophisticated commercial parties, particularly if the other party chooses to involve its legal advisers on a limited basis to save costs.

Marking-up and circulating drafts

When proposing revisions to a draft agreement, it is conventional to mark-up the changes on the draft. This can be done either by using the review functions of most modern word processing software, or by using a document comparison function or third-party software which will produce a version which shows the changes made.

If the review function is used, the drafter should be very careful to ensure that all changes have been made with this function switched on. Sometimes drafts are circulated which highlight only some of the changes that have been made.[76] In the authors' view, this is very bad practice. Although the side receiving the reviewed document has a responsibility for checking what they receive, because of the modern realities of negotiating agreements the time available to a drafter is limited and he or she will usually rely on what is received. Although often done carelessly rather than deliberately (eg if several people within an organisation have been involved in making changes to a draft), it can lead to very bad feeling between the negotiating parties if discovered, and extra care should be taken to ensure this does not happen.

---

75 This will apply to solicitors who are external to a party but also to those who are employees of a party (ie 'in-house solicitors'). This latter point which can sometimes be overlooked by commercial negotiators in their use of lawyers (whether in-house or not); that lawyers have a separate code they must abide with.
76 Unless a word-by-word comparison is carried out, such changes are in effect hidden.

Sometimes a party will send out a draft in a pdf format that cannot be easily revised,[77] and this can be done deliberately to discourage changes to the draft.[78] In the authors' view this is a short-sighted approach, and the authors' practice when faced with this is to request the original word-processed version of the document, which is rarely if ever refused. Alternatively the text of the pdf can be extracted (where possible) and reformatted in a word-processing program, then marked-up (but having to go through this process is likely to cause bad feeling).[79]

The signing process – different methods

The most secure method of signing an agreement is to have both parties physically present at the same location at the same time, and have them sign the agreement there.

However, many agreements are signed by parties where they are at different locations. In such cases, the parties may wish the agreement to be executed quickly, and without waiting for copies to be sent by post or courier between them so that each party can sign. Different methods are used to enable the agreement to be executed in a short space of time.

A common method, once the full terms are agreed informally, is to have the parties scan and email (or send by facsimile), the signed signature pages to one another, to indicate their final agreement. Under English law, this is generally an acceptable method of executing an agreement. Typically, parties will follow this up with hard copies (originals) of the signatures, but the agreement is made when the signatures are exchanged by fax or email.[80]

Nowadays, parties sometimes choose to enter into contracts by means of electronic signatures, including digital signatures. The term 'electronic signature' covers a wide range of types of signature and, for certain purposes, has been held to include a typed name at the bottom of an email. Digital signatures are a specific, more secure example of electronic signatures.[81] In

---

77 It is possible to disable the ability to add comments etc to a pdf file with a password.

78 Although the full version of Adobe Acrobat and other programs such as PDFX-change allow documents to have comments put on them (unless the document is password protected), this is not ideal as the comments, if accepted, have to be manually entered into the original word-processing document.

79 The worst-case scenario is to use a printed version of the document, scan the document, convert to text and reformat in word-processing software and then engage in extensive proof-reading.

80 In effect this is adaption of the traditional approach used by English solicitors in house sales, where the solicitors agree a telephone exchange of contracts by one of the methods laid down by the Law Society. This approach depends on each solicitor having a version of the agreement signed by his or her client in front of him or her when speaking to the other solicitor by telephone to make the exchange. Once the exchange has taken place, each solicitor undertakes to hold his or her client's signed agreement 'to the order' of the other solicitor, and sends it to the other solicitor by post or courier. In principle, this method could be adapted for use in the execution of technology transfer agreements, but this is rarely done.

81 Digital signatures are, in effect, a piece of computer code that is encrypted, and which a party applies to an electronic document to signify his or her 'signature' of it.

the authors' experience, these methods are rarely encountered in technology transfer or other commercial agreements. The authors' preference is to see a traditional signature (even if scanned and emailed or faxed), which may be more difficult to forge than some types of electronic signature that rely on use of passwords and email accounts; the latter may be at risk of access by third parties who are given the relevant passwords.

For the benefit of readers who are not experienced in English contract law, many agreements, including many technology transfer agreements, can be binding under English law without having a formal written agreement signed.[82] The above comments assume that the parties intended that their agreement would only become binding once both parties had signed and sent the agreement (or at least the signature page) to the other party. Legal advice should be sought on all proposed methods of signature, particularly if they are unusual, or if an agreement is to become legally binding other than at the time the parties sign the agreement.

Verifying that proper execution of the agreement has occurred

Each party should consider whether the individuals signing the agreement (on both sides of the transaction) have the necessary authority to do so. For English companies, this may raise questions of agency law and whether the individual has 'apparent authority' to sign the agreement. A party may need to seek advice from its lawyers as to what degree of due diligence is appropriate in an individual case to ensure that the individual is authorised.

In very large or important transactions involving English companies, a party may require the other party to produce a certified copy of a board of directors' resolution, authorising the signing of the agreement and giving a named individual authority to sign it on the company's behalf.[83]

---

82 It is possible, as in most contracts made in England, to have a verbal technology transfer agreement (although, of course, this is never recommended or suggested as ever being desirable or practical!).

83 However, sometimes, almost irrespective of the size of the deal it may not be possible to do so. Obtaining a board resolution from a large multinational pharmaceutical company whose head office is based in another country is unlikely to be achieved other than for the most substantial deal (ie one worth several hundred million euros); or within a timescale which is realistic, ie the pharmaceutical company's procedure may require that a request for a board resolution needs to go through several stages of management in different countries and it could take several months before it reaches the top. Or to take another example, a commercial organisation has a standard procedure that all deals it enters into above a certain value require the other party to demonstrate that the person signing has authority to do so via a specially passed board resolution; but if the other party is a university, the procedures and timing of meeting of its council simply cannot accommodate such as request.

There is a separate issue as to whether the organisation has the legal capacity to enter into the type of agreement contemplated. It is extremely rare for an English corporate entity to be able to avoid contractual obligations by arguing that it lacked the necessary legal capacity.[84] The position in other countries may vary. This point is often covered by warranties, particularly in agreements based on US templates, although the legal effectiveness of such warranties may be doubted if the agreement in which they are contained is ultra vires.

Keeping and archiving original versions of the agreement

Even today, with the widespread use of the internet for the purchase of items using electronic funds, and the absence of a conventional signature, commercial agreements of any value are routinely still signed with a physical signature. Partly this is convention (and perhaps old-fashioned), but also, a physical signature is much easier to test as being related to a particular person than an electronic or a digital signature on a document sent electronically from one computer through the internet (through many different computers/servers located around the world) and received at another computer.[85]

It is highly desirable to keep the signed original of an agreement in a safe place, and in addition to scan the signed original and keep an electronic copy of it or make a photocopy and store that separately from the original. If the original is lost, the English court is likely to accept the scanned copy or photocopy as evidence of the agreement's existence. But there may be situations in which the original version is much more useful, eg if forgery is alleged or there is doubt as to what is the final (agreed) version of the agreement. The position in other countries may vary.

To facilitate review of existing agreements, all related agreements, including amendments, termination agreements, etc, file notes, emails and letters should be kept in one place. If advice is sought on an agreement, it is very important to provide the signed version (or a scanned or photocopied reproduction of the signed version) rather than an unsigned document that 'we are pretty sure

---

84　Sometimes known by the Latin expression 'ultra vires'.

85　At least in the English courts, the calling of expert evidence to establish whether a particular signature is that of a particular person is tried and tested over many centuries. That of an electronic signature (ie a typed name on an email accepting a contract) requires much more evidence that the person who bears the typed name actually typed it, and the email containing the signature was actually sent by that person, and so on. For an understanding of the complexities in establishing the provenance, see Mason (ed), *Electronic Evidence: Disclosure, Discovery and Admissibility* (LexisNexis Butterworths, 2007).

is the final version' (more often than one would like it turns out that last-minute changes were made or that the agreement was never fully signed). These housekeeping points are often overlooked.[86]

---

86   In addition, a company which has poor housekeeping procedures for its documentation could have its case undermined in the event of a dispute. The other side in the dispute could argue that poor housekeeping procedures (ie not knowing which document is definitive or not having versions of an agreement which support the company's arguments) are demonstrative of the weaknesses in the company's case.

CHAPTER 3

Overview of Intellectual Property

INTRODUCTION

Ways in which intellectual property laws affect technology-related agreements

It is possible to draft a legally enforceable technology transfer agreement with very little knowledge of intellectual property law. Ignorance of intellectual property law may damage a party's commercial and legal interests, but the basic agreement may still 'work' as a legally binding contract. A few examples illustrate how this can happen:

- *Commercial parties enter into an agreement under which one party grants manufacturing rights to the other.* Neither party considers in detail the intellectual property rights that protect the manufacturing technology, the assumption being that the licensor is licensing all relevant rights that it owns. A vague statement is included in the agreement to this effect. Perhaps a patent number is mentioned, or there is a passing reference to copyright in a licensed (software) product, or a paragraph is included which describes relevant know-how. Otherwise little attention is given to intellectual property issues.

- *Development of computer software.* A company wishes to commission a software developer to write a specialist business computer program. The company wishes to automate part of its business and spends a considerable amount of time specifying what the computer program is to do and how it will interact with other programs it owns. But the agreement does not address the issue of who is to own the resulting computer program (because the company assumes that since it is paying for the computer program, it will own it). On that assumption the company believes others can use it on its behalf (for example because the company wishes to out-source part of its operations).

- *A company owns a portfolio of patents.* The company's assets are made the subject of a fixed and floating charge in favour of a bank, as security for providing the company with an overdraft. The bank's standard form of charge creates a mortgage over the patents,[1] as part of its charge over all the company's assets. The bank fails to register this mortgage at the UK Intellectual Property Office, relying instead on the protection given by registration of the charge with the Registrar of Companies,[2] and it does not specifically address the legal issues which arise out of the fact that the assets over which it has a charge include patents.

In these examples the parties may be fortunate: no harm may result from their failure to take account of intellectual property law issues. Transactions involving intellectual property are often legally effective despite the parties' ignorance of intellectual property laws. This is partly because much of the law governing transactions in intellectual property is the same as for transactions in other kinds of personal property.[3] A party who is familiar with the general requirements of commercial law, and the ways in which personal property may be traded,[4] may apply its understanding to intellectual property transactions, sometimes without adverse consequences.

However, the parties may be unlucky. Through failure to take account of intellectual property laws, they may find that their transaction is not legally effective or, more commonly, they may not be able to take advantage of protection that would have been available if appropriate steps had been taken, such as registration of the transaction with the UK Intellectual Property Office.[5] Or they may simply have failed to address in their agreement issues which arise in the context of intellectual property transactions.[6]

The laws governing intellectual property transactions are a mixture of general laws governing commercial transactions in personal property – intellectual property being (for most purposes) a type of personal property[7]– and specific laws which are mostly to be found in the intellectual property legislation. To take one example: under English law it is possible to transfer title to most

---

1 Assuming the mortgage is in writing and signed on behalf of the mortgagor: see Patents Act 1977, s 30(6).
2 See Companies Act 2006, ss 860, 861 and 874.
3 In essence, the term 'personal property' covers virtually all types of property, eg anything from Mars bars to complex machinery, but not land and buildings, which are 'real property'.
4 See further Ch 9.
5 Eg the protection given under Patents Act 1977, s 68 if an assignment or exclusive licence is registered within six months of the transaction taking place. See Ch 4 under 'Proceedings for infringement'.
6 Eg in the case of a licence, who should be responsible for taking action against infringers of the licensed intellectual property. In the example of the commissioned software, who will own it because if this issue is not addressed, the company who commissioned it may not be able to use it as they wish, as the default position is likely to be they will not be the owners, but only have the right to use it.
7 See Ch 9. In broad terms, personal property comprises all types of property other than *real* property (ie land and buildings). This is a different issue as to whether intellectual property is considered to be 'goods' or 'services' (See Ch 10 under 'Is a sale (assignment) of patents a sale of "goods"?').

kinds of personal property under an oral contract – no writing is required.[8] By contrast, most UK intellectual property laws provide that an assignment (transfer) of title (ie ownership) is void unless it is in writing and signed by or on behalf of the assignor.[9]

In other areas, the laws governing transactions are the same whether one is dealing with intellectual property or other subject matter. For example, the requirement under English law that each party should give *consideration* (ie something of value) in order for a contract to be legally binding on that party[10] applies equally to contracts involving intellectual property as to other types of personal property.[11]

Thus, to be sure of fully protecting rights arising from an intellectual property transaction, it is necessary to be familiar with both the laws governing commercial transactions generally (particularly transactions involving personal property) and the specific laws that apply to the type of intellectual property under consideration, and in some cases override the general law.[12]

Issues of contract law of particular relevance to intellectual property transactions are considered in Chapter 10. This chapter will provide an overview of intellectual property laws that are relevant to technology transfer. Later chapters will consider those laws in more detail.

Some of the laws governing intellectual property transactions are concerned with the fact that title to the property in question is registrable. A party who fails to take this into account when negotiating the terms of an intellectual property transaction may be prejudiced. For example, if the purchaser of a UK patent fails to register the transfer of title to the patent (ie the assignment) within six months of the date of the assignment, the right to claim costs and expenses for infringements which take place between the date of the assignment and the date on which it is registered are lost.[13] If the purchaser fails to register the assignment at the UK Intellectual Property Office at all, and the original seller purports to sell the patent to another person who registers her/his assignment, the second purchaser may acquire better rights to the patent than the original purchaser.[14]

---

8   This contrasts with the position under US law, where contracts for the sale of goods over a certain value must be in writing.

9   See Patents Act 1977, s 30(6); Copyright, Designs and Patents Act 1988, s 90(3); and Registered Designs Act 1949, s 15B(3).

10 Unless, of course, the contract is executed as a deed. See Anderson and Warner, *Drafting and Negotiating Contracts* (2nd edn, Tottel Publishing, 2007).

11 Although, in the absence of consideration under a licence agreement, the licensee might still have what is known as a 'bare licence' under the intellectual property.

12 Not to mention the other areas of English law that may be relevant.

13 See Patents Act 1977, s 68.

14 See Patents Act 1977, s 33.

Some of the main ways in which intellectual property laws affect commercial transactions relating to technology are as follows:

- **Ownership of rights.** The intellectual property legislation defines who will be the first owner of an item of intellectual property, and deals specifically with the position of employees, employers and persons commissioning works. The rules are different for each type of intellectual property and include traps for the unwary.[15] Some legislation also addresses some of the rights of co-owners,[16] but in this area co-owners are well advised to agree their rights and obligations to one another specifically, rather than rely on the statutory provisions.

- **Methods of transferring rights.** The main methods of transfer of intellectual property rights under English law are:

  — *assignment* (ie transfer of title/ownership, eg by way of contract or as gift);[17]

  — *licence* (ie one person is giving permission to another to use the intellectual property – analogous in some ways to a lease of a building – only limited rights are granted by the owner, such as the right to use the building for a particular period of time or indefinitely, but not to own the building); and

  — *mortgage* (ie lending money to the owner of the intellectual property, with the lender having the right to own or sell the intellectual property if the owner fails to make payments).

---

15 For example, the commissioner of a design consisting of a semiconductor topography will be the first owner of design right in the design, unless there is a written agreement in place between the designer and commissioner which provides otherwise. For other types of design, it seems the commissioner will always be the first owner of design right – the legislation does not appear to allow the parties to agree otherwise (see Copyright, Designs and Patents Act 1988, s 215(2)), although there is nothing in the legislation to prevent the first owner agreeing to assign his rights to the commissioner, and in most cases it is unlikely to be important whether one is the first or second owner. By contrast, the position for registered designs is that the commissioner will only be the first owner of the design if the commission is 'for money or money's worth'. In the case of copyright, the commissioner will not own the copyright in the commissioned work unless this is specifically agreed with the author or his employer (see Copyright, Designs and Patents Act 1988, s 11). Thus where the author and commissioner of a work fail to address the question of ownership in an appropriate form of agreement, the parties' rights will differ depending on the type of right in question.

16 In reality only the Patents Act 1977 has any meaningful provisions regarding co-owners (albeit limited).

17 An 'assignment' in reality has two meanings: one is the document whose only function is to transfer title (similar to the formal document which formally notifies the Land Registry in England that title in a house has been transferred from one person to another); and a second meaning whereby there is an agreement which records the details on which the property is sold or gifted. In the second meaning the word is merely used, by convention, instead of 'sell', 'sale' or 'gift' etc.

These methods of transfer are specifically provided for in, or recognised by, intellectual property legislation.[18]

- **Formalities for transferring rights.** Unlike the position for transactions in most other types of personal property, it is in some cases necessary for the transaction (eg an assignment) to be in writing.[19] In most cases such transactions can be simply signed by one or more of the parties, although the transaction may also be executed as a deed according to general contract law principles.[20]

- **Registration of rights.** Although generally not compulsory,[21] there are often advantages, as described in the intellectual property legislation, in registering the transaction with the appropriate intellectual property authority (eg UK Intellectual Property Office)[22] where available.[23] Registration with Registrar of Companies may also be appropriate in some cases (eg in the case of a mortgage over intellectual property rights owned by a company).

- **Rights provided by statute.** In some cases the legislation describes certain rights that the transferee of the intellectual property right will have. For example, the Patents Act 1977 describes certain rights of co-owners of a patent,[24] and provides for specific rights for an exclusive licensee.[25] Generally, these rights may be overridden by contract, but they will operate in the absence of contract terms to the contrary. Where the legislation is silent as to the rights and duties of parties to a transfer of intellectual property rights, the contract may specify particular rights and duties of the parties, or it may be possible for a term to be implied, in accordance with normal contract law rules.[26]

- **Contractual issues arising from the nature of intellectual property.** The transfer of intellectual property rights raises a number of issues that may not arise when other types of personal property are transferred. It may be desirable to address these issues in the contract (although not all will be relevant in all situations). For example:

---

18 See Ch 4 under 'Nature of patents and patent applications'; Ch 5 under 'Nature of copyright'; and Ch 7 under 'Nature of design right' and 'Community design'.

19 See Ch 4 under 'Nature of patents and patent applications'; Ch 5 under 'Nature of copyright'; and Ch 7 under 'Nature of design right' and 'Community design'.

20 See Ch 9 under 'Execution of deeds and agreements concerning property'. Assignments of intellectual property are often signed as deeds, usually as a precautionary measure. Ie if there is any doubt that anything of value is being provided by the party who is to become the owner (assignee) of the assigned intellectual property.

21 Strangely, Registered Designs Act 1949, s 19(1) (as amended) *requires* the assignee of a registered design to register the transaction. This is discussed in Chs 4, 5 and 6.

22 See Ch 4 under 'Registration of patents and interests in patents'.

23 It is not possible to register any form of transaction at the UK Intellectual Property Office where copyright or the design right is involved.

24 See Ch 4 under 'Co-ownership of patents and patent application'.

25 See Ch 4 under 'When must the application be made'.

26 See Ch 10 under 'Interpretation and construction of licences and other agreements'.

— who may/must register the transaction;

— who is responsible for maintaining the intellectual property in force (eg by paying renewal fees);

— who may/must deal with infringers;

— who may/must deal with challenges to the intellectual property (eg applications for revocation); and

— (in the case of assignments particularly) who may sue in respect of infringements which occurred prior to the date of the assignment.

Meaning of the term 'intellectual property'

There is no universally accepted meaning for the term 'intellectual property'. It is generally understood to refer to:

- patents (including supplementary protection certificates);

- registered designs;

- the separate protection known as design right;

- community registered and unregistered designs;

- copyright;

- database right;

- trade marks (whether registered or not);

- community trade marks; and

- similar property, including applications for registered intellectual property.

In other countries there are other forms of protection for intellectual property, particularly utility models (a lesser form of patent protection).

Know-how is sometimes treated as a type of intellectual property – it is commonly licensed and sold in the same way as the above types of intellectual property. However, it is not, strictly speaking, a form of property; it may be more accurate to describe know-how as information (particularly technical information) which may be protected under the law of confidence.[27] The law of confidence will be considered in Chapter 8.

Intellectual property is defined for specific purposes in the Companies Act 2006 as meaning:

---

27 See eg the analysis of the nature of know-how in Ch 8 under 'Meanings of the term 'know-how'.

'(a) any patent, trade mark, registered design, copyright or design right;

(b) any licence under or in respect of any such right'.[28]

This definition seems to confuse types of intellectual property (patents, trade marks etc) with licences under intellectual property. A similar confusion arises in some other legislation; for example the Value Added Tax Act 1994 referred to:

'transfers and assignments of copyright, patents, licences, trade marks and similar rights…'.

Peculiar definitions of intellectual property feature in other non-intellectual property legislation. For example, the Corporation Tax 2009 defines intellectual property as:

'(a) industrial information or techniques likely to assist in—

(i) the manufacture or processing of goods or materials, or

(ii) the working of a mine, oil well or other source of mineral deposits or the winning of access to them, or

(iii) the carrying out of any agricultural, forestry or fishing operations,

(b) a patent, trade mark, registered design, copyright, design right or plant breeder's right, and

(c) a right under the law of a country outside the United Kingdom which corresponds or is similar to any of those falling within paragraph (b)'.[29]

This definition includes a (very narrow) description of know-how (relating to products or extraction and does not cover the use of know-how where services are provided). The definition also does not cover a licence under the forms of intellectual property stated.

This 'lumping together' of intellectual property and rights in or under intellectual property is not uncommon in legislation which is not primarily concerned with intellectual property, reflecting, in part, the absence of a generally recognised definition.

---

28 Companies Act 2006, s 861(4). This definition does not appear to include some of the newer intellectual property, eg community designs or the database right and is being used in the specific context of the type of charges that a company can create (and what the company must do once it has created one).

29 Corporation Tax Act 2009, s 1139.

The term *industrial property* is sometimes used, although this term has largely been superseded by the term intellectual property. Industrial property is sometimes understood to mean patents and industrial designs, but not copyright (or at least not copyright for non-industrial items, for example literary works).[30]

The law does not protect intellectual property as a general category; it is necessary to consider the specific protection given for each type of property, patent, copyright etc and then how each one is protected in a particular country. The rules governing transactions in each type are not uniform; this may be a consequence of the fact that the legislation governing the different types of property was drafted at different times – sometimes decades apart. The rules will be considered in the following chapters.

Sources of UK intellectual property law

The main sources of the UK intellectual property laws[31] which directly protect technology are statutes and statutory instruments, including:

- **Patents**. Patents Act 1977.

- **Supplementary protection certificates.** Council Regulation (EEC) 1768/92 of 18 June 1992 concerning the creation of a supplementary protection certificate for medicinal products.[32]

- **Copyright (including copyright protection for computer programs and databases and measures to prevent removal, or circumvention, of copy-protection devices).** Part I of the Copyright, Designs and Patents Act 1988.

- **Database right.** Copyright and Rights in Databases Regulations 1997.[33]

- **Design Right (including semi-conductor right).** Part III of the Copyright, Designs and Patents Act 1988, as amended. In relation to design right protection for semi-conductor topographies (where special rules apply), see also particularly the Design Rights (Semiconductor Topographies) Regulations 1989.[34]

---

30 For example, the EU divides intellectual property into two categories, industrial property (covering patents, utility models, designs, trade marks etc) and copyright and related rights. See http://ec.europa.euinternal_market/index_en.htm; http://ec.europa.eu/internal_market/indprop/index_en.htm; and http://europa.eu.int/comm/internal_market/en /intprop/index.htm.
31 Despite the devolving of many powers to Scotland and Wales, intellectual property legislation still covers, with some minor exceptions, the whole of the UK.
32 Patents Act 1977, s 128B and Sch 4A.
33 SI 1997/3032.
34 SI 1989/1100.

- **Registered designs.** Registered Designs Act 1949 (particularly Part IV of the Copyright, Designs and Patents Act 1988; see the full text of the Registered Designs Act 1949, as amended by the 1988 Act and earlier legislation, and by the Registered Designs Regulations 2001,[35] set out in Schedule 4 of the 1988 Act (as amended).Community designs. Council Regulation (EC) 6/2002 of 12 December 2001 on Community designs (both registered and unregistered).

This book does not consider other types of intellectual property, such as trade marks and several types of copyright protection, such as sound recordings, performance or broadcasting rights, nor the non-statutory law of 'passing off'. These areas of law do not directly protect technology, although they are part of the larger subject of intellectual property. Confidential information is considered in Chapter 8.

NATIONAL AND INTERNATIONAL INTELLECTUAL PROPERTY LAWS: CURRENT LAWS AND PROPOSALS[36]

Current laws

Transactions in relation to technology are often international in nature. For example, a licence is often granted to exploit technology in more than one country. On the other hand, most of the rights that protect technology are national, rather than international, rights.[37]

Licence agreements are frequently concerned with a portfolio of national intellectual property rights which protect the licensed technology in different countries. An agreement may need to take account of separate legal requirements governing transactions in intellectual property, in each country of the licensed territory. The fact that the agreement is stated to be made under one country's laws may not override national laws in other countries.[38] Particularly in cases where such national laws concern matters of public

---

35 SI 2001/3949, implementing Directive 98/71/EC on the legal protection of designs.
36 For developments in intellectual property laws in the European Union, consult the following websites of the EU: http://europa.eu/internal_market/indprop/index_en.htm and http://europa. eu/internal_market/copyright/index_en.htm. Also, a useful summary table of the current status of all EU laws and proposals for new laws is provided on a monthly basis in European Intellectual Property Review.
37 Although there may be an international treaty or law underlying the national laws. The point being is that although many countries have signed up to a treaty, the implementation of the treaty will be on a country by country basis.
38 See eg *Chiron v Organon Teknika Ltd (No 2)* [1993] FSR 567 where the court held that the provisions of then in force Patents Act 1977, s 44 applied to a patent licence covering both UK and non-UK patents even though the agreement was expressed to be made under US laws. (s 44 has since been repealed (see Ch 4 under 'Anti-competitive provisions in agreements relating to patents').

policy (for example competition or tax law), it may not be possible to override those laws by private agreements.

In order to be certain that the agreement complies with the legal requirements of all parts of the territory covered by the transaction, it may be necessary to take legal advice on the transaction in more than one jurisdiction, particularly if it is intended to register the transaction, for example with national patent offices.[39] Where the cost of doing so is not thought to be justified, the agreement is sometimes drafted so that it is merely an agreement to execute a transfer or to license rights, rather than an immediate transfer or licence of those rights. The parties may then agree that they will execute further documents for each part of the contract territory, which may need modification to comply with any local legal requirements.[40]

The main areas in which there is currently a degree of international harmonisation of intellectual property systems in respect of technology are considered below.

Patents

Domestic UK patent applications

The application for and granting of patents in the UK[41] are subject to the same basic regime as patents applied for under the European Patent Convention.

Applications under the European Patent Convention

Where a person wishes to make applications for a patent for the same invention in several countries, as an alternative to making applications to each individual national patent office, it is possible to make a single application to the European Patent Office (EPO) in Munich.[42] A successful application leads to a 'bundle' of national patents in identical form. The consideration of

---

39 Which often will involve the use of local agents, if the parties do not have a sufficiently large presence in a particular jurisdiction to be able to handle such activities themselves. In practice, a party will usually have a patent/trade mark agent who will handle their registrable intellectual property, and the patent/trade mark agent will instruct a local agent to deal with such matters as formal registrations, etc. In many jurisdictions it is a requirement that specific forms are used when making a registration (ie the parties cannot use something of their own devising).

40 Although such steps will not guarantee that the agreement is legally enforceable in all parts of the licensed territory, they may help to ensure that the form of licence executed is appropriate for registration in the relevant jurisdiction.

41 Those that are not applied for under the European Patent Convention or the Patent Co-operation Treaty).

42 See http://www.epo.org/patents/law/legal-texts/epc.html for the latest version of the EPC (currently that in effect from 13 December 2007) for details on making applications and the procedure used by the EPO, etc.

an application and procedure up to grant is dealt with by the EPO not by each country's patent office.

Most European countries are members of the European Patent Convention (EPC), but membership is completely distinct from membership of the European Union; there are some notable differences in the respective membership of these organisations.[43]

If the UK is designated by the applicant as one of the countries in which the applicant wishes the EPC application to take effect, the UK patent resulting from the application is known as a European patent (UK), and is then governed by the Patents Act 1977.[44]

Applications under the Patent Co-operation Treaty

It is also possible to make an application under the Patent Co-operation Treaty (PCT)[45] to which most countries of the world are party. The application is processed through its early stages by the World Intellectual Property Organisation (WIPO) in Geneva,[46] and then converts to national applications which are processed to grant or rejection in national patent offices.[47]

Membership of the PCT currently extends to 142 countries and includes the countries of the EU, the United States of America, many Latin American countries, China and Japan.[48]

Supplementary protection certificates and patent term extension

Supplementary protection certificates (SPC)[49] are, for practical purposes, but not in law, a type of patent term extension. As they were introduced under EC Regulations the substantive law creating them is the same throughout the EU.[50] These are available for pharmaceutical products and plant protection products which have also received government approval for marketing in the

---

43 There are currently 36 members of the EPC, but 9 are not members of the European Union (for example, Norway, Switzerland and Turkey).
44 See Patents Act 1977, ss 77–81 for how a European patent (UK) takes effect under UK law.
45 See http://www.wipo.int/pct/en/texts/articles/atoc.htm for the text of the PCT.
46 It is also possible for an application to be made to an applicant's national patent office (or in some cases the EPO). The circumstances in which an application can be made to a particular patent office (national or international) can be found at http://www.wipo.int/pct/en/treaty/about.htm.
47 Patents Act 1977, ss 89, 89A and 89B concern the application of the Patents Act to PCT applications.
48 The current membership list can be found at http://www.wipo.int/treaties/en/ShowResults.jsp?lang=en&treaty_id=6. Reference was made above to Norway, Turkey and Switzerland not being members of the EPC – they are all members of the PCT.
49 See Ch 4 under 'Supplementary Protection Certificates'.
50 Council Regulation (EC) 1768/92; Council Regulation (EC) 1610/96.

country in which the SPC is sought. The period of time a SPC is granted for is limited to five years.

Patent term extension generally

Patent term extension laws exist in other countries, including the USA, Australia, New Zealand and Japan. However there is currently no harmonisation as to how and when a patent term may be extended (for example an international treaty or law such as for the application of a patent under PCT).

The basic idea behind patent term extension law is to allow an additional period of protection for certain inventions (particularly pharmaceuticals) which in practice do not enjoy the full period of patent monopoly. For example, in the case of a pharmaceutical drug it can take eight or more years to obtain regulatory approval to market the drug (in addition to the lengthy period which is necessary for the research, development and testing of it, which can often last ten to twenty years). As a result, the effective period of monopoly of a patent covering such a drug can often be reduced to under ten years. Patent term extensions seek to bring the effective monopoly period up towards the full twenty-year patent period.[51]

Patents for biotechnological inventions

The EC Directive on the legal protection of biotechnological inventions[52] was implemented in the UK by the Patents Regulations 2000. The principal aim of the Directive is to provide an indication of what, in relation to biotechnological inventions, is considered to be patentable. As such, the scheme of patent protection within the UK is not altered, but merely refined to take account of the increasing importance of biotechnology and genetic engineering in a wide range of industries within the European Community, and the need to establish clear indications for protection.

Utility models

In addition to the protection provided by patents for inventions there is also a lesser form of protection available, the utility model. The protection available to patents (and most other major forms of intellectual property) is now based to a large extent on detailed international treaties. The same is not yet true for that of utility models.

---

51 The life of a European patent being generally 20 years from the application date; the life of a US patent is also now 20 years from the date of grant.

52 Directive 98/44/EC ([1998]) OJ L213/13) on the legal protection of biotechnological inventions; implemented into law in the UK by the Patents Regulations 2000 (SI 2000/2037). This is considered in Ch 4 under 'Patents for biotechnological inventions'.

The procedures for the application for protection of an invention by a utility model, and the criteria by which such an invention can be protected, vary from country to country.[53] However, some generalisations can be made:

- a utility model provides protection for an invention for a shorter period than a patent (often for a period of between six and ten years, rather than the 20-year period for a patent);

- an application for a utility model is not examined as exhaustively by a patent office as for a patent (the substance of the application is often not examined prior to registration of the utility model);

- the length of time it takes to register a utility model is often significantly quicker than for a patent (taking an average of six months) and the costs involved are often substantially less;

- the criteria for inventiveness of a utility model are less than for a patent (while there is usually a requirement for 'novelty' in an invention, the requirement for the invention to contain an inventive step or be non-obvious is sometimes not required at all or is of a lower standard than for an application for a patent);

- a utility model is not always available for every type of invention or technology; it is often only available for products but not processes; and

- utility models appear to be confined to situations where there are improvements made to an existing product, or where an invention is minor or there is an adaptation.

The utility model is available in many EU countries (including France, Germany, Italy and Spain but significantly, not in the UK or Sweden for example). It is also not available in the US. However it is available in other countries which are now more likely to be encountered where mainstream commercial transactions involving technology transfer are involved, such as China, Japan and South Korea (but apparently not India).

In practice, the use of a utility model is therefore not usually encountered in the UK where intellectual property transactions are involved, particularly where the licensed territories are the UK or the US and only a significant intellectual property is being licensed, such as a patent. However a utility model could be useful in a number of situations. For example, a company has developed a product which is protected by one or more patents. The company has licensed the patent(s) to a manufacturer to make and sell the

---

53   This lack of harmonising also extends to the name chosen. Other names sometimes used are: 'innovation patent' (Australia), 'short term patent' (Ireland, South Korea, Netherlands), 'utility model patent' (China), or 'petty patent' (Indonesia).

product throughout the EU. The company then makes a minor improvement to the product, which its patent agent indicates is not significant enough to be patentable. If not patentable then the company would normally license this improvement to the product as know-how to the manufacturer (whether under an existing obligation under the patent agreement or under a further agreement entered into by the parties). The danger with know-how is that it is only enforceable where it is supplied under obligations of confidentiality and those obligations have not been breached.[54] However, the company could apply in certain European countries for protection for the improvement as a utility model and therefore not have to ensure the improvement is disclosed or used only under obligations of confidentiality. A utility model would be a more secure form of protection. On the downside, just as with patents, the company would have to go through the process of making one or more applications, country by country, for protection together with the costs involved in making such applications.[55]

Copyright

International treaties, most notably the Berne Convention for the Protection of Literary and Artistic Works, have led to a degree of consistency between national copyright laws as well as reciprocal protection for copyright created in other countries, although there are still wide divergences in some respects. Most of the major economies, including the countries of the EU (including of course the UK), the US, China, Japan, Korea and India are members of the Berne Convention.

Another treaty, the Universal Copyright Convention (UCC) also provides protection for copyright and was instigated by the United Nations Educational, Scientific and Cultural Organisation (UNESCO) as an alternative to the Berne Convention. It was created for countries which did not agree with certain provisions of the Berne Convention but wished to have a form of international protection available for copyright material. These countries included developing countries and the now former Soviet Union and took the view that the Berne Convention was designed to favour developed Western countries that exported their copyright material. The UCC is of less significance now, as many of the countries that are signatories of it are now also contracting states to the Berne Convention.

---

54   Once the know-how is revealed, in breach of an obligation of confidentiality its value is lost, even where the licensor, in this example, takes prompt legal action. See Ch 8 for further consideration of this topic.
55   Another negative factor with utility models is that the licensor would not be making one application to the EPO for example, specifying several countries, in the same way as for patent applications.

The requirements for copyright notices, for example 'all rights reserved' under UCC rules, are generally not necessary to obtain protection in Berne Convention countries.[56]

EC legislation is making increasing attempts to harmonise intellectual property law within the EC member states. In the copyright field, of most relevance for this book are the following:

- *Computer programs*: the Computer Program Directive providing that computer programs are protected as literary works.[57]

- *Databases*: the Database Directive providing that databases are protected as copyright works and also under a new right, the database right (the latter right, which provides a lesser but distinct form of protection than copyright, and which recognises the 'substantial investment in obtaining, verifying or presenting the contents of the database').[58]

- *Standardising length of protection offered by copyright*: the Term Directive harmonises the length of protection that copyrights provide, a period of the life of the author plus 70 years.

- *Removal of copy protection devices etc*: the Information Society Directive[59] has:

    — restricted the 'fair dealing' provisions for research, so that they will only apply when research is done for a non-commercial purpose;

    — introduced measures to prevent the circumvention of anti-copying devices; and

    — introduced measures to prevent the removal of digital rights information.

There have been a considerable number of other EU-wide copyright-related measures, including European Council Directives on rental rights,[60] on

---

56 As to copyright statements for computer programs, see Ch 5 under 'Presumptions as to authorship and ownership'.

57 Council Directive 91/250/EEC [1991] OJ L122/42 on the legal protection of computer programs. It was implemented in the UK by the Copyright (Computer Programs) Regulations 1992 (SI 1992/3233).

58 Directive 96/9/EC on the legal protection of databases. It was implemented by the Copyright and Rights in Databases Regulations 1997(SI 1997/3032).

59 Directive 2001/29//EC ([2001] OJ L167/10) on the harmonization of certain aspects of copyright and related rights in the information society. It was implemented by the Copyright and Related Rights Regulations 2003 (SI 2003/2498). The Directive has made far-reaching changes to the Copyright, Designs and Patents Act 1988, the most important of which are set out in Ch 5.

60 Directive 92/100/EEC.

satellite broadcasting and cable transmission, on electronic commerce,[61] on broadcasts, (electronic) communications to the public and rights in performances,[62] on resale rights of authors of works of art[63] and the enforcement of intellectual property rights.[64] These laws sometimes affect technology-related transactions, but are not relevant in most cases.

Semiconductor topographies

EC member states were required to harmonise the protection given to semiconductor topographies by an EC Directive.[65]

Designs

Many countries protect industrial designs, although there is not the same degree of international harmonisation of design laws as there is in the case of patents. In most countries little searching is carried out and registration of the design is virtually automatic. However, in the US applications for 'design patents' are processed in a similar way to patents, making such applications more costly than in many other countries.

A measure of harmonisation has now been achieved in the EU through:

- a Directive[66] which has harmonised the law in relation to what can be a registered design;[67] and

- a Regulation[68] which has created a Community-wide registered and unregistered design right, which in terms of what is protected as a design is almost identical to the Directive. Registered Community designs receive greater protection than unregistered Community designs.

There is also a separate UK-only (unregistered) design right.

---

61 Directive 2000/31/EC on certain legal aspects of information society services, in particular electronic commerce, in the Internal Market.
62 Directive 2001/29//EC ([2001] OJ L167/10) on the harmonization of certain aspects of copyright and related rights in the information society.
63 Directive 2001/84/EC ([2001] OJ L272/32) on the resale right for the benefit of the author of an original work of art.
64 Directive 2004/48/EC ([2004] OJ L195/16) on the enforcement of intellectual property rights.
65 Directive 87/54/EEC; implemented in the UK by what is now the Design Right (Semiconductor Topographies) Regulations 1989 (SI 1989/1100) as a modified form of design right: see Ch 6 under 'Semiconductor topographies'.
66 Directive 98/71/EC on the legal protection of designs.
67 Implemented by Registered Designs Regulations 2001 (SI 2001/3950), extensively modifying the Registered Designs Act 1949. The Act has subsequently been further amended following the adoption of the Directive on the enforcement of intellectual property rights (2004/48/EC), implemented by the Regulatory Reform (Registered Designs) Order 2006 (SI 2006/1974) and the Intellectual Property (Enforcement, etc) Regulations 2006 (SI 2006/1028).
68 Council Regulation (EC) 6/2002 on Community designs.

Proposals for (further) harmonisation of intellectual property laws

Europe-wide patent

There have been proposals for the creation of a EU-wide patent much in the same way as for community-registered designs or community trade marks. These proposals date back to the early 1970s, and include a 'Community Patent Convention' signed in 1975. Since 1975 these proposals have been the subject of considerable debate and amendment.[69] Following the adoption of the Lisbon Treaty in December 2009, the Competition Council of the EU published a draft Regulation in December 2009 for a EU-wide patent. The main provisions relating to commercial transactions involving intellectual property include:

- a new type of patent would be created, the EU patent, covering the EU and which would have equal effect throughout the EU;

- the EU patent would be only be granted, transferred, declared invalid or lapse for the whole of the EU;

- the EU patent would be granted by the EPO under the provisions of the EPC;

- a transfer of ownership would require the signature of the 'parties to the contract' and then registration with the EPC;[70]

- an EU patent can be licensed for the whole or only part of the EU.[71] An EU patent licence can be granted on an exclusive or non-exclusive basis;

- provisions concerning the right to be granted a patent, who is to be owner of the patent (ie employee or employer), who has the right to work the EU patent, who has the right to use the patent without the permission of the patent owner, licences of right etc are similar or the same as those under the EPC and/or the Patents Act 1977.

Other features of the proposal put forward by the Competition Council include matters which have featured in previous proposals for a EU patent, such as a unified litigation system. However, the latest proposals continue to fail to address the issue of language, that is with regard to which languages

---

69   For an overview of some of the ideas and proposals, see the previous edition of this book. In this edition, consideration will be given only to the specific draft provisions which relate to commercial transactions involving intellectual property.

70   In line with Art 72 of the EPC, unlike the position under the Patents Act 1977, where only the signature of the assignor is required (and then registration with the UK Intellectual Property Office).

71   The draft Regulation does not state whether a license for part of the EU has to cover a particular country (eg the UK or France) or can cover a particular area (eg a specific region of a country, such as specific counties in England or administrative areas in France).

an application can be filed in and processed to grant. The latest proposal puts off this issue and indicates that it would be addressed in a separate EU Regulation (in effect indicating, still, that no decision has yet been made on this point). Also not addressed is the issue of the necessary revisions to be made to the EPC to allow for applications to be made to the EPO (presumably as this is a matter for the EPO rather than the EU).

Utility models

Utility models are considered above. The EU has put forward proposals either to harmonise national protection procedures regarding utility models or to create a Community protection right. The EC published a proposal for a Directive on approximating the legal arrangements for the protection of inventions by utility model in 1997, which was revised in 1999.[72] There was a further consultation in 2001.[73]

The main features proposed for a Community utility model were:

- invention for both products and methods would be protected;

- inventions would need to satisfy the criteria of absolute novelty, suitability for industrial application and a certain degree of inventiveness (the latter being fixed at a lower level than for patents);

- applications for a Community utility model would be subject only to a formal verification, and the utility model would be granted without prior examination of the conditions for obtaining protection with regard to novelty and inventive step;

- there would be no limit on the number of claims;

- a search report on the state of the art could be requested by the applicant or by third parties; the search report would be added to the file and would become compulsory in the event of legal proceedings;

- the rights conferred by a Community utility model would be identical to those conferred by a patent;

- the duration of protection would be a non-renewal maximum of ten years from the date of filing of the application;

- dual protection (application for a patent and for a utility model) would be permitted, but in the event of a dispute, successive proceedings under both sets of protection arrangements would not be allowed;

72   12 December 1997 (COM(97)691).
73   Consultations on the impact of the Community utility model to update the Green Paper on the Protection of Utility Models in the Single Market (SEC(2001)1307).

- the Community utility model would not replace national arrangements for the protection of utility models but would be additional right to them.[74]

The principle economic aim of the Community utility model is to provide a more flexible and less burdensome form of protection than for patents, and the model would be suitable for inventions which have a limited degree of inventiveness and a relatively short lifespan.

The result of the consultation mentioned above was that the respondents were not in favour of a Community utility model at all, but rather that any relevant EU legislation should be directed to harmonising the laws of different member states regarding this form of protection.[75] Since 2002 there appears to have been no activity at the EU level regarding utility models, whether for a Community utility model or for legislation to harmonise national laws.

Other means of protecting technology

Other intellectual property rights

Some countries give legal protection to varieties of intellectual property which have no direct equivalent under UK law.[76] For example under Italian law, protection is given to 'industrial models', a type of design protection.[77] Local advice should be obtained on the ways in which the technology is, or can be, protected under the relevant laws of other countries.

Confidentiality obligations in respect of know-how

Technology is often protected by keeping it secret or disclosing it only under obligations of confidence.[78] This is not a 'safe' method, as this form of protection will only last as long as everyone who is under an obligation of confidence continues to keep to the obligation.

---

74 Drawn from 'Summary report of replies to the questionnaire on the impact of the Community utility model with a view to updating the Green Paper on the protection by the utility mode in the internal market (SEC(2001)1307)'.

75 This consultation provided 47 responses, most from governmental organisations. It seems that larger companies that responded preferred a central office to deal with utility models (less cost involved for them), but smaller companies preferred national offices which were perceived as closer to them.

76 The utility model which is described above is a common example of one.

77 See Italian Industrial Models Act, Royal Decree No 1411 of 25/8/40, Royal Decree No 1354 of 31/10/41, and Arts 2592–2594 of the Civil Code.

78 See Ch 8.

'Data exclusivity' for medicinal products

Under EC laws relating to applications to regulatory bodies for approval to market medicinal products (market authorisation), it is generally necessary to submit the results of pre-clinical and clinical trials on the product with the market authorisation application.

If a person ('new producer') wishes to make and sell a medicinal product which has already been put on the market by another producer then the new person, in certain circumstances, does not need to provide new pre-clinical and clinical trial results; he or she can use the data which has already been provided by the producer who originally put the medicinal product on the market. However the new producer cannot do so for a period of ten years from when the original medicinal product was first approved for marketing in the EC.[79] This ten-year period is known as the period of 'data exclusivity' and may provide valuable protection to the producer that originally submitted the data, particularly if patent protection is weak or absent.

Although a new producer may not be able to use existing data, there is nothing to stop it generating its own pre-clinical and clinical data if it wishes to obtain market authorisation within the ten-year period mentioned above.

Orphan drug status

The US Orphan Drug Act of 1983 established a means of obtaining, from the United States' Food and Drug Administration (FDA), the exclusive right to market a medicinal product for a period of seven years from the date of the FDA's approval to market it. 'Orphan drug status' is available for products which treat rare conditions or diseases, defined as affecting less than 200,000 people in the US (with some exceptions). The intention behind the legislation is to give drug manufacturers an incentive to develop products which would otherwise be uneconomic to produce, because the market for the product is too small.

Similar orphan drug protection has become available in the EU (where the number of persons affected is not more than 5 in 10,000 in the Community).[80]

Compulsory licensing regime (for pharmaceutical products)

In particular circumstances a person can acquire the right to manufacture and sell pharmaceutical products protected by the patent of another. This can occur under the compulsory licensing regime for the manufacture and

---

79 See Directive 2004/27/EC amending Directive 2001/83/EC on the Community code relating to medicinal products for human use. In some circumstances the period can be 11 years. This Directive harmonised the law throughout the EU (where previously until 2004 the period in some countries was six years, while in others it was ten years).

80 Regulation (EC) 141/2000 on orphan medicinal products.

licensing of pharmaceutical products in countries with public health problems under EU Regulation 816/2006.[81] There are extensive provisions as to when this is permitted and what level of royalty needs to be paid for such a licence.

Regulatory measures

In some areas of technology, regulatory approval can have the effect of giving the holder of the approval a form of monopoly, as in the case of the data exclusivity provisions referred to above under '"Data exclusivity" for medicinal products'. The telecommunications field is also extensively regulated.

Traditional property laws, and contractual rights

Some protection is given to the products of technology, for example genetically modified organisms, under traditional property laws.[82] Contractual rights can also protect technology.[83]

Plant breeders' rights

Protection is given to plant varieties under, for example, the Plant Varieties Act 1964 and the Plant Varieties Act 1997, and similar legislation in other countries. There is also an EC Council Regulation on Community plant variety rights.[84]

Trade marks

Trade marks do not protect technology as such. Instead, they provide a form of protection for the symbols and names under which the products of technology are marketed and sold (and in some cases the services that the industry is reliant on). A trade mark can be a very effective means of protection, and in some cases may be more valuable than patents or other rights protecting the technology as such.[85]

---

81 Regulation (EC) 816/2006 on compulsory licensing of patents relating to the manufacture of pharmaceutical products for export to countries with public health problems. The Regulation is directly applicable. The Compulsory Licensing Regulation also covers supplementary protection certificates (Regulation (EC) 816/2006, Art 1).

82 See Ch 9 for whether such material can amount to and be owned as material; and Ch 11, which describes some of the regulatory regimes affecting such material.

83 See Ch 10.

84 Regulation (EC) 2100/94 on Community plant variety rights.

85 Eg it is understood that when the patents for the sugar substitute aspartame expired, the patent owners were able to continue to maintain their favourable position in the market by continuing to license manufacture of aspartame under their trade mark 'Nutrasweet', which by this time was well known.

Passing off

The laws of passing off (in the UK) and unfair competition (in some European countries in particular) can prevent an organisation from getting a 'free ride' on the reputation of another organisation. As with the law of trade marks, such laws do not protect technology as such, but may protect the products of technology when they are marketed and sold.

COMMERCIAL TRANSACTIONS AND INTELLECTUAL PROPERTY LAW

Which intellectual property?

The following paragraphs consider some practical aspects of intellectual property law which are relevant to commercial transactions concerned with or relating to technology transfer.

An important first step in any intellectual property transaction is to identify the intellectual property and other rights which are to be subject to the agreement. Often the technology is protected or protectable by a variety of different rights in different countries, and which may be owned by different persons. For example:

- a pharmaceutical preparation may be protected by patents and patent applications in some countries, by utility models in those countries which have that form of protection, by orphan drug laws in other countries, by data exclusivity provisions in Europe and Japan, and some aspects may also be protected by trade secrets laws;

- a computer software product for the retail market (for example a computer game) may incorporate a number of different copyright works: a computer program, one or more musical works, artistic designs (such as icons which are displayed on the screen), and a separate literary work in the manual; it may also incorporate one or more design works, such as protection of any icons (in addition to qualifying as artistic works) being suitable for protection under the Registered Designs Act 1949, or as a registered and/or unregistered Community design; and it may also incorporate one or more trade secrets, depending on the way in which the program is provided. Furthermore, if the computer program consists of a large number of interconnected programs, then the database right and copyright may also be relevant for that.

Each of these is a separate item of property, and the parties to the transaction should be clear as to which properties are covered by the agreement.

Who owns, or has other rights in, the intellectual property?

Having identified the relevant intellectual property and other property, it is necessary to establish who the owners of rights in these properties are. Some of the questions needing consideration are listed below. In some cases, the transferee (assignee) or licensee under the agreement may be content to rely on warranties from the transferor (assignor or licensor) on some of these issues. In others, the transferee will wish to check the position itself and may require further steps to be taken, such as requiring the transferor's employees to execute confirmatory assignments in favour of their employer or by making checks with relevant regulatory or government organisations (eg patent offices), to ensure that the transferor owns the relevant rights. The main issues are the following:

- *Who created or developed the rights?* Was it the party who is transferring rights under the present agreement (transferor), or some other person?

- *If the transferor created the rights.* Did the transferor do so under any contract of employment or other contract or arrangement which might cause the rights to be owned by some other person (such as a sub-contractor or consultant)?

- *If another person developed the rights.* Where another has created the rights, what rights does the transferor have?

- *As employer.* If the transferor is the employer of the developer, is he or she clearly the owner under relevant intellectual property laws for the right in question? For example, in the case of an invention made by an employee where Patents Act 1977, s 39 is applicable, does the invention belong to the employer or employee? If an agreement is in existence which would override the position under the relevant intellectual property legislation (for example an assignment from the developer to the transferor under the present agreement), is that agreement legally effective?[86]

- *As commissioner.* If the transferor commissioned work which led to the creation of the rights, does he or she own those rights under relevant intellectual property laws or under any agreement with the creator? The position is different for different types of intellectual property. For example, in relation to commissioned works, the commissioner of a design will own design right in that design,[87] but the author will generally own copyright in a commissioned copyright work subject to

---

86 Eg in relation to patents, in the light of Patents Act 1977, s 42.
87 Copyright, Designs and Patents Act 1988, s 215(2).

any agreement to the contrary.[88] Thus, the ownership position must be established for each type of intellectual property right.[89]

- *As assignee, licensee etc.* If the transferor has acquired the rights under an agreement, does that agreement enable the transferor to enter into the present transaction? For example, if the transferor is an exclusive licensee and proposes to grant a sub-licence in the present transaction, does the agreement with the rights owner permit sub-licensing?

- *If the transferor is the owner of the relevant rights, has he or she entered into any agreement which might prevent him or her from entering into the present agreement?* For example, has he or she already licensed the rights to another, or granted an option over the rights to another?

- *Are there any third-party rights which may affect the transferee's ability to exploit the transferred rights?* For example, are the transferred rights the original work of the transferor or did he or she copy or draw inspiration from someone else's work, such that a third party may own rights in the transferred technology?[90] Irrespective of whether plagiarising has occurred, does any third party own rights which may be infringed when the transferred rights are exercised (for example a dominating patent)? Have any allegations to this effect been made? Also, is it necessary to obtain a licence from a third party for the transferred rights to be exploited?

- *How much protection do the transferred rights give to the transferee?* If they are only applications for rights, how likely is it that they will be granted? Are the rights valid and enforceable, or are they likely to be revoked or held invalid by a court? Is there any pending or threatened litigation which might have that result? Are the transferred rights proving to be a deterrent to competitors, or are infringing articles already available in the marketplace?

Which rights are to be transferred?

It is possible to divide up intellectual rights in a number of different ways. The owner of an item of intellectual property, such as a patent, has the right

---

88 Copyright, Designs and Patents Act 1988, s 11.
89 And there should always be a written agreement between the commissioner and the person who makes the intellectual property which clearly indicates that the commissioner is the owner of that intellectual property.
90 This point is likely to be more important to those rights, when registered, that give its owner a monopoly position concerning it. Also it is important to distinguish some forms of copyright from others, particularly literary copyright (which includes computer programs), where it is entirely possible to create, for example, a computer program which operates and does almost exactly the same as another computer program without infringing the intellectual property rights of the owner of the other computer program (as long as no code has been copied and/ or there has not been any access to the code of the other computer program). See Ch 5 under 'Protecting the ideas or concepts contained in computer programs with copyright'.

to prevent others from doing infringing acts, for example making, disposing of, using and importing the product.[91] The owner of a patent may wish to license another to do some, but not all, of these things. In the case of a licence covering more than one country, the owner of the licensed patents may wish to reserve different rights in different territories, for example restricting the licensee's right of manufacture to one country, but permitting sale in several countries.[92]

The rights to be granted may be exclusive, sole or non-exclusive. The terms 'exclusive' and 'sole' are sometimes confused. Although there is no general statutory definition of them, an exclusive licence is generally understood to be one where only the licensee is entitled to exploit the subject matter of the licence, ie even the licensor is excluded from doing so. By contrast, under a sole licence, the licensor merely undertakes not to appoint any other licensee in respect of such subject matter; the licensor may exploit the licensed technology directly himself or herself.[93]

The transferor of the rights may also wish to reserve rights for himself in particular technical fields or applications of the technology, for example granting rights to a chemical compound for human but not animal healthcare applications. There may be improvements or new uses of the original technology that were not envisaged when the agreement was made, which may be included in the package of transferred rights or not, as appropriate. The parties may also wish to divide up particular product markets or customers between them. In all cases (but particularly in relation to product or customer sharing) their ability to do so may be constrained (or prohibited) by competition law.

In some areas of technology, there are even more ways to 'slice the cake'. For example, in the area of computer games software, a successful game may lead to merchandising opportunities, sequel products, and film and broadcasting opportunities. The owner of rights in the games software may wish to license one company to publish the game and another to make a film based on the characters in the game. As new technology becomes available and affordable, it may be desirable to produce an 'interactive' or other version of the original

---

91   Patents Act 1977, s 60(1).

92   The patent owner may, however, be prevented from doing this under competition laws: see Ch 12.

93   There are definitions of 'exclusive licence' in the intellectual property legislation which are consistent with the above explanation (Patents Act 1977, s 130; Copyright, Designs and Patents Act 1988, s 92), but those definitions have no general application; they only have statutory force in relation to their use in the relevant parts of the legislation.

     The definition for Patents Act 1977, s 130 reads:

       "exclusive licence' means a licence from the proprietor of or applicant for a patent conferring on the licensee, or on him and persons authorised by him, to the exclusion of all other persons (including the proprietor or applicant), and right in respect of the invention to which the patent or application relates, and 'exclusive licensee' and 'non-exclusive licence' shall be construed accordingly;'.

game. Thus different rights may be granted in different industries, or in the same industry at different times, under the same basic intellectual property.

Intellectual property is a relatively flexible commodity that can accommodate many sophisticated types of commercial arrangement. The important point for the drafter of a contract is that the contract should clearly identify the scope and extent of the rights granted.

How may/must these rights be transferred?

Methods of transfer of rights

The main types of transaction in intellectual property which are recognised under intellectual property law in the UK (and most other industrially developed countries) are:

- assignments (including partial assignment);
- licences;
- mortgages; and
- vesting by operation of law (for example transfer under a will).

Where there is a partial grant of rights, for example the exclusive right to manufacture and sell articles for a limited period of time, the more conventional method of giving effect to such an arrangement is by means of a licence. However, the possibility of making a partial assignment of rights should not be overlooked in appropriate cases.

Other types of transaction may, in effect, lead to one of the above types of transaction. For example, the 'sale' of a patent might, depending on the form and content of the sale agreement, be construed as an assignment, or as imposing a legally enforceable obligation on the parties to execute an assignment. It should be noted that under the Patents Act 1977[94] and the Registered Designs Act 1949[95] no notice of any trust, whether express, implied or constructive, may be entered in the registers of patents or designs.

Formalities for the transfer of rights

Some intellectual property transactions must be in writing. However they need not be executed as deeds. Assignments of intellectual property (and

---

94 Patents Act 1977, s 32(3).
95 Registered Designs Act 1949, s 17(2).

mortgages of patents) must be in writing, as must some exclusive licences[96] if they are to benefit from certain statutory rights.[97]

Where there is no legal requirement for an intellectual property transaction to be in writing it will, nevertheless, always be desirable for the transaction to be recorded so as to provide evidence that it has taken place. The most obvious way of doing this is by a written agreement. Where it is intended to register the transaction in the relevant intellectual property register, some form of written evidence of the transaction is generally needed to persuade the comptroller or registrar to register the transaction. In some cases, registration is compulsory; in other cases merely highly desirable.

The requirements as to who must sign the document which executes or records the transaction also vary from one type of intellectual property to another. In most cases, the assignor/transferor must sign it.[98]

In some situations, failure to comply with the statutory requirements as to writing may not be fatal to the intended transaction if a court can be persuaded to use its discretion to provide a remedy.[99] However, such remedies are discretionary, and recent cases in the real property field suggest that the courts are reluctant to use their discretionary jurisdiction to (effectively) override statutory requirements as to writing formalities. It is therefore recommended that intellectual property transactions are made in writing and signed by both parties to the transaction.

In the case of non-UK intellectual property (for example a foreign patent), the formalities for executing and recording transactions vary from country to country, and local legal advice should be sought as to the required form of any transaction.

Often, parties to an agreement concerned with the intellectual property of more than one country include a provision in the agreement under which they will execute further documents if they are subsequently advised that this is necessary to comply with local laws.

What restrictions are there on the transaction?

There are relatively few constraints on the scope and content of intellectual property transactions under UK intellectual property law itself. Such constraints are more likely to arise under:

---

96 See eg the definition of 'exclusive licence' in respect of copyright in Copyright, Designs and Patents Act 1988, s 92.

97 Principally the right to sue an infringer for most forms of intellectual property.

98 Eg in respect of copyright assignments: see Copyright, Designs and Patents Act 1988, s 90(3); and in respect of patent assignments, see Patents Act 1977, s 30(5).

99 The person making an application to a grant does not have a right to the remedy it is seeking, but is relying on the discretionary remedies a court has, ie the court will apply the rules of equity.

- competition law,[100] particularly under EC Treaty, Art 81 (Art 101, following adoption of the Lisbon Treaty); UK competition law (principally the Competition Act 1988) or other national competition law (for example in the case of a licence in respect of that country) may also be relevant; or

- regulatory law affecting use of certain materials which sometimes feature in technology transfer agreements (such as that which controls the use of human and animal tissue);[101] or

- regulatory law affecting the use of products resulting from the exploitation of technology, such as pharmaceuticals (controls on the testing of and sale of pharmaceuticals) and particular technology (controls on the export of certain technology);[102] or

- regulatory law affecting the use of material generated from the creation or exploitation of technology, particularly data protection provisions, such as data concerning individuals who are subject to a clinical trial.[103]

In the special case of an agreement with an employee inventor, where the agreement might diminish the rights of the inventor in the invention, it is important to consider the provisions concerning enforceability of contracts relating to employees' inventions.[104]

What rights will the parties have under intellectual property laws?

UK intellectual property legislation addresses the rights and obligations of parties who have interests in intellectual property (for example, there are provisions governing the rights of an exclusive licensee under copyright to bring infringement proceedings[105]). Some of these provisions are concerned with the mutual rights and obligations of the holders of rights in the same item of intellectual property. In most cases, it is possible to override by contract between the parties holding the rights in the intellectual property, for example between the co-owners of a patent.[106] In many cases this is desirable for the following reasons:

- the statutory provisions are not always appropriate or do not address the important commercial issues in a transaction. For example, the Patents Act 1977 provides that each co-owner of a UK patent may manufacture

---

100 See Ch 12.
101 Such as Human Tissue Act 2004 and Human Fertilisation and Embryology Act 1990. See Ch 11.
102 Such as items which have a dual use (eg which are capable of both military and non-military uses. See Ch 11 under 'import and export regulation'.
103 Data Protection Act 1998: see Ch 11.
104 Patents Act 1977, s 42.
105 Copyright, Designs and Patents Act 1988, s 101.
106 Patents Act 1977, s 36(2).

products in accordance with the patented invention, but neither may grant a licence under the patent without the consent of the other co-owners.[107] Where an academic institution and a manufacturing company are co-owners of a UK patent, in practice only the company is in a position to manufacture and sell products in accordance with the patent. Thus the company is able to exploit the patent without paying the institution a royalty. This inequality of opportunity may not be what one or both of the parties would have intended had they considered the point. Or, a copyright owner and a licensee may wish to make special arrangements as to how any litigation over the patents is to be handled and funded, and therefore may wish to modify the statutory provisions concerning the rights of the licensee to sue infringers.[108]

• the statutory provisions vary as between different types of intellectual property and as between the same type of intellectual property in different countries. For example, it is apparently the case that under some countries' laws a co-owner of intellectual property may grant a non-exclusive licence under the intellectual property without the consent of the other co-owner, but must obtain the other co-owner's consent before granting an exclusive licence. Thus, in an agreement concerned with the intellectual property of more than one country, relying on the provisions of national intellectual property legislation may lead to the parties having different rights in each country.

Must the transaction be registered?

Is registration possible?

There are registers of patents (including supplementary protection certificates), registered designs, registered Community designs (and registered trade marks and Community trade marks). Most types of transaction in such property are registrable, including assignments, licences and mortgages. As there is no register of copyright or design right, it is not possible to register transactions in these rights in the UK. (Registers of copyright do exist in some other countries, most notably in the US.)

Advantages of registration

There are several potential advantages in registering a transaction (such as an assignment or licence):

• in the event of conflicting claims to an interest in the property, for example two parties claiming to have an exclusive licence under

---

107 Patents Act 1977, s 36.
108 Copyright, Designs and Patents Act 1988, ss 101, 102.

the same patent, the registered party often has superior rights to the unregistered party;[109]

- registration of an interest, for example a patent licence, acts as public notice of that interest. Thus, where a patent licence is registered:

  — a subsequent purchaser of the patent could not disclaim the licence under general contract law principles on the ground that he was a 'bona fide purchaser without notice of the interest'; or

  — a potential licensee could check whether the potential licensor has granted other licences to other parties, and thus may make a better evaluation as to the likelihood of it being able to successfully exploit any licence it is granted;

- in some cases, registration gives the registered party positive rights – for example, registration of an exclusive patent licence within six months of the grant of the licence gives the licensee the right, in certain cases, to claim costs and expenses in respect of infringements which took place before the date of registration;[110]

- in the case of registered designs, registration of transactions such as assignments and licences would seem to be compulsory.[111]

Registration of title of or interest in intellectual property does not guarantee that it will remain registered. There are provisions enabling the register to be rectified in appropriate cases.

The registration process

The procedures for registration with the UK Intellectual Property Office of transactions concerning patents and registered designs in the UK are set out in regulations.[112] The procedures normally include forms to be completed and fees to be paid.

Pitfalls under intellectual property law

One major pitfall arises in the case of old intellectual property which came into existence before the passing of the current legislation for that type of property. The law in force at the time the old intellectual property came into existence may still apply to it. This is most likely to apply in relation to works protected by copyright. For example, it is possible that a work created in 1914

---

109 Patents Act 1977, s 33.
110 Patents Act 1977, s 68.
111 Registered Designs Act 1949, s 19(1), as amended by Copyright, Designs and Patents Act 1988, s 272.
112 See eg Patents Rules 2007 (SI 2007/3291); and Registered Designs Rules 2006 (SI 2006/1975).

but whose author died after 1940 would still be protected by copyright in 2010.[113] In that case, the work may originally have attracted copyright under the Copyright Act 1911 on terms which may be significantly different to those which apply in the case of new works created after 1 August 1989. (The Patents Act 1977 and the Copyright, Designs and Patents Act 1988 contain transitional provisions dealing with the legal position for old patents and old copyright works in existence before the commencement of these Acts.)

---

113 Copyright for literary (including computer programs), dramatic, musical or artistic works lasts for 70 years after the death of the author. There are numerous complications and details which means the statement in the previous sentence must be treated with caution and each work needs careful consideration as to when it was created, its type, when it was published etc to establish whether it is protected by copyright. To add to the complication, in 1995 the terms of protection for literary and some other forms of copyright were extended from 50 years to 70 in the European Union. There are complex transitional measures for works which had lost their copyright protection at 50 years but would qualify for protection under the new 70-year period.

CHAPTER 4

Patents

HISTORICAL BACKGROUND AND OVERVIEW OF LEGISLATION

Modern UK patent law can be traced from 1883,[1] with the establishment in that year of the UK Patent Office (now known as the UK Intellectual Property Office) and a number of other changes to patent law, including the abolition of jury trials for patent cases.[2] The present law is found in Patents Act 1977[3] ('the Act' in this chapter). The Act has been subject to extensive revision. It was passed, in part, to bring the law in the UK in line with the provisions of the European Patent Convention,[4] the Patent Co-operation Treaty[5] and the Community Patent Convention.[6] This chapter will discuss the provisions of the Act. At the end of the chapter there are separate sections discussing two areas which have become of increasing importance to industry, research organisations and universities and the economy in general – biotechnology and computer software.[7]

For technology transfer, traditionally the protection offered by patent law has been the form of intellectual property which is of most importance and which is why it is the focus of more extensive treatment. This is due for a number of reasons. First, it is still true that most transactions involving intellectual

---

1   Until the passing of the most recent Patents Act, in 1977, patents were officially known as 'letters patent', a name that had been in use for centuries. This name was originally used for any type of trading monopoly awarded by the English monarch. The award was confirmed by the issue of letters patent, literally an 'open' letter bearing the royal seal. The grant of letters patent formed part of the monarch's prerogative powers.

     Concern at abuses of this royal prerogative, as well as the increasing power of the House of Commons, led to the passing of the Statute of Monopolies in 1624. The monarch's powers to grant letters patent were largely removed. One major exception remained: by s 6 of that statute, letters patent could be granted for a period of 14 years for 'any manner of new manufacture'. This exception was designed to encourage the introduction of new technologies into Britain, by giving the person introducing the new technology a monopoly over its commercial application. The original term of 14 years is thought to equate to the period it took to train up two apprentices in the technology, one after another.

2   Patents, Designs, and Trade Marks Act 1883.

3   Previous Patents Acts were passed in 1907, 1919, 1932 and 1949. All patents granted under the Patents Act 1949 have now expired.

4   See Ch 3 under 'Applications under the European Patent Convention'.

5   See Ch 3 under 'Applications under the Patent Co-operation Treaty'.

6   See Ch 3 under 'Europe-wide patent'.

7   Biotechnology and biotechnological innovations have been subject to an EC Directive (Directive 98/44/EC ([1998] OJ L213/13) on the legal protection of biotechnological inventions).

     Computer software, although almost always protected by copyright, can also, in certain circumstances, be protected by patents. At the time of the 2nd edition of this book (2003), the European Commission had proposed a Directive aimed at harmonising the law as to the patentability of software. The then proposed Directive has not in reality progressed further in the form originally proposed, and appears stalled at the time material for this edition is being prepared. See 'Patenting and software' below for an outline of the current position regarding when software can be protected by patent law, based on the case law.

property and which can be defined as 'technology transfer' have involved the licensing of patents, or less often the assignment of patents. Other forms of intellectual property have traditionally played more of a 'supporting' role. Secondly, patent law is perhaps the oldest form of intellectual property, and has a formal procedure in place for obtaining its protection. Therefore it has had longer to build up detailed commentary and case law as to how it works in practice. Thirdly, at least in the UK, it is the form of intellectual property, as expressed in its statutory form, which has the most detail concerning provisions which are most likely to be relevant to commercial transactions.[8]

PROVISIONS OF UK PATENT LAW WHICH ARE DIRECTLY RELEVANT TO COMMERCIAL TRANSACTIONS

Introduction

The first part of this chapter considers provisions of UK patent law which are directly relevant to commercial transactions, and in particular sections 30–59 of the Act. These sections deal with:

- the nature of patents as personal property and the types of transactions in patents which are recognised by the Act;

- the rights of owners and co-owners and the effect of registration of rights;

- ownership of employees' inventions and the statutory right of employees to receive compensation from their employers;

- the effect of including certain anti-competitive provisions in patent agreements;

- licences of right and compulsory licences; and

- rights to use patented inventions for the services of the Crown, the so-called Crown user provisions.

The section entitled 'Other fundamental provisions of UK patent law which may affect parties to a patent transaction' will consider other provisions of UK patent law which are not so directly relevant to commercial transactions but which are nevertheless important for an understanding of the nature of UK patents.

---

8   Also, the provisions (which are not reflected in the statutory law) of commercial agreements which have come before the courts for interpretation have most often involved patents.

Nature of patents and patent applications

Section 30 of the Act describes the nature of patents as personal property.[9]

In summary, the position in England and Wales and in Northern Ireland is as follows:

(a) *Patents are personal property:* a patent or patent application is personal property but is not a 'thing in action' (also known as a 'chose in action').[10] For practical purposes, the issue of whether or not a patent is a chose in action is unlikely to be significant in commercial transactions. Of greater significance is the provision that a patent is personal property; the effect of this is that the law of personal property will generally apply to patents, except where overridden by specific laws which apply to patents.[11]

(b) *Assignment, mortgage, etc of patents:* a patent or patent application, or any right in it:[12]

   (i) may be assigned (ie ownerships transferred) or mortgaged;[13]

   (ii) will vest by operation of law in the same way as other personal property, eg on death or bankruptcy;[14] and

   (iii) may be vested by an assent of personal representatives (eg by one's executors, following death, ie where an owner is an individual).[15]

   However, any such assignment, mortgage or assent will be void unless it is in writing and is signed by or on behalf of the assignor or mortga-

---

9 Section 31 (as modified by the Requirements of Writing (Scotland) Act 1995) describes the equivalent position in Scotland, modified to reflect Scots law and practice. The differences between ss 30 and 31 arise because the systems of property law and contract law are in some respects fundamentally different in (1) England and Wales, and (2) Scotland respectively, and the law relating to patent transactions must fit within the overall legal structure in each jurisdiction. This may be contrasted with most of the other provisions of the Act which apply equally to England and Wales and Scotland (and Northern Ireland). For Northern Ireland see s 131 of the Act.

10 Section 30(1) of the Act. For a definition of a chose in action: 'The meaning of the expression "chose in action" or "thing in action" has expanded over time, and it is now used to describe all personal rights of property which can only be claimed or enforced by action, and not by taking physical possession. It is used in respect of both corporeal and incorporeal personal property which is not in possession' (13 *Halsbury's Laws of England* (5th edn, LexisNexis, 2009) para 1).

11 See further Ch 9 under 'Does the LPA apply to intellectual property?'.

12 The phrase 'or any right in it' does not to refer to a licence under a patent, not least because licences under patents are dealt with in a later subsection (section 30(4)). See also *Insituform v Inliner* [1992] RPC 83. The phrase would, presumably, cover the rights of a co-owner of a patent, which are further dealt with in s 36.

13 Subject to the rights of co-owners, where the patent is jointly owned – see further under 'Co-ownership of patents and patent applications' below.

14 Section 90(3); it may also vest by an assent of personal representatives (ie following death).

15 Section 30(3) of the Act.

gor to the transaction[16] or, in the case of an incorporated party ('body corporate' as defined), is signed by that party or is under the seal[17] of that party.

(c)   *Licences:* licences may be granted under a patent or patent application.[18] They need not be in writing.

(d)   *Sub-licences:* to the extent the licence so provides, a sub-licence may be granted under a patent licence.[19]

(e)   *Assignment, mortgage, etc of licences and sub-licences:* a licence or permitted sub-licence may be assigned or mortgaged (to the extent the licence so provides), and will vest by operation of law in the same way as other personal property.[20]

(f)   *Rights of assignee or exclusive licensee:* an assignment of a patent or patent application, or a share in it, and any exclusive licence under a patent or patent application, may confer on the assignee or licensee the right to bring proceedings for infringements which occurred prior to the date of the assignment or licence.[21] It is a common practice in UK intellectual property assignments to state (where appropriate) that the assignee shall have the right to bring proceedings in respect of past infringements[22] and to retain any damages awarded in respect of such infringements.

---

16   Section 30(4) of the Act. In the case of an assent by personal representatives, by or on behalf of the personal representative. Failure to follow all the requirements may not be fatal to the assignment, etc of a patent. An assignment executed only by the assignor has been held to pass the equitable ownership to the assignee (when the law required both parties sign the assignment): *Baxter International Inc v Nederlands Produktielaboratorium* [1998] RPC 250. In the case of companies, it is important that a director (or directors) who sign(s)the assignment on behalf of the company are correctly appointed (see *European Environmental Recycling's International Application* (SRIS O/316/99)). The word 'assignment' does not need to appear in the document, as a court would look at the reality of a transaction (*Thorn Security Limited v Siemens Schweltz AG* [2008] EWCA Civ 1161). This case is also authority for the proposition that an assignment can include an assignment by operation of law. Prior to the amendment of the Act in 2004, assignments had to be signed by all the parties to the transaction.

17   Under Companies Act 2006, s 45, a company is no longer required to have a company seal; documents which are stated to be executed by the company and which are signed by a director in the presence of a witness, two directors, or by a director and the secretary (if the company has one), take effect as if executed under seal. A body corporate will include a company formed or regulated by one of the Companies Acts (2006, 1985, 1948), and other organisations which are not governed by the Companies Act 2006, such as universities, NHS trusts, government departments, and regulatory authorities (eg the Human Tissue Authority), some of which are important players in the technology transfer sector.

18   Section 30(4) of the Act.

19   Section 30(4)(a) of the Act.

20   As to whether a licence under intellectual property amounts to a property interest, see Ch 10 under 'Nature and extent of licences'.

21   The section specifically refers to the right to bring proceedings under sections 58, 61 or 69 of the Act.

22   Although it is uncertain whether such assignments are effective to assign past causes of action; each case will depend on its merits and the factual situation involved.

Co-ownership of patents and patent applications

Rights of co-owners – basic position

Section 36 of the Act defines the rights of co-owners of a UK patent or patent application. These rights may be overridden by a contract between the co-owners which can provide for different arrangements.[23] The section also considers the rights of third parties who have dealings with one or more of the co-owners. The main elements of section 36 are as follows:

(a) *Property:* each of the co-owners is entitled to an equal, undivided share in the patent, unless otherwise agreed.[24]

(b) *Use of invention by co-owner:* each of the co-owners is entitled, by himself or herself or through his agents,[25] for his or her own benefit to do any act which would otherwise infringe the patent,[26] without the consent of or the need to account to the other co-owners. In other words, the co-owner may exploit the patent directly. For example, the co-owner will not need the permission of the other co-owners to manufacture, use or sell products which are within the scope of the patent. Nor will he or she be required, for example, to share any profits obtained from sale of such products, unless otherwise agreed. However, any licensing of rights under the patent to third parties will require the consent of the other co-owners – (see the following paragraph).

(c) *Licensing, assignment and mortgaging by co-owner:* a co-owner may not, without the consent of the other co-owners, grant a licence under the patent or assign or mortgage a share in the patent.[27]

(d) *Supply of items to co-owner which would otherwise infringe patent:* it is not an infringement of the patent to provide one of the co-owners

---

23   Note: the phrases 'subject to any agreement to the contrary' which appears in sub-ss (1), (2), and 'subject ... to any agreement for the time being in force' in sub-s (3). Subsections (4) and (5), which deal with the rights of third parties, are not affected by an agreement between the co-owners, as one might expect.

24   The legal implications of the phrase 'equal, undivided share', also known as ownership in common, and possible alternatives under UK property law, are considered further in Ch 9. Although if they hold the patent as trustees, they may/will hold as joint tenants; this is allowed for by s 36(6) of the Act.

25   Section 36(2) of the Act. The expression 'agent' does not include subcontractors, partners, or companies formed by the co-owner, unless they act strictly as agents (see *Howard & Bullough v Tweedale & Smalley* (1895) 12 RPC 519). In *Henry Bros (Magherafelt) Ltd v Ministry of Defence* [1997] RPC 693, it was held that the word 'agent' in s 36(2) of the Act does not have a strict legal meaning, but a co-owner may have the patented product made for that co-owner, to protect home use. This point is also explored in more detail below under 'Agents and subcontractors'.

26   Section 36(2) of the Act; the subsection is made subject to s 55 of the Act, which concerns Crown use of inventions.

27   Section 36(3) of the Act; the subsection is made subject to sections 8, 12 and 37 of the Act, which broadly concern disputes over entitlement.

with the means, relating to an essential element of the invention, for putting the patented invention into effect.[28] Such an act would otherwise amount to contributory infringement.[29] This provision is consistent with the principle described in (b) above, that each co-owner is entitled to exploit the patent directly without the consent of the other co-owners.

(e)   *Dealing in patented products supplied by a co-owner:* where a patented product is disposed of by a co-owner of the patent, the co-owner and any person claiming through him or her is entitled to deal with the product as if it had been disposed of by a sole registered proprietor.[30] Thus, a purchaser of a patented product from a co-owner will generally not infringe the rights of the other co-owners.

Aspects of multi-ownership of intellectual property

Agents and subcontractors

Section 36 of the Act provides:

> Where two or more persons are proprietors of a patent [...] each of them shall be entitled by himself, or his agents, to do in respect of the invention concerned, for his own benefit and without the consent of or the need to account to the other or others, any act which would apart from this subsection and section 55, amount, an infringement of the patent concerned ...'.

'Any act' would mean such an activity as making or selling a patented article by an agent of one co-owner.

How far exactly this provision ranges is not entirely clear,[31] but what is clear is that the right to appoint an agent is not a means of allowing a co-owner the right to grant a commercial licence.[32]

There is only limited case law regarding the meaning of an 'agent', and what there is deals with Crown's user rights. It appears that the use of the term 'agent' in the Act is not that of its normal legal meaning.[33] It has been held that the word 'agent' when used in this context, would include subcontractors,

---

28   Section 36(4) of the Act.
29   Section 60(2) of the Act.
30   Section 36(5) of the Act.
31   See *CIPA Guide to the Patents Acts* (6th edn, Sweet & Maxwell, 2009) para 36.04.
32   As to what acts require the permission of the other co-owners, see 'When the consent of a co-owner is required' below, as well as *Hughes v Paxman* [2006] EWCA Civ 818, [2006] All ER (D) 279 (Jun) at para 7.
33   *Howard Bros (Magherafelt) Ltd v Ministry of Defence and Northern Ireland Office* [1997] RPC 693, [1999] RPC 442, CA.

partners or companies formed by a co-owner, unless any of them was acting in the strict legal sense of an agent of the co-owner.[34]

The question of whether a co-owner can appoint a subcontractor is not expressly mentioned or prohibited in the Act,[35] although it can be argued:

- that the appointment of a subcontractor would in effect be the granting of a licence, one of the activities that requires the consent of the other co-owner or co-owners;[36]

- that the activities of a subcontractor would constitute infringement of the patent. Although a person who supplies an 'essential element' of an invention to a co-owner is protected from an action for infringement,[37] the protection would not cover the subcontractor making the whole of a product.

The following points may be put forward in the situation where an agent or subcontractor might be involved:

- if a co-owner makes a product, and uses a commercial agent to sell the product and any sales are made in the name of the co-owner, the co-owner's action is likely to fall within the protection of section 36(2) of the Act, but:

- if a co-owner has the product made by a subcontractor and the subcontractor supplies the product only to the co-owner in order for the co-owner to sell the product, the making of the product may not have the protection of section 36(2) of the Act.

When the consent of a co-owner is required

For the sake of completeness the full list of what a co-owner cannot do without the agreement of the other co-owner(s) (unless the co-owners agree otherwise) is as follows:

- grant a licence under a patent;

- assign a share in a patent;

- mortgage a share in a patent;

- amend the specification of a patent;

---

34   *Howard & Bullough Ltd v Tweedales and Smalley* (1895) 12 RPC 519, but decided under the former common law. For what amounts to manufacturing by a licensee, see 79 *Halsbury's Laws of England*('Patents and Registered Designs') (5th edn, LexisNexis, 2008) para 382.

35   Such as a co-owner appointing a subcontractor and the subcontractor manufacturing a product which is to be sold by a co-owner.

36   Under s 36(3) of the Act.

37   Under s 36(4) of the Act.

- apply for an amendment to the specification of a patent to be allowed;
- apply for a patent to be revoked.

Whether consent has in fact been given or can be implied has been considered by the courts.[38]

The effect of section 36(2) of the Act can mean that unless the co-owners agree otherwise, then the co-owner which has the resources (whether financial or physical) in place or can obtain them, could manufacture and sell products without the permission or knowledge of the other co-owner(s), and also keep any financial returns that derive from such exploitation of the patent. In this situation the other co-owner which did not have the resources and was not able to obtain the resources (eg through borrowing), would lose out financially. This second co-owner would also be unable to licence or otherwise exploit the patent (if it could not obtain the consent of the first co-owner).

However a co-owner without the resources to exploit the patent can apply to the comptroller for a licence to be granted.[39] However, if both parties cannot exploit a patent themselves and also cannot agree on how it should be exploited then there will be deadlock.[40]

Concluding points: provisions relating to co-ownership

The provisions found in the Act regarding co-ownership have attracted criticism in cases which have been before the courts.[41]

Regardless of the quality of the drafting used in the Act regarding co-owners, the provisions do not cover all the commercial issues which co-owners should include in an agreement.

Employee inventions

Sections 39–43 of the Act provide a code for determining:

---

38 *Whitehead & Poole Ltd v Sir James Farmer & Sons Ltd* (1918) 35 RPC 241. In this case an earlier Patents Act was under consideration: Patents and Designs Act 1907, s 37.

39 Under s 37(1) of the Act. See *Hughes v Paxman* [2006] EWCA Civ 818, [2006] All ER (D) 279 (Jun).

40 As happened in *Hughes v Paxman* [2006] EWCA Civ 818, [2006] All ER (D) 279 (Jun), Jacobs LJ noting: 'I cannot imagine for a moment that Parliament could have intended it to be possible that exploitation of an invention could be frustrated by a deadlock situation. The whole point of the patent system was and is to encourage innovation and the exploitation of invention. That is indeed why, where patented inventions have not been exploited, subject to certain conditions, there is a provision for compulsory licences'.

41 See *Henry Bros (Magherafelt) Ltd v Ministry of Defence* [1997] RPC 693, and most recently *Hughes v Paxman* [2006] EWCA Civ 818, [2006] All ER (D) 279 (Jun), where the drafting of s 36 of the Act was labelled 'turgid'.

- when an employee will own an invention made by him;

- the circumstances in which he will be entitled to compensation from his employer for patented inventions made by him which are of 'outstanding benefit' to his employer; and

- the limited circumstances in which it is possible to 'contract out' of these ownership and compensation provisions.

Ownership of employee inventions

Section 39 of the Act provides, in effect, three alternative circumstances in which an invention made by an employee will belong to his employer. If none of these circumstances exists, the invention will belong to the employee.[42]

An invention[43] made by an employee[44] will, as between him and his employer,[45] belong to his employer[46] if:

(a) it was made in the course of his *normal duties*;[47] or

---

42   The language of s 39 of the Act is more complex than the equivalent test for copyright ownership (ie was the work made in the course of the employee's employment?). In some situations the more complex language of s 39 of the Act may lead to a different ownership position than if the 'course of employment' test were applied. This is tacitly recognised by s 39(3) of the Act (as amended) which provides, inter alia, that the working of an employee-owned invention will not be taken to infringe any copyright or design right owned by the employer in any model or document relating to the invention.

43   The term 'invention' is not defined, although the requirements for a *patentable* invention are described in s 1 of the Act (as amended by SI 2000/2037). By implication, s 39 applies also to unpatentable inventions. However, to say that an invention 'belongs' to someone would appear to be meaningless unless an enforceable property right attaches to the ownership, eg through patents or some other form of property, including the right to apply for such property. Also, only the person who is the actual deviser of an invention will be entitled to a grant of a patent (see s 7(3) of the Act). It must be the 'natural person who "came up with the inventive concept" […] the contribution must be the formulation of the inventive concept' (*Yeda Research v Rhone-Poulenc Rorer* [2007] UKHL 43, [2008] RPC 1, at para 20).

44   The provisions relating to employee inventions, sections 39–42 of the Act (as amended) will not apply unless at the time the employee made the invention, he was mainly employed in the UK, or he was not mainly employed anywhere, or his place of employment could not be determined, but his employer had a place of business in the UK to which the employee was attached, whether or not he was also attached elsewhere.

45   Ie the invention could belong to a third party if, for example, the employee sold it; but see para (c) in relation to the enforceability of an agreement by the employee to assign his inventions.

46   Section 39(1) of the Act.

47   Section 39(1)(a) of the Act. See *Szewczyk's Application* BL 0/301/04 for a case which considered the meaning of 'normal duties'. The inventor was both an employee as well as a director. One of his duties was labelled 'product development'. The inventor made an invention while working on an on-going project. In this case it was held that the invention belonged to the employer under s 39(1)(a) of the Act. An invention can also belong to an employer even if the normal duties which an employee carries out are not of the type where an invention is likely to be made (*Paul Auckland and Enderby Construction Ltd* BL 043/06). In this case the invention made belonged to the employee.

(b) it was made in the course of *duties specifically assigned to him*, even though these fell outside his normal duties;

and in either case the circumstances were such that an invention might reasonably be expected to result from the carrying out of his duties;[48] or

(c) it was made in the course of the *duties* of the employee and, at the time of making the invention, because of the nature of his duties and the particular responsibilities arising from the nature of his duties he had *a special obligation to further the interests of the employer's undertaking.*[49]

Any other invention made by an employee in any other circumstances will, as between him and his employer, belong to the employee.[50]

Clearly, it will be easier to apply the first of these three tests – the normal duties test[51] – if the employee's normal duties are recorded, for example in her contract of employment.[52] However, contracts of employment are apt to change as the employee's job changes, and there is no legal requirement for a contract of employment to contain a list of the 'normal duties' of the employee. It is possible, during the course of an employee's employment, by either the actions of the employer and/or the employee, for the duties of the employee to expand or contract, as described in one case, 'by a continuous process of subtle variation', and for an employee to be given extra or different tasks, which would have been duties which are 'specially assigned' but in time become 'normal duties'.[53]

Similarly, it will be a matter of evidence as to what duties were specifically assigned to the employee. The third test may be more difficult to apply. Scientific staffsenior management or directors[54] who make inventions may

---

48   Section 39(1)(a) of the Act.
49   Section 39(1)(b) of the Act. If the invention is made by a director (who is not an employee) then any invention made will normally not fall within this provision of the Act.
50   Section 39(2) of the Act.
51   Ie the actual duties he or she is employed to do (see *Harris's Patent* [1985] RPC 19).
52   Eg where research facilities were made available to a clinical hospital registrar, it was held that his normal duties were limited to clinical responsibilities and not to inventorship, such as the modifying of existing equipment he used (see *Greater Glasgow Health Boards Application* [1996] RPC 207).
53   *LIFFE Administration & Management v Pinkava* [2007] RPC 30. In determining what an employee's normal duties are, a court is not limited to seeing what an employee does day-by-day. An invention could still belong to the employer even if it was made by an employee in the course of work which was a departure from what the employee normally did: 'As between the employer and employee the primary sources of a duty are the terms of the contract. What is it that he is employed to do must be the key question. That is not the same thing as [...] what his day-to-day work [is]. Take for instance a research chemist working on a cancer cure for the last 10 years. Suppose he came up with a cure for arthritis. He could not seriously contend that he owned the invention because he was day-to-day working on a cancer cure. His duty as a research chemist is clearly wider than his day-to-day work'.
54   Directors also have fiduciary duties to their company, as directors, which may in some cases affect their rights to exploit their inventions.

169

be more likely to be caught by item (c) than junior administrative staff, but it may be difficult to predict whether this test applies to a particular individual without a detailed review of his duties and responsibilities; much will depend on the circumstances of each case. It might, for example, apply to a works manager even though he had been instructed not to involve himself in his employer's R&D activities.[55]

Rights of employee to claim compensation for making invention

An employee who has made an invention for which a patent has been granted may be awarded compensation where the invention initially belongs to the employer or, where it initially belongs to the employee but he has assigned or exclusively licensed it to the employer.[56] The employee must apply to the court or comptroller[57] for compensation within a prescribed period (normally from the date of grant of the patent until one year after it has expired).[58] In summary, for a claim to succeed, the following must be established:

Employer-owned inventions

(a) the employee has made an invention belonging to the employer, for which a patent has been granted;

(b) the *invention and/or the patent* is (having regard among other things to the size and nature of the employer's undertaking) of *outstanding benefit* to the employer; and

(c) by reason of those facts, the court or comptroller finds that it is *just* that the employee should be awarded compensation to be paid by the employer.

Employee-owned inventions

(a) the employee has made an invention belonging to him, for which a patent has been granted;

(b) he has assigned, or exclusively licensed, his rights in the invention or patent to the employer;[59]

(c) the benefit derived by the employee from the assignment or licence or any ancillary contract ('the relevant contract') is *inadequate* in relation to the benefit derived by the employer from the *patent*; and

---

55   See *Peart's Patent* (SRIS O/209/87) cited in *CIPA Guide to the Patents Acts* (6th edn, Sweet & Maxwell, 2009) para 39.11.
56   Section 40 of the Act.
57   The head of the UK Intellectual Property Office.
58   See s 40(2) of the Act; Pt 7 and Rule 91, the Patents Rules 2007.
59   And this took place after 1 June 1978 – see reference in s 40(2)(b) of the Act to the 'appointed day'.

(d) by reason of those facts, the court or comptroller finds that it is *just* that the employee should be awarded compensation to be paid by the employer in addition to the benefit derived from the relevant contract.

In practice, very few awards have been made to employees under section 40, partly because of the high hurdles which the wording of the section imposes. Prior to the Patents Act 2004, section 40 of the Act required that the patent (rather than the invention) must benefit the employer (a much narrower entitlement for an employee), and that (in the case of employer-owned inventions) the benefit to the employer should be *outstanding*, which in the case of a company with a very large turnover may be very difficult to establish.[60]

As noted above, with the introduction of the changes made by the Patents Act 2004, where an employee wishes to make a claim for compensation, the employee can include not only the benefit from the patent but also the benefit obtained from the invention (or just the invention if the employee wishes). This change provides a simplification for employees, as they no longer need to establish whether the benefit that the employer has derived relates just to the invention or to the patent (or determine what amount of benefit relates to the invention or the patent).

However, although the change made by the Patents Act 2004 can potentially improve the likelihood that an employee can obtain compensation, it should be noted that the invention still has to be subject of a patent. Therefore the employee can only benefit from that part of an invention which is patented. Secondly, the change applies only from 1 January 2005; it is not retrospective.

Irrespective of any legal entitlement under the Act, many academic institutions in the UK have policies in place to share any revenue obtained by those academic institutions for inventions commercially exploited with the academic responsible for the invention.[61]

---

60 See *GEC Avionics Ltd's Patent* (1992) RPC 107; *British Steel plc's Patent* [1992] RPC 117 and *Memco-Med Ltd's Patent* (1992) RPC 403. In *Garrison's Patent* (SRIS O/44/97) it was held that an employers' benefit from an invention was not outstanding where the patent contributed 2–3 per cent of the total turnover of a small manufacturing company. *Memco-Med Ltd's Patent* was applied in *Kelly and another v GE Healthcare Ltd* [2009] EWHC 181 (Pat), [2009] All ER (D) 114 (Feb).

61 Although academic institutions may have revenue-sharing schemes in place, following the change made by the Patents Act 2004 as noted above, they still may wish to review such schemes so that they cover both the invention and patent and not just the patent. Of interest, in *Kelly and another v GE Healthcare Ltd* [2009] EWHC 181 (Pat), [2009] All ER (D) 114 (Feb) reference is made to an academic benefiting under a revenue-sharing scheme operated by his university and the method of calculating the reward.

Collective agreements

The above sections do not apply where there is a 'relevant collective agreement'[62] which provides for the payment of compensation in relation to such inventions.[63]

Amount of compensation

The amount of any compensation awarded by the court or comptroller is governed by section 41 of the Act. The wording of section 41 is complex, but the main requirement is that the employee should receive a *fair share* of the benefit which the employer derives from the patent.[64] The court or comptroller must take certain matters into account, including:[65]

- the nature of the employee's duties;

- the benefits the employee derives from his employment or from the invention;

- the effort and skill the employee contributed to making the invention;

- the effort and skill that others contributed;

- the employer's contribution (for example in providing facilities or commercial skills);

- in the case of a claim for additional compensation where the employee has previously assigned or licensed the invention to his employer, any conditions in any licences granted in respect of the invention or patent.[66]

Assignment or licensing of patent by employer to a connected person

There are special provisions to deal with the situation where the employer assigns or licenses the patent to a connected person (eg, in the case of a company employer, a company which is under common control with the employing company).[67]

---

62 Ie within the meaning of the Trade Union and Labour Relations (Consolidation) Act 1992, made between the employee's trade union and the employer or employers' association.
63 Section 40(3) of the Act.
64 Section 41(1) of the Act. There are special provisions to deal with the situation where the employer assigns or licences the patent to a connected person: s 41(2) of the Act.
65 Section 41(4) of the Act.
66 The wording of sub-ss 41(4) and (5) of the Act expands on these matters and mentions other matters to be taken into account.
67 See s 43(8) of the Act, which applies the definition of 'connected person' set out in s 839 of the Income and Corporation Taxes Act 1988.

Where the employer is the Crown or a Research Council

There are also special provisions for calculating the benefit to the employer where it is the Crown or a Research Council[68] and it has assigned the invention for no consideration or only nominal consideration to 'a body having among its functions that of developing or exploiting inventions resulting from public research'.[69]

Enforceability of contracts which remove employee's rights of ownership or compensation

The provisions of section 42 of the Act are designed to prevent employees from signing away their rights to future inventions. The section provides that in certain situations a term in a contract, which would diminish an employee's rights to his inventions, will be unenforceable against him. Without such a provision, section 39 of the Act (which determines when an employee will own an invention made by him) could be easily circumvented by an employer. All that the employer would need to do would be to include in the contract of employment a term providing that all employee-owned inventions would be assigned to the employer.

The circumstances in which section 42 of the Act applies may be summarised as follows:

- the section applies to any contract entered into by the employee, a term of which relates to inventions made by him. The contract could be with the employer, or with some other person at the employer's request or as required by the contract of employment (eg an obligation to assign inventions to the employer's parent company);

- the section applies only to inventions, patent applications or patents made by the employee after the date of the contract[70] (referred to below as 'Future Inventions'). Thus, the section will not prevent an employee, for example, from assigning to his employer a patent which is already in existence at the date of the assignment;

- the section provides that any term in such a contract which diminishes the employee's rights in or under Future Inventions will be unenforceable against him. The term may be enforceable for other purposes, depending on its wording;[71]

---

68   Ie for the purposes of the Science and Technology Act 1965 (see s 41(3) of the Act).
69   This provision was designed to deal with inventions assigned to the NRDC, then the British Technology Group, and now 3i. The extent of its application today, given the abolition of 3i's automatic right to certain inventions and the privatisation of 3i, may be uncertain.
70   Note that under s 42(2) of the Act the invention must also be made after the 'appointed day' (ie 1 June 1978).
71   See the wording of s 42(2) of the Act, and the general law of contract on severability, including the 'blue pencil test'.

- any duty of confidentiality which the employee may owe to his employer will not be affected by the above provisions.[72]

Whilst on the subject of unenforceable provisions in contracts, section 40(4) of the Act should be borne in mind. This provides that the provisions of section 40(2) of the Act, under which the court or comptroller may award additional compensation to an employee who has assigned or exclusively licensed his invention to his employer, shall have effect notwithstanding anything in the relevant contract or any agreement applicable to the invention.[73] Thus it is not possible to contract out of section 40(2) of the Act. However, there is no equivalent provision in relation to compensation awarded under section 40(1) of the Act (ie in respect of employer-owned inventions).[74]

Extent of UK law on employee inventions

Section 43 of the Act sets out some supplementary provisions which define the extent to which the code on employee inventions, set out in sections 39–42 of the Act, will apply. The main points[75] are:

(a) sections 39–42 of the Act do not apply to inventions made before 1 June 1978;[76]

(b) sections 39–42 of the Act will not apply unless at the time the employee made the invention, either:

  (i) he was mainly employed in the UK, or

  (ii) he was not mainly employed anywhere or his place of employment could not be determined, but his employer had a place of business in the UK to which the employee was attached, whether or not he was also attached elsewhere;

(c) references in sections 39–43 of the Act to the making of an invention apply to both sole and joint inventions, but do not refer to merely contributing advice or other assistance in the making of an invention by another employee;

(d) references in sections 39–42 of the Act to a patent and to a patent being granted refer to a patent *or other protection* and its being granted in the UK or elsewhere. Thus foreign patents and similar rights (eg

---

72 Section 42(3) of the Act.

73 There is an exception in the case of collective agreements, as to which see 'Collective agreements'.

74 See the discussion on this point in *CIPA Guide to the Patents Acts* (6th edn, Sweet & Maxwell, 2009) para 40.11. It is unlikely, in the author's view, that any attempt to contract out of s 40(1) of the Act would be legally enforceable.

75 There are also important provisions clarifying that 'benefit' means benefit in money or money's worth, and dealing with the situation where the employee dies.

76 For the position prior to that date, see Schs 1–4 of the Act.

petty patents and supplementary protection certificates) are covered; it is debatable whether this extends sections 39–42 to other types of intellectual property which might be said to protect inventions, such as trade marks.[77]

Summary of the law illustrating how entitlement is determined

A recent case has provided a convenient summary of the law concerning the employee's entitlement under the Act and is worth quoting in full:[78]

'i)   Section 40 is available to an inventor in the sense of the 'actual deviser' of the invention, but not to those who merely contribute to the invention without being joint inventors;

ii)   Section 40 is available to an employee who makes an invention (which is subsequently patented by the employer) in the ordinary course of his employment or in the course of duties specifically assigned to him;

iii)   Under the section prior to its amendment, it is the patent (as opposed to the invention) which must be of outstanding benefit to the employer, having regard to the size and nature of the employer's undertaking;

iv)   'Outstanding' means 'something special' or 'out of the ordinary' and more than 'substantial', 'significant' or 'good'. The benefit must be something more than one would normally expect to arise from the duties for which the employee is paid;

v)   On the other hand it is not necessary to show that the benefit from the patent could not have been exceeded;

vi)   Section 40 is not concerned with whether the invention is outstanding, although the nature of the employee's contribution may fall to be considered at the section 41 stage, if it is reached;

vii)   It will normally be useful to consider what would have been the position of the company if a patent had not been granted, and compare this with the company's position with the benefit of the patent;

viii) The patent must have been a cause of the benefit, although it does not have to be the only cause. The existence of multiple causes for a benefit does not exclude the benefit from consideration, although the benefit may have to be apportioned to isolate the benefit derived from the patent;

---

77   See the discussion of this point in *CIPA Guide to the Patents Acts* (6th edn, Sweet & Maxwell, 2009) para 43.05.
78   *Kelly and another v GE Healthcare Ltd* [2009] EWHC 181 (Pat), [2009] All ER (D) 114 at para 60.

ix) "Patent" in section 40 does not include regulatory data exclusivity ["RDE"].[79] Thus the scenario without patent protection is one where RDE nevertheless exists;

x) It must be "just" to make an award: the consideration of what is just is not limited to the facts set out in section 40;

xi) It is not a requirement of obtaining compensation that the employee can prove a loss (for example by reference to inadequate remuneration for his employment) or by the expenditure of effort and skill beyond the call of duty. These are nevertheless factors to take into account under section 41;

xii) The valuation of any benefit is to be performed ex post and in the light of all the available evidence as to benefit derived from the patent: not "ex-ante";

xiii) Where the employee shows that the invention has been of outstanding benefit, the amount of compensation is to be determined in the light of all the available evidence in accordance with section 41 so as to secure a just and fair reward to the employee, neither limiting him to compensation for loss or damage, nor placing him in as strong a position as an external patentee or licensor'.

This case was decided on the version of the Act prior to its amendment,[80] and therefore only the benefit derived from the patent was available for consideration by the court. The court awarded the 2 claimants £1.5 million. When considering whether the patents were of outstanding benefit to the employer, the judge considered the size and nature of the employer's undertaking (amongst other factors). He found that the patents were of outstanding benefit to the employer of the claimants having regard to all the circumstances:

'I have come to the conclusion that the patents were of outstanding benefit to Amersham having regard to all the circumstances, including the size and nature of its undertaking: The benefits went far beyond anything which one could normally expect to arise from the sort of work the employees were doing'.

Of particular interest is the judge's analysis:

'The first and most obvious contribution the patents have made to [the drug company] is in protecting the business against generic competition

---

79 RDE 'guarantees additional market protection for originator pharmaceuticals by preventing health authorities from accepting applications for generic medicines during the period of exclusivity' (from the European Generic Medicines Association website: http://www.egagenerics.com/gen-dataex.htm).

80 See 'Rights of employee to claim compensation for making invention' above.

and reduced profits after the expiry of RDE. The expiry of the patents in about 2008 and the advent of generic competition was one of the major issues facing the [drug] company from 2000 onwards. If the patents had not existed in 2000, and [the drug company] had been facing the expiry of RDE in 2002, this would not simply have been a major issue, it would have been a crisis for [the drug company].

The benefit of patent protection is not limited to profits from sales. As I have held, the fact that [the drug company] had a patented blockbuster radiopharmaceutical has been a major factor in achieving the corporate deals. In this way the patents have helped transform [the drug company]. Considering the totality of the evidence I had no difficulty in recognising that the patents were of outstanding benefit to [the drug company]'.

Anti-competitive provisions in agreements relating to patents

The Competition Act 1998 repealed the competition law provisions, ie sections 44 and 45, in the Act.[81] Under these provisions, certain types of tying clauses and post-patent expiry restrictions were void. Those provisions still apply to agreements[82] and applications[83] made before 1 March 2000. Contract provisions which breach these sections may also breach EC and UK competition law.[84]

There are no provisions equivalent to section 44 in any of the other UK intellectual property statutes. Under Article 81 of the EC Treaty and the Competition Act 1998, tying clauses are just one example of a large number

---

81   Perhaps as a consequence, the wording of ss 44, 45 of the Act (repealed by ss 70, 74 of the Competition Act 1998) was relatively intricate. The scope of s 44 of the Act was considered in *Chiron v Murex* [1996] RPC 535 which should be considered when drafting any tying clause, particularly if the agreement relates to both UK and non-UK activities.

82   Section 44 of the Act still applies to agreements entered into before 1 March 2000 (where the agreements contain conditions or terms for the supply of a patented product or of a licence to work a patented invention, or of a contract relating to any such supply or licence): Competition Act 1998 (Transitional, Consequential and Supplemental Provisions) Order 2000 (SI 2000/311), Art 3(a). Section 44 is dealt with in more detail in the first edition of this book.

83   Section 45 of the Act continues to apply to:
      '(a) notices to terminate an agreement relating to patents on three months notice after the expiry or revocation of those patents notwithstanding anything to the contrary in the agreement (the types of agreements are those described in section 44); or
      (b) applications made to a court to vary the terms of an agreement of the type envisaged by (a) where the patents have ceased to be in force and it would be unjust to require the applicant to continue to comply with the existing terms'.
      Where the notice was given and/or application was made before 1 March 2000: Competition Act 1998 (Transitional, Consequential and Supplemental Provisions) Order 2000 (SI 2000/311), Art 3(b). Section 45 is dealt with in more detail in the first edition of this book.

84   See Ch 14.

of types of contract clause which may be void if included in agreements concerned with intellectual property.[85]

Licences of right

At any time after a patent is granted, the proprietor may apply to the comptroller for an entry to be made in the register to the effect that licences under the patent are to be available to the public as of right.[86] If the comptroller is satisfied that the proprietor is not precluded by contract from granting licences (eg, because an exclusive licence has already been granted), he usually makes such an entry in the register.

Where an entry is made, any person is entitled as of right to the grant of a licence under the patent on terms to be agreed with the proprietor or, if agreement cannot be reached, on terms settled by the comptroller, following an application by either the potential licensee or the proprietor.[87]

Existing licensees and defendants in infringement proceedings can also apply for such licences.[88] For example, an existing licensee who has been granted its licence prior to a patent being endorsed (so that licences under it are available as of right) may apply to the comptroller so that its licence be swapped for a licence of right on the same terms as the terms on which a licence of right is settled by the comptroller.[89]

The main advantages to the proprietor of having the patent made subject to licences of right are that the renewal fees are halved, and the entry in the register provides some limited advertising of the fact that the proprietor is willing to grant licences under the patent.[90]

The licensee under a licence of right may request the proprietor to take proceedings against an infringer, and if he fails to do so the licensee may do so in his own name.[91] The proprietor may apply to cancel the licence of

---

85 Competition law is considered in greater detail in Chs 14 (Guidelines and Regulation on R&D Agreements) and 15 (UK Compeititon Law).

86 Section 46(1) of the Act.

87 Section 46(3)(a) of the Act. If the proprietor and the proposed licensee cannot settle the terms of the licence, then the application must be made on Patents Form 2 with two copies of the terms of the draft licence. The comptroller must notify the proprietor and provide a copy of the application and proposed draft licence, with the proprietor having the right to file a statement. Thereafter the new procedure for applications before the comptroller is followed. See Patent Rules 2007 (SI 2007/3291), r 89 and Pt 7.

88 Section 46(3) of the Act.

89 Section 46(3)(b) of the Act.

90 Section 45(3)(d) of the Act. There may be other advantages in having the patent made subject to licences of right in some situations, eg where there is a risk of a compulsory licence being ordered by the comptroller (eg under s 51 of the Act).

91 Section 46(4), (5) of the Act.

right designation at any time, provided there are no current licensees, or all licensees consent to the cancellation.[92] In addition, a person can apply for the cancellation of a licence of right, if that person can satisfy the comptroller that the proprietor had entered into a contract with that person and the contract precludes the proprietor granting licences.[93]

There have been many reported cases in which the terms of licences of right have been contested, most of which were concerned with new existing patents, ie patents which on 1 June 1978 had more than five years of their 16-year term still to run.[94] The Act extended the term of these patents from 16 years to 20 years to bring them in line with new patents granted under the Act, on condition that during the last four years they would be deemed to be subject to licences of right. This led to a considerable amount of litigation for a few years, as parties contested the terms on which such licences were to be granted.[95] As well as being of relevance to licences of right under patents, these cases are likely to be of particular interest in future years in relation to design right and copyright in designs, as licence of right provisions were introduced for those rights in the Copyright, Designs and Patents Act 1988.[96]

Compulsory licences

General

The Act sets out grounds for granting compulsory licences. The procedure, and grounds for obtaining a compulsory licence, underwent heavy revision in 1999 in order to comply with the TRIPS (the Trade-Related Aspects of Intellectual Property Rights) agreement.[97] The provisions are now different depending on whether the patent in question has a proprietor who is considered to be a 'WTO proprietor' or not. A proprietor of a patent is a WTO proprietor if:

---

92 Section 47 of the Act.
93 Section 47(3) of the Act. Such an application has to be done within two months of an entry in the register that licences under the patent are to be available to the public as of right.
94 As distinct from old existing patents, the date of which fell 11 years or more before 1 June 1978, and which were not given automatic extension to a 20-year term.
95 The deemed licence of right provisions were, in effect, cancelled for some patents in respect of pharmaceutical uses of medicinal products in 1988, and in respect of pesticidal uses of products in 1989 (see Copyright Designs and Patents Act 1988, s 293 and the Patent (Licences of Right) (Exception of Pesticidal Uses) Order 1989 (SI 1989/1202)).
96 Copyright, Designs and Patents Act 1988, s 237 (in relation to design right – applicable for the last five years of the design-right term); Copyright, Designs and Patents Act 1988, Sch 1, para 19 (in relation to copyrights existing before 1 August 1989). After that date copyright is not available for most industrial designs.
97 Section 48 of the Act, as substituted by SI 1999/1899 with effect from 2 July 1999. These Regulations replaced ss 48, 51, 52 of the Act, added two new sections, ss 48A and 49B to the Act, and made revisions to other sections and several changes to the rules made under the Patent Rules 1995 (SI 1995/2093) (which are now revoked and replaced by the Patent Rules 2007 (SI 2007/3291)).

(a) he is a national or is domiciled in a country which is a member of the World Trade organisation; or

(b) he has a real and effective industrial or commercial establishment in such a country.[98]

Time at which the grant of a compulsory licence etc can be sought and grounds for licence

Any person may, at any time after the expiration of three years from the date of the grant of a patent, apply on the prescribed form[99] to the comptroller:[100]

(a) for a licence under the patent; or

(b) for an entry to be made in the register to the effect that licences under the patent are available as of right; or

(c) if the applicant is a government department, for the grant to any person specified in the application of a licence under the patent.

If the comptroller is satisfied that the relevant grounds are satisfied[101] then the comptroller may

(i) for (a) above, grant a licence to the applicant on such terms as the comptroller considers fit;

(ii) for (b) above, make an entry in the register that licences are available of right; and

(iii) for (c) above, grant a licence on such terms as the comptroller considers fit to the government department (or any person specified in the government department's application).

Where the comptroller is satisfied the use of items is unfairly prejudiced by conditions placed by the proprietor of a patent on the grant of a licence (or other disposal of the items) then the comptroller can grant a licence to an applicant or to the applicant's customers. This is subject to two conditions:

(a) the items are not protected by the patent; and

(b) the patent is the subject of application for a compulsory licence or entry of a licence of right.[102]

---

98 Section 48(5) of the Act, as substituted by SI 1999/1899. The UK is a member of the World Trade Organisation. Most other countries are also members.

99 Patents Form 2. The application will need to comply with the procedure for applications in Patent Rules 2007 (SI 2007/3291), Pt 7.

100 Section 48(1)(a)–(c) of the Act. The applicant can be an existing holder of a licence under the patent, section 48(3) of the Act.

101 The relevant grounds are (i) if the application is made where the proprietor of a patent is a WTO proprietor, the relevant grounds are those set out in s 48A(1) of the Act (see under 'WTO proprietor' below ; (ii) in any other case, the relevant grounds set out in s 48B(1) of the Act (see under 'Non-WTO proprietor' below (s 48(4) of the Act, as amended by SI 1999/1899 with effect from 2 July 1999).

102 Section 49(1) of the Act. 'Items' means 'the manufacture, use or disposal of materials'.

Where a person makes an application for a compulsory licence or entry of a licence of right concerning a patent, but that person already has a licence under the patent, the comptroller can cancel the existing licence and grant another or amend the provisions of the existing licence.[103]

A licensee under a compulsory licence or a licence by virtue of a compulsory entry 'licences of right' has the same power to require the proprietor to take infringement proceedings, and in default to take proceedings in his own name, making the proprietor a defendant, as has a licensee under a voluntary entry.[104]

WTO proprietor

For an application in respect of a patent whose proprietor is a WTO proprietor, the relevant grounds are:

(a) where the patented invention is a product, that a demand for the product in the UK is not being met on reasonable terms;

(b) that by reason of the refusal of the proprietor of the patent concerned to grant licence(s) on reasonable terms; and

  (i) the exploitation in the UK of any other patent which involves an important technical advance of considerable economic significance in relation to the invention for which the patent concerned was granted is prevented or hindered;[105] or

  (ii) the establishment or development of commercial or industrial activities in the UK is unfairly prejudiced;

(c) that by reason of conditions imposed by the proprietor of the patent:

  (i) on the grant of licence(s) under the patent; or

  (ii) on the disposal or use of the patent product; or

  (iii) on the use of the patented process.

  The manufacture, use or disposal of materials not protected by the patent, or the establishment or development of commercial activities in the UK is unfairly prejudiced.[106]

Before an applicant can make an application the applicant has to have made efforts to obtain a licence from the proprietor of the patent on reasonable commercial terms and conditions and has been unable to do so within a reasonable period.[107]

---

103 Section 49(2) of the Act.
104 Section 46(4), (5) of the Act are applied to compulsory licences by s 49(4) of the Act.
105 This ground will not apply if the comptroller is satisfied that the proprietor of the patent for the other invention is able and willing to grant to the proprietor of the patent concerned and his licensees a licence under the patent for the other invention on reasonable terms (s 48A(4) of the Act, as inserted by SI 1999/1899).
106 Section 48A(1) of the Act, as inserted by SI 1999/1899.
107 Section 48A(2) of the Act, as inserted by SI 1999/1899.

Non-WTO proprietor

For an application in respect of a patent whose proprietor is a non-WTO proprietor the relevant grounds are:

(a) the patented invention is not being commercially worked in the UK, or not to the fullest extent that is reasonably practicable;

(b) demand for a patented product in the UK is not being met on reasonable terms, or is being met to a substantial extent by importation from a country which is not a member state;

(c) the patented invention is being prevented from being commercially worked in the UK by importation of the patented product from a country which is not a member state, or where the invention is a process, by importation of the product produced by the process from such a country of a product obtained directly by means of the process or to which the process has been applied;

(d) by reason of the refusal of the proprietor of the patent to grant licence(s) on reasonable terms:

    (i) a market for the export of any patented product made in the UK is not being supplied;

    (ii) the working in the UK of any other patented invention which makes a substantial contribution to the art is prevented or hindered; or

    (iii) the establishment or development of commercial or industrial activities in the UK is unfairly prejudiced; or

    (iv) by reason of conditions imposed by the proprietor on the grant of licences, or on the disposal or use of the patented product or on the use of the patented process, the manufacture, use or disposal of materials not protected by the patent, or the establishment or development of commercial or industrial activities in the UK is unfairly prejudiced.[108]

The comptroller must exercise his powers with a view to securing, inter alia, the prompt and full working of inventions in the UK, and reasonable remuneration for the proprietor of the patent, and with a view to not unfairly prejudicing the interests of any person developing or working a patented invention.[109]

Restrictions on grant of licence where the proprietor of the patent in question is a World Trade Organisation ('WTO') proprietor

Certain restrictions are placed on the type of licence that can be granted in pursuance of an order in respect of a patent whose proprietor is a WTO proprietor:

---

108 Section 48B(1) of the Act, as inserted by SI 1999/1899.
109 Section s 50(1) of the Act, as amended by SI 1999/1899.

(a) it shall not be exclusive;

(b) it can only be assigned to a person to whom there is also assigned the part of the enterprise that enjoys the use of the patented invention or the part of the goodwill that belongs to that party;

(c) it shall be predominantly for the supply of the market in the UK;

(d) it shall allow the proprietor adequate remuneration, taking into account the economic value of the licence; and

(d) it shall be limited in scope and duration to the purpose for which the licence was granted.[110]

Purpose of powers to grant compulsory licences proprietor is a non-WTO proprietor

The comptroller must, when deciding whether to make an order for the grant of a compulsory licence or an entry 'licences of right', where the proprietor is a non-WTO proprietor, seek to achieve the following general purposes:

'(a) that inventions which can be worked on a commercial scale in the United Kingdom and which should in the public interest be so worked shall be worked there without undue delay and to the fullest extent that is reasonably practicable;

(b) that the inventor or other person beneficially entitled to a patent shall receive reasonable remuneration having regard to the nature of the invention;

(c) that the interests of any person for the time being working or developing an invention in the United Kingdom under the protection of a patent shall not be unfairly prejudiced.'[111]

The comptroller shall take the following matters into account whether to grant a compulsory licence or make a licence available of right:

(a) the nature of the invention, the time which has elapsed since the patent was granted and the measures already taken by the patent owner or any licensee to make full use of his invention;

(b) the ability of any person to whom a licence would be granted under the order concerned to work the invention to the public advantage; and

(c) the risks to be undertaken by that person in providing capital and working the invention if the application for an order is granted.[112]

---

110 Section 48A(6) of the Act, as inserted by SI 1999/1899 with effect from 2 July 1999.
111 Section 50(1) of the Act, as amended by SI 1999/1899 with effect from 2 July 1999.
112 Section 50(2) of the Act, as amended by SI 1999/1899 with effect from 2 July 1999.

Once an application has been made, the comptroller is not required to take account of any matters which have arisen after the date of the making of the application although he may do so if he wishes.[113]

Competition Commission report

If the Competition Commission has produced a report and provided it to Parliament

(a) 'on a competition reference, that a person was engaged in an anti-competitive practice which operated or may be expected to operate against the public interest, or

(b) on a reference under section 11 of the Competition Act 1980 (reference of public bodies and certain other persons), that a person is pursuing a course of conduct which operates against the public interest',

then a minister can make an application to the comptroller asking the comptroller to take action under section 51 of the Act.[114]

If the comptroller considers that the matters appearing in the Commission's report (which in the opinion of the Commission) operate (or are likely to operate) against the public interest include:

(a) conditions in a licence granted under a patent and those conditions restrict

    (i) the licensee's use of the invention; or

    (ii) the power of the patentee to grant other licences;

    or

(b) the proprietor refusing to grant licences on reasonable terms;

then the comptroller has the power to remove or modify such conditions or enter a licence of right in the register of patents.[115]

There is similar procedure involved and powers provided to the comptroller following market and merger investigations.[116]

---

113 Section 50(2) of the Act, as amended by SI 1999/1899 with effect from 2 July 1999.
114 Section 51(1) of the Act, as substituted by SI 1999/1899. Before making the application the minister has to consult, including publishing a notice which sets out the proposed application, and consider any representations: see s 51 of the Act.
115 Section 51(3) of the Act, as substituted by SI 1999/1899.
116 Section 50A of the Act, inserted by the Enterprise Act 2002.

Rights of the Crown to use patented inventions

Any government department, and any person authorised in writing by a government department,[117] may 'use' a patented invention 'for the services of the Crown'.[118] It is thought that such authorisation may be express or implied.

Use: the term 'use' is defined[119] to include manufacture, importation and keeping of patented products, including products produced by patented processes, and some sales of patented products, but including all sales of 'specified drugs and medicines'.[120]

For the services of the Crown: the term 'for the services of the Crown' is defined[121] to include:

(a)   the supply of anything for foreign defence purposes;

(b)   the production or supply of specified drugs and medicines; and

(c)   such purposes relating to the production or use of atomic energy or research into matters connected therewith as the Secretary of State thinks necessary or expedient.

These items are further defined[122] and need reading in conjunction with the Defence Contracts Act 1958 (as amended). Separate powers exist for a government department and its nominees to use inventions during times of emergency.[123]

Compensation is generally payable by the relevant government department to the proprietor or the proprietor's exclusive licensee in respect of Crown use of his invention. In some cases the compensation is calculated by reference to the loss of profit the proprietor suffers as a result of not being awarded a contract to supply the patented product or perform the patented process.[124] Third parties who are adversely affected by the Crown's use of the invention

---

117   Such persons may include, for example, companies supplying goods or services to the Government.
118   Section 55 of the Act.
119   See n 118.
120   As defined in s 56(4) of the Act.
121   Section 56(2) of the Act.
122   Section 56(3), (4) of the Act.
123   Section 59 of the Act.
124   Section 57A of the Act; subject to detailed criteria set out in this section, eg that the contract could have been fulfilled from his existing manufacturing capacity. See also the separate compensation provisions of ss 55(4), 57(4) of the Act and the criteria for compensation in s 58 of the Act.

(eg a licensee under the patent, a person who assigned the patent to the proprietor in return for royalties, or the owner of related copyright or design right) may also be entitled to compensation.[125] Disputes over Crown user provisions may be referred to the court.[126]

OTHER FUNDAMENTAL PROVISIONS OF UK PATENT LAW WHICH MAY AFFECT PARTIES TO A PATENT TRANSACTION

Introduction

The following sections consider provisions which are important for an understanding of UK patents, including obtaining, registering, infringing, challenging and revoking UK patents. As has already been mentioned, these sections do not consider aspects which are unlikely to affect commercial transactions, eg the detailed procedures for obtaining or challenging patents (which are more likely to be of interest to drafters of patent specifications or litigators).[127]

Applications for patents and other procedural matters

What is a patentable invention?[128]

The word 'invention' is not defined in the Act.[129] Instead of attempting a definition which might have a restrictive effect on the granting of patent protection to inventions or processes resulting from changes in technology, the Act sets out criteria, in general terms by which an invention is to be tested in order that it should be patentable, and specifically excludes certain things from being inventions for the purposes of the Act.

---

125 Section 57 of the Act.
126 Section 58 of the Act.
127 Much of which is contained in the Patent Rules 2007 (SI 2007/3291).
128 See ss 1–6 of the Act.
129 However, the Act does provide a description of what is considered an invention for the purposes of the Act: an 'invention for a patent for which an application has been made or for which a patent has been granted shall, unless the context otherwise requires, be taken to be that specified in a claim of the specification of the application or patent, as the case may be, as interpreted by the description and any drawings contained in that specification, and the extent of the protection conferred by a patent or application for a patent shall be determined accordingly' (s 125(1) of the Act).

To be patentable, an invention must satisfy three positive requirements and must not fall within a category excluded from patentability by the Act:

(a) it is new (novelty);

(b) it involves an inventive step (inventiveness);

(c) it is capable of industrial application (utility); and

(d) it is not excluded on account of its falling within the specified exceptions, prohibitions on grant.

In more detail:

(a) *Novelty:* the invention must be new, that is to say it must not form part of the state of the art (as defined).[130] The state of the art includes all matter which has been made available to the public anywhere in the world before the invention's priority date.[131] The priority date is also defined; this is generally the date of filing of the patent application, or in some limited cases is the date of filing by the same person of an earlier application claiming the same invention. Disclosures made prior to the priority date may be disregarded in very limited circumstances.[132] There is not, however, a one-year grace period equivalent to that which has traditionally been available in the US. Thus, in order to obtain patent protection it is generally essential that the invention should not be publicly disclosed prior to making the patent application.

(b) *Inventiveness:* the invention must involve an inventive step, that is to say it must not be obvious to those skilled in the art (technical field) to which it relates, as defined,[133] having regard to any matter which forms part[134] of the known technical field of the invention (the prior art).[135]

---

130 Section 2 of the Act.
131 Section 2(2) of the Act. A disclosure made in confidence is not likely to be considered as being made available to the public. In EPO Decision T 300/86, a report made available to licensees on loan, with the report having 'confidential' marked on it, was held as not being published to the public. Where confidentiality is raised as an issue, then it is for the party who is arguing that the information in question is subject to confidentiality obligations to argue that the recipient was bound by those obligations (whether in law or in equity): see *Kavanagh Ballons v Cameron Ballons* [2004] RPC 97[5] (decision of the Patents County Court).
132 See s 2(4) of the Act – some disclosures made in breach of confidence during a six-month grace period are disregarded, as are disclosures made at a very limited number of major international exhibitions (see s 130(2) of the Act and Patent Rules, r 5(3), (4)).
133 Section 3 of the Act.
134 Ie by virtue of s 2(2) of the Act, and ignoring s 2(3) of the Act.
135 Section 3 of the Act. Matter in a concurrent application treated as published, does not form part of the prior art for this purpose (s 3 of the Act).

Thus an invention has to be more than simply new to justify the grant of a patent. Under the Act the UK Intellectual Property Office has to consider whether the invention involves an inventive step in addition to examining for novelty.

(c) *Utility:* the invention must be capable of industrial or agricultural application.[136] Methods of treatment of humans or animals by surgery, therapy or diagnosis are excluded.[137] However, substances or compositions invented for use in such methods of treatment may be capable of industrial application.[138]

(d) *Excluded categories:* in addition to the above three positive requirements, the invention must also not be within any of the excluded categories.[139] Patents are not available[140] for:

(i) a discovery, scientific theory or mathematical method;

(ii) a literary, dramatic, musical or artistic work or any other aesthetic creation;

(iii) a scheme, rule or method for performing a mental act, playing a game or doing business, or a program for a computer;

(iv) the presentation of information;

Items (i) to (iv) are only excluded 'as such' from being granted patent protection.[141]

(e) *Treatment or diagnosis of/on human or animal body:* a patent will not be granted for an invention for:[142]

(i) a method of treatment of the human or animal body by surgery or therapy; or

(ii) a method of diagnosis practised on the human or animal body.

---

136 Section 4(1) of the Act. In *Chiron Corpn v Murex Diagnostics Ltd* [1996] RPC 535, the Court of Appeal held that the invention had to be capable of being used in any kind of industry. The court went on to say that the word 'industry' had to be useful: that industry 'does not exist to make or use that which is useless for any known purpose', and intellectual property rights should be restricted to those inventions which are useful, and industrial application does not necessarily mean that a profit should be achieved or desired.

137 Section 4(2) of the Act.

138 Section 4(3) of the Act.

139 Sections 1–4 of the Act.

140 See s 1(2) of the Act.

141 Section 1(2) of the Act.

142 Section 4A(1) of the Act (inserted by the Patents Act 2004, in force from 13 December 2007, SI 2007/3396). Prior to the Patents Act 2004, these provisions were considered to be inventions not capable of industrial application (under s 4 of the Act).

The exclusion from patentability of (i) and (ii) will not apply to an invention consisting of substances or compositions for use in such methods.[143]

The excluded items are capable of variation; the Secretary of State may by order vary these exclusions for the purposes of maintaining them in conformity with developments in science and technology.[144]

In addition a patent will not be granted for an invention where the commercial exploitation of the invention would be contrary to public policy or morality.[145] This phrase is not explained further in section 1 of the Act, but the exploitation of an invention shall not be regarded as contrary to public policy or morality only because it is prohibited by any law of the UK or any part of it.[146]

The exclusion of computer programs prevents computer programs as such from being patented.[147] However, an invention which includes the use of a computer program may be patentable. Thus a method or process satisfying other requirements for patentability and carried out under control of a computer program may be granted a patent.[148] If an applicant for a patent

---

143 Section 4A(2) of the Act, inserted by Patents Act 2004 from 13 December 2007 (SI 2007/3396). However, if the invention consists of a substance or composition in one of these excluded methods (whether generally or for a specific use), although the substance or composition may be part of the state of the art, the invention may still be considered new if the substance's or composition's use in such a method is not part of the state of the art (s 4A(2), (3) of the Act).

144 Section 1(5) of the Act.

145 Section 1(3) of the Act, as amended by SI 2000/2037. Article 6(2) of the Biotechnology Directive states what is considered to be contrary to *ordre public* or morality:
1. processes for cloning human beings;
2. processes for modifying the germ-line genetic identity of human beings;
3. use of human embryos for industrial or commercial purposes; and
4. processes for modifying the genetic identity of animals which are likely to cause them suffering without any substantial medical benefit to man or animal, and also animals resulting from such processes.

These four items are also found in para 3(b)–(f), Sch A2 to the Act; they are in that Schedule held not to be patentable inventions, together with:
'... the human body, at the various stages of its formation and development and the simple discovery of one of its elements, including the sequence or partial sequence of a gene' (Sch A2, para 3(a)).

The invention per se may be innocuous; it is what it may encourage that is considered to be the reason for not making it a patentable invention. What is offence under this provision may change with the attitudes of future times; thus in 1926 a patent was refused in respect of contraceptive invention as being against public policy, but contraceptive inventions have been granted patent protection since 1956.

146 Section 1(4) of the Act, as amended by SI 2000/2037.

147 The patentability of computer programs is discussed in more detail under 'Patenting and software' below.

148 See *Merill Lynch Inc's Application* [1988] RPC 1 and more recent cases (eg *Fujitsu Ltd's Application* [1996] RPC 511) with regard to the exclusion under s 1(2)(c) of the Act, in general, and 'schemes for doing business' in particular. The UK courts continue to regard many software-related inventions as unpatentable by virtue of s 1(2)(c) of the Act, taking a stricter view than either the European Patent Office or the US patent authorities.

describes a method of applying a new idea to a manufacture, then it may be possible to protect the idea when related to the manufacture.

Biological material[149] and other products, which are produced by biological techniques, are not excluded from patentability.[150]

Biotechnological inventions are now specifically addressed in the Act.[151] An invention is not considered unpatentable solely on the ground that it concerns a product consisting of or containing biological material or a process by which biological material is produced, processed or used.[152] Biotechnological invention[153] can be patentable whether it is obtained from the natural environment or by means of a technical process[154] and can include elements obtained from a human body, including the sequence or partial sequence of a gene (even identical to that of a natural element).[155]

Established criteria for a new invention

Whilst the enactment of requirements for an invention to be patentable, set out above,[156] clarifies the statute law, it is thought that the general principles for patentable inventions established by the courts under previous patent legislation still apply under the Act. The statutory criteria mentioned above are sometimes difficult to apply, but the following principles have been established under the previous law, which, it is submitted, remain the same under the Act:

(a) smallness or apparent simplicity does not render an improvement unpatentable, as long as invention is involved;

(b) the actual history of the mental process of the inventor is not material, the product of the inventor's mind being judged upon its merits in the light of the prior art;

(c) the application of a well-known thing in a manner or to a purpose analogous to that in or to which it has previously been applied is not

---

149 Biological material (formerly micro-organism) is any material containing genetic information and capable of reproducing itself or being reproduced in a biological system (s 130 of the Act, as inserted by SI 2000/2037).

150 But is subject to s 76A, Sch A2 of the Act (as inserted by SI 2000/2037).

151 Section 76A and Sch 2A of the Act (inserted by the Patents Regulations 2000 (SI 2000/2037)) to give effect to Directive 98/44/EC ([1998] OJ L213/13) on the legal protection of biotechnological inventions.

152 Sch 2A, para 1 of the Act, as inserted by the Patents Regulations 2000 (SI 2000/2037). Biological material is defined in s 130(1) of the Act.

153 A biotechnological invention is defined as meaning an invention which concerns a product consisting of or containing biological material or a process by means of which biological material is produced, processed or used: s 130(1) of the Act.

154 Sch A2, para 2 of the Act.

155 Sch A2, para 5 of the Act.

156 See under 'What is a patentable invention'.

invention, unless that application involves the exercise of ingenuity in overcoming some difficulty;

(d) where the perception of the idea which is at the basis of a patent involves ingenuity, it does not matter that the application of the idea involves no difficulty;

(e) commercial success or the fulfilment of a long-felt want may indicate ingenuity, but does not necessarily do so; commercial success may be due to other causes;[157]

(f) a combination of known integers arranged so that they produce a new result may involve invention, but this is not so if the result produced is merely the duplication of the several results which the integers used separately were previously known to produce.

These pre-1977 Act principles are summarised here to give a general flavour of some of the issues which may be considered by the courts when assessing whether an invention is patentable. The formal criteria for patentability are those set out in the Act, as interpreted by court decisions.[158]

Prior disclosures which do not invalidate a patent

There are certain exceptional cases where a patent is not held to be invalid despite previous disclosure of the subject matter of the invention. If a patent application is made not later than six months after the disclosure, the disclosure must be disregarded provided that the disclosure was made in breach of confidence or information concerning it was obtained unlawfully,[159] or that the disclosure was made at an international exhibition and the applicant states, on filing the application, that the invention has been so displayed and also, within four months of filing the application, files written evidence in support.[160] The number of international exhibitions qualifying is very limited.[161]

157 See *Technograph Printed Circuits Ltd v Mills and Rockley (Electronics) Ltd* [1972] RPC 346, HL.

158 See further *CIPA Guide to the Patents Act* (6th edn, 2009), particularly paras 1.02–5.21, for a detailed review of the UK law as to patentability.

159 See s 2(4)(a), (b) of the Act. The six-month period is calculated from the actual filing date of the application, and not any claimed priority date. The corresponding European Patent Convention (EPC) provision appears to be less restrictive (EPC, Art 55(1)): the six-month period is calculated from the priority date rather than the filing date (*PASSONI/Strand Structure* [1992] EPOR 79). In a later case the European Patent Office (EPO) Enlarged Board of Appeal agreed with the *PASSONI* decision (Decision T 3777/95).

160 See s 2(4)(c) of the Act and the Patents Rules 2007 (SI 2007/3291). The written evidence consists of a certificate issued by the authority responsible for the international exhibition as well as a statement duly authenticated by that authority. The statement must identify the invention as being the invention displayed at the exhibition and the certificate must include the opening date of the exhibition (or the date on which the invention was first displayed if this date is later): see Patents Rules 2007, r 5(4), (5).

161 See s 130(1), (2) of the Act.

Capable of industrial application

As noted above, for an invention to be patentable it must be capable of 'industrial application' which according to the Act means that the invention is capable or susceptible to be made or used in any kind of industry or agriculture. In a recent case the meaning of industrial application was set out at some length and is worth quoting in full as it illustrates how the meaning of 'industrial application' can be understood in practice (and is a convenient summary of other case law on this point):[162]

'i)   The notion of industry must be construed broadly. It includes all manufacturing, extracting and processing activities of enterprises that are carried out continuously, independently and for commercial gain [...]. However, it need not necessarily be conducted for profit [...] and a product which is shown to be useful to cure a rare or orphan disease may be considered capable of industrial application even if it is not intended for use in any trade at all [...].

ii)   The capability of industrial exploitation must be derivable by the skilled person from the description read with the benefit of the common general knowledge [...].

iii)   The description, so read, must disclose a practical way of exploiting the invention in at least one field of industrial activity [...].

iv)   More recently, this has been re-formulated as an enquiry as to whether there is a sound and concrete basis for recognising that the contribution could lead to practical application in industry. Nevertheless, there remains a need to disclose in definite technical terms the purpose of the invention and how it can be used to solve a given technical problem. Moreover, there must be a real prospect of exploitation which is derivable directly from the specification, if not already obvious from the nature of the invention or the background art [...].

v)   Conversely, the requirement will not be satisfied if what is described is merely an interesting research result that might yield a yet to be identified industrial application [...]. A speculative indication of possible objectives that might or might not be achievable by carrying out research is not sufficient [...]. Similarly, it should not be left to the skilled reader to find out how to exploit the invention by carrying out a research programme [...].

vi)   It follows that the purpose of granting a patent is not to reserve an unexplored field of research for the applicant [...] nor to give the patentee unjustified control over others who are actively investigating in that area and who might eventually find ways actually to exploit it [...].

---

162   *Eli Lilly & Co v Human Genome Sciences Inc* [2008] EWHC 1903 (Pat), [2008] All ER (D) 410 (Jul), from para 226.

vii) If a substance is disclosed and its function is essential for human health then the identification of the substance having that function will immediately suggest a practical application. If, on the other hand, the function of that substance is not known or is incompletely understood, and no disease has been identified which is attributable to an excess or a deficiency of it, and no other practical use is suggested for it, then the requirement of industrial applicability is not satisfied. This will be so even though the disclosure may be a scientific achievement of considerable merit [...].

viii) Using the claimed invention to find out more about its own activities is not in itself an industrial application [...]'.

Biological material

Since 1945, the science of biotechnology has become one of the major features of the chemical and pharmaceutical industry. Today, many medicines are devised with the use of biotechnology (which may involve the use of biological material).

These biological materials, being living matter, are bred in certain material, and the whole is known as 'material'. An invention may require for its performance the use of biological materials, which is capable of forming the subject of patent protection provided that it is not available to the public at the date of filing of the application. A specification disclosing use of biological material will be treated for the purposes of the Act as disclosing the invention in such a manner as to enable the invention to be performed by a person skilled in the art[163] only if two requirements are met in the specification of the application as filed:[164]

(a) *The first requirement:* on or before the date of filing the application biological material has been deposited in a depositary institution which is able to furnish a sample of the biological material.

(b) *The second requirement:* on or before the relevant period:

(i) the name of the depositary institution, the date when the culture was deposited and the accession number of the deposit are given in the specification of the application; and

(ii) where the biological material has been deposited by a person other than the applicant:

(A) a statement is provided which identifies the name and address of the depositor; and

163 Section 125A of the Act.
164 See Patents Rules 2007, r 13(1), Sch 1, para 2(2). The application is to contain such information as is available to the applicant on the characteristics of the biological material.

   (B) a statement is filed which authorises the applicant to refer to the biological material in his application and authorises the making available to the public of the biological material.[165]

The information referred to in (b) above may be added to the application within 16 months of the declared priority date or, if none, the date of filing.[166]

The comptroller can issue an authorisation certificate following a request from any person.[167] With the application, there must be given undertakings:

(a) not to make the material, or any material derived from it, available to any other person; and

(b) not to use the material, or any material derived from it, otherwise than for experimental purposes relating to the subject matter of the invention.[168]

Both these undertakings shall cease to have effect when an application for a patent is terminated or has been withdrawn or the patent ceases to have effect.[169]

It is possible to restrict the availability of biological materials to experts as long as certain conditions, including that such a request is made to the comptroller and that the request is made prior to preparations for the publication of the patent application, are met.[170]

Any person can also apply for biological materials to be made available to an expert. The comptroller is required to notify the applicant and can decide whether the materials are released (even if the applicant objects) or not.[171]There are rules as to when fresh biological material should be deposited to replace biological material already deposited under the Patents Rules in

165 Patents Rules 2007, r 13(1), Sch 1, para 3(1), (2). The second requirement is also met with application being filed properly with the European Patent Office or the Patent Co-operation Treaty (Patents Rules 2007, r 13(1), Sch 1, para 3(2)).

166 See SI 1995/2093, r 17, Sch 2, para 1(3) as substituted by Patents Rules 2007, r 13(1), Sch 1, para 3(3). Other periods are also specified under s 16(1) of the Act and r 52(2) of the Patents Rules 2007. (Patents Rules 2007, r 13(1), Sch 1, para 3(3)). Other periods are also specified under s 16(1) of the Act and r 52(2) of the Patents Rules 2007.

167 Patents Rules 2007, r 13(1), Sch 1, para 4. An 'authorisation certificate' authorises a depositary institution to make available samples of biological material (Patents Rules 2007, r 13(1), Sch 1, para 1).

168 Patents Rules 2007, r 13(1), Sch 1, para 5(1).

169 Patents Rules 2007, r 13(1), Sch 1, para 5(3). If a government department (or a person authorised by a government department) makes a request (for the purpose of using the invention) for the service of the Crown, an undertaking does not need to be given (and if given, will have no effect) (Patents Rules 2007, r 13(1), Sch 1, para 3(4)).

170 Patents Rules 2007, r 13(1), Sch 1, para 6. A second condition is in relation to an international application for a patent (UK): the applicant needs to make a reference to the deposited biological material in accordance with the Patent Co-operation Treaty (Patents Rules 2007, r 13(1), Sch 1, para 6).

171 Patents Rules 2007, r 13(1), Sch 1, para 7.

particular circumstances, such as where it is no longer viable, or for any other reason the institution is unable to supply samples, or the institution has transferred the material to another depositary institution.[172]

Who may apply for and obtain a patent[173]

The Act makes a distinction between the ownership and inventorship of a patent. Both owner and inventor are named on a UK patent. Being named as inventor does not imply that one has any rights over the patent. Most patents are applied for, and owned, by companies, the inventions having been made by their employees.[174] Where an invention is made by someone who is not an employee, the inventor will often be the first owner. Any person may apply for a patent either alone or jointly with another.[175] The UK operates a 'first to file' principle for inventions, so that if two persons, separately, make the same invention then the first person to file will be entitled to the patent.[176] The applicant need not be the inventor, and is commonly the employer of the inventor.

Grant of patent

A patent may only be granted to:[177]

(a) the inventor(s);[178]

(b) any person other than the inventor(s) who is entitled to the whole of the property in it (for example the inventor's employer); or

(c) any successor in title to a person within (a) or (b) above.

---

172 Patents Rules 2007, r 13(1), Sch 1, para 8.
173 See ss 7–13 of the Act.
174 As to employee inventions see 'Employee inventions' above.
175 Section 7(1) of the Act. This contrasts with the position in the US where the initial application is generally made by the inventor and assigned to the employer where appropriate.
176 If a person wished to show that he was entitled to a grant of a patent arising from an application of another person, he had to indicate his entitlement arose other than from the provisions of s 7 of the Act, such as from a breach of contract or confidence (see *Markem Corporation and another v Zipher Ltd* [2005] EWCA Civ 267, [2005] All ER (D) 377 (Mar), paras 77–79).
177 Section 7(2) of the Act.
178 It seems that only the person or persons making the invention should be named on the patent application. In *Xaar's International Application* (BL O/257/98) patent agents were cautioned to name only the true devisers of the invention, and not name persons who did not make any contribution to devising the inventive concept for which a patent is sought. In *BNOS Electronics Ltd* (BL O/270/98) it was held that a patent agent merely naming a research team was too casual, if regard was not given to who had actually made the invention.

'Inventor' means the actual deviser of the invention, and 'joint inventor' is to be construed accordingly.[179]

Mention of inventor

The inventor(s) of an invention have the right to be mentioned in any patent granted in respect of their invention, and have similar rights in respect of applications.[180] An inventor whose name has been omitted may apply to the comptroller for an order to rectify the position.[181] The applicant is required to identify the inventors in the application.[182] A person who considers that another has been wrongly identified as inventor may apply to the comptroller for a certificate to that effect.[183] Whether the patent or patent application is valid is not a relevant issue as far as these types of proceedings are concerned.[184] The courts have emphasised that only the true inventors should be identified, and that particular responsibility lay with patent agents to ensure that all employees (current and past) who contributed to the actual devising of the claimed subject matter should be named as inventors.[185]

The main advantage of being named as inventor is probably the kudos that this brings; there may also be career advantages, particularly for academic inventors. In the special case of employees who are entitled to financial compensation for their inventions[186] (for example under specific provisions of their contracts of employment), being named as an inventor may be a prerequisite to participate in such schemes.[187]

---

179 Section 7(3) of the Act. *Henry Bros (Magherafelt) Ltd v Ministry of Defence* [1997] RPC 693, [1999] RPC 442, CA provided some guidance as to the meaning of an inventor. Inventorship was held to be carried out by the person who contributed the underlying inventive concept. In *IDA Ltd and others v University of Southampton and others* [2006] EWCA Civ 145 the CA applied *Markem and Henry Bros (Magherafelt) Ltd.* Where a person carried out tests to determine whether another's invention would work, such testing 'was a matter of simple routine experimentation – mere verification' (from para 32 of the judgment). The testing was a contribution which amounted to no more than adding to the common general knowledge in the art.

180 Section 13(1) of the Act.

181 Section 13 of the Act.

182 Section 13(2) of the Act.

183 Section 13(3) of the Act.

184 See *Monk Constructions Patent* (SRIS 0/119/98).

185 See *Xaars International Application* (SRIS 0/257/98).

186 Eg employees of universities, most of whom are entitled to receive a share of any royalties or other payments received by their employing institution from the exploitation of their inventions. In *BNOS Electronics Patent* (SRIS 0/270/98) it was held that naming an entire research team without identifying who actually carried out or was responsible for the invention was too casual an approach.

187 As to statutory compensation for employee inventors, see 'Rights of employee to claim compensation for making invention'.

It is also possible for an inventor *not* to be named on (or have their address mentioned in) a patent application.[188]

Disputes

Disputes over entitlement to a patent (including any entitlement arising by virtue of a commercial agreement)[189] may be referred at any time before grant[190] or after the grant[191] of the patent to the comptroller, who has wide powers to determine such entitlement.[192] Alternatively, he may refer the matter to the court.[193] Disputes between joint applicants over how the application should be pursued may also be referred to the comptroller.[194]

How to apply for a patent

Detailed rules exist on the form in which the application must be made, the fees payable, time limits for filing documents etc. Every application must include a specification containing a description of the invention, a claim or claims, any drawing referred to in the description or any claim, and an abstract. There are broadly three types of claim: apparatus (or device) claims; process (or method) claims; and product claims. More than one claim, and more than one type of claim, may be included in a single application provided that they claim inventions which are so linked as to form a single inventive concept.

Where the invention requires the use of a biological material for its performance, the applicant is required to make samples of biological material available to the public. In most cases, a sample must be deposited with a depositary institution (ie an authorised culture collection) on terms which will allow the institution to make the culture available to third parties.

---

188 Patents Rules 2007 (SI 2007/3291), r 11.
189 The comptroller does not have the power to deal with contractual or breach of confidence disputes as such, but if there is a dispute arising under s 8 of the Act concerning entitlement and there are issues relating to breach of contract or confidence then the comptroller will have the power to deal with them. If there is a dispute under s 8 of the Act, parties cannot issue separate proceedings to deal with the other legal disputes between them where they could all be dealt with under s 8 proceedings. If they do so then such separate proceedings may be struck out as an abuse of process (*Markem Corporation and another v Zipher Ltd* [2005] EWCA Civ 267, [2005] All ER (D) 377).
190 Section 8 of the Act.
191 Sections 8, 37 of the Act for disputes arising after grant may be referred under the Act; see also s 9 of the Act, where the dispute straddles the date of grant.
192 Section 8(2) of the Act.
193 Section 8(7) of the Act.
194 Section 10 of the Act.

Processing of applications to grant (or refusal)

Once an application has been filed and various procedures have been complied with, it is given a date of filing.[195] Unless it is withdrawn or refused in the meantime, the application is published 18 months after the declared priority date or (if there is no declared priority date) the date of filing.[196]

Once the application has a date of filing, the applicant may request a preliminary examination and search.[197] If the application survives this stage of the procedure, an application may be made for a substantive examination.[198] At the end of the substantive examination stage, a patent is either granted or refused. At any time before a patent is granted, the applicant may amend the application, for example to take account of objections raised by the examiner.[199] There is however a maximum period within which an application must be put in order, failing which it is deemed to be refused.[200] It is possible for an application to be reinstated if it is refused (or withdrawn) where the refusal is caused by the applicant not complying with the Act or the Rules.[201]

Where a patent application has been published but not yet granted, any person other than the applicant may make observations in writing to the comptroller on whether the application is a patentable invention.[202]

Restrictions on applications: for the defence of the realm or public safety

The Act includes two provisions designed to protect the defence of the realm and public safety:

(a) *Secrecy orders:* the first of these provisions gives the comptroller the power to make orders (sometimes known as 'secrecy' or 'prohibition' orders) to prohibit or restrict the publication of any information contained in a patent application which might be prejudicial to the national security or public safety.[203] The comptroller can prevent publication for specified periods or indefinitely depending on the circumstances. Breach of the terms of a secrecy order is a criminal offence.

---

195 Section 15 of the Act, as substituted by Patents Act 2004, from 1 January 2005 (SI 2004/2357).
196 Section 16 of the Act.
197 Sections 15A and 17 of the Act; s 15A inserted by the Patents Act 2004 from 1 January 2005 (SI 2004/2357), and s 17 as amended by Patents Act 2004 and other legislation.
198 Section 18 of the Act, as amended by Patents Act 2004 and other legislation.
199 Section 19 of the Act.
200 Section 20 of the Act.
201 Sections 20A, 20B of the Act, inserted by Patents Act 2004, from 1 January 2005 (SI 2004/2357).
202 Section 21 of the Act.
203 Section 22 of the Act.

(b) *Restrictions on applications abroad by UK residents:* it is a criminal offence, in certain circumstances, for a person resident in the UK to file a patent application, or cause one to be filed, outside the UK.[204] In view of the importance of this section, it is worth repeating it virtually in full:

'(1) Subject to the following provisions of this section , no person resident in the United Kingdom shall, without written authority granted by the comptroller, file or cause to be filed outside the United Kingdom an application for a patent for an invention [if subsection (1A) below applies to that application,] unless–

(a) an application for a patent for the same invention has been filed in the UK Intellectual Property Office (whether before, on or after the appointed day) not less than six weeks before the application outside the United Kingdom; and

(b) either no directions have been given under section 22 above [ie no secrecy order has been made] in relation to the application in the United Kingdom or all such directions have been revoked.

(1A) This subsection applies to an application if–

(a) the application contains information which relates to military technology or for any other reason publication of the information might be prejudicial to national security; or

(b) the application contains information the publication of which might be prejudicial to the safety of the public.

(2) Subsection (1) above does not apply to an application for a patent for an invention for which an application for a patent has first been filed (whether before or after the appointed day) in a country outside the United Kingdom by a person resident outside the United Kingdom.

(3) A person who files or causes to be filed an application for the grant of a patent in contravention of this section shall be liable–

(a) on summary conviction, to a fine not exceeding the prescribed sum [; or

(b) on conviction on indictment, to imprisonment for a term not exceeding two years or a fine, or both.

(3A) A person is liable under subsection (3) above only if–

(a) he knows that filing the application, or causing it to be filed, would contravene this section; or

(b) he is reckless as to whether filing the application, or causing it to be filed, would contravene this section.

---

204 Section 23 of the Act, as amended principally by Patents Act 2004, from 1 January 2005 (SI 2004/3205).

(4) In this section–

(a)   any reference to an application for a patent includes a reference to an application for other protection for an invention;

(b)   any reference to either kind of application is a reference to an application under this Act, under the law of any country other than the United Kingdom or under any treaty or international convention to which the United Kingdom is a party'.

Applications for clearance to file a foreign application are made to the UK Intellectual Property Office.[205] It is recommended that a UK resident (or anyone who considers he might arguably be a UK resident – the term is not defined for present purposes) take professional advice before making a foreign application, so as to avoid committing a criminal offence.

Post-grant procedural matters

Once a patent has been granted, the comptroller is required to:

(a)   publish a notice to this effect in the Official Journal and also publish the specification and the names of the proprietor and inventor; and

(b)   send a certificate in the prescribed form to the proprietor.[206]

The patent is treated as having been granted, and takes effect, on the date on which notice of its grant is published in the Official Journal. The proprietor's rights to bring proceedings against infringers are then, in effect, backdated to the date on which the application was published, subject to some qualifications.

The term of the patent is 20 years from the date of filing.[207] It will, however, cease to have effect if renewal fees are not paid, subject to certain rights of the former proprietor to apply to restore the lapsed patent.[208] The proprietor may apply to the comptroller to amend the specification[209] or offer to surrender the patent at any time.[210] A third party may give notice of objections to the proposed amendment or offer to surrender.[211] The decision as to whether to accept the offer is for the comptroller.

---

205 The current address for applications for clearance and enquiries is: The UK Intellectual Property Office, Room GR 70, Concept House, Newport, Gwent (tel: 01633 813588). Website: http://www.ipo.gov.uk.

206 Section 24 of the Act. The information to be included will be the name of the proprietor of the patent and the inventor (if different), unless the inventor has waived his right to be named (s 24(4) of the Act, as inserted by Patents Act 2004 from 1 October 2005 (SI 2005/2471)).

207 Section 25(1) of the Act.

208 Sections 25(3), 28 of the Act, as amended.

209 Section 27 of the Act.

210 Section 29 of the Act.

211 See n 210.

Registration of patents and interests in patents

Register

The comptroller maintains the register of patents.[212] The Act includes provisions describing how the register will be maintained, what information may be placed in the register, and the extent of the public's right of access to it.[213] Of particular interest in relation to commercial transactions in patents are the following provisions:

(a) The Patents Rules 2007[214] set out the detailed requirements for registration of various matters relating to patents, including details of the patent or patent application, and any transactions or interests in the patent, as well as various other matters including the correction of any errors in the register. The Rules specify, for example, which forms must be completed when applying to register a transaction, which documents must accompany the application, and which documents will appear on the public file. There are provisions allowing for confidential treatment of some documents and information.

(b) No notice of any trust, whether express, implied or constructive, may be entered in the register and the comptroller will not be affected by any such notice.[215]

(c) As well as giving the public the right to inspect the register,[216] the section enables applications to be made to the comptroller for a certified copy of an entry in the register, subject to detailed rules,[217] and such certified copies may be produced in evidence in Court.[218]

Effect of non-registration of transactions etc

The Act includes provisions relating to conflicting claims to a patent or an interest in a patent, by virtue of conflicting 'transactions, instruments or events'[219] (eg an assignment, mortgage, licence or sub-licence).[220] Such a situation might arise, for example, where the original owner of a patent purports to sell it twice, and the first purchaser fails to register the assignment before the second sale takes place. The provisions describe the circumstances

---

212   Section 32(1) of the Act.
213   Section 32 of the Act.
214   Section 32(2) of the Act. The rules are found in the Patent Rules 2007 (SI 2007/3291).
215   Section 32(5) of the Act.
216   Section 32(5) of the Act.
217   Section 32(6) of the Act.
218   Section 32(11) of the Act.
219   The types of conflicting 'transaction, instrument or event' to which the section applies include assignments and mortgages of patents, the grant, assignment or mortgage of patent licences or sub-licences, transfers on death and transfers by order of a court.
220   Section 33 of the Act.

in which, to take the above example, the second purchaser's rights to the patent would take priority over the first purchaser's.

Under the Act, the second person claiming the rights (the section is not limited to acquisition by purchase) will be entitled to those rights as against the first person if, at the time of the later transaction, the earlier transaction was not registered and the second person did not know of the earlier transaction.[221]

The section applies both to acquisitions of the property in a patent or patent application, and acquisitions of any right in or under a patent or patent application, including a licence.

In view of these provisions it is highly desirable to register transactions immediately.[222]

Rectification of the register

An application may be made to the court by any 'person aggrieved' to rectify the register by making, varying or deleting any entry in it.[223] It is also possible to apply to the comptroller to correct any error in the register,[224] and to refer to the comptroller any dispute over entitlement to a patent (see below).

Disputes over entitlement to patents

Determination of right to patent

After grant of the patent, any person who claims a proprietary interest in or under it may refer to the comptroller the following questions:[225]

(a) who is (are) the true proprietor(s) of the patent;

(b) whether the patent should have been granted to the person(s) to whom it was granted; or

(c) whether any right in or under the patent should be transferred to any other person or persons.

The comptroller may order, inter alia, a transfer of ownership of the patent, the grant of a licence or other rights in or under the patent, the registration of transactions, and such orders may be coupled with the revocation of the

---

221 See further the wording of s 33 (including provision dealing with the position in respect of unpublished applications).
222 As to the effect of non-registration on infringement proceedings, see s 68 of the Act, referred to under 'Effect of non-registration on infringement proceedings'.
223 Section 34 of the Act.
224 Section 32(2)(d) of the Act.
225 Section 38(1)–(3) of the Act.

patent in some circumstances.[226] There is a two-year time limit, from the date of the grant of the patent, after which such an order may not be made unless it is shown that the registered proprietor knew at the time of the patent (or time of transfer of the patent to him) that he was not entitled to the patent.[227]

The comptroller may decline to deal with the matter if he considers it would more properly be dealt with by the court.[228]

Effect of transfer of patents on licences

The effects on licences of an order by the comptroller transferring ownership of patents may be summarised as follows:[229]

(a) Any licences or other rights granted or created by the old proprietor(s) continue in force as if granted by the new proprietor(s),[230] provided at least one of the new proprietor(s) was also one of the old proprietor(s), so that there is some continuity of ownership.

(b) Where ownership of the patent is transferred to a completely new proprietor, none of whom was an old proprietor,[231] any licences or other rights lapse on the registration of the new proprietor, subject to (c) below.

(c) Where the old proprietor or a licensee, acting in good faith, worked the invention in the UK or made effective and serious preparations to do so before the entitlement dispute was referred to the comptroller, the old proprietor or the licensee is entitled to be granted a licence (but not an exclusive licence) by the new proprietor to continue working or work the invention.

(d) Any such licence must be granted for a reasonable period and on reasonable terms.[232]

(e) Disputes over the entitlement to, or the terms of, such licences may be referred to the comptroller for determination.[233]

Opinion as to validity or infringement of a patent

The comptroller has the power to provide an opinion (non-binding) as to whether:

---

226 Section 37(2)–(4) of the Act, and the powers for revocations under s 72 of the Act.
227 Section 37(5) of the Act.
228 Section 37(8) of the Act.
229 Section 38(1)–(3) of the Act.
230 Subject to s 33 of the Act and the provisions of the comptroller's order.
231 Ie on the ground that the patent was granted to a person not entitled to be granted the patent – see wording of the section 38 of the Act.
232 Section 38(4) of the Act.
233 Section 38(5) of the Act.

(a) an act constitutes (or if not done, would constitute) an infringement of patent;

(b) an invention is not patentable (or the extent to which an invention is not patentable).[234]

The proprietor or any other person can request the opinion.[235] The comptroller is required to notify interested parties that an opinion has been requested, including the patent holder, exclusive and other (sub-) licencees if their interest has been registered in the register of patents.[236] The fact that an opinion has been requested, refused or provided will be noted in the register of patents.[237]

Infringement of patents

Meaning of infringement and exceptions

Section 60 of the Act defines the acts which infringe a UK patent, subject to the limitations and exceptions provided in that section and elsewhere in the Act. There are two main types of infringement: direct, also known as substantive, infringement; and indirect, also known as contributory, infringement. The infringing acts will be considered below. Examples of substantive infringement are manufacture, use or sale of a patented product; an example of contributory infringement is selling an essential ingredient for making a patented product, intending that the ingredient will be used by the purchaser to make the patented product. Non-infringing acts under this section include private, non-commercial use and use for experimental purposes.

Substantive infringement

It is an infringement of a UK patent to do any of the following things in the UK[238] without the consent of the proprietor while the patent is in force:

---

234 Section 74A(1), (4) of the Act, inserted by Patents Act 2004 from 1 October 2005 (SI 2005/2471). The request can be made even if the patent has expired or been surrendered (s 74A(2) of the Act, inserted by Patents Act 2004 from 1 October 2005 (SI 2005/2471)).

235 Section 74A(1) of the Act, inserted by Patents Act 2004 from 1 October 2005 (SI 2005/2471).

236 Patent Rules 2007 (SI 2007/3291), rr 92, 95(1).

237 Patent Rules 2007 (SI 2007/3291), r 44(5).

238 As to the extent of the UK for these purposes, see s 132 – it includes England and Wales, Scotland, Northern Ireland, Isle of Man, territorial waters, designated Continental Shelf and some other designated areas.

(a) *Product patents:*[239] where the invention is a product, to make, dispose of, offer to dispose of, use, or import the product or keep it whether for disposal or otherwise.

(b) *Process patents:*[240] where the invention is a process:

    (i) *Use etc of the process itself:* to use the process or offer it for use when one knows, or it is obvious to a reasonable person in the circumstances, that its use there without the consent of the proprietor would be an infringement of the patent; or

    (ii) *Use etc of products obtained by the process:* to dispose of, or offer to dispose of, use or import any product obtained directly by means of that process or keep any such product whether for disposal or otherwise.

Contributory infringement

It is also an infringement of a UK patent to do the following in relation to the patented invention, without the consent of the proprietor, while the patent is in force:

- supply or offer to supply in the UK;

- a person other than a licensee or other person entitled to work the invention;

- with any of the means, relating to an essential element of the invention, for putting the invention into effect;

- when one knows, or it is obvious to a reasonable person in the circumstances, that those means are suitable for putting, and are intended to put, the invention into effect in the UK.[241]

It is not, however, a contributory infringement to supply or offer to supply a *staple commercial product* (not defined in the Act; it may mean a generally available raw product or commodity of commerce suitable for uses some of which (perhaps) must be non-infringing), unless this is done for the purpose of inducing the recipient to (substantively) infringe the patent.[242]

Exceptions to the infringing acts

Certain acts will not infringe a patent.[243] It is convenient to repeat the provisions of the Act which deal with the permitted acts in full (with added headings):

---

239 Section 60(1)(a) of the Act.
240 Section 60(1)(b), (c) of the Act.
241 Section 60(2) of the Act – for the original wording and layout please refer to the section.
242 Section 60(3) of the Act.
243 Section 60(5) of the Act, as amended by SI 2000/2037 and SI 2005/2759.

'(5) An act which, apart from this subsection, would constitute an infringement of a patent for an invention shall not do so if–

private and non-commercial

(a)   it is done privately and for purposes which are not commercial;

experimental

(b)   it is done for experimental purposes relating to the subject-matter of the invention;[244]

extemporaneous preparation in pharmacy

(c)   it consists of the extemporaneous preparation in a pharmacy of a medicine for an individual in accordance with a prescription given by a registered medical or dental practitioner or consists of dealing with a medicine so prepared;

use on ship temporarily in UK waters

(d)   it consists of the use, exclusively for the needs of a relevant[245] ship, of a product or process in the body of such a ship or in its machinery, tackle, apparatus or other accessories, in a case where the ship has temporarily or accidentally entered the internal or territorial waters of the United Kingdom;

use on aircraft, hovercraft or vehicle temporarily in UK

(e)   it consists of the use of a product or process in the body or operation of a relevant[246] aircraft, hovercraft or vehicle which has temporarily or accidentally entered or is crossing the United Kingdom (including the air space above it and its territorial waters) or the use of accessories for such a relevant aircraft, hovercraft or vehicle;

use of exempted aircraft

(f)   it consists of the use of an exempted[247] aircraft which has lawfully entered or is lawfully crossing the United Kingdom as aforesaid or of the importation into the United Kingdom, or the use or storage there, of any part or accessory for such an aircraft.

---

244 See *Monsanto Co v Stauffer Chemical Co and Another* [1985] RPC 515 where the limits of what would constitute an experiment were set out: 'Trials carried out in order to discover something unknown or to test a hypothesis or even in order to find out whether something which is known to work in specific conditions can fairly, in my judgment, be regarded as experiments. But trials carried out in order to demonstrate to a third party that a product works or, in order to amass information to satisfy a third party, whether a customer or a [regulatory] body [...], that the product works as its maker claims are not, in my judgment, to be regarded as acts done "for experimental purposes"' (from p 542 of the judgment).

245 As to the meaning of 'relevant' ship, aircraft, hovercraft or vehicle, and 'exempted aircraft', see s 60(7) of the Act.

246 See n 245.

247 See n 245.

use of plant propagating material

(g) it consists of the use by a farmer of the product of his harvest for propagation or multiplication by him on his own holding, where there has been a sale of plant propagating material to the farmer by the proprietor of the patent or with his consent for agricultural use;

use of animal or animal reproductive material

(h) it consists of the use of an animal or animal reproductive material by a farmer for an agricultural purpose following a sale to the farmer, by the proprietor of the patent or with his consent, of breeding stock or other animal reproductive material which constitutes or contains the patented invention];

permitting clinical or veterinary trials of medicinal products

for any act done in conducting a study, test or trial necessary in regards to Directive 2001/82/EC (medicinal products for human use) or Directive 2001/83/EC (veterinary medicinal products)'.

The first two of these exceptions are the ones most commonly encountered in practice. There is case law on the extent of the exceptions;[248] before relying on an exception it is recommended that advice be sought as to whether the particular activities under consideration fall within the exception.

Reform of the research exemption

The Gowers Review[249] has criticised the wording of the exemption from infringement which is 'done privately and for purposes which are not commercial' (section 60(5)(a) of the Act) and/or 'it is done for experimental purposes relating to the subject-matter of the invention' (section 60(5)(b) of the Act). The criticisms include:

- difficulty in describing what uses of a patent fall within the scope of the experimental use exception;

- a use within the scope of the subject matter would be covered by the exemption, but not uses of different subject matter;

---

248 See eg *Smith Kline & French v Evans Medical* [1989] FSR 513; *Monsanto v Stauffer (No 2)* [1985] RPC 515, CA.
249 The Gowers Review of Intellectual Property, November 2006, available at http://www.hm-treasury.gov.uk/gowers_review_index.htm. See in particular paras 4.3–4.12.

- that there is no defined meaning of 'relating to the subject-matter' in section 60(5)(b) of the Act;

- that because of the uncertainty of the scope of the exception, smaller research groups are not able to carry out research work in case they have to defend expensive litigation regarding alleged infringement by the research group;

- that seeking a licence to carry out research is often refused or a licence is only available at too great a cost;

- the requirement that research is done 'privately' is not in tune with the modern practice at universities, where research is increasingly done in collaboration with private research organisations; and

- if research (in order to be 'private' (section 60(5)(a) of the Act)) has to be not disclosed in order to come within the exception, then any publicly funded research (which as a condition of its funding has to be disclosed) would not come within the exception.

The Gowers Review suggests that in order to facilitate experimentation, innovation and education the research exception in section 60(5) of the Act is amended in line with the research exception used in Switzerland:

'The effects of a patent do not extend:

(a) to acts undertaken in the private sphere for non-commercial purposes

(b) to acts undertaken for experimental and research purposes in order to obtain knowledge about the object of the invention, including its possible utilities; in particular all scientific research concerning the object of the invention is permitted

(c) to acts necessary to obtain a marketing authorisation for a medicament according to the provisions of the law of 15 December 2000 on therapeutic products

(d) to the use of the invention for the purpose of teaching in teaching establishments

(e) to the use of biological material for the purposes of selection or the discovery and development of a plant variety

(f) to biological material obtained in the field of agriculture which was due to chance or which was technically unavoidable'.

Proceedings for infringement[250]

In England and Wales, proceedings for infringement may be brought in the Patents Court[251] (part of the High Court, and presided over by one or more specialist patents judges)[252] or in the Patents County Court[253] (which also has a specialist patents judge)[254].

In such proceedings[255] a claim may be made:[256]

(a) for an injunction (including an interlocutory (ie interim) injunction);

(b) for an order requiring the defendant to deliver up or destroy any infringing product or any article in which that product is 'inextricably comprised';

(c) for damages;

(d) for an account of the profits derived by the defendant from the infringement;[257]

(e) for a declaration that the patent is valid and has been infringed by the defendant.

There are restrictions on the recovery of damages or an account of profits where the infringement was innocent, ie the infringer was not aware and had no reasonable grounds for supposing that the patent existed.[258] Marking the patented product with the word 'patented' is insufficient to make the infringer aware of the patent; the number of the patent should also be stated.[259]

Where a patent is jointly owned, any of the joint owners may bring infringement proceedings without the consent of the others. The others must be joined as parties to the proceedings, but will not be liable for any costs or expenses if

---

250 As to the right to bring proceedings in respect of the period between publication of the application and grant of the patent, see s 69 of the Act.

251 See ss 61(1), 130(1) of the Act.

252 See the *Patents Court Guide*, which supplements the normal court rules for conducting litigation with details of who are the judges serving the court as well as an online court diary and court listings (http://www.hmcourts-service.gov.uk/infoabout/patents/crt_guide.htm).

253 See Copyright, Designs and Patents Act 1988, ss 287–292. The Patents County Court was 'revived' from 25 October 2001 ([2002] FSR 79).

254 See n 253 for details.

255 Parties may by agreement refer the case to the comptroller instead of the court, although the comptroller may decline to deal with the case if he considers it should be dealt with by the court (s 61(3), (5) of the Act).

256 Section 61(1) of the Act.

257 However, the proprietor cannot be awarded both damages and an account of profit – s 61(2) of the Act.

258 Section 62 of the Act.

259 See s 62(1) of the Act.

made defendants unless they take part in the proceedings.[260] In principle, the joint owners may agree different arrangements amongst themselves as to how they will bring infringement proceedings.

An exclusive licensee[261] under a patent may bring infringement proceedings in the same way as the proprietor of a patent.[262] The proprietor must be joined as a party to the proceedings but will not be liable for any costs or expenses if made a defendant unless the proprietor takes part in the proceedings. In principle, the proprietor and licensee may agree different arrangements between them as to how proceedings will be brought.

Effect of non-registration of interests on infringement proceedings

Section 68[263] deals with the consequences of failing to register an assignment, licence or other 'transaction, instrument or event'[264] (referred to below as a transaction) with the UK Intellectual Property Office within six months of the date of the transaction.[265] The section provides that where a person becomes the proprietor, joint proprietor or exclusive licensee of a patent by virtue of a transaction, that person will not be entitled to costs or expenses in respect of infringements which occurred *before* the date of registration of the transaction with the UK Intellectual Property Office, unless:

(a) the transaction is registered within six months of its date; or

(b) the court or comptroller is satisfied that it was not practicable to register the transaction within that period and it was registered as soon as practicable thereafter.

Thus one may register the transaction with the UK Intellectual Property Office at any time and claim costs and expenses profits in respect of infringements which take place after the date of registration. But in order to obtain costs and expenses in respect of infringements which take place before the date of registration, it is generally necessary to register the transaction within six months of its date. There is therefore every incentive for registering such transactions promptly.

---

260 Section 66 of the Act; as to the position of joint proprietors generally see s 36 of the Act, discussed under 'Register' above.

261 For definition of exclusive licensee see s 130(1) of the Act, referred to under 'Miscellaneous and administrative provisions' below.

262 Section 67(1) of the Act.

263 As amended from 29 April 2006 by SI 2006/1028.

264 As defined in s 33 of the Act – the relevant transactions include assignments, licences and mortgages of patents.

265 As to other possible consequences of failure to register, see s 33 of the Act discussed under 'Effect of non-registration of transactions etc'.

Remedies for groundless threats of infringement proceedings

Where a person[266] threatens[267] another with patent infringement proceedings, a person aggrieved by the threats[268] may bring proceedings for:

(a)   a declaration that the threats are unjustifiable;

(b)   an injunction against the continuance of the threats; and

(c)   damages in respect of any loss sustained by the threats.[269]

The aggrieved person will be entitled to this relief if he proves that the threats were made and he was aggrieved.[270] The aggrieved person will not be entitled to the relief if the defendant can show that the acts (in respect of which the proceedings are threatened or pursued) are an infringement of a patent but the infringed patent is invalid in a relevant respect.[271] Also the aggrieved person will not be entitled to any relief if the defendant can show that he did not know (and had no reason to suspect) that the patent was invalid in that respect.[272]

Proceedings may not be brought under this provision in respect of threats:

(a)   concerning bringing proceedings for an infringement alleged to consist of making or importing a product for disposal or of using a process; or

(b)   made to a person who has imported a product for disposal or used a process, concerning bringing proceedings for an infringement alleged to consist of doing anything else in relation to that product or process.[273]

Thus the provision is mainly concerned with infringement by sale or other disposal, using patented products and contributory infringement.

Providing information about a patent, or making enquiries solely for the purpose of determining whether a person has infringed (a) immediately

---

266   Not necessarily the patent owner – s 70(1) of the Act.
267   According to s 70(1) of the Act, the threat may be by 'circulars, advertisements or otherwise'.
268   Not necessarily the person threatened – s 70(1) of the Act.
269   Section 70(3) of the Act.
270   Section 70(2) of the Act, as substituted by Patents Act 2004, from 1 January 2005. (SI 2004/3205).
271   Section 702A(a) of the Act, as inserted by Patents Act 2004, from 1 January 2005 (SI 2004/3205).
272   Section 702A(b) of the Act, as inserted by Patents Act 2004, from 1 January 2005 (SI 2004/3205).
273   Section 70(4) of the Act, as substituted by Patents Act 2004, from 1 January 2005 (SI 2004/3205).

above or making an assertion about a patent for the purpose of making such enquiries will not constitute a threat of proceedings.[274]

A patent owner or its representatives will have defence for any threats made for infringement against another if it can show that best endeavours have been used to identify the person who, for example, made or imported a product for disposal, as long as details of such endeavours are provided when the threats are made.[275]

The Patents Act 2004 has made it easier for patent owners and their representatives to inform people of the existence of a patent. However they still need to be careful as to how to 'warn people off' from infringing a patent before threats are made. Legal advice should be sought before doing this.

Non-infringement, revocation, invalidity and amendment of patents

The Act includes provisions under which a person may apply to the comptroller or court for an order or declaration (as applicable):

(a)   that an act or proposed act does not infringe a patent;[276]

(b)   to revoke the patent;[277]

(c)   that the patent is invalid;[278] or

(d)   to allow the proprietor to amend the specification of the patent in the course of proceedings in which the validity of the patent is challenged.[279]

Application of UK patent law to European applications, Community patents etc

Part II (sections 77–95) of the Act includes provisions which, inter alia:

---

274   Section 70(5) of the Act, as substituted by Patents Act 2004, from 1 January 2005 (SI 2004/3205).

275   Section 70(6) of the Act, as inserted by Patents Act 2004, from 1 January 2005 (SI 2004/3205).

276   Section 71 of the Act.

277   Section 72(1) of the Act, as amended by the Patents Act 2004 from 1 October 2005 (SI 2005/2471). Key grounds are: on one or more of a number of grounds, including that the invention is not a patentable invention, or was granted to a person not entitled to be granted that patent, or the invention is not sufficiently disclosed in the specification. The comptroller also has powers to revoke a patent on his own initiative (s 73 of the Act).

278   Section 74 of the Act, as amended by the Patents Act 2004 from 1 October 2005 (SI 2005/2471); but only in the circumstances described in this section.

279   Section 75 of the Act; in relation to amendment other than in the course of such proceedings, see ss 27, 19 of the Act, discussed at 'Post-grant procedural matters' and 'Processing of applications to grant (or refusal)' respectively.

(a) Give effect under UK patent law to patent applications which are made under the European Patent Convention (EPC)[280] and which designate the UK as a country in respect of which the application is made. In many situations the UK element of such an application is treated as if it were an application made under the Act. However, many of the powers which are vested in the comptroller in the case of domestic UK applications are, in the case of EPC applications, vested in the European Patent Office (EPO).

(b) Give effect under UK patent law to patent applications made under the Patent Cooperation Treaty (PCT) to the extent they designate the UK.

(c) Would give effect to the Community Patent Convention (CPC) in the UK. The Community Patent Convention has yet to come into force.[281] If it does, it will enable a single patent to be applied for which will have effect throughout the European Community.

Criminal offences

Falsification of register

Three offences are created by section 109 of the Act. These are:

(a) to make (or cause to be made):

    (i) a false entry in the register [of patents]; or

    (ii) a writing falsely purporting to be a copy or reproduction of an entry in any such register

(b) to produce or tender (or cause to be produced or tendered) in evidence any such writing,

knowing the entry or writing to be false.

The maximum penalty on summary conviction is 'the prescribed sum'; on conviction on indictment the maximum penalty is imprisonment for up to two years or an unlimited fine, or both.[282]

Unauthorised claim that product is patented

It is an offence for a person falsely to represent that anything disposed of by him for value is a patented product. Where a person disposes of a product

---

280 As to which see Ch 3 under 'Patents'.
281 However, in December 2009 the EU brought forward new proposals for a Europe-wide patent (see Ch 3 under 'Europe-wide patent').
282 Section 109 of the Act. The 'prescribed sum' for the fine on summary conviction is currently £1,000. This amount can change from time to time.

for value and the product has stamped, engraved or impressed upon it or otherwise applied to it the word 'patent' or 'patented' or anything expressing or implying that the article is a patented product, that person is taken to represent that the article is patented.[283]

Such an offence is only triable summarily (ie in the Magistrates Court) and attracts a fine. Such a false representation is not an offence where:

(a)   it is made after expiry or revocation of the patent but 'before the end of a period which is reasonably sufficient to enable the accused to take steps to ensure that the representation is not made (or does not continue to be made)';[284]

(b)   the accused proves that he used due diligence to prevent the commission of the offence.[285]

Unauthorised claim that application has been made

It is an offence[286] for a person to represent that a patent has been applied for in respect of an article disposed of by him for value, where no such application has been made or any such application has been refused or withdrawn. The offence is very similar to that of making an unauthorised claim that a product is patented, with the same maximum penalty (see previous paragraphs), and with equivalent defences to those indicated above. Use of the words 'patent applied for' or 'patent pending' is taken to be a representation that a patent has been applied for, in the same way that the words 'patent' or 'patented' are in respect of the latter offence.

Misuse of the words 'Patents Office' etc in documents etc

It is an offence[287] for a person to use on his place of business, or on any document issued by him, or otherwise, the words 'Patents Office' or any other words suggesting that his place of business is, or is officially connected with, the Patents Office. The offence is only triable summarily and attracts a fine.

Personal liability of officers, managers etc for offences committed by company

Where an offence has been committed under the Patents Act by a body corporate (ie a limited company and certain other incorporated bodies) and it is proved that the offence was committed:

---

283   Section 110 of the Act.
284   Section 110(3) of the Act.
285   Section 110(4) of the Act.
286   Section 111 of the Act.
287   Section 112 of the Act. As stated at the beginning of this chapter, the Patents Office is now known as the UK Intellectual Property Office, but its official name is, and continues to be, the Patents Office, which is reflected in this section of the Act.

'... with the consent or connivance of, or [was] attributable to any neglect on the part of, a director, manager, secretary or other similar officer of the body corporate, or anyone who was purporting to act in any such capacity, he, as well as the body corporate, shall be guilty of that offence and shall be liable to be proceeded against and punished accordingly'.[288]

Note that the category of persons who may commit the offence extends beyond directors and the company secretary, to include a 'manager'.

Miscellaneous and administrative provisions

The Patents Act includes a number of administrative provisions including such matters as the immunity of UK Intellectual Property Office officials,[289] the correction of errors in patents[290] and inspection of documents on the patent register.[291] Section 130 of the Act defines a large number of terms used in the Act, including for example 'exclusive licence' which is defined for the purposes of the Act as:

'[A] licence from the proprietor of or applicant for a patent conferring on the licensee, or on him and persons authorised by him, to the exclusion of all other persons (including the proprietor or applicant), any right in respect of the invention to which the patent or application relates, and 'exclusive licensee' and 'non-exclusive licence' shall be construed accordingly'.

SUPPLEMENTARY PROTECTION CERTIFICATES

Introduction

A Supplementary Protection Certificate (SPC) provides an extended period of protection for a patented medicinal product or a patented plant protection product, after the patent expires. It is similar to patent term extension under US and Japanese laws.

Although SPCs can be thought of as a form of patent term extension, technically they are a new form of intellectual property, as will be discussed below. However, the practical effect of having an SPC is that certain patent rights continue after the patent has expired. SPCs were initially introduced for medicinal products only in 1993, but further provision was made for SPCs

---

288 Section 113 of the Act.
289 Section 116 of the Act.
290 Section 117 of the Act.
291 Section 118 of the Act.

for plant protection in 1996, both directly into the laws of all EC member states by EC Regulations.[292]

SPCs are available on a country-by-country basis in all the countries of the EC. In the UK, the EC Regulations are implemented by a section which has been inserted into the Act as well as the application of certain sections of the Act to SPCs.[293]

The official reasoning behind the introduction of SPCs is given in the Recitals to the Regulation. Essentially, there was concern that whilst US and Japanese laws provided for extended patent terms for certain pharmaceutical products, EC countries did not do so, or not in any uniform way. This was commercially disadvantageous to the EC pharmaceutical industry, and could have led to research work moving to the US or Japan. The argument for an extended term for pharmaceuticals is essentially that, because it takes several years to obtain government approval to market a pharmaceutical product, the effective duration of a patent monopoly is reduced, compared with the position in other areas of technology which are not so strictly regulated. This may make it uneconomic to develop important new pharmaceutical products, as the high costs of researching and developing such products cannot be recovered over the shorter period of protection.

The structure and wording of the EC Regulations are complex, not helped by the political negotiations which led to their introduction. The main provisions of the Regulations will now be summarised.

Types of product for which an SPC is available

In summary, SPCs are available for certain types of medicinal and plant protection products which are patented and have also received government approval for marketing in the country in which the SPC is sought. An SPC will cover only a product for which marketing approval has been obtained. Thus, if a patent covers more than one product, several SPCs may be needed

---

292 For *medicinal products*: Council Regulation (EEC) 1768/92 ([1992] OJ L182/1) concerning the creation of a supplementary protection certificate for medicinal products, and originally implemented in the UK by Patents (Supplementary Protection Certificate for Medicinal Products) Regulations 1992 (SI 1992/3091). For *plant protection*: Council Regulation (EC) 1610/96 ([1996] OJ L198/30) concerning the creation of a supplementary protection certificate for plant production products, originally implemented in the UK by Patents (Supplementary Protection Certificate for Plant Production Products) Regulations 1996 (SI 1996/3120). These Regulations were reproduced as Sch 1 and Sch 2 respectively in the Patents (Supplementary Protection Certificate) Rules 1997 (SI 1997/64). All these Regulations have been revoked from 17 December 2007 (SI 2007/3293).
293 Section 128B, Sch 4A of the Act, inserted by the Patents (Compulsory Licensing and Supplementary Protection Certificates) Regulations 2007 (SI 2007/3293) from 17 December 2007.

to 'extend' the patent in respect of all those products. Moreover, in view of the definitions of 'basic patent' and 'product' referred to below, it appears that some patented products may not qualify for SPC protection.

The EC Regulations provide that an SPC may be obtained for a 'product' which at the date of application for the SPC:

(a)   is protected by a 'basic patent' which is in force in the country of application; and

(b)   is validly authorised[294] for marketing[295] as a 'medicinal product' or a 'plant protection product'; and

(c)   has not already been covered by an SPC; and

(d)   the authorisation referred to in (b) above, is the first authorisation to place the product on the market as a medicinal product or a plant protection product as the case may be.[296]

The terms 'medicinal product', 'plant protection product', 'product' and 'basic patent' are defined in the Regulations as follows:

●   'Medicinal product' means any substance or combination of substances presented for treating or preventing disease in human beings or animals and any substance or combination of substances which may be administered to human beings or animals with a view to making a medical diagnosis or to restoring, correcting or modifying physiological functions in humans or in animals.[297]

●   'Plant protection product' means active substances and preparations containing one or more active substances, put up in the form in which they are supplied to the user, intended to:

—   protect plants or plant products against all harmful organisms or prevent the action of such organisms, in so far as such substances or preparations are not otherwise defined below;

—   influence the life processes of plants, other than as a nutrient (eg plant growth regulators);

---

294   Ie pursuant to Directive 65/65/EEC ([1965] OJ 022/369) or Directive 81/851/EEC ([1981] OJ L317/1) for medicinal products and Directive 91/414/EEC ([1991] OJ L230/1) for plant protection products.

295   For medicinal products the marketing authorisation has to be full marketing authorisation – permission to conduct clinical trials is not sufficient (*British Technology Group Ltd's SPC Application* [1997] RPC 118). For plant protection products, a provisional marketing authorisation may be acceptable if it is followed directly 'by a definitive authorisation concerning the same product' (EC Council Regulation 1610/96 art 13(3)).

296   The Regulations are both expressed in the same terms except for the use of the different type of products. The wording is found at Art 3 for both.

297   Council Regulation (EEC) 1768/92 ([1992] OJ L182/1), Art 1(a).

- — preserve plant products, in so far as such substances or products are not subject to special Council or Commission provisions on preservatives;

- — destroy undesirable plants; or

- — destroy parts of plants, check or prevent undesirable growth of plants.[298]

● 'Product' means, for a medicinal product, the active ingredient or combination of active ingredients of a medicinal product,[299] and for a plant protection product, the active substance as defined in the definition of active substances or combination of active substances of a plant protection product.[300]

● 'Basic patent' means a patent which protects a product as defined for a medicinal or plant protection product (as the case may be) as such, a process to obtain a product or an application of a product, and which is designated by its holder for the purpose of the procedure for grant of an SPC.[301]

Who may apply for an SPC?

An SPC may be granted only to 'the holder of the basic patent or his successor in title'.[302] Licensees are not eligible to apply.

How to apply for an SPC; procedural provisions

The Regulations set out certain procedural requirements for the making and processing of applications for an SPC.[303] In the UK these procedures are supplemented by the application of the Act and the Patents Rules 2007 to

---

298 Council Regulation (EC) 1610/96, Art 1(1). Further definitions based on this definition are provided in Article 1: '"substances": chemical elements and their compounds, as they occur naturally or by manufacture, including any impurity inevitably resulting from the manufacturing process; "active substances" means substances or micro-organisms including viruses, having general or specific action: (a) against harmful organisms; or (b) on plants, parts of plants or plant products; "preparations": mixtures or solutions composed of two or more substances, of which at least one is an active substance, intended for use as plant protection products; "plants": live plants and live parts of plants, including fresh fruit and seeds; "plant products": products in the unprocessed state or having undergone only simple preparation such as milling, drying or pressing, derived from plants, but excluding plants themselves as defined in "plants"; "harmful organisms": pests of plants or plant products belonging to the animal or plant kingdom, and also viruses, bacteria and mycoplasmas and other pathogens'.

299 Regulation 1768/92, Art 1(b).

300 Regulation 1610/96, Art 1(1).

301 The definition of a basic patent is the same for both medicinal or plant protection products, but both definitions are predicated on the individual definitions for 'products'.

302 Regulation 1768/92, Art 6, and Regulation 1610/96, Art 6.

303 See Regulation 1768/92, Arts 7–10, and Regulation 1610/96, Arts 7–10.

SPCs, which specify matters such as the forms that must be completed in applications made to the UK Intellectual Property Office.[304] In situations where neither the Regulation nor the Rules make specific provision, the procedural provisions of national patent law are generally to apply, but it is specifically provided that there will be no opposition procedure for SPCs.[305]

When must the application be made?

The application for an SPC must be made within six months of the date on which authorisation was given to place the product on the market as a medicinal product or a plant protection product, unless this took place before the basic patent was granted, in which case the application must be made within six months of the date of grant of the basic patent.[306]

Protection given by an SPC

The protection given by an SPC is limited in two respects. First, it is limited to the product for which marketing approval was given, and for any use of the product as a medicinal or plant protection product (as the case may be) that was authorised before the expiry of the SPC. Secondly, it is limited to the protection given by the basic patent. Only if the product meets both these tests will it be protected by the SPC.[307]

Subject to these limitations, an SPC 'shall confer the same rights as conferred by the basic patent and shall be subject to the same limitations and the same obligations'.[308] In this respect at least, an SPC can be considered as an extension of the term of the basic patent.

Duration of the SPC

The question of the duration of SPCs was the subject of considerable political debate. The final compromise position, as provided for by the Regulations, limits the duration of SPCs to a maximum of five years. The rather complicated formula for determining the duration is as follows:[309]

---

304 Certain provisions of the Act are to include a reference to an SPC (for example, a reference to a proprietor of a patent shall also be a reference to a holder of an SPC (para 1(1), Sch 4A to the Act). For the list of which sections of the Act apply to SPCs, see Sch 4A to the Act.
305 See Regulation 1768/92, Art 18, and Regulation 1610/96, Art 18.
306 Regulation 1768/92, Art 7, and Regulation 1610/96, Art 7.
307 See Regulation 1768/92, Art 4, and Regulation 1610/96, Art 4.
308 See Regulation 1768/92, Art 5, and Regulation 1610/96, Art 5.
309 See Regulation 1768/92, Art 13. Regulation 1610/96, Art 13 is expressed in exactly the same terms.

'The [SPC] shall take effect at the end of the lawful term of the basic patent for a period equal to the period which elapsed between the date on which the application for a basic patent was lodged and the date of the first authorisation to place the product on the market in the Community reduced by a period of five years.

Notwithstanding [the above] paragraph, the duration of the [SPC] may not exceed five years from the date on which it takes effect'.

Thus, to take some examples: if the application for a basic patent was lodged in 1990, and the first marketing authorisation is granted in 1996, the SPC will last for one year (six years less five years) from the expiry of the basic patent. If the first marketing authorisation is granted in 1999, the SPC will last for four years (nine years less five years). If the first marketing authorisation is granted in 2002, the SPC will last for five years (twelve years less five years equals seven years, but this is subject to the five-year maximum).

Commencement and transitional provisions

For medicinal products, SPCs were available from 2 January 1993 and for plant protection products from 8 February 1997. The latest set of rules governing both medicinal and plant protection products came into force on 17 December 2007.[310]

Implementation for other EC states has taken place on different dates. In addition there have been transitional provisions resulting in different provisions applying to different member states. In some EC countries, such as France and Italy, there were already SPCs in place prior to the introduction of the Medicinal Product Regulations.

Commercial transactions involving Supplementary Protection Certificates

There are no specific provisions concerning dealings with SPCs in either the Regulations or the UK Rules. It can therefore be assumed that the dealing provisions of UK patent law apply to UK SPCs. The effects of SPCs on patent licences have not been finally established. For example, does a licence which is stated to continue for the life of the licensed patent continue for the duration of the corresponding SPC? It is understood that the UK Intellectual Property Office's intention is to treat such licences as continuing on the same terms until expiry of the SPC. In other words, at least in the context of UK

---

310 Patents (Compulsory Licensing and Supplementary Protection Certificates) Regulations 2007 (SI 2007/3293), r 1(2).

Intellectual Property Office practice, SPCs will be regarded as extensions of the basic patent, even though technically a separate right.

Whether such an approach will be upheld by the courts has yet to be finally decided. It has been held that an SPC is subject to licences of right in the same way as the underlying patent.[311] The judge commented that an SPC gives no more and no less rights than those which existed under the basic patent.

PATENTS FOR BIOTECHNOLOGICAL INVENTIONS[312]

General

In 2000 and 2001 amendments were made to the Act (and the Patent Rules) to implement the Biotechnology Directive.[313]

The aim of the Directive is to harmonise national patent laws as regards the protection of biotechnological inventions. If an invention is new, involves an inventive step and is capable of industrial application it shall be patentable although the invention concerns a product consisting of or containing biological material or a process by means of which biological material is produced, processed or used. The new provisions provide a series of criteria of what in terms of biological material is considered patentable and what is not patentable. That is, making what was implicit and could be derived from other sources, explicit.

Summary of changes made to implement the Biotechnology Directive into UK law

The implementation of the Directive into the UK introduced a new section and a new Schedule[314] in the Act in regard to biotechnological inventions, as well as making certain other changes such as changing the meaning of the general prohibition on the granting of patents and indicating that all patents and patent applications are subject to this new Schedule.

---

311 *Research Corpn's Supplementary Protection Certificate* [1994] RPC 387 and 667. The *CIPA Guide to the Patents Acts* (6th edn, 2009) suggests at para B11 that by analogy, based on this case, a licence agreement 'which grants a licence under a patent should be construed as extending to a SPC which becomes effective upon expiry of that patent', unless there are clear words to the contrary. If this view is not taken, they suggest, a licensee would become an infringer of the SPC upon expiry of the patent and the expiry of the licence.
312 This section provides an outline of the law regarding biotechnological inventions as found in the Patents Act 1977. For background on the introduction and controversy of this matter see previous editions of the book.
313 Council Directive 98/44/EC ([1998] OJ L213/13) on the legal protection of biotechnological inventions.
314 Section 76A and Sch 2A, inserted by SI 2000/2037, from 28 July 2000.

221

It should be noted that the general requirements for patentable inventions described earlier in this chapter have not changed a(that the invention is new, involves an inventive step and is capable of industrial application).[315]

Meaning of biotechnological inventions and biological material

Definitions are now specifically provided for a biotechnological invention and for biological material:

(a) A biotechnological invention is defined as an invention which concerns a product consisting of or containing biological material or a process by means of which biological material is produced, processed or used.[316]

(b) Biological material is any material containing genetic information and capable of reproducing itself or being reproduced in a biological system.[317]

Biotechnological inventions containing biological materials

Biotechnological inventions are not unpatentable solely on the grounds that they concern:

(a) a product consisting of or containing biological materials; or

(b) a process by which biological material is produced, processed or used.[318]

Biological materials which are isolated from their natural environment or produced by a technical process may be subject of an invention, even if the biological material previously occurred in nature.[319]

Although the human body, plants and animals are generally not patentable inventions (see section below), they may constitute a patentable invention if:

(a) *For a human body:* an element is isolated from the human body or otherwise produced by means of a technical process. This can include the sequence or partial sequence of a gene.[320] The element can constitute

---

315 See 'What is a patentable invention?' above.
316 Section 130 of the Act.
317 Section 130 of the Act.
318 Paragraph 1, Sch A2 to the Act. Biological material which is isolated from its natural environment or produced by means of a technical process may be the subject of an invention if it previously occurred in nature (para 2, Sch A2 to the Act).
319 Paragraph 2, Sch 2A to the Act.
320 Paragraph 5, Sch A2 to the Act.

a patentable invention if the structure of that element is identical to that of a natural element.

(b) *For a plant or animal:* the technical feasibility (of the invention) is not confined to a particular plant or animal variety.[321]

Inventions not capable of being patentable

The following inventions are not capable of being patentable:[322]

(a) the human body, at the various stages of its formation and development, and the simple discovery of one of its elements, including the sequence or partial sequence of a gene;

(b) processes for cloning human beings;

(c) processes for modifying the germ-line genetic identity of human beings;

(d) uses of human embryos for industrial or commercial purposes;

(e) processes for modifying the genetic identity of animals which are likely to cause them suffering without any substantial medical benefit to man or animal, and also animals resulting from such processes;

(f) any variety of animal or plant or any essentially biological process for the production of animals or plants, not being a micro-biological or other technical process of the product of such a process.[323]

Applications for patents involving biotechnological inventions and other provisions of the Act made under the Act

All patent applications and patents (and other provisions of the Act) involving biotechnological inventions are to be subject to the Act.[324]

---

321 Paragraph 4, Sch A2 to the Act.
322 Paragraph 3, Sch A2 to the Act.
323 See *Leland Stanford/Modified Animal* [2002] EPOR 2, European Patent Office (Opposition Division). A European patent held by an American University, for a mouse implanted with human tissue. It was stated to have potential significance in relation to human transplants and the development of anti-AIDS remedies. The opponent in these proceedings attacked the patent on the grounds that it was unethical and against the general moral principles of Western society to grant patents on life. In particular it was unethical to use human foetal cells, which would cause suffering to animals and posed an ethical risk.
324 Section 76A of the Act.

Additional information to be provided when making an application for a patent involving or concerning a sequence or partial sequence of a gene

The industrial application of a sequence or partial sequence of a gene must be disclosed in the patent application as filed.[325]

Extension of protection to patents

The protection provided by a patent on a biological material processing specific characteristics as a result of the invention shall extend to any biological material derived from that biological material through propagation or multiplication in an identical or divergent form and possessing those same characteristics.[326] Also protected are the biological material and its progeny directly obtained through a process that enables a biological material to be produced processing specific characteristics as a result of the invention.[327]

This protection is extended to products which contain or consist of genetic information and all material in which the patented product is incorporated and in which the genetic information is contained and performs its function.[328] This particular protection does not extend to the human body at its various stages of formation and development, and the simple discovery of one of its elements, including the sequence or partial sequence of a gene.[329]

In relation to a farmer, an act that would otherwise constitute an infringement of a patent for an invention shall not do so if:[330]

(a) it consists of the use by a farmer of the product of the farmer's harvest for propagation or multiplication by him on his own holding, where there has been a sale of plant-propagating material to the farmer by the proprietor of the patent or with his consent for agricultural use; and

(b) it consists of the use of an animal or animal reproductive material by a farmer for an agricultural purpose following a sale to the farmer, by the

---

325 Paragraph 6, Sch A2 to the Act.
326 Paragraph 7, Sch A2 to the Act
327 Paragraph 8, Sch A2 to the Act.
328 Paragraph 9, Sch A2 to the Act. The *CIPA Guide to the Patents Acts* (6th edn, Sweet & Maxwell, 2009) states at 125.25 that paras 8 and 9 mean:
  '... that, if the claimed invention is directed to biological material (or the production of biological material) which is characterised by having a particular amino acid protein sequence, or is a material replicated by a particular DNA sequence, then (if that sequence is specified in the patent) the extent of protection provided by such a patent extends to any material which continues to possess that same sequence data'.
329 Paragraphs 9, 3(a), Sch A2 to the Act.
330 SI 2000/2037, reg 4.

proprietor of the patent or with his consent, of breeding stock or other animal reproductive material which constitutes or contains the patented invention.

PATENTING AND SOFTWARE

Patenting software inside the EC and the UK

The patenting of software is a topic which has caused and continues to cause confusion, uncertainty and difficulty:

- *confusion* as to whether patent law covers computer software;

- *uncertainty* as to the extent to which patent law will allow the patenting of computer software; and

- *difficulty* as to understanding the current law (and in particular the case law which has grappled with the issue of the patenting of software).

Computer software is nowadays of great importance whether as the principal aim of development of commercial products or as a tool in other activities such as research and development. This section addresses whether computer software (as inventions) can be patented.

Since the first and second editions of this book there have been important case decisions[331] which led to successive attempts by the UK Intellectual Property Office to revise the criteria as to what types of claims regarding applications for patents are acceptable

Since the second edition, although the main criteria of whether software can be patented have been reasonably consistent (the software must have a 'technical effect' or 'technical character' beyond the mere running of the software on a computer), much remains uncertain and the boundaries or the precise meaning of a 'technical effect' or a 'technical character' are still not firmly established. What follows can be no more than a snapshot of the current position, which may well change during the lifetime of this book.

Why patent software?

Computer software is normally protected by copyright.[332] The principal extra 'benefit' provided by the patenting of software would be to protect the idea and principles behind the software. Generally, copyright only prevents

---

331 *IBM Computer program product* (EPO Decision T1173/97) and *IBM Computer programs* (EPO Decision T935/97), [1999] RPC 861. Both decisions were handed down in 1999.
332 Copyright, Designs and Patents Act 1988, ss 1, 3.

copying,[333] but does not protect' the ideas and principles behind the software. As long as the code or the structure of the software is not copied (or is not copied too closely), another person can recreate the idea and principles behind the software using different programming code . In such a case the copyright owner of the original software may be able to do little about this.[334] However, if the copyright holder also held a patent he or she would be able to restrict such activity. In addition, it can be argued that if some developments in software are not protected by copyright, then if they are not protected by patent law, the originator of the development would not have any protection from it being used by others.

What does the Patents Act 1977 provide for computer software?

The Act indicates that a program for a computer is not considered to be an invention but only to the extent that a patent or application for a patent relates to a computer program 'as such'.[335] The meaning and extent of 'as such' has been of extensive discussion, interpretation and doubt (both in the UK and the EU).

The current position

Besides the normal criteria for a patent to be granted for invention,[336] the software invention must also have a 'technical character' or make a 'technical advance/contribution'. These phrases are not found in the Act or the Patent Rules 2007 (or indeed the European Patent Convention). Whether (and the extent to which) a computer program can be patentable is largely a creation of case law (particularly and initially by European Patent Office case law), in particular:

- *Vicom*,[337] where it was held that a claim directed to a technical process which is carried out under the control of a program (whether by means of hardware or software) cannot be regarded as relating to a computer program as such; and

---

333 And the other prohibitions and restrictions provided for under the Copyright, Designs and Patents Act 1988.
334 The extent to which copyright protects all aspects of a computer program is considered in Ch 5 under 'Protecting the ideas or concepts contained in computer programs with copyright'.
335 Section 1(2) of the Act: 'It is hereby declared that the following (among other things) are not inventions for the purposes of this Act ... a program for a computer ... but the foregoing provisions shall prevent anything from being treated as an invention for the purposes of this Act only to the extent that a patent or application for a patent relates to that thing as such'.
336 That the invention is new, it involves an inventive step, it is acceptable of industrial application and that the grant of a patent is not in an excluded category (s 1(1) of the Act). A program for a computer being one of the excluded categories, for example (s 1(2) of the Act).
337 *Re Vicom* [1987] 2 EPOR 74.

- *IBM,*[338] where a computer program can itself be claimed if it is running on a computer where it brings about a technical effect going beyond the normal interactions between the computer program and the computer.

The requirement for an invention to have a 'technical character' is found, other than in case law, in the *Guidelines for Examination in the European Patent Office*[339] That the presence or absence of a 'technical character' or 'technical contribution' is often key in determining whether or not an invention is excluded from patentability, particularly under EPC, Art 52(2), (3), has been adopted by the European Office Board of Appeal[340] and been approved by the Court of Appeal.[341]

Subsequent to these decisions there has been a significant amount of case law, and this has emphasised the need for a computer program invention to make a technical contribution in order to be eligible for protection by a patent.[342]

The relevant principles in the EPO guidelines and case law appear to be as follows:

(a) a contribution to the art by what is inside a computer program itself: that contribution, or its subject matter, is not patentable;

(b) a computer program which merely runs on a computer (such as a word-processing program or a spreadsheet) and which does not make any changes or improvements to the computer (hardware or other software) is also not patentable;

(c) where the computer program is able to bring about a further technical effect, when running on a computer, which goes beyond the normal physical effect, the further technical effect will not be excluded from patentability;

(d) a computer program which is provided on disc or CD-ROM or loaded into the computer or the computer's memory is not patentable (if the computer program merely loads and runs the program);

---

338 *IBM Computer programs* (EPO Decision T935/97), [1999] RPC 861.
339 At para 2.36, 'Programs for Computers', in the April 2009 edition of the Guidelines.
340 *Re Vicom* [1987] 2 EPOR 74: 'Generally speaking, an invention which would be patentable in accordance with conventional patentability criteria should not be excluded from protection by the mere fact that for its implementation modern technical means in the form of a computer program are used. Decisive is what technical contribution the invention as defined in the claim when considered as a whole makes to the known art'.
341 *Merrill Lynch's Application* [1989] RPC 561; Fox LJ said at p 569: '... it seems to me to be clear, for the reasons indicated by Dillon LJ, that it cannot be permissible to patent an item excluded by section 1(2) [of the Act] under the guise of an article which contains that item – that is to say, in the case of a computer program, the patenting of a conventional computer containing that program. Something further is necessary. The nature of that addition is, I think, to be found in the *Vicom* case where it is stated: "Decisive is what technical contribution the invention makes to the known art". There must, I think, be some technical advance on the prior art in the form of a new result (eg a substantial increase in processing speed as in *Vicom*)'.
342 Such as *Merrill Lynch's Application* [1989] RPC 561; *Gale's Application* [1991] RPC 305; and *Fujitsu Ltd's Application* [1997] RPC 608.

(e) however, if the computer program as regards its subject matter as claimed does make a technical contribution to the known art, then patentability should not be denied merely on the ground that a computer program is involved in its implementation.

Current case law

The most recent English case law, while broadly following the above points, has developed a new, structured way of establishing whether a computer program can be protected by a patent:[343]

(a) properly construe the claim;

(b) identify the actual contribution made (examining what problem is being solved by the computer program, how the invention works, what its advantages are and what has the inventor really added to human knowledge);

(c) ask whether it fell solely within the excluded subject matter (whether the contribution made by the computer-program invention falls within the 'as such' exclusion); and

(d) check whether the actual or alleged contribution was actually technical in nature (in effect applying the earlier English case law as to the technical nature of the contribution that needs to be made).[344]

In the case where this four-step approach was approved it was not decided whether a computer program (whether on its own or on a disc (carrier)) can be claimed in a patent application. The four-step approach has also been applied in further English cases:

(a) In a case applying the four-step approach it was held, in principle, that a computer program could be claimed by itself. However the claim made

---

343 *Aerotel Ltd v Telco Holdings Ltd (and others) and Macrossan's Application* [2006] EWCA Civ 1731, [2006] All ER (D) 346 (Oct). The Court of Appeal indicated that their approach in this case was merely re-ordering the questions to be asked as to whether a computer program invention was patentable from *Fujitsu Ltd's Application* [1997] RPC 608: '*Fujitsu Ltd's Application* asks first whether there is a technical contribution (which involves two questions: what is the contribution? Is it technical?) and then added the rider that a contribution which consists solely of excluded matter will not count as a technical contribution'. (see para 46). The Court of Appeal based their judgment not on section 1 of the Act but on the provisions of Art 52, EPC (which the Patents Act 1977 aims to be the equivalent of). The relevant wording from Art 52: '(1) European patents shall be granted for any inventions, in all fields of technology, provided that they are new, involve an inventive step and are susceptible of industrial application. (2) The following in particular shall not be regarded as inventions within the meaning of paragraph 1: (a) discoveries, scientific theories and mathematical methods; (b) aesthetic creations; (c) schemes, rules and methods for performing mental acts, playing games or doing business, and programs for computers; (d) presentations of information. (3) Paragraph 2 shall exclude the patentability of the subject-matter or activities referred to therein only to the extent to which a European patent application or European patent relates to such subject-matter or activities as such'.

344 The court held that this step may be necessary if the claim failed at the third stage (see para 46 of the judgment).

in the patent application 'must be drawn to reflect the features of the invention which would ensure the patentability of the method which the program is intended to carry out when it is run'.[345]

(b) It was held in another case that a computer program which solved a problem in a computer (reducing the likelihood of the unreliability of a computer's file system) did make a technical contribution by solving a technical problem. The court, applying the third step of the four-step approach, found that the computer program was not solely excluded matter, as it had a knock-on effect by making the computer on which it ran work better as a matter of practical reality.[346]

The effect of the latter decision is to widen the meaning of what constitutes a technical contribution, by potentially allowing claims for where a computer program improves the running or stability of a computer through programming, but which has not directly appreciable effect outside the computer or directly affects other parts of the computer hardware.[347]

Further developments

There appears to be divergence between UK and European case law regarding the patentability of software (based, it appears, on the EPO concentrating on whether software claimed as an invention is novel or involves an inventive step, rather than the UK approach, which attempts to determine whether the software is making the 'right' kind of inventive step). This has led the President of the European Patent Office referring a number of questions to the Enlarged Board of Appeal for consideration:

'Question 1 – Can a computer program only be excluded as a computer program as such if it is explicitly claimed as a computer program?

[...]

---

345 *Astron Clinica Ltd and others v Comptroller General of Patents, Designs and Trade Marks* [2008] EWHC 85 (Pat), [2008] 2 All ER 742, from para 54.

346 *Symbian Ltd v Comptroller General of Patents* [2008] EWCA Civ 1066, [2008] All ER (D) 75 (Oct). The patent application in this case concerned a computer program which provided a method for better accessing other electronic (dynamic link library) files. The computer program could be used on conventional computers as well as a range of electronic, communication and digital devices.

347 See the UK Intellectual Property Office Practice Note of 8 December 2008 for more on this. In essence an invention which either solved a technical problem external to a computer or inside the computer would not be excluded from patentability, and in particular: 'The Intellectual Property Office has previously recognised that an invention which either solves a technical problem external to the computer or solves "a technical problem within the computer" is not excluded. What *Symbian* has now shown is that improving the operation of a computer by solving a problem arising from the way the computer was programmed – for example, a tendency to crash due to conflicting library program calls – can also be regarded as solving "a technical problem within the computer" if it leads to a more reliable computer. Thus, a program that results in a computer running faster or more reliably may be considered to provide a technical contribution even if the invention solely addresses a problem in the programming'.

Question 2 – (A) Can a claim in the area of computer programs avoid exclusion under Art 52(2)(c) and (3)[348] merely by explicitly mentioning the use of a computer or a computer-readable data storage medium?

(B) If question 2(A) is answered in the negative, is a further technical effect necessary to avoid exclusion, said effect going beyond those effects inherent in the use of a computer or data storage medium to respectively execute or store a computer program?

[…]

Question 3 – (A) must a claimed feature cause a technical effect on a physical entity in the real world in order to contribute to the technical character of the claim?

(B) If question 3(A) is answered in the positive, is it sufficient that the physical entity be an unspecified computer?

(C) If question 3(A) is answered in the negative, can features contribute to the technical character of the claim if the only effects to which they contribute are independent of any particular hardware that may be used?

[…]

Question 4 – (A) Does the activity of programming a computer necessarily involve technical considerations?

(B) If question 4(A) is answered in the positive, do all features resulting from programming thus contribute to the technical character of the claim?

(C) If question 4(A) is answered in the negative, can features resulting from programming contribute to the technical character of a claim only when they contribute to a further technical effect when the program is executed?'.[349]

---

348 This is a reference to the following: Art 52 of the European Patent Convention. Section 1(2) is the equivalent provision in UK law: 'It is hereby declared that the following (among other things) are not inventions for the purposes of this Act, that is to say, anything which consists of– […] (c) a scheme, rule or method for performing a mental act, playing a game or doing business, or a program for a computer; […] but the foregoing provision shall prevent anything from being treated as an invention for the purposes of this Act only to the extent that a patent or application for a patent relates to that thing as such'. See 'What is a patentable invention?' above.

349 The referral to the EPO Board of Appeal was made under reference G/08 in October 2008. Just as the proofs for this book were being returned to the publisher the EPO (Enlarged) Board of Appeal published an opinion, dated 12 May 2010 (http://www.epo.org/topics/news/2010/20100512.html). Technically, the Board of Appeal decided that the referral was inadmissible because the legal requirement for making a referral to it was not met (it did not consider there was a real difference in opinions of different EPO Board of Appeals). However, the opinion appears to confirm the current EPO approach concerning whether software is patentable, which is seen as less strict then that of the UK Intellectual Property Office. Commentary on the opinion will appear on the website which accompanies this book.

CHAPTER 5

Copyright

INTRODUCTION

Current statutory basis for copyright law

The current statutory basis of UK copyright law relevant to this book is Part I of the Copyright, Designs and Patents Act 1988 (referred to in this chapter as 'the Act').[1] There are important Schedules to the Act which deal with, among other things, the legal position for works which were in existence prior to the coming into force of the Act. Given the very long duration of copyright protection (unlike the much shorter duration period for patents), these provisions are often relevant in practice, and will continue to be relevant for many years.

International legislative basis for modern copyright law

Some of the Act's provisions reflect the requirements of the Berne Convention,[2] WIPO Treaties,[3] TRIPS[4] and several EC Directives and Regulations. Some provisions of UK copyright law reflect other international obligations. In recent years new provisions have been introduced in the Act concerning:

- copyright protection for computer programs;[5]

- extending copyright protection to databases;[6]

- creating a separate, new form of protection, the database right (which is a lesser right than copyright);[7]

- various mandatory and optional exceptions to the rights of copyright owners by users of copyrighted works and material;

- the restriction on circumvention of anti-copying devices;[8] and

- the prevention of removal of copyright information placed in copyrighted works and material.[9]

---

1   The remainder of the Act (Ps II–VII) is concerned with other matters: performance rights, design rights (see Ch 6), registered designs (see Ch 6), provisions relating to patent agents and trade mark agents, provisions relating to the setting up of the Patents County Court, amendments to the licence of right provisions under UK patent law, and other miscellaneous matters.

2   To which the UK is a party. Countries, which are parties to the Convention, undertake to implement copyright laws which reflect the requirements of the Convention, thus ensuring a degree of international harmonisation of national copyright laws.

3   For example WIPO Copyright Treaty (1996), WIPO Performances and Phonograms Treaty (1996).

4   Agreement on Trade-Related Aspects of Intellectual Property Rights (see http://www.wto.org/english/docs_e/legal_e/27-trips_01_e.htm).

5   Council Directive 91/250/EEC ([1991] OJ L122/42) on the legal protection of computer programs.

6   Directive 96/9/EC ([1996] OJ L077/20)on the legal protection of databases.

7   See n 6.The database right is considered in Ch 6.

8   Directive 2001/29/EC ([2001] OJ L167/10) on the harmonisation of certain aspects of copyright and related rights in the information society.

9   The Copyright and Related Rights Regulations 2003 (SI 2003/2498) in force from 31 October 2003 and implementing Directive 2001/29/EC (see n 8). This Directive implements the 1996 World Intellectual Property Organisation treaties on copyright and performances and phonograms.

In summary, UK law provides a system of copyright protection where:

- protection is given to literary works (which includes computer programs and databases), dramatic, musical and artistic works, sound recordings and films, broadcasts, cable programmes, and the typographical arrangement of published editions;

- registration is not required to protect a literary work by copyright, merely that it be expressed in a permanent form (which can include an electronic form, such as in a computer file);[10]

- copyright protection normally lasts for the life of the author plus an additional 70-year period;[11]

- the protection offered by copyright relates to the form or expression of the work, rather than any ideas or concepts which are contained in the work. It is possible to copy the ideas or concepts contained in a work without infringing copyright;[12]

- the owner of copyright may bring civil proceedings to prevent infringement of his or her copyright and claim other relief, particularly damages. There are also criminal offences associated with copyright infringement;

- certain authors of copyright works (whether or not they own the copyright) have 'moral rights'. A moral right includes the right to be identified as the author and to object to 'derogatory treatment' of the work;[13]

- a person who is not the copyright owner (or having permission from the copyright owner) can use a copyright work without the permission of the copyright owner. Such use can be for such purposes as non-commercial research, private study, criticism and review and educational purposes.[14]

---

10 There is no general register of copyright works in the UK. Compare the position in the US, for example, where copyright works may be registered at the Library of Congress and certain legal benefits may result from such registration. In the UK, there are commercial companies who, for a fee, maintain a register of copyright works. But this is purely voluntary. One of the proposals of the Gowers Review (see under 'Gowers Review and other proposals' below) is that the UK IPO maintains a voluntary copyright register.

11 Changed from life of the author plus 50 years, pursuant to the EC Copyright Term Directive (SI 1995/3297), by the Duration of Copyright and Performers Rights Regulations 1995 Directive 93/98, OJ L77/20.

12 Unlike the idea contained in an invention, which once protected by a patent, cannot be copied while the patent is in force. That the ideas or concepts cannot normally be protected by copyright has been emphasised repeatedly by the courts in England in relation to computer programs (see 'Protecting the ideas or concepts contained in computer programs' below, which sets out case law on this point).

13 It is possible to waive moral rights. Authors who are employees do not have moral rights; also moral rights do not arise where a work is created by a computer program.

14 Sections 28–76 of the Act, as amended.

SOME RECENT DEVELOPMENTS IN COPYRIGHT LAW

- Of particular note since the second edition of this book has been the introduction into UK law of the Information Society Directive[15] and the report of the Gowers Review, the relevant parts of which will be outlined in this section.

- Also of note is the continual struggle for greater protection for computer programs in England and Europe. For patents, the struggle surrounds whether and the extent to which a patent can protect a computer program (in particular whether and the extent to which a computer program has a 'technical effect'). Where copyright is concerned, this struggle is expressed in a different way. Although a computer program will be protected by copyright, it does not protect the ideas and principles contained in a computer program. A section at the end of this chapter has been added to explore the implications of this, particularly in regard to the latest case law.

The Information Society Directive

General

The Information Society Directive[16] was brought into force in the UK from 1 October 2003.[17] The Directive was passed to harmonise copyright and related laws among member states of the European union, and focuses on three main areas:

- the rights that authors have in relation to their work;

- measures to prevent the circumvention of anti-copying devices; and

- measures to prevent the removal of any copyright and author-specific information contained in a work.

The Information Society Directive does not deal with many issues relevant to this book, such as what works qualify for copyright protection, the length of protection provided to copyright, who can qualify for protection or the assignment (ie transfer of ownership) or licensing of copyright works.

---

15 The second edition of the book contained a detailed outline of this Directive.
16 Directive 2001/29/EC ([2001] OJ L167/10) on the harmonisation of certain aspects of copyright and related rights in the information society.
17 The Information Society Directive was implemented by the Copyright and Related Rights Regulations 2003 (SI 2003/2498). The Regulations have made extensive changes to the Act, but many of the changes relate to matters which are not relevant to the subject matter of this book, such as broadcasts, (electronic) communications to the public and rights in performances.

Objective of the Information Society Directive

An important objective of the Directive concerns the protection of digital information through the use of copy circumvention devices and digital rights management. These provisions proved controversial prior to the passing of the Directive, because the provisions give greater powers to copyright owners (and especially large corporations owning large amounts of copyright material) to control access to their material. Measures in the US similar to those of the Information Society Directive have also been introduced.[18]

Non-application of the Information Society Directive to computer programs and databases

The Information Society Directive does not affect certain existing EU provisions relating to computer programs and databases,[19] including:

- the legal protection of computer programs;

- the term of protection of copyright and certain related rights; and

- the legal protection of databases.

The Directive does not apply to computer programs and databases as there are corresponding provisions to those found in the Directives relating to them.[20]

Summary of changes made to the Act by the Information Society Directive

The changes that the Information Society Directive made to the Act which are most relevant to the subject of this book include:

- copyright is not infringed in literary works by the making of a temporary copy which is transient or incidental but is an integral or essential part

---

18 Digital Millennium Copyright Act 1998.

19 Article 1 and Recital 20 of the Information Society Directive:

'The Directive is based on principles and rules already laid down in the Directive currently in force in this area, in particular [the Directives providing protection to computers and databases] and it develops those principles and rules and places them in the context of the information society. The provisions of this Directive should be without prejudice to the provisions of those Directives, unless otherwise provided in this Directive.'

20 The Patent Office Consultation document issued at the time implementation of the Information Society Directive was being undertaken underlined this point:

'No specific action is needed as a direct result of [Article 1]. For example, Article 6 of the Directive [the legal protection against the circumvention of any effective technological measures] cannot apply to computer programs since [s 296(2A) of the Act] deals with technological protection devices … Similarly, Article 5.1 of the Directive [regarding temporary acts of copying which are transient or incidental] does not apply to computer programs or databases, since [the relevant Directives] specifically provide lists of exceptions to rights in respect of such works …'.

of a technological process. For example to enable such a work to be transmitted or otherwise be lawfully used (such as over the internet).[21] This provision does not apply to computer programs or databases;

- restricting the fair dealing provisions for research so that they are only available where the research is done for a non-commercial purpose and sufficient acknowledgement is given;[22]

- permitting a lawful user of a computer program to observe, study or test the function of the program in order to determine the ideas and principles which underlie any element of the program. These activities can be carried out while loading, displaying, running, transmitting or storing the computer program. Any term or condition which purports to prohibit this right is void;[23]

- restricting the removal or circumvention of technical devices (for computers) or technological measures (for other copyright works);[24]

- permitting a non-exclusive licensee to bring an action for infringement of copyright subject to conditions. The conditions are that the infringing act was directly connected to the prior licensed act of the licensee, and the licence was signed by or on behalf of the copyright owner and that the licence expressly permitted the licensee a right of action under the Act.[25]

Gowers Review and other proposals[26]

The Gowers Review was set up by the Government to consider whether the current intellectual property system in the UK was 'fit for purpose'. The outcome of the Review was largely positive and many of the recommendations involved matters which are not within the subject matter of this book. The main thrust of the proposals concerned:

- strengthening enforcement of IP rights (such as introducing stronger measures for stopping piracy or the trade in counterfeit goods);

---

21 Copyright and Related Rights Regulations 2003 (SI 2003/2498), inserting s 28A into the Act. A similar exception is introduced for performances: insertion of para 1A into Sch 2 to the Act. This exception to infringement also applies to dramatic, musical or artistic works, films, sound recordings and typographical arrangements of published works.
22 Copyright and Related Rights Regulations 2003 (SI 2003/2498), amending s 29 of the Act. The other 'fair dealing' provisions in the Act are also amended in ss 30, 32, 35, 36, 38 and 39 of the Act.
23 Copyright and Related Rights Regulations 2003 (SI 2003/2498), inserting s 50BA into the Act.
24 Copyright and Related Rights Regulations 2003 (SI 2003/2498), substituting s 296 and adding ss 296ZA–296ZG into the Act.
25 Copyright and Related Rights Regulations 2003 (SI 2003/2498), inserting s 101A into the Act.
26 Gowers Review of Intellectual Property, November 2006, http://www.hm-treasury.gov.uk/independent_reviews/gowers_review_intellectual_property/gowersreview_index.cfm.

- reducing the cost of registering intellectual property rights;

- reducing the cost of enforcing intellectual property rights through litigation; and

- providing better access to intellectual property material to individuals, businesses and institutions taking account that much material is now in a digital format.

Therefore the Review was concerned with much more than copyright, and thus the proposals that were contained in the final report are limited as to the subject matter of this book. Those most relevant to copyright are set out here:

- in addition to the existing 'fair dealing' provisions for educational purposes and to improve access to copyright materials, educational institutes should be allowed to provide copies of materials to students who study by distance learning;[27]

- allow libraries to make copies of all forms of materials (including film) as well as to copy materials to another format (usually to a digital format);[28]

- extend the 'fair dealing' provisions for non-commercial research and private study to cover all materials (such as sound recordings and film);[29]

- allow for an exception to copyright for the creation of creative, transformative or derivative works (within the Berne three-step test as well as for the creation of works which are caricatures, parodies or pastiches);

- permit the use of a work by a person where the copyright owner of the work cannot be found or traced (so-called 'orphan works')[30] based on using 'reasonable endeavours' to trace the copyright rights holder;

27 For example, a lecturer may copy an article and provide copies to students who attend a class with the lecturer. However, under the current law, if some of the students were enrolled on a distance learning course the lecturer would not be able to provide those copies by email and come within the current exceptions to copyright infringement for educational purposes.

28 The Gowers Review (see n 26) noted that many libraries hold vast archives of film and sound recordings which are deteriorating, but since they are not able to trace the copyright owner or those who have rights over it (or it is too expensive to do so) such material will no longer be usable by the time copyright runs out on them. Also, some material is held in a format which relies on obsolete technology and therefore by the time copyright runs out there may no longer be a working version of the technology. This is likely to apply to computer programs too in the future.

29 Note the Gowers Review (see n 26) did not appear to address the change made by the Copyright Directive which changed the fair dealing provision for research so that it can only be for non-commercial purposes.

30 This point is more than an author not being found, but can include where an author of a report has died but it is not possible to establish whether he or she assigned or licensed his or her copyright. Or the author has assigned the copyright to a company and the company has gone bankrupt, or cannot be found, or has not kept records of what materials they have rights over, etc. In all these cases, under the current law it is not possible to copy such a work legally even though the person with the rights to the copyright work cannot be traced.

- the Intellectual Property Office should start a voluntary register of copyright;

- where digital rights management prevents copying of material which a person can lawfully use (such as under the 'fair dealing' provisions) then the present system of making a complaint to the Secretary of State be simplified; for example by providing a page on the Intellectual Property Office website for doing so.

- make the fines payable by online infringers the same as those paid by 'offline' infringers.

These proposals largely do not affect the main topics covered in this chapter except peripherally, as there are no proposals as to how the law should be changed as to creation of new copyright works, or as to licensing or assignment or other commercial provisions which affect technology transfer. The proposals are aimed to increase access to (or reduce restrictions of) a wider range of material to legitimate users within the current law. If all of these changes were made, a likely consequence would be that academics and researchers involved in *non-commercial*, early-stage, research would have greater access to and use of a wider range of material.

At the time material for this volume was being prepared, none of the above recommendations had been implemented. However, the UK Intellectual Property Office has carried out consultation based on the findings of the Gowers Report. The proposed changes (out of those set out above from the Gowers Report) to be taken forward appeared very limited and principally centre around:[31]

- extending the fair dealing exception to copyright for non-commercial research and private study to sound recording, film or broadcast material, but only where the person who wishes to carry out the research or private study is a member of an educational establishment and the research is authorised by the educational establishment. This proposed exception is more limited than that for literary works, where the person carrying out the research does not need to be a member of an educational establishment; and

- permitting the provision of copyright materials to students who study by distance learning provided that a student is authorised by an educational establishment to receive the materials. The students need to be specifically authorised for a particular communication they are to receive or be authorised for a particular type of communication;

---

31 Taking Forward the Gowers Review of Intellectual Property: Second Stage Consultation on Copyright Exceptions, December 2009, UK Intellectual Property Office (see http://www.ipo. gov.uk/pro-policy/consult/consult-closed/consult-closed-2009/consult-2009-gowers2.htm.

These proposals (and the other proposals for legislative change) are modest. Many recommendations in the Gowers Report appear not to have been taken forward by the UK Intellectual Property Office, or have been put off pending further consultation, or needing change at EU level. For example, the issue that digital rights management (DRM) can impede the legitimate use of copyright materials reflects this point. The consultation issued by the UK Intellectual Property Office notes that the EU legislative framework provides for a voluntary scheme and that further consideration is needed because of the impact of any change that might result from a more effective method to overcome DRM where a person has a legitimate right to use the protected copyright material.[32]

Some of the issues dealt with by the Gowers Report are taken up in another report on copyright in the digital age (the Digital Report).[33] Although the Digital Report focuses, rightly, on the importance and profound changes brought by modern, digital, means of creating and distributing copyright works, it has little to say about practical changes that might be made to improve matters. However some of the points the Digital Report makes are of general interest and relevance to those who create and license copyright works as well as those who seek licenses for such works:

- copyright law is complex, mostly because it consists of additions to deal with technological changes, including new rights and restrictions for new types of work and for increasingly complex ways of distribution and exploitation of copyright works;

- whether the exceptions to copyright works found in law can override any contractual terms agreed by the parties and in particular that many contractual terms on which licenses to copyright material were available were not in accordance with the fair dealing provisions found in the Act;

- whether the permitted exceptions for fair dealing for non-commercial purposes have kept up with the latest methods of creating, storing and using copyright works (such as downloading various copyright works and adapting and putting them together for a non-commercial use).[34] The discussion in the Report does not focus on the use of copyright works for carrying out research or technology transfer (or business use);

---

32   As n 31, paras 22–24.
33   © the way ahead: A strategy for copyright in the digital age, October 2009, UK Intellectual Property Office and Department for Business Innovation and Skills (see http://ns2.ipo.gov.uk/pro-types/pro-copy/c-policy.htm).
34   Such as buying a music track from an online store and combining the music with photographs and video obtained elsewhere, for a person's own private enjoyment.

- the complexity in licensing of copyright works whether they are available at or on acceptable terms is examined, particularly from the consumer's point of view. The expense and time taken to obtain clearance rights in order to access copyright works can be a major financial burden. This can be significant to those carrying out research (whether on a commercial or non-commercial basis) where they wish to access a variety of material from different copyright owners. Non-commercial organisations may not have the resources to deal with this. The Report favours a collective licensing scheme[35] where a potential licensee can obtain a licence for a broad range of works without having to negotiate individual licenses.

The issue with the Digital Report is that, as it notes, much of the change sought is dependent on changes being made to European legislation (which in turn, in many cases, would be dependent on changes to international treaties such as TRIPS and WIPO).

COMMERCIAL TRANSACTIONS INVOLVING COPYRIGHT WORKS

The Act addresses a number of issues of direct relevance to transactions in copyright, some of them of a technical legal nature, which are discussed in this section. In addition, there are many other aspects of copyright law that need to be taken into account when structuring or advising upon a copyright transaction, and which are summarised in later sections of this chapter. The provisions that are directly relevant to transactions may be summarised as follows:

Nature of copyright

Copyright is treated as 'personal or moveable property'. Thus, the general law of (personal) property applies to copyright and transactions in copyright,[36] except where overridden by specific provisions in the Act.

---

35   © the way ahead: A strategy for copyright in the digital age, October 2009, UK Intellectual Property Office and Department for Business Innovation and Skills: see paras 85–89 (see http://ns2.ipo.gov.uk/pro-types/pro-copy/c-policy.htm).

36   Section 90(1) of the Act. See Ch 9 for further consideration of the law relating to personal property.

Transfer of copyright[37]

The Act provides for three methods of transfer of copyright:

- by assignment;[38]
- by testamentary disposition;[39] or
- by operation of law.[40]

In a commercial transaction, transfer of copyright will generally be by means of an assignment. Transfer of copyright should be distinguished from the more limited grant of rights under copyright by means of a licence. Where a licence is granted, the person granting the licence retains ownership of the copyright and gives the licensee permission to do certain of the acts restricted by copyright.

Assignments

An assignment of copyright is not effective unless it is in writing signed by or on behalf of the assignor.[41] It need not be in the form of a deed or any other particular form[42] nor need the word 'copyright' be mentioned.[43] But if there is no consideration for the assignment, then under the law of contract a deed may be necessary to make the transaction legally effective. An assignment which is defective, ie is not signed by or on behalf of the assignor, is usually considered to be an agreement to assign. The assignee is the equitable, not the legal, owner of the copyrighted work, provided that the defective assignment allows the assignee to specifically enforce the assignment, and consideration is present. An equitable assignment does not need to be in writing.[44] Alternatively, if the wording of the assignment is not clear, it may, in reality, also be an agreement to assign.

---

37 The provisions relating to the transfer of copyright as detailed below equally apply to databases and the database right: Copyright and Rights in Databases Regulations 1997 (SI 1997/3032), reg 23.
38 Section 90(1) of the Act.
39 Copyright passes under the will with an unpublished work, unless the will provides otherwise: s 93 of the Act.
40 Section 90(1) of the Act.
41 Section 90(3) of the Act.
42 See eg *London Printing and Publishing Alliance Ltd v Cox* [1891] 3 Ch 291, CA. There are a number of old cases on this point. The obvious danger if there is not clear wording that there is an assignment of copyright then a court may decide to interpret the wording as not providing for an assignment.
43 In *Murray v King* [1986] FSR 116 where it was held that the assignment of 'interest, property, benefit' of the seller plus the goodwill in the business being sold was sufficient to transfer the copyright.
44 *Lakeview Computers plc v Steadman* (unreported, 26 November 1999, CA), *Bookmakers' Afternoon Greyhound Services Ltd v Wilf Gilbert (Staffordshire) Ltd* [1994] FSR 723.

An assignment, or other transmission of copyright, may be of limited scope and duration; it may apply to one or more, but not all, of the things the copyright has the exclusive right to do; or to part, but not the whole, of the period for which the copyright is to subsist.[45]

An assignment of future copyright[46] (for example an assignment which relates to a literary work which has yet to be written) is often legally effective, such that no further assignment is required to transfer title when the copyright comes into existence. The Act provides as follows:

> 'Where by an agreement made in relation to future copyright,[47] and signed by or on behalf of the prospective owner of the copyright,[48] the prospective owner purports to assign the future copyright (wholly or partially) to another person, then if, on the copyright coming into existence, the assignee or another person claiming under him would be entitled as against all other persons to require the copyright to be vested in him, the copyright shall vest in the assignee or his successor in title by virtue of this subsection.'[49]

Licences

(a) There is no general requirement that licences must be in writing,[50] although for an exclusive licensee to obtain the benefit of certain statutory rights the licence has to be in writing. In practice, most licences are in writing.

(b) Licences generally continue when copyright in the licensed work is transferred (ie assigned); the only exception to this is that a licence is not binding upon:

> '... a purchaser in good faith [of the copyright owner's interest in the copyright] for valuable consideration and without notice (actual or constructive) of the licence, or a person deriving title from such a purchaser.'[51]

---

45 Section 90(2) of the Act.
46 Future copyright is copyright which will or may come into existence in respect of a future work or class of works or on the occurrence of a future event: s 91(2) of the Act.
47 As defined in s 91(2) of the Act.
48 See n 47.
49 Section 90(2) of the Act.
50 Ie a licence can be implied, or arise from a course of conduct: see *R Griggs Group Ltd v Evans* [2005] EWHC 1487 (Ch), [2006] FSR 21, [2005] All ER (D) 172 (July) for a recent case where this point was considered.
51 Section 90(4) of the Act.

As there is no official register of copyright in the UK, a licensee under copyright is not able to register his or her licence and thereby give notice to the world of his or her interest (unlike the position in relation to patents). There is therefore an increased risk of a licensee losing his or her rights under a copyright licence if the copyright is sold to a purchaser who comes within the category described above.[52]

(c) Similarly, a licence granted by a *prospective* owner of copyright is binding on persons to whom he or she transfers his or her interest in the copyright, except for a purchaser in good faith.[53]

An exclusive licensee has the same rights against a successor in title to the copyright who is bound by the licence, as he or she does against the person who originally granted the licence to him or her.[54] The question of whether a successor in title is bound by the licence is dealt with in paragraphs (b) and (c) above. The special rights of an exclusive licensee are referred to below. An *exclusive licence* is defined as follows:

> 'In this Part [ie Part I of the Act, which sets out the new law on copyright] an 'exclusive licence' means a licence in writing signed by or on behalf of the copyright owner authorising the licensee to the exclusion of all other persons, including the person granting the licence, to exercise a right which would otherwise be exercisable exclusively by copyright owner.'[55]

OTHER FUNDAMENTAL ASPECTS OF UK COPYRIGHT LAW WHICH MAY AFFECT THE PARTIES TO COMMERCIAL TRANSACTIONS, INCLUDING 'MORAL RIGHTS' PROVISIONS

Types of work protected by copyright

Copyright subsists in various kinds of original work:[56]

---

52 There is no failsafe way of dealing with this situation, except for carrying out adequate due diligence prior to entering a deal (which assumes the provider of the information will tell the complete truth, or if willing to tell the complete truth, or has adequate records, which is not always the case). Other methods to deal with this situation are: to include warranties in an agreement (so that if a licence is discovered after the deal is signed, then the party in breach can be sued); or making the party in breach deposit a sum of money (for a limited period of time) against such an eventuality.
53 Section 91(3) of the Act.
54 See n 53.
55 Section 92(1) of the Act.
56 Section 1(1) of the Act.

- original literary works (defined[57] as meaning any work other than a dramatic or musical work, which is written, spoken or sung, and including a table or compilation[58] (other than a database[59]), a computer program, the preparatory design material for a computer program, a database);

- original dramatic, musical or artistic works;

- sound recordings, films or broadcasts;[60] and

- the typographical arrangement of published editions.[61]

This section of the book focuses mainly on the provisions of copyright law which apply to literary and artistic copyright. In practice, literary and artistic copyright are more often relevant to transactions involving technology transfer and research and development than other types of copyright.[62].

Copyright will not subsist in a literary, dramatic or musical work unless and until it is recorded, in writing or otherwise.[63]

A literary or artistic work must be original[64] if it is to be protected by copyright. This does not mean that any ideas contained in the work must be original. Rather, the work itself must not have been copied from any other work and must pass a relatively low threshold of creativity, in the

---

57 Section 3(1) of the Act.
58 For example, a complex software program which comprises many individual programs which are linked together can be protected by a separate copyright as a compilation: *Ibcos Computers Ltd v Barclays Mercantile Highland Finance Ltd* [1994] FSR 275.
59 Although a database is considered a literary work, it has its own definition: a database is a collection of independent works, data or other materials which: (a) are arranged in a systematic or methodical way, and (b) are individually accessible by electronic or other means: s 3A(1) of the Act, as inserted by SI 1997/3032. Therefore it is possible that each of the independent works have their own copyright protection, while the database is a separate, distinct, copyright.
60 Section 1(1)(b) of the Act, as amended by SI 2003/2498 from 31 October 2003.
61 Section 1(1)(c) of the Act.
62 Although with the increasing importance of software in itself being the focus of research and further development work, as well as the increasing importance of graphical, sound and video aspects of software, it is more likely that the types of copyright likely to come under consideration will include sound recordings, film and possibly broadcasting copyright.
63 Section 3(2) of the Act. '"Writing" means "any form of notation or code, whether by hand or otherwise and regardless of the method by which, or medium in or on which, it is recorded"; and "written" is to be construed accordingly' (s 178 of the Act).
64 This is considered further under 'Protecting the ideas or concepts contained in computer' particularly in relation to computer programs.

sense that the author(s) must have expended a degree of skill and labour in creating the work, regardless of the level of quality or style.[65]

There is a slightly different, and higher, test for originality concerning copyright in databases (not the database right). A database is original if the selection or arrangement of its contents constitute the author's own intellectual creation.[66]

In order to qualify for UK copyright protection, there must be a defined connection between the work and the UK or another country with which the UK has a reciprocal agreement. In summary, either:

• the author of the work must be a citizen of, or domiciled or resident in, such a country when the work was created; or

• the work must be first published in such a country.[67]

Authorship of copyright

The Act makes a distinction between authorship and ownership of copyright. The author is defined as the person who creates the work.[68]

The Act recognises that some works have more than one author, and includes provisions which deal with the rights of joint authors,[69] although not all the

---

65 *University of London Press Ltd v University Tutorial Press* [1916] 2 Ch 601 at 608. This point has been subject to extensive case law. Many types of works have been held to be literary works, however 'mundane' they appear or lacking in creativity. The following have all been considered literary works by the courts: business letters (*Tett Bros Ltd v Drake & Gorham Ltd* [1928-35] Mac CC 492); a booklet of instructions for use of a toy (*Meccano Ltd v Anthony Horden & Sons* [1918] SR (NSW) 696); rules of a trade association (*Co-operative Union Ltd v Kilmore, etc Ltd* (1912) 47 ILT 7); formulas which use symbols and numbers (*Bookmakers' Afternoon Greyhound Services Ltd v Wilf Gilbert (Staffordshire) Ltd* [1994] FSR 723) but not the results produced by using the formulas. A single word is generally not capable of protection (*Exxon Corpn v Exxon Insurance Consultants International Ltd* [1982] Ch 119, [1981] 3 All ER 241, CA), nor a collection of words where there was no skill in assembling them (unless they qualify as a compilation). However a single word could be capable of protection as a trade mark.
66 Section 3A(2) of the Act, as inserted by the Copyright and Rights in Databases Regulations 1997 (SI 1997/3032). The individual items can be subject of copyright (and possibly owned by others), which would not affect whether a person who creates a database would own his or her own copyright for the database.
67 Sections 153–156 of the Act.
68 Section 9 of the Act.
69 Section 10 of the Act, as amended by the Copyright and Related Rights Regulations 1996 (SI 1996/2967).

authors need to have collaborated to the same extent[70] or in the same way[71] to the creation of a work.[72] A work of joint authorship means:

> '... a work produced by the collaboration of two or more authors in which the contribution of each author is not distinct from that of the other author or authors'.[73]

Some works are sometimes referred to as works of joint authorship, when in fact the work is a collection of separate works, with each work created by a separate author.[74] A recent case has summarised recent case law as to the meaning of what amounts to joint authorship:[75]

- for a person to be joint author of a work his or her contribution to the creation of the work has to be significant and original, although it does not have to be of equal magnitude to the contribution of the other joint author.[76] A slight contribution is unlikely ever to be sufficient as the effect of a person being a joint author is that the person has an equal share in the copyright.[77]

- the contribution which is made must be a contribution to the creation of the work. A significant contribution of a different kind will not make the person a joint author. For example:

  — extensive and technically sophisticated testing by one person of software written by another would not make the first person a joint author of the software;[78] or

  — the performance of a musical work, however skilful or inventive, would not be contributing to the creation of the musical work.[79]

The 'right kind of skill and labour' would have to be used, which in these two examples would not be the case.

---

70 *Levy v Rutley* (1871) LR 6 CP.
71 *Godfrey v Lees* [1995] EMLR 307.
72 It will be a matter of fact and degree whether a person's contribution was large enough to allow him or her to be a joint author: *Stuart v Barrett* [1994] EMLR 448; *Fylde Microsystems v Key Radio Systems* [1998] FSR 449. The contribution needs to be significant and original: *Godfrey v Lees* [1995] EMLR 307. In *Hadley v Kemp* [1999] the contribution required was divided into four parts: 1. the claimant must make a contribution of some sort; 2. it must have been significant; 3. it must have been original; and 4. it must have been a contribution to the creation of the work.
73 Section 10(1) of the Act.
74 Each author making a distinct contribution, or in which works or parts of works of different authors are incorporated into one larger work. See second part of section 178, Copyright, Designs and Patents Act 1988.
75 Brighton and another *v* Jones [2004] EWHC 1157 (Ch); [2004] All ER (D) 247 (May).
76 Held in *Godfrey v Lees* [1995] EMLR 307 at p 325.
77 Held in *Hadley v Kemp* [1999] EMLR 589.
78 Eg in *Fylde Microsystems v Key Radio Systems* [1998] FSR 449.
79 Eg in *Hadley v Kemp* [1999] EMLR 589.

A person can be a joint author even if he or she does not actually write or create the work itself. For example a second person writing what the first person has created. However, there has to be a very close relationship between the creation and its expression, such as the person who is claiming to be a joint author having to instruct the person writing. The first person has to have a direct responsibility for what appears on paper. However, this situation, where a person who will be considered a joint author but has not been involved in the actual creation of the copyright work, is likely to arise only in exceptional situations.[80]

In the case of a computer-generated work where there is no human author, the author is taken to be 'the person by whom the arrangements necessary for the creation of the work are undertaken'.[81] 'Computer-generated' means more than, for example, simply printing out a document which is stored in a computer. For example, where a computer is programmed to interpret data from weather satellites and generate maps of weather patterns using such data without direct human intervention, the maps are computer-generated works.

Ownership

Works produced on or after 1 August 1989

The first owner of the copyright in a work is generally the author,[82] except for:

- **Employee works**: where a literary, dramatic, musical or artistic work is made by an employee in the course of his or her employment,[83] his or her employer is the first owner of any copyright in the work subject to any agreement to the contrary;[84]

- **Crown copyright etc**: special rules apply to Crown copyright, Parliamentary copyright and copyright in works produced by some international organisations.[85]

If the work was produced in the course of employment, the employer owns it unless there is an agreement to the contrary. Unlike the position for design right, a party who commissions the creation of a copyright work is not entitled to own it unless the contract so provides.

---

80 Based on the judgments in *Cala Homes (South) Ltd v Alfred McAlpine Homes East Ltd* [1995] FSR 818, and *Robin Ray v Classic FM plc* [1998] FSR 622.
81 Section 9(3) of the Act.
82 Section 11(1) of the Act.
83 The 'standard' test for whether a person is an employee, ie whether there is a 'contract of service', in *Ready Mixed Concrete (South East) Ltd v Minister of Pensions and National Insurance* [1968] 2 QB 497, will usually apply: see *Ultraframe (UK) Ltd v Fielding* [2003] EWCA Civ 1805, [2004] RPC 24.
84 Section 11(2) of the Act, as amended by SI 1996/2967.
85 Sections 11(3), 163 and 165 of the Act.

It is sometimes argued, in relation to contracts where one person commissions another to create a copyright work, that there is an implied term that the commissioner will own the copyright. The trend of case law in this area is usually against such a proposition;[86] for example:

- in one case[87] which concerned commissioned computer software, it was held that the commissioner did not have equitable title to the copyright in the software by virtue of any implied term;

- another case confirmed this view,[88] which indicates that if the issue of ownership of copyright has not been expressly dealt with, a term will be implied only to the extent necessary to close the gap left by the express terms of the contract.

That is, a licence will usually be sufficient, rather than an assignment of the copyright, and the licence will be limited to only the necessary uses of the commissioner of the software.

- in a further case, also concerning software, all that was necessary to be implied, based on the facts of the case, was a non-exclusive, perpetual, irrevocable royalty-free licence (but with no right to sub-licence but with the right to repair the software code). Based on the facts to give 'business efficacy' to the contract and to protect the commissioner's operating procedures from being used by the software developer, all that was necessary to be implied was a non-exclusive licence.[89]

- In another recent case[90] where a software developer was commissioned to write code in return for a royalty, an exclusive licence was implied into the contract, as an outright assignment to the commissioner would leave the software developer with no rights,[91] whereas an exclusive licence could be terminated on an accepted repudiation.

---

86 For a case which found that the commissioner of a work had a right to own the copyright (and not a licence), see *R Griggs Group Limited and others v Evans and others* [2005] EWCA Civ 11, [2005] All ER (D) 213 (Jan).

87 *Saphena Computing Ltd v Allied Collection Agencies Ltd* [1995] FSR 616, CA.

88 *Robin Ray v Classic FM plc* [1998] FSR 622.

89 *Clearsprings Management Ltd v BusinessLinx Ltd* [2005] EWHC 1487 (Ch), [2005] All ER (D) 172 (Jul).

90 *Wrenn v Landamore* [2007] EWHC 1833 (Ch), [2007] All ER (D) 361 (Jul), and upheld on this point on appeal: [2008] EWCA Civ 496.

91 Ie if there is a further assignment. The judgment referred to *Barker v Stickney* [1919] 1 KB 121 in support of this proposition.

Works produced before 1 August 1989

Given the very long duration of copyright protection, it is sometimes necessary to consider the provisions of earlier legislation in respect of older works.[92] In respect of works in existence before 1 August 1989, the question of who was the first owner of copyright in the work is determined in accordance with the law in force at the time the work was made.[93] In most cases, the position is the same as under the Act, but it may be necessary to check the earlier legislation.

Duration of copyright

Copyright in a literary, dramatic, musical or artistic work[94] generally expires 70 years after the end of the year in which the author dies.[95] The main exceptions and qualifications to this general position which are likely to be relevant to technology transfer are:[96]

- if the work is of unknown authorship, copyright expires 70 years after the end of the year in which the work was first made available to the public;

- if the work is computer generated, copyright expires 50 years after the end of the year in which the work was made. However, the copyright in computer programs which have a known human author continues for the life of the author plus 70 years, as above;

- if there was more than one author of the work, copyright expires 70 years after the end of the year of death of the last of them to die.

The above provisions do not apply to Crown copyright, Parliamentary copyright or the copyright of certain international organisations. Copyright protection in respect of articles produced to designs is in some cases abolished altogether and in other cases reduced to a maximum period of 25, 15 or 10 years.[97]

---

92 For example, a research programme that was carried out in the 1970s which led to an invention later subject to patent protection. By now the patent protection may have expired but any reports or other documentation would still be subject to copyright protection, and if created before 1 August 1989 would still be subject to the previous version of the Act.

93 Schedule 1 to the Act.

94 There are separate rules for sound recordings, films, broadcasts, cable programmes and the typographical arrangement of published editions. In the last of these cases, the copyright lasts for a period of 25 years. For the database right (rather than copyright in databases) the protection afforded by the right lasts for 15 years.

95 Section 12(1) of the Act. The Duration of Copyright and Rights in Performances Regulations 1995 (SI 1995/3297) extended the period from 50 years after the end of the year in which the author dies.

96 Section 12(2)–(4) of the Act.

97 Sections 51–53 of the Act.

Infringement

Restricted acts

The Act gives the owner of copyright in a work the exclusive right to do certain 'acts restricted by the copyright'.[98]

Infringement of copyright takes place when a person does any of these acts, or authorises another to do them, without the licence of the copyright owner.[99] The restricted acts are:

- to copy the work;[100]

- to issue copies of the work to the public.[101] this would include, for example, where a copyright owner grants a manufacturing licence to a company, terminable on liquidation and the company goes into liquidation with unsold stocks. Although manufactured under licence, sale of such stocks would be an infringement of the right to issue copies to the public.

- to rent or lend the work to the public;

- in the case of literary, dramatic or musical works, to perform, show or play the work in public;

- to communicate the work to the public;[102]

- to make an adaptation (including a translation[103]) of the work or do any of the above in relation to an adaptation.

---

98 Section 16, and ss 17–27 of the Act. These sections have been amended at various points by the Copyright (Computer Programs) Regulations 1992 (SI 1992/3233), the Copyright and Related Rights Regulations 1996 (SI 1996/2967), the Copyright and Rights in Database Regulations 1997 (SI 1997/3032) and the Copyright and Related Rights Regulations 2003 (SI 2003/2498) in force from 31 October 2003.

99 Section 16(2) of the Act.

100 In relation to a literary, dramatic, musical or artistic work, copying means reproducing the work in any material form, including storing the work in any medium by electronic means: s 17(2) of the Act. Such copying can include making permanent copies or copies which are transient or are incidental to some other use of the work: s 17(6) of the Act.

101 Section 18, Copyright, Designs and Patents Act 1988. The section was amended in relation to computer programs only by the Copyright (Computer Programs) Regulations 1992, SI 1992/3233 to accommodate EC 'exhaustion of right' principles as required by the EC Software Directive

102 Section 20 of the Act. 'Communication to the public' means 'communication to the public by electronic transmission, and in relation to a [copyright] work includes: (a) the broadcasting of the work; (b) inclusion of the work in an on-demand service or other interactive service' (from s 20(2) of the Act); 'on-demand service' means an 'interactive service for making a work available to the public by electronic transmission in such a way that members of the public may access the work from a place and at a time individually chosen by them' (s 20(3) of the Act.

103 Section 21(3) of the Act.

Infringement takes place when any of the restricted acts are done in relation to the whole of the work, or any substantial part of it, directly or indirectly.[104] What is substantial will very much depend on what has been copied. Generally, whether the copying of a part of a work will amount to a substantial part will depend much more on the quality of what is taken than the quantity that has been taken.[105] Further case law on this point has also emphasised whether a substantial part of the independent skill and labour of the author of the original copyright work has been used or incorporated by the person who made the infringing copy.[106]

Secondary infringement

Certain acts amount to secondary infringement of copyright in a work. These include:

- importing an infringing copy into the UK, knowing or having reason to believe it is an infringing copy.[107] In the case of computer programs, the definition of infringing copy was amended[108] to exclude copies which had previously been sold in another member state of the European Union with the consent of the copyright owner;

- possessing in the course of business or dealing with (selling, hiring etc) an infringing copy, knowing or having reason to believe it is an infringing copy;[109]

- manufacturing, importing, possessing in the course of business or dealing with an article specifically designed or adapted for making copies of the work, knowing or having reason to believe they are infringing copies;[110]

- transmitting the work by means of a telecommunications system (other than by communication to the public), knowing or having reason to believe that infringing copies will be made by the recipient of the transmission.[111]

For secondary infringement, the copyright owner needs to show that the infringer had knowledge or reason to believe that he or she was dealing in an

---

104 Section 16(3) of the Act.
105 See *Ladbroke (Football) Ltd v William Hill (Football) Ltd* [1964] 1 WLR 273, [1964] 1 All ER 465.
106 *Designers Guild v Russell Williams* [2001] FSR 113, [2000] All ER (D) 1950, HL, approving the lower courts' definition of the problem.
107 Section 22 of the Act.
108 By the Copyright (Computer Programs) Regulations 1992 (SI 1992/3233).
109 Section 23 of the Act.
110 Section 24 of the Act.
111 Section 24(2) of the Act, as amended by the Copyright and Related Rights Regulations 2003 (SI 2003/2498) in force from 31 October 2003. For the meaning of 'communicating to the public' see n 102.

infring copy. In one case,[112] the Court of Appeal held that an objective test was to be used as to the existence of knowledge.

Computers and computer programs

The Act explains what is meant by some restricted acts in relation to computer programs. The meaning of a 'computer program' is not defined in the Act or in the Information Society Directive.[113] One definition is:

> 'A set of instructions which, when incorporated in a machine-readable medium, is capable of causing a machine having information-processing abilities to indicate, perform, or achieve a particular function.'[114]

Of particular interest in this context are the following provisions:

- The Act confirms that the term 'literary work' means a work (other than a dramatic or musical work) which is written, spoken or sung, and accordingly, includes a computer program and preparatory design material for a computer program.[115] Although the term 'computer program' is not defined, the term 'writing' includes 'any form of notation or code, whether by hand or otherwise and regardless of the method by which, or the medium in or on which, it is recorded'.[116] Direct keying of a work into a computer would therefore seem to be 'writing' for the purposes of the Act.

- The restricted act of copying includes 'storing the work in any medium by electronic means'.[117] This would include storing a computer program or document on a hard or floppy disk or USB key, and probably includes loading a copy of the program from such a disk into the computer, resulting in temporary storage of the program in the computer's central memory in the course of running the program. Copying also includes

---

112 *LA Gear Inc v Hi-Tech Sports plc* [1992] FSR 121, CA.
113 Council Directive 91/250/EEC ([1991] OJ L122/ 42) on the legal protection of computer programs.
114 WIPO Model Provisions on the Protection of Computer Programs, s 1.
115 Section 3(1)(b) and (c) of the Act, as inserted by the Copyright (Computer Programs) Regulations 1992 (SI 1992/3233).
116 Section 178 of the Act.. As stated above, a 'computer program' is not defined in the Act, but Council Directive 91/250/EEC ([1991] OJ L122/ 42) on the legal protection of computer programs (as implemented by Copyright (Computer Programs) Regulations 1992 (SI 1992/3233)) does provide some further guidance as indicating that protection is afforded a computer program which is expressed in any form. Article 1(2) also goes on to indicate that 'ideas and principles which underlie any element of a computer program, including those which underlie its interfaces' are not to be protected by copyright.
117 Section 17(2) of the Act.

'the making of copies which are transient or are incidental to some other use of the work.[118]

● In the case of computer programs, the restricted act of issuing copies to the public includes rental of copies of the program to the public, subject to the right of the Secretary of State to order that licences will be available as of right.[119]

● The restricted act of adaptation of a work includes making any arrangement or altered version of the program or a translation of it.[120] In the case of computer programs, a translation includes 'a version of the program in which it is converted into or out of a computer language or code or into a different computer language or code'.[121] Such translation is likely to occur when the program is run.

● Certain acts are, for computer programs only, specifically permitted:[122]

(i) a lawful user can decompile a program in order to allow another program to operate with it;

(ii) a lawful user can observe, study or test the functioning of a computer program in order to determine the ideas and principles which underlie any element of the computer program;

(iii) a lawful user can copy or adapt a computer program to correct errors in it.

As for copyright generally, in order for copyright infringement to occur, what is copied must be substantial. It has been held that copyright protects the skill and labour of the author used in creation of the work and what is substantial will need to be considered against what was copied.[123] A starting point will be examining the entirety of what has been copied and then assessing whether what has been copied is a substantial part, and regard can be taken of the program structure as well as design features.[124] However, ideas, principles or functions (rather than their implementation) are not protected.[125]

---

118 Section 17(6) of the Act.
119 Sections 18A(2), and 66, the Copyright, Designs and Patents Act 1988, as amended by SI 1996/2967
120 Section 21(3) of the Act.
121 Section 21(4) of the Act.
122 These three points are considered further below under 'Computer programs'.
123 *Cantor Fitzgerald International and another v Tradition (UK) Ltd and others* [2000] RPC 95, [1999] All ER (D) 389.
124 See eg *John Richardson Computers v Flanders* [1993] FSR 49; *Ibcos Computers Ltd v Barclays Mercantile Highland Finance Ltd* [1994] FSR 275; and *Cantor Fitzgerald International and another v Tradition (UK) Ltd and others* [2000] RPC 95, [1999] All ER (D) 389.
125 This point is considered further below under 'Computer Software'.

The source code used for a computer program will be protected[126] as well as, most probably, the object code. A large number of programs collected together as a suite, or where it is necessary for all of them to be present in order to create a functioning unit, may qualify as a compilation.[127]

Consequently, loading a program from a disk into the memory of a computer, saving the program to disk[128] or running the program without the permission of the owner are all likely to infringe copyright, and all of these acts generally require a licence from the copyright owner.

Permitted acts

The Act permits persons[129] to carry out acts in certain circumstances which would otherwise infringe copyright. The permitted acts are to be considered separately from each other, so that if an act cannot enjoy the protection provided by one of the permitted acts it may nevertheless benefit from the protection provided by another.[130] The permitted acts only relate to acts which would otherwise infringe copyright. Such acts may breach some other obligation or right which restricts such acts, such as a contract between the copyright owner and a licensee, which might have a provision not permitting the licensee to copy the work concerned for the purposes of research.

Research or private study

Literary works generally

'Fair dealing' of a literary work or a dramatic, musical or artistic work for the purposes of research for a non-commercial purpose and with sufficient acknowledgement being given [131] does not generally infringe copyright.

---

126 *John Richardson Computers v Flanders* [1993] FSR 49; *Ibcos Computers Ltd v Barclays Mercantile Highland Finance Ltd* [1994] FSR 275.
127 *Ibcos Computers Ltd v Barclays Mercantile Highland Finance Ltd* [1994] FSR 275.
128 *Occular Sciences Ltd v Aspect Vision Care Ltd, Geoffrey Harrison Galley v Ocular Sciences Ltd* [1997] RPC 289 at 418.
129 Other than the copyright owner or a person permitted by him or her.
130 Section 28(4) of the Act.
131 Section 29(1) of the Act, as amended by SI 1997/3032 and the Copyright and Related Rights Regulations 2003 (SI 2003/2498) in force from 31 October 2003. An acknowledgement is not required if it is not possible practically to do so (s 29(1B) of the Act.)
      The wording before 1 October 2003 did not have the restriction that the research had to be for a non-commercial purpose. This represents a significant reduction in what can be done under the heading of 'research'. Before the change, a commercial research and development company might be able to ask one of its researchers to use the copyright material of another for a commercial research project (subject to the use being 'fair dealing') in the preparation of a report for a commercial purpose; but from 31 October 2003 such use would no longer be permitted (unless a licence was obtained).

In addition 'fair dealing' of a literary, dramatic, musical or artistic work for the purposes of private study does not infringe any copyright in the work.[132]

The distinction between 'research' and 'private study' is not spelt out in the Act, and the distinction is hard to understand as both have to be for a non-commercial purpose.

Computer programs

In regard to computer programs, it is not fair dealing:

- in relation to a computer program to convert it from a low-level language to a higher level language or, incidentally in the course of so doing, to copy the program;[133] or

- in order to determine the ideas and principles which underlie any element of a computer, to observe, study or test the functioning of a computer program.[134]

Other points

The fair dealing exception is generally understood to allow copying of a limited extract from a publication. As noted above copying for research can no longer be for a commercial purpose. The position until October 2003 was, at least by implication, that the fair dealing provision probably allowed limited copying for the purposes of commercial research in commercial organisations.

The making of multiple copies is generally not fair dealing, particularly if the person making the copy is not the researcher or student.[135]

It should also be noted that this permitted act does not extend to all forms of works which can be the subject of copyright, such as sound recordings, films, broadcasts and cable programs. These media, together with the restrictions on the use of computer programs for research and private study, may increasingly

---

132 Section 29(1C) of the Act, as inserted by the Copyright and Related Rights Regulations 2003 (SI 2003/2498) in force from 31 October 2003. Unlike the case of research, an acknowledgement is not required, however, as in the case of research it cannot be done for any commercial purpose, whether directly or indirectly (s 178 of the Act, as inserted by the Copyright and Related Rights Regulations 2003 (SI 2003/2498) in force from 31 October 2003.

133 Section 29(4) of the Act, inserted by Copyright (Computer Programs) Regulations 1992 (SI 1992/3233). These acts can be done if done for the purpose of 'decompilation' in accordance with s 50B of the Act.

134 Section 29(4B) of the Act, as inserted by the Copyright and Related Rights Regulations 2003 (SI 2003/2498) in force from 31 October 2003. These acts can be done if done in accordance with s 50BA of the Act.

135 Section 29(3) of the Act.

mean that this permitted act will be of less relevance and application as more works become available only in electronic format.[136]

Criticism, review

Fair dealing with a work[137] for the purposes of criticism or review, or for the purpose of reporting current events, provided that it is accompanied by a sufficient acknowledgement and that the work has been made available to the public, does not infringe copyright.[138] The requirement that the work be made available to the public includes that the copies have been issued to the public, that they are available by means of an electronic retrieval system, or that copies have been rented by or lent to the public.[139]

In limited cases, this exception may be relevant to research and development, for example where a scientific paper quotes from another scientific paper for the purposes of criticism or review.

Meaning of 'fair'

'Fair dealing' does not have a statutory definition in the Act.[140] However, in one case it was held[141] that there are three factors to be considered in whether a particular use is fair:

---

136 But see the suggestions of the Gowers review, and the latest proposals from the UK Intellectual Property Office that the fair dealing provisions would extend to such material (see 'Gowers Review and other proposals' above.

137 The work which is being criticised or reviewed must be a work in which copyright subsists: *Fraser-Woodward Ltd v British Broadcasting Corpn* [2005] EWHC 472 (Ch), [2005] FSR 762.

138 Section 30(1) of the Act, as amended by the Copyright and Related Rights Regulations 2003 (SI 2003/2498) in force from 31 October 2003. Prior to the amendment it was possible to engage in criticism of a copyright work even if it had not been issued to the public.

139 Section 30(1A) of the Act, as inserted by the Copyright and Related Rights Regulations 2003 (SI 2003/2498) in force from 31 October 2003.

140 This can be contrasted with the approach taken in US law: Copyright Act 1976, s 107 where the meaning of fair dealing is spelt out:

'...the fair use of a copyrighted work, including such use by reproduction in copies or phonorecords or by any other means specified by that section, for purposes such as criticism, comment, news reporting, teaching (including multiple copies for classroom use), scholarship, or research, is not an infringement of copyright. In determining whether the use made of a work in any particular case is a fair use the factors to be considered shall include—

(1) the purpose and character of the use, including whether such use is of a commercial nature or is for nonprofit educational purposes;
(2) the nature of the copyrighted work;
(3) the amount and substantiality of the portion used in relation to the copyrighted work as a whole; and
(4) the effect of the use upon the potential market for or value of the copyrighted work.

The fact that a work is unpublished shall not itself bar a finding of fair use if such finding is made upon consideration of all the above factors'.

141 *Hubbard v Vosper* [1972] 2 QB 84 at 92–95.

- the number and extent of the quotations and the extracts should be considered;

- the use that has been made of the quotations and the extracts should be considered (if used for a rival purpose then they may be unfair);

- the proportion of the work consisting of quotations and extracts should be compared to the proportion of the work consisting of comment and analysis (not relevant for private study and research).

An objective standard to be used in determining whether the copying of a copyright work is fair[142]

Temporary copies

The copyright in a literary work[143] will not be infringed where a temporary copy is made. This will only apply where the temporary copy:

- is incidental and transient;

- is an integral and essential part of a technological process;

- has a sole purpose that is:

    — to enable a transmission in a network between third parties by an intermediary; or

    — a lawful use of the work;

- has no independent economic significance.[144]

This exception from infringement does not apply to computer programs or databases.

This exception will apply where, for example, a person accesses a web page and some elements of that page are stored (cached) temporarily on the person's computer.

Abstracts

The copying of an abstract (or issuing copies of it to the public) from articles on scientific or technical subjects is permitted. The exception does not apply if, or to the extent that, there is a certified licensing scheme in place.[145]

---

142 See *Hyde Park Residence v Yelland* [2001] Ch 257: '... Thus the court must judge the fairness by the objective standard of whether a fair minded person would have dealt with the copyright work in the manner that [defendant] did...' (from para 38).

143 Including dramatic, artistic, musical works or typographical arrangements of published works, plus sound recordings and films.

144 Section 28A of the Act.

145 Section 60 of the Act.

None of these factors by itself is conclusive of the question of fairness. In certain circumstances it may be fair to quote a whole work (especially if short).

Designs

Designs which are not artistic works

There are important exceptions in relation to designs, which strictly limit the copyright protection available. It is not an infringement of copyright in a design document, or in a model recording, or in embodying a design for anything other than an artistic work or a typeface, to make an article to the design or copy an article made to the design.[146] This exception should be read in conjunction with the provisions of the Act which create the new design right;[147] design right largely replaces copyright protection for non-artistic designs.

Designs which are derived from artistic works

This exception applies where an artistic work has been exploited, by or with the licence of the copyright owner, by making in an industrial process articles which are copies of the work, or by marketing such articles.[148]

Works in electronic form

There is an important exception in the case of a work in electronic form (for example a computer program on disk) which has been purchased on terms which allow the purchaser to copy or adapt the work in connection with his or her use of it.[149] Such terms may be express or implied, or arise by virtue of any rule of law.[150] The purchaser of a computer program generally comes within this category as he or she needs to copy the work in order to use it. Where such a purchaser transfers his or her purchased copy to another person, the transferee has the same rights to copy or adapt the work as the original purchaser had. However, any copies which the purchaser does not transfer are treated as infringing copies after the transfer. This is, in effect, a resale right.

This exception does not apply where there are express contractual terms which: (a) prohibit transfer; (b) impose obligations which continue after transfer; (c) prohibit the assignment of any licence; (d) terminate any licence

---

146   Sections 51–53 of the Act.
147   Sections 213–235 of the Act.
148   Section 52 of the Act. In such cases, copyright protection in respect of such articles expires 25 years after the end of the year in which the articles are first marketed.
149   Section 56 of the Act.
150   Eg the Copyright (Computer Programs) Regulations 1992 (SI 1992/3233).

on a transfer; or (e) provide for the terms on which a transferee may do the things which the purchaser was permitted to do.[151]

Computer programs

Lending

The Secretary of State may order that lending to the public of copies of literary, dramatic, musical or artistic works, sound recordings or films shall be treated as licensed by the copyright owner subject to payment of a reasonable royalty.[152]

Back-up copies

It is not an infringement of copyright for a lawful user (for example a licensee or purchaser directly or indirectly from the copyright owner)[153] of a copy of a computer program to make any back-up copy of it which is necessary for him or her to have for the purposes of his or her lawful use.[154] Any contract provision which conflicts with this right is void.[155]

Decompilation of computer programs

The lawful user[156] of a computer program has the right to decompile a computer program in order to obtain information which would enable him or her to write another program which would work with the first program (the

---

151 Section 56(2) of the Act.

152 As may be agreed or determined in default of agreement by the Copyright Tribunal: s 66 of the Act, as substituted by Copyright and Related Rights Regulations 1996 (SI 1996/2967). 'Literary work' includes a computer program: s 3 of the Act, as amended.

153 A lawful user of a computer program is one who has the right to use the program (whether under a licence to do any acts restricted by copyright in the program or otherwise): s 50A(2) of the Act, as inserted by the Copyright (Computer Programs) Regulations 1992 (SI 1992/3233).

154 Section 50A of the Act, as inserted by the Copyright (Computer Programs) Regulations 1992 (SI 1992/3233). The meaning of a 'back-up' is not further defined in the Act, or in the Directive on which this section (and others) are based. The European Commission, in its communication on the effect of the Software Directive 91/250 (COM/2000/0199 final), has indicated its opinion that the relevant Art 5(2) in that Directive contains wording relating to, and with the objective of, allowing only one copy being made, and that the purpose of the back-up is to ensure that the normal use of the program can continue in the event of loss or defect of the original. The making of unauthorised copies for private use would not be permitted, and amount to software privacy. See also *Kabushiki Kaisha Sony Computer Entertainment Inc and others v Ball and others* [2004] EWHC 1738 (Ch) at paras 29–30, where the judge considered whether a back-up was 'necessary' where a computer program is provided in a robust form such as a DVD or CD and where the supplier of the computer program is willing to provide a replacement DVD or CD.

155 Section 296A of the Act, as inserted by the Copyright (Computer Programs) Regulations 1992 (SI 1992/3233).

156 For the meaning of 'lawful user' see n 153.

right to achieve inter-operability). This right is subject to certain conditions, including that the user does not have ready access to the necessary information without decompiling the program. Any contract provision which conflicts with this right is void.[157]

In view of the complexity of this subject, it is useful to quote the section of the Act which defines the scope of the decompilation right:[158]

'(1) It is not an infringement of copyright for a lawful user of a copy of a computer program expressed in a low level language—

    (a) to convert it into a version expressed in a higher level language, or

    (b) incidentally in the course of so converting the program, to copy it, (that is, to 'decompile' it), provided that the conditions in subsection (2) are met.

(2) The conditions are that—

    (a) it is necessary to decompile the program to obtain the information necessary to create an independent program which can be operated with the program decompiled or with another program ('the permitted objective'); and

    (b) the information so obtained is not used for any purpose other than the permitted objective.

(3) In particular, the conditions in subsection (2) are not met if the lawful user—

    (a) has readily available to him the information necessary to achieve the permitted objective;

    (b) does not confine the decompiling to such acts as are necessary to achieve the permitted objective;

    (c) supplies the information obtained by the decompiling to any person to whom it is not necessary to supply it in order to achieve the permitted objective; or

    (d) uses the information to create a program which is substantially similar in its expression to the program decompiled or to do any act restricted by copyright.

(4) Where an act is permitted under this section, it is irrelevant whether or not there exists any term or condition in an agreement which purports to prohibit or restrict the act (such terms being, by virtue of section 296A, void).'

---

157 Section 296A of the Act, as inserted by the Copyright (Computer Programs) Regulations 1992 (SI 1992/3233).
158 Section 50B of the Act, as inserted by the Copyright (Computer Programs) Regulations 1992 (SI 1992/3233).

Observing, studying and testing of computer programs

A lawful user will not infringe copyright where he or she copies a computer program and his or her purpose for so doing is to 'observe, study or test the functioning' of the computer program.[159] The copying can only be done where the lawful user wishes to determine the ideas and principles which underlie any element of the computer program and then only while he or she is doing acts which he or she is permitted to do (such as loading, displaying, running, transmitting or storing the computer program).

Any contract provision which conflicts with this right is void.[160]

Databases

A lawful user of a database, whether by licence or otherwise, does not infringe the database's copyright by using the database (or any part of it) and doing anything, in exercise of a right, which is necessary for the purposes of access to and use of the contents of the database (or any part of it),[161] for example if a lawful user is forbidden to copy the database but needs to do so in order to use the database and access the contents. In addition, any act permitted by this provision cannot be excluded by any term or condition in a contract.[162]

Other exceptions

The Act sets out the circumstances in which acts done for the purposes of education[163] and public administration[164] do not infringe copyright. It also provides for copying by libraries and archives.[165] There is a further exception in the case of works of unknown authorship and where it is reasonable to assume that the copyright has expired.[166]

---

159 Section 50(BA) of the Act, as inserted by the Copyright and Related Rights Regulations 2003 (SI 2003/2498) in force from 31 October 2003. For the meaning of a 'lawful user' see n 153. This right does not permit the user to use the program for 'fair dealing' purposes (see 'Computer programs' above).

160 Section 50BA(2) of the Act, as inserted by the Copyright and Related Rights Regulations 2003 (SI 2003/2498) in force from 31 October 2003.

161 Section 50D of the Act, as inserted by the Copyright and Rights in Databases Regulations 1997 (SI 1997/3032).

162 Section 50D(2) of the Act, as inserted by the Copyright and Rights in Databases Regulations 1997 (SI 1997/3032).

163 Sections 32–36 of the Act, as amended. Following the introduction made by the Copyright and Related Rights Regulations 2003 (SI 2003/2498), in force from 31 October 2003, these and the following categories of exceptions to infringement of copyright have been restricted. If the copyright material is likely to be used for any of these uses the wording of the Act should be examined and advice taken.

164 Sections 45–50 of the Act.

165 Sections 37–44 of the Act.

166 Section 57 of the Act.

Moral rights

General

The Act introduced for the first time into UK law two new rights which have become known as the 'paternity right' (the right to be identified as the author of a copyright work) and the 'integrity right' (the right of the author not to have his or her work subjected to derogatory treatment).[167] These rights are independent of ownership of copyright and may exist even where copyright has been transferred to another person. The rights cannot be assigned or licensed (they are 'inalienable') but they may be waived. In addition, the Act continues to provide that a person has the right not to have a work falsely attributed to him, and provides for a right of privacy of certain privately commissioned photographs and films. Together these rights are described in the Act as moral rights, although some people use the term 'moral rights' to refer only to the paternity and integrity rights.

Moral rights are sometimes of less importance in the case of copyright works concerned with technology than they are in the case of other copyright works. There are two main reasons for this:

- employees have considerably fewer moral rights in works produced by them in the course of their employment, and technology is often developed by employees, whether in industry or at academic establishments; and

- the paternity and integrity rights do not apply to computer programs.

Nevertheless, moral rights remain relevant to many copyright works concerned with technology and should not be overlooked.

Paternity right

The author of a copyright literary, dramatic, musical or artistic work has the right (the paternity right) to be identified as the author, in certain circumstances.[168] The author of a literary or artistic work has the right to be identified whenever the work is published commercially, and whenever an adaptation of the work is published.[169] The paternity right is not infringed unless the right has been asserted (either generally or in relation to any specified act or description of acts) in one of the following ways:[170]

---

167 Sections 77–89 of the Act.
168 Section 77(1) of the Act. The right of a person is to be identified as the author of the work, not to be identified as, eg the source of the ideas which is contained in the literary work.
169 Section 77(2) of the Act.
170 Section 78 of the Act.

- on an assignment of copyright in the work, by including in the assignment a statement that the author asserts his or her right to be identified as the author of that work; or

- by instrument in writing signed by the author.

Once assertion is made by a person then the identification made in the copyright work must be sufficient to identify the person as the author[171] (ie not as something else in relation to the work).

The persons bound by an assertion of the paternity right are:[172]

- where the assertion is made in an assignment, the assignee and anyone claiming copyright through the assignee;

- where the assignment is made by instrument in writing, anyone to whose notice the assertion is brought.

Paternity right does not apply to

- a computer program;

- the design of a typeface; or

- any computer-generated work.[173]

Where the work was produced in the course of the author's employment, such that copyright in the work originally vested in the author's employer, the paternity right does not apply to anything done by or with the authority of the copyright owner.[174] Thus, the right is not abolished entirely for employees, and applies in the case of acts done without the authority of the copyright owner.

In some limited cases,[175] the paternity right is not infringed by an act which would not infringe copyright in the work; for example, the right is not infringed by an act which would be fair dealing for the purpose of reporting current events by means of a sound recording, film, broadcast or cable programme. The right does not apply to the publication, in some periodicals and collective works of reference, of works made for the purposes of such a publication or made available for such publication with the consent of the author.[176]

---

171 *Sawkins v Hyperion Records Ltd* [2005] EWCA Civ 565, [2005] 3 All ER 636.
172 Section 78 of the Act.
173 Section 79(2) of the Act.
174 Section 79(3) of the Act, as amended by the Copyright and Related Rights Regulations 2003 (SI 2003/2498) in force from 31 October 2003.
175 Section 79(4) of the Act.
176 Section 79(6) of the Act.

Integrity right

The author of a copyright literary, dramatic, musical or artistic work has the right (the integrity right) not to have his or her work subjected to derogatory treatment, in certain circumstances.[177] It is perhaps easier to understand the need for such a right in the arts than the sciences; for example a film director whose film is altered by the film studio before it is released to such an extent that the director wishes to disown it as his or her work. In the field of technology an example may be the scientific paper which is written under a commission from a company, and the company alters the conclusions of the paper before it is published without the permission of the author.

The main aspects of integrity right which are most likely to be relevant to works concerned with technology may be summarised as follows:

- Derogatory treatment is defined as treatment which amounts to distortion or mutilation of the work or is otherwise prejudicial to the honour or reputation of the author.[178] Treatment means any addition to, deletion from or alteration to or adaptation of the work, other than (in relation to literary works) a translation of the work.[179]

- The integrity right is infringed, inter alia, by the commercial publication of a derogatory treatment of the work.[180] It is not enough that the author must be aggrieved by any alterations to his or her work, there must be prejudice to the author's reputation.[181]

- The integrity right does not apply to:[182]

  — a computer program or computer-generated work;

  — any work made for the purpose of reporting current events;

  — publication in certain periodicals and collective works of reference, of a work made for the purposes of such publication, or made available with the consent of the author for such publication.

- Where the work was created by the author in the course of his or her employment, the right is not infringed by anything done by or with the authority of the copyright owner, unless the author is identified at the time of the infringing act, or has previously been identified in or on published copies of the work and there is not a sufficient disclaimer.[183] A sufficient disclaimer is a clear and reasonably prominent indication

---

177 Sections 77–79, 80–83 of the Act.
178 Section 80(2)(b) of the Act.
179 Section 80(2)(a) of the Act.
180 Section 80(3) and (4) of the Act.
181 *Pasterfield v Denham* [1999] FSR 168.
182 Section 81 of the Act.
183 Section 82(2) of the Act.

that the work has been subjected to treatment to which the author has not consented.[184]

● It is also an infringement of the integrity right to possess or deal with an infringing article.[185]

Provisions applicable to moral rights

The paternity right and the integrity right continue as long as the copyright exists in the work.[186] The rights are not infringed where the author has consented to the acts in question[187] and may be waived by an instrument in writing signed by the author.[188] A waiver may relate to a specific work, works of a specified description, works generally, or to existing or future works; it may be conditional or unconditional.[189] If made in favour of the owner or prospective owner of the copyright in the work or works to which it relates, it is presumed to extend to his or her licensees and successors in title unless a contrary intention is expressed.[190] Although the Act requires waivers to be in writing, the possibility of informal (ie non-written) waivers being binding under the general law of contract or estoppel is specifically not excluded.[191] In the case of works which have more than one author, the general position is that each joint author has his or her own rights, and assertion or waiver of the right by one of the joint authors does not affect the rights of the other joint authors.[192]

The integrity right applies in relation to the whole or any part of the work.[193] By contrast, the paternity right applies only to the whole or any substantial part of the work in question. Thus, the paternity right is not infringed by failure to acknowledge the author of an insubstantial part of that author's work.

Moral rights are not assignable.[194] They are intended to be a personal right for the author, rather than an economic right which can be traded (as in the case of copyright). On the death of the author the rights pass to whomever the author directs in his or her will; there are detailed provisions in the Act

---

184 Section 178 of the Act.
185 Section 83 of the Act.
186 Section 86 of the Act.
187 Section 87(1) of the Act.
188 Section 87(2) of the Act.
189 Section 87(3) of the Act.
190 Section 87(3) of the Act.
191 Section 87(4) of the Act.
192 Section 88 of the Act.
193 Section 89 of the Act.
194 Section 94 of the Act.

which address the position on death, including what happens if the author's will makes no mention of his or her moral rights, or if there is no will.[195]

Infringement of a person's moral rights is actionable as a breach of statutory duty.[196] In the case of a breach of the integrity right, a court may grant an injunction prohibiting the breach unless a disclaimer is made in terms approved by the court.[197]

Remedies for infringement

The main general remedies for infringement of copyright are:[198]

- an injunction (ie an order of the court prohibiting further infringement, breach of which would be a contempt of court);
- damages;
- as an alternative to damages, an account of profits. That is an award of the amount of profits the defendant received from his or her infringing acts;
- an order for delivery up to the claimant of infringing copies (or articles used to make infringing copies) in the possession of the defendant. It is also possible to apply to the court for destruction or forfeiture to the copyright owner of infringing goods in some circumstances;
- seizure and detention of infringing goods which are being offered for sale (eg by a street trader).[199]

These remedies fall outside the scope of this title. An exclusive licensee has, in general, the same remedies against infringers as the copyright owner.[200] Where a non-exclusive licensee has a written licence which is signed by or

---

195 Section 95 of the Act.
196 Section 103(1) of the Act.
197 Section 103((2) of the Act.
198 Sections 96–100 of the Act, as amended by Copyright (Computer Programs) Regulations 1992 (SI 1992/3233).
199 This remedy is in addition to the relief known as the search order whereby a court will sometimes grant an intellectual property owner what is in effect a civil search warrant, entitling his or her solicitors to search a defendant's premises without prior warning, for evidence of infringement.
200 Section 101 of the Act.

on behalf of the copyright owner, and the licence expressly grants a right of action, then the licensee may bring an action for infringement.[201]

Presumptions as to authorship and ownership

Where a person is named as the author on a copyright literary, dramatic, musical or artistic work, there is a statutory presumption that he or she is the author and first owner of copyright in the work, for the purposes, inter alia, of infringement proceedings, unless the contrary is proved.[202] In relation to computer programs, there is an additional presumption which applies, inter alia, in copyright infringement proceedings. Where copies of the program are issued to the public bearing a copyright statement (name of owner on issue date, or year of first publication in a specified country or issue of copies), the statement is admissible as evidence of the facts stated and is presumed to be correct until the contrary is proved.[203] It is therefore recommended that a copyright statement is included on the work including (in the case of a computer program) on the disk and appearing on the screen when the program is run.[204] Failure to do so does not prevent a copyright owner from bringing infringement proceedings, but it means that copyright ownership has to be proved rather than relying on the statutory presumption. The onus is then on the defendant to disprove ownership.

There are further presumptions which apply in the cases of unknown or dead authors, and in the case of other types of copyright work (for example sound recordings and Crown copyright).

Devices designed to circumvent copy-protection

Generally

Where a copyright work is published in electronic form the Act contains a number of provisions concerning it where it is 'copy-protected' (or protected by 'technological measures', to use current terminology). These provisions are designed to stop a person who markets a device which can be used to by-pass the copy-protection of a work (where the use of such devices makes it possible to make infringing copies of the work).

---

201 Section 101A of the Act, as inserted by the Copyright and Related Rights Regulations 2003 (SI 2003/2498) in force from 31 October 2003. The phrase 'non-exclusive licensee' means 'the holder of a licence authorising the licensee to exercise a right which remains exercisable by the copyright owner' (s 101A(6) of the Act, as inserted by the Copyright and Related Rights Regulations 2003 (SI 2003/2498) in force from 31 October 2003).
202 Section 104(2) of the Act.
203 Section 105(3) of the Act.
204 Such a statement also helps to counter an argument by a defendant to infringement proceedings that he or she was an innocent infringer.

The latest version of these provisions provides one set of them for computer programs and another set for works other than computer programs (such as a document published in an electronic format and which is protected from being opened or copied unless a password or similar is provided).

Computer programs

A copyright owner, an exclusive licensee and certain others ('Owner')[205] have rights to take action against a person ('Infringer') who carries out certain actions designed to remove or circumvent technical devices which are applied to computer programs.

The actions which an Infringer carries out and which incur liability are:

'(i)   manufactures for sale or hire, imports, distributes, sells or lets for hire, offers or exposes for sale or hire, advertises for sale or hire or has in his possession for commercial purposes any means the sole intended purpose of which is to facilitate the unauthorised removal or circumvention of the technical device; or

(ii)   publishes information intended to enable or assist persons to remove or circumvent the technical device.'[206]

The Infringer must know or have reason to believe that the technical device will be used to make infringing copies of the computer program to which the technical device has been attached.[207] The wording used in this part of the Act does not suggest that:

- the means or information need to actually have been used; or

- the technical device has to be contained within the computer program (ie it could be located on or in a computer itself).[208]

---

205   Section 296(2) of the Act, as substituted by the Copyright and Related Rights Regulations 2003 (SI 2003/2498) in force from 31 October 2003. These include a person who issues to the public copies of (or communicates to the public) the computer program to which a technical device has been attached, or the owner or exclusive licensee of any intellectual property right in a technical device applied to a computer program. Each of them have concurrent rights (s 296(3) of the Act, as substituted by the Copyright and Related Rights Regulations 2003 (SI 2003/2498) in force from 31 October 2003.

206   Section 296A of the Act, as inserted by the Copyright and Related Rights Regulations 2003 (SI 2003/2498) in force from 31 October 2003.

207   Section 296A(1) of the Act, as inserted by the Copyright and Related Rights Regulations 2003 (SI 2003/2498) in force from 31 October 2003.

208   See *Sony Computer Entertainment Inc v Ball* [2004] EWHC 1738 (Ch).

Copyright works other than computer programs[209]

If 'effective technological measures'[210] are applied to a copyright work an Infringer will face civil liability if he or she does anything which circumvents them knowing or having reasonable grounds to know that he or she is pursuing that object.

An Infringer will not face liability where he or she circumvents the effective technological measure when conducting research into cryptography. This exception will not apply if when carrying out the research he or she affects prejudicially the rights of the copyright owner (including if he or she issues information derived from the research and it creates such prejudice).

The rights of an Owner who is entitled to take action against such an Infringer are similar to those where a computer program is involved.[211]

The Owner who is entitled to take action can also take action where technological measures have been applied to a copyright work other than a computer and where an Infringer:

'... manufactures, imports, distributes, sells or lets for hire, offers or exposes for sale or hire, advertises for sale or hire, or has in his possession for commercial purposes any device, product or component, or provides services which—

(i)   are promoted, advertised or marketed for the purpose of the circumvention of, or

(ii)   have only a limited commercially significant purpose or use other than to circumvent, or

---

209   The provisions of the Act applying to the non-copyright works is lengthy and outside the scope of this book. Interested readers should consult the previous edition of this book.

210   'Technological measures' means 'any technology, device or component which is designed, in the normal course of its operation, to protect a copyright work other than a computer program' (s 296ZF(1) of the Act, as inserted by the Copyright and Related Rights Regulations 2003 (SI 2003/2498) in force from 31 October 2003). A measure is effective if 'the use of the work is controlled by the copyright owner through – (a)   an access control or protection process such as encryption, scrambling or other transformation of the work, or (b) a copy control mechanism, which achieves the intended protection' (s 296ZF(2) of the Act, as inserted by the Copyright and Related Rights Regulations 2003 (SI 2003/2498) in force from 31 October 2003).

211   Section 296ZA of the Act, as inserted by the Copyright and Related Rights Regulations 2003 (SI 2003/2498) in force from 31 October 2003. See 'Computer programs' and n 205 above.

(iii)   are primarily designed, produced, adapted or performed for the purpose of enabling or facilitating the circumvention of,

those measures'.[212]

The 'fair dealing' provisions, on the whole, equally apply to copyright works to which technological measures have been applied but those technological measures prevent a person from carrying out a permitted act[213] in relation to that work. A person who cannot exercise a permitted act will need to issue a complaint to the Secretary of State, who can, in appropriate circumstances, require the copyright owner (or his/her exclusive licensee, etc) to allow the person to access the copyright work which is the subject of the complaint.[214] This procedure does not apply to copyright works provided 'on-demand'.[215]

In addition to civil liability it is also possible for an Infringer circumventing a technological measure to face criminal sanctions including fines, imprisonment and forfeiture.[216]

Copyright licensing schemes and licensing bodies

The Act provides for the setting up of statutory licensing schemes and licensing bodies, and the resolution of disputes (generally by the Copyright Tribunal) in relation to such schemes and bodies.[217] A licensing body would typically enter into agreements with individual authors permitting it to offer licences on the author's behalf. The licensing body would have a portfolio of copyright works which it made available for licence, and would collect royalties on the author's behalf.

---

212   Section 296ZD(1) of the Act, as inserted by the Copyright and Related Rights Regulations 2003 (SI 2003/2498) in force from 31 October 2003. The procedure outlined appears time-consuming and is likely to involve lengthy delay for someone who has lawful access to a work subject to the technological measures. The Gowers Review suggested that it should be easier to make a complaint, via the UK Intellectual Property Office website (para 4.106, p 73).

213   These are listed in Sch 5A to the Act, as inserted by the Copyright and Related Rights Regulations 2003 (SI 2003/2498) in force from 31 October 2003, and include most of the acts which are listed above [eg 'Research and private study' above].

214   See s 296ZE of the Act, as inserted by the Copyright and Related Rights Regulations 2003 (SI 2003/2498) in force from 31 October 2003.

215   Section 296ZE(9) of the Act, as inserted by the Copyright and Related Rights Regulations 2003 (SI 2003/2498) in force from 31 October 2003: 'This section does not apply to copyright works made available to the public on agreed contractual terms in such a way that members of the public may access them from a place and at a time individually chosen by them.' This would mean that interactive use of the internet (such as accessing a TV programme at the time a consumer wished to access it) would not be covered by s 296ZE of the Act, but a user of a non-interactive service would be covered.

216   Sections 296ZB, 296ZC of the Act, as inserted by the Copyright and Related Rights Regulations 2003 (SI 2003/2498) in force from 31 October 2003.

217   Section 116 of the Act.

Competition Commission report[218]

The Act enables the relevant Government Minister to make certain orders where the Competition Commission has reported that either of the following matters are against the public interest:[219]

- conditions in licences granted by the owner of copyright in a work restricting the use of the work by the licensee or the right of the copyright owner to grant other licences; or

- a refusal of a copyright owner to grant licences on reasonable terms.

The Government Minister may cancel or modify those conditions and, instead or in addition, provide that licences in respect of the copyright shall be available as of right.

The last power may provide a disincentive to copyright owners who wish to include very onerous conditions in their licences. However, the power only arises in cases where the Competition Commission has issued a report in relation to the copyright owner's activities – a rare event in practice. These provisions bolster existing powers under the Competition Act 1998 in relation to anti-competitive behaviour; it remains to be seen whether these provisions have much effect on copyright licensing activities. The Act introduces similar powers in relation to other intellectual property rights.

Copyright tribunal

The Act establishes a constitution and jurisdiction for the Copyright Tribunal. The function of the Tribunal is to hear and determine proceedings in relation to statutory licensing schemes and licensing bodies, and the settling of licence terms in relation, inter alia, to licences of right, rental right and other matters.

Qualification for copyright protection

General

In order for a literary or artistic work to qualify for copyright protection, either the author must be a 'qualifying person' (ie having a defined connection with the UK or another specified country) or the work must be first published in the UK or in another qualifying country.[220] The rules on qualification for copyright protection are detailed and complex, particularly in respect of the

---

218 Competition law relating to intellectual property transactions is dealt with generally in Chs 12 and 15.
219 Section 144 of the Act, as amended by the Competition Act 1998 and the Enterprise Act 2002.
220 Section 153 of the Act.

protection given to works first published outside the UK or whose author was not a British citizen at the 'material time'.[221] The most common examples of qualifying persons and countries are discussed below.

Foreign, existing works can be brought into protection for the first time by a country joining the Berne Convention. Some works whose copyright has expired may be brought back into copyright protection for the remainder of the 'life of the author plus 70 years' copyright period previously mentioned.[222]

Qualification by reference to author

A work qualifies for copyright protection if the author was at the material time a qualifying person.[223] The most common examples of a qualifying person are:

- a British citizen;

- an individual domiciled or resident in the UK;

- a body incorporated under the law of a part of the UK.

There are special rules dealing with the position of works of joint authorship where not all of the authors are qualifying persons.[224]

Material time, in relation to literary, dramatic, musical and artistic works,[225] is:

- in the case of an unpublished work, when the work was made or, if the making of the work extended over a period, a substantial part of that period;

- in the case of a published work, when the work was first published or, if the author had died before that time, immediately before his or her death.

Qualification by reference to country of first publication

A literary, dramatic, musical or artistic work, and some other types of work, qualifies for copyright protection if it is first published in the UK, or

---

221 Sections 153–162 of the Act, as amended to determine any such entitlement to copyright protection, and the statutory instruments made pursuant to the Act which, inter alia, list qualifying countries for the purposes and reflect, inter alia, the reciprocal protection given to citizens of other countries under the Berne Convention as well as the position of former British colonies.

222 Duration of Copyright and Rights in Performances Regulations 1995 (SI 1995/3297).

223 Section 154(1) of the Act.

224 Section 154(3) of the Act, as amended by the Duration of Copyright and Rights in Performances Regulations 1995 (SI 1995/3297).

225 Section 154(4) of the Act.

in another country which meets special criteria.[226] Where the work is first published outside a qualifying country, but within 30 days of that publication is published in a qualifying country, protection under the above provisions is still available.[227]

Protecting the ideas or concepts contained in computer programs with copyright

A question which is frequently asked is whether it is possible to stop one person 'copying' another person's computer program. Often what is being asked is 'can I stop you using the ideas or concepts I have regarding my computer program as well as stop you using my code?'. The aim, like with patents, is to create a monopoly position in regard to the idea or concept of the person who has created or written a computer program.

If a patent can protect a computer program, the answer will be 'yes'.[228] But in the current position where a computer program is protected 'only' by copyright then the answer will be 'no', based on the current case law, at least in England.

Therefore, one person can lawfully obtain a copy of a computer program developed by another person, study, examine and run the computer program and thereafter create an exact functional copy. In such a case, the other person will normally have no remedy against the first person for copyright infringement.[229]

The requirement for originality

Any literary work (which will include a computer program) must be 'original' in order to receive protection by copyright. The word 'original' is not defined or explained in the Act as such; however there has been considerable case law on this point.

The essential point is that the cases which have come before the courts in England have emphasised the current position in law, ie the dichotomy between:

- the ideas or thoughts which are contained in a literary work; and

- the expression of those ideas and thoughts.

---

226 Section 155(1) of the Act.
227 Section 155(3) of the Act.
228 See Ch 4 under 'Patenting software' on the current position regarding the patenting of computer software.
229 As long as the first person does not have access to the software code or if he or she does not make any use of it.

It is only the latter which is protected or is capable of being protected by copyright. Only the 'original skill or labour in execution of the work',[230] that is the expression of the thought and/or idea in printing and writing, will be protected[231]. This point is perhaps best expressed in a judgment from a recent case:

> '29. The important point is that copyright can be used to prevent copying of a substantial part of the relevant form of expression, but it does not prevent use of the information, thoughts or emotions expressed in the copyright work. It does not prevent another person from coincidentally creating a similar work by his own independent efforts. It is not an intellectual property monopoly in the same sense as a patent or a registered design. There is no infringement of copyright in the absence of a direct or indirect causal link between the copyright work and the alleged copy.
>
> [...]
>
> 31. The policy of copyright protection and its limited scope explain why the threshold requirement of an "original" work has been interpreted as not imposing objective standards of novelty, usefulness, inventiveness, aesthetic merit, quality or value. A work may be complete rubbish and utterly worthless, but copyright protection may be available for it, just as it is for the great masterpieces of imaginative literature, art and music. A work need only be 'original' in the limited sense that the author originated it by his efforts rather than slavishly copying it from the work produced by the efforts of another person.'[232]

Computer software

There will generally be no problem in establishing that a computer program is not 'original' if a substantial part of the code of another program is copied. In most cases, the direct copying of code can be easily identified (with the right tools) just as text in one written report can be compared to another. However, software authors look to copyright protection for things other than just whether their code is copied. For example, a software programmer may design and seek protection for the following things:

- the way a computer program looks, how its interface operates or how a user interacts with it; or

---

230 From Copinger & Skone, *James on Copyright* (15th edn, Sweet & Maxwell, 2005) Vol 1 at 3-129.
231 *University of London Press Ltd v University Tutorial Press Ltd* [1916] 2 Ch 601 at 608.
232 *Sawkins v Hyperion Records Ltd* [2005] EWCA Civ 565, [2005] 3 All ER 636.

- the structure and implementation of the structure of the software program; or

- the particular functions it carries out.

All of these are likely to involve substantial investment on the part of a software programmer, in some cases more so than the actual writing of code.[233]

First principles

The requirement for originality is, in principle, no different for a computer program than for any other literary work, in order for the work to be capable of protection by copyright.

It is perhaps useful to start with what law there is specifically in place regarding computer programs; that is the Software Directive:[234]

- computer programs are capable of protection by copyright as literary works;

- the protection is for the *expression* of the computer program in any form;

- the ideas and principles which underlie any element of a computer program cannot be protected by copyright. This exclusion from protection includes a computer program's interface;

- a computer program shall be protected by copyright if it is original. Original is to be taken as meaning that the computer program is the author's own intellectual creation;

- programming languages, logic and algorithms are not protected by copyright, but only to the extent that they comprise ideas and principles;[235]

- it is the expression of the ideas and principles which are protected by copyright.[236]

A key problem has been where to set the dividing line between what is an idea or principle and what is its expression. For example, in one case it was held that, by analogy with a novel (where its plot may sometimes be protected), the architecture of a computer program can be protected if 'a substantial part of the programmer's skill, labour and judgement went into it',[237] the judge finding that in a computer program the algorithms or sequences of operations

---

233   There are now software programs which can write, once various parameters and settings are entered, the actual code for another software program (or at least parts of it).
234   Council Directive 91/250/EEC ([1991] OJ L122/42) on the legal protection of computer programs.
235   Council Directive 91/250 (see n 234), Rectial 14.
236   Council Directive 91/250 (see n 234), Rectial 15.
237   *Cantor Fitzgerald International v Tradition (UK) Ltd* [2000] RPC 95 at p134.

decided on by the programmer to achieve the programmer's object are closest to the plot of a novel. But the same judge in a later case decided that the analogy with the plot of a novel was unhelpful, primarily because it is possible to write a computer program which performs the same functions as another computer program without having any access to the code of the first. The judge compared a computer program to a book of instructions which:

'... has no theme, no events, and does not have a narrative flow. Nor does a computer program, particularly one whose behaviour depends upon the history of its inputs in any given transaction. It does not have a plot, merely a series of pre-defined operations intended to achieve the desired result in response to the requests of the customer'.[238]

There has only been a limited amount of case law regarding computer software, which has focussed on the dichotomy between thought/ideas and expression.

The current leading case considered whether the 'reproduction' of one computer program by another amounted to infringement even though no code was copied (and there was no suggestion that there was any access to the code of the first, allegedly, infringed computer program). It is worth examining this case in a little detail as it illustrates the boundaries of what can and cannot be 'copied' from a computer program.

Key facts

- the claimant had developed a computer reservation system which was used by the first defendant;

- the first defendant wished to replace the claimant's computer program with another company's computer program (developed by the second defendant);

- the first defendant wanted the new software to be substantially indistinguishable from the claimant's computer program, in terms of its functions, how they were carried out and in respect of the new software 'user interface'. This was achieved although none of the new computer program's code resembled the claimant's computer program in any way, except that it acted upon identical or very similar inputs and produced very similar results;

- the claimant alleged that the copyright in its computer program was infringed by what was called 'non-textual copying';

- the alleged infringement consisted of three aspects:

---

238 *Navitaire Inc v Easyjet Airline Co and another* [2004] EWHC 1725 (Ch), [2004] All ER (D) 162 (Dec) at para 125.

— the use of the 'business logic' of (ie the functions carried by) the claimant's computer program;

— the copying of the commands (keystrokes) which a user needed to type in order to get the new computer program to perform its functions;

— the copying of reports and screen displays including graphical elements.

The judge found no infringement in each of these cases,[239] for the following reasons:

● *Copying of commands*. There were three elements to this point:

● *Individual keystrokes*: copyright was found not to subsist in the individual command names as literary works. They did not have the necessary qualities of a literary work.[240]

● *Complex commands*: there was also a category of keystrokes which amounted to complex commands to operate or use the computer program.[241] These were also not protected by copyright as they in effect represented a programming language and thus were excluded from protection by the Software Directive.[242]

● *Combination of commands being a compilation*: also considered was whether if all the commands were put together in the form of a compilation they were capable of protection. It was held that they were either a computer programming language or not a compilation in the sense envisaged by the Act.

● *Screen displays and graphic elements*. it was held that certain graphic elements when displayed during the operation of the software were capable of protection not as literary but as artistic works.[243] This was the sole ground on which the claimant succeeded. However, those screens which were text-based were considered to be tables and 'are properly to be viewed as tables and so literary in character for the purposes of

239 Except in one respect of the last aspect, and then there was no infringement in relation to the computer program itself (as a literary work), but concerning icons which were considered to be graphical works (ie protected by copyright as artistic, not literary, works).
240 As single words normally cannot be a work of copyright, the case cites *Exxon Corporation Insurance Consultants International v Control Systems Technology Ltd* [1982] RPC 69 in support of this proposition.
241 That is commands that had a syntax; ones which have one or more arguments that must be expressed in a particular way.
242 SeeCouncil Directive 250/90/EEC ([1991] OJ L122/42) on the legal protection of computer programs, Recital 14.
243 Screen displays which were more than the display of textual elements were capable of protection as artistic works, ie they would be protected by copyright as artistic works (but not as literary works), and thus not within the provisions of the Software Directive (Council Directive 250/90/EEC ([1991] OJ L122/42) on the legal protection of computer programs).

copyright (s 3(1)(a), [the Act]). They are, in my view, "ideas which underlie its interfaces" in the sense used in Article 1(2) of the Directive: they provide the static framework for the display of the dynamic data which it is the task of the software to produce'.

- *'Business logic'*: the argument here that the functions ('business logic') of the claimant's software and the second defendant's software were identical[244] and amounted to infringement was rejected by the judge, as the business logic was the ideas and principles of the computer program and therefore not capable of protection by copyright:

> '129. The questions in the present case are both a lack of substantiality and the nature of the skill and labour to be protected. Navitaire's computer program invites input in a manner excluded from copyright protection, outputs its results in a form excluded from copyright protection and creates a record of a reservation in the name of a particular passenger on a particular flight. What is left when the interface aspects of the case are disregarded is the business function of carrying out the transaction and creating the record, because none of the code was read or copied by the defendants. It is right that those responsible for devising [the claimant's software] envisaged this as the end result for their program: but that is not relevant skill and labour. In my judgment, this claim for non-textual copying should fail.

> 130. I do not come to this conclusion with any regret. If it is the policy of the Software Directive to exclude both computer languages and the underlying ideas of the interfaces from protection, then it should not be possible to circumvent these exclusions by seeking to identify some overall function or functions that it is the sole purpose of the interface to invoke and relying on those instead. As a matter of policy also, it seems to me that to permit the "business logic" of a program to attract protection through the literary copyright afforded to the program itself is an unjustifiable extension of copyright protection into a field where I am far from satisfied that it is appropriate.'

This approach in this case has been followed in a later case.[245] The latter case concerned a computer game owned by the claimant. The defendant had developed a similar game. Again there was no copying of the software code of the claimant, but the features were similar, and in particular the defendant had used the claimant's game as inspiration for its game.

The court held that literary features did not protect the features of one game which inspired the use of them in another as being too general to amount to

---

244 In this case concerning such functions as checking availability of flights, making reservations, obtaining passengers' details and taking payments for tickets.
245 *Nova Productions Ltd v Mazooma Games Ltd and others* [2007] EWCA Civ 219, [2007] IP & T 899.

a substantial part of the claimant's game and quoted with approval a passage from the lower court's judgment:

> 'They are ideas which have little to do with the skill and effort expended by the programmer and do not constitute the form of expression of the literary works relied upon.'[246]

The court went on to state that a written description of the features/functions of the game would be protected by copyright, but the features/functions themselves were in effect ideas and were not protected:

> [51] ... a written work consisting of a specification of the functions of an intended computer program will attract protection as a literary work. But the functions themselves do not. Of course to someone familiar with the prior English law it is self-evident that copyright could subsist in such a description. The fact that a work can get copyright even if mundane, is old and familiar to an English lawyer. But the [Software] Directive needed to say that protection as a literary work should be provided for preparatory design work because not all member states under their existing laws necessarily provided that. That is the whole point of the Directive – and the clear reason for it is recited in art 1.

> [52] ... The reasoning in [*Navitaire Inc v Easyjet Airline Co* [2004] EWHC 1725 (Ch), [2006] RPC 111] provides a second reason for dismissing this appeal. [The judge in that case] was quite right to say that merely making a program which will emulate another but which in no way involves copying the program code or any of the program's graphics is legitimate.

---

246 See *Nova Productions Ltd* above, at para 44.

CHAPTER 6

Protection of databases

GENERALLY

Databases are provided with two forms of protection – copyright, and a separate form of protection, the database right. Prior to 1997 databases were sometimes protected, by copyright only, as a table or compilation.[1] With the coming into force of the Copyright and Rights in Databases Regulations[2] (the 'Database Regulations') two distinct rights were created in regard to databases:

---

1   For example, material such as football-fixture listings (*Football League v Littlewoods* [1959] Ch 637), listings of information (*Blacklock v Pearson* [1915] 2 Ch 376), trade directories (*Morris v Ashbee* (1868–69) LR 7 Eq 34), a compilation of music tracks (*Robin Ray v Classic FM plc* [1998] FSR 622) or a directory of solicitors and barristers (*Waterlow Publishers Ltd v Reed Information Services Ltd* [1992] FSR 409). They have all been classified as being protected by copyright.

2   The Copyright and Rights in Databases Regulations 1997 (SI 1997/3032) implementing Directive 96/9/EC ([1996] OJ L077/20) on the legal protection of databases ('Database Directive').

- **Copyright:** the extension of copyright protection to some types of databases, ie those that meet the test of originality for databases.[3] But the definition of 'originality' for a database in order for the database to be protected by copyright has a particular meaning (which is slightly different to that for other material protected by copyright): the database must constitute the author's own intellectual creation in regard to the selection of the contents of the database;[4] and

- **Database right:** the creation of a database right if the database has been the result of 'a substantial investment in obtaining, verifying or presenting the contents of the database'.[5]

The meaning of a 'database' is the same for both the database right and for copyright.[6] A database can be protected both by copyright and the database right.[7] The database right is a separate, new additional form of right to copyright. It is a property right. The Database Regulations amended the Copyright, Designs and Patents Act 1988 by extending copyright protection to databases (as another form of literary work). However the provisions regarding the database right are only to be found in the Database Regulations.

MEANING OF A DATABASE

Legal definition of a database

Both for the purposes of copyright and the database right a 'database' means:

'... a collection of independent works, data or other materials which are arranged in a systematic or methodical way and are individually accessible by electronic or other means'.[8]

Forms that a database can take

The database right is a new distinct right, which is not comparable to copyright. The recitals to the Database Directive provide a useful list of what

---

3 Copyright and Rights in Databases Regulations 1997 (SI 1997/3032), reg 5.
4 Copyright, Designs and Patents Act 1988, s 3A(2), as inserted by the Copyright and Rights in Databases Regulations 1997 (SI 1997/3032).
5 Copyright and Rights in Databases Regulations 1997 (SI 1997/3032), reg 13(1).
6 Copyright and Rights in Databases Regulations 1997 (SI 1997/3032), reg 12(1).
7 Copyright and Rights in Databases Regulations 1997 (SI 1997/3032), reg 13(4).
8 Database Directive, Art 1, implemented as Copyright, Designs and Patents Act 1988, s 3A(1), as inserted by the Copyright and Rights in Databases Regulations 1997 (SI 1997/3032). The meaning of a database has been further explained in an ECJ case as '... any collection of works, data or other materials, separable from one another without the value of their contents being affected, including a method or system of some sort for the retrieval of each of its constituent materials' (*Fixtures Marketing Ltd v Organismos Prognostikon Agonon Podosfairou*, Case C-444/02, [2004] ECR I-10549, [2005] ECDR 3).

is considered to be covered by the database right, as well as the meaning of a database:

- the Database Directive protects collections of work, data or other material which are arranged, stored and accessed by means which include electronic, electromagnetic or electro-optical processes or analogous means;[9]

- protection extends to electronic *and* non-electronic databases;[10]

- an electronic database may include devices such as CD-ROM and CD-I;[11]

- the meaning of a 'database' includes:

  — literary, artistic, musical or other collections of works; or

  — collections of other material such as text, sound images, numbers, facts and data; or

  — collections of independent works, data or other materials which are systematically or methodically arranged and can be individually accessed;

  but would not include a recording or an audiovisual, cinematographic, literary or musical work itself;[12]

- protection will extend to the materials necessary for the operation or consultation of certain databases such as thesaurus and indexation services;[13]

- works, data, or other materials comprised in a database which are arranged systematically or methodically, do not have to be physically stored in an organised manner;[14]

- the term 'database' does not extend to computer programs used in the making of or operation of a database;[15]

- the compilation of several recordings of musical performances on a CD, as a rule, does not come within the scope of the Database Directive, because as a compilation, it does not meet the conditions for copyright protection and because it does not represent a substantial enough investment to be eligible as a database right.[16]

---

9 Database Directive, Recital 13.
10 Database Directive, Recital 14.
11 Recital 22. Directive of the European Parliament and of the Council of 11 March 1996 on the legal protection of databases (96/9/EC).
12 Database Directive, Recital 17.
13 Database Directive, Recital 20.
14 Database Directive, Recital 21.
15 Database Directive, Recital 23.
16 Database Directive, Recital 19.

LEGAL POSITION OF CONTENTS OF A DATABASE

A database can or will include or contain a series of other copyright or non-copyright works (whether they be documents, software code, film, recordings of sound, etc). The legal status of the database itself (not its contents) is a separate right (whether protected by copyright and/or the database right) and is distinct from the copyright position of each of the contents. Also, the copyright position of the contents of the database will remain unaffected by the copyright in a database.[17] Consequently, before a database can be licensed the licensor may need to acquire licences to all of the contents.

Database as a copyright work

As noted above and in Chapter 5, a database is protectable as a copyright work, being a literary work.[18] An adaptation of a database is also protectable as a copyright work.[19] As such it will be subject to the same provisions regarding the protection of other literary works as set out in Chapter 5, including those concerning assignment and licensing, creation, authorship, ownership and duration, infringement and fair dealing.[20]

For other literary works the test of whether they qualify for copyright protection is whether they are 'original' (which is not further explained in the Copyright, Designs and Patents Act 1988). However a database, in order for it to qualify for copyright protection, is only 'original':

> '… if, and only if, by reason of the selection or arrangement of the contents of the database the database constitutes the author's own intellectual creation'.[21]

---

17   See Database Directive, Art 3(2).
18   Copyright, Designs and Patents Act 1988, s 3(1)(d), as amended by the Copyright and Rights in Databases Regulations 1997 (SI 1997/3032).
19   Copyright, Designs and Patents Act 1988, s 21(2). 'Adaptation' means an arrangement or altered version of the database, or a translation of it.
20   The provisions relating to copyright in databases are set out in Ch 5, together with the small amount of amendments to the Copyright, Designs and Patents Act 1988 where the copyright position of databases is different compared to other literary works.
21   Copyright, Designs and Patents Act 1988, s 3(2) as inserted by the Copyright and Rights in Databases Regulations 1997 (SI 1997/3032).

DATABASE RIGHT

Assignment and licensing of the database right

The provisions which apply to copyright concerning assignment and licensing in the Copyright, Designs and Patents Act 1988 equally apply to the database right (as well as copyright in databases).[22]

Qualification for protection

A database right will subsist in a database if there has been a substantial investment in obtaining, verifying or presenting the contents of the database.[23] The investment can be financial, human or technical. 'Substantial' in relation to any investment means substantial in terms of quantity or quality or a combination of both.[24]

The protection offered by the database right relates primarily to its economic value rather than its originality (the latter being necessary for a database to qualify for copyright protection). Guidance has been provided as to the meaning of certain words used in relation to the law applying to the database right,[25] in particular:

- *Obtaining* means the 'resources used to seek out existing independent materials and collect them into the database'. Obtaining will not mean the resources which are used to create the independent materials which make up the contents of the database.

---

22 Copyright and Rights in Databases Regulations 1997 (SI 1997/3032), reg 23, which applies certain provisions of the Copyright, Designs and Patents Act 1988 to the database right. Concerning the provisions regarding assignments and licensing found in the Copyright, Designs and Patents Act 1988, see Ch 5 under 'Commercial transactions involving copyright works'.
23 Copyright and Rights in Databases Regulations 1997 (SI 1997/3032), reg 13(1).
24 Copyright and Rights in Databases Regulations 1997 (SI 1997/3032), reg 12(1). In *Fixtures Marketing Ltd v Organismos Prognostikon Agonon Podosfairou*, Case C-444/02, [2004] ECR I-10549, [2005] ECDR 3, the meaning of 'quantity' and 'quality' were further elaborated: 'Investment in the creation of a database may consist in the deployment of human, financial or technical resources but it must be substantial in quantitative or qualitative terms. The quantitative assessment refers to quantifiable resources and the qualitative assessment to efforts which cannot be quantified, such as intellectual effort or energy, according to the 7th, 39th and 40th recitals of the preamble to [Directive 96/6/EC]'.
25 *Case C-203/002 Reference for a preliminary hearing under Article 234 EC, from the Court of Appeal on the case of British Horseracing Board Ltd and others v the William Hill Organisation Ltd.* The case is based on the wording of the Directive rather than the Copyright and Rights in Databases Regulations 1997 (SI 1997/3032). Art 7(1) provides: 'Member States shall provide for a right for the maker of a database which shows that there has been qualitatively and/or quantitatively a substantial investment in either the obtaining, verification or presentation of the contents to prevent extraction and/or re-utilization of the whole or of a substantial part, evaluated qualitatively and/or quantitatively, of the contents of that database.'
   The decision of the Court of Appeal was set out in detail in the previous edition of this book.

- *Verification* means the use of resources to ensure 'the reliability of the information contained in the database, to monitor the accuracy of the materials collected when the database was created and during its operation'. However verification will not mean those resources used for verifying the independent materials at the stage they are created.

Ownership

The maker of the database, ie the 'person who takes the initiative in obtaining, verifying or presenting the contents' is the first owner of the database.[26] A database is made jointly if two or more persons acting in collaboration take the initiative in obtaining, verifying or presenting the contents of the database and assume the risk of investing in that obtaining, verification, or presentation.[27] Like copyright works, a database made in the course of employment by an employee is considered to be made by the employer (unless they agree otherwise).[28]

For the database right to subsist in a database, at the material time the maker needs to be:[29]

- an individual who is a national of, or habitually resident within, an EEA[30] state; or

- a body incorporated under the laws of an EEA state, provided:

  — its principal place of business or its central administration is within an EEA state; or

  — its registered office is within an EEA state and its operations are linked on an ongoing basis with the economy of an EEA state;

- a partnership or other unincorporated body formed under the law of an EEA state, with its principal place of business or its central administration within an EEA state.

---

26 Copyright and Rights in Databases Regulations 1997 (SI 1997/3032), reg 15.
27 Copyright and Rights in Databases Regulations 1997 (SI 1997/3032), reg 14(6).
28 Copyright and Rights in Databases Regulations 1997 (SI 1997/3032), reg 14(2). This point was considered in *Cureton v Mark Insulations Ltd* [2006] EWHC 2279 (QB), [2006] All ER (D) 85 (Mar), where a database was created by the sales agent claimant to enable it to sell products for the defendant. The database contained details of the defendant's customers, orders made or not made, telephone calls made by the claimant, etc. The court held that the database belonged to the sales agent claimant and rejected the defendant's argument, that a database made by an employee belongs to the employer, and therefore, in accordance with the Copyright and Rights in Databases Regulations 1997 (SI 1997/3032), reg 14, by analogy, a database made by agent should also be owned by the principal. See also *PennWell Publishing (UK) Limited v Isles and others* [2007] EWHC 1570 (QB), [2007] All ER (D) 180 (Jun).
29 Copyright and Rights in Databases Regulations 1997 (SI 1997/3032), reg 18.
30 For the meaning of EEA, see Ch 12 under 'European Economic Area Agreement'.

Duration of the database right

The database right lasts for 15 years from the end of the year after:[31]

- the database was made; or

- the database was made available to the public (as long as this is within 15 years of the database being made).

If the database is changed (by additions, deletions or alteration) a new database right is created, as long as the changed database is considered to be a substantial new investment.[32]

Infringement

The database right in a database is infringed if a person extracts or re-utilises all or a substantial part of the contents of the database without the consent of the owner of the right.[33] Where insubstantial parts of the contents of a database are repeatedly and systematically extracted or re-utilised then such activity may amount to the extraction or re-utilisation of a substantial part of those contents.[34]

Extraction is the 'permanent or temporary transfer of those contents to another medium by any means or in any form', while re-utilisation is 'making those contents available to the public by any means'.[35]

Meaning of 'extraction' and 're-utilisation'

The leading case referred to above also provided guidance as to the meaning of 'extraction' and 're-utilisation'.[36] The words:

- are to be given a wide definition;

- are to be taken as referring to any act of appropriating and making available to the public without the consent of the maker of the database the contents of the whole or a part of the contents of the database, the result of the maker's investment which deprives the maker of revenue;

- will not imply direct access to the database concerned;

31 Copyright and Rights in Databases Regulations 1997 (SI 1997/3032), reg 17.
32 Copyright and Rights in Databases Regulations 1997 (SI 1997/3032), reg 17(3).
33 Copyright and Rights in Databases Regulations 1997 (SI 1997/3032), reg 16(1).
34 Copyright and Rights in Databases Regulations 1997 (SI 1997/3032), reg 16(2).
35 Copyright and Rights in Databases Regulations 1997 (SI 1997/3032), reg 12(1).
36 *Case C-203/002 Reference for a preliminary hearing under Article 234 EC, from the Court of Appeal on the case of British Horseracing Board Ltd and others v the William Hill Organisation Ltd.*

- will include extraction and re-utilisation by a third party which is carried out from a source other than the database, just as much as such acts carried out directly from that database, which prejudice the investment of the maker of the database;

- do not cover consultation of the database; if the maker makes the content of the database available (or a part of it) to the public, his or her sui generis right does not allow the maker to prevent third parties consulting the database.

And:

- the fact that the contents of a database were made accessible to the public by its maker or with his or her consent does not affect the right of the maker to prevent acts of extraction and/or re-utilisation of the whole or a substantial part of the contents of a database.

The meaning of 'extraction' has also been considered in a recent case, and can be found where a person transfers:

'… material from a protected database to another database following an on-screen consultation of the first database and an individual assessment of the material contained in that first database is capable of constituting an 'extraction''.[37]

Meaning of 'substantial parts of the contents of that database'

The case also provided guidance as to the meaning of 'substantial part of the contents of that database':

- whether there has been extraction or re-utilisation of a substantial part must be evaluated qualitatively or quantitatively;

- to decide whether the part which has been extracted or re-utilised is substantial quantitatively it is necessary to refer to the volume of the data extracted from the database or re-utilised, and that must be assessed against the total volume of the contents of the database;

---

37 *Directmedia Publishing GmbH v Albert-Ludwigs-Universitat Freiburg* Case C-304/07, [2009] IP & T 69, [2008] All ER (D) 88 (Oct). In this case, the database consisted of a number of verse titles and was published on the internet (it was based on statistical analysis of the most popular German poetry, using more than 20,000 poems to select the verse titles, with the project taking 2½ years and costing some 35,000 Euros). A commercial company (who published a CD-Rom under the title '1000 poems everyone should have') consulted the internet database as a guide for poems to put on its CD-Rom, but the commercial company used the actual text of the poems which it obtained from its own resources. There was an overlap in the poems included on the internet database and the CD-Rom. All the poems appear to have been out of copyright. No poetry appeared to have been written later than 1900. The claim before the court was for copyright infringement and infringement of the database right.

- to decide whether the part which has been extracted or re-utilised is substantial qualitatively reference needs to be made to the scale of the investment in the obtaining, verification or presentation of the contents of what has been extracted or re-utilised; this is regardless of whether the extract or re-utilised contents represent a quantitatively substantial part of the total database;

- the intrinsic value of the independent parts of the database which are affected by the act of extraction and/or re-utilisation does not constitute a relevant criterion for the assessment of whether the part at issue is substantial.

If the part of the database which is extracted or re-utilised does not fall within the definition of being quantitatively or qualitatively substantial then it will fall within the definition of an insubstantial part of the contents of the database.

Meaning of 'repeated and systematic extraction or re-utilisation of insubstantial parts'

The case also provided guidance as to where there is repeated and systematic extraction or re-utilisation of insubstantial parts of the contents of the database, which will be taken to mean:

- unauthorised acts of extraction or re-utilisation;

- the cumulative effect of which is to reconstitute and/or make available to the public the whole or a substantial part of the contents of the database;

- where the reconstitution and/or making available to the public is done without the authorisation of the maker of the database; and

- which seriously prejudice(s) the investment of the maker in the database.

Fair dealing

There are no specific fair dealing provisions as such for the database right in the same way as for copyright (for example for criticism, (non-commercial) research, private study etc). However, if a database qualifies as a copyright work, fair dealing is permitted (as modified).[38] But if the database only qualifies for the lesser database right, a (very) limited fair dealing exception applies if a substantial part of the database is extracted and:[39]

---

38 Copyright, Designs and Patents Act 1988, s 29(1A), as inserted by the Copyright and Rights in Databases Regulations 1997 (SI 1997/3032).
39 Copyright and Rights in Databases Regulations 1997 (SI 1997/3032), reg 20.

- the database has been issued to the public; and

- that part has been extracted by a person who is otherwise a lawful user (has a licence from the maker of the database); and

- the extraction is for illustration in teaching or research; and

- is not for any commercial purpose; and

- the source is indicated.

In addition, the database right is not infringed if anything is done for the purposes of public administration (such as judicial or parliamentary proceedings, communication to the Crown in the course of public business, etc).[40] There is no infringement by extraction or re-utilisation of a substantial part of the database if it is not possible to identify the maker (by making reasonable enquires) or it is reasonable to assume that the database right has expired.[41]

Avoidance of certain terms

Any term or condition which prevents a person who has a right to use a database (or part of a database) from extracting or re-utilising insubstantial parts of the contents of the database (or of that part of the database) for any purpose is void.[42]

Transfer of database right

A database right can be dealt with in the same way as copyright works, such as by assignment and licence.[43]

Remedies

The same remedies are available for database right infringement as for copyright infringement, except that the owner cannot apply for an order that the infringing article be delivered up to him, or seize infringing copies.[44] Exclusive licensees of the database right have the same remedies available to them as for copyright.[45] There appear to be no criminal sanctions or remedies in regard to the database right.

---

40   Copyright and Rights in Databases Regulations 1997 (SI 1997/3032), reg 20(2).
41   Copyright and Rights in Databases Regulations 1997 (SI 1997/3032), reg 21.
42   Copyright and Rights in Databases Regulations 1997 (SI 1997/3032), reg 19.
43   Copyright and Rights in Databases Regulations 1997 (SI 1997/3032), reg 23.
44   See n 43.
45   See n 43.

CHAPTER 7

Designs

GENERAL

This chapter considers the legislation covering the protection of designs. In recent years the legal protection afforded to designs has undergone substantial transformation.

The protection offered for designs is now seemingly more complicated with the introduction of two new forms of protection available for designs, due to EU legislation (the 'Design Directive' and the 'Design Regulation').[1] However, the reality is that the criteria for protection are now more uniform as regards:

- the existing protection offered to UK-registered designs; and

- the new protection offered to registered Community Designs and unregistered Community Designs.

The changes, however, still leave one anomaly in that for the UK unregistered design right the criteria for protection are now defined in a different way to those of the Design Directive and the Design Regulation.

---

1   Directive 98/71/EC ([1998] OJ L289/28) on the legal protection of Designs (in this chapter, the 'Design Directive'); and Council Regulation (EC) 6/2002 ([2002] OJ L3/1) on Community designs (in this chapter, the 'Design Regulation').

There are now up to four possible protections available for a design:

Name of right	Legislative measure	How obtained/comes into being	Area of protection
Design right	Copyright, Designs and Patents Act 1988	Once the design is recorded in a design document	UK
Registered designs	Registered Designs Act (incorporated into the Copyright, Designs and Patents Act 1988) following implementation of the Design Directive	On registration	UK
Registered Community Design	Design Regulation	On registration	EU
Unregistered Community Design	Design Regulation	On making design available to the public	EU

The following sections consider, separately:

● UK design right;

● UK registered designs; and

● Community Designs (both unregistered and registered together).

At the end of these sections, there is a table summarising the main provisions regarding each of these protections available for design.

DESIGN RIGHT

Introduction

Design right and copyright

The design right was introduced by the Copyright, Designs and Patents Act 1988 (the '1988 Act'). It provides protection against the copying of industrial designs for commercial purposes. Many aspects of design right law are similar, or identical, to copyright law. A design can be protected by both copyright and, separately and in addition to copyright, by design right.

It is perhaps not surprising that the design right, as an unregistered right replaces some of the protection given by copyright to designs before the passing of the Act. However there are still some important differences between design right and copyright including the following:

● *Ownership of commissioned designs*: in the absence of express or implied contract terms to the contrary, the commissioner of a design is normally the first owner of design right, rather than the party which produced the design. Under copyright law, the author of a copyright work (or his or her employer) is normally the first owner of the copyright in that work, even where the work is commissioned,[2] subject to any contract term to the contrary.

- *Duration*: design right normally lasts for a period of between 10 and 15 years, with slightly different provisions in the special case of design right in semiconductor topographies. There is a minimum 50- or 70-year period for copyright protection.[3]

- *Licences of right*: in the last five years of design right protection for an article, licences are available (for example to the competitors of the design right owner) as of right on commercial terms.[4] (These provisions do not apply to design right in semiconductor topographies.) There are automatic licence of right provisions which apply in the case of copyright (as distinct from the provisions enabling licences of right to be ordered following a Competition Commission report).

- *Must fit/intended to match exceptions*: although design right is available for functional (ie non-aesthetic) designs, it is not available in certain cases for designs which are pre-determined by the need for the designed article to fit with another article (for example the design of an electrical plug and socket) or to match with another article so as to form an integrated whole (for example some car body parts). The scope of these exceptions is becoming clearer as litigation over design right reaches the courts. There are also some further complex exceptions to design right in the special case of semiconductor topographies, particularly those relating to 'reverse engineering'.

- *Qualification for design right protection*: the first owner of copyright in a work may qualify for UK copyright protection on the basis of a defined connection with the UK or other qualifying country, or on the basis of where the copyright work is first published. These rules are complex and different to those which apply in the case of design right; for example in the case of design right, protection may also be available on the basis of where the design is first marketed. However, in general, foreign designs are less likely to receive protection under UK law than foreign copyright works. It should be pointed out that the international treaties providing for international recognition of copyright (for example the Berne Convention) do not apply to design right; indeed relatively few countries have design right as such. Some countries (the EU and the US) give protection to semiconductor topographies, which are protected in the UK by a special category of design right, and mutual recognition provisions are in place between a number of such countries.

---

2   Copyright, Designs and Patents Act 1988, s 11 (as amended by SI 1996/2967).
3   See Ch 5 under 'Duration of Copyright'.
4   Copyright, Designs and Patents Act 1988, s 237.

Provisions of design right law of direct relevance to commercial transactions

As is mentioned further below, design right is defined as being a property right, which is consistent with the position of other types of intellectual property.[5]

The provisions of the 1988 Act concerned with dealings[6] in design right are in most cases identical to the equivalent provisions in respect of copyright.[7] These include recognised methods of transfer (assignment, testamentary disposition or by operation of law), requirements for an assignment to be in writing, provision for assignments to be limited in scope or duration, assignment of future design right, the lack of a general requirement for licences to be in writing, and the rights of a licensee against subsequent owners of design right.

Other provisions of design right law which may directly affect the parties to a commercial transaction involving design right, and which are discussed in more detail later in this chapter, include the following:

- the provisions relating to ownership of commissioned designs, which differ from those which apply to copyright;

- the licence of right provisions which apply in the last five years of design right protection, including the special provisions that apply if a defendant in design right infringement proceedings undertakes to take a licence;

- the provisions relating to Crown use of designs;

- in addition to the general exceptions to the design right (eg must fit, must match etc), the special exceptions that apply only to design right in semiconductor topographies, eg in relation to 'reverse engineering'.

Fundamental aspects of design right law which may affect the parties to a commercial transaction

Nature of design right

Design right is a property right which subsists in an 'original design' in accordance with the provisions of the 1988 Act.[8] The terms 'original' and

---

5   See Ch 9 under 'Relevant provisions of intellectual property statutes'.
6   Copyright, Designs and Patents Act 1988, ss 222–225.
7   Copyright, Designs and Patents Act 1988, ss 90–92; but s 93 (where copyright to pass under will with an unpublished work) is not reproduced in ss 222–225.
8   Copyright, Designs and Patents Act 1988, s 213(1). 'Original' is defined in s 213(1), except as noted below, but it has the same meaning as 'original' in Copyright, Designs and Patents Act 1988, s 1(1) (that is the requirement for a copyright to subsist in a literary or artistic work) and must be 'namely not copied but the independent work of the designer': *C & H Engineering v Klucznik & Sons* [1992] FSR 421. This case went on to note that 'original' had to be contrasted with 'novelty' which is a requirement of registration of a registered design.

'design' are defined and the circumstances in which design right subsists are explained in the 1988 Act as follows.[9]

Design

'Design' means the

'design of any aspect[10] of the shape or configuration[11] (whether internal or external) of the whole or part of an article'.[12]

This has been held to include an individual part, combinations of parts and the parts made up into a whole 'machine'.[13]

Original

'A design is not "original" ... if it is commonplace in the design field in question at the time of its creation.'[14]

---

9   Copyright, Designs and Patents Act 1988, ss 213, 214.

10 The word 'aspect' in the phrase 'design of any aspect of the shape or configuration of the whole or part of an article' has been held to mean it is 'discernible' or 'recognisable': *A Fulton Company Ltd v Totes Isotoner (UK) Ltd* [2003] EWCA Civ 1514, [2003] All ER (D) 33 (Nov).

11 An article which is merely coloured in a new way will not amount to 'shape or configuration': *Lambretta Clothing Co Ltd v Teddy Smith (UK) Ltd and another* [2004] EWCA Civ 886, [2004] All ER (D) 269 (Jul).

12 Copyright, Designs and Patents Act 1988, s 213(2). This has been held to mean that an article 'may and generally will embody a multitude of "designs" – as many "aspects" of the whole or part of the article as can be': *Dyson Ltd v Qualtex (UK) Ltd* [2006] EWCA Civ 166, [2006] All ER (D) 101 (Mar).

13 *Farmers Build Ltd v Carier Bulk Materials Handling Ltd and others* [1999] RPC 461: 'The definition of "design" in Section 213(2) is wide enough to include the shape or configuration of the individual parts of the [machine in question in this case] and of the [machine in question in this case] as a whole: the individual parts, combinations of parts and the parts made up into a whole machine are all "articles" with a shape and a configuration'. (from the judgment of Mummery LJ).

14 Copyright, Designs and Patents Act 1988, s 213(4). 'Commonplace' has been interpreted as meaning 'any design which is trite, trivial, common-or-garden, hackneyed or of the type which would excite no peculiar attention in those in the relevant art': *Ocular Sciences Ltd v Aspect Vision Care Ltd* [1997] RPC 289 at 429, and adopted in *Parker & Parker v Tidball* [1997] FSR 680 at 793. In *Farmers Build Ltd v Carier Bulk Materials Handling Ltd* [1999] RPC 461, CA, a two-step test was developed for originality: first, originality should be considered like copyright, ie whether the design was copied from another design; secondly, if it was not, then the court has to decide whether it is 'commonplace'. For the second step, the design in consideration has to be examined to see how similar it is to other designs of similar articles in the same field of design made by persons other than the parties or persons unconnected with the parties.

Excluded types of design: method of construction/must fit/must match/ surface decoration

'Design right does not subsist in–

(a)   a method or principle of construction,

(b)   features of shape or configuration of an article which–

>   (i)   enable the article to be connected to, or placed in, around or against, another article so that either article may perform its function, or

>   (ii)   which are dependent upon the appearance of another article of which the article is intended by the designer to form an integral part, or

(c)   surface decoration.'[15]

Subsistence of design right

Design right does not subsist unless and until the design has been recorded in a design document or an article has been made to the design.

'Design document' is defined as:

>   '… any record of a design, whether in the form of a drawing, a written description, a photograph, data stored in a computer or otherwise'.[16]

Commencement of design right law

'Design right does not subsist in a design which was recorded, or to which an article was made, before the commencement of this Part [ie before 1 August 1989].'

Transfer of design right

The 1988 Act provides for three methods of transfer of design right:

•   by assignment;

•   by testamentary disposition; or

•   by operation of law.[17]

---

15   Copyright, Designs and Patents Act 1988, s 213(3).

16   Copyright, Designs and Patents Act 1988, s 263(1). The categories of design document defined in this section are examples of possible ways in which the record of an aspect of design can be made, and are not to be limiting: *Mackie Designs Inc. v Behringer Specialised Studio Equipment (UK) Ltd* [1999] RPC 717 at 721.

17   Copyright, Designs and Patents Act 1988, s 222(1).

In a commercial transaction, the transfer of design right will generally be by means of an assignment. Transfer of design right should be distinguished from the more limited grant of rights under design right by means of a licence. Where a licence is granted, the person granting the licence retains ownership of the design right and gives the licensee permission to do certain of the acts restricted by design right.

Assignments

An assignment of design right is not effective unless it is in writing signed by or on behalf of the assignor.[18] It need not be in the form of a deed, but if there is no consideration for the assignment, then under the law of contract a deed may be necessary to make the transaction legally effective. An assignment which is defective, ie is not signed by or on behalf of the assignor, is usually considered to be an agreement to assign. The assignee is the equitable, not the legal, owner of the design right work, provided that the defective assignment allows the assignee to specifically enforce the assignment, and consideration is present. Alternatively, if the wording of the assignment is not clear, it may, in reality, also be an agreement to assign.

An assignment, or other transmission of design right, may be of limited scope and duration; it may apply to one or more, but not all, of the things the design right owner has the exclusive right to do; or to part, but not the whole, of the period for which the design right is to subsist.[19]

An assignment of future design right[20] (for example an assignment which relates to a design right which has not yet been created) is often legally effective, such that no further assignment is required to transfer title when the design comes into existence. The 1988 Act provides as follows:[21]

> 'Where by an agreement made in relation to future design right, and signed by or on behalf of the prospective owner of the design right, the prospective owner purports to assign the future design right (wholly or partially) to another person, then if, on the design right coming into existence, the assignee or another person claiming under him would be entitled as against all other persons to require the design right to be vested in him, the design right shall vest in the assignee or his successor in title by virtue of this subsection.'

---

18 Copyright, Designs and Patents Act 1988, s 90(3).
19 Copyright, Designs and Patents Act 1988, s 222(2).
20 Future design right means design right which will or may come into existence in respect of a future design or class of designs on the occurrence of a future event: Copyright, Designs and Patents Act 1988, s 223(2).
21 Copyright, Designs and Patents Act 1988, s 223(1).

Licences

(a) There is no general requirement that licences must be in writing, although for an exclusive licensee to obtain the benefit of certain statutory rights the licence should be in writing. In practice, most licences are in writing.[22]

(b) Licences generally continue when the design right in the licensed work is transferred (ie assigned); the only exception to this is that a licence is not binding upon:

> '... a purchaser in good faith [of the design right owner's interest in the design right] for valuable consideration and without notice (actual or constructive) of the licence, or a person deriving title from such a purchaser'.[23]

> As there is no official register of design right in the UK, a licensee under design right is not able to register his or her licence and thereby give notice to the world of his or her interest (unlike the position in relation to registered designs or patents). There is therefore an increased risk of a licensee losing its rights under a design right licence if the design right is sold to a purchaser who comes within the category described above.[24]

(c) Similarly, a licence granted by a prospective owner of design right is binding on persons to whom he or she transfers his or her interest in the copyright, except for a purchaser in good faith.[25]

(d) An exclusive licensee has the same rights against a successor in title to the design right who is bound by the licence, as he or she does against the person who originally granted the licence to him or her.[26] The question of whether a successor in title is bound by the licence is dealt with in (b) and (c) above. The special rights of an exclusive licensee are referred to below. An exclusive licence is defined as follows:

> 'In this Part [ie Part III of the Copyright, Designs and Patents Act 1988] an "exclusive licence" means a licence in writing signed by or on behalf of the design right owner authorising the licensee to the exclusion of all other persons, including the person granting the

---

22 Copyright, Designs and Patents Act 1988, s 225.
23 Copyright, Designs and Patents Act 1988, s 222(4).
24 There is no failsafe way of dealing with this situation, except for carrying out adequate due diligence prior to entering a deal (which assumes the provider of the information will tell the complete truth), or adding warranties to the agreement (so that if a licence is discovered after the deal is signed then the party in breach can be sued), or making the party in breach deposit a sum of money (for a limited period of time) against such an eventuality.
25 Copyright, Designs and Patents Act 1988, s 223(3).
26 Copyright, Designs and Patents Act 1988, s 225(2).

licence, to exercise a right which would otherwise be exercisable exclusively by the design right owner'.[27]

First owner of design right: designer/commissioner/ employer/first marketer?

The provisions of design right law as to who is the first owner of design right, have some similarities to the position under copyright law and some important differences, particularly where the design is commissioned.

The designer (analogous to the author in copyright law) will be the first owner, unless:

- the work was commissioned; or

- the work was produced in the course of the designer's employment; or

- the work benefits from design right protection only because it was first marketed in a relevant country.

The 'designer' is defined in very similar terms to the definition of 'author' under copyright law:

'(1) In this Part the 'designer', in relation to a design, means the person who creates it.

(2) In the case of a computer-generated design the person by whom the arrangements necessary for the creation of the design are undertaken shall be taken to be the designer'.[28]

Designer as first owner

The designer is the first owner of any design right in a design which is not created in pursuance of a commission or in the course of employment.[29]

Commissioner as first owner

Where a design is created in pursuance of a commission, the person commissioning the design is the first owner of any design right in it.[30]

---

27 Copyright, Designs and Patents Act 1988, s 225(1).
28 Copyright, Designs and Patents Act 1988, s 214.
29 Copyright, Designs and Patents Act 1988, s 215(1).
30 Copyright, Designs and Patents Act 1988, s 215(2). See *Ultraframe (UK) Ltd v Fielding* [2003] EWCA Civ 1805, [2004] RPC 479, [2003] All ER (D) 232 (Dec).

This provision can be contrasted with the position under copyright law, where the commissioner of a work will not own copyright in the work unless the contract so provides.[31]

Employer as first owner

'Where, in a case not falling within subsection (2) [ie where the design is not commissioned], a design is created by an employee in the course of his employment, his employer is the first owner of any design right in the design.'[32]

First marketer as first owner

'If a design qualifies for design right protection by virtue of section 220 [of the 1988 Act] (qualification by reference to first marketing of articles made to the design), the above rules do not apply and the person by whom the articles in question are marketed is the first owner of the design right.'[33]

The circumstances in which a design qualifies for design right protection are discussed below.[34] It should perhaps be emphasised that the first marketer will be the first owner only where the design benefits from design right protection solely because the article was first marketed in a qualifying country, ie neither the designer, employer nor commissioner was a qualifying person.

Duration of design right

The provisions on duration of design right are complicated; they provide for a maximum 15 years of protection, with a reduced period (down to a minimum of ten years) where articles made to the design are first put on the market within five years of the design right in that design coming into existence.[35] Separate provisions apply in the case of design right in semiconductor topographies.[36]

The relevant section of the 1988 Act reads as follows:

'(1) Design right expires–

(a)   fifteen years from the end of the calendar year in which the design was first recorded in a design document or an article was first made to the design, whichever first occurred, or

---

31   See under Ch 5 'Ownership' above for the position under copyright law.
32   Copyright, Designs and Patents Act 1988, s 215(3).
33   Copyright, Designs and Patents Act 1988, s 215(4).
34   See under 'Qualification for design right' below.
35   See Copyright, Designs and Patents Act 1988, s 216.
36   See 'Semiconductor topographies: special provisions of design right law' below.

(b) if articles made to the design are made available for sale or hire within five years from the end of that calendar year, ten years from the end of the calendar year in which that first occurred.

(2) The reference in subsection (1) to articles being made available for sale or hire is to their being made so available anywhere in the world by or with the licence of the design right owner.'[37]

To put it another way, if articles made to a design are made available in the same calendar year as the year in which the design right came into existence (which for convenience is referred to below as the Commencement Year), the period of design right protection is ten years from the end of the Commencement Year. If such articles are first made available in the year after the Commencement Year, the period of protection is 11 years from the end of the Commencement Year, and so on, subject to a maximum period of 15 years from the end of the Commencement Year.

Qualification for design right

A design may qualify for design right protection in a number of different ways, which may be summarised as follows:

(a) *Qualifying designer:* if the design was not made under a commission, nor in the course of the designer's employment, and the designer was a 'qualifying individual'.[38]

(b) *Qualifying commissioner/employer:* if the design was made under a commission or in the course of the designer's employment, and the commissioner or employer was a 'qualifying person'.[39]

(c) *Qualifying first marketer:* if the design does not qualify for design right protection under (a) or (b) above, it will still qualify for design right protection if the first marketing of articles made to the design: (i) is by a qualifying person who is exclusively authorised[40] to put the articles on the market in the UK; and (ii) takes place in the UK or elsewhere in the EC or in certain other countries.[41]

(d) *Further categories of qualification:* the 1988 Act enables Orders in Council to be made to extend the categories of qualification for design

---

37 Copyright, Designs and Patents Act 1988, s 216.
38 Copyright, Designs and Patents Act 1988, s 218; the section also deals with the position of computer-generated designs and joint designs.
39 Copyright, Designs and Patents Act 1988, s 219; the section also deals with the position of joint commissioners and joint employers.
40 As defined in Copyright, Designs and Patents Act 1988, s 220(4).
41 That is countries included by virtue of an Order in Council under s 255; s 220 also addresses the question of joint first marketing.

303

right protection 'with a view to fulfilling an international obligation of the United Kingdom'. This might, for example, occur if the UK enters into a treaty with one or more other countries to provide for reciprocal protection to each other's nationals, as occurs under copyright laws.[42]

The terms 'qualifying person' and 'qualifying individual' are defined in the 1988 Act.[43] The definitions are complex, and need to be read in conjunction with Orders in Council (which are updated from time to time) which list other countries whose nationals receive the benefit of UK design right protection. The most common examples of qualifying individuals and qualifying persons provided for by the 1988 Act are the following:

(i) citizens and habitual residents of the UK or another EC country;

(ii) companies incorporated under the law of the UK or another EC country, which have in the EC a place of business at which substantial business is carried on.

Infringement of design right

There are two categories of infringement of design right: primary infringement and secondary infringement. Each type of infringement is concerned with acts done for 'commercial purposes' or in the course of a business.[44] Acts done for commercial purposes are defined[45] as acts done 'with a view to the article in question being sold or hired in the course of a business'.[46] Acts which are not done for commercial purposes do not infringe design right. The infringing acts are also subject to the exceptions described below.[47]

Primary infringement

Primary infringement occurs[48] when a person does, or authorises another to do, any of the following acts[49] without the licence of the design right owner:

'... reproduce the design for commercial purposes–

(a) by making articles to that design (ie copying the design directly or indirectly so as to produce articles exactly or substantially to that design[50]), or

---

42   See eg SI 1989/1294 and more recent SIs.
43   Copyright, Designs and Patents Act 1988, s 217.
44   See wording of Copyright, Designs and Patents Act 1988, ss 226(1), 227.
45   Copyright, Designs and Patents Act 1988, s 263(3).
46   See wording of Copyright, Designs and Patents Act 1988, ss 226(1), 227.
47   At 'Exceptions to rights of design right owner'.
48   Copyright, Designs and Patents Act 1988, s 226(3).
49   Copyright, Designs and Patents Act 1988, s 226(1).
50   Copyright, Designs and Patents Act 1988, s 226(2), (4).

(b)　by making a design document recording the design for the purpose of enabling such articles to be made'.

Secondary infringement

Secondary infringement occurs[51] when a person, without the licence of the copyright owner:

'(a)　imports into the United Kingdom for commercial purposes, or

(b)　has in his possession for commercial purposes, or

(c)　sells, lets for hire, or exposes for sale or hire, in the course of a business,

an article which is, and which he knows or has reason to believe is, an infringing article'.[52]

Remedies for infringement

The remedies for infringement of design right are similar, but not always identical, to those for infringement of copyright.[53] The provisions of the 1988 Act should be consulted concerning the detailed circumstances in which the remedies are available.[54]

Exceptions to rights of design right owner

The 1988 Act provides for a number of exceptions to the rights of the design right owner. Some of these exceptions are similar to those which apply in the case of copyright; others (eg the Crown user provisions) are similar to the exceptions which apply under UK patent law; some are unique to design law.

Infringement of copyright

The 1988 Act seeks to ensure there is no overlap between copyright and design right protection. In some situations a copyright work may include or consist of a design in which design right also subsists. It is expressly not an infringement of design right under the 1988 Act[55] to do anything which is an infringement of copyright in that work.[56]

51　Copyright, Designs and Patents Act 1988, s 227.
52　Infringing article being defined in Copyright, Designs and Patents Act 1988, s 228; design documents are excluded from the definition.
53　As to which see Ch 5 under 'Infringement – restricted acts'.
54　See Copyright, Designs and Patents Act 1988, ss 226–235.
55　Copyright, Designs and Patents Act 1988, s 236.
56　There are also provisions in the Part of the Act dealing with copyright works which provide that in certain circumstances it is not an infringement of copyright in, inter alia, a design document, to copy an article made to the design: see Copyright, Designs and Patents Act 1988, s 51.

Licences of right in last five years of design right

In the last five years of design right for a design, licences are available as of right. The comptroller of designs settles the terms of the licence if the parties cannot agree upon them. The licence of right provisions for patents, and the reported cases on patent licences of right, may provide some guidance as to the approach the comptroller will take in exercising these powers.[57] The relevant provisions of the 1988 Act[58] read as follows:

'(1) Any person is entitled as of right to a licence to do in the last five years of the design right term anything which would otherwise infringe the design right.

(2) The terms of the licence shall, in default of agreement, be settled by the comptroller'.

The Act also includes powers for the Secretary of State to remove the licence of right provisions for particular types of design in certain circumstances, eg to comply with international treaty obligations.[59]

Powers exercisable following Competition Commission report

The 1988 Act includes powers similar to those applicable in the case of patents and copyright,[60] for the protection of the public interest, including:

'(a) conditions in licences granted by a design right owner restricting the use of the design by the licensee or the right of the design right owner to grant other licences, or

(b) a refusal of a design right owner to grant licences on reasonable terms'.[61]

The power includes the power to cancel or modify those conditions and/or to provide that licences in respect of the design right shall be available as of right.

Undertaking to take licence in infringement proceedings

Where a person is sued for infringement of design right, and where licences of right are available in respect of that design, as described in the two previous paragraphs, the defendant may undertake to take a licence under that design.

---

57   See Ch 4 under 'Licences of right'.
58   Copyright, Designs and Patents Act 1988, s 237.
59   Copyright, Designs and Patents Act 1988, s 237(3), (4).
60   See Ch 4 under 'Licences of right' and Ch 5 under 'Copyright licensing schemes and licensing bodies'.
61   Copyright, Designs and Patents 1988, s 238, as amended by the Competition Act 1998 (Competition Commission) Transitional, Consequential and Supplemental Provisions Order 1999 (SI 1999/506), art 23.

If he or she does so, no injunction or order for delivery up can be awarded against him or her and the maximum damages for the past infringements during the period in which licences of right were available, will be twice the amount which would have been payable if a licence of right had been held throughout that period.[62]

Crown use of designs

There are detailed provisions concerning the rights of a government department, or a person authorised in writing by a government department, to do the following without the licence of the design right owner:

(a) do anything for the purpose of supplying articles for the services of the Crown; or

(b) dispose of articles no longer required for the services of the Crown.

The Crown user provisions in relation to design right are similar to those which apply in the case of patents.[63] The relevant provisions of the 1988 Act should be consulted if a question of Crown user in relation to design right arises.[64]

Other exceptions

The 1988 Act enables the Secretary of State to introduce further exceptions to design right by statutory instrument, if necessary in the context of international treaty or other arrangements.[65]

Terms of licences of right

The 1988 Act includes provisions which determine how applications may be made to the comptroller to settle the terms of a licence of right, and how such terms will be determined, as well as how appeals may be brought against the comptroller's decision. The powers of the comptroller in other proceedings are also described.[66]

Miscellaneous

Remedies for groundless threats of infringement proceedings

The provisions of the relevant section[67] are relatively clear:

---

62 Copyright, Designs and Patents Act 1988, s 239.
63 As to which see under 'Rights of the Crown to use Patented Inventions' above.
64 Copyright, Designs and Patents Act 1988, ss 240–244.
65 Copyright, Designs and Patents Act 1988, s 245.
66 Copyright, Designs and Patents Act 1988, ss 247–252.
67 Copyright, Designs and Patents Act 1988, s 253.

'(1) Where a person threatens another person with proceedings for infringement of design right, a person aggrieved by the threats may bring an action against him claiming–

(a)   a declaration to the effect that the threats are unjustifiable;

(b)   an injunction against the continuance of the threats;

(c)   damages in respect of any loss which he has sustained by the threats.

(2) If the plaintiff proves that the threats were made and that he is a person aggrieved by them, he is entitled to the relief claimed unless the defendant shows that the acts in respect of which proceedings were threatened did constitute, or if done would have constituted, an infringement of the design right concerned.

(3) Proceedings may not be brought under this section in respect of a threat to bring proceedings for an infringement alleged to consist of making or importing anything.

(4) Mere notification that a design is protected by design right does not constitute a threat of proceedings for the purposes of this section'.

Licensees of right not to claim connection with design right owner

The 1988 Act prohibits a licensee of right from applying to licensed goods, or using in an advertisement, a trade description that he or she is the licensee of the design right owner, without the consent of the design right owner.[68]

Articles in kit form

The 1988 Act confirms that the design right provisions of the Act apply:

'in relation to a kit, that is, a complete or substantially complete set of components intended to be assembled into an article, as they apply to the assembled article'.[69]

---

68   Copyright, Designs and Patents Act 1988, s 254.
69   Copyright, Designs and Patents Act 1988, s 260. This section also allows for the possibility that design right might subsist in the design of components of the kit as well as the complete article.

Semiconductor topographies: special provisions of design right law

Background to legislation

Since 1987, UK law has provided specific protection against the copying of semiconductor topographies. Originally, these laws were introduced in the UK by a statutory instrument[70] which was designed to implement an EC Directive.[71] These laws were free-standing, in the sense that they were not based on any traditional form of intellectual property protection. Part of the reason for the passing of the underlying EC Directive was to ensure reciprocal protection for EC citizens under US laws for protection of semiconductors; the US Government had threatened not to give reciprocal protection to EC citizens under such laws unless equivalent laws were introduced throughout the EC which also gave protection to US citizens. Thus the UK laws initially protected, inter alia, citizens of the EC and US.

When the 1988 Act introduced the new form of protection for designs known as design right,[72] the protection given to semiconductor topographies was re-formulated as a modified version of design right.[73] This change was largely a matter of re-categorising the topography right as a form of design right. The substance of the law protecting semiconductor topographies remained similar to what it had been previously, albeit extended to give reciprocal protection to a larger number of countries. There are, however, some significant differences between design right law for semiconductor topographies and design right law for other types of designs, which will be referred to below. For convenience, the design right applicable to semiconductor topographies will be referred to in the following paragraphs as 'topography right'.

The most recent amendments to the law in respect of semiconductor topographies have extended this reciprocal protection to a larger number of countries (most notably Japan, Australia and most non-EC western European countries), as the EC has negotiated reciprocal arrangements with other countries.[74]

The Regulations are notoriously difficult to understand, and their precise scope may not be known for many years, until case law has resolved a number of difficult issues of interpretation (even though they have now been in force for many years). The following paragraphs will attempt no more than a brief summary of what is covered by the Regulations and how the protection differs

---

70 Semiconductor Products (Protection of Topographies) Regulations 1987 (SI 1987/ 1497).
71 Directive 87/54/EEC ([1987] OJ L24/36).
72 With effect from 1 August 1989.
73 By the Design Right (Semiconductor Topographies) Regulations 1989 (SI 1989/1100).
74 See SI 1989/2147, SI 1990/1003, SI 1991/2237, SI 1992/400, SI 1993/2497 and SI 2006/1833.

from design right law for other types of design. They should therefore be read together with the above paragraphs which describe design right generally.

Scope of topography right

The topography right legislation[75] (which for convenience is referred to below as 'the Regulations') takes the form of a series of amendments to the design right provisions of the 1988 Act (ie Part III of that Act). The Regulations give protection under Part III of the Act to designs which are semiconductor topographies (as defined) and articles made to such designs which are semiconductor products (as defined), subject to the amendments set out in the Regulations. Thus in principle (subject to the amendments which will be summarised below), references in Part III of the 1988 Act to designs can be read as including semiconductor topographies, and references to articles in Part III can be read as including semiconductor products. These terms are defined[76] as follows:

- 'semiconductor product' means an article the purpose, or one of the purposes, of which is the performance of an electronic function and which consists of two or more layers, at least one of which is composed of semiconducting material and in or upon one or more of which is fixed a pattern appertaining to that or another function; and

- 'semiconductor topography' means a design within the meaning of s 213(2) of the Act which is a design of either of the following:

    (a) the pattern fixed, or intended to be fixed, in or upon–

        (i) a layer of semiconductor product, or

        (ii) a layer of material in the course of and for the purpose of the manufacture of a semiconductor product, or

    (b) the arrangement of the patterns fixed, or intended to be fixed, in or upon the layers of a semiconductor product in relation to one another.

The definition of semiconductor product makes clear that mainstream chips will be covered by the Regulations, as will many other types of product which contain a semiconducting layer and perform an electronic function. Products which are not covered by the Regulations (eg possibly some types of optoelectronic product) may be covered by the general law of design right.

Qualification for topography right

The Regulations amend the definitions of 'qualifying individual', 'qualifying person' and 'qualifying country' set out in Part III of the

---

75   Ie the Design Right (Semiconductor Topographies) Regulations 1989 (SI 1989/1100).
76   Design Right (Semiconductor Topographies) Regulations 1989 (SI 1989/1100), reg 2.

1988 Act.[77] In effect, the Regulations establish a separate set of rules on qualification for protection, reflecting the fact that there have been international negotiations on reciprocal protection for semiconductor topographies which have not been concerned with other types of design right. The number of countries which are recognised is increasing from year to year; at the date of writing, reciprocal protection is given to individuals and companies in other EC countries, the US, Japan, Australia and most other western European countries.

Ownership of topography right

The provisions governing ownership of designs of topographies are similar to those governing other types of designs.[78] The main differences are the addition of the phrase 'subject to any agreement in writing to the contrary'[79] in the provisions which provide for ownership by: (i) the commissioner of the design; or (ii) the designer's employer;[80] and amendment of the provisions which provide for ownership by the 'first marketer' to take account particularly of regulation 7 which is concerned with the marketing of articles in confidence (as to which see below).

Duration of topography right

The duration of topography right is ten years from the end of the year in which the semiconductor topography or articles made to it were first made available for sale or hire, but the right expires if such 'making available' does not take place within 15 years of the right coming into existence.[81] The provisions differ from those which apply to other types of design (and generally provide for a longer period of protection), but are no less complex. The modified wording reads as follows:

'216. The design right in a semiconductor topography expires–

(a)   ten years from the end of the calendar year in which the topography or articles made to the topography were first made available for sale or hire anywhere in the world by or with the licence of the design right owner, or

---

77   As to which see 'Qualification for design right' above.
78   As to which see 'Scope of topography right' above.
79   It seems surprising that this phrase was not included in the general design right provisions concerned with ownership, particularly as equivalent wording has for a long time been included in the closest equivalent copyright law provision – see Copyright, Designs and Patents Act 1988, s 11(2) which provides for ownership by the author's employer but states this to be 'subject to any agreement to the contrary' (note this wording does not require the agreement to be in writing, unlike the rules for semiconductor topographies).
80   See Design Right (Semiconductor Topographies) Regulations 1989 (SI 1989/1100), regs 5, 6.
81   Design Right (Semiconductor Topographies) Regulations 1989 (SI 1989/1100), reg 6.

    (b)   if neither the topography nor articles made to the topography are so made available within a period of fifteen years commencing with the earliest of the time when the topography was first recorded in a design document or the time when an article was made to the topography, at the end of that period.

The [above provisions are] ... subject to regulation 7 below. [see paragraph (f)]'.

Marketing of products subject to confidentiality obligations

Regulation 7 provides, in effect, that marketing which is done subject to confidentiality obligations will not be considered for the purposes of determining when articles were first marketed or made available for sale or hire. Thus it may be possible to extend the duration of the right by marketing products subject to confidentiality obligations. Regulation 7 should be treated with caution until its scope has been more clearly established by case law.

Infringement

The Regulations amend the provisions of design right law to make additional exceptions to the infringing acts in the case of semiconductor topographies. The exceptions are difficult to understand. The main ones[82] are:

- the reproduction of a design privately for non-commercial aims;

- the reproduction of a design for the purpose of analysing or evaluating the design or analysing, evaluating or teaching the concepts, processes, systems or techniques embodied in it.

The rules on secondary infringement are also amended to provide for an 'exhaustion of rights' where the article has been sold by or with the consent of the right-holder in the EC.[83]

There is also a kind of reverse engineering exception[84] which is expressed as follows:

    'It is not an infringement of design right in a semiconductor topography to–

    (a)   create another original semiconductor topography as a result of an analysis or evaluation of the first topography or of the concepts, processes, systems or techniques embodied in it, or

    (b)   reproduce that other topography'.

---

82   Design Right (Semiconductor Topographies) Regulations 1989 (SI 1989/1100), reg 8, substituting a new s 226(1A), Copyright, Designs and Patents Act 1988.

83   Design Right (Semiconductor Topographies) Regulations 1989 (SI 1989/1100), reg 8, amending s 227 of the Act.

84   Design Right (Semiconductor Topographies) Regulations 1989 (SI 1989/1100), reg 8(4).

Licences of right

The licence of right provisions which apply to other types of design right in the last five years of the right[85] do *not* apply to semiconductor topographies.[86]

Transitional provisions

The Regulations amend the complex transitional provisions set out in Schedule 1 to the 1988 Act in respect of any continuing copyright protection[87] for designs produced prior to commencement of the Regulations (ie 31 July 1989).

Dealing with topography right

The rules governing dealing in topography right are identical to those for other types of design in which design right subsists.[88]

REGISTERED DESIGNS

Introduction

Background

Compared with patents, relatively few registrations of designs under the Registered Designs Act 1949 (in this section referred to as 'the 1949 Act') have been made over the years. The reasons for this may be partly historical: until the law was changed by the 1988 Act, the maximum duration of registered designs was 15 years (now 25 years).[89] Another reason may have been lack of uniformity in protection of designs throughout the EU, which has now been addressed with a Directive[90] aiming to harmonise the law among member states and a Regulation to provide a community-wide registered and unregistered design.[91]

85　Copyright, Designs and Patents Act 1988, s 237.
86　Design Right (Semiconductor Topographies) Regulations 1989 (SI 1989/1100), reg 9.
87　Although it is doubtful whether, in most cases, there would have been any copyright protection for topographies.
88　As to which see 'Provisions of design right law of direct relevance to commercial transactions' above.
89　Five years initially, and renewal for further periods of five years up to a maximum of twenty-five years.
90　Directive 98/71/EC ([1998] OJ L289/28) on the legal protection of Designs ('Design Directive'), implemented in the UK by the Registered Designs Regulations 2001 (SI 2001/3949), as from 9 December 2001.
91　Council Regulation (EC) 6/2002 ([2002] OJ L3/1) on Community designs ('Design Regulation').

Historically, copyright protection was available for some industrial designs, and was the preferred route for protection in many cases. The main alternative to registration of designs under the new law is the unregistered design right (in the UK only), which lasts for between ten and fifteen years, or the unregistered Community design right (across the whole EU), which lasts for three years.

Considerable amendment of the 1949 Act has taken place, principally in 1989 by the 1988 Act, in 2001 following implementation of the Design Directive[92] and most recently, as far as this book is concerned, in 2006.[93]

The 1949 Act provides a form of monopoly protection to the owner of a registered design for a period of up to 25 years.[94] To be registrable, a design must, among other things, be new and have individual character, and applies to the appearance of the whole or a part of a product (whether an industrial item or individual, handicraft item). A product can include packaging, get-up, graphics symbols (including computer desktop icons), and typographic typefaces. The design itself is protected, and need not be associated with some physical item,[95] although not if dictated solely by a product's technical function. Computer programs are specifically excluded as being protected by

92 Implemented to harmonise the protection offer to designs (which are protected by registration); implemented in the UK by the Registered Designs Regulations 2001 (SI 2001/3949). This led to a number of amendments as to what constitutes the definition of a design, including expanding the definition so that it covers non-aesthetic products as well as component products. Other changes included expanding the list of infringing and permitted acts, a revised concept of novelty as well as a new concept of 'individual character in making an application.

93 These changes followed the introduction of the Design Regulation (which appears to have led to a substantial drop in applications for registered designs) and Directive 2004/48/EC ([2004] OJ L157/32; [2004] OJ L195/16) on the enforcement of intellectual property rights, implemented in the UK by the Regulatory Reform (Registered Designs) Order 2006 (SI 2006/1974) and the Intellectual Property (Enforcement, etc) Regulations 2006 (SI 2006/1028). The changes aimed to reduce the complexity of making an application for a registered design, including simplifying the criteria for protection, allowing one application to cover more than one design, making it easier to restore a registered design if the renewal fee is not paid and allowing an applicant to delay publication and registration for a period of up to 12 months. The other changes included setting out more modern provisions relating to the nature of a registered design (as personal property) and the transmission of registered design.

94 The text that follows in this section deals only with the Act as amended by the Directive. The 1949 Act, as amended by the Copyright, Designs and Patents Act 1988 is still of relevance to those applications for a registered design made up to 8 December 2001.

95 Guidance issued by the UK Intellectual Property Office provides as follows:
'(1) It will be the design which is protected, not an article bearing a design. Currently [under the Act before the implementation of the Directive] a plate bearing a floral pattern would be protected, and if at a later date that floral pattern were applied to table linen or curtains, a new registration would be required. Under the new regime [following implementation of the Directive] it is the floral pattern itself which is protected, irrespective of the product to which it is applied. Even graphic (computer desktop icons) will now be registrable'. (*Protecting your Designs – the Law is Changing*, available at http://www.patent.gov.uk/about/ippd/issues/faq.htm).

a registered design, but elements of what appear on a computer screen may be protectable, such as computer desktop icons.

In view of the emphasis in the 1949 Act on the appearance aspects of designs, it is at least arguable that the registration of a design does not protect technology as such, but may overlap with copyright protection and unregistered design right.

Provisions of registered design law which are of direct relevance to commercial transactions

The Act until 2006 contained few references to commercial transactions in registered designs.[96] This historically may be related to the fact that the 1949 Act originates from the late 1940s, much earlier than any of the other current versions of intellectual property legislation. As noted above, the 1949 Act is now extensively amended, but its basic structure remains unchanged. Although now containing more provisions concerning commercial transactions, they are still 'light' compared to the provisions found in the Patents Act 1977.[97]

Registered designs as personal property

A registered design (and an application for a registered design) is personal property.[98]

Transmission of registered designs

A registered design (or an application for a registered design) may be assigned (or vest by assent or by mortgage). However such an assignment or assent will not be effective unless it is in writing and is signed by or on behalf of the assignor (or the personal representative).[99]

---

96   Before the amendment by the Directive, the Registered Designs Act 1949 provided that a person could apply to the registrar for the grant of a compulsory licence in respect of a registered design (Registered Designs Act 1949, s 10, before amendment). This has now been removed by Registered Designs Regulations 2001 (SI 2001/3949), reg 6(1).

97   For example, the Registered Designs Act 1949 has nothing to say about sub-licences or the right of co-owners, although by implication, rather than explicit provision, it appears that a registered design can be owned by co-proprietors and in shares (although not stated as whether as tenants in common or joint tenants): see Registered Designs Act 1949, s 19(1).

98   Registered Designs Act 1949, s 15A, inserted by the Intellectual Property (Enforcement, etc) Regulations 2006 (SI 2006/1028) from 1 October 2006.

99   Registered Designs Act 1949, ss 15B(3), (5), as inserted by the Intellectual Property (Enforcement, etc) Regulations 2006 (SI 2006/1028) from 1 October 2006. Where the assignor is a body corporate, the requirement for signing is satisfied by the application of the corporate seal of the body corporate: Registered Designs Act 1949, s 15(4), as inserted by the Intellectual Property (Enforcement, etc) Regulations 2006 (SI 2006/1028) from 1 October 2006.

Licences

A licence may be granted under a registered design.[100] However there is no specific mention of whether:

- a licence can be granted where there is an application for a registered design; or
- a sub-licence can be granted.[101]

Despite these omissions, it seems likely that similar rules apply to commercial transactions in registered designs as apply to transactions in other types of UK intellectual property, but are not stated explicitly in the 1949 Act.

The other main provisions of the Act which are likely to affect commercial transactions, and which are discussed further below, are:

- the provision dealing with first ownership of registered designs – note that the commissioner of a design is the first owner (or, to use the language of the 1949 Act, 'proprietor'), but only if the design is commissioned 'for money or money's worth' (these last words do not appear in the equivalent provisions relating to unregistered design right);
- transactions in registered designs must normally be registered;
- registered designs continue for an initial five-year period, then may be renewed up to a maximum total period of 25 years;
- damages may not be awarded against an innocent infringer, as defined. There are advantages in this context in including a statement on articles produced according to a registered design, stating that the design is registered and the number of the registration;
- there are Crown user provisions.

Aspects of registered design law which may affect the parties to commercial transactions

Registrable designs

The Act describes the criteria that a design must satisfy in order to qualify for registration. The main criteria are as follows.

---

100 Registered Designs Act 1949, s 15(7), as inserted by the Intellectual Property (Enforcement, etc) Regulations 2006 (SI 2006/1028) from 1 October 2006.
101 Contrast the position with the Patents Act 1977, s 30(4).

Appearance

The Act permits registration of certain features of design relating to the appearance of a product or part of a product.

Definition of a 'design'

'Design' is defined in the 1949 Act[102] as follows:

> '(2) In this Act, "design" means the appearance of the whole or a part of a product resulting from the features, of, in particular, the lines, contours, colours, shape, texture or materials of the product or its ornamentation'.

A 'Product' (and the related definition of 'Complex Product') are defined in the 1949 Act[103] as follows:

> '(3) In this Act—
>
> "complex product" means a product which is composed of at least two replaceable components permitting disassembly and reassembly of the product; and
>
> "product" means any industrial or handicraft item other than a computer program; and in particular, includes packaging, get-up, graphic symbols, typographic type-faces and parts intended to be assembled into a complex product'.

Points to note from this definition

- a design can apply to an industrial item (ie where a number of items are to be produced) or a handicraft item (ie where individual, one-off, items are to be produced);

- a design can be related to a complete product or part of a product;[104]

---

102 Registered Designs Act 1949, s 1(2), as substituted by the Registered Design Regulations 2001 (SI 2001/3949).

103 Registered Designs Act 1949, s 1(3), as substituted by the Registered Design Regulations 2001 (SI 2001/3949).

104 In the UK Intellectual Property Office document *The Registered Designs Regulations 2001: The Effect of the Amendments to the Registered Designs Act 1949* guidance is given on the meaning of this: 'As indicated by the European Commission in an Explanatory Memorandum accompanying their 14 March 1996 proposal for a Directive, "part" in this context means an individual feature which may be an integral piece of a product, as distinct from a "component part", which is an item which, although intended as a constituent of a larger product which can be removed or replaced within that product, is treated as a separate product in its own right. Consequently it will remain the case that a registration may, for example, protect specifically the design of the head of a toothbrush even though that head may be integral with the handle'.

- the design can be the product or the ornamentation of that product;

- protection is provided to the design itself, and will extend to any product in which the design is incorporated;[105]

- the design need not relate to one particular product or item, but to different products.[106]

Novelty and individual character

A design may be protected by a right in a registered design to the extent that the design is new and has individual character.[107]

Novelty

A design is to be considered new if no identical design (or no design whose features differ only in immaterial details) has been made available to the public before the relevant date.[108]

Individual character

A design has individual character if the overall impression it produces on the informed user is different to the overall impression produced on that user by another design made available to the public before the relevant

---

105 In the UK Intellectual Property Office document *The Registered Designs Regulations 2001: The Effect of the Amendments to the Registered Designs Act 1949* guidance is given on the meaning of this: 'It is a design itself which may be registered, not features of a design as applied to a specified article or set of articles. The protection will extend to any product in which the design is incorporated. In many cases the design will be the product itself'.

106 In the UK Intellectual Property Office document *The Registered Designs Regulations 2001: The Effect of the Amendments to the Registered Designs Act 1949* guidance is given on the meaning of this: 'However some designs, for example some forms of ornamentation, will be applicable to many different types of product. Furthermore some products are specifically intended to look like a different type of product (eg novelty goods or models, eg of vehicles). In these cases the protection should now extend to any product which incorporates that design'.

107 Registered Designs Act 1949, s 1B(1), as substituted by Registered Design Regulations 2001 (SI 2001/3949), reg 2.

108 Registered Designs Act 1949, s 1B(2), as substituted by Registered Design Regulations 2001 (SI 2001/3949), reg 2. The 'relevant date' being the date on which the application for the registration was made or is being treated as having been made by other sections of the Act: s 1B(7), as substituted by reg 2 of the Registered Design Regulations 2001.

date.[109] In determining the extent to which a design has individual character, the degree of freedom of the author in creating the design shall be taken into consideration.[110]

Making available to the public before the relevant date

A design is considered to be prior art if it has been made available to the public before the relevant date[111] and:

- if the design has been published, exhibited, used in trade or otherwise disclosed before the relevant date (whether following registration or otherwise) to the public;[112] or

- if such disclosure does not fall within five exceptions.[113]

The exceptions are set out in the 1949 Act[114] as follows:

---

109 Section 1B(3) as substituted by the Registered Design Regulations 2001 (SI 2001/3949), reg 2. 'Informed user' is not defined in the Directive or the Act. In the UK Intellectual Property Office document *The Registered Designs Regulations 2001: The Effect of the Amendments to the Registered Designs Act 1949* guidance is given (at para 18, p 9) on the meaning of 'informed user', quoting part of an Explanatory Memorandum by the European Commission: '18. The term "informed user" is not defined in the Act or the Directive, but an indication of the Commission's intention can be seen from the Explanatory Memorandum on their original proposal for a regulation, which stated that: "The person on whom an overall impression of dissimilarity must be made is an 'informed user'. This may be, but is not necessarily, the end consumer who may be totally unaware of the appearance of a product, for example if it is the internal part of a machine or a mechanical device replaced in the course of a repair. In such cases, the 'informed user' is the person replacing the part. A certain level of knowledge or design awareness is presupposed depending on the character of the design. But the term 'informed user' should indicate also that the similarity is not to be assessed at the level of 'design experts'".'
(See also n 133 below regarding the meaning of 'informed user'.)

110 Registered Designs Act 1949, s 1B(4) as substituted by the Registered Design Regulations 2001 (SI 2001/3949). The UK Intellectual Property Office document *The Registered Designs Regulations 2001: The Effect of the Amendments to the Registered Designs Act 1949* reproduces (at para 20, p 9) part of a commentary by the European Commission on (at the time) the equivalent wording to Registered Designs Act 1949, s 1C(4), in the draft Community Design Regulation: 'Highly functional designs where the designer must respect given parameters are likely to be more similar than designs in respect of which the designer enjoys total freedom. Therefore, paragraph 2 also establishes the principle that the freedom of the designer must be taken into consideration when the similarity between an earlier and a later design is being assessed'.

111 For the meaning of 'relevant date', see n 107.

112 Registered Designs Act 1949, s 1B(5), as substituted by the Registered Design Regulations 2001 (SI 2001/3949). For the meaning of 'relevant date', see n 107.

113 Registered Designs Act 1949, s 1B(5)(b), as substituted by the Registered Design Regulations 2001 (SI 2001/3949).

114 Registered Designs Act 1949, s 1B(6), as substituted by the Registered Design Regulations 2001 (SI 2001/3949). For the meaning of 'relevant date', see n 107.

'(6) A disclosure falls within the subsection:–

(a) it could not reasonably have become known before the relevant date in the normal course of business to persons carrying on business in the European Economic Area and specialising in the sector concerned;[115]

(b) it was made to a person other than the designer, or any successor in title of his, under conditions of confidentiality (whether express or implied);

(c) it was made by the designer, or any successor in title of his, during the period of 12 months immediately preceding the relevant date;

(d) it was made by a person other than the designer, or any successor in title of his, during the period of 12 months immediately preceding the relevant date in consequence of information provided or other action taken by the designer or any successor in title of his; or

(e) it was made during the period of 12 months immediately preceding the relevant date as a consequence of an abuse in relation to the designer or any successor in title of his'.

These exceptions provide a 'safeguard clause' which allows for prior art which could not have been reasonably known to persons in the normal course of their business in the specialised area covered by the design, within the

---

115 The equivalent provision in the Design Regulation has been recently considered in a Court of Appeal case, *Green Lane Products Ltd v PMS International Group Ltd and others* [2008] EWCA Civ 358, [2008] All ER (D) 313 (Apr), particularly the words 'sector concerned' (the wording in the Design Regulation is 'the circles specialised in the sector concerned operating within the Community' (Art 7)) and was held to mean 'the sector of the alleged prior art'. The following words from the judgment of the High Court in this case were upheld: '1. "The sector concerned" within the meaning of Article 7 of the Regulation is the sector that consists of or includes the sector of the alleged prior art. 2. "The circles specialised in the sector concerned, operating within the Community" within the meaning of Article 7 of the Regulation are capable of consisting of all individuals who conduct trade in relation to products in the sector concerned, including those who design, make, advertise, market, distribute and sell such products in the course of trade in the Community'. Although this is a judgement concerning the Design Regulation and not concerning the Registered Designs Act 1949, as the wording between the two are for all purposes to be taken as identical, if this matter was to arise in the UK, it can be reasonably argued that a similar view would be taken as in this case. See also the judgments of *Procter & Gamble Co v Reckitt Benckiser (UK) Ltd* [2007] EWCA Civ 936, [2008] FSR 208, [2007] All ER (D) 133 (Oct) and *Woodhouse UK plc v Architectural Lighting Systems* [2006] RPC 1 (a case heard in the Patents County Court).

territory of the European Economic Area[116] and allowing a grace period for the designer and others to disclose the design for a period of 12 months be the relevant date without harming the right to make an application for registration as a registered design, as well as for disclosures of designs made in confidence. The equivalent provision for patents is much stricter, with no equivalent provision to a 'safeguard clause', and the grace period being restricted to six months.[117]

Grounds for refusal of registration

The 1949 Act sets out the grounds on which a design will not be protected by registration under the Act:

- where the appearance of a product is solely dictated by the product's technic al function;[118]

- where the features of appearance of a product which must necessarily be reproduced in their exact form and dimensions so as to permit the product in which the design is incorporated or to which it is applied to

116 In the UK Intellectual Property Office document *The Registered Designs Regulations 2001, The Effect of the Amendments to the Registered Designs Act 1949* guidance is given on the meaning of this exception, at para 23, p 10:
      '23. The rider of "could not reasonably have become known" is not intended to break up designs into different industrial sectors – since the design is protected and not the product, this would not make sense for designs (e.g. ornamentation designs) which can be used on a wide variety of products. The intention can be seen in the Commission's Explanatory Memorandum on their second proposal for the Design Directive, which explained that:
      "The Article 6 has further been amended in accordance with the wishes of the European Parliament and the Economic and Social Committee through the introduction of what is commonly known as the 'safeguard clause'. Its aim is to protect the design industry from claims that a design right is not valid because there was an earlier design in use somewhere in the world where the European industry could not possibly have been aware of it. The intention of this provision is to avoid the situation where design rights can be invalidated by infringers claiming that antecedents can be found in remote places or museums"'.
117 Patents Act 1977, s 2.
118 Registered Designs Act 1949, s 1C, as substituted by Registered Design Regulations 2001 (SI 2001/3949), reg 2.

be mechanically connected to, or placed in, around or against, another product so that either product performs its function;[119]

- where it is contrary to public policy or to accepted principles of morality.[120]

Ownership of designs

The first owner of a registered design may be the author of the design (the 'original proprietor')[121], the commissioner of the design, or the employer of the author. The position is similar to that for design right, with some important exceptions, referred to below.

Author as owner

The author of a design is defined as 'the person who creates it' or, in the case of a computer-generated design which has no human author, the 'person by whom the arrangements necessary for the creation of the design are made'.[122]

Unless the design was created in the course of the author's employment or pursuant to a commission, the author is the first owner of the property in the design.[123]

---

119 Registered Designs Act 1949, s 1C(2), as substituted by Registered Design Regulations 2001 (SI 2001/3949), reg 2. The 'must fit' exception. But does not include a design serving the purpose of allowing multiple assembly or connection of mutually interchangeable products within a modular system, which can be protected as a registered design (Registered Designs Act 1949, s 1C(3), as substituted by the Registered Design Regulations 2001 (SI 2001/3949). In the UK Intellectual Property Office document *The Registered Designs Regulations 2001: The Effect of the Amendments to the Registered Designs Act 1949* guidance is given (at para 33, p 11) on the meaning of the type of items which might be covered by s 1C(3) as including interlocking seating systems or shelving arrangements which can be built up to any size. In addition, Recitals 14 and 15 of the Design Directive provide help in understanding the reasoning for the inclusion of s 1(3):

'(14) Whereas technological innovation should not be hampered by granting design protection to features dictated solely by a technical function; whereas it is understood that this does not entail that a design must have an aesthetic quality; whereas, likewise, the interoperability of products of different makes should not be hindered by extending protection to the design of mechanical fittings; whereas features of a design which are excluded from protection for these reasons should not be taken into consideration for the purpose of assessing whether other features of the design fulfil the requirements for protection;

(15) Whereas the mechanical fittings of modular products may nevertheless constitute an important element of the innovative characteristics of modular products and present a major marketing asset and therefore should be eligible for protection'.

120 Registered Designs Act 1949, s 1D, as substituted by Registered Design Regulations 2001 (SI 2001/3949), reg 2.

121 Registered Designs Act 1949, s 2(1), as amended by Copyright, Designs and Patents Act 1988, s 267.

122 Registered Designs Act 1949, ss 2(3), (4), as amended above.

123 Registered Designs Act 1949, s 2(1), as amended above.

Commissioner of design as owner

'If one person (the commissioner) asks another to create a design for money or money's worth, then the first person shall be treated as the original proprietor of the design.[124]

This provision is similar to a provision concerning ownership of design right.[125] In the case of designs protected under the 1949 Act, the commissioner does not own the property in the design unless the commission is 'for money or money's worth'. By contrast, the commissioner of a copyright work, eg a computer program, does not own the copyright unless this is provided for by contract, ie there is no mention of money. Thus, different rules apply in the case of copyright, design right and registrable designs.

Employer of author as owner

Where a design is created by an employee in the course of his or her employment, and it is not owned by a commissioner, the employer is the first owner of the property in the design.[126]

Subsequent owners and formalities of transfer

The 1949 Act recognises the possibility of a design being assigned or otherwise transferred to another person.[127]

It now requires an assignment to be in writing[128] as well as the assignee registering the assignment[129] in a prescribed form. It is the registration of the assignment that gives rise to the ownership right, rather than the assignment itself, unlike the position in the case of patents.[130]

---

124 Registered Designs Act 1949, s 2(1)(A), as amended by Copyright, Designs and Patents Act 1988, s 267.
125 Copyright, Designs and Patents Act 1988, s 215(2).
126 Registered Designs Act 1949, s 2(2), as amended by the Copyright, Designs and Patents Act 1988, s 267. However, it is important that the formalities are properly complied with as to the original proprietor: see *Woodhouse UK plc v Architectural Lighting Systems* [2006] RPC 1 (a decision of the Patents County Court), where the commissioner of a design did not register the design under the Registered Designs Act 1949 (but the design was registered by one of the companies commissioned to make the design, the application being made by someone who is not the proprietor).
127 Registered Designs Act 1949, s 2, as amended by Registered Design Regulations 2001 (SI 2001/3949), reg 9(2).
128 Registered Designs Act 1949, s 15B.
129 Registered Designs Act 1949, s 19(1).
130 See Registered Designs Act 1949, ss 7, 7A (s 7 substituted, and s 7A inserted, by the Registered Design Regulations 2001 (SI 2001/3949). Also see s 19(5), and, compared with Patents Act 1977, s 33. Sections 7 and 7A describe the rights given by registration as such, while s 19(5) indicates that a document (eg an assignment) will not be admitted in evidence in court unless (with some exceptions) an entry is made in the registrar of that document. But Patents Act 1977, s 33 sets out the benefits of registration, but does not make registration compulsory.

Applications for registration or cancellation of registration

The Registered Designs Act 1949 outlines the proceedings for registration of a design.[131] The Secretary of State may supplement these provisions with more detailed rules.[132] Once a design is registered, the proprietor or any other person interested may apply to the registrar to cancel the registration.[133]

Exclusive rights given by registration

The registration of a design gives the registered proprietor the exclusive right to use the design and any design which does not produce on the informed user[134] a different overall impression.[135] This right is subject to any limitation

---

131 Registered Designs Act 1949, ss 3, 3A, 3B, 3C, 3D; s 3 as substituted, and ss 3A, 3B, 3C, 3D as inserted, by the Registered Design Regulations 2001 (SI 2001/3949) and further amended by the Regulatory Reform (Registered Designs) Order 2006 (SI 2006/1974). The principal amendment is to allow several designs to be included in one application for a design.

132 Registered Designs Act 1949, ss 36, amended by the Copyright, Designs and Patents Act 1988 and Registered Design Regulations 2001 (SI 2001/3949). There are new rules governing the processing of applications for a registered design: Registered Designs Rules 2006 (SI 2006/1975). A summary of the changes the rules made can be found on the UK Intellectual Property Office website, at http://www.ipo.gov.uk/pro-types/pro-design/d-law/d-dpn/d-dpn-506.htm.

133 Registered Designs Act 1949, ss 11, 11ZA, 11ZB, 11ZC, 11ZD, 11ZE, 11ZF; s 11 substituted by, and ss 11ZA, 11ZB, 11ZC, 11ZD, 11ZE, 11ZF inserted by, the Registered Design Regulations 2001 (SI 2001/3949), and as amended by the Regulatory Reform (Registered Designs) Order 2006 (SI 2006/1974) and the Designs (International Registrations Designating the European Community) Regulations 2007 (SI 2007/3378).

134 The Registered Designs Act 1949 does not provide a definition or explanation of the meaning of 'informed user' (but see the view of the UK Intellectual Property Office at n 108 above). However, the section in which this phrase is used was introduced to implement the provisions of the Design Directive. In *Rolawn Ltd and another v Turfmech Machinery Ltd* [2008] EWHC 989 (Pat), [2008] All ER (D) 77 (May) the meaning of the informed use was analysed, partly on the basis of Recital 13 from the Design Directive:
   'Whereas the assessment as to whether a design has individual character should be based on whether the overall impression produced on an informed user viewing the design clearly differs from that produced on him by the existing design corpus, taking into consideration the nature of the product to which the design is applied or in which it is incorporated, and in particular the industrial sector to which it belongs and the degree of freedom of the designer in developing the design.'
   And specifically in relation to the informed user the following is quoted from a case heard in Austria: 'The "informed user" will, in the view of the Appeals Court, have more extensive knowledge than an "average consumer in possession of average information, awareness and understanding" ... in particular he will be open to design issues and will be fairly familiar with them ...' (see footnote 110 in this document for a discussion on 'informed user').

135 Registered Designs Act 1949, s 7(1), as substituted by the Registered Design Regulations 2001 (SI 2001/3949). In determining whether a design produces a different overall impression on the informed user, the degree of freedom of the author in creating his design shall be taken into consideration (Registered Designs Act 1949, s 7(3), as substituted by the Registered Design Regulations 2001 (SI 2001/3949)).

attaching to the registration in question (such as any partial disclaimer or a declaration of partial invalidity made by a court or the registrar).[136]

The 'use of a design' is further defined by the Act as to include a reference to:

'(a) the making, offering, putting on the market, importing, exporting or using of a product in which the design is incorporated or to which it is applied; or

(b) stocking such a product for those purposes'.[137]

Infringement

A registered design is infringed by a person who, without the permission of the registered proprietor, does anything which is the proprietor's exclusive right.[138]

The 1949 Act lists a range of activities which are not considered to be infringements of a registered design and include[139] (other than with the consent of the registered proprietor):

- an act which is done privately and for purposes which are not commercial;

- an act which is done for experimental purposes;

- an act of reproduction for teaching purposes or for the purpose of making citations provided that the act for reproduction is compatible with fair trade practice and does not unduly prejudice the normal exploitation of the design, and mention has to be made of the source;

- the use of equipment on ships or aircraft which are registered in another country but which are temporarily in the UK;

- the importation into the UK of spare parts or accessories for the purpose of repairing such ships or aircraft; or

- the carrying out of repairs on such ships or aircraft.

---

136 Including any partial disclaimer or any declaration by the registrar or a court of partial invalidity: Registered Designs Act 1949, s 7, as substituted by the Registered Design Regulations 2001 (SI 2001/3949).
137 Registered Designs Act 1949, s 7(1), as substituted by the Registered Design Regulations 2001 (SI 2001/3949).
138 Registered Designs Act, s 7A(1), as inserted by the Registered Design Regulations 2001 (SI 2001/3949).
139 Registered Designs Act 1949, ss 7A(2), (3), as inserted by the Registered Design Regulations 2001 (SI 2001/3949).

Exhaustion of rights

Once a product which has a design protected by registration (or a registered design applied to it) and which is put on the market within the European Economic Area by the registered proprietor (or with his or her consent), then the registered design is not infringed by any acts in relation to it.[140]

'Must-match' spare parts

A further exception is provided for a right in a registered design of a component part which may be used for the purpose of the repair of a complex product so as to restore its original appearance is not infringed by the use for that purpose of any design protected by the registration.[141]

Duration of rights

Registered designs continue, in the first instance, for five years from the date of registration.[142] They may be renewed for further periods of five years, up to a maximum total period of 25 years.[143] There are detailed provisions dealing with the position where renewal fees are not paid.[144]

Crown user provisions

The Act includes Crown user provisions which are similar (but not identical) to those for patents.[145]

---

140 Registered Designs Act 1949, s 7A(4), as inserted by the Registered Design Regulations 2001 (SI 2001/3949).
141 Registered Designs Act 1949, s 7A(5), as inserted by the Registered Design Regulations 2001 (SI 2001/3949). In the UK Intellectual Property Office document *The Registered Designs Regulations 2001: The Effect of the Amendments to the Registered Designs Act 1949*, para 53, p 14, the meaning of 'use' is related to Registered Designs Act 1949, s 7(2), and 'consequently includes the full range of actions which would otherwise be an infringement, including making, importing, stocking product for the design itself' (Registered Designs Act 1949, s 7(2)); see 'Exclusive rights given by registration' above.
142 Registered Designs Act 1949, s 8(1).
143 Registered Designs Act 1949, s 8(2).
144 Registered Designs Act 1949, ss 8(4), 8A, 8B, as amended by the Registered Design Regulations 2001 (SI 2001/3949) and the Regulatory Reform (Registered Designs) Order 2006 (SI 2006/1974).
145 Registered Designs Act 1949, s 12.

Register of designs

The Act includes provisions relating to the maintenance of the register of designs, including provisions concerning the public right of access to the register and the status of entries on the register.[146]

Obligation on transferee or licensee to register transaction

The Act requires the transferee or licensee of a registered design to apply to the registrar for registration of his or her title, or notice of his or her interest, on the register.[147]

Transferor may register

The obligation upon the transferee to register the transaction does not prevent the transferor from doing so.[148]

Duties of the registrar

The Act sets out the obligations of the registrar to register transactions notified to him or her.[149] The registrar may not register any interest in a registered design in which a national unregistered design right also subsists unless he or she is satisfied that the holder of the interest is also entitled to a corresponding right in the design right.[150]

Deemed assignment of design right

Where the registered design and national unregistered design right are owned by the same person, an assignment of the registered design is deemed to be also an assignment of the design right 'unless a contrary intention appears'.[151]

Consequences of failure to register

There are no direct penalties for failure to register a transaction. However, failure to register a document such as an assignment or licence in respect of a design may result in one's rights being unenforceable. A document in respect of which no entry has been made on the register shall not be admitted in any

---

146 Registered Designs Act 1949, s 17, as amended by the Youth Justice and Criminal Evidence Act 1999 and the Criminal Justice Act 2003.
147 Registered Designs Act 1949, s 19(1).
148 Registered Designs Act 1949, s 19(2).
149 Registered Designs Act 1949, s 19(3); Registered Design Regulations 2001 (SI 2001/3949).
150 Registered Designs Act 1949, s 19(3A), as amended by the Registered Design Regulations 2001 (SI 2001/3949).
151 Registered Designs Act 1949, s 19(3B), as amended by the Registered Design Regulations 2001 (SI 2001/3949).

court as evidence of the title of any person to a registered design or share of a registered design unless the court otherwise directs.[152] It is therefore very important to register transactions involving registered designs.

Rectification of the register

Applications may be made to the court to rectify the register, ie change the details contained in the register in respect of a design, including the name of the proprietor.[153]

Miscellaneous provisions

Groundless threats of infringement proceedings

As in the case of patents, there is a civil wrong of making groundless threats of infringement proceedings.[154]

Criminal offences

Breach of secrecy orders for defence purposes

The Act includes provisions under which the registrar may make certain orders that information concerning a design shall be kept secret 'for the defence of the realm'.[155] Failure to comply with such an order is a criminal offence.[156] The provisions may be compared with the equivalent provisions in respect of patents.[157]

Falsification of the register

An offence is committed where a person:

> '... makes or causes to be made a false entry in the register of designs, or a writing falsely purporting to be a copy of an entry in that register,

---

152 Registered Designs Act 1949, s 19(5).
153 Registered Designs Act 1949, s 20, as amended by the Registered Design Regulations 2001 (SI 2001/3949) and the Regulatory Reform (Registered Designs) Order 2006 (SI 2006/1974).
154 Registered Designs Act 1949, s 26. For a description of the similar provisions applicable to patents, see Ch 4 under 'Proceedings for infringement'.
155 Registered Designs Act 1949, s 5, as amended by Copyright, Designs and Patents Act 1988, s 273, and Registered Design Regulations 2001 (SI 2001/3949), reg 9(2) and Sch 2. Whilst the equivalent provisions in respect of patents may be sensible, it is difficult to imagine that the country's security interests would normally be harmed by the disclosure of a registered design.
156 Registered Designs Act 1949, s 33.
157 See Ch 4.

or produces or tenders or causes to be produced or tendered in evidence any such writing, knowing the entry to be false ...'.[158]

False representations that a design is registered

An offence is also committed[159] where a person:

'(1) ... falsely represents that a design applied to, or incorporated in, any product sold by him is registered ... and for the purposes of this provision a person who sells a product having stamped, engraved or impressed thereon or otherwise applied thereto the word "registered", or any other word expressing or implying that the design applied to, or incorporated in, the product is registered, shall be deemed to represent that the design applied to, or incorporated in, the product is registered ...

(2) ... after the right in a registered design has expired, marks any product to which the design has been applied or in which it has been incorporated with the word "registered", or any word or words implying that there is a subsisting right in the design under this Act, or causes any such product to be so marked ...'.

Liability of directors, officers etc

The 1949 Act includes provisions[160] which make a 'director, manager, secretary or other similar officer' of an organisation criminally liable for offences committed under the Act by the organisation, in certain limited circumstances.

COMMUNITY DESIGN

General

In 2001 the EU introduced Europe-wide protection for designs[161] (in this section referred to as the 'Design Regulation'). In summary, the Design

---

158 Registered Designs Act 1949, s 34. These provisions are similar to the equivalent provisions in respect of patents; see Ch 4 under 'Falsification of register'.
159 Registered Designs Act 1949, s 35, as amended by Registered Design Regulations 2001 (SI 2001/3949), reg 9(1) and Sch 1, paras 10(1)–(3). For the equivalent provisions in respect of patents, see Ch 4 under 'Unauthorised claim that product is patented'.
160 Registered Designs Act 1949, s 35A, as inserted by the Copyright, Designs and Patents Act 1988. The provisions are identical to those which apply in the case of patents and are discussed in Ch 4 under 'Personal liability of officers, managers for offences committed by company' in Ch 4.
161 Council Regulation (EC) 6/2002 ([2002] OJ L3/1) on Community designs ('Design Regulation').

Regulation provides for the following:

- The introduction of two new types of design protection directly applicable in each member state:[162]

    — a Registered Community Design ('RCD');[163] and

    — an Unregistered Community Design ('UCD');[164]

    (together, 'Community Design(s)').

- These Community Designs are to be effective throughout the EU.[165]

- The RCD is administered by the Office for Harmonisation in the Internal Market (OHIM) and the UK Intellectual Property Office.[166]

- The criteria for protection are expressed in similar terms as in the Design Directive and as implemented in the Registered Designs Act 1949.[167] These criteria are the same whether the design is a RCD or UCD.

- The length of protection provided to each type of Community Design is different:

    — for the RCD, five years initially from the date of filing an application, and then renewal for further five-year periods up to a maximum of 25 years from the date of filing;[168] and

---

162 Design Regulation, Art 1(2).
163 Available from 1 April 2003.
164 Available from 6 March 2002.
165 Design Regulation, Art 1(1). Design Regulation, Art 1(3) provides that a Community Design shall 'have a unitary character. It shall have equal effect throughout the Community. It shall not be registered, transferred or surrendered or be the subject of a decision declaring it invalid, nor shall its use be prohibited, save in respect of the whole Community. This principle and its implications shall apply unless otherwise provided in this Regulation'.
166 Design Regulation, Art 12. It will now be known as the Office for Harmonisation in the Internal Market (Trade Marks and Designs).
167 Most of the elements concerning registered designs are set out under 'Registrable designs' above. In Recital 3 of the Design Regulation it is noted that there are substantially different member state design laws and the Design Directive is to remedy this situation; Recital 3 states that the 'substantive provisions of this Regulation on design should be aligned with the respective provisions in the [Directive]'.
   Compare Arts 3–10 of the Design Regulation to Arts 1–8 of the Design Directive to see the similarity of the wording. However, not all of the provisions between the Design Regulation and the Design Directive are expressed in the same way; for example, concerning ownership, under the Design Directive a commissioner of a design 'for money or money's worth' can register a design whereas under the Design Regulation such a provision is not incorporated (Art 14).
168 Design Regulation, Art 12.

— for the UCD, 3 years from the date on which the design was made available to the public within the EC.[169] Protection for the UCD only commences from the date on which the design was made available to the public within the EC.

● The main rights of the Community Design are the exclusive right to use it and to prevent any third party, not having consent from the proprietor, from using it.[170] The proprietor of a RCD or UCD receives the same level of protection and rights except that for a UCD[171] the rights are only infringed where there is copying of the protected design.[172]

● The 'fair dealing' provisions are almost identical for the Design Regulation as for the Design Directive.[173] There is one substantial difference between the Design Regulation and the Design Directive: in regard to a RCD, a third party, if he or she can establish that before the date an application for a RCD is filed (or priority is claimed), that he or she has in good faith commenced use within the EU (or has made serious and effective preparations to that end) of a design which is included in the scope of protection of a registered Community Design which has not been copied from the latter, he or she shall have a right of prior use.[174] This right shall entitle the third party to exploit the design but not to grant a licence to another person to exploit the design.[175]

● The Design Regulation sets out detailed provisions for the application for, and practice and procedure concerning, a RCD.[176]

---

169 Design Regulation, Art 11(1); 'made available to the public within the European Community' means that the design 'has been published, exhibited, used in trade or otherwise disclosed in such a way that, in the normal course of business, these events could reasonably have become known to the circles specialised in the sector concerned, operating within the Community. The design shall not, however, be deemed to have been made available to the public for the sole reason that it has been disclosed to a third person under explicit or implicit conditions of confidentiality'.

    The creation of two types of Community Designs is prompted by the need to serve all sections of the industry in the Community. One should be to provide short-term protection for designs where the design would be incorporated in products which have a short market life. Therefore, to require registration would be too great a burden for the owner/designer of the design: Recitals 15–17 of the Regulation.

170 Design Regulation, Arts 19(1), (2). The right is spelt in the same terms as the Design Directive and as implemented in Registered Designs Act 1949, s 7.

171 Design Regulation, Art 19(1). See 'Community, Design, General' above for a description of some of the rights conferred by the Directive and the Regulation.

172 Design Regulation, Art 19(2). The Article goes further by stating what is not deemed to be copying: 'The contested use shall not be deemed to result from copying the protected design if its results fixed from an independent work of creation by a designer who may be reasonably thought not to be familiar with the design made available to the public by the holder'.

173 See 'Infringement' above for an outline of them as they have been implemented in the Registered Designs Act 1949 by the Design Directive.

174 Design Regulation, Art 22.

175 Design Regulation, Art 22(2), (3).

176 Design Regulation, Arts 35–78.

- The Community Design shall vest in the designer, or the designer's employer, where the designer created the design in the execution of his or her duties or following the instructions given by the employer.[177]

- Provides sanctions in actions for infringements[178] which can be enforced in the UK courts.[179]

Provisions of a Community Design which are of direct relevance to commercial transactions

Nature of Community Design

Subject to certain articles,[180] a Community Design is 'an object of property' which shall be dealt with in its entirety, and for the whole area of the Community, as a national design right of the member state in which the holder has domicile or is established.[181] As the 1949 Act has been amended so that a registered design is now clearly stated to be personal property, and this amendment and others were made to bring this Act in line with the Design Directive, it can be reasonably assumed that a Community Design is also personal property.[182]

Licensing

A Community Design can be licensed, exclusively or non-exclusively, for the whole or part of the Community.[183] A holder:

- can invoke the rights provided by the Community Design against a licensee who contravenes any provision in his or her licensing contract

---

177 Design Regulation, Art 14(1), (3). It should be noted that unlike UK Design Right and UK Registered Design, title does not automatically vest in the commissioner.

178 Design Regulation, Art 89(1)(a)–(c), which provides for (i) injunctions, (ii) an order to seize infringing products, and (iii) an order to seize materials and implements which are primarily for use in the manufacture of infringing goods. Also available are damages, accounts, orders for delivery up and disposal of infringing articles etc; see Community Design Regulations 2005 (SI 2005/2339), as amended.

179 The High Court and the Patents County Court have been designated as 'Community Design courts' which can deal with Community Design infringements; see Community Designs (Designation of Community Design Courts) Regulations 2005 (SI 2005/696).

180 For example, the article concerning licensing; see further below.

181 Design Regulation, Art 27(1).

182 See 'Registered designs as personal property' above.

183 Design Regulation, Art 32. But other than this provision, and certain other provisions concerning the transfer of a RCD (its being given as security, being levied in execution and a Community Design being involved in insolvency proceedings), a Community Design can only be dealt with in its entirety and for the whole area of the Community (Community Design Regulation, Art 27).

with regard to its duration, the form in which the design may be used, the range of products for which the licence is granted and the quality of products manufactured by the licensee;[184]

- has to give his or her consent if a licensee wishes to bring proceedings for infringement of a Community Design.[185]

Transfer

The Design Regulation does not have any specific provisions regarding the transfer (eg assignment) of a Community Design other than that to acknowledge that once a transfer has taken place regarding a RCD, then it is required to be entered into the register of registered Community Designs.[186]

Actions against a licensee

A proprietor of a Community Design can invoke the rights conferred by a Community Design against a licensee who contravenes any provision in his or her licensing contract in regard to:

- its duration;
- the form in which the design may be used;
- the range of products for which the licence is granted; and
- the quality of products manufactured.

A licensee requires the consent of the rights holder to bring infringement proceedings unless the licensee has an exclusive licence, in which case he or she can bring infringement proceedings, if after notice the rights holder refuses to do so.[187]

Applications

Applications for RCDs could be made from 1 January 2003, but the first RCD was not available until 1 April 2003. Applications can be made direct to the OHM or the UK Intellectual Property Office, who will forward an application on to the OHM (for a fee).

---

184 This provision is without prejudice to any legal proceedings which would be based on the law of contract.
185 Again this provision is without prejudice to any licensing contract. An exclusive licensee can bring an action, but only if the holder does not do so within the relevant time limits.
186 Community Design Regulation, Art 28.
187 Community Design Regulation, Art 32.

COMPARISON OF FEATURES OF THE VARIOUS FORMS OF DESIGN PROTECTION

Protection	Design Right	Registered Design	Registered Community Design	Unregistered Community Design
Length of protection	15 years from end of calendar year in which the design was first recorded or an article was first made (whichever comes first); or 10 years from the end of the calendar year if the designs are made available for sale or hire within 5 years	5 years from the date of registration, renewable in 5-year periods, up to a total of 25 years	5 years from the date of filing of an application, renewable in 5-year periods, up to a total of 25 years	3 years from the date on which the design was first made available to the public
First owner	Designer, unless created in course of employment or a commission, then employer or commissioner	The author of the design, unless created in the course of employment or a commission, then the employer or commissioner	The designer, unless created in the course of employment, then the employer	Same as for RCD
Meaning of design	The design of any aspect of the shape or configuration (whether internal or external) of the whole or part of an article.	The appearance of the whole or a part of a product resulting from the features of, in particular, the lines, contours, colours, shape, texture or materials of the product or its ornamentation	Same as for Registered Design	Same as for Registered Design
Criteria for protection	That the design be original	That the design: (a) is new (b) has individual character (c) is not dictated solely by its technical function (d) is not contrary to public policy or morality	Same as for Registered Design	Same as for Registered Design
Exclusion from protection	That the design: (a) is common-place in the design field in question (b) is a method or principle of construction (c) contains features of shape or configuration of an article which allow it to be connected to/placed in/around/	(a) features of appearance of a product which are solely dictated by the product's technical function (b) features of appearance which must necessarily be reproduced in their exact form and dimension in order to permit the	Same as for Registered Design	Same as for Registered Design

Protection	Design Right	Registered Design	Registered Community Design	Unregistered Community Design
Exclusion from protection – *contd*	against another article to allow either to function ('must-fit') or is dependent on appearance of another article of which it is intended to form an integral part ('must-match') (d) is surface decoration	designed product to be mechanically connected to, or placed in, around or against another product so that either product may perform its function (c) a design which is contrary to public policy or to accepted principles of morality		
Formalities	None – but design needs to be recorded in a design document for protection to arise	Registration	Registration	None – but protection will arise on making design available to the public
Rights	The owner of the design right has the exclusive right to reproduce (ie copy) the design: (a) by making articles to that design, or (b) by making a design document recording the design for the purpose of enabling such articles to be made	Exclusive right of the registered proprietor to use the design and any design which does not produce on the informed user a different overall impression	Exclusive right for the registered holder of a RCD to use it and to prevent any third party not having his or her consent from using it. The use shall cover: (a) making (b) offering (c) putting on the market (d) importing (e) exporting, or (f) using of a product in which the design is incorporated or to which it is applied, or stocking such a product for those purposes	Same as for RCD, but: (a) only if the contested use results from copying the protected design; And (b) the contested use is deemed not to result from copying the protected design if it results from an independent work of creation by a designer who may be reasonably thought is not familiar with the design made available to the public
Extent of protection	UK	UK	EU	EU
Date of implement-ation	1 January 1989	1950 (9 December 2001, for applications following implementation of the Design Directive)	6 March 2002 (but the date on which applications can be made is still awaited)	6 March 2002

CHAPTER 8

The Law of Confidence and Technology Transfer

INTRODUCTION

The area of law that protects confidential information, sometimes known as the law of confidence, is central to any discussion of the laws relating to the exploitation or transfer of technology. The law of confidence is relevant in a number of different commercial situations. The most commonly encountered may be the following:

Confidential information as a tradable asset: it is common for confidential 'know-how'[1] to be licensed in a similar way to patents and other types of intellectual property. The most obvious official recognition of this practice (if official recognition is needed) is in an EC block exemption regulation, the Technology Transfer Regulation.[2]

Strictly, know-how is not a type of intellectual property, in the way that patents and copyright are intellectual property.[3] Yet the law of confidence gives sufficient protection to know-how for commercial organisations to regard it as a valuable asset and suitable for licensing on commercial terms. The nature of this protection is in some respects quite different from the protection given by a patent, copyright, design right, registered design or registered trade mark. Perhaps, this difference is best characterised in this way: that the protection will generally only exist where the know-how is and remains secret, while the protection for the other forms of intellectual property will exist, regardless of whether it is secret or not.

Preventing the misuse or disclosure of business secrets: the owner or licensee of business secrets (which may include manufacturing know-how) may need to take action to prevent misuse or disclosure of those secrets by others. As is discussed below, it is not always necessary for a confidentiality agreement to be in place for obligations of confidence to arise.

A common example of this is where an employee leaves a company and joins a rival company, with the employee taking information learnt whilst

---

1   The meaning of the term 'know-how' is discussed under 'meanings of the term "know-how"' below.

2   Commission Regulation (EC) 772/2004 ([2004] OJ L123/11) on the application of Article 81(3) of the Treaty to categories of technology transfer agreements, which is discussed in Ch 13.

3   Lawyers have discussed the nature of confidential information, and in particular whether it is protected under the law of property, the law of equity, trusts, contract etc. See eg *Gurry on Breach of Confidence: The Protection of Confidential Information* (1st edn, Oxford, 1984 (2nd edn expected December 2010)). The best view seems to be that confidential information is not property (a proposition which is still supported by recent case law: see eg *Douglas v Hello! Ltd (No 3)* [2005] EWCA Civ 595; [2006] QB 125 at paras 119, 126–127). Commonly, confidentiality obligations arise under the law of contract, as in the case of written confidentiality agreements. But in the absence of a formal agreement, a person may still owe legally enforceable duties of confidence under the law of equity. An important feature of the law of equity is that its remedies are generally in the discretion of the court. There are also various 'rules' of equity which may be invoked by the court and adversely affect a party. Eg, 'he who comes to equity must come with clean hands'. It is generally recommendable that parties decide the extent of their duties to one another for themselves, by contractual terms.

working for the former employer. In certain circumstances it will be possible to obtain an injunction to prevent the employee or his or her new employer from misusing such information and/or obtain damages in respect of any misuse.[4] The law in this area affects a broader category of information than just technical know-how.

Some of the leading court decisions in this field are not concerned with technical information, but concern more general business secrets, including sales and customer information.[5] There have been a number of cases directly concerned with technology-related businesses.[6] The law of confidence is often extremely important to prevent misuse of know-how, whether by employees or others who are considered to have a legal duty not to use or disclose that know-how.

This chapter briefly summarises the law of confidence as it applies to technical information and technology transfer. In technology-based industries, confidentiality obligations are often derived from (sometimes detailed) written confidentiality agreements. Chapter 2 includes a discussion of the commercial and practice issues that commonly arise in confidentiality agreements.

PROTECTION OF TECHNICAL INFORMATION

Patents

It is useful to compare the protection afforded to confidential information with that provided by patents. In the area of technical ideas, confidence cannot really play a long-term role unless the information can be put to commercial use without at the same time becoming public.[7] For example, a mechanical device will almost always reveal its workings to experts once it is marketed, whilst a process of manufacture may not be similarly detectable. In the short

---

4   See most recently an application of this point in *Crowson Fabrics Ltd v Rider* [2007] EWHC 2942 (Ch), [2008] FSR 17. This case is considered further below, see n 10.

5   *Faccenda Chicken v Fowler* [1987] Ch 117, [1986] FSR 291 (CA) (a leading case which concerned the misuse of customer lists by a frozen chicken salesman). This case has been applied in a number of decisions, such as *Wallace Bogan & Company v Cove* [1997] IRLR 453 (involving solicitors canvassing clients of their ex-employer); *AT Poeton (Gloucester Plating) Ltd v Michael Ikem Horton* [2001] FSR 169 (involving a sales engineer employee of the claimant setting up in competition to the claimant and allegedly misusing confidential information concerning the technical process used by the claimant in its business, as well as customer lists).

6   Eg *Searle v Celltech* [1982] FSR 92.

7   In one case it was suggested that a duty of confidence will not be implied (ie where the parties have not expressly agreed that there is a duty of confidence) where it would be reasonable to expect that the subject matter of what is claimed to be protected, an implied duty of confidence could be legally protected in another way (such as making an application for a patent, registered design or registered trade mark) (*Carflow Products (UK) Ltd v Linwood Securities (Birmingham) Ltd* [1996] FSR 424).

term, until a patent application can be filed, obligations of confidence prevent the possibility that revealing details of the invention will destroy its novelty.

In practice, patents are often secured for a central invention, while information relating to the process of bringing it into commercial production is tied up as secret 'know-how' by means of confidentiality undertakings. Thus an invention, and the product developed from that invention, may be protected by both patents and know-how.

Copyright

In the field of computer software, copyright and know-how may be more relevant than patents. For example:

- if software is commercialised by making only the object code available, but the underlying source code is kept secret, there may be a competitive value in the secret know-how comprised in the source code; or

- a programmer may make use of or have knowledge of computer and programming techniques and methodologies which are not known either generally or specifically to other programmers. Such techniques and methodologies, although perhaps not reflected in the final code, will have a commercial value if known as they could speed up the work on a computer program or produce better code.

The 'protection' given by any know-how will only last as long as it remains secret, ie for as long as competitors of the owner or licensee of the know-how do not have access to it.[8]

Employees

Problems can often arise when managers or other employees try to take the know-how off to a rival organisation – the know-how in question may not amount to more than an employee is entitled to treat as his or her general skill and knowledge,[9] and breach of confidence proceedings would be hard to maintain against such employees. Generally, courts are reluctant to burden ex-employees with obligations that will prevent them using their general knowledge and skill to their best advantage.

---

8   Or perhaps decompile it to obtain interoperability information (where a person is lawfully entitled to do this) (see Ch 5). Of course software can be decompiled by persons not entitled to do so, and in such information they could access any confidential information contained in the decompiled code, but they would be infringing the copyright of the owner of the software.

9   *Yates Circuit Foil v Electrofoils* [1976] FSR 345.

For example, in a case concerning the taking of a range of information by employees prior to their leaving their employment, what could or could not be used by ex-employees was examined by the court.[10] The employees set up in competition to the employer. It was held that the employees had a duty of fidelity and a fiduciary duty to their employer. The information copied was confidential while the employees where in employment with the employer. However, once the employment was ended any of the information which had been copied and which was in fact not confidential would not be subject, as far as the employees were concerned, to obligations of confidentiality, *as long as such information could be used in a legitimate way*:

> 'It is well established that if an ex-employee deliberately copies or even deliberately memorises information for use post termination that is illegitimate and the ex-employees can be restrained from so acting. It is no defence to a claim for breach of an implied obligation of good faith and fidelity and breach of confidence for an employee who has taken a customer list to say that some or all of the information on the list is publicly available ...'[11]

Consequently, if information is copied which is in the public domain it can be used by the employees so long as the information is obtainable in the public domain.[12] Although an ex employee, using the expertise and skills he or she earned during his or her employment, and using his or her memory and skills of recall, cannot be prevented from using that information he or she recalls but which is confidential.[13] The judge distinguished between information which was only confidential as opposed to information which was confidential and constituted a trade secret. If it amounted to a trade secret it appears it would be protected. However the judge did not further elaborate on the precise meaning of a trade secret.[14] Of particular interest is that the employers also claimed that there was a breach of their database right in the copying of some of their material. This part of the claim was upheld by the judge.

---

10   *Crowson Fabrics Ltd v Rider* [2007] EWHC 2942 (Ch), [2008] FSR 17. The case was a trial only concerning the issue of liability. The information taken included customer details, sales figures for the employer's customers, profit margins for its customers and details of goods ordered by the employer's customers.
11   *Crowson Fabrics* (see n 10) at para 107.
12   *Crowson Fabrics* (see n 10) at para 99, quoting in support of this proposition a passage from the judgment of Lord Denning in *Seager v Copydex Ltd (No 1)* [1967] RPC 349 at p 368.
13   *Crowson Fabrics* (see n 10) at para 101, and citing *Faccenda Chicken Ltd v Fowler* [1987] Ch 117, [1986] FSR 291 (CA).
14   *Crowson Fabrics* (see n 10) at para 101.

THE LAW OF CONFIDENCE AND ITS APPLICATION TO TECHNICAL INFORMATION

Meanings of the term 'know-how'

The term 'know-how' has different meanings in different situations. The term has been defined for specific purposes in UK tax legislation[15] and in EC Regulations.[16] In certain other legislation the term is not used at all – instead expressions such as 'technical information'[17] or trade secret (used in US legislation)[18] are used.

In some employment law cases, the term 'know-how' has been used in a very specific sense to refer to the general skill and knowledge of an employee, which may have been learnt whilst an employee of X, but which he or she may be entitled to use after leaving the employment of X. In this sense, the term is contrasted with 'trade secrets' which the employee may not use after ceasing to be an employee of X. In one case the Court of Appeal held:

> 'It appears to me that the problem is one of definition: what are trade secrets, and how do they differ (if at all) from confidential information? [the advocate for the defendant] suggested that a trade secret is information which, if disclosed to a competitor, would be liable to cause real (or significant) harm to the owner of the secret. I would add first, that it must be information used in a trade or business, and secondly that the owner must limit the dissemination of it or at least not encourage or permit widespread publication.

> That is my preferred view of the meaning of trade secret in this context.

---

15 For example, Income and Corporation Taxes Act 1988, s 533(7) which defines know-how as 'any industrial information and techniques likely to assist in the manufacture or processing of goods or materials ...'. Tax legislation also uses the term 'show-how', which has a slightly different meaning.

16 For example Commission Regulation (EC) 772/2004 ([2004] OJ L123/11) on the application of Article 81(3) of the Treaty to categories of technology transfer agreements, which defines know-how as 'a package of non-patented practical information, resulting from experience and testing, which is: (a) secret, that is to say, not generally known or easily accessible; (b) substantial, that is to say, significant and useful for the production of the contract products; and (c) identified, that is to say, described in a sufficiently comprehensive manner so as to make it possible to verify that it fulfils the criteria of secrecy and substantiality'.

17 For example, see Unfair Contract Terms Act 1977, Sch 1, which states that certain sections of that Act do not apply to: 'any contract so far as it relates to the creation or transfer of a right or interest in any patent ... technical or commercial information ...'.

18 The Uniform Trade Secrets Act (adopted by many states in the US) defines a 'Trade Secret' as 'information including a formula, pattern, compilation, program device, method, technique, or process, that: (i) derives independent economic value, actual or potential, from not being generally known to, and not being readily ascertainable by proper means by, other persons who can obtain economic value from its disclosure or use, and (ii) is the subject of efforts that are reasonable under the circumstances to maintain its secrecy'. This Act has not been adopted, it is believed, in New York but has been in California.

It can thus include not only secret formulae for the manufacture of products but also, in an appropriate case, the names of customers and the goods which they buy. But some may say that not all such information is a trade secret in ordinary parlance. If that view be adopted, the class of information which can justify a restriction is wider, and extends to some confidential information which would not ordinarily be called a trade secret.'[19]

It is understood that a similar distinction may be made under certain Federal or State laws in the US. In some cases, it appears that a distinction is also made between confidential information and trade secrets, the latter being the more important and 'proprietary' to the employer.

In the authors' experience, the distinctions between know-how, confidential information and trade secrets which have been made in some employment cases are not normally made by business people in licence and other commercial agreements involving technology; accordingly they should not normally be applied by a court in a dispute involving the interpretation of a technology-related commercial agreement.[20] The term 'confidential information' should be understood in a commercial context to mean any information which the law will protect under the law of confidence, as to which see below, whilst the term 'know-how' has various meanings, discussed in the following paragraphs. In the authors' experience the term 'trade secrets' is not commonly used in licence agreements made under English law.

Sometimes the term 'know-how' is used in technology-related agreements to refer to all technical information disclosed under the agreement. In licence agreements where both patents and know-how are licensed, the term is:

● used to mean technical information that the licensee is entitled to use but which is not within the claims of the licensed patents; or

● is applied only to *confidential* technical information, to which competitors do not have access; or

● is applied to both *confidential* and *non-confidential* technical information; or

● is used more broadly, and may include some non-technical information, eg customer lists, business methods or practises, financial projections, marketing and sales plans and data, pricing information and so on.

---

19 *Lansing Linde Ltd v Kerr* [1991] 1 All ER 418 at pp 425–426, approved in *FSS Travel and Leisure Systems v Johnson* [1998] IRLR 382 and applied in *Sectrack NV v Satamatics Ltd and another* [2007] EWHC 3003 (Comm), [2007] All ER (D) 312 (Dec). For another case which considers this distinction, see *Poly Lina Limited v Finch* [1995] FSR 751.

20 Unless of course the dispute involves the misuse of technology-type information by an (ex-) employee or perhaps a consultant.

In summary, although the precise meaning of the term know-how will vary from agreement to agreement, it is suggested that the most common meanings are as follows:

(a) technical information (as distinct from marketing or other commercial information); or

(b) confidential, technical information; or

(c) confidential, technical information relating to a manufacturing process.

Scope of the law of confidence

The are two main areas of English law that protect confidential information: the law of equity and the law of contract.[21] This may be contrasted with other countries; for example many states in the US have adopted the Uniform Trade Secrets Act,[22] whilst in Continental Europe there are unfair competition laws which may give an additional form of protection. By contrast, it is understood that some countries (eg in South East Asia) do not give any legal protection to confidential information, or only very limited protection. There is no international harmonisation of confidentiality laws in the way that there is, for example, to a greater or lesser extent, in the case of patents.

This section will focus on the protection given under the English law of equity.

As with the common law, the law (or rules) of equity have developed over centuries, mainly through court decisions. The remedies for breach of confidence form only a small part of such laws, which also cover many other areas. For example, when determining whether to order 'specific performance' of a contract, the court will apply equitable principles.

There is no single, reported case or other source that definitively states all aspects of the law of confidence. This may be contrasted with, for example, the law of patents or law of copyright. Although there have been many reported cases which have considered questions of patent or copyright law, the basic principles of current UK patent and copyright law are set out in one main source for each: the Patents Act 1977 and the Copyright, Designs and Patents Act 1988 respectively.

---

21 For completeness it should also be mentioned that an obligation of confidence can be protected in other ways: as a tort, bailment or by specific legislation.

22 As noted above (see n 20). New York, it is believed, continues, like England, with an entirely common law approach to confidence.

The remainder of this section provides a very brief summary of the law of confidence in its current state of development. The following paragraphs concentrate on issues that are likely to arise in relation to confidential information concerning technology. Most of this law is based on reported court decisions. For a fuller treatment of this subject, the reader is referred to the books cited in the bibliography at the end of this book.

Protection of know-how under the law of confidence

The extent of protection for know-how under the law of confidence will depend in part on the sense in which the term 'know-how' is used. In principle, technical information is as likely to qualify for protection under the law of confidence as any other type of information; the same rules normally apply whatever the subject matter of the information. In the absence of patents, copyright or other intellectual property, the law of confidence may give the only available means of protection to an item of know-how, under English law.

Circumstances in which a breach of confidence arises

In order to bring a successful action for breach of confidence, it is necessary, generally, to establish three things:[23]

(a)   that the information in question has the 'necessary quality of confidence';

(b)   that it was disclosed in circumstances which 'imported an obligation of confidence'; and

(c)   that the defendant made unauthorised use of the information to the detriment of the claimant.

The necessary quality of confidence

Information will not have the necessary quality of confidence if it is 'public property and public knowledge'. But it may be possible for a package of information to be confidential even if individual elements of the package are publicly known, for example if substantial work is needed to recreate the

---

23   See *Coco v Clark (AN) (Engineers) Limited* [1969] RPC 41 and subsequent cases. The three elements stated by Megarry J in this case were confirmed by Knox J in *De Maudsley v Palumbo* [1996] FSR 447 and were also considered in the case of *Mars UK Limited v Teknowledge Limited (No 1)* [2000] ECDR 99, and referred to in the recent cases of *Inline Logistics Ltd v UCI Logistics Ltd* [2002] RPC 611 and *Collag Corpn v Merck & Co Inc* [2003] FSR 16.

package.[24] It is important to note that information is not confidential if it is common knowledge either among the general public, or among that part of the general public interested in the field to which the information in question relates, for example researchers working in a particular area of science or engineering. The following, rather subjective test has been suggested in a case[25] to determine whether (in a business context) information has the necessary quality of confidence:

(a) the owner must believe that the release of the information would be advantageous to the rivals of the owner or injurious to him or her; and

(b) the owner must believe that the information is not in the public domain; and

(c) the owner's beliefs (in (a) and (b) above) must be reasonable; and

(d) the information must be judged in the light of the usage and practices of the particular trade or industry concerned.[26]

There have been many cases which have considered the necessary quality of confidence; it is difficult to draw brief conclusions from those cases, except that many types of information, including customer lists, names and addresses of employees, simple ideas and detailed technical data have all been held to have the necessary quality of confidence in particular situations. For a couple of instances where information relevant to technology transfer has been considered:

• in a recent case it was held that the core inventive concept (for a patentable invention) has the necessary quality of confidence where it was used by another person in making a patent application;[27]

• in another case[28] a technique for testing computer software was not protected as a trade secret (and therefore could be used by an ex-employee after termination of the ex-employee's employment). It could be readily reproduced by a skilled person using publicly available sources. But

---

24 See Lord Greene MR in *Saltman Engineering Co v Campbell Engineering Co Ltd* [1963] RPC 203, where it was held that a document may be confidential if it is the result of work done by its maker, even if the matters on which he or she worked were matters of public knowledge. See also *Ocular Sciences Ltd v Aspect Vision Care Ltd* [1997] RPC 289 where a list of publicly available design features relating to contact lenses was held not to be confidential, because the effort shown was that of simply packaging the features together. The judge found in this case that no relevant skills were employed.

25 In *Marshall (Thomas) (Exports) v Guinle* [1979] Ch 227, [1978] 3 All ER 193, [1978] 3 WLR 116, [1979] FSR 208, by Megarry V-C, which was referred to in *American Home Products Corporation v Novartis Pharmaceuticals (UK) Ltd (No 2)* [2001] EWCA Civ 165, [2001] FSR 784, [2001] All ER (D) 141 (Feb).

26 See *Ibcos Computers Ltd v Barclays Mercantile Highland Finance Ltd* [1994] FSR 275.

27 *Stanelco Fibre Optics Ltd's Application* [2004] EWHC 2263, [2005] RPC 15, [2004] All ER (D) 06 (Oct).

28 *Cantor Fitzgerald International v Tradition (UK) Ltd* [2000] RPC 95.

the use of the claimant's software source code by the defendants was considered to be a breach of obligation of confidentiality (even if the use was no more than to check that the defendants' computer program operated correctly).

In certain cases, the courts have not been prepared to treat information as confidential, if this is not in the public interest (eg if the information concerns criminal activity or other wrongdoing). Even though the obligation of confidence may be part of a contract of employment, it should be noted that there is no duty to keep a secret about the employer's wrongful or unlawful act.[29] Also, if the information comes within an exceptional category (eg information disclosed on discovery in litigation) the courts may not be prepared to treat such information as confidential.

Circumstances importing a duty of confidence

An obligation of confidence can arise for example by express agreement between persons (such as by contract), by implication, by the nature of the relationship between persons (such as between a lawyer and the lawyer's client, a doctor and the doctor's patient, an employer and an employee) and by statute. The following are some common ways in which a duty of confidence can arise or be implied and which are most likely to be encountered in commercial situations.

Marking a document or information as confidential

Whether a document or information is marked as 'confidential' (or similar) or not will in itself not make the document or information confidential. In one case a technical document was labelled as being 'confidential', but the court held that it was not in fact confidential, as it had been provided to many members of a trade association.[30] In another case,[31] operators of manufacturing processes were of the view that the processes that they used to manufacture a type of pesticide were confidential. They had procedures in place to keep the processes secret, which included imposing obligations of confidence on persons such as suppliers. The court held that all these efforts were not enough to make the processes confidential. The three points listed under 'Circumstances in which a breach of confidence arises' (at p 345 above) had to be established.

Agreement to keep information confidential

The cases which have come before the courts do not support a simple, general definition of when a duty of confidence is 'imported'. Where the defendant

---

29   *Initial Services v Putterill* [1968] 1 QB 396.
30   *Dalrymple's Application* [1957] RPC 449.
31   *Collag Corpn v Merck & Co Inc* [2003] FSR 16.

has agreed to keep the information confidential, he or she will normally have such a duty. In cases where the defendant has not given specific undertakings to keep the information in confidence, the courts have some discretion in determining whether the defendant is under a duty to keep the information confidential. In one case,[32] the test applied by the court was that if a reasonable person, standing in the shoes of the recipient of the information, would have realised that upon reasonable grounds the information was being given to him in confidence, then this should suffice to impose upon him the equitable obligation of confidence. Or put another way (in more simplistic terms), should the recipient have realised that the information was being disclosed to him in confidence? The duty of confidence may arise even where words such as 'keep this information confidential' are not used. For example, in one case a product was provided to the recipient subject to a condition that the recipient would not examine the mechanism. This was held to be sufficient to make information relating to the mechanism confidential.[33]

Manner in which information is acquired

Where confidential information is innocently acquired, as in the case of an overheard conversation or where it is seen on the premises of a company,[34] the acquirer may not be under a duty of confidence, even if he or she realises that the information he or she has heard or seen is meant to be confidential. If the acquirer acted in an underhand way the court may be more likely to find against him or her, as it did in a case involving illegal telephone tapping.[35] If the acquirer of the information acted with all propriety, he or she may well not have a duty of confidence, although much will depend on the circumstances of the case and the view taken by the court. In one case with rather unusual facts, a barrister intended to send papers containing confidential information to the solicitors instructing that barrister. The barrister's administrator made a mistake: the papers were sent to the opposing side's solicitors. It was held that those solicitors, even though they were an innocent acquirer of the confidential information, could be restrained from using it to the benefit of

---

32   *Coco v Clark (AN) (Engineers) Limited* [1969] RPC 41.
33   *Paul (KS) (Printing Instruments) Ltd v Southern Instruments (Communications) Ltd and EP Ellis* [1964] RPC 118.
34   See *Folding Attic Stairs Ltd v Loft Stairs Co Ltd* [2009] EWHC 1221 (Pat); [2009] FSR 24 at paras 81–83, where a visit by the Irish Minister of Trade and Tourism with a photographer was made without an obligation of confidence being imposed on them. Unsurprisingly the judge held they were under no obligation of confidence and were free to disclose whatever they saw. This case was not primarily about confidentiality but concerned patent infringement and whether there was prior disclosure of art.
35   See *Francome v Mirror Group Newspapers Ltd* [1984] 2 All ER 408 (CA; interlocutory) and the earlier *Malone v Commissioner of Metropolitan Police (No 2)* [1979] 2 All ER 620 (referred to in *Douglas v Hello! Ltd* [2001] FSR 732). *Francome v Mirror Group* was referred to in *Imutran Ltd v Uncaged Campaigns Ltd* [2002] FSR 20. The latter case involved the defendants receiving leaked documents from the claimant pharmaceutical drug company. The defendants published the documents on websites and provided them to various government and non-governmental organisations.

their client because they had become 'improperly implicated in the leakage of the information' contained in the papers that they had received.[36] That is they had taken overt acts in relation to the papers by taking copies of them.

Unsolicited information

It is unlikely that one person could oblige another to respect confidence by sending the other person unsolicited information in a letter or email marked 'Confidential' (ie an inventor sending unsolicited details of his or her invention to a company and asking the company to develop the invention into a commercial product). If this was the case, one organisation could send confidential information to another in order to put difficulties in the way of the latter using it, should it be discovered by them independently. The recipient of such unsolicited confidential information should, for the recipient's own protection, return the material at once (unless the supplier of the information is willing to sign a waiver disclaiming its rights in respect of confidentiality) making it clear that he or she regards himself or herself as being under no obligation.[37]

Information disclosed in the course of negotiations

In some cases, it has been held that information disclosed in the course of negotiations had been disclosed in confidence, even where no confidentiality undertaking was given. For example, it has been held that obligations of confidence arose in respect of details of an unpatented invention, where these details were disclosed in the course of negotiations concerning another, patented invention.[38] It would be unwise to assume that such obligations would be found to arise in all negotiations concerning inventions. It is suggested that this and other cases illustrate the point that, if a confidentiality agreement is not signed, it *may* still be possible to persuade a court to find an equitable duty of confidence in the particular circumstances of the negotiations. It is generally much, much safer, though, to enter into a written confidentiality agreement which identifies clearly the extent of any confidentiality obligations.

Information disclosed under a contract

Obligations of confidence may also be implied in relation to information disclosed under a contract. In one case,[39] an obligation of confidentiality was implied in relation to information disclosed by a contractor to a manufacturing

---

36 *English & American Insurance Co Ltd v Herbert Smith* [1988] FSR 232.
37 Sometimes commercial organisations who are in the habit of receiving information of this kind develop policies for dealing with such a situation, ie designating one role to deal with all correspondence of this nature and sending a standard letter back.
38 *Seager v Copydex Ltd* [1967] 1 WLR 923.
39 *Saltman Engineering Co Ltd and others v Campbell Engineering Co Ltd* (1948) 65 RPC 203, CA.

subcontractor. The information in question included drawings of tools for the manufacture of metal punches, which were provided by the contractor to enable the subcontractor to manufacture the tools for the contractor. The subcontractor used the drawings to manufacture tools which it sold to third parties. In that case the Court of Appeal observed that:

> 'if two parties make a contract, under which one of them obtains for the purpose of the contract, or in connection with it, some confidential matter, then, even though the contract is silent on the matter of confidence, the law will imply an obligation to treat such confidential matter in a confidential way. If a defendant is proved to have used confidential information, obtained directly or indirectly from a plaintiff, without the consent, express or implied, of the plaintiff, he will be guilty of an infringement of the plaintiff's rights'.

In another case[40] the question arose at a preliminary hearing as to whether a licensee was permitted to use confidential information disclosed to the licensee by the licensor for purposes other than the manufacture of licensed products. It was held, construing the agreement and applying general principles, that the licensee could be restrained from deriving any advantage from the information which it had received exclusively for the purposes of the agreement.

These cases may illustrate a wider principle, namely that information disclosed for a limited purpose may be subject to an implied obligation on the recipient to use the information only for that limited purpose, and not to disclose it to third parties or use it on the recipient's own account.

Use of the information outside limits of authorisation

Clearly, if no use is permitted, then all uses are unauthorised. Similarly, if only limited uses are permitted, as in the cases referred to in the previous paragraphs, then any use outside those limits is unauthorised.

The defendant's state of mind

It does not seem to matter that the defendant acts out of some misguided or well-meaning motive,[41] or does not appreciate the confidentiality of a document from which he or she takes the information,[42] or the defendant has forgotten the source of the information and thinks he or she has thought of it himself or herself. One case[43] involved subconscious copying of this last

40   *Torrington Manufacturing Company v Smith and Sons (England) Ltd* [1966] RPC 285.
41   *Nichrotherm v Percy* [1956] RPC 272.
42   *National Broach v Churchill Gear* [1965] RPC 61.
43   *Seager v Copydex (No 1)* [1967] 2 All ER 415.

kind: the defendant's employees were found to have worked out how to make a carpet grip incorporating a basic idea which they had forgotten being shown by the claimant.

Form in which the information is disclosed

For an obligation of confidentiality to arise it does not need to be in any special form. The obligation can arise in writing or orally; it can be expressly agreed or by implication. However disclosing the information in a particular form will by itself not make the information confidential. In one case, certain information was encrypted and provided in a coin receiving and changing mechanism. The defendant decrypted that information in order to determine how to recalibrate the devices. The claimants argued that the fact of encrypting the information made it confidential. The judge was not persuaded and considered the fact that information is encrypted can mean no more than that the encrypter wanted to stop others having access to the information. As to confidentiality, the judge held:

> '[A customer of the mechanism] is the intended recipient of the article containing the information ... There is nothing obviously confidential about the machine he gets. There is no marking 'confidential' and indeed there is not even any indication of encryption. By the time one gets to find out about the encryption it is, in my judgment, far too late to impose a duty of confidence.'

Who is bound by a duty of confidence, and to whom is the duty owed?

A discloses information to B

In a simple case where A (an inventor) discloses an invention in confidence to B (a manufacturing company), the position of A and B is clear: B owes a duty of confidence to A. Difficulties arise where other parties become involved, as in the situations considered below.

Third party proposes to disclose information

Where a third party, C learns of the invention and proposes to disclose it in a scientific paper and B brings proceedings against C for breach of confidence, difficult issues arise. First of all, in what circumstances did C learn of the invention? If it was disclosed to him or her in breach of confidence and C knew this, then it seems he or she will have a duty of confidence.[44] If C acquired the information innocently, ie he or she did not know the information was confidential, it is not certain whether he or she will have any duty of confidence. If C acquired the information innocently from someone who was

---

44   See eg *Albert v Strange* (1849) 1 Mac & G 25 and *Schering Chemicals v Falkman* [1981] 2 WLR 848.

bound by a duty of confidence, then it seems he or she may not be liable until he or she becomes aware that the information is confidential.[45]

The other main question is whether B has the right to sue C. In one case, the claimant produced a report for the Greek Government under a contract that required the claimant (but not the Greek Government) to keep the contents of the report confidential. A newspaper obtained a copy of the report from an unauthorised government source and proposed to publish an article based on the report. It was held that the claimant's claim against the editor of the newspaper must fail because the duty of confidence was owed to the Greek Government and not to the claimant.[46]

In this scenario, B may not have legal standing or the right to sue C, and A may need to be the claimant or co-claimant.

A assigns his or her rights in the invention to D

B proposes to publish. A possible scenario is that A assigns to D his or her rights in the invention, which are stated in the assignment to include his or her rights in respect of confidential information. B proposes to publish details of the invention and D brings proceedings against B to obtain an injunction. It would seem that D now 'owns' the confidential information and would have the legal standing or right to sue for breach of confidence.[47] If B's duty of confidence arose under a contract with A, there may be an argument that D is not a party to that contract and therefore has no right to sue. Even if this argument were technically correct in contract law, the parallel remedies under the law of equity would probably enable a court to find in D's favour. However, it may again be desirable to join A as co-claimant.

Consequences of breaching a duty of confidence

The enforcement of commercial confidentiality obligations

In order to obtain an injunction or damages for misuse of confidential information, it will generally be necessary for the claimant to show that he or she has suffered detriment from the breach of confidence. The remedies available where a breach of confidentiality obligations has been proved are:

---

45 See the judgment of Lord Denning in *Fraser v Evans* [1969] 1 QB 349.

46 See *Fraser v Evans* [1969] 1 QB 349, referred to in *Ashdown v Telegraph Group Ltd* [2002] RPC 235; the same result arose in *Broadmoor Special Hospital Authority v Robinson* [2000] QB 775 (although on very different facts).

47 There is case law which would appear to entitle the legitimate recipient of confidential information (under an assignment of intellectual property or the sale of the assets of a business) to sue for mis-use of the confidential information: *Morrison v Moat* (1851) 9 Hare 241; *Gilbert v Star Newspaper Co. Ltd* (1894) 11 TLR 4; *Douglas v Hello! Ltd (No. 3)* [2005] EWCA Civ 595; [2006] QB 125, para 129.

- a permanent injunction restraining further breaches; and/or

- damages based on the value of the confidential information; and/or

- an account of profits in respect of past or anticipated future breaches.

The court may also in certain cases order the recipient to destroy or return to the donor documents or other items in his or her possession containing or embodying the confidential information in question.

The remedy of an interlocutory (ie temporary) injunction to restrain the misuse or disclosure of confidential information pending a full trial on the merits is also available, subject to the principles laid down in one leading case.[48] Interlocutory decisions turn ultimately on the particular balance of convenience. In another leading case[49] no injunction was ordered, as the court was reluctant to destroy the tools in question. The confidential information was of no great value, and could have been easily recreated by an independent consultant. The defendants had also not behaved dishonestly. They were thus only ordered to pay damages, calculated on the basis of a royalty, for products already manufactured, and to be manufactured in the future, with the aid of confidential information.

In another case,[50] where an interlocutory injunction was felt inappropriate in the absence of a seriously arguable case, it was held that where a claimant made indiscriminate claims of confidence in relation to a wide range of information, without attempting to disentangle the obviously public domain material from the confidential, he or she should not be surprised if the court was wary of granting interlocutory relief.

The problem of remedies can become quite complex when dealing with the use of information as what has been described as a 'springboard' (see below), particularly where the body of information is partly public and partly private. In the leading case on what it was necessary to establish in order to bring a successful action for breach of confidence,[51] concern was expressed over the issue of the duty of the recipient in such a situation. An interlocutory injunction was granted, in large part because the court was satisfied that the defendant had made an offer to pay royalties at a reasonable rate into a suspense account pending outcome of the trial on the merits. In another case,[52] the information in question was valuable and there was also the added element of a serious breach of duty by the claimant's ex-managing director.

---

48 *American Cyanamid Co v Ethicon* [1975] AC 396.
49 *Saltman Engineering Co Ltd v Campbell Engineering Co Ltd.*
50 *CMI Centres for Medical Innovation GmbH v Phytopharm plc* [1999] FSR 235, referred to in the *Gadget Shop Ltd v The Bug.Com Ltd* [2001] FSR 383.
51 See *Coco v Clark (AN) (Engineers) Limited* [1969] RPC 41. See under 'Circumstances in which a breach of confidence arises' above.
52 *Cranleigh Precision Engineering v Bryant* [1966] RPC 81.

In this case, the court said that not to grant an injunction 'would involve putting a premium upon dishonesty by managing directors'.

It has also been noted[53] that the courts consider a wider range of factors in deciding whether to grant a final injunction in a breach of confidence case than in patent or copyright cases.

Where the misuse of the technical information is not accompanied by any independent development, so that in substance it amounts to a mere copying, the remedy will be a final injunction, to prevent the continued marketing of the 'copied' product, even though the confidential information in question has become common knowledge, whether or not because of the wrongful act of the defendant. Here the duty is 'no use at all', even if third parties are free to use the information.[54]

The springboard doctrine

The springboard doctrine affects the obligations of confidentiality covering technical information, particularly where a product to which that information relates has been put on the market. The springboard cases illustrate that it is a misuse of confidential technical information not only to use it to reproduce an existing product marketed by the donor of that confidential information but also to use such information as a springboard, that is 'as a starting point for a new design', even if 'in the end the design wholly or partially discards the information from which it was originally built up'.[55]

Where only part of the information is or remains confidential, that part of the information remains subject to obligations of confidentiality, and the fact that another part of the information has ceased to be is irrelevant. This can happen in a number of ways, for example the originator can disclose part of it in a patent specification, but still retain confidentiality in 'ancillary secrets',[56] or can publish part of the information in a manner making it common knowledge, for instance by producing a description in a product brochure.[57]

Where the technical information has been used as a springboard to develop a new product, or even to assist in the manufacture of an existing product, particularly where the whole body of information is partly public and partly private, the correct remedy is not an injunction but damages based upon the worth of the information used as a springboard. Here the duty is 'not to use

---

53   See *Cadbury Schweppes v FBI Foods* (1999) 83 CPR (3d) 289 (SC Canada), [2000] FSR 491.
54   See *Lancashire Fires Ltd v SA Lyons & Co Ltd* [1996] FSR 629; *Ocular Sciences v Aspect Vision Care* [1997] RPC 289. *Lancashire Fires Ltd v SA Lyons & Co Ltd* was also referred to in *Cantor Fitzgerald International v Tradition (UK) Ltd* [2000] RPC 95.
55   *Terrapin Ltd v Builders' Supply Co (Hayes) Ltd* [1967] RPC 375, referred to in *Sun Valley Foods Ltd v John Philip Vincent* [2000] FSR 825.
56   *O Mustad & Son v S Allcock & Co Ltd and Dosen* [1963] RPC 41, HL.
57   *Terrapin Ltd v Builders' Supply Co (Hayes) Ltd* [1967] RPC 375.

without paying', although a duty not to further disclose might in appropriate cases also be imposed by injunction.[58] Only the part of the confidential information relating to the product which, either at once or at some later date, becomes common knowledge as a result of the putting of the product on the market, will, at the time that it does become common knowledge, cease to be confidential. This is the basis for the judge's dicta in a case in which although:

> 'it might be possible for an expert ... to infer from the finished product the general nature of the processes used to produce it, this is a far cry from detailed knowledge of the processes such as would enable them to be replicated'.[59]

It is important to be able to ascertain the point in time at which information becomes common knowledge once a product is put on the market. At any rate initially, and perhaps after some lapse of time, if the product is not marketed very widely, then only the 'features' of the product which are ascertainable by visual inspection and the information about it published in product brochures, will become common knowledge once enough people have bought or seen the product or read the brochures.[60] The fact that more knowledge is potentially available to anyone who is prepared to take the time and effort to dismantle or analyse the product does not mean that this information is in fact common knowledge, unless and until either a large number of people actually carry out the process, or one person does so, and publishes the information so that it becomes common knowledge in some other way, such as an article in a learned journal.[61]

STRENGTHS AND WEAKNESSES OF THE LAW OF CONFIDENCE

This chapter has already referred to some of the strengths and weaknesses of this area of law as a means of protecting technology, whilst discussing other topics. In some industries (eg the pharmaceutical industry) there is more of a tendency to patent inventions, particularly in the case of new drugs whose chemical structure can be quickly determined by competitors once the drug reaches the market (if not earlier). In other industries (eg in some parts of the engineering industry), there is more of a tendency to rely on the protection given by keeping the technology secret, particularly if those secrets cannot be discovered by reverse engineering the product. In other

---

58   See *Lancashire Fires Ltd v SA Lyons & Co Ltd* [1996] FSR 629, *Ocular Sciences v Aspect Vision Care* [1997] RPC 289.

59   *Lancashire Fires Ltd v SA Lyons & Co Ltd.*

60   *Terrapin Ltd v Builders' Supply Co (Hayes) Ltd* [1967] RPC 375, *Seager v Copydex Ltd* [1967] 1 WLR 923.

61   *Yates Circuit Foil v Electrofoils Ltd* [1976] FSR 345.

industries, eg software, the restrictions on what can be patented may also influence companies in the direction of trade secret protection. The following is a summary of the main strengths and weaknesses (without reference to specific industries) as they appear to the author.

Strengths of the law of confidence

The main strengths of the law of confidence are:

- there is no need to register confidential information (unlike patents) or even put the information in writing (unlike copyright);

- as long as the information is kept confidential, rivals do not have access to it (unless they develop it independently), unlike patents which are published or copyright material once made available;

- the remedies available in a court are such that the court can show some flexibility to treat parties 'fairly' even in the absence of a contractual relationship (ie the court has an equitable, that is discretionary, jurisdiction);

- it can protect:

    — the applicant for a patent by allowing him or her to impose an obligation of confidence on those who are in a position to know, or who need to know, the details of the invention before a patent application has been filed. This is important because if the details of an invention are made public before the patent application is made, it could fail for lack of novelty. Patents Act 1977, s 2(4)(b) states that publication made in breach of confidence will not invalidate the patent application; or

    — the creator of a copyright work by allowing him or her to impose an obligation of confidence on those who know the details of (and in particular the ideas/principles contained in) the copyright work. Once the copyright work is made available (eg leaked or licensed) the ideas or principles contained in it cannot be protected;

- an idea for something yet to be elaborated may attract protection as confidential information where there is nothing that generates copyright.

Weaknesses of the law of confidence

The main weaknesses of the law of confidence are:

- once the information 'leaks out' and becomes public knowledge, further protection will not generally be available under the law of confidence (the main exception being where the 'springboard doctrine' applies – see above);

- there may be difficulties in identifying exactly what is confidential information – compare with patents where the claims of the patent are precisely defined;

- unlike patents or copyright, there is no monopoly over confidential information: others may develop the same information independently and then use or disclose it;

- once patented information is published, protection for the published information under the law of confidence is lost. Similarly, when a copyright work is made available, the ideas and principles contained in the work will no longer be protected, only in the way they are expressed;

- where there is a misuse of the confidential information of one person by another person, the first person:

  — has to act quickly (via the courts) to seek a remedy or else he or she will lose the right to seek a remedy in relation to it (generally not the case with patents or copyright material); and

  — is dependent on a judge agreeing with him or her that the confidential information is in fact confidential;

- even where information is clearly confidential and clearly has been misused, a court may still not stop the misuser using it or award the innocent party sufficient or any damages.[62]

---

62 Ie as the remedies available are discretionary. For example, in *Seager v Copydex (No 1)* [1967] 2 All ER 415 the court refused to grant an injunction, and assessed the loss of the claimant based on the value of the misused information, rather than assessing on the basis of the profits lost. There is also case law in which the assessment of damages has been on the basis of loss of profits (such as in *Dowson & Mason Ltd v Potter* [1986] 1 WLR 1419).

CHAPTER 9

Personal Property

INTRODUCTION

The application of personal property laws to intellectual property

The main forms of intellectual property – patents, designs and copyright – are part of that broad category of property under English law known as 'personal' property (such as goods, rights to sue) as distinct from 'real' property (ie land).

Except where intellectual property laws provide differently, the general law of personal property applies to patents, copyright, designs and the like. The most familiar example of this, for the purposes of this book, may be the provisions of ss 2–5 of the Law of Property (Miscellaneous Provisions)

Act 1994 ('the 1994 Act', in this chapter).[1] These sections imply certain covenants[2] into conveyances[3] of property that are expressed to be made by a person 'with full title guarantee' or 'with limited title guarantee'.

As will be discussed below, it is considered by many intellectual property lawyers that these implied covenants are applicable to assignments of intellectual property.[4] But if these provisions can apply to intellectual property transactions, are there also other provisions of property statutes – particularly the Law of Property Act 1925 ('the LPA', in this chapter) – and of property law generally, which affect such transactions?[5] In the authors' view there are several areas where this is so, including some that are rarely considered. It may be unwise to be too dogmatic – the application of traditional property laws to intellectual property transactions has not received much attention from the courts. Moreover, the LPA largely consolidated 19th century laws and it is unlikely that intellectual property was a significant consideration for the drafters of the LPA. This chapter considers some areas of traditional property law which, in the authors' view, may significantly affect agreements concerned with intellectual property (especially if those areas are not specifically addressed in an agreement).

Note that due to the frequency of references to gender in this chapter, the masculine is understood as including the feminine.

Bailment

The law of personal property may also be relevant to technology-related agreements where the technology is not protected by intellectual property. In the biotechnology field, agreements sometimes provide for the supply of materials such as cell lines, monoclonal antibodies or genetically modified organisms which are not protected or protectable by patents or other intellectual property rights. 'Exclusive licences' to use such materials are not uncommon; in the absence of intellectual property rights such exclusivity is often based on the assumption that the cell line or other property is unique,

---

1 Which replaced LPA, s 76.
2 A covenant is essentially a binding, contractual, promise or undertaking. Traditionally, a covenant was only used in 'real' property transactions, under deed. They are also commonly encountered in employment contracts (eg 'restrictive covenants'), although other terminology could just as easily be used to describe such binding promises.
3 The formal transference of ownership (or the document that transfers ownership) of property from one person to another. In intellectual property transactions 'assignment' is the word used rather than conveyance.
4 See under 'Implied covenants of title, freedom from encumbrances etc.' below.
5 An example of where intellectual property laws do provide differently is Patents Act 1977, s 30(6) which provides that an assignment of a patent must be in writing signed by the assignor (or mortgagor) to the transaction. By contrast, LPA, s 52 provides only that conveyances of *land* must be by deed; there is no requirement that a conveyance of personal property be by deed or in writing.

and cannot be obtained from any source other than the licensor. The licensee is, in effect, granted exclusive access to personal property.

The agreement may provide that the materials may only be used for limited purposes and must be returned when the agreement comes to an end. Such an agreement may give rise to a *bailment* of the materials, in which case the long-established common law of bailment will apply.[6]

This chapter will consider the main areas where personal property laws may affect technology-related agreements. It does not consider the law of property as it applies to land and buildings as such. But the law of property will be considered to the extent that it is the same for both real and personal property. As noted above, much of it is found in the LPA or in the 1994 Act. Also dealt with in this chapter are specific areas dealing with the highly topical issue of whether human tissue is property or can be 'owned'.[7]

IMPLIED COVENANTS UNDER THE LAW OF PROPERTY ACT 1925 ('THE LPA') AND THE LAW OF PROPERTY (MISCELLANEOUS PROVISIONS) ACT 1994

Does the LPA apply to intellectual property?

Relevant provisions of the LPA

In order to establish that the LPA (as amended) applies to intellectual property assignments at all, and its effect on such assignments, it is necessary to consider a number of provisions and definitions in the LPA. First, some indications can be obtained from the now repealed LPA, s 76 which introduced the covenants into English law, including the following words:

> '(1) In a conveyance there shall, in the several cases in this section mentioned, be deemed to be included, and there shall in those several cases, by virtue of this Act, be implied, a covenant to the effect in this section stated, by the person or by each person who conveys, as far as regards the subject matter or share of subject matter expressed to be conveyed by him, with the person, if one, to whom the conveyance is made, or with the persons jointly, if more than one, to whom the conveyance is made as joint tenants, or with each of the persons, of more than one to whom the conveyance is (when the law permits) made as tenants in common, that is to say:

---

6   See under 'Bailment' below.
7   The laws which govern the issue of the obtaining, retention and use of (as well as requirement to or obtain consent for the use of) human tissue (and bodies and body parts) is considered in Ch 11.

(A)   In a *conveyance for valuable consideration* [emphasis added], other than a mortgage, a covenant by a person who conveys and is expressed to convey *as beneficial owner* [emphasis added] in the terms set out in Part I of the Second Schedule to this Act...

[...]

(C)   In a *conveyance by way of mortgage* [emphasis added] (including a charge) a covenant by a person who conveys or charges and is expressed to convey or charge *as beneficial owner* [emphasis added] in the terms set out in Part III of the Second Schedule to this Act...'

By LPA, s 205, 'conveyance' is defined to *include*:

'a mortgage, charge, lease, assent, vesting declaration, vesting instrument, disclaimer, release and every other assurance of *property* (emphasis added) or of an interest therein by any instrument, except a will'.

The term 'property' is defined by the same section of the LPA to *include*:

'any thing in action, and any interest in real or personal property'.

Thus a transfer of legal title to real or personal property, or transfer of an interest in real or personal property, would seem to be a conveyance for the purposes of the LPA. Clearly, intellectual property is not real property (ie land and buildings). The argument in favour of LPA, s 76 applying to intellectual property transactions therefore depends partly on whether intellectual property is *personal property*.

It also depends on whether the LPA applies to personal property. After all, the LPA was introduced as part of a major reform of *land* law in the 1920s.[8] Although the LPA does not specifically state that its provisions apply to personal property, it seems clear that some of them do. This can be seen from the fact that some sections of the LPA state that they apply only to *land* (eg s 1), whilst other sections (including s 76) are not so limited. However, the LPA only applies to property situated in England and Wales.[9] Thus, even if intellectual property is property for the purposes of the LPA, it is likely that the LPA only applies to UK intellectual property, eg a UK patent.

---

8   See the commentary in 39(2) *Halsbury's Laws of England* (4th edn, LexisNexis, 2003 reissue) Real Property, para 43 ff.

9   LPA, s 209.

Relevant provisions of intellectual property statutes

The key question is whether intellectual property can properly be classified as *personal property*. Most of the statutory forms of intellectual property contain statements on this point. Each will be examined in turn.

In the case of patents, the position is clear. The Patents Act 1977 states:

> 'Any patent or application for a patent is personal property (without being a thing in action)...'[10]

For registered trade marks, the position is equally clear. The Trade Marks Act 1994 states:

> 'A registered trade mark is personal property...'[11]

For registered designs, the position is now also equally clear. The Registered Designs Act 1949 states:

> 'A registered design or an application for a registered design is personal property...'[12]

For copyright and design right, the position is almost as clear. Under the Copyright, Designs and Patents Act 1988:

> 'Copyright is transmissible by assignment, by testamentary disposition or by operation of law, as personal or moveable property.'[13]

Whilst for design right:

> 'Design right is transmissible by assignment, by testamentary disposition or by operation of law, as personal or moveable property.'[14]

In the case of the database right, it is stated:

> 'A property right ('database right') subsists, in accordance with this Part, in a database if there has been a substantial investment in obtaining, verifying or presenting the contents of the database.'[15]

---

10   Patents Act 1977, s 30(1). A definition of a 'thing in action' (or a *chose in action*): 'The meaning of the expression "chose in action" or "thing in action" has expanded over time and is now used to describe all personal rights of property which can only be claimed or enforced by action, and not by taking physical possession. It is used in respect of both corporeal and incorporeal personal property which is not in possession': 13 *Halsbury's Laws of England* (5th edn, LexisNexis, 2009) para 1.
11   Trade Marks Act 1994, s 22.
12   Registered Designs Act 1949, s 15A, as amended by SI 2006/1028.
13   Copyright, Designs and Patents Act 1988, s 90.
14   Copyright, Designs and Patents Act 1988, s 222.
15   Copyright and Rights in Databases Regulations 1997 (SI 1997/3032), reg 13(1).

Conclusions

It seems clear that most if not all types of intellectual property, particularly patents, trade marks, copyright, design right, registered designs and database right, are examples of personal property.

An assignment of such intellectual property will generally transfer the legal title to that property.[16] Thus, it seems that an assignment of intellectual property could be a conveyance of property for the purposes of the LPA and the 1994 Act.

It is less likely that an intellectual property licence would be regarded as a conveyance or disposition of property. A licence is regarded as a right *under* the intellectual property, rather than a right or interest *in* the property.[17] There may be an argument that certain kinds of exclusive licence give the licensee a property interest in the intellectual property, as distinct from a mere contractual right; certainly an exclusive licence can give the licensee statutory rights, which may be thought of as going beyond mere contractual rights.[18]

Implied covenants of title, freedom from encumbrances etc

The 1994 Act created a new regime[19] for dispositions of property that are expressed to be made:

- 'with full title guarantee'; or

- 'with limited title guarantee'.[20]

Where these expressions are used then a set of covenants will be implied into the conveyance/assignment of property.

'Property' is defined as before to include any interest in personal property, whilst 'disposition' (the equivalent of 'conveyance' under LPA, s 76) is

---

16 Subject to compliance with any formalities, eg a patent, assignment must be in writing signed by or on behalf of the assignor (Patents Act 1977, s 30(6)) and should be registered (see Patents Act 1977, s 33); for a registered design, a registered design assignment, like for a patent , must be in writing signed for or on behalf of the assignor (Registered Designs Act 1949, s 15B(3)) and should be registered (Registered Designs Act 1949, s 15B(3)).

17 See eg *Insituform Technical Services Ltd v Inliner UK plc* [1992] RPC 83 at p 105.

18 See eg the rights of an exclusive licensee of a patent, under Patents Act 1977, s 67 (the right to bring infringement proceedings after the date a licence under a patent has been granted).

19 1994 Act, s 10 repealed LPA, s 76 'as regards dispositions of property made after commencement of this Part'; commencement was on 1 July 1994 by statutory instrument.

20 1994 Act, s 2 ff.

defined as including the creation of a term of years (essentially, under the law of *real* property, a lease).[21]

The covenants are to be implied:

'whether or not the disposition is for valuable consideration'[22]

unlike the position under LPA, s 76.[23]

It is possible to limit or extend the operation of any of the implied covenants by wording in the disposition/assignment which contains the expressions 'with full title guarantee' or 'limited title guarantee'.[24] In addition, the person making the disposition/assignment has no liability under a covenant in respect of:

- any matter to which the disposition is expressly made subject; or

- any matter which is within the actual knowledge of the person to whom the disposition/assignment is made.[25]

The benefit of these implied covenants is stated to go with the estate or interest of the person to whom the disposition/assignment is made.[26] It can be enforced by every person in whom that estate or interest is (in whole or in part) for the time being vested.[27]

In summary, the following covenants are to be implied[28] (covenants relevant only to land are not mentioned here).

Covenants applicable to Full Title Guarantee and Limited Title Guarantee

- The person disposing of the property ('seller') has the right to dispose of that property.

- The seller will at his own cost do all he reasonably can to give to the person to whom he disposes of the property ('buyer') the title he purports to give. And

- Where the disposition is a mortgage of property subject to a rentcharge, the mortgagor will fully and promptly observe and perform all the

---

21   1994 Act, s 1(4).
22   1994 Act, s 1(1).
23   See under 'Does the LPA apply to intellectual property?' above.
24   1994 Act, s 8(1).
25   1994 Act, s 6.
26   1994 Act, s 7.
27   See n 26.
28   By 1994 Act, ss 2, 3, 5.

obligations under the instrument creating the rentcharge that are enforceable by the owner of the rentcharge.[29]

Covenants applicable to Full Title Guarantee only

- The seller is disposing of the property free from all charges, encumbrances (whether monetary or not) and third party rights, other than charges, encumbrances and rights he does not and could not reasonably be expected to know about.[30]

Covenants applicable to Limited Guarantee only

- The seller has not, since the last disposition for value of that property, charged or encumbered it by any charge or encumbrance which subsists at the time of the present disposition, nor granted any third party rights in relation to the property which subsist at the time of the present disposition; nor has he allowed ('suffered') anyone else to do so; nor is he aware that anyone else has done so since the last disposition for value.

Implied conveyance of all rights held

A provision of the LPA confirms that a conveyance is effective to transfer all the rights in the property held by the party conveying the property. This provision appears to have been intended to remove doubts based on 19th century case authority.

In the intellectual property field, there is case law[31] on a similar point, namely that following an assignment of a patent, no rights are retained by the assignor. Therefore where an assignment of a patent merely states that a party assigns a named patent to another, the effect of the above provision would seem to be that all his right, title, interest, claims and demands in the patent are assigned.

---

29 It is not clear whether this provision is relevant to mortgages of intellectual property, but it is included for the sake of completeness (as a 'rentcharge' is an annual or periodic sum arising from land (other than the rent reserved by a lease or tenancy etc)). New rentcharges cannot be created (Rent Charges Act 1977, ss 2(1), 2(3)), with existing ones ceasing to exist within 60 years of 1978.

30 This implied covenant is also stated to apply, by 1994 Act, s 3(2), to liabilities imposed and rights conferred by or under any enactment unless, because they are only potential liabilities and rights in relation to that property, or apply to property generally, they do not constitute defects in title.

31 See *In the matter of Scott and Beard's Patent* 45 RPC 31 (1927), where a former owner unsuccessfully tried to object to an application by the assignees to extend the term of the patent, on the grounds that he had not assigned the right to apply for an extension. See also *Massmann v Massmann and the Custodian of Enemy Property* 61 RPC 13 (1943) (CA) and 60 RPC 45 (1943).

Often, assignments will specifically state that all 'right, title and interest' is transferred. Although this would seem not to be strictly necessary by virtue of the above provisions, it may be prudent to state expressly the extent of rights transferred, particularly where non-UK intellectual property is included in the assignment. Note that this provision does not mention the right to sue in respect of infringements which occurred prior to the date of the infringement, although it does refer to claims and demands that have already been made. If the right to sue in respect of past infringements is intended to be transferred, it should certainly be stated in the assignment.[32]

OTHER PROVISIONS OF THE LAW OF PROPERTY ACT 1925 WHICH COULD APPLY TO INTELLECTUAL PROPERTY TRANSACTIONS

Introduction

The main intention of the LPA was to consolidate previous law on transactions in land although, as has already been mentioned, many of its provisions apply also to transactions in personal property.[33] The following paragraphs concentrate on those provisions of the LPA that appear to have a direct impact on intellectual property transactions, for example provisions which may alter the interpretation of an assignment or licence agreement. Other provisions of the LPA, which are not described here, may be applicable to intellectual property transactions but do not seem to affect such transactions significantly.

---

32   For example Patents Act 1977, s 30(7), which provides that an assignment of a patent 'may' confer on the assignee the right to bring proceedings for a previous infringement, ie this is not automatically implied into such an assignment. Often an assignment of intellectual property will include multiple sets of provisions to cover this and other eventualities, 21(1) *Encyclopaedia of Forms of Precedents* 1997: see (LexisNexis) Patents and Technology Transfer, Form 29 [275].

33   Primarily because some provisions of the LPA are stated to apply to real property, while others are to 'property' but without further elaboration or restriction as to the type of property which is meant.

Use of expressions

It is common in commercial agreements to state specifically that certain expressions, when used in the agreement, are to be interpreted broadly. For example, it is common to state that references to a person include a firm, company or other organisation. In the absence of such express terms, LPA, s 61[34] provides that the following words have the following meanings:

'In all deeds, wills, orders and other instruments executed, made or coming into operation after the commencement of this Act [ie 1st January 1926], unless the context otherwise requires:

(a)   'Month' means calendar month;[35]

(b)   'Person' includes a corporation;

(c)   The singular includes the plural and vice versa;

(d)   The masculine includes the feminine and vice versa.'

It is not expressly stated that these provisions apply only to deeds and instruments (eg written agreements) concerning property, but this may be implicit given the general purpose of the LPA. It would seem that such provisions apply to assignments of intellectual property, whether or not executed as deeds, and possibly also to licences and other agreements concerning intellectual property.

In relation to the interpretation of implied covenants, LPA, s 83 implies some further provisions which appear to repeat parts of LPA, s 61:

'In the construction of a covenant or proviso, or other provision, implied in a deed or assent by virtue of this Act, words importing the singular or plural number, or the masculine gender, shall be read as also importing the plural or singular number, or as extending to females, as the case may require.'

---

34   See also the equivalent provisions in Interpretation Act 1978, ss 5, 6 and Sch 1.
35   97 *Halsburys Laws of England* (5th edn, LexisNexis, 2010) Time, paras 307–311, 345, the latter paragraph dealing with fractions of days, which are normally disregarded in any calculation of time.

Notices

It is generally desirable in commercial agreements to include a provision stating the method(s) by which communications by one party to another can be sent and whether and when any communication which is sent is taken to be received.

In the absence of such a provision, the notice provisions set out in LPA, s 196 may be taken to apply to any 'instrument affecting property'; this phrase would appear to cover most agreements in respect of intellectual property, including licences and assignments. LPA, s 196 can be a major trap for the unwary, as failure to serve a notice in the required manner could invalidate the notice.[36] For example, the termination provisions in a licence agreement sometimes provide that termination for breach may only take place after the defaulting party has been given notice of the breach and given an opportunity to remedy it. Failure to give notice of the breach in the correct way could invalidate any subsequent purported termination of the contract.

LPA, s 196(5) implies certain notices provisions into any:

> 'instrument affecting property executed or coming into operation after the commencement of this Act [ie 1st January 1926] unless a contrary intention appears'.

The notices provisions are set out in LPA, s 196(1)–(5), the relevant parts of which read as follows:

> 'Any notice required or authorised to be served or given by this Act shall be in writing.
>
> [...]
>
> (3) Any notice required or authorised by this Act to be served shall be sufficiently served if it is left at the last known place of abode or business in the United Kingdom of the ... person to be served ...
>
> (4) Any notice required or authorised by this Act to be served shall also be sufficiently served, if it is sent by post in a registered letter addressed to the ... person to be served, by name, at the aforesaid place of abode or business, office or counting house, and if that letter is not returned by

---

36 See *Orchard (Developments) Holdings plc v Reuters Ltd* [2009] EWCA Civ 6 for a recent example (in a commercial landlord and tenant case), where failure to follow contractual provisions for providing a notice by a particular method made the notice of no effect. This case did not deal with a failure to follow the method specified in s 196, but is a recent illustrative example of the consequences of failure to follow the specified method, although it can often seem a bureaucratic impediment or of technical insignificance if a notice is communicated one way rather than another (if the recipient of the notice did receive the notice and was aware of its contents).

the postal operator (within the meaning of the Postal Services Act 2000) concerned undelivered; and that service shall be deemed to be made at the time at which the registered letter would in the ordinary course be delivered.

(5) The provisions of this section shall extend to notices required to be served by any instrument affecting property executed or coming into operation after the commencement of this Act unless a contrary intention appears.'

Fraudulent concealment of material matters

LPA, s 183 includes provisions which affect not only the parties to a property transaction, but also their agents. The provision is designed to prevent a person, when disposing of property, from concealing or falsifying matters which are material to the title to the property, and may go further than the general law of fraud. In that sense it may be regarded as an exception to the principle of caveat emptor – let the buyer beware!

Unusually, the provision mentions specifically the solicitor acting for a party disposing of property. The section provides for both a criminal offence and a civil wrong where matters, which are material to the title to the property, are concealed or falsified. LPA, s 183(1) provides as follows:

'Any person disposing of property or any interest therein for money or money's worth to a purchaser, or the solicitor or other agent of such person, who:

(a) conceals from the purchaser any instrument or incumbrance material to the title; or

(b) falsifies any pedigree upon which the title may depend in order to induce the purchaser to accept the title offered or produced;

with intent in any of such cases to defraud, is guilty of a misdemeanour [ie criminal offence] punishable by fine, or by imprisonment for a term not exceeding two years, or by both.'

LPA, s 183(2) provides for a similar civil cause of action giving a right to damages.

Purchaser's constructive notice

LPA, s 199 limits the circumstances in which a purchaser is prejudicially affected by notice of any instrument or matter or any fact or thing relating to the property being purchased by him. In brief summary, he is not so affected unless he or his counsel, solicitor or other agent knew or would have known if he had made reasonable enquiries.

Execution of deeds and contracts concerning property[37]

The law on execution of deeds and other documents has been extensively revised since the LPA was passed, both:

- for *individuals* (by the Law of Property (Miscellaneous Provisions) Act 1989); and

- for *companies* (by the Companies Act 2006);

- *BUT NOT FOR companies or other organisations who are not covered by the Companies Act 2006.*

In summary (and excluding mention of requirements that relate only to land transactions):

Individuals who sign deeds[38]

(a) there is no longer any requirement for a deed executed by an individual to be sealed;

(b) it must be made clear on the document that it is intended to be a deed (ie by stating that it is a deed or that it is executed as deed);

(c) it must be signed *by the individual* (or a person authorised to execute it in the name of or on behalf of that individual):

    (i) in the presence of a witness who attests the signature; or

    (ii) *at his direction* and in his presence by someone else, and in the presence of two witnesses who each attest the signature.

(d) to be valid the deed must also be *delivered as a deed* by him or a person authorised to do so on his behalf.

UK companies signing contracts and deeds

The following rules apply to companies incorporated under, or otherwise covered by, a UK Companies Act.[39] In relation to overseas companies, see below. Furthermore, the following rules only apply to deeds or other documents executed under English law.

---

37 The execution of documents is considered in greater depth, and with practical examples, in Anderson and Warner, *The Execution of Documents* (2nd edn, Law Society Publishing, 2008).

38 Law of Property (Miscellaneous Provisions) Act 1989, ss 1(2), (2A).

39 Companies can be incorporated under a number of Companies Acts, including 1948, 1985 and from October 2009, 2006.

Contracts (which are not deeds)

(a) a contract may be made

    (i) *by* a company,

        (A) by writing under its common seal (if it has one); or

        (B) by two authorised signatories (which are all directors and the company secretary (if the company has one)) or by a director signing in the presence of a witness);[40] or

    (ii) *on behalf of* a company, by any person acting under its authority, express or implied (ie the person signing on behalf of the company does not need to be a director or the company secretary).[41]

Deeds (or other documents signed by the company)

(a) A deed *can* be executed by a company:

    (i) affixing its common seal; or

    (ii) by two authorised signatories (which are all directors and the company secretary (if the company has one)) or by a director signing in the presence of a witness).[42]

(b) The document signed in the way stated above, where it is intended that it be a deed, will also:

    (i) make clear on its face that it is intended to be executed as a deed.[43]

    (ii) have to be delivered as a deed. It is presumed, unless a contrary intention is proved, that it is automatically 'delivered' upon being executed.[44]

(c) In favour of a 'purchaser', a document is deemed to have been duly executed by a company if it purports to be signed by two authorised signatories (which are all directors and the company secretary (if the company has one)) or by a director signing in the presence of a witness).[45]

---

40 Companies Act 2006, ss 44(1)–(4).
41 Companies Act 2006, s 43.
42 Companies Act 2006, ss 44(1), (2), (3), 46(1)(a). The way the seal is used will also be governed by the provisions of the company's Articles of Association, which will specify how many directors (or other persons authorised) have to be present when the seal is applied.
43 Law of Property (Miscellaneous Provisions) Act 1989, s 1(2)(a).
44 Companies Act 2006, s 46(1)(b), (2).
45 Section 44(5). 'Purchaser' means a purchaser in good faith for valuable consideration and includes a lessee, mortgagee, or other person who for valuable consideration acquires an interest in property.

Foreign companies

(a) In the case of companies incorporated outside the United Kingdom, the provisions relating to UK companies summarised above are applied with applicable modifications.[46]

(b) In essence a contract can be executed by or on behalf of the foreign company, either by applying its common seal, or by any manner permitted by the laws of the territory in which the company is incorporated for the execution of documents by such a company; the document should also state that it is executed by the company.

(c) A deed may be executed by the foreign company, either by applying its common seal, or by any manner permitted by the laws of the territory in which the company is incorporated for the execution of documents by such a company.

Other bodies, academic institutions and government departments and organisations

The LPA as regards the signing of various documents (such as contracts, assignments, etc) is still of relevance to bodies and organisations which do not fall within the above categories. Many academic institutions, research organisations and governmental departments and other similar organisations are still bound by the provisions of the LPA as to the execution of documents, particularly the use of a seal for the execution of documents.[47] They are a form of incorporated body, a 'corporation aggregate' (but without requirement to register as companies under, or be regulated by, the Companies Act 2006). They have distinct legal identities, some being formed by Royal Charter (such as most universities), others by statute (such as NHS Trusts, under the National Health Service Act 2006).[48]

Signing of a document by a corporation aggregate

Either by

(a) the affixing of the seal of the corporation aggregate on the document in the presence of and attested by:

(i) two members of the board of directors, council or governing body of the corporation aggregate; or

(ii) one member of the board of directors, council or governing body of the corporation aggregate and the clerk, secretary or other permanent officer of the corporation or his deputy.

---

46 Overseas Companies (Execution of Documents and Registration of Charges) Regulations 2009 (SI 2009/1917), with effect from October 2009. For documents executed prior to 1 October 2009, readers should consult the law as stated in the 2nd edition of this book.

47 LPA, s 74.

48 The LPA calls such forms of incorporated body a 'corporation aggregate'.

Or by

(b)   such method of execution or attestation which is authorised by the corporation aggregate's charter, statute, etc that regulates its affairs.[49]

Signing of a document on behalf of a corporation aggregate

A corporation aggregate can appoint someone on their behalf to sign documents (other than deeds), either by resolution or by some other method.

Signing of deeds by corporation aggregates

(a)   this will follow the same procedure as described under 'Signing of a document by a corporation aggregate';

and

(b)   the document signed will also:

(i)   make clear on its face that it is intended to be executed as a deed;[50]

(ii)   have to be delivered as a deed. It is presumed, unless a contrary intention is proved, that it is automatically 'delivered' upon being executed.[51]

Witnessing of conveyances

Another provision which appears designed to protect the purchaser of property is to be found in LPA, s 75. It deals with the situation where the conveyancing document is signed in counterparts,[52] often without both parties being present at signature. LPA, s 75 includes the following provision:

> 'On a sale, the purchaser … shall be entitled to have, at his own cost, the execution of the conveyance [ie by the seller] attested [ie witnessed] by some person appointed by him, who may, if he thinks fit, be his solicitor.'

In the case of an assignment of intellectual property and where the validity of a signature may be in doubt, this may provide some protection for the purchaser. Alternatively the parties could always arrange to sign together at a completion meeting.

---

49   LPA, s 74(6).
50   Law of Property (Miscellaneous Provisions) Act 1989, s 1(2)(a).
51   LPA, ss 74A(1)(b), (2).
52   The traditional practice where each party to an agreement signs a copy of the agreement, and then the parties exchange copies, so that each party holds the copy signed by the other party. The contract comes into being at the time the copies of the agreements are exchanged. This is the way contracts have, traditionally, been entered into for conveyancing (no party holds a copy of the agreement signed by both parties).

Relief from forfeiture

In one case,[53] a court was prepared to override a provision in an agreement between co-owners of a patent, which provided that if a party failed to reimburse the other one half of certain patent expenses within a period of 30 days, the other party could require the defaulting party to assign to it its rights in the patent. The court held that its equitable jurisdiction to grant relief against forfeiture (more frequently encountered in real property disputes, eg cases concerning attempts to evict a tenant for failure to comply with the terms of the lease) is available for all kinds of proprietary or possessory rights. The court extended the time period in which the defaulting party was required to reimburse the other party for the patent costs.

That case was distinguished in a more recent case concerning a trade mark licence,[54] on the grounds that the licensee's rights were contractual, rather than being an interest in property. Accordingly, the principle of relief against forfeiture was not available.[55]

For the sake of completeness, it may be worth mentioning that the principle of relief against forfeiture is also established in statutory form in LPA, s 146(2). Under that section a lessee can apply to the court for relief from forfeiture of the lease, even though he has been in breach of the lease, and the lease provides that it may be terminated in the event of such a breach. However, LPA, s 146 is stated to apply to 'leases'; it is not clear whether this term could apply to intellectual property licences, but it seems unlikely on reading the section.[56]

MULTIPLE OWNERSHIP OF PROPERTY

Introduction

Multiple ownership of intellectual property can lead to significant problems for the owners, particularly if their rights and obligations towards one another in respect of that property are not fully agreed. Some of the reasons why problems can arise are described in this section.

---

53 *BICC v Burndy Corporation* [1985] RPC 273 (CA), referred to in *On Demand Information plc (in administrative receivership) and another v Michael Gerson (Finance) plc and another* [2000] 4 All ER 734.
54 *Crittall Windows Limited v Stormseal (UPVC) Window Systems Limited and Another* [1991] RPC 265.
55 See Ch 10 under 'Nature and extent of licences', 'Licence or agreement to grant licence?'.
56 See LPA, ss 146(5), 205 for definitions of lease and lessee.

Patents in the UK

The Patents Act 1977 determines certain rights and obligations of co-owners of a UK patent, in the absence of any agreement between them to the contrary.[57] In brief summary, each co-owner is entitled to an equal, undivided share in the patent; each co-owner may manufacture and sell products using the patented invention without the consent of the other co-owner(s); but a co-owner may not grant any licence under the patent, nor assign his share in the patent without the consent of the other co-owner(s).

Parties who agree to co-own a patent are not always aware of these provisions and their implications. For example, if an academic institution and a manufacturing company agree that they will co-own a patent, it will often be the case that the manufacturing company can exploit the patent without paying the academic institution any royalty, if it manufactures the patented products itself. By contrast, the academic institution will generally not be in a position to manufacture the products and in order to exploit the patent it will need to grant licences under it. It will not be able to do this unless the other co-owner agrees; even where the other co-owner does agree it may demand a royalty or other payment as the price for its consent. Unless there is agreement beforehand, the manufacturer could work the patent itself without needing to ask the permission of the academic institution, and thus keep all the financial revenue from so doing (unless the parties have entered into an agreement which varies the default position provided by the Patents Act 1977).

The position in regard to other UK intellectual property

The nature of co-owners' rights in other types of UK intellectual property is not as clearly stated in the legislation as it is in the case of patents. The position appears to be similar to that governing patents, in relation to the granting of licences.[58] However, it is noticeable that the legislation for copyright and design right refers to *joint* owners rather than co-owners;[59] as will be discussed below, the law of property makes a distinction between joint tenancy and tenancy in common, and it may be, therefore, that the ownership rules in respect of jointly owned copyright and design right differ from those for co-ownership of patents.

---

57   See Patents Act 1977, s 36, and Ch 14 under 'Co-ownership of patents and patent applications'.

58   For example in the case of copyright, see Copyright, Designs and Patents Act 1988, s 173(2) which provides that in the case of jointly owned copyright, any requirement of the licence of the copyright owner requires the licence of all of them. Section 259 of that Act makes similar provision in the case of jointly owned design right. In the case of registered designs, there is now specific provision addressing this point. The provision formerly to be found in the Registered Designs Act 1949 has been repealed, and in any case did not deal with the issue of co-owners.

59   See the heading to Patents Act 1977, s 36.

The position in regard to non-UK intellectual property

The rights and obligations of co-owners under the patent laws of other countries are in many cases different to those which apply to UK patents. It is understood, for example, that it may be possible for a co-owner of a US patent to grant a non-exclusive licence under the patent without the consent of the other co-owner(s). Thus if parties co-own a portfolio of patents in several countries, and fail to agree their respective rights in those patents, they may find that their rights vary depending on the country of the patent. Misunderstandings may arise where the co-owners are from different countries which have different rules: each co-owner may imagine that the patent laws of his country apply worldwide, and may intend that his country's laws on co-ownership would apply to all the patents.

Comment

It may therefore be advisable either to avoid co-ownership of intellectual property wherever possible, or to agree in advance (and in detail) what each co-owner may do with the intellectual property. Issues to consider include:

- who is responsible for obtaining and maintaining (eg paying renewal fees) the property;
- defending it against challenges;
- enforcing it against infringers;
- deciding on any amendments to its scope;
- licensing it, enforcing licence provisions; and
- when the consent of a co-owner is required, and what happens if it is not forthcoming.

The remainder of this section will consider how the traditional laws of personal property may affect the rights and obligations of multiple owners of intellectual property.

Joint ownership and ownership in common

Distinction between joint ownership and ownership in common

The most common situation in which people encounter joint ownership and ownership in common, is where spouses or civil partners co-own their house. They may agree to do so either jointly or in common. For the reasons referred to below, the legal mechanism for doing this will generally involve them in holding the property on trust for themselves as either joint tenants or tenants in common. The essential difference between these two methods of ownership can be seen where one of the co-owners dies. In the case of:

- *a joint tenancy*, on the death of one of the joint tenants, the house becomes the sole property of the surviving joint tenant;

- *a tenancy in common*, on the death of one of the tenants his or her share of the property passes under his or her will or under the intestacy rules.[60]

Tenants in common each have what is known as an undivided share in the property. A husband and wife who own a house as tenants in common will generally have equal, undivided shares in the property. This terminology becomes relevant when considering the statutory rights of co-owners of patents. Patents Act 1977, s 36(1) provides as follows:

'Where a patent is granted to two or more persons, each of them shall, subject to any agreement to the contrary, be entitled to an equal undivided share in the patent.'

The rights of co-owners of a patent are thus defined by statute, as quoted above, rather than under the general law of personal property. Nevertheless it seems clear from the statutory wording that the owners of a patent are to be considered as owners (tenants) in common rather than joint owners (tenancy), subject to any agreement to the contrary. The general law governing ownership in common may therefore be applicable to co-ownership of patents, except to the extent that such law has been modified by the statutory provisions.

By contrast, the Copyright, Designs and Patents Act 1988 ('the CDPA') does not include any wording equivalent to Patents Act 1977, s 36(1). The CDPA refers to joint owners of copyright and design right.[61] It is not clear whether use of the word 'joint' implies joint ownership in the traditional property law sense. The Registered Designs Act 1949 makes no reference to joint ownership or ownership in common.[62]

In cases of doubt, it may be desirable to include in an agreement between the co-owners of intellectual property a statement indicating whether ownership in common or joint ownership is intended. In practice, owners of intellectual property tend to prefer to be owners in common.

Prohibition on legal ownership in common

LPA, s 34(1) made it impossible to create an undivided share in land (ie ownership in common) except under a settlement or a trust for sale. One effect of this provision is that if two people (eg spouses or civil partners) wish to own their house in common, they may only do so by holding the

---

60   For example, the deceased tenant could leave a will stating that his or her share of the property could go to someone other than the surviving spouse/civil partner, such as a third person or a charity. If there is no will, then there are rules to decide the amount the surviving spouse will have, depending on whether there are children and other family members.

61   See eg Copyright, Designs and Patents Act 1988, s 173(2) (in relation to copyright), and s 258(2) (in relation to design right).

62   See ss 15A, 15B, as inserted by SI 2006/1028.

house as joint legal owners, and on trust for themselves as *beneficial* tenants in common.

This prohibition on *legal* ownership in common does not apply to patents, by virtue of Patents Act 1977, s 36(1). Nevertheless, in view of the general approach of English property law in distinguishing between legal and beneficial co-ownership, it may be desirable to indicate, in agreements between co-owners of intellectual property, that they own the property as *beneficial* owners in common (if that is intended), as well as the respective shares that they hold in the property (eg equal shares, or two-thirds to one-third etc).

Ability of companies to hold as joint tenants

For the sake of completeness, the following matter should be mentioned. Until the end of the 19th century it was not possible for a 'body corporate'[63] to own property as joint tenants. This prohibition was removed by the Bodies Corporate (Joint Tenancy) Act 1899. Section 1 of that Act includes the following provisions:

'(1) A body corporate shall be capable of acquiring and holding any real or personal property in joint tenancy in the same manner as if it were an individual ...

(2) Where a body corporate is joint tenant of any property then on its dissolution the property shall devolve on the other joint tenant.'

Thus, there is no legal constraint on companies owning intellectual property as joint beneficial owners (or, for that matter, as beneficial owners in common). However, it is hardly conceivable that two commercial organisations would wish to own any form of intellectual property as joint tenants (ie that if one ceases to exist, then its interest in the intellectual property would automatically be owned by the 'surviving' commercial organisation).

BAILMENT

Introduction

In certain circumstances, the possession of physical items by one person which are owned by another person may give rise to the legal relationship known as bailment,[64] and which can exist independently from any contract. Common examples of bailment are the hire of goods (eg a car), the deposit of valuables with a bank for safe custody, leaving a coat with a laundry for

---

63   The legal name for companies and other types of organisation which have a separate legal status from the persons owning them or responsible for their running, such as universities, government departments, regulatory authorities, NHS trusts and so on.

64   See (2) *Chitty on Contracts* (30th edn, Sweet & Maxwell, 2008) Ch 32, and Bell, *Modern Law of Personal Property in England and Ireland* (Butterworths, 1989) Ch 5.

drying cleaning, the transport of goods[65] and the loan of a garden mower. There appears to be no universally accepted definition of bailment. One definition[66] suggests the following:

'A bailment arises when one person (the bailee) is willingly and with authority in possession of goods to which another (the bailor) retains better title; and the necessary authority to possess may be supplied either by the bailor's consent, actual or implied, or by operation of law.'

Note that the bailor does not need to be the owner of the goods; he merely has to have a 'better title' to the goods. For example, if a pharmaceutical company wishes to have some compounds tested by a contractor, but the contractor needs to use equipment which the pharmaceutical company has. However the pharmaceutical company does not own the equipment but has leased the equipment from the manufacturer of the equipment before providing it to the contractor. In this example, the pharmaceutical company would have the better title to the equipment (having the right to possess and use the equipment directly from the owner).

Where a bailment relationship exists, there is a considerable amount of (case) law governing the rights and obligations of the parties to that relationship – the bailor and the bailee.[67] That relationship is different from a contractual relationship and, for example, may give the bailor and bailee rights against third parties.[68] This section will consider ways in which such rights may be used by an owner of technology.

Goods are sometimes provided under a technology transfer agreement, or other agreement concerning technology, in circumstances which may give rise to a bailment. For example:

- It is common in the biotechnology field for samples of biological materials to be provided by one scientist to another, or by one company to another, to enable the recipient to carry out research work using the materials. The materials may be self-reproducing, eg a cell line.

- Sometimes, a contract research organisation will be provided with equipment to carry out the research work by the other party contracting with it.

The parties may agree that property to the materials or equipment remains with the provider. In such circumstances, under English law the recipient may hold the materials as bailee for the provider (independent and in addition

---

65 See *East West Corporation v DKBS 1912 A/S and another; Utaniko Ltd v P & O Nedlloyd BV* [2003] EWCA Civ 83; [2003] 2 All ER 700 for the application of the law of bailment to a modern commercial contract (although not related to intellectual property).

66 See n 65. See also 3(1) *Halsbury's Laws of England* (4th edn, LexisNexis, 2005 reissue) Bailment, para 1 for an outline of the meaning of bailment.

67 This area of law is almost entirely developed by case law.

68 See (2) *Chitty on Contracts* (30th edn, Sweet & Maxwell, 2008) para 33-011.

to any contractual arrangement between the parties). It seems this may also be the position under US laws.[69]

The same relationship may exist in other fields of technology; however, the topic is of particular importance in the biotechnology field. Sometimes materials are provided in circumstances where there are no intellectual property rights protecting them and they do not embody any confidential information. In such cases, the protection given under the laws of personal property, including the law of bailment, may be the only legal protection available[70] to the owner of the materials to prevent use of the materials by third parties.

The following paragraphs will briefly summarise the main legal implications of a relationship of bailment and consider how it may apply to the supply of materials under a technology-related agreement such as a research collaboration agreement. The terms implied into a contract of hire (a type of bailment) under the Supply of Goods and Services Act 1982 are discussed in Chapter 10.

Circumstances in which bailment may arise

The rights and duties of bailor and bailee vary, depending on the circumstances in which the bailment arose. The main categories of bailment that may be relevant to the supply of materials are:

gratuitous bailment, ie where one party is merely doing the other party a favour. Examples of this in relation to supply of materials would be (i) where the owner of the materials is asked to provide a sample to enable someone else to carry out research; and (ii) where the owner requests another person to carry out tasks using the materials;

bailment for reward, where the bailment is mutually beneficial, eg under a contract. An example of this in the technology transfer field could be where the owner of materials provides a sample to another person, and the owner and the other person agree to share the financial proceeds from the exploitation of any intellectual property created or developed from carrying out research work on the sample.

Rights of the bailor

The bailor remains the owner of (or the person having a better title to) the goods during the period of bailment, but his rights as owner may be restricted.

---

69   See eg Kirn in 9(3) *Licensing Law and Business Report* (1986).
70   Except for eg contractual rights against the recipient, where a contract has been made.

For example, he may not be able to sue third parties for conversion[71] of his property during the period of the bailment.

Rights of the bailee

The bailee has a *special property* in the goods; the nature of his rights varies depending on the circumstances of the bailment. All bailees have rights against third parties who interfere with the goods, and for example are able to sue third parties for conversion and in negligence. A bailee has a proprietary interest in the goods. The bailee may also have rights against the bailor, eg if the bailee is storing the materials for reward and the bailor fails to pay the storage charges.

Duties of the bailee

The main duties of a bailee, which appear relevant to the supply of materials under a technology transfer agreement, are the following:

Take care of the goods: the bailee has a duty to take care of the goods whilst they are in his possession, including the duty to protect the goods from third parties. This duty may go further than under the general law of negligence. The extent of the common law duty may vary depending on the circumstances of the bailment, although there is conflicting case authority on this point. In addition, there is the statutory duty on the provider of a service, under a contract (which may involve a bailment of goods),[72] to carry out the service with reasonable care – see Supply of Goods and Services Act 1982, s 13.

Exercise skills: where the bailee holds himself out as having particular skills, he will be liable for failure to exercise them. Conversely the bailor's knowledge of the bailee's inexperience and infirmities may lower the standard of care required.

Use of facilities: a bailee must exercise due care to protect the goods entrusted to him against the risks inherent in his premises, although he may be exonerated if he complies with specific instructions from the bailor.

Duty not to convert: unsurprisingly, a bailee must not 'convert' the goods, eg by selling them or appropriating them for himself.

Duty not to deviate: it is a serious breach of the bailment to 'deviate' from the bailment. This expression covers all failures to comply with the conditions

71 Where a person deals with goods (which do not belong to him) in a manner which is inconsistent with the rights of the owner of the goods.
72 See Supply of Goods and Services Act 1982, s 12(3).

imposed on the bailee's possession of the goods. For example it would cover keeping the goods for longer than the agreed period, or at a different location from that agreed, or providing them to third parties without permission. The bailee is liable for any harm that the goods receive during the deviation, without the need to prove further default by the bailee. Apparently this head of liability does not extend to financial loss suffered as a result of the deviation, in respect of which the normal rules of causation apply. Deviation is regarded as a repudiatory breach, giving the bailor the immediate right to the return of the goods.

Duty to redeliver: generally, the bailee will be under an obligation to redeliver the goods to the bailor or to his order, at the agreed time and place. Prima facie, this duty is passive: the bailee merely has to make the goods available for collection at his own premises within a reasonable time as and when the bailor calls upon him to do so, unless otherwise agreed.

Duties of the bailor

The main duties of a bailor, which seem relevant to the supply of materials under a technology transfer agreement, are the following:

Right to bail: in general it is an implied term of the bailment, at common law, that the bailor has the right to bail the goods.[73]

Safety and fitness of the goods: it seems that in gratuitous bailments (eg, where there is no contractual relationship between the bailor and the bailee), the bailor's common law duty of care towards the bailee may be similar to that which operates under the law of negligence, with possibly a higher standard where the gratuitous bailment is for the benefit of the bailor. It seems that in the case of bailments for reward, eg under a contract of hire or carriage, the standards may be higher still.[74]

Other common law duties: a number of other duties may arise in particular situations, eg a duty to reimburse the bailee for expenses incurred by him in preserving the goods from harm.[75]

Statutory duties: for a discussion of the implied terms in a contract of hire, under the Supply of Goods and Services Act 1982, see Chapter 10.

---

73   For the statutory provision to this effect contained in the Supply of Goods and Services Act 1982, see Ch 10.

74   For the statutory provisions, see Ch 10 under 'Supply of materials'.

75   This duty was held to arise where the expense was caused by the bailor's failure to give adequate instructions regarding disposal of a salvaged cargo – see *China-Pacific SA v Food Corpn of India, The Winson* [1982] AC 939 at 960, [1981] 3 All ER 688.

Sub-bailment

It seems that a bailee may in some circumstances sub-bail the goods unless the contract is a personal one, or he has agreed not to do so, or on the circumstances of the bailment. For example, it has been held that all warehousing contracts are personal, as they rely on the personal skills of the bailee.[76] If the bailee is entitled to sub-bail, then the sub-bailment must be consistent with the purposes for which the goods were originally bailed. It is for the bailee to justify any sub-bailment. The bailee will be liable if he is negligent in selecting the sub-bailee, and for the sub-bailee's failure to carry out his delegated duties.

Where materials are sub-bailed (ie bailed by the bailee to another person), it seems the sub-bailee owes the duties of a bailee to both his bailor and the main bailor, despite the lack of privity of contract with the latter.[77] The bailee acts as agent for the bailor to create a collateral bailment between the bailor and the sub-bailee. Normally the sub-bailee can only look to the bailee for any agreed payment.

Commercial implications of the law of bailment

The above summary demonstrates that there is an extensive amount of law on the rights and duties of the parties to a bailment. That law may be applicable to a transfer of biological or other materials, for example to enable research to be carried out on those materials by the bailee. However, the law has evolved to deal with quite different factual situations, and may not be considered appropriate in the biotechnology field. For example, the rules on sub-bailment may seem too permissive – often the owner of materials will wish the materials to be kept in confidence by the recipient, and he will not be prepared to allow them to be transferred to a third party. Under the law of bailment it seems that the recipient might be entitled to transfer the materials to a third party unless the bailment was personal to him.

The danger for a party where a written agreement stating specifically what their rights and duties are to be is not entered into, is that some of the implied 'terms' of a bailment may apply and in ways which the party does not intend or want. Even in contracts where the possession of materials is transferred from one party to another, although such matters as liability arising from any personal damage caused by the materials, who is to own intellectual property arising from the use of the material, and how the materials are to be held are often addressed, many of the other 'terms' implied by the law of bailment are not addressed.

---

76 *Edwards v Newland & Co (E Burchett Ltd, third party)* [1950] 2 KB 534, [1950] 1 All ER 1072, CA.
77 See Bell, *Modern Law of Personal Property in England and Ireland* (Butterworths, 1989), p 96.

Non-derogation from grant

The case of British Leyland Motor Corporation Ltd Armstrong Patents Co Ltd

The principle of non-derogation from grant (also known as the rule against derogation) is a traditional property law principle, normally encountered in relation to real property (land and buildings). To the surprise of many intellectual property lawyers it formed the basis of a judgment of the senior court (House of Lords, now the Supreme Court) in England and Wales in 1985, in a case concerning copyright law. The case illustrates that traditional property laws can be applied to intellectual property matters by the courts, sometimes in unexpected ways.

This may be true particularly in the appeal courts, where judges tend not to be intellectual property specialists and tend to have less experience of the practical application of intellectual property laws than, for example, judges in the Patents Court.[78] This section briefly discusses the *British Leyland* case and the property law principle which was relied upon in one of its leading judgments, as well as some related legal principles.

In the case;[79] the principle of non-derogation from grant was referred to in one judgment. The case concerned copyright in drawings of the exhaust pipes of the Morris Marina car. The central issue was whether a purchaser of such a car had the right to buy replacement exhaust pipes to the same design from someone other than the original manufacturer of the car, British Leyland (BL); BL also held the copyright in the drawings. On appeal to the most senior court in England and Wales, the leading judgment held that the purchaser of a car had the right to have his car repaired, including the right to purchase replacement exhaust pipes from someone other than the car manufacturer. In this judgment, the basis of the decision was as follows:

> 'For my part, I base the right to repair on the principle of non-derogation from grant rather than implied licence and I see no difficulty in concluding that suppliers such as Armstrong may make exhaust pipes to be supplied to those cars of BL [British Leyland] which require to be repaired by the replacement of exhaust pipes. Every owner of a car has the right to repair it. That right would be useless if suppliers of spare parts were not entitled to anticipate the need for repair. The right cannot,

---

78 With the increasingly specialist nature of the judiciary, cases will sometimes be assigned to a specialist judge. For example, now many Court of Appeal cases involving intellectual property matter will have at least one judge who is a specialist in an aspect of intellectual property law.

79 *British Leyland Motor Corporation Ltd and another v Armstrong Patents Co Ltd and another* [1986] 1 AC 577, [1986] RPC 279, referred to in *United Wire Ltd v Screen Repair Services (Scotland) Ltd* [2000] FSR 204; *Newspaper Licensing Agency Ltd v Marks and Spencer plc* [2001] 3 All ER 977; *Dyson Ltd v Qualtex (UK) Ltd* [2006] EWCA Civ 166, [2006] All ER (D) 101 (Mar) (see paras 5–12).

in my view, be withheld by the manufacturer of the car by contract with the first purchaser and cannot be withheld from any subsequent owner.'

Earlier in this judgment,[80] it was considered how the principle might apply to the sale of a car:

'I see no reason why the principle that a grantor will not be allowed to derogate from his grant by using property retained by him in such a way as to render property granted by him unfit or materially unfit for the purpose for which the grant was made should not apply to the sale of a car. … The principle applied to a motor car manufactured in accordance with engineering drawings and sold with components which are bound to fail during the life of the car prohibits the copyright owner from exercising his copyright powers in such a way as to prevent the car from functioning unless the owner of the car buys replacement parts from the copyright owner or his licensee.'

The judgment also considered the implied licence to repair a purchaser of a patented article has to carry out repairs without being held liable for infringement. The judgment reviewed cases on this issue which address the difficult question of when repair becomes so extensive as to amount to reconstruction, and therefore the production of a new, infringing item.[81] There is no suggestion in the judgment that any of the judgments in these earlier patent cases were based on the rule against derogation; they were concerned simply with the law of patents, which could not be directly applied to a case concerning copyright.[82] Instead, the judgment turned to the general law of property, and the rule against derogation in particular, as the basis of a purchaser's right to have repaired an article protected by copyright. It appears that this principle has not been widely followed in cases which came after.[83]

In one case[84] (a copyright case concerning computer software), it was held that the right to repair referred to in *British Leyland Motor Corporation Ltd v Armstrong Patents Co Ltd* did not give a right to copy computer file layouts from the source code of a suite of computer programs.

---

80 [1986] 1 AC at 641.
81 See [1986] 1 AC 642–643. The cases considered include *Dunlop Pneumatic Tyre Co Ltd v Neal* [1899] 1 Ch 807; *Dunlop Pneumatic Tyre Co Ltd v Holborn Tyre Co Ltd* (1901) 18 RPC 222; *Dunlop Pneumatic Tyre Co Ltd v David Moseley & Sons Ltd* [1904] 1 Ch 612 (CA); *Sirdar Rubber Co Ltd v Wallington, Weston & Co* (1905) 22 RPC 257, (1907) 24 RPC 539 at 543 (HL); and *Solar Thomson Engineering Co Ltd v Barton* [1977] RPC 537. See also 79 *Halsbury's Laws of England* (5th edn, LexisNexis) Patents, para 507.
82 See [1986] 1 AC at 644B.
83 *British Leyland Motor Corporation Ltd v Armstrong Patents Co Ltd* appears to have been cited in only a few cases since.
84 *IBCOS Computers v Barclays Mercantile Highland Finance Limited* [1994] FSR 275, referred to in *Cantor Fitzgerald International (an unlimited company) and another v Tradition (UK) Ltd and others* [2000] RPC 95, and also in *Stoddard International plc v William Lomas Carpets Ltd* [2001] FSR 848.

It is important to note that the scope of the right to repair has also been reduced by the decision in *Canon Kabushiki Kaisha v Green Cartridge Co (Hong Kong) Limited*[85] to situations where overriding public policy would prevent a manufacturer from using copyright to control a market in spare parts.

This case concerned a claim by Canon Kabushiki Kaisha for copyright infringement against Green, which manufactured and sold printer and photocopier cartridges that were detailed imitations of, and interchangeable with those of, Canon Kabushiki Kaisha. The defendant denied infringement and claimed that the claimant was not entitled to enforce its rights in so far as such enforcement interfered with an inherent right to repair. Allowing Canon Kabushiki Kaisha's appeal, the court held that the decision in *British Leyland Motor Corporation Ltd v Armstrong Patents Co Ltd* was founded on unfairness to the customer and abuse of monopoly power. Where these features were not obvious, the jurisprudential and economic basis for the doctrine was greatly undermined. In the *Canon Kabushiki Kaisha* case, the analogy with the sort of repair that a person who bought an item would assume he could do for himself was much weaker, as when the cartridge was replaced nothing in the machine would need to be repaired.

Equally, the competition argument was held to be far less compelling in that the cost of replacement toner cartridges was significant, and it could not be assumed that customers did not take account of such costs when choosing a machine, which did introduce an element of competitiveness into the aftermarket as well as for the market in photocopiers and printers itself. Further, it was felt that there was competition between the manufacturers of replacement cartridges and those who refilled existing cartridges, such that it could not be said without proof that Canon's use of its intellectual property rights had allowed it to obtain a dominant position in the market, much less to abuse that position.

The remainder of this section will consider the rule against derogation and similar laws, and briefly indicate some general implications for intellectual property transactions.

Traditional formulation of the rule against derogation

Halsbury's Laws[86] describes the rule against derogation in the following terms, using an example from the land law field:

> 'It is a well-established rule that a grantor cannot be permitted to derogate from his grant. Though usually applied to sales and leases of

---

85   [1997] AC 728; [1997] FSR 817, PC, a Privy Council decision of a Hong Kong case.
86   13 *Halsbury's Laws of England* (4th edn, LexisNexis, 2007 reissue) Deeds and other instruments, para 58.

land, it is of wider application. The principle is that if one man agrees to confer a particular benefit on another, he must not do anything which substantially deprives the other of the enjoyment of that benefit, because that would be to take away with one hand what is given with the other. Hence, on the grant by the owner of a tenement of part of that tenement there will pass to the grantee all those easements which are necessary in order that the property may be enjoyed reasonably for the purpose for which it was granted. On the other hand, if the grantor intends to reserve any right over the tenement granted, he must do so expressly, though to this rule there are certain exceptions, notably in cases of what are known as ways of necessity.'

The principle, as defined in these terms, is stated to go wider than real (land and buildings) property law. However the case law cited (except for *British Leyland Motor Corporation Ltd v Armstrong Patents Co Ltd*) seems to be concerned with the transfer of property, where rights over neighbouring property are retained by the transferor, and therefore is not relevant to the sale of goods protected by copyright. On the sale of goods, there is generally no 'neighbouring' property. If the goods are protected by intellectual property rights owned by the seller, there is an implied licence by the seller under those rights to enable the purchaser to use the goods. The principle of non-derogation would not seem to be applicable. The principle would seem more relevant, if at all, to a partial assignment of copyright, or a licence under copyright. A possible example of this might arise in relation to registered intellectual property under which a licence has been granted; arguably the owner's failure to renew the registration might be regarded as a 'derogation', giving his licensee a right of action against the owner.

Elsewhere in the leading judgment in *British Leyland Motor Corporation Ltd v Armstrong Patents Co Ltd*,[87] there is quoted an extract from an earlier case,[88] on the extent of the rule against derogation:

'... the implications usually explained by the maxim that no one can derogate from his own grant do not stop short with easements. Under certain circumstances there will be implied on the part of the grantor or lessor obligations which restrict the user of the land retained by him further than can be explained by the implication of any easement known to the law. Thus, if the grant or demise be made for a particular purpose, the grantor or lessor comes under an obligation not to use the land retained by him in such a way as to render the land granted or demised unfit or materially less fit for the particular purpose for which the grant or demise was made.'

87   [1986] 1 AC at 641.
88   *Browne v Flower* [1911] 1 Ch 219 at 225.

Expressed in this way, the principle seems closer to an implied covenant of quiet possession or quiet enjoyment.[89] In the leading judgment from *British Leyland Motor Corporation Ltd v Armstrong Patents Co Ltd* this formulation of the principle was regarded as applicable to the sale of a car. If the principle can be extended to cover personal as well as real property, and new factual situations, without obvious limits on how far it can be extended, it is difficult to predict how far a court might extend the principle in the future in the intellectual property field.

Related legal principles

The rule against derogation also has similarities with the principle of exhaustion of rights, ie the principle that once one has put a product on the market one's rights in that product are exhausted. This principle has been developed under EC law in a number of cases concerned with the free movement of goods rules contained in EC Treaty, Arts 28–30.[90] It is also understood that the intellectual property laws of some countries may incorporate specific 'non-derogation' or 'exhaustion of rights' rules into the relevant legislation.[91]

Different, but related, legal principles operate where a licensor of intellectual property requires his licensee to purchase from him, or use, certain products (eg by means of a tying provision in a licence agreement). Such a provision may be unlawful under EC and/or UK competition laws (unless that product must be used for valid technical reasons).[92]

Conclusion

The decision in *British Leyland Motor Corporation Ltd v Armstrong Patents Co Ltd* was not concerned with agreements for the exploitation or transfer of technology, except in the broader sense that a sale of a product, which is protected by intellectual property rights, may be considered as a technology transfer agreement. However, the leading judgment does suggest, by implication, that certain provisions in licences and similar agreements may not be enforceable. For example, a provision in a licence agreement, under which a licensee agreed not to offer spare parts to customers of other licensees or of the licensor, might well offend against the principle of non-derogation from grant.[93]

---

89   Compare Supply of Goods and Services Act 1982, s 12.
90   Following adoption of the Lisbon Treaty in December 2009, these Article numbers will be renumbered as 34–36.
91   For example, it is understood that US copyright statutes may include such a principle.
92   See Chs 12 and 15.
93   As well as possibly breaching EC or other competition laws.

In a broader sense, the case indicates that the traditional law of property is indeed applicable to the exploitation and enforcement of intellectual property rights, and should not be overlooked by intellectual property law practitioners.

IMPACT OF EC LAWS ON UK PROPERTY LAW

In principle, EU laws do not affect national property laws in EU member states. EC Treaty, Art 295[94] is apparently unambiguous:

> 'This Treaty shall in no way prejudice the rules in Member States governing the system of property ownership.'

In other words, property is a matter of national law, and not within the jurisdiction of the European Community. However, the European Court has distinguished, in a number of cases,[95] between the *existence* of a national right, which is not subject to EC laws, and the *exercise* of that right, which may be subject to EC laws. In a series of cases involving the rules on the free movement of goods contained in EC Treaty, Arts 28–30,[96] the European Court has held that transactions in national property may be caught by EC laws if in the *exercise* of the property right there is a breach of a provision of the Treaty.

This principle has been applied in intellectual property cases, and there would seem to be no reason in principle why it would not apply also to other types of property, if an effect on inter-state trade can be established. (It may be more difficult to establish such an effect in the case of land.) Thus, Article 295[97] probably does not enable transactions in UK property to be exempted from EC competition laws.

OWNERSHIP OF HUMAN TISSUE AND BIOTECHNOLOGICAL PRODUCTS ORIGINATING FROM HUMAN TISSUE

Introduction

The phenomenal rate of progress in the biosciences in general and the biomedical sciences in particular and the fact that the related legal issues are also now in a similar state of flux, necessitate an understanding of relevant surrounding legal issues with respect to intellectual property contracts in

---

94   Following adoption of the Lisbon Treaty in 2009, this Article number will be renumbered 345.
95   Most famously in *Consten and Grundig v Commission* [1966] ECR 299.
96   See n 95.
97   To become Art 345 (see n 100).

medicine and the biosciences, particularly regarding ownership and use of materials generated by or made available to, these scientific areas.[98]

Human tissue as property

Common law and statutory provisions

Since an Australian case in 1908,[99] it has been clear that no one can have proprietary rights in the body of another person *as such*.

The case also expresses an important exception to the long-established common law rule mentioned in the previous paragraph that there is no property in a corpse. Where a corpse, or part of a corpse, had undergone a process or application of human skill designed to preserve it for medical or scientific examination, it acquired a value and became property. This exception has been confirmed in recent case law.[100]

With the rise of tissue banks, biotechnological engineering and human reproductive technology as major users of human tissue, the situation has now changed dramatically from the days when human tissue was only relevant from the point of view of the treatment of corpses and cadaveric specimens. At common law, since a donor could not bequeath his body, it followed that there could be no consent to the removal of tissue at death for transplantation or therapeutic purposes.[101]

There has been recent legislation concerning (and much larger regulatory control and licensing of) obtaining, use and disposal of bodies, body parts and human tissue ('tissue')[102] – principally, the Human Fertilisation and Embryology Act 1990[103] and Human Tissue Act 2004.[104] These modern statements of law have, however, not specifically addressed the issue of property rights in (let alone ownership of) materials, fluids and human tissue.

---

98 Chapter 11 provides a brief introduction to the background to the scientific matters dealt with by this area as well as outlining the regulatory control of and the need for consent where bodies, body parts or human tissue are involved, principally now through the Human Fertilisation and Embryology Act 1990 (as amended by the Human Fertilisation and Embryology Act 2008) and the Human Tissue Act 2004. This part of this chapter focuses entirely on issues of whether such things as bodies, body parts and human tissue can be property and whether they can be owned by anyone.

99 *Doodeward v Spence* (1908) 6 CLR 406.

100 *R v Kelly* [1999] 2 WLR 384, [1999] QB 621, [1998] 3 All ER 741, CA. This case concerned the theft of human body parts from the Royal College of Surgeons.

101 See *Williams v Williams* (1882) 20 ChD 659.

102 And as noted at n 99, regulatory control and licensing, and the requirement for consent matters, are dealt with in Ch 11.

103 As amended by the Human Fertilisation and Embryology Act 2008, from 1 October 2009.

104 This Act has repealed the Human Tissue Act 1961, the Human Organ Transplant Act 1989 and other relevant Acts (which were dealt with in the second edition of this book), and was largely brought into force from 1 September 2009.

Criminal law

There are a small number of decisions on theft offences in which certain materials, fluids or human tissue has been treated as property:

- *Urine*: in one case a defendant was convicted of theft of a urine sample collected at a police station for the purposes of an alcohol level test.[105] Having initially provided the sample, the defendant poured it down the sink while the constable was temporarily absent from the room. On appeal to the Court of Appeal on sentence only, the court noted that theft of urine was 'in its way a technical offence', but otherwise cast no doubt on its correctness.

- *Blood*: in another case a similar decision was reached, where a defendant had provided a blood sample for a blood alcohol test.[106] He was then released and he left, taking the sample with him, having removed it while the officer's back was turned. He was convicted of both theft and failing to provide a specimen under the Road Traffic Act 1972. On appeal, the Court of Appeal quashed the conviction for the offence under the Road Traffic Act. The conviction for theft was not in issue, although the judgment of the court, delivered by Scarman LJ, appeared to recognise its correctness and freely spoke of the removal of the blood sample as 'theft'.

It should follow from the above decisions that statutes which require the provision of human tissue samples for police-related forensic investigation effectively require the donor of the tissue to transfer his or her proprietary interests in the sample to the police. Such interests presumably come into existence as soon as the sample is removed from the body. In the absence of legislation, sample removal by consent could be regarded as a gift. This may be compared with the situation under a bailment model, for example, where a donor might place legal restrictions on the kind of diagnostic tests which could be performed on tissue samples.

Ownership of the products of biotechnological engineering

Biotechnology generally involves the development of techniques for the application of biological processes to the production of materials for use in medicine and industry. Therefore it encompasses not only genetic engineering but also the use of materials, fluids and human tissue, obtained from living or dead bodies, transplants, and in vitro fertilisation, as well as the production of antibiotics.

In the biotechnology industry huge sums are spent on research and development, as well as manufacture and marketing, relating to novel

---

105   In *R v Welsh* [1974] RTR 478.
106   *R v Rothery* [1976] RTR 550, CA.

cell lines, bacterial strains, drugs, biologic probes and other products of biotechnological engineering. One issue which arises concerns property rights in human tissue used in these manufacturing processes. Much of the case law appears not to decide whether a person is the owner of some materials, fluid or human tissue, but whether it is capable of patent protection (within the current law governing patent protection).

For example in the US the Supreme Court granted patent protection to a living, genetically engineered microorganism capable of breaking down the components of crude oil,[107] a decision which stimulated large-scale capital investment in the biotechnology sector.

In relation to the human genome, its patentability has generated complex case law not only in the UK, but also in the US and elsewhere.

Patent protection is available for products synthesised from human cells or containing cloned human DNA.[108] Also, in the US, patents for DNA sequences controlling Alzheimer's disease, multiple sclerosis and diabetes have been granted. Patent rights in living things, including microorganisms, and cloned human DNA, can also exist under the laws of the UK. A patent has been granted for the genetic structure of the hepatitis C virus.

How biotechnology uses human tissue: legal rights

While cloned human DNA sequences may be patentable, it is highly likely that 'human patents' would be excluded under the Patents Act 1977, s 1(3) (as amended by SI 2000/2037), which provides that a patent may not be granted for an invention, the publication or exploitation of which would be contrary to public policy or morality. This is further reflected in the Biotechnology Directive,[109] which provides that the human body, at any stage in its formation or development, cannot be patented.[110]

While the issue of patentability of much biotechnological and tissue material is set out and being tested in the courts, and therefore capable of forming the basis of profitable businesses, the issue of whether the provider of the material and tissue can have a share in profits is a different matter. It appears that the provider of the material and/or tissue will not have any rights to a

---

107 *Diamond v Chakrabarty* (1980) 65 L Ed 2d 144.
108 See *Kirin-Amgen Inc and others v Hoechst Marion Roussel Ltd and others; Hoechst Marion Roussel Ltd and others v Kirin-Amgen and others* [2004] UKHL 46, [2005] 1 All ER 667.
109 Council Directive 98/44/EC.
110 The precise scope of this is constantly being tested as new and further uses are being applied. For example, such as a case heard in the European Patents Office, the EPO Opposition Division, University of Edinburgh/Stem Cells, European Patent Number 0695351, where claims directed to or embracing human embryonic stem cells were unpatentable as contrary to *ordre public* and morality.

share. For example in a US case[111] a conversion claim was brought against a physician at the University of California at Los Angeles (UCLA) Medical Center who, in the course of treating the plaintiff for leukaemia, developed a unique cell line using tissue (which was obtained without the plaintiff's consent). The Regents of the University of California patented the cell line together with methods of production for various products derived from it, and the physician negotiated agreements for commercial development of the cell line.

The Court of Appeals held that the plaintiff had a cause of action for conversion;[112] this was reversed by the Supreme Court of California, which held that there was no judicial precedent recognising conversion liability for unauthorised use of human cells in biotechnological research. It seems that this decision in effect requires that the removal of tissue be treated (under relevant US law) as a gift by the donor to the removing institution and that the plaintiff had no rights in the material removed.

Although the position under English law would be different as far as the removal of the material, following the passing of the Human Tissue Act 2004, the US case appears to confirm the position under English law that a person will not have any rights in the commercial application (and the profits arising from such application) of his or her human tissue.

This brings us back to the relationship between the use of tissue in biotechnological research and human tissue legislation, discussed earlier. Such legislation provides for the donor's consent to use donated tissue for scientific and medical purposes, and this presumably includes biotechnological research.[113] However, the legislation is only effective if property rights are acknowledged in severed tissue. Otherwise the researcher (or the researcher's employing organisation) would have no better right to the tissue than the tissue donor, or anybody else for that matter.

Proprietary rights could, of course, be regarded as being created through the process of biotechnological research, rather than at the time the tissue was removed from the donor. This would provide a basis for enforcing a researcher's right to possession of tissue, even if the tissue at the time of donation had no legal status. Following this line of reasoning would seem to lead to the conclusion that the proprietary status of tissue in the products of manufacture is unlikely in reality to be seriously challenged, although the issue of the tissue donor having a possible share in any commercialisation seems more open and perhaps an area from which further case law will emanate over the coming years.

---

111 *Moore v Regents of the University of California* (P 2d 479 (1990) (Supreme Court)).
112 'Conversion' is, very simply, where a person deals with the goods (which do not belong to that person) in a manner that is consistent with the rights of the owner.
113 A position reinforced, following the bringing into force of the Human Tissue Act 2006.

Human Fertilisation and Embryology Act 1990 and Human Tissue Act 2004[114]

As indicated above, both of these Acts have little or nothing to say, substantially, about the issue of ownership (or other proprietary rights of the material which is their subject matter). For the purposes of this book both Acts permit research to be carried out in a controlled and a licensed fashion or with the provision of consent of the person from whom material is obtained. For example:

- Human Fertilisation and Embryology Act 1990: the authority established under this Act grants separate licences in respect of treatment, storage and research activities in respect of gametes and embryos;[115] and

- *Human Tissue Act 2004*: the removal (in some circumstances), storage and use of a human material for particular purposes are only lawful if done with appropriate consent.[116] To carry out these activities without consent is an offence.[117] For example, the purposes relevant to this book that require consent include:

  — obtaining scientific or medical information about a living or deceased person which may be relevant to any other person (including a future person);

  — research in connection with disorders, or the functioning, of the human body.[118]

The issue of consent is subject to exceptions and in any case needs to be seen in the context of the numerous Codes on Consent issued by the Human Tissue Authority, in particular the Code on carrying out research[119] (which among other things indicates when licensing is required, when consent is required and how the Human Tissue Act 2004 interacts with other legislation or requirements to conduct research on human tissue (such as the need to obtain ethical approval for such research)).

---

114 Chapter 11 provides an outline of these Acts.
115 In respect of licensing activities, see ss 11(1)(c) , 15 and Sch 2, para 3.
116 Human Tissue Act 2004, s 1. 'Relevant material' means material other than gametes, which consist of human cells, but will not include in any case embryos outside the human body or hair and nail from the body of a living person (Human Tissue Act 2004, s 53). 'Appropriate consent' depends on whether the tissue or body part is coming from a person who is living or dead or whether the person is a child. In the case of a living adult the consent has to come from him or her. See Human Tissue Act 2004, ss 2–4.
117 Human Tissue Act 2004, s 5.
118 Human Tissue Act 2004, Sch 1, Pt I.
119 In particular Code of Practice 9 on research, which illustrates the complex and heavily regulated nature of undertaking research on human tissue. The Code of Practice is available from http://www.hta.gov.uk.

There is one statutory exception to the requirement for consent for the use and/or storage of human tissue:

• the human tissue has to come from a living person; and

• the researcher is not in possession, and not likely to come into possession, of information that identifies the person from whom the human tissue has come; and

• the research has been ethically approved, eg by a recognised research ethics committee.[120]

The modern law as expressed in these two Acts makes commercial dealing in human tissue an offence. For example, the Human Tissue Act 2004 makes it an offence to supply human tissue for any financial or other material award for transplantation.[121] Certain material is exempt from this restriction. These are gametes and embryos[122] and 'material which is the subject of property because of an application of human skill'.[123] This latter phrase is not further explained but does raise the possibility that in some circumstances it might be possible for limited commercial dealings to take place:

• where a researcher has legitimate access to human tissue; and

• has carried out work on the human tissue (presumably within the appropriate licensing scheme and receiving ethical approval from the appropriate body); and

• wishes to sell the material.

---

120 Human Tissue Act 2004, ss 1(8), (9).
121 Human Tissue Act 2004, s 32. The way an offence can be committed under the Act goes wider, including initiating or negotiating involving the giving of a financial or material award for the supply of human tissue, issuing an advertisement inviting persons to supply human tissue, and finding a person willing to supply human tissue. There are exceptions where a person is authorised to store or use material and payments are made for legitimately incurred expenses such as transporting, preparing or storing the human tissue. The human tissue covered by this section is tissue that (i) consists of or includes human cells; (ii) is, or is intended to be, removed from a human body; (iii) is intended to be used for the purpose of a transplant and is not excepted (see next sentence of paragraph in text).
122 Presumably because they would be covered by the Human Fertilisation and Embryology Act 1990.
123 Human Tissue Act 2004, s 32(9)(c).

CHAPTER 10

Contract Law

INTRODUCTION

Intellectual property transactions and contract law

The law of contract is a large subject; much of it applies equally to commercial transactions involving intellectual property as it does to other types of commercial agreement. There are only a small number of areas where there are special rules for intellectual property transactions.

The extent of contract law can be seen from examining the standard legal practitioner's work on contract law, *Chitty on Contracts*.[1] This book runs to two volumes, each of more than 2,000 pages. It does not, however, include a section on intellectual property transactions.[2] Moreover, its discussion of general principles of contract law in Volume 1 does not focus on examples from the intellectual property field.[3] There are a number of reasons for this omission, including:

- There is relatively little legislation in the UK specifically directed towards commercial transactions in intellectual property.[4] There is no general codifying statute for intellectual property licences in the way that there is for the sale of goods.[5] The laws that govern contracts generally also govern intellectual property transactions, although sometimes commercial legislation contains modified provisions for intellectual property transactions. For example, the Unfair Contract Terms Act 1977[6] applies in principle to commercial agreements concerned with intellectual property as it does to commercial agreements with other subject matter. However, the Act includes provisions which modify the general regime in the case of certain types of intellectual property transaction.[7] Such modifying provisions form only a small (and sometimes overlooked) part of the statutes in question. Moreover, the application of such legislation to intellectual property transactions remains relatively untested in the courts.

---

1   30th edn, Sweet & Maxwell, 2009.
2   In the latest edition there is only one mention of intellectual property in the index for Vol 1 at 14–105, and then only in relation to the Unfair Contract Terms Act 1977 (see below). Volume 2 of Chitty deals with particular types of contract (eg building contracts), and intellectual property is not dealt with at all.
3   Other books on contract law are similarly brief in their discussion of intellectual property matters (if they mention them at all).
4   This chapter does not consider those provisions of intellectual property legislation which affect commercial agreements concerned with intellectual property. It is fair to say that such provisions deal with a limited number of contract law issues and do not provide a general codification of commercial law in the area of agreements concerned with intellectual property. See further Ch 3.
5   Ie Sale of Goods Act 1979. Other legislation, particularly the Supply of Goods and Services Act 1982, may be relevant in particular situations. See under 'Supply of materials etc'.
6   See Unfair Contract Terms Act 1977, Sch 1.
7   However, in both these examples the precise scope of the special provisions for intellectual property remains, in some respects, unclear.

- Historically, intellectual property transactions have formed a relatively small proportion of the total number of commercial transactions. Fewer cases in this field have reached the higher courts than in some other fields, such as shipping or insurance. As the judges have developed the law of contract through court decisions, the facts of the cases in which such decisions were made have tended not to be concerned with intellectual property. Of course there are exceptions: for example the case of *Martin Baker Aircraft Co Ltd v Canadian Flight Equipment Ltd*[8] was concerned with a patent and know-how licence in respect of aircraft ejector seat technology.[9] It is likely that the courts will hear more commercial cases concerned with technology in the future, as technology becomes more and more central to our economy.

- A further practical matter, which should not be overlooked, is the way in which cases concerned with intellectual property are dealt with by the English court system. Most cases concerned with patents or involving complex technology, including contract disputes, will be referred to the Patents Court (part of the Chancery Division of the High Court).[10] By contrast, many major commercial cases are referred to the Commercial Court (part of the Queen's Bench Division of the High Court). Until recently, cases in the Patents Court tended to be reported only in specialist law reports.[11] But now cases in the High Court and higher level courts are all made available electronically, and therefore are more easily accessible by lawyers and non-lawyers alike.[12] One possible consequence of the historical division in the court system is that patent- (or other intellectual-property-) related commercial cases do not form part of the mainstream of commercial cases cited in the higher courts and in leading textbooks on contract law. It is too early to say whether

---

8   *Martin Baker Aircraft Co Ltd v Canadian Flight Equipment Ltd* [1955] 2 QB 556. This case is often cited as a general authority for the right to terminate certain types of contract on reasonable notice.

9   For example, Chitty cites the case both in the agency and employment chapters of vol 2 of that work, but its relevance to intellectual property matters is not mentioned.

10   Pursuant to CPR 49 and Practice Direction 49E. Sometimes these cases are referred to the Patents County Court or to a judge of the (ordinary) Chancery Division who has a scientific background. See also the *Patents Court Guide* (http://www.hmcourts-service.gov. uk/infoabout/patents/crt_guide.htm). Some technically complex contract disputes, eg in relation to the supply of computer hardware or software, are referred to the Technology and Construction Court pursuant to CPR 49 and Practice Direction 49C.

11   Particularly the Reports of Patent, Design and Trade Mark Cases (RPCs) and the Fleet Street Reports (FSRs).

12   The judgments of the High Court, Court of Appeal and Supreme Court (the latter formerly, until 30 September 2009, the House of Lords) are available in electronic format on http://www. bailii.org/. The use of the bailii website allows a user to view all the reports of a particular court, for example it is possible to see all the cases decided on one page for the Patents Court in any particular year. However cases which pre-date (currently) the late 1990s that involve intellectual property matters are likely to be confined to the specialist reports mentioned in n 11. One advantage of having access to traditional law reports is that each has a summary of the facts and the key points from the judgment at the beginning of the report, something which is not present for the judgments made available on bailii.

the change in the way law reports are made available will lead to any change in coverage by leading textbooks.

To summarise, in a few areas of commercial law there is specific legislation for intellectual property transactions. In most areas, general principles of contract law, including contract legislation, apply to intellectual property transactions as they do to most other types of commercial transaction. However, there is relatively little case law which gives authoritative guidance on the application of these laws to intellectual property agreements.

Scope of this chapter

A complete book could be written on the subject of English contract law from the perspective of intellectual property transactions. This chapter has more a limited purpose. It will focus on the following distinct areas:

- Case law which has concerned the interpretation of provisions of licences and other types of agreements, (including those concerning ownership of intellectual property).[13]

- Statute law in the contract law field of particular relevance to intellectual property transactions. The provisions of intellectual property legislation, which affect commercial transactions, are dealt with elsewhere,[14] as are the provisions of competition legislation;[15] to avoid repetition they are not considered in this chapter.

This chapter assumes that the reader is familiar with English contract law. The topics discussed below should be read in the light of general English contract law principles.[16]

---

13 These sections are based on a review of the specialist intellectual property law reports referred to above. They also draw on cases cited in various texts, particularly those listed in 'Interpretation and construction of licences and other agreements'below. Particular mention should be made of 79 *Halsbury's Laws of England* (5th edn, LexisNexis, 2008), 'Patents and Registered Designs', paras 378–391, which provided supplementary material for these sections.

   As well as referring to recent cases, *Halsbury* cites a number of 19th century authorities for propositions concerning patent licences. In the absence of more recent authority, many of these cases and the principles they establish have been repeated in this chapter, for the sake of completeness, although sometimes with 'health warnings'.

14 See Ch 3.

15 See Ch 12.

16 For readers wishing to refresh their knowledge of contract law, the books listed in the Bibliography (p xi) are suggested as useful starting points. Mention is made above of *Chitty* (see n 1). For those wishing to obtain an overview or even a moderately detailed outline of English contract law, *Chitty* is not the place to start as it is too detailed for that purpose.

INTERPRETATION AND CONSTRUCTION OF LICENCES AND OTHER AGREEMENTS

Introduction

This section reviews cases where the English courts have interpreted the wording (or lack of wording) of agreements concerning commercial transactions involving intellectual property, particularly, and most frequently patent (and sometimes know-how) licences. Such cases give guidance as to how a court would be likely to interpret similar wording in similar circumstances in the future (or what would happen if wording was not found in an agreement). However, it may not be safe to place too much reliance on some of these cases noted below. For the benefit of readers who are not familiar with English contract law it may be useful to mention a couple of significant reasons for this:

- The proper construction of an agreement may depend to a considerable extent on the circumstances in which the agreement was made – the 'factual matrix' as it is sometimes known. A court may depart from an earlier court's ruling on the meaning of particular words.[17]

- In some respects, cases specifically about agreements concerning commercial transactions involving intellectual property form a backwater of English commercial law. Sometimes, this means there are very few reported cases of direct relevance to a point in issue. In other areas the cases are old and may be thought out of line with modern commercial practice. Often, the highest authority on a point is at High Court level (often by a specialist patents judge rather than a Commercial Court judge), and even where it is binding on another judge in the High Court, it can be overruled by the Court of Appeal or the Supreme Court (formerly the House of Lords).

Despite these caveats, it is hoped that the following paragraphs will provide a useful brief summary of English court decisions in the areas discussed. In general, when drafting an agreement concerning a commercial transaction involving intellectual property such as a licence, the best course may be for the rights and obligations of the parties to be stated specifically, rather than relying on some of these court decisions. For example, if it is intended that interest will be payable on late payment of royalties it would be prudent to state this in the agreement, rather than rely on the leading authority for the proposition that interest is payable on patent royalties, which was decided over 100 years ago.[18]

---

17   See further Lewison, *Interpretation of Contracts* (4th edn, Sweet & Maxwell, 2007) Ch 3.
18   *Redges v Mulliner* (1892) 10 RPC 21. Which in any case may now be superseded by the Late Payment of Commercial Debts (Interest) Act 1998 (see 'Late Payment of Commercial Debts (Interest) Act 1998' below.

Most of the cases referred to in this chapter are concerned with patent (or patent and know-how) licence agreements or agreements concerning confidential information. This is perhaps inevitable, given that historically these have been the main types of intellectual property right protecting technology.

In recent years, copyright and design right have become more important as means of protecting technology – copyright being particularly important for protecting computer software. However, to date there have been relatively few major cases in the English courts concerned with commercial transactions involving these types of intellectual property. This may be partly because it takes a number of years, after a new technology has emerged and become commercially important, before a significant body of case law develops – the widespread use of information technology, for example, is relatively recent. In the last few years there have been some notable cases in relation to computer software, particularly in the area of liability for defective software.[19]

This chapter focuses on cases which are concerned with technology-related transactions. There is a body of case law on the interpretation of agreements concerned with 'arts'-related copyright which, it might be argued, is applicable to the licensing of copyright in computer programs. In the authors' view this would be a dangerous assumption to make. For example, take the issue of whether a party can unilaterally terminate an intellectual property licence agreement which includes no termination provisions. In relation to:

- *Patents and know-how:* the leading case[20] suggests that such a licence may be terminated on reasonable notice, the law being similar to that for distribution agreements.

- *Copyright:* by contrast there is case law[21] which indicates that a licence which does not include a termination provision could not be so terminated.

It is suggested that, in the case of a licence of a bespoke computer program which has 'industrial' applications, the leading case referred to above in relation to patents may provide a more reliable guide than the copyright cases, even though the intellectual property right protecting the software may be copyright. The factual circumstances of patent licences are generally much closer to the circumstances of software licences than the facts of many arts-related copyright cases.

---

19 Particularly *St Albans City and District Council v International Computers Ltd* [1996] 4 All ER 481, *Salvage Association v CAP Financial Services Limited* [1995] FSR 654 and *Watford Electronics Ltd v Sanderson CFL Ltd* [2001] EWCA Civ 317, discussed below under 'Unfair Contract Terms Act 1977 (as amended)'.

20 *Martin Baker Aircraft Co Ltd v Canadian Flight Equipment Ltd* [1959] 2QB 556.

21 Eg *Reade v Bentley* (1858) 4 K & J 656; *Re Berker Sportcraft* (1947) LT 420.

One area where this hypothesis may break down is in the area of 'multimedia' licences, traditionally concerned both with information technology and entertainment subject matter.[22] This book does not consider the arts/entertainment aspects of 'media law', which is a subject in itself.

What is not covered in this chapter

As noted above, this chapter deals with cases concerning commercial agreements involving intellectual property. It does not deal with the many other cases which do not involve intellectual property but involve interpretations of wording which are also of relevance where an agreement is being negotiated.[23] The section below also does not examine in any detail issues which usually involve, in the authors' experience, considerable concern and effort in the negotiation of commercial agreements involving intellectual property: warranties, limitations and exclusion of liability and indemnities. This is primarily because such issues are of general application in commercial agreements in many areas, not only those involving technology transfer or intellectual property.[24]

Nature and extent of licences

Licence or agreement to grant licence?

It is possible to draw a distinction between:

- a licence; and

- an agreement to grant a licence.

In written licence agreements the former might be drafted to include words such as 'X hereby grants Y a licence', while the latter with words such as 'X shall grant Y a licence in the form attached as Schedule 1 to this Agreement'.

A court has held that an agreement to grant a licence is enforceable by a court by an order for specific performance, if the licensor fails to do so.[25]

---

22   Although this point is less likely to continue to be true in the future.
23   For readers who wish to consult a source which contains examination of other wording interpreted by the courts, see Anderson and Warner, *A-Z Guide to Boilerplate and Commercial Clauses* (2nd edn, Tottel Publishing, 2006).
24   See Anderson and Warner *Drafting and Negotiating Commercial Contracts* (2nd edn, Tottel Publishing, 2007) for consideration of negotiating these issues.
25   *Brake v Radermacher* (1903) 20 RPC 631; *British Nylon Spinners Ltd v Imperial Chemical Industries Ltd* [1952] 2 All ER 780, 69 RPC 288, CA.

The following are further propositions in relation to forms of licence that can be derived from mainly old cases:[26]

- an agreement to grant a licence, if the parties act upon it, is treated in equity as a licence;[27]

- an agreement to renew a licence on the same terms as originally applied to it is presumed where a licensee continues to manufacture and pay royalties after the expiration of his or her licence;[28]

- an agreement for a licence is presumed where use of an invention has been permitted during negotiations for a licence;[29]

- a parol (ie non-written) licence, in order to be enforceable, must be certain in its terms;[30]

- a licence can be made orally, in writing, or implied from the conduct of the parties.[31]

Nature of a licence

Normally, a patent licence is not a right *in* the licensed patent, rather it is a right *under* the patent.[32] In other words it is a contractual right rather than

---

26 Halsbury's Laws (see n 13) para 379.
27 See *Ward v Livesey* (1887) 5 RPC 102; *Postcard Automatic Supply Co v Samuel* (1889) 6 RPC 560; but see *Henderson v Shiels* (1906) 24 RPC 108.
28 *Warwick v Hooper* (1850) 3 Mac & G 60; *Goucher v Clayton* (1865) 13 LT 115.
29 *Tweedale v Howard and Bullough Ltd* (1896) 13 RPC 522. In some cases the proposed licensee may be in a position to elect whether or not he or she will be treated as a licensee: *Postcard Automatic Supply Co v Samuel* (1889) 6 RPC 560. Where the negotiations for a licence fell through, damages were refused for acts done with the patentee's knowledge during such negotiations: *Coslett Anti-Rust Syndicate Ltd v Lennox* (1912) 29 RPC 477 at 481. The licence may preclude the proprietor of the patent from suing for infringement prior to the licence: *Campbell v G Hopkins & Sons (Clerkenwell) Ltd* (1931) 49 RPC 38.
30 An oral agreement to grant a licence at royalties to be fixed by arbitration was upheld, and in default of arbitration royalties were fixed by the Official Referee: see *Fleming v JS Doig (Grimsby) Ltd* (1921) 38 RPC 57; *Mellor v William Beardmore & Co Ltd* (1926) 43 RPC 361; varied (1927) 44 RPC 175; *Brake v Radermacher* (1903) 20 RPC 631.
31 *Chanter v Dewhurst* (1844) 13 LJ Ex 198; *Chanter v Johnson* (1845) 14 LJ Ex 289; *Crossley v Dixon* (1863) 10 HL Cas 293. Where a licence is made orally the terms and conditions which are to bind the parties have to be certain (or that the methods by which terms and conditions are fixed must be certain). For example, if the parties orally agree that a licence be granted by one party to another and that royalties should be paid but the amount to be paid was to be settled by arbitration. The method chosen where arbitration was not able to settle the amount was that the amount would be fixed by the official referee. This was held as being sufficiently certain to be binding: *Fleming v JS Doig (Grimsby) Ltd* (1921) 38 RPC 57; see also *Mellor v William Beardmore & Co Ltd* (1926) 43 RPC 361 (varied (1927) 44 RPC 175); *Brake v Radermacher* (1903) 20 RPC 631.
32 *Insituform Technical Services Ltd v Inliner UK plc* [1992] RPC 83; see also *Crittall Windows Ltd v Stormseal (UPVC) Window Systems Ltd and another* [1991] RPC 265.

being an interest in property.[33] On this basis, in order to determine the rights and obligations of a licensee, and in the absence of statutory provision, it may be more appropriate to look to the law of contract for guidance rather than precedents from the law of property.[34] By contrast, an assignee of a patent clearly does have property rights in the patent.[35] In the special case of an exclusive licence, it is likely that the licensee does have a property interest in the intellectual property, although this does not seem to have been finally resolved.[36]

Extent of licence

A licence should make clear what activities are licensed, and in particular which of the acts, which would otherwise infringe the licensed intellectual property, may be carried out by the licensee.

It is possible to split the permitted activities between more than one licensee, such as one licensee having the right to make, another having the right to sell, for example. Other matters that may need consideration include:

---

33 See eg Bell, *Modern Law of Personal Property in England and Ireland* (Butterworths, 1989). Part II of that work discusses in detail the different types of right in personal property. Bell indicates that one test of whether a right in property exists is whether the holder of the right has rights against the world rather than just eg contractual rights (see pp 6–7 of that work). On this test, an exclusive licensee under eg a patent, whose licence is registered, may be said to have property rights in the patent, by virtue of his or her statutory right to bring proceedings against infringers of the patent under Patents Act 1977, s 67. This may be regarded as an exception to the general principle that a licensee has merely contractual rights. For a case which indicates that a licensee has no rights against the world, see eg *Gillette Safety Razor Co Ltd v AW Gamage Ltd* (1908) 25 RPC 492, 25 RPC 782, CA.

34 See *Allen & Hanbury v Generics* [1986] RPC 203, HL at 264 (the speech of Lord Diplock); *Instituform Technical Services Ltd v Inline UK plc* [1992] RPC 265 and *Crittal Windows Ltd v Stormseal (UPVC) Windows Systems Ltd and another* [1991] RPC 265. However there has also been case law which suggests that a licensee may have a proprietary interest in the licensed patent – see *British Nylon Spinners Ltd v Imperial Chemical Industries Limited* [1952] 2 All ER 780 at 783, 69 RPC 288 at 294, CA: 'An English Patent is a species of English property of the nature of a chose in action, and peculiar in character. A person who has an enforceable right to a licence under an English patent appears, therefore, to me to have, at least, some kind of proprietary interest which it is the duty of the Courts to protect'. Also, see similar comments of Romer LJ in *National Carbonising Co Ltd v British Coal Distillation Ltd* (1937) 54 RPC 41. In the case of an exclusive, irrevocable licence under a patent which is registered, the licensee effectively 'owns' all remaining rights under the patent and almost certainly does have property rights in the patent. This is consistent with the former treatment of such licences for stamp duty purposes (ie prior to the abolition of stamp duty on most IP transactions) – they were regarded in the same category as outright assignments.

35 The terms 'assignment' and 'licence' are sometimes confused. Assignment of a patent may be regarded as a 'sale' of the patent. See further Ch 4.

36 For a case concerning the rights of an exclusive licensee of trade marks, see the comments of Jacobs J in *Northern & Shell plc v Conde Nast* [1995] RPC 117. In that case, it was held that a licensee was not entitled to sue a third party for infringement where the proprietor had given consent.

- the duration of the licence;
- the geographical area it covers;
- technical or field limitations;
- whether manufacture and/or sales are permitted;
- whether any form of payment is required (such as royalties, set amounts or assets such as equity); and
- the number of units/items which can be made, sold or used.

Traditionally, licences under UK intellectual property law used the language of the relevant statute, eg a patent licence might be drafted so as to permit the licensee to:

'make, use, exercise and vend'

products falling within the claims of the patent, the quoted words being those used in the Patents Act 1949. The equivalent infringing acts in the language of the Patents Act 1977[37] include, in the case of products, to:

'make, dispose of, offer to dispose of, use, import or keep the product whether for disposal or otherwise'.[38]

The extent of the licence granted and the wording used can be important where a licensee is defending an action for infringement brought by a licensor that the licensee is using the patent outside the terms of the licence.[39]

However, modern licences tend not to track the language of a statute so closely, not least because:

- licences frequently extend to more than one country;
- the statutory language in each country varies; and
- it is common to grant licences under more than one type of intellectual property, eg one licence agreement granting licences under several types of intellectual property, such as patents, copyright and designs, and the statutory language differs according to the type of right under consideration.

Thus more general wording tends to be used, eg a licence might permit the licensee to 'manufacture, have manufactured, use and sell' the licensed products.

---

37 Patents Act 1977, s 60.
38 Which is similar to the wording used in TRIPS, Art 28: 'making, using, offering for sale, selling or importing'.
39 *Apple Computer Inc v Articulate Systems Inc* 44 USPQ 2d 1369 (ND Cal 1997), quoted by Melville: *Forms and Agreements on Intellectual Property and International Licensing* (3rd edn, Sweet & Maxwell) a licence to use, modify and compile a patentee's source code in a particular software product, can if paid-up, offer a complete defence to allegations of patent infringement.

Sometimes, licences are not clear as to which acts are permitted. In a number of reported cases it has been decided that particular rights should be implied into particular licence agreements (eg that a licence to manufacture included a right to use the patented invention). Even though the typical wording used in licences may have changed over the years, and the cases were decided in relation to provisions not commonly used in modern licences, they give some useful guidance. It has been decided[40] (in some cases on the particular facts) that:

- a licence to manufacture implies the right to use;[41]

- a licence to 'vend' (ie sell) gives the right to license purchasers to use, or sell again, the article purchased;[42]

- a licence merely to 'use and exercise' may be extended so as to authorise manufacture and sale,[43] or import for subsequent sale and distribution;[44]

- a personal licence to use certain goods, the property of the licensor, does not give the power to license others to use them;[45] and

- if a licence only permits the making of an article of a particular kind, proceedings for infringement will lie against the licensee for making articles within the patent and not within the licence.[46]

Meaning of 'invention' and 'improvements'

The courts have considered the meaning of the expressions 'invention' and 'improvement', as used in licence agreements on more than one occasion. Sometimes, the meaning can only be ascertained with difficulty. This is often due to the lack of precision in the drafting of the agreement. Where these terms are not clearly defined, the court may have difficulty in determining the intentions of the parties.

Meaning of 'invention'

A number of cases have considered the meaning of 'invention', including:

---

40 The following cases are all taken from *Halsbury's Laws* (see n 13). 'Patents', para 384.
41 The footnote to this statement referring to *Basset v Graydon* (1897) 14 RPC 701, HL; and *National Phonographic Co of Australia Ltd v Menck* [1911] AC 336, 28 RPC 229, PC.
42 *Thomas v Hunt* (1864) 17 CBNS 183; *National Phonographic Co of Australia Ltd v Menck* [1911] AC 336, 28 RPC 229, PC.
43 *Dunlop Pneumatic Tyre Co Ltd v North British Rubber Co Ltd* (1904) 21 RPC 161, CA.
44 *Pfizer Corpn v Ministry of Health* [1965] AC 512, [1965] RPC 261, HL.
45 *British Mutoscope and Biograph Co Ltd v Homer* [1901] 1 Ch 671, 18 RPC 177.
46 *SA pour la Fabrication d'Appareils d'Eclairage v Midland Lighting Co* (1897) 14 RPC 419; *Dunlop Pneumatic Tyre Co Ltd v Buckingham and Adams Cycle and Motor Co Ltd* (1901) 18 RPC 423, CA.

- the mere disclosure by a licensor to his licensee of a chemical formula was held not to amount to making an 'invention'. If it had amounted to an invention, the licence agreement would have required the licensor to extend the licence to cover such additional invention;[47]

- on the other hand, in a case involving a dispute over the scope of a licence, the licensed invention was held to include the subject matter of patent applications which had not been filed at the time the licence agreement was made, and whose claims were broader than the inventions disclosed by the licensor to the licensee at the time the licence agreement was made;[48]

- an obligation to pay royalties on products 'falling within any claim of the patents' included products made under patents no longer subsisting, interpreting earlier patents legislation.[49] However, it may be unsafe to assume that this case would have general application today.

Meaning of 'improvement'

The meaning of the term 'improvement' will be a matter of interpretation of the agreement and the sense in which the term is used in the agreement. Generally, an improvement is a technical advance to the patents or other technology provided under a licence agreement, including such items as new inventions, know-how protectable by intellectual property law, or modifications to software.

In cases where the term has been considered the following points emerge:

- An improvement was limited to a technical advance of the functions of the licensed invention, and that if there was no licence in place then there would an infringement:

  'The way to treat the question whether any particular powder would be an addition to, or an improvement on, the plaintiff's invention, would be to see whether, assuming the plaintiff's patent to be valid, and assuming a person to be using it without licence from the patentee, it would be an infringement'.

---

47   *Beecham Group Limited v Bristol Laboratories International SA* [1978] RPC 521, HL.
48   *Fluflon Limited v William Frost & Son Limited* [1968] RPC 508, HL; this case illustrates the dangers of not defining key terms in a patent licence. The meaning of an invention was set out in the Recitals. The meaning was stated as being 'The said processes, apparatus and the yarns produced (to the extent that said yarns are new and patentable) are hereinafter sometimes referred to as the invention'. Lord Pearson in his speech noted that the word which stopped this sentence being a true definition was 'sometimes': 'The insertion of the word 'sometimes' renders the application of the definition uncertain and is apt to create ambiguities'.
49   *Bristol Repetition v Fomento* [1961] RPC 222.

- It has been held in an old case that:

  'an improvement of a patented machine includes any machine which, while retaining some of those essential or characteristic parts of the machine which are the subject of the monopoly claims, yet by addition, omission or alteration better achieves the same or better results, whether such improvement infringes the monopoly claims for the patented machine or not'.[50]

- However, an important advance created by a licensee to a licensor's patents may still be considered to be an 'improvement' and therefore need communicating to and/or to be owned by the licensor (subject to the provisions of the licence agreement) unless the invention created by the technical advance was so radical as to make the invention quite 'distinct'.[51]

- The meaning of 'improvements' is to be interpreted through the technically orientated eyes of the reasonable man in the area to which the technology/patent relates.[52]

When must improvements be communicated?

There appears to be no definite time when an improvement, once made, needs communicating to the licensor in the absence of clear wording in the agreement. In one case it was held:[53]

- that the time at which the obligation to communicate an improvement could vary; and

- it would be early in the case of a major advance, for which the licensor might want to secure the earliest possible patent priority; and

- it would be later in the case of a minor workshop improvement which might require extensive trial to establish whether it was an improvement or not.

Extent of licence of improvements

On the question of whether a licence of improvements, with no express duration, arising under a patent licence agreement, continued after expiry

---

50   *Linotype and Machinery Limited v Hopkins* (1910) 27 RPC 109 , HL; quoted extract from Court of Appeal judgment.

51   *Buchanan v Alba Diagnostics Ltd* [2000] RPC 367 at 384, Lord Hamilton, Court of Session, Outer House, quoting the words of PO Lawrence J in *Sadgrove v Godfrey* (1919) 37 RPC 7.

52   As above, p 110-111.

53   *National Broach and Machine Company v Churchill Gear Machines Limited* [1967] RPC 99, HL. See also the different answers to this question given by the Court of Appeal [1965] RPC 516 and by the High Court [1965] RPC 61, respectively. A clause of the kind under consideration in this case would probably breach EC Treaty, Art 81 today. See further Ch 12.

of the main licence, in one case it was held, construing the wording of the agreement, that the licence did continue without limit of time.[54]

On the consequences of assignment by a licensor of a patent licence in respect of an obligation on the licensee to communicate improvements, see 'Rights to assign, sublicense, subcontract etc a licence' below.

As for competition law issues in improvement clauses, see further Chapters 12 and 15.

Exclusive, non-exclusive or sole[55]

Exclusive licence

It is generally understood, under English law, that the grant of an exclusive licence means that the licensor:

- will not license anyone else under the licensed intellectual property within the scope of the licensee's licence; and

- will not exercise those rights himself.

For example, if a manufacturing licence under a patent for a chemical compound is stated to be exclusive within the human healthcare field in a defined territory, the patent owner agrees in effect:

- not to license anyone else under that patent to manufacture within that field within that territory; and

- not to manufacture himself within that field within that territory;

for as long as the licence continues.

He would, however, be entitled to license the patents in another field, such as animal health, or outside the licensed territory, or to exploit the patents directly outside the licensed field and territory. The impact of competition laws upon such arrangements should not be overlooked.[56]

---

54 *Regina Glass Fibre Ltd v Werner Schuller* [1972] RPC 229, CA. This case is also interesting for a further reason: it was held that there was no general proposition of law that when confidential information was given under an agreement and that agreement came to an end, the right to use the confidential information also came to an end.
55 For a case in which arguments were presented as to whether a licence was exclusive or sole, see *PCUK v Diamond Shamrock Industrial Chemicals Ltd* [1981] FSR 427.
56 See Ch 12.

Disputes over whether a party is an exclusive licensee under a patent have reached the courts. In one case,[57] albeit decided under earlier patent legislation, it was held that no particular document or form of grant was required to constitute an exclusive patent licence; the position was in each case a mixed question of law and fact as to whether a licence is in fact exclusive. Clearly, a written agreement which makes it clear whether an exclusive licence is granted, is desirable.

It has been held (not surprisingly) that it is a breach of contract, in the case of an exclusive licence, if the patent owner himself or herself uses or works the patent.[58]

Non-exclusive licence

A non-exclusive licence allows the licensor both to license others and exercise the licensed rights himself or herself, within (and, for that matter, outside) the scope of the licensee's licence.

Sole licence

By contrast, a sole licence means only that the licensor will not grant anyone a licence within the scope of the licensed rights. The licensor remains free to exercise those rights directly himself or herself in competition to the sole licensee (or through his or her agents or assigns).[59]

Statutory meaning of exclusive, non-exclusive or sole licences

There is no statutory definition of exclusive, non-exclusive or sole licences which is generally applicable under English law. There are, however, definitions for specific statutory purposes which are consistent with the above explanation. These will be referred to below.

In general, intellectual property licences, whether exclusive, sole or non-exclusive, do not have to be in writing in order to be legally enforceable.[60] However, in order to take advantage of certain statutory rights of an exclusive licensee under patent, copyright and design right legislation, in particular the right to sue infringers,[61] the exclusive licence must meet the definitions of an 'exclusive licence' as set out in the legislation. In the

---

57 *Morton-Norwich Products Inc and Others v Intercen Ltd (No 2)* and *Morton-Norwich Products Inc and Others v United Chemicals (London) Ltd* [1981] FSR 337.
58 *Rapid Steel Co v Blankstone* (1907) 24 RPC 529, at 541.
59 *Murray (HM Inspector of Taxes) v Imperial Chemical Industries Ltd* [1967] RPC 216, CA.
60 See *Crossley v Dixon* (1863) 10 HL Cas 293, HL; *Morton-Norwich Products Inc v Intercen Ltd (No 2)*; and *Morton-Norwich Products Inc v United Chemicals (London) Ltd* [1981] FSR 337.
61 See eg Ch 4 from 'Meaning of infringement and exceptions' to 'Remedies for groundless threats of infringement proceedings.'

case of copyright and design right, 'exclusive licence' is defined[62] for these purposes as follows:

> 'In this Part an "exclusive licence" means a licence in writing signed by or on behalf of the [copyright/design right] owner authorising the licensee to the exclusion of all other persons, including the person granting the licence, to exercise a right which would otherwise be exercisable exclusively by the [copyright/design right owner]'.

The equivalent definition of an exclusive licence under the Patents Act 1977 makes no mention of the licence being in writing:[63]

> '"exclusive licence" means a licence from the proprietor of or applicant for a patent conferring on the licensee, or on him and persons authorised by him, to the exclusion of all other persons (including the proprietor or applicant), any right in respect of the invention to which the patent or application relates, and "exclusive licensee" and "non-exclusive licence" shall be construed accordingly'.

There is a similar definition in respect of registered designs as for patents:[64]

> 'In this Act an "exclusive licence" means a licence in writing signed by or on behalf of the proprietor of the registered design authorising the licensee to the exclusion of all other persons, including the person granting the licence, to exercise a right which would otherwise be exercisable exclusively by the proprietor of the registered design'.

In the leading case on whether a patent licence can be terminated on reasonable notice, referred to in 'Duration of licence and termination; effect of termination' below, the licensee conceded in court that a term in a licence to manufacture and sell 'not to make any similar agreement with any other party ... nor ... permit anyone else to manufacture or sell' did not exclude manufacture by the patent owner, ie it was a sole licence.

Rights to assign, sublicense, subcontract etc a licence

A licence under a UK patent or patent application may be assigned, and a licensee may grant sub-licences, but only 'to the extent that the licence so

---

62   See Copyright, Designs and Patents Act 1988, s 225(1) for the definition in respect of designs, and s 92(1) of that Act for the equivalent definition in respect of copyright. The definitions are identical save for the substitution of the word 'copyright' or 'design' in the places shown in square brackets in the quoted text.

63   Patents Act 1977, s 130(1). An exclusive licence does not mean all the rights that a licensor may have, but can be one or more, therefore it is possible to grant several exclusive licences under a patent (*Courtauld's Application* [1956] RPC 208).

64   Registered Designs Act 1949, s 15C, as inserted by SI 2006/1028.

provides'.[65] This statutory wording from the Patents Act 1977 is not entirely clear, however. It could be interpreted as referring to implied as well as express provisions of a licence.

It has been held that a licence of patents is personal to the licensee and may not be assigned or sublicensed by him or her without the consent of the licensor, unless there is evidence which shows that there was an intention that the licence should not be limited to the original licensee, eg an express term in the licence permitting assignment or sublicensing.[66] There is no equivalent statutory language regarding the rights of a licensee under copyright or designs. But in one case a court held that, in the absence of express terms to the contrary, a licence of copyright (including copyright in designs) was personal to the licensee and not assignable.[67]

Where a patent licence agreement includes an obligation on the licensee to communicate improvements, it has been held that following an assignment (by the liquidator of the patent owner) of the patents and the benefit of the licence, the obligation to communicate improvements continues on the licensee towards the assignee.[68]

Sub-licensing

Without specific provision a licensee is not able to grant sub-licenses, even if the licensee has an exclusive licence.[69] In one case the court stated:[70]

> 'The general rule is clearly that a licensee under a patent has, in the absence of provision to the contrary in his licence, no power to grant sub-licences. That means not merely that he cannot grant sub-licences

---

65 Patents Act 1977, s 30(4).

66 *Lawson v Donald Macpherson & Co Ltd* (1897) 14 RPC 696; *National Carbonising Co Ltd v British Coal Distillation Ltd* (1937) 54 RPC 41 (this case considers in detail the rights of an assignee from a liquidator). See also *British Mutoscope and Biograph Co Ltd v Homer* [1901] 1 Ch 671, 18 RPC 177.

67 *Dorling v Honnor and Honnor Marine Limited* [1963] RPC 205.

68 *National Carbonizing Company Ltd v British Coal Distillation Ltd* (1937) 54 RPC 41. It was argued in this case that because the agreement only referred to the 'Patentee' and not the 'Patentee and his assigns', the obligation to communicate improvements did not extend to the Patentee's assigns. The Court of Appeal rejected this argument on the basis that it was settled law that no such reference was necessary if it were ascertained 'that the intention of the contract is that it should be assigned'.

69 *Howard Bullough v Tweedles & Smalley* [1895] 12 RPC 519.

70 *Allen & Hanbury Ltd's (Salbutamol) Patent* [1987] RPC 327, CA. See the comments of Dillon LJ at 379–380. What terms would be implied into a licensee agreement (whether sub-licensing or sub-contracting) will be a matter of construction. See also *Clearsprings Management Ltd v Businesslink Ltd and another* [2005] EWHC 1487 (Ch), [2005] All ER (D) 172 (Jul) where what was necessary to be implied was the minimum type of licence, which did not include the right to sub-licence. The case concerned copyright and dealt with whether an exclusive licence or an assignment of the copyright should be implied into a software development agreement.

to third parties to enable the third parties to operate the patent for the third parties' own purposes, but he cannot sub-contract to third parties the making of the patented articles for the licensee himself[71] ... The licensee can work the patent, but he cannot sub-contract to others to work it for him'.

Where there is a grant of a sub-licence a court held that the sub-licence will terminate when the main licence terminates, unless the contrary can be implied.[72]

In a case relating to the licensing of gene technology,[73] which contained a term permitting sub-licensing to a consortium, and where the licence indicated that the consortium must have as a principle objective the development of products, it was held insufficient that only one member of the consortium 'majored' on the product.

In a case where there was one provision in a patent licence permitting the grant of a sub-licence as well as another provision which restricted the right to sub-licence, it was held that the restriction should be removed.[74]

The right to sub-contract

It is arguable that a patent licensee is not permitted to subcontract his or her rights (eg a right to manufacture licensed products) except with the consent of the licensor.[75]

General points

It may not be safe to rely on the propositions stated immediately above in all situations. These would appear to be an exception to the general rule that a contractual *right* can be assigned by a party (unless the other party contracted with him or her on the basis of his or her personal skill and reputation). However, the cases do not appear to affect the general principle

---

71 The judge cited *Dixon v The London Small Arms Company Ltd* (1871–1876) 1 App Cas 632.
72 *Austin Baldwin & Co Ltd v Greenwood Batley Ltd* (1925) RPC 454.
73 *Oxford Gene Technology Ltd v Affymetrix Inc* [2000] FSR 12, CA.
74 *JR French Ltd v Redbus LMDS Ltd* [2005] EWHC 1436 (Ch), [2006] FSR 13. In this case the judge was prepared to go beyond the wording of the agreement to find the objective intentions of the parties. Of particular interest was the observation of the judge that if he had considered only the wording of the agreement he would have decided the other way, ie he would have given preference to the wording which restricted the right to sub-licence, as that wording dealt with the scope of the grant of licence.
75 *Dixon v The London Small Arms Co Ltd* (1876) 1 App Cas 632, HL; *Allen & Hanbury Ltd's (Salbutamol) Patent* [1987] RPC 327 at 380, CA, per Dillon LJ. Also *Henry Bros (Magherafelt) Ltd v Ministry of Defence and Northern Ireland Office* [1997] RPC 693. On the question of what is and is not manufacture by a licensee, Halsbury's Laws (see n 13), at 'Patents', para 382, n 4, cites *Dunlop Pneumatic Tyre Co Ltd v Holborn Tyre Co Ltd* (1901) 18 RPC 222; *Dunlop v Cresswell Cheshire Rubber Co* (1901) 18 RPC 473; and *Dunlop v North British Rubber Co Ltd* (1904) 21 RPC 161, CA.

that it is not possible to assign a contractual *obligation* without the other party's consent. Where all rights and obligations under a contract are assigned (ie with the consent of the other party) there will, in effect, be a novation of the contract.[76]

Other cases have held:

- That an assignment of a patent licence was intended by the licensee to, and did, include an assignment of the benefit of a sub-licence previously granted by him, even though no mention of the sub-licence was made in the deed of assignment.[77] Consequently the deed was rectified accordingly. It appears that the court approached the issue on ordinary contract law principles rather than on the basis that any special rule applied to the construction of patent assignments.

- That an assignment of all the interest of an assignor in a patent passes everything there is to pass including the right to apply for an extension of the term of the patent, and the joint inventor/joint owner had no continuing rights.[78]

Duration of licence and termination; effect of termination

Where a licence is granted for a fixed period

Where a licence is stated to be for a fixed term, it is likely to be construed as not being terminable:

- before the end of that term except under an express termination provision; or

- except with the consent of all parties.[79]

---

76 *Linden Gardens Trust Limited v Lenesta Sludge Disposals Limited* [1994] 1 AC 85, HL.

77 *Massmann v Massmann and the Custodian of Enemy Property* (1943) 61 RPC 13, CA overturning the High Court decision reported at (1943) 60 RPC 45. This case was heard during the Second World War. The exceptional circumstances of that case involved a licensee who was a German national and resident. He assigned the licence to his UK-resident son in 1939 to provide him with an income in case war broke out. These unusual circumstances may undermine the authority of the decision, in so far as it states a general principle of law.

78 *In the matter of Scott and Beard's Patent* (1927) 45 RPC 31. In this case the joint-owners of a patent assigned the patent to a company. The company and one of the former joint-owners applied to have the term of the patent extended under the then current patent legislation (Patents and Designs Act 1907 and 1919, s 18(6)). The other former joint-owner objected on the grounds, among others, that he had not assigned the right to obtain an extension of the patent.

79 See eg *Cutlan v Dawson* (1897) 14 RPC 249, CA and *Guyot v Thomson* [1894] 3 Ch 388, (1894) 11 RPC 541, CA.

Where a licence is granted without termination provisions or for a fixed period and whether termination possible on reasonable notice

Sometimes, though, licences are granted under an agreement with no express provision for their termination. The question then arises as to whether the licence is perpetual, or can be terminated.[80]

The leading intellectual property case on this subject held that a patent and know-how licence agreement which contained no provision as to the period for which the licence was to remain in force was terminable on reasonable notice (although there were provisions allowing termination in very specific situations).[81]

Other cases which have held that an agreement is terminable on reasonable notice include:

- In a case concerning copyright (including copyright in designs) it was held that a manufacturing licence which did not include express provisions for termination without cause, was terminable on notice by the licensor after a reasonable time.[82]

- In a (non-intellectual property) case where the licence contained no express provision for termination of the licence by the licensors, it was held that it was terminable on reasonable notice.[83]

- In another case, there was no mention in the agreement between a gas supplier and its customer of the period for which it was to run, and no mention in the agreement of any right to terminate it.[84] The court held that an agreement which, although indefinite in point of time, was merely one by which the supplier company obtained a customer for its gas on particular terms, and from its very nature introduced an implication that either party could determine it by notice.

---

80 The law is different for licences which do not form part of a contract: such licences may be terminable at will, unless coupled with an interest. See *Wood v Leadbitter* (1845) 13 M & W 838; *Winter Garden Theatre v Millennium Productions* [1984] AC 173, HL.

81 *Martin-Baker Aircraft Co Ltd and another v Canadian Flight Equipment Ltd* (1955) 72 RPC 236, [1955] 2 QB 556, [1955] 2 All ER 722. The case involved the licensing of aircraft ejector seat technology. The licensor sought a declaration from the court that the agreement was terminable on reasonable notice; the licensee opposed the application, arguing that the licence could only be terminated by mutual consent.

82 *Dorling v Honnor and Honnor Marine Limited* [1963] RPC 205, [1963] 2 All ER 495. A case concerning a licence to use designs to manufacture a sailing dinghy.

83 *Winter Garden Theatre (London) Ltd v Millennium Productions Ltd* [1948] AC 173, HL. A case concerning a licence to use a theatre.

84 *Crediton Gas Company v Crediton Urban District Council* [1928] 1 Ch 174. The agreement concerned a contract entered into between a gas supplier and a local council, under which the supplier agreed to light all the public lamps in a district from September to May each year.

In contrast to these cases, there are cases concerning copyright where licences had no provision for termination without cause but have been held not to be terminable on notice.[85] It is thought that this line of cases does not represent the law in respect of agreements concerned with the exploitation of technology, ie such agreements *are* terminable on reasonable notice. However, there would seem to be no reason in principle why one type of intellectual property licence should be treated differently than another.

Older case law provides the following propositions:[86]

- If a licence is expressed to be for a definite time, it cannot legally be revoked,[87] except for acts bringing about forfeiture,[88] nor can the licensee disclaim it.[89]

- If there is a provision that a licence is determinable on a certain date if certain provisions have not been complied with, acceptance of royalties after that date may estop (ie, prevent) the licensor from terminating it.[90]

What is reasonable notice?

Where a contract is terminable on reasonable notice, the question then arises as to what is a reasonable notice period. This will vary from contract to contract. Some guidance was given in one case[91] where it was held that an agreement included an implied term that it was terminable on reasonable notice, and that it could not be so terminated on notice of less than 12 months.

Other cases have held:

- On 'rather scanty' evidence before the court that a reasonable period in the circumstances of that case was 12 months.[92] The court observed

---

85   *Re Berker Sportcraft* (1947) LT 420.
86   The cases listed below are cited in Halsbury's Laws (see n 13), at 'Patents and Registered Designs', para 390. Because of their age and in the absence of modern authority, they should be treated with caution.
87   *Guyot v Thomson* [1894] 3 Ch 388, (1894) 11 RPC 541, CA; *Ward v Livesey* (1887) 5 RPC 102.
88   Halsbury's Laws states that a mere breach of covenant, for example to pay renewal fees (*Mills v Carson* (1892) 9 TLR 80, (1892) 10 RPC 9, CA) or to sue infringers (*Huntoon Co v Kolynos (Inc)* [1930] 1 Ch 528, 47 RPC 403) or to provide working instructions (*Cheetham v Nuthall* (1893) 10 RPC 321) does not give rise to forfeiture. The relevance of the rules against relief from forfeiture to modern intellectual property contracts may be queried, although see later in this chapter for further discussion of this topic. Moreover, the law on the circumstances in which a breach of contract may allow the innocent party to terminate the contract has developed considerably since these cases were decided.
89   *Cutlan v Dawson* (1897) 14 RPC 249, CA.
90   *Warwick v Hooper* (1850) 3 Mac & G 60.
91   *Decro-Wall International SA v Practitioners in Marketing Ltd* [1971] 1 WLR 361, CA. The case concerned an exclusive supply agreement relating to decorative tiles.
92   *Martin-Baker Aircraft Co Ltd v Canadian Flight Equipment Ltd* [1955] 2 QB 556, [1955] 2 All ER, 722, [1955] 3 WLR 212, (1955) 72 RPC 236, at 245.

that, in determining what is reasonable notice to determine a contract, consideration should be given to the circumstances at the time of the notice, rather than to those existing at the time the contract was made.

- That six months was a reasonable period on the facts of that case.[93]

- That nine months was a reasonable period, again on the facts of the case.[94]

Termination for breach and relief from forfeiture

Where a party holds a proprietary or possessory right then a court may grant relief from forfeiture by exercising its equitable jurisdiction. For example in one case a court was prepared to override a provision in an agreement between joint owners of a patent, providing that if a party failed to reimburse to the other one half of certain patent expenses within a period of 30 days, the other party could require the defaulting party to assign to the other its rights in the jointly owned patents.[95] The court held that its equitable jurisdiction to grant relief against forfeiture (more normally encountered in cases involving evictions from domestic property) is available for all kinds of proprietary or possessory rights. In the circumstances the court was prepared to grant relief by extending the time in which the defaulting party was to reimburse the other party under the agreement.

Where only a contractual right is available a party's rights would not be eligible for relief. For example, it has been held that the defendant's rights under a licence agreement were contractual; it had no proprietary or possessory rights.[96] Accordingly, the defendant's rights were ineligible for relief from forfeiture. This decision is consistent with the principle mentioned earlier that, although a joint owner of a patent has a property right in the patent, a licensee has no right *in* the licensed property; instead he or she has a contractual right.[97]

On the question of whether breach of an obligation to provide information to the licensor's auditors entitled the licensor to terminate a licence, see 'Auditing of records' below. On the question of whether a breach of an obligation to sue infringers went to the root of a licence agreement, see 'Maintaining the patents – bringing and defending legal proceedings' below.

93   *Dorling v Honnor and Honnor Marine Limited* [1963] RPC 205, [1963] 2 All ER 495. A case concerning a licence to use designs to manufacture a sailing dinghy.

94   *Jackson Distribution Limited v Tum Yeto Inc* [2009] EWHC 982. A case involving a distributorship.

95   *BICC plc v Burndy Corporation and BICC-Burndy Limited* [1985] RPC 273, CA.

96   *Crittall Windows Limited v Stormseal (UPVC) Window Systems Limited and another* [1991] RPC 265.

97   See also *Sport International Bussomm BV v Inter-footwear Limited* [1984] 1 WLR 776.

In a case concerning licences of right arising under the Patents Act 1977, the Patents Court was asked to settle the terms of such a licence.[98] The Patents Court refused a request of the patent owner that the licence should be terminable:

- immediately without prior warning if the licensee committed a fundamental breach of any of its terms; or

- if the licensee was in breach of its terms.

The Patents Court decided that the penalty of allowing immediate termination of the licence without prior warning was too severe if it could apply even to trivial and accidental breaches. A warning period would be required in all cases where the patent owner sought termination for breach. Although this case was concerned with the special circumstances of licence of right disputes, it may provide some clues as to the likely attitude of the Patents Court to the question of a patent owner's right to terminate a licence in the event of breach by the licensee, particularly in the absence of express terms in the licence dealing with the issue.

Also a court has held that a licensor can terminate a patent licence where a licensee has ceased to carry on a business (or the licensee is threatening to cease to carry on business).[99] But the licensor could only terminate if at the date the notice is given the licensee has in fact ceased to carry on a business (or the threat to cease to carry on the business is active).

When does notice of termination take effect?

A provision permitting either party to terminate a licence on six months' notice has been held to mean, having regard to the context, six calendar months rather than six lunar months.[100] This approach is no different than that for other types of commercial agreements.[101]

---

98 *American Cyanamid Co's (Fenbufen) Patent* [1990] RPC 309; appealed (but only on the question of the level of royalty that should be paid) and reported at [1991] RPC 409.

99 *JR French Ltd v Redbus LMDS Ltd* [2005] EWHC 1436 (Ch), [2006] FSR 13. The court held that the words 'carry on business' had to be construed in the context of the agreement and was not a term of art. The case concerned an agreement to exploit the intellectual property of the claimant.

100 *Erith Engineering Company Ltd v Sanford Riley Stoker Company and Babcock & Wilcox Ltd* 37 RPC 217 (Supplement, 1920).

101 As well as being a 'statutory default' position, see Law of Property Act 1925, s 61. See also Anderson & Warner, *A-Z Guide to Boilerplate and Commercial Clauses* (2nd edn, Tottel Publishing, 2006) 347–357.

Effect of termination of licence on sub-licences

On termination of a licence, any sub-licence granted under the licence will also terminate unless the parties agreed otherwise, expressly or by implication.

In one case on this issue a court held[102] that:

- the relations of the parties were to be determined by the contract into which the parties had entered;

- the sub-licensee had probably known what was in the licence under which the head licensee had purported to grant the sub-licence;

- the terms of the deeds by which the head licence had been granted showed that none of the parties contemplated that, if an intermediate licence was dropped out, the antecedent licensor was subjected to the obligations created in favour of the sub-licensee; and

- in the events that had happened, the sub-licences had ceased to operate simultaneously with the putting to an end of the head licence.

In another case concerning the right of a patent owner to obtain an interlocutory (ie temporary) injunction against the former sub-licensee the court at first instance held that, assuming that the sub-licence was revoked, the claimants were not entitled to relief since their alleged cause of action arose out of their own acts.[103]

Consequences of termination

After a licence agreement is terminated, either party may call for an account of any matter still outstanding under the agreement, even where the agreement is silent as to such rights.[104]

Termination by expiry of the patent

In some licence agreements there are provisions that the licence for the patent will terminate when the patent expires, or if the patent is held in different countries, the dates of termination will be the dates of expiry in each country (or, if there is only one termination date, the date on which the last of the patents expires). There is authority for the proposition that where a licence

---

102 *Austin Baldwin & Co Ltd v Greenwood & Batley Ltd*; and *Austin Baldwin & Co Ltd v Magnetic Car Company Ltd* (1925) 42 RPC 454.

103 *Fomento (Sterling Area) Limited and Another v Refill Improvements (Ri-Co) Co Ltd* [1963] RPC 163. The decision was upheld on appeal but for different reasons.

104 *Anglo-American Asphalt Co v Crowley Russell* [1945] 2 All ER 324. In this case a clause permitted the licensor to inspect the licensee's books and accounts. On the facts of the case the judge held that the right of inspection should not run for longer than six years prior to the date when the case started. Also of interest is that although the licensor had signed a receipt for the payment of royalties by the licensee, the licensor was not prevented from inspecting books and accounts etc in relation to those royalties which had been paid and receipted.

terminates when the last patent expires, the date of expiry is found in the law at the date of expiry not at the date of grant.[105]

Effect of invalidity of licensed rights on licence

It has been held that a patent licence granted 'on the understanding that the patent rights are sound' was not a guarantee of the validity of the licensed patents.[106] In that case, the defendant argued that the claimant was not entitled to the patents, but it was held that the defendant's manufacture of licensed products meant that he was not entitled to deny the claimant's title.

In another case, under a patent licence, the defendant agreed to pay royalties based on the defendant selling a guaranteed minimum number of machines. The claimant guaranteed the validity of the patent and to protect the licensee from infringement. The patent was invalid, and it was admitted that it was invalid. It was held that the whole basis of the agreement was the validity of the patent and therefore the agreement could be rescinded.[107]

Rights of purchasers of licensed products; implied warranty by seller

A purchaser of a patented article, who buys the article:

- from the patent owner;
- from the patent owner's licensee; or
- from any co-owner of the patent; or
- in a direct chain from any of the above

has an implied licence under the patent to use the article and resell it.[108] In the absence of express terms to the contrary, the licence obtained by a purchaser from the patent owner in one country extends to all other countries where the latter owns the patents.[109]

---

105 *BJM Inc v Melport Corp*, 18 F Supp 2d 704, 48 USPQ 2d 1537 (WD KY 1988), quoted by Melville *Forms and Agreements on Intellectual Property and International Licensing* (3rd edn, Sweet & Maxwell) at 3.09[6].

106 *RFH Suhr v Crofts (Engineers) Ltd* (1932) 49 RPC 359. See also *Lyle-Meller v A Lewis & Co (Westminster) Ltd* [1956] RPC 14 and *IMH Investments Ltd v Trinidad Home Developers Ltd* [1994] FSR 616 (case in Trinidad Court of Appeal).

107 *Henderson v Shiels* (1907) 24 RPC 108.

108 *Incandescent Gas Light Co Ltd v Cantelo* (1895) 11 TLR 381, 12 RPC 262; *Scottish Vacuum Cleaner Co Ltd v Provincial Cinematograph Theatres Ltd* (1915) 32 RPC 353.

109 *Betts v Willmott* (1871) 6 Ch App 239, CA; *National Phonograph Co of Australia Ltd v Menck* [1911] AC 336, (1911) 28 RPC 229, PC; such implied licence does not, apparently, extend to other countries where the purchaser bought from a licensee whose licence did not extend to those other countries: *Halsbury's Laws* (see n 13), 'Patents and Registered Designs', para 385, including n 14 to that paragraph.

Sometimes a patent owner seeks to impose restrictions on the use that can be made of the article by purchasers. Under domestic English law, if at the time of sale the purchaser has notice of a restriction imposed by or on behalf of the patent owner, the restriction will bind the purchaser.[110] However, such restrictions would nowadays frequently be in breach of EC competition laws, and in particular the free movement of goods rules set out in Articles 28–30 (now 34–36) of the Treaty.[111]

Under the Sale of Goods Act 1979, a number of terms are implied into a contract of sale, including an implied warranty that (in most circumstances) the buyer will enjoy 'quiet possession' of the goods.[112] If the buyer is unable to use the goods because of third-party patent rights, this warranty is breached. It has even been held that this warranty is breached by publication of a patent after the date of sale which could render the goods unusable in the future.[113] Similarly, in a case involving third-party trade-mark rights, it was held that if a buyer's full possession of goods is disturbed by a third party acting within his or her rights, the buyer is entitled to be indemnified by the seller.[114]

Other contractual rights and obligations

Obligation to exploit licence

The ordinary rules of construction of contracts apply as to implying terms in a patent licence.[115] There is ordinarily no implied term that a licensee will manufacture or use his or her licence.[116]

Unless a licence agreement includes provisions which address what a licensee is to do to exploit the licensed intellectual property, then the owner and/or licensor of the intellectual property will not be protected from a failure by the licensee to work the licence. Such provisions might include:

---

110 See Halsbury's Laws (see n 13), para 385 for discussion of the extent of this rule.

111 See further Ch 12 (and texts referred to in bibliography at p **XX**. These Articles will be renumbered as 34–36 following the adoption of the Lisbon Treaty.

112 Sale of Goods Act 1979, s 12, particularly s 12(2)(b).

113 *Microbeads AC v Vinhurst Road Markings Ltd* [1975] 1 WLR 218, CA.

114 *Niblett Ltd v Confectioners' Materials Co* [1921] 3 KB 387, [1921] All ER Rep 459, CA.

115 *The Moorcock* (1889) 14 PD 64, CA at 68, ie the courts will imply terms which express the presumed intention of the parties (the 'business efficacy' test): 'the law is raising an implication from the presumed intention of the parties, with the object of giving to the transaction such efficacy as both parties must have intended that at all events it should have. In business transactions such as this what the law desires to effect by the implication is to give such business efficacy to the transaction as must have been intended at all events by both parties' (*Campbell v G Hopkins & Sons (Clerkenwell) Ltd* (1931) 49 RPC 38, at 45). The efficacy to be implied will only be so far as the appropriate terms for the contract in question (*Express Newspapers v Silverstone Circuits* (1989) The Independent, 16 June, CA).

116 Asserted in Halsbury's Laws (see n 13), 'Patents and Registered Designs', para 386 and cases cited at that paragraph. See also *Re Railway and Electrical Appliances Co* (1888) 38 Ch D 597, at 608; *Cheetham v Nuthall* (1893) 10 RPC 321, at 333.

- what level of effort the licensee is to use in exploiting the intellectual property (see below);

- payments that the licensee needs to make (such as a minimum royalty to be paid for particular periods);

- what is to happen if the licence is not worked at all or at a sufficient level to satisfy the licensor (such as termination of the licence).

Meaning of 'best endeavours' and 'reasonable endeavours'

A licence agreement can contain provisions as to what a licensee is required to do to work a licence; this can normally be addressed in two ways:

- *An absolute obligation:* the licensee will face an obligation, for example, to sell a certain number of a product produced under a licensed patent within a particular period.[117]

- *An evaluative obligation:* the licensee will be required to undertake a certain amount of effort into working the licence but the level of effort is expressed in evaluative terms.

In this section the latter type of obligation is examined. Often the wording used is expressed in the following ways:

- best endeavours;
- reasonable endeavours;
- all reasonable endeavours;
- commercially reasonable efforts;
- to be diligent in undertaking; and
- best efforts.

These phrases do not have a specific meaning. The meanings that have been established are derived from a series of cases, all of which have addressed different subject matters, and most of which have not concerned commercial intellectual property transactions. However, at least under English law, a 'best endeavours' obligation appears to require a higher level of obligation than one expressed as 'reasonable endeavours'.

Best endeavours

Licence agreements sometimes include an obligation on the licensee to use his or her best endeavours to do certain things, such as maximise sales of

---

117 Eg: 'The Licensee shall sell 450 Licensed Products during each Year in the Territory during each calendar year of the Term of the Agreement'.

licensed products. Licensees often resist the inclusion of such an obligation in the agreement, on the basis that it imposes a heavy obligation on them.

The case[118] traditionally cited on the meaning of 'best endeavours' concerned two licence agreements relating to inventions and designs. The agreements contained clauses requiring the licensees to use 'all diligence' to promote sales of the inventions and designs, and to use their 'best endeavours' to exploit these. It was held that the licensees' obligation was:

> '... at least that of taking reasonable steps to exploit the inventions and designs, having regard both to the interests of their shareholders and their contractual obligations to their shareholders ... but that the licensees' financial and commercial position and capabilities, and the chance that the inventions would prove commercially successful, were relevant in assessing the amount of damages'.

The judge went on to give some contextual explanation as to the meaning of a best endeavours obligation:

> 'In my opinion contractual obligations to use due diligence and their best endeavours to promote sales under such contracts as these would not require the directors to carry on the manufacture and attempted sale to the certain ruin of the Company and utter disregard of the interest of the shareholders; but before that extreme position could be reached ... there would arise questions, some of which have arisen here, as to the amount of money to be expended on the production and on advertisement and vending of the goods and how far money is to be borrowed for that purpose, if it could be and what is already available'.

In another case (which concerned the sale of land), a contract of sale included an obligation on the purchaser to use its best endeavours to obtain planning permission. The court stated:

> 'These words (best endeavours) oblige the purchaser to take all reasonable steps which a prudent and determined man acting in his own interests and anxious to obtain planning permission would have taken'.[119]

---

118 *Terrell v Mabie Todd & Co Ltd* (1952) 69 RPC 234; also briefly reported in the Court of Appeal where the appeal was dismissed by consent ((1952) 70 RPC 97). In the earlier case the obligation was stated to be 'to leave no stone unturned', but this probably overstates the position. See *Sheffield District Railway v Great Central Railway* (1911) 14 Ry & Can Tr Cas 299 27 TLR 451. See also *B Davis v Tooth & Co* [1937] 4 All ER 118; and *Western Geophysical Co v Bolt Associates* 200 USPQ 1 (2d Cir 1978).

119 *IBM United Kingdom Ltd v Rockware Glass Ltd* [1980] FSR 335, CA. For a case where an obligation to use best endeavours was considered in a preliminary motion before the court, see *Imasa Ltd v Technic Incorporated* [1981] FSR 554.

In this case, by failing to appeal against a refusal of planning permission the purchaser was held not to have used his best endeavours.

The amount of effort required to meet a best endeavours obligation cannot be compared to a person under a contractual obligation. The correct comparison is to a person acting in their own interest, but the level of effort in a best endeavours obligation does not mean that no account can be taken of the reasonableness of the effort required:[120]

> '"Best endeavours" are something less than the efforts which go beyond the bounds of reason, but are considerably more than intermittent activities. They must at least be doing all that a reasonable person reasonably could do in the circumstances'.

Other cases have held that:

- if there is obligation to use best endeavours to deliver something (but the agreement is silent as to a date) it has been held to mean that the obligation is to use best endeavours to secure delivery within a reasonable time;[121]

- a 'best endeavours' obligation may not extend to the provision of bad advice;[122]

- a 'best endeavours' obligation to negotiate and agree a settlement within a particular period of time will not require the parties to enter into any particular form of actual agreement;[123]

- in order for a best endeavours obligation to exist it is not necessary to use the phrase 'best endeavours'.[124]

Reasonable endeavours

It is a common understanding among English commercial lawyers that an undertaking to use 'reasonable endeavours' is less onerous than an undertaking to use 'best endeavours'. In one case it was held that an obligation to use 'reasonable endeavours' was 'considerably less' onerous than an obligation

---

120 *Pips (Leisure Products) Ltd v Walton* [1990] BCLC 895.
121 *Monkland v Jack Barclay Ltd* [1951] 2 KB 252.
122 *Rackham v Peek Foods Ltd* [1990] BCLC 895. In this case a company had covenanted to use its best endeavours to ensure that its shareholders voted in favour of acquiring another company; it was held, following an intervening event (a change in the law regarding taxation and other matters), that not to recommend to, or procure the approval of, shareholders to acquire the other company, would not amount to a breach of the best endeavours clause if it amounted to giving bad advice.
123 *Beta Investment SA v Transmedia Europe Inc* [2003] EWHC 3066 (Ch), [2003] All ER (D) 133 (May).
124 *Days Medical Aids Ltd v Pihsiang Machinery Manufacturing Co Ltd and others* [2004] EWHC 44 (Comm), [2004] 1 All ER (Comm) 991. This case involved a distributorship agreement with an obligation to 'promote sales to the best of its ability in the UK and all countries in the schedule'. The comments of the judge were obiter.

to use 'best endeavours'[125] and would lie at the lowest end of a spectrum.[126] Where an agreement contains a reasonable endeavours obligation:

- a party is able to factor in other commercial considerations;[127]

- a party would not be in breach of such an obligation if it did something which was financially disadvantageous;[128]

- a party is not required to take all reasonable courses of action but just one of them.[129]

All reasonable endeavours

Sometimes a party is required to use 'all reasonable endeavours' – there is very little case law as to its meaning. There is conflicting case law as to its meaning so that an all reasonable endeavours obligation:

- occupies a middle ground between best endeavours and reasonable endeavours;[130] or

- amounts to a best endeavours obligation.[131]

Right to promote competing products?

It has been held that an implied term in a contract, that a company would use its best endeavours to promote another's products, was to be construed in the context of the circumstances of the contract. Such a term was not inconsistent with the company being at liberty to promote, and promoting,

---

125 *UBH (Mechanical Services) Ltd v Standard Life Assurance Co* (1986) The Times, 13 November. A lessee undertook to his landlord to use reasonable endeavours; the lessee could take into account other commercial considerations as well as his obligation to the landlord. This involved 'a balancing act whereby the [defendants] were obliged to put in one scale the weight of the contractual obligation to [the claimants], and in the other all relevant commercial considerations'. The judge was persuaded that an obligation to use 'all reasonable endeavours' 'probably' lay between best and reasonable endeavours.

126 *Jolley v Carmel* [2000] 2 EGLR 153; see also *Rhodia International Holdings Ltd and another v Huntsman International LLC* [2007] EWHC 292 (Comm), para 35.

127 *UBH (Mechanical Services) Ltd v Standard Life Assurance Co* (1986) The Times, 13 November.

128 *Phillips Petroleum Co (UK) Ltd v ENRON (Europe) Ltd* [1977] CLC 329, CA. It seems that the courts are prepared to allow a party to take some account of its own interests when using its 'reasonable endeavours'.

129 *Rhodia International Holdings Ltd and another v Huntsman International LLC* [2007] EWHC 292 (Comm), para 33.

130 *UBH (Mechanical Services) Ltd v Standard Life Assurance Co* (1986) The Times, 13 November.

131 In *Rhodia International Holdings Ltd and another v Huntsman International LLC* [2007] EWHC 292 (Comm) the judge stated: 'An obligation to use reasonable endeavours to achieve the aim probably only requires a party to take one reasonable course, not all of them, whereas an obligation to use best endeavours probably requires a party to take all the reasonable courses he can. In that context, it may well be that an obligation to use all reasonable endeavours equates with using best endeavours ...'.

similar products made by competitors of the other, but required the company to treat the other at least as well as it treated the competitors.[132]

In an Australian case[133] (not binding on an English court) a licence agreement contained an obligation on the licensee:

'... at all times to use his best endeavours in and towards the design fabrication installation and selling of the [licensed product] throughout the licensed territory and to energetically promote and develop the greatest possible market for the [licensed product]'.

The five judges hearing the case on appeal in the High Court reached different conclusions on whether this obligation, by implication, prohibited the sale of competing products by the licensee.

Warranties and implied terms

Ordinarily, there is *no* implied covenant or warranty by a licensor in a licence agreement:

- as to his or her title to the intellectual property or the absence of encumbrances, nor that the technology does not infringe the rights of a third party,[134] nor

- that the licensed intellectual property is valid,[135] and nor do the statutory 'beneficial owner' covenants imply such a covenant.[136]

However, it will be necessary to construe the agreement in each case to determine whether any such term should be implied. This means that a court could find that such a term is implied in an appropriate case.[137] Similarly,

---

132 *Ault & Wiborg Paints Ltd v Sure Service Ltd* (1983) The Times, 2 July, High Court.
133 *Transfield Pty Ltd v Arlo International Ltd* [1981] RPC 141.
134 Asserted in *Encyclopedia of Information Technology Law* (Sweet & Maxwell), para 4.11; and asserted in relation to there being no implied covenants for validity or non-infringement of third-party rights in Halsbury's Laws (see n 13), paras 386, 387. If no such terms are expressly stated, they are unlikely to be implied.
135 *Bessimer v Wright* (1858) 31 LTOS 213; *Suhr v Crofts (Engineers) Limited* (1932) 49 RPC 359.
136 The covenants that are implied into conveyances (ie a transfer of ownership), under the Law of Property (Miscellaneous Provisions) Act 1994, which repealed and replaced Law of Property Act 1925, s 76. These covenants cannot in any event be implied into licences, as these generally are not 'conveyances' or 'dispositions of property' for the purposes of these statutes.
137 Eg a warranty that the licensor has the right to grant the licence could be implied in the circumstances of the grant of a licence, or that due to the wording and context of a licence agreement a licensee might have an implied warranty of freedom of use in the absence of an express warranty of use (*Frayling Furniture Limited v Premier Upholstery Limited* (1999) 22(5) IPD 22051, Ch D).

there is no implied warranty of validity when a patent is assigned.[138] An assignor is estopped (ie prevented) from denying validity as against his or her assignee.[139]

A covenant (ie a form of binding promise or obligation) for quiet enjoyment probably imports a limited covenant that the proprietor has not done anything invalidating the patent, eg omitting to pay renewal fees.[140] Moreover, where a patent owner undertook to his licensee 'by all means in his power to protect and defend the said letters patent from all infringements', it was held that he was required to maintain the patent in force by payment of the renewal fee.[141] In some circumstances a licensee may even be required to pay royalties when the recitals to a licence agreement refer to patent rights which are later discovered never to have existed.[142]

As to terms that may be implied by statute into intellectual property agreements, see 'Sale of Goods Act 1979' and 'Supply of Goods and Services Act 1982' below (in relation to contract law statutes) and Chapter 9 (in relation to property law statutes).

Interference and threats by licensor

It appears that a court will normally imply into any licence agreement a term that the licensor will not impede the licensee's working of the licence.[143] Similarly a licensor will be restrained from using threats of infringement proceedings against the licensee.[144]

Most favoured licensee clauses

A clause which requires a licensor to offer to a non-exclusive licensee any better terms that are given to his or her other non-exclusive licensees, has

---

138 *Hall v Conder* (1857) 26 LJCP 138, 288, Ex Ch; *Smith v Neale* (1857) 26 LJCP 143. The same rule applies to agreements to assign: *Hall v Conder*; and *Smith v Buckingham* (1870) 18 WR 314; *Liardet v Hammond Electric Light and Power Co* (1883) 31 WR 710.

139 *Walton v Lavater* (1860) 8 CBNS 162, at 180, 186, Ex Ch, cited in Halsbury's Laws (see n 13), para 375, n 4; see the further cases cited in that note.

140 See *Halsbury's Laws* (see n 13), para 387 which discusses various aspects of quiet enjoyment covenants in licences. 'Letters patent' is the former name for a patent under older versions of the Patents Acts

141 *Lines v Usher* (1897) 14 RPC 206: cited in *Encyclopedia of Information Technology Law* (Sweet & Maxwell), para 4.11.

142 *IMH Investments v Trinidad Home Developers* [1994] FSR 616 (a case in the Trinidad courts).

143 See *Acrow v Rex* [1971] 1 WLR 1676, CA, at 1680, 1683, cited by *Encyclopedia of United Kingdom and European Patent Law* (Sweet & Maxwell), para 8–410, where a covenant for quiet enjoyment was implied into a patent licence contract.

144 *Clark v Adie* (1873) 21 WLR 456, 21 WLR 764; *SA des Manufacturers de Glaces v Tilghman's Patent Sand Blast Co* (1883) 25 Ch D 1, CA.

been construed by the court[145]. Such a clause may need further provisions to be effective, such as the licensor must notify the licensee of the more favourable terms, and allow the licensee to consider them.

Normal terms of a patent licence – uncertainty of terms

It is a general principle of contract law that an agreement will be void if its terms are not sufficiently certain.[146]

On the other hand, where parties have agreed the important terms of a contract, the fact that further terms have yet to be added or further formalities to be fulfilled does not prevent there being a binding contract between them in respect of the terms that have been agreed.[147] If the further

---

145 *Fomento (Sterling Area) Ltd v Selsdon Fountain Pen Co Ltd* [1958] RPC 8, HL where the relevant clause stated: 'Should the sub-licensor grant a licence under the said patents at a lower royalty, that lower royalty shall apply in substitution for the royalty herein agreed'. The case concerned a 'deed of terms' whereby a full but non-exclusive sub-licence was granted by the appellants to the respondents for the manufacture, use and selling of writing instruments. The writing instruments were fully or partially protected by patents. Royalties were payable on a sliding scale (from 6 per cent to 3 per cent). A provision in the deed of terms provided that if a licence was granted to a third party by the appellants at a lower royalty then that lower royalty would be substituted for the royalty in the deed of terms. The appellants in the case granted a non-exclusive sub-licence to a third party allowing the third party to sell patented articles at a royalty of 5 per cent. The respondents argued that the new royalty rate (of 5 per cent) should be paid. The appellants argued that since respondents paid royalties at different percentages, it was only possible at the end of any particular period to decide whether the respondents were receiving less favourable terms, an argument which was rejected by the House of Lords.

There was considerable discussion in the House of Lords as to whether the flat rate of a 5 per cent royalty granted to the third party was more favourable than that paid by the respondents (ie the range from 6 per cent to 3 per cent). The House of Lords was required to interpret the clause quoted in the previous paragraph and it was found that the word 'royalty' did not mean the total sum payable for all articles produced under the licence. It was interpreted as meaning the relevant royalty for articles in a comparable category, with the implication of this meaning being drawn in one of the speeches: 'Thus, if the agreed royalty on articles under £1 is six per cent and the new royalty on like articles is five per cent, then five per cent is to be substituted for six per cent. Whereas, if the agreed royalty on articles between £1 and £2 is four per cent and the new royalty on a like article is five per cent, there is no substitution and the four per cent prevails. Any other view would mean that, by the simple device of altering the structure on which royalties are paid, the licensor could avoid the clause altogether; which would not, I am sure, commend itself to your Lordships, seeing that the whole object of the clause is to ensure that the respondents are not exposed to unfair competition' (from the speech of Lord Denning, at p 25).

146 *Scammell v Ouston* [1941] AC 251.

147 *Pagnan SpA v Feed Productions* [1987] 2 Lloyd's Rep 601, CA. See also *Simtech v Jasmin Simtec Limited* [1995] FSR 475 and *Dalgety v DEB-ITS Limited* [1994] FSR 125 where earlier cases in this area were reviewed, including *Donwin v EMI Films* (1984) The Times, 9 May, and *Edward v Skyways Limited* [1964] 1 WLR 355.

terms or formalities are not agreed or fulfilled, the contract will not be invalidated unless such failure renders the contract unworkable or void for uncertainty.

In a case[148] which would appear to illustrate this principle, the parties entered into an agreement to settle patent litigation. The agreement provided that the patent owner would grant the other party a licence under the patent. Certain important terms were agreed, eg royalties, duration etc. The agreement also included a provision that as to the remaining terms, the licence:

> '... shall be in the normal terms of a patent licence. In the event of dispute the terms shall be referred to Counsel at the Patent Bar to be agreed by [the parties to the agreement]'.

A dispute arose between the parties on another provision of the agreement which led to litigation. The court observed that it is a question of law, what are the normal terms of a patent licence. The case is of interest in that it appears that a clause of the kind quoted above would be legally enforceable. The court also stayed the action on the grounds that the arbitration clause, quoted above, covered disputes as to all terms of the proposed licence.

An exception to the general principle that an agreement will be void if its terms are uncertain, apparently arises where a licence is granted and the parties do not fix a royalty: it may be implied that a reasonable royalty is payable by the licensee.[149] This exception apparently arises by analogy with land law – a similar exception operates where a property lease has been granted, and where the amount of rent has not been agreed: in such cases a reasonable rent will be payable.[150]

This case is also interesting in that it confirms that the courts will sometimes apply legal principles from the 'real' property field, particularly where the law in respect of intellectual property transactions is uncertain.[151] (See further Chapter 9.)

---

148 *The Miles-Martin Pen Co Ltd and Martin v the Selsdon Fountain Pen Co Ltd, Ralph Selsdon and Rebecca Selsdon (No 2)* (1950) 67 RPC 64, CA.

149 The issue being what is reasonable in the light of the circumstances operating when the licence was granted. In this case it was observed that on the question of the necessity of all terms in a contract being set out, the rules for licences resembled those for leases (for real property) rather than those for ordinary contracts. On that basis and in the absence of any provision in the agreement as to royalties, a term was implied into the licence that a royalty at a reasonable rate was payable. See *Chadwick v Bridges (SN) & Co Ltd* [1960] RPC 85, per Lloyd-Jacob J.

150 See eg *Brown v Gould* [1972] 1 Ch 53 where the court reviewed certain authorities in the real property field.

151 An extreme example of this arose in the case of *British Leyland Motor Corporation Ltd and Another v Armstrong Patents Co Ltd and Another* [1986] 1 AC 577, [1986] RPC 279. This case is considered in detail in Ch 9 under 'Non-derogation from grant'.

Royalties, interest, payment terms, advance payment, milestone payments and currency provisions

Implied obligation to pay reasonable royalty

Where a licence agreement does not state whether royalties are payable or not then a term may be implied whereby a reasonable royalty will be payable.[152] That this term is implied is based on an analogy with a proposition found in land law – that if the rent has not been agreed then a reasonable rent will be payable.[153]

Interest payable on royalties

Interest is apparently payable on a patent royalty in the event of late payment, even in the absence of any express provision to this effect.[154]

But this may be no longer good law. In any case the point may no longer be relevant with the passing of the Late Payment of Commercial Debts (Interest) Act 1998 (see below). Before the passing of this Act, the case represented an exception to the general rule that interest is not automatically payable on contract debts, prior to the commencement of legal proceedings.

Time not of the essence for payment terms

Breach of an obligation to pay royalties by a certain date will not allow the licensor to terminate the licence, unless the date of payment is expressly stated to be of the essence of the contract.[155]

Milestone payments not deductible from royalties

Normally, an upfront or milestone payment will not be deductible from royalties unless the agreement so provides. By contrast, it is suggested that a payment expressed to be an 'advance' will normally be deductible from royalties.

---

152 See *Chadwick v Bridges (SN) & Co Ltd* [1960] RPC 85, per Lloyd-Jacob J. In this case the licence was not in writing. The court held that in determining what were the terms for the licence, the rules for so doing were similar to those for leases of real property rather than those for an ordinary contract. Based on this proposition, and as the oral agreement in this case was silent as to whether royalties were payable, a term would be implied into the oral licence agreement that a royalty was payable and at a reasonable rate.

153 In *Brown v Gould* [1972] 1 Ch 52. In this case the judge reviewed other cases dealing with real property.

154 *Redges v Mulliner* (1892) 10 RPC 21, at 23; *Gill v Stone & Co Ltd* (1911) 28 RPC 329.

155 *Patchett v Sterling Engineering Co* (1953) 70 RPC 269; (1954) 71 RPC 63; (1955) 72 RPC 50.

Currency terms

On the question of whether a reference to a currency, eg 'pounds', means UK pounds sterling or another currency, it has been held[156] that such an expression must be determined in accordance with the proper law of the contract. In other words if the proper law is English law, and the contract refers to pounds, UK pounds sterling would normally be inferred.

Payment of royalties beyond the scope of a patent, after a patent has expired or a licence is terminated

Other case law has decided the following on royalties:[157]

- that royalties may be paid on products whether within or outside the scope of the patent;[158]

- that royalties may continue to be payable whether or not the patent is valid and until such time as the licence is terminated;[159]

- whether a licensee's obligation to pay full royalties after some patents had expired has also been considered by the courts.[160]

However, these cases predate the UK's membership of the European Community, and such arrangements would be likely to contravene Article 81 (101) of the EC Treaty[161] nowadays, where Article 81 (101) applied to the agreement.

Royalty stacking (royalty sharing)

In modern intellectual property licences, to reflect the increasingly complex position where intellectual property is licensed, a licensee's obligation to pay a royalty at a certain rate to the licensor will often be reduced if the licensee has to obtain licences to intellectual property of a third party in order to work the licensed intellectual property.

---

156 *John Lavington Bonython and Others v Commonwealth of Australia* [1951] AC 201. Decided by the Privy Council (the House of Lords (now the Supreme Court) by another name), which hears appeals from some Commonwealth countries.
157 These cases are mentioned in Halsbury's Laws (see n 13), para 389.
158 *Baird v Nelson* (1842) 8 Cl & Fin 726, HL.
159 *Mills v Carson* (1892) 89 TLR 80, (1892) 10 RPC 9, CA; *African Gold Recovery Co Ltd v Sheba Gold Mining Co Ltd* (1897) 2 Com Cas 277, (1897) 14 RPC 660.
160 *Hansen v Magnavox Electronics Co Ltd* [1977] RPC 301; *Bristol Repetition Ltd v Fomento (Sterling Area) Ltd* [1961] RPC 222; *Siemans v Taylor* (1892) 9 RPC 393. The impact of EC competition laws in this area should not be overlooked. See further Ch 12.
161 See further Ch 12.

This point has come under consideration in one case,[162] particularly the following wording:

'Royalties paid to third parties [...] in order to license rights needed to practise or to have practiced the technology claimed in the Patents, will be borne equally by the parties provided that [the Claimant]'s royalty pursuant to [Clause] 5.01 [of the development and licensing agreement] is not less than 2% (two percent) of Net Sales'.[163]

In order for the defendants to make products which incorporated the claimant's technology, they also had to licence patents from third parties. The defendants argued that such third-party licensing (and the payment of royalties to third parties) meant that the royalty they would pay to the claimant would be reduced to 2 per cent, in accordance with the quoted clause above.

The defendants also argued that the words 'to practise or to have practiced the technology claimed in the Patents' in the above-quoted clause meant more than just the technology of the claimant but needed to be interpreted in relation to the claims of the patent, which contained so-called 'reach through' claims for the production of antibodies which comprise the product and in which the antibodies themselves fall.

The claimants looked at the matter differently. Their position was that:

- the quoted clause related only to royalties which the defendants had to pay in order to work the claimant's technology; and

- the quoted clause did not cover the situation which the defendants were in, which was that the licenses required for third-party intellectual property was for parts of the processing for producing products and not to the claimant's technology.

---

162 *Cambridge Antibody Technology v Abbott Biotechnology Ltd and another* [2004] EWHC 2974 (Pat); [2004] All ER (D) 323 (Dec). The case concerned a development and licensing agreement concerning the production of antibodies, and is one of the few recent cases which deals with a modern intellectual property licensing agreement. Also notable are: (i) the thorough analysis of the evidence of witnesses by the judge and their recollections about the negotiations which led to the development and licensing agreement; (ii) the dangers of not defining precisely what is meant by words and phrases, such as the phrase 'license rights needed to practise or to have practiced the technology claimed in the Patents', which is the heart of the dispute and the amount of technical (scientific) analysis needed by the judge to attempt to discern which party view of the phrase was correct; (iii) the length of the judgment (193 paras); (iv) the lack of consistency in some of the terms used in the licensing and development agreement (see para 78); (v) the agreement reflects a modern trend whereby a small start-up company which has potentially valuable technology and research expertise licenses them to a multinational company, but third-party intellectual property was needed at various stages of the development of a product (see paras 40–44); and (vi) perhaps less seriously (unless the cost is counted), the number of lawyers involved in arguing the case in court.

163 See n 162 – from para 64 of the judgment.

The court found in favour of the claimants after construing the provisions of the agreement, finding that the claimant's construction of the agreement was not only consistent with the wording used in the agreement but also made commercial sense. The court also determined the following points:

- the claimant was only involved in bringing its technology under the agreement;

- the claimant was not involved in the development of the product;

- the claimant had no right to be involved in or know about downstream developments (such as what third-party licences the defendants were considering taking or what royalties they would pay to third parties for so doing).

Consequently any royalty sharing between the claimant and defendants would be limited to the part of the project for which the claimant was responsible.

At what date a payment of a (minimum) royalty is to start

The date when a royalty may start becoming payable under a licence agreement may be dependent on an event as agreed between the parties; for example:

- when a licensee starts licensing the licensed intellectual property to third parties; or

- the date when the licensee has successfully made a sellable product using the licensed intellectual property; or

- on a particular date.

In one case[164] such a situation came under consideration, and in particular in relation to the following clause:

> 'Within sixty (60) days at the end of (a) the first two Years under this Agreement (b) each Year thereafter, the Licensee shall, in the manner provided in Clause 3.6 below, pay to [the Claimant] the shortfall (if any) between the royalties paid in accordance with Clause 3.1 above and the Minimum Royalty payable with respect to the period in question'.

The defined terms were set out in the recitals to the agreement as follows:

- 'Year' was defined as 'the period of twelve months from the Effective Date and each subsequent consecutive period of twelve months during the period of this Agreement'.

---

164 *Cambridge Display Technology Ltd v El Dupont de Nemours & Co* [2004] EWHC 1415 (Ch); [2004] All ER (D) 186 (June).

- 'Minimum Royalty' was defined as meaning 'in relation to each Year after January 1, 2003, US 1 million'. And

- 'Effective Date' was defined as 'the date of the last signature to the Agreement which in any event was 16th October 2001'.

The court held, in construing the wording used in the agreement, that the defendant would start paying royalties from 16 October 2004 and not, as the claimant contended, from 16 October 2003. The judge held that 'each Year after January 1, 2003' (as used in the definition of 'Minimum Royalty') meant each complete period of 12 months from 16 October which took place after 1 January 2003.[165]

On what are royalties payable?

Unlike the position where a specific good is being sold it can be harder to determine on what precisely a royalty *is* payable where intellectual property is licensed. For example, a patent may be licensed, and the licensee may have to carry out further research and/or development work to create a product which can be sold. A key question will be, is the resulting product covered by the licensed patent? Typically, wording in modern patent licences[166] follows this type of structure, with the obligation to pay a royalty being expressed as:

'The Licensee shall pay to the Owner a royalty being a percentage of the Net Sales Value of all Licensed Products [or any part thereof] sold by the Licensee'.

And the definition of Licensed Products being:

'Any and all products that are manufactured, sold or otherwise supplied by the Licensee or its sub-licensee and which (a) are within any Valid Claim of the Patents and/or (b) incorporate, or their development makes use of, any of the Know-how'.

---

165   The judge in this case found the drafting of the agreement poor: 'It goes without saying that the Agreement as signed has not been well drafted, and the careful draftsman would undoubtedly have reworked [the clause quoted above] so as to incorporate the "not before" provision which the definition of Minimum Royalty imposes. It looks to me very much as if a short cut has been taken, using the definition as the vehicle for imposing a further restriction on the clause which it was intended to interpret. But the language used makes it impossible, as I see it, to treat the reference to 1st January 2003 as a mere imitation of the opening words of [the clause quoted above]'. (Good drafting practice suggests that definitions of terms should not be used as the place for imposing obligations. See the section 'Definitions' in Anderson and Warner, *A-Z Guide to Boilerplate and Commercial Clauses* (2nd edn, Tottel Publishing, 2006).)

166   The quotes here are drawn from the patent and know-how licence which appeared in the second edition of this book.

And a Valid Claim being defined as:

'A claim of a patent[167] or patent application that has not expired or been held invalid or unenforceable by a court of competent jurisdiction in a final and non-appealable judgement'.

The courts have recently considered the issue of whether a product fell within the claims of a patent and/or patent application[168] and in particular whether the royalty should be payable on the claims made in a patent application or those made in the granted patent. Sometimes between the time of the making of the application and the time the patent is granted the applicant can withdraw some of the claims made for the invention (or the relevant patent office may 'disallow' a claim). In this case that is what appeared to happen. What fell to be considered by the court, based on the wording used by the parties: whether the royalty should be for a product which fell within the claims made in the patent application or that the product did not fall within the claims made in the granted patent.

The judgment of the court repeatedly criticised the quality of the drafting, but it is one of the few cases reported involving technology transfer and the

---

167 A claim 'is a definition in words of the invention that you want to protect' and 'should list all of the main technical features of your invention including those that distinguish it from what already exists. Subsidiary or preferred features, which are not crucial to your invention, should be set out in dependent claims that can refer to one or more of the previous claims'. You must write each claim as a single sentence.

168 *Oxonica Energy Limited v Neuftec Limited* [2009] EWCA Civ 668. This case could easily be held as being an example of the need to check the meaning of defined words (eg whether they cover the facts of a deal, or whether the meaning is what is intended by the parties, etc); or how the courts will construe the provisions of a modern commercial agreement to ascertain the meaning; or just an example of poor-quality drafting (not only on how wording in the agreement was used but also whether a 'sanity check' was undertaken). For example the court applying the now famous words (at least among lawyers) of Lord Hoffman in *Investors Compensation Scheme v West Bromwich Building Society* [1997] UKHL 2, [1998] 1 WLR 896, at 912–913: 'the ascertainment of the meaning which the document would convey to a reasonable person having all the background knowledge which would reasonably have been available to the parties in the situation in which they were at the time of the contract'. This exercise, the court noted, was more difficult if 'it is apparent to the reader that the draftsman of the document was inept or did not fully understand the legal background – as was the case here' (from para 11 of the judgment). In constructing the meaning of a contract the judgment also relied on the guidance given in another case (*Mitsui Construction Co Ltd v A-G of Hong Kong* (1986) 33 BLR 14) that poor drafting itself provides 'no reason to depart from the fundamental rule of construction of contractual documents that the intention of the parties must be ascertained from the language that they have used interpreted in the light of the relevant factual situation in which the contract was made. But the poorer the quality of the drafting, the less willing the court should be to be driven by semantic niceties to attribute to the parties an improbable and unbusinesslike intention, if the language used, whatever it may lack in precision, is reasonably capable of an interpretation which attributes to the parties an intention to make provision for contingencies inherent in the work contracted for on a sensible and businesslike basis'. Because of the poor quality of the drafting and the ambiguity in the meaning of a definition, the court felt able to in effect rewrite part of the contract to arrive at a meaning in keeping with good business sense.

licensing of patents and know-how, and it is worth setting out the judgment in some detail.

The defendant filed a patent application for technology it had developed. The application was filed under the Patent Co-operation Treaty.[169]

The defendant wished to exploit the technology and granted, to simplify the facts, an exclusive patent and know-how licence to a spin-out company of Oxford University, the claimant.

The licence provided that the claimant would pay royalties to the defendant on the sale of 'Licensed Products'. The defined meaning of 'Licensed Products' was:

> '... any product, process or use falling within the scope of claims in the Licensed Application or Licensed Patent'.[170]

After the signing of the patent and know-how licence agreement the defendant's patent applications proceeded through the application processes in a number of countries. The patents granted had claims which were narrower than those of the patent applications.

The claimant took over research and its scientists developed a commercial product (Envirox), made sales and paid royalties to the defendant. It then developed a further product (Envirox 2) which was outside the claims of the patents granted, at least in Europe. The claimant refused to pay any royalties on Envirox 2.

However, Envirox 2 fell within the claims of the PCT application (but not that of the granted patents). Therefore the dispute between the parties and the decision in the case fell on the precise meaning of the definition quoted above. The judgment of the court noted that the section of the agreement containing definitions (including the one quoted above) started with the phrase 'unless the context otherwise requires', which meant that in different contexts a definition could have different meanings.

The court noted that interpreting the quoted definition could lead to three possible results:

● any product covered by the claims of the PCT patent application (ie the widest claims); or

---

169   See Ch 3 under 'Applications under the Patent Co-operation Treaty'.
170   'Licensed Application' was defined as 'the PCT and 'any continuation, continuation-in-part or divisional applications thereof as well as foreign counterparts and re-issues thereof'; and 'Licensed Patent' was defined as 'any patent issuing from the Licensed Application thereof as well as foreign counterparts and reissues thereof'.

- any product covered by the claims of the PCT patent application or a patent and therefore could be a later patent claim wider than the claim of an application; or

- any product covered by the claims of a national application when and if it superseded the PCT application, and if in turn the national application was superseded by a granted patent, then the claims of the granted patent. In effect the words 'as the case may be' would be added to the quoted definition above, and the royalty payable would be dependent on the particular patent position in each country.

The claimant argued that the third result applied, so that in a particular territory if a national patent with a narrower claim superseded a PCT application, royalties would be paid only on a product which fell within that narrower claim.

The claimant further argued that if the first or second results applied it would have to pay royalties on products which did not have any patent protection where they were sold, and such a position would not make any business sense (and the claimant would face competition from others who would not be paying royalties). If the first result was correct, then the phrase 'or Licensed Patent' in the quoted definition would make no sense. The claimant argued that to do so would mean that the court was rewriting the contract for the parties, which normally is not permissible.

The defendant argued that the claimant was not only getting a patent licence but also a worldwide licence to the defendant's know-how and a world-wide non-competition clause. There was no reason in logic or business sense why royalties should be confined to the scope of the patents or patent applications at any one place or time. It was reasonable, it was argued, that the claimant's payment of royalties should reflect that it was getting the benefit of the defendant's know-how rather than leave the claimant free of all royalty if it could find a way around a narrowed patent claim. Also the defendant argued that the third result above would be difficult to deal with as with every sale it would have to consider the patent position in the country concerned, involving not only accountants but also an examination of the state of the patent or patent application locally.

The court decided that the first result was the correct approach to take, and found that 'it offends one's business sense' that the claimant could use the defendant's know-how without making a payment for it in every country where there was no patent or a restricted patent (ie a patent whose claims were narrower than the know-how). While the claimant may have to compete with third parties in those countries where there was no patent or who got around the patent (if the patent was restricted), those third parties would have to develop their own know-how. The court, in interpreting the provisions of the agreement, found that the know-how to be provided by the defendant was significant and valuable.

The claimant's argument that the first result would mean that the words 'or Licensed Patents' would have no meaning was rejected. However the court found that the words at the start of the definition section of the agreement stated that the defined terms would have the meanings given 'except where the context otherwise requires'. The court distinguished the two primary purposes of the patent and know-how license:

- to license all and any patents and know-how; and

- to provide for the payment of royalties.

The contexts of licensing and payment were different. For licensing it was essential that the claimant got everything so that all applications and patents should be licensed. But for payments, it was not necessary to tie payment to what was being licensed. The court noted that payments not only covered the licensed patents but know-how and the non-competition clause. Therefore in the context of the payment of royalties the alternative of 'or Licensed Patent' should be read as not being applicable and in this context it makes no sense or an unreasonable sense. The court was initially not comfortable with disregarding the phrase 'or Licensed Patent' in the definition of 'Licensed Products' for deciding what was royalty-bearing, but it was necessary to do so to make rational senses of an 'appallingly drafted document'.

Other points regarding the payment of royalties

The following propositions can be derived from a number of 19th century cases concerning royalties:

- Money paid for royalties under a licence cannot be recovered on the ground that the patent was invalid, unless the licence so provides.[171]

- Where a licence is given under an application for a patent but no patent is granted, money paid cannot be recovered, as the licensee has been protected from possible proceedings for infringement from the date of publication of the specification.[172]

- An assignee of the share of the profits from a patent can have an account of royalties taken against the licensee, provided the account is taken in such circumstances as will bind the assignor.[173]

---

171 *Taylor v Hare* (1805) 1 Bos & PNR 260. In *Celltech R & D Ltd v Medimmune Inc* [2004] EWCA Civ 1331, Jacob LJ observed at para 12 that royalties are to be paid under a (valid) patent claim even if the claim later turns out to be invalid (ie the royalties will no longer be payable once the claim has definitely been held to be invalid).

172 *Otto v Singer* (1889) 7 RPC 7; the same applies if the granted patent covers less than the original application: *Hadden v Smith* (1847) 20 LTOS 154.

173 *Bergmann v Macmillan* (1881) 17 Ch D 423.

- A covenant to render accounts is generally only auxiliary to the covenant to pay.[174] However, failure to keep proper books may be a material breach of the conditions and lead to forfeiture of the licence.[175]

- A covenant to pay a sum out of the profits derived from use of the invention or by way of royalty runs with the patent and is binding on a legal assignee of the patent with notice of the covenant.[176]

These propositions are mentioned here for the sake of completeness but should, it is suggested, be treated with caution in the absence of modern authority.

Auditing of records

Breach of an obligation to allow auditing of the licensee's activities under a licence may entitle the licensor to terminate the licence.[177]

Apparently, a licensor may query whether the books offered for inspection are the only relevant ones, and he or she may demand that other books be produced which he or she has reason to believe contain relevant information.[178]

A contractual obligation to permit the grantor to inspect accounts will ordinarily continue in force even if the agreement is terminated.[179] In this case the licensee was ordered to give inspection of books for six years back from the date of the writ, although royalty statements and payments had been accepted by the licensor throughout the life of the agreement.

---

174 *Bower v Hodges* (1853) 22 LJCP 194.
175 *Ward v Livesey* (1887) 5 RPC 102.
176 *Werderman v Societe Generale d'Electricite* (1881) 19 Ch D 246, CA, followed in *Dansk Rekylriffel Syndikat Akt v Snell* [1908] 2 Ch 127, (1908) 25 RPC 421, and explained in *Bagot Pneumatic Tyre Co v Clipper Pneumatic Tyre Co* [1902] 1 Ch 146, (1902) 19 RPC 69, CA where it was held that equitable assignees are not so bound.
177 *Fomento Ltd v Selsdon* [1958] RPC 8, HL. This case concerned patents for ball-pointed pens. There was a licence agreement which included obligations on the licensee to permit the licensor's auditors to examine the licensee's records and make extracts from them as well as an obligation on the licensee to give the auditors all such other information as might be necessary or appropriate to enable the amount of the royalties payable to be ascertained. The licensees claimed that certain articles were not covered by the licensed patents and they refused the request of the auditors for samples of such articles so that they might form an opinion as to whether the claim for exemption from royalties was justified. The licensors successfully applied to the High Court for a declaration that this was a breach of contract and entitled them to terminate the licence. On appeal, the House of Lords by a majority of 3 to 2 upheld the High Court's decision.
178 *Fomento v Selsdon* [1958] 1 WLR 45; *Peter Pan Manufacturing v Corset Silhouette* (1963) RPC 45.
179 *Anglo-American Asphalt Co Ltd v Crowley Russell & Co Ltd* [1945] 2 All ER 324.

Maintaining the patents – bringing and defending legal proceedings

Apparently, a licensee may recover royalties paid during any period when patents have not been renewed or allowed to lapse.[180]

It has been held[181] on appeal that breach by the licensor of an obligation to take proceedings, at the request of the licensee, in respect of infringements of the licensed patent, did not go to the root of the contract and therefore did not relieve the licensee of obligations under the licence.

In one case[182] a licence agreement required the licensee to notify the licensor of any infringement of the patent, whereupon the licensor was required within six weeks to take steps to prevent such infringement. The licensee claimed that the licensor had not taken proper steps as required by the licence. It was held that the licensor was required to take such steps as a reasonably energetic patentee would take to protect what he or she thought was a valuable patent, and that the licensor had not taken the necessary steps to prevent the infringement.

No challenge clauses – implied terms under English law as against prohibition under EC competition law

Contractual provisions which prohibit a licensee from challenging the validity of the licensed intellectual property, eg by instituting revocation proceedings, are condemned under Article 81 (101) of the EC Treaty.[183] Within the UK under the Competition Act 1998, which aims to provide similar provisions to those under the EC Treaty, it is likely the courts will interpret such issues in the same way.

But these laws will only apply to agreements which are caught by them. Where Article 81 (101) of the EC Treaty and Chapter I of the Competition Act 1998 do not apply then the traditional approach of the English courts to this issue may still apply. Where EC or UK statutory competition law does apply, they will override any inconsistent domestic English laws on this topic.

The traditional approach of the English courts can be seen in a case[184] concerning trade marks and the validity of a 'no challenge' clause.

---

180 *Lines v Usher* (1896) 13 RPC 685, (1897) 14 RPC 206.
181 *The Huntoon Company v Kolynos (Incorporated)* (1930) 47 RPC 403, CA.
182 *N v 'Splendor' Gloeilampen Fabrieken v Omega Lampworks Ltd* (1933) 50 RPC 393. A case involving the licensing of a patent for electric lightbulbs.
183 See Ch 12 under 'When does Article 81(1) (101(1)) apply?'. This Article is renumbered as Article 101 on implementation of the Lisbon Treaty.
184 *Apple Corps Ltd and Another v Apple Computer Inc and Others* [1992] FSR 431.

The case concerned an agreement between Apple Corps Ltd, publishers of Beatles records, and Apple Computer Inc, the US computer company, each of which owned trade marks which included the word 'Apple'. The agreement was made under English law and the parties submitted to the exclusive jurisdiction of the English courts, though the agreement concerned trade marks registered in many different countries of the world. Each party agreed, among other things, not to use its 'Apple' trade marks in the other party's field of business, and not to lodge opposition to or apply to cancel any of each other's trade-mark applications and registrations.

Apple Corps Ltd sued Apple Computer Inc, alleging breach of the agreement. Apple Computer Inc claimed, inter alia, that the no challenge clauses were unenforceable under English law and under the laws of certain other countries in which the agreement operated. The court held that the no challenge clauses were enforceable under English law (leaving aside questions of restraint of trade and Article 81(101) of the EC Treaty).[185] Furthermore, the fact that such clauses might be unenforceable under other countries' laws was irrelevant to the enforcement by an English court of a no challenge clause.

The Apple decision is consistent with some older English cases[186] where the courts have been called upon to construe the wording of no challenge clauses, and where it appears to have been assumed by all concerned that such clauses were enforceable in principle. In one old case[187] an injunction was ordered against a licensee who sought to impeach the validity of the licensed patent. This was in breach of an agreement between the licensee and the licensor that he would not 'impeach or deny the Letters Patent of [the licensor] while in force'.

There also appears to be a principle of English law that a licensee will be prevented from denying the validity of the licensed intellectual property by virtue of his or her status as licensee, even though the agreement may contain no express no challenge clause. In one case[188] such an argument was raised in a preliminary hearing and, although not accepted in its entirety, appears not to have been dismissed out of hand. In another case[189] the judge based part of his decision on the basis that a licensee was precluded from contesting the validity of patents under which the licence was granted.[190] Whether any such general principles exist today, in the light of Article 81

---

185 This Article will be renumbered as Article 101 on implementation of the Lisbon Treaty.
186 *Bristol Repetition Ltd v Fomento (Sterling Area) Ltd* [1960] RPC 163; *Campbell v G Hopkins & Sons (Clerkenwell) Ltd* (1931) 49 RPC 38, overturned on appeal for different reasons and reported at 50 RPC 213.
187 *Watts v Everitt Press Manufacturing Company* (1910) RPC 718, CA, upholding the High Court's decision.
188 *Fuel Economy Co Ltd v Murray* (1930) 47 RPC 346, CA.
189 *Lyle-Meller v A Lewis & Co (Westminster) Ltd* (1955) 72 RPC 307, decision upheld on appeal and reported at [1956] RPC 14.
190 See report of the High Court judgment cited above, lines 28–30, p 307.

(101) of the EC Treaty, must be uncertain. There is also old authority for the proposition that a plea of invalidity is not a defence to an action to recover royalties, although this case was decided prior to the introduction of Patents Act 1977, s 74(2).[191]

The question of the enforceability of no challenge clauses in agreements which are subject to Article 81 (101) of the EC Treaty has been considered in a number of cases before the European Court of Justice and the European Commission.[192] For a discussion of the way in which such clauses are treated in the Technology Transfer Regulation, see Chapter 13.

Anti-competitive provisions – generally

Under domestic English law, a provision may be unenforceable for being in breach of competition legislation, such as the Competition Act 1998,[193] or common law rules on restraint of trade. These subjects are discussed further in Chapter 15.

A contractual provision will also be unenforceable if it is in breach of Article 81(1) (101(1)) of the EC Treaty and it does not benefit from an exemption under Article 81(3) (101(3)). This subject is discussed in Chapter 12.

The English courts have from time to time considered the effect of an unenforceable provision on the contract as a whole. For example in one case[194] the court held that in applying Article 81 (101) to an English contract, consideration has to be given as to whether, after any excisions required by the Article had been made, the contract remaining would fail for lack of consideration or because of a fundamental change in its character. This approach is broadly consistent with pronouncements by the European Court of Justice on this issue.

Confidentiality obligations

For a general discussion of the law of confidentiality, and its application to the exploitation and transfer of technology, see Chapter 8. The following

---

191 *Fuel Economy Co Ltd v Murray* [1930] 2 Ch 93, at 106, (1930) 47 RPC 346, at 359, CA; see also Patents Act 1977, s 74(2).

192 See eg *Bayer AG and Maschinenfabrik Hennecke GmbH v Sullhofer* [1990] FSR 300 (ECJ) which confirms that such a clause may infringe Art 81(1) (101(1)), but does not do so in two very limited situations: (a) when the licence is a free licence; and (b) when the licence relates to a technically outdated process which the licensee does not use.

193 Although with the coming into force of the Competition Act 1998, it is expected that UK competition law will follow EC law more closely.

194 *Chemidus Wavin Limited v Societe pour la Transformation etc* [1977] FSR 181, CA.

paragraphs consider case law on the use and disclosure of confidential information provided under licence agreements.

It has been held that there is no general proposition of law that when confidential information was given under an agreement and that agreement came to an end, the right to use the confidential information also came to an end.[195]

In one case,[196] the court held that an obligation of confidentiality was implied in a manufacturing agreement. It was also held that a document may be confidential if it is the result of work done by its maker, even if the matters on which he worked were matters of public knowledge. In this case the court observed that:

> '[I]f two parties make a contract, under which one of them obtains for the purpose of the contract, or in connection with it, some confidential matter, then, even though the contract is silent on the matter of confidence, the law will imply an obligation to treat such confidential matter in a confidential way. If a defendant is proved to have used confidential information, obtained directly or indirectly from a plaintiff, without the consent, express or implied, of the plaintiff, he will be guilty of an infringement of the plaintiff's rights'.

In another case[197] the question arose, at a preliminary hearing, as to whether a licensee was permitted to use confidential information disclosed to him by the licensor for purposes other than the manufacture of licensed products. It was held, construing the agreement and applying general principles, that the licensee could be restrained from deriving any advantage from the information which it had received exclusively for the purposes of the agreement.

There have been many reported cases in which misuse of confidential information has been alleged, including cases involving ex-employees.[198] It has been held that an innocent acquirer of confidential information can be restrained from using it[199] probably only once he or she has knowledge of its confidential status.[200]

---

195 *Regina Glass Fibre Ltd v Werner Schuller* [1972] RPC 229, CA.
196 *Saltman Engineering Co Ltd and others v Campbell Engineering Co Ltd* (1948) 65 RPC 203, CA.
197 *Torrington Manufacturing Company v Smith and Sons (England) Ltd* [1966] RPC 285.
198 See for example *Seager v Copydex Ltd* [1969] RPC 250, CA, [1967] RPC 349; *Coco v AN Clark (Engineers) Ltd* [1969] RPC 41; *Cranleigh Precision Engineering Ltd v Bryant* [1966] RPC 81; *Printers & Finishers Ltd v Holloway* [1965] RPC 239.
199 For a case dealing with the position of information mistakenly sent to the other side's solicitors in litigation, see *English & American Insurance Co Ltd v Herbert Smith* [1988] FSR 232.
200 *Stevenson Jordan and Harrison Ltd v Macdonald and Evans* [1952] RPC 10.

Meaning of 'business' in a licence agreement

A usual provision in many commercial agreements is the one restricting one or all parties assigning, transferring or otherwise dealing with their rights and obligations under the agreement. Sometimes a party is permitted to assign and transfer all its rights and obligations when it assigns and transfers all of its business.

In one case the meaning of a 'business' was considered.[201] It was held that some of the assets only of a party would be enough to be 'business' even though there was no ongoing business operation or any products or processes which could be sold or any revenues which were being generated. The reasoning of the court (both at first instance and on appeal) is particularly interesting and relevant to commercial transactions involving intellectual property, and is set out in some detail:

- The claimant was the owner of certain patents, and it granted a licence under them to the third defendant to develop and exploit them (including making products, and manufacturing and selling them). The assignment clause provided:

  'LICENSEE'S [the third defendant, Beckman Coulter Inc] rights under this Agreement and the licences herein granted shall pass to any person, firm or corporation succeeding to its business in products licensed hereunder as a result of sale, consolidation, re-organisation or otherwise, provided, such person, firm or corporation shall without delay, undertake directly with LICENSOR [the claimant, Oxford Gene Technology Ltd] to comply with the provisions of this Agreement and to become in all respects bound thereby in the place and stead of LICENSEE'.

- To simplify somewhat the facts of this long-running and complicated case, the third defendant purported to sell the 'business in products' including the licence to the first and second defendants, Affymetrix Inc and Affymetrix Ltd.

- It was the wording of the phrase 'business in products' which came under particular scrutiny by the court.

- The third defendant undertook some development work, which included obtaining some further patents, but had not, it appears, created any products based on the patents licensed by the claimant or the new patents.

- What was sold by the third defendant to the first and second defendants included the benefit of the licence and some laboratory equipment, notebooks, and computer software.

---

201 *Oxford Gene Technology v Affymetrix Inc* [2001] IP & T 93, CA (overturning the High Court decision, [2000] IP & T 1006).

- At first instance it was held that the activities undertaken by the third defendant under the licence from the claimant could not be described as a 'business':[202]

> 'I think that the true meaning of "business" in clause 16.2 is simply that conveyed by the normal meaning of the words. No one would normally describe a few patents and some incomplete research work, even if the latter were modestly ongoing, as a "business". Still less would they describe the mere transfer of the rights to such, without any associated transfer of any actual activity, as a "business". Moreover where does the submission stop? Suppose that the [third defendant] had done even less research then they had – a few test tubes and the odd notebook – would that amount to a "business" too? Could they have assigned them after only a few months of research? The incomplete research is no more a "business" than a half-built factory and probably less.
>
> ... the business begins broadly when the sales start. I do not think, however, that the line is that sharp. If a factory existed, and samples were on trial, that might have been enough to constitute a business in embryonic form. To some extent the question is one of degree. What I am clear about however, is that whatever was passed, or supposed to be passed, to the [first and second defendant] did not amount to the transfer of a business'.

- The first instance judgment was overturned on appeal. In addition to analysing the contract, a business was held not to start at the point active commercialisation had started or where products were ready or nearly ready to be sold, and the appeal court relied on a dictum quoted by the first and second defendants from an earlier case:

> '... anything which occupies the time and attention and labour of man for the purpose of profit is a business. It is a word of extensive use and indefinite signification' (*Smith v Anderson* (1880) 15 Ch D 247 at 258, per Jessel MR).

- The appeal court rejected the submissions put forward by the claimant that the meaning of the phrase 'business in products' meant that the third defendant had to have products that were available for sale, and to have moved on from mere research and development. The appeal court interpreted the assignment clause (quoted above) by examining one of the recitals to the licence agreement:

> '[the third defendant] is in the business of designing, developing, manufacturing and selling bioanalytical instrument systems and is interested in acquiring rights in and to the Licensed Patent Rights and related Technical Information' (the "Second Recital")'.

---

202   As Jacob J stated in the High Court in *Oxford Gene Technology v Affymetrix Inc* (see n 200), at paras 53, 54.

- As held by the appeal court, the phrase 'business in products' was used, not to restrict assignment of the licence granted by the claimant to the third defendant to a third party as provided by the Assignment Clause, but 'to distinguish those assets and activities of [the third defendant] from other assets and activities of [the third defendant]'.[203]

- The appeal court stated that the phrase 'business in products licensed hereunder' found in the assignment clause needed to be construed in the context of the whole agreement, and the court recited that the claimant's aim was to have its patents licensed and that the claimant and the third defendant both realised that a substantial amount of research and development would need to be done to commercialise the licensed patents. Having a restriction that limited transfer of the business (including the licence granted by the claimant to the third defendant) of the third defendant to the situation where the third defendant had developed products, was not something that would have been in the contemplation of either party. Furthermore, the court held that there was no:

  '... limitation as to the type of business in products that are licensed. The products licensed are those referred to in Clause 5.1 which grants the licence. They are all products covered by a claim asserted in good faith in the Licensed Patent Rights. Thus the licence covers the manufacture, use, sale and offer for sale of products. There is no requirement that such activity has to have reached the stage of commercialisation. That is made by Clause 6. Clause 6 requires an upfront advance and also provides for royalties after commercialisation. Thus the licence covers the period both before commercialisation and thereafter so that the words "products licensed hereunder" in [the assignment clause] include products made other than for commercial use. [The assignment clause] appears to provide for transfer of the licence upon a succession of the business of [the third defendant] even before commercialisation. That conclusion is, I believe supported by the recitals. [The Second Recital] records that the [third defendant] is in the business of "designing, developing and manufacturing and selling ...". Thus the parties accepted that there can be a business in designing and developing'.[204]

Service of notices

Failure to give notices in the correct manner as required by the agreement could be fatal for the exercise or enforcement of a right.[205] In many cases the statutory provisions concerning notices set out in Law of Property Act 1925, s 196[206] will apply, if this issue is not addressed in the agreement.

---

203   As above, at para 37.
204   As n 201, at para 44.
205   See eg *UDT (Commercial) Ltd v Eagle Aircraft Ltd* [1968] 1 WLR 74.
206   See Ch 9 under 'Notices'.

Law and jurisdiction

The question of which country's laws should be applied to a contract, and which courts have jurisdiction to hear cases concerning a contract, is a large and complex one and beyond the scope of this book. There have been some cases in the intellectual property field addressing specific issues, which it may be useful to mention:

- In a dispute concerning a licence agreement, that as a matter of public policy, in a contract by British subjects to be performed in Britain, it was held that it was undesirable that litigation that turned on it should be determined in a foreign country without express provision to that effect in the contract.[207] An injunction was granted to restrain the defendant from prosecuting a claim in the US arising out of an agreement with the claimants, an English subsidiary of a US corporation.

- In a case concerning the application of the Arbitration Act 1950[208] to an arbitration clause, in an agreement between a Swiss company and an English company concerning the exploitation of certain inventions owned jointly by the parties, where the relevant clause stated that

  'all disputes ... between the parties to this agreement with respect of any matter ... arising out of or relating to this agreement shall be referred to arbitration',

  it was held[209] that this arbitration clause amounted to an agreement to submit disputes to arbitration in the terms required by section 4(2) of the Act.

- In a case[210] involving a patent licence agreement which contained law and jurisdiction clauses as follows:

  'The validity, construction and performance of this Agreement shall be governed by English law'.

---

207 *Smith Kline & French Laboratories Ltd and another v Bloch* (1981) 125 Sol Jo 81. See also the following cases cited in Melville *Forms and Agreements on Intellectual Property and International Licensing* (3rd edn, Sweet & Maxwell), paras 9.15, 9.16: *James Miller & Partners v Whitworth Street Estates* [1970] All ER 768; *Re United Railways of Havana* [1960] 2 All ER 332; *The Assunzione* [1954] 1 All ER 278; *Compagnie Tunisienne de Navigation SA* [1970] 3 All ER 71.

208 Now the Arbitration Act 1996.

209 *Unipat AG v Dowty Hydraulic Units Limited* [1967] RPC 401.

210 *Celltech R & D Ltd v Medimmune Inc* [2004] EWCA Civ 1331. The case involved consideration by the court of a patent licence agreement and the defendant's refusal to pay royalties following the defendant's manufacture and sale of products in the US. The defendant started proceedings in the US courts for a declaration that the claimant's patent under which the goods were made was invalid. The claimant argued that the law and jurisdiction clause conferred jurisdiction on the courts of England and Wales on the question whether or not a licensed product is covered by the patent. The court did not decide the question whether the English courts had exclusive or non-exclusive jurisdiction.

'All disputes, claims or proceedings between the parties relating to the validity, construction or performance of this Agreement shall be subject to the jurisdiction of the laws of England to the jurisdiction of whose courts the parties hereto submit. Each of the parties consents to the award or grant of any relief in any such proceedings before the High Court of Justice in England. Either party shall have the right to take proceedings in any other jurisdiction for the purposes of enforcing a judgment or order obtained from a Court of Justice in England'.

The court held that the English courts were able to hear a dispute which involved a US patent and where products were sold in the US under the US patent.

OWNERSHIP RIGHTS

Rights of co-owners

Section 36(1) of the Patents Act 1977 provides that:

'[W]here a patent is granted to two or more persons, each of them shall, subject to any agreement to the contrary, be entitled to an equal undivided share in the patent'.

In a case[211] heard in the UK Intellectual Property Office (and not, therefore, binding on the High Court), and predating the passing of the Patents Act 1977, it was held that the equal undivided shares held by joint owners of a patent prima facie implied a right to share equally in any money received for the patent.

Under UK patent law a co-owner of a patent may manufacture and sell products made in accordance with the claims of the patent without the consent of the other co-owner(s), but may not grant any license under the patent without the consent of the other co-owner(s).[212] In one case the question arose as to whether in fact any such consent had been given or could be implied.[213]

See further Chapter 4 under 'Co-ownership of patents and patent applications' (in relation to the rights of co-owners under intellectual property legislation) and Chapter 9 under 'Multiple ownership of property' (for a discussion of the rights of co-owners under traditional property laws, and the application of these laws to co-ownership of intellectual property).

---

211 *Florey & Others' Patent* [1962] RPC 186.
212 Patents Act 1977, ss 36(2), (3).
213 *Whitehead & Poole Ltd v Sir James Farmer & Sons Ltd* (1918) 35 RPC 241; the decision was based on the provisions of Patents and Designs Act 1907, s 37.

Rights of employees

The rights of an employee in inventions made by him or her are nowadays governed by Patents Act 1977, ss 39–43.[214]

As is discussed in more detail in Chapter 4, it is not possible to contract out of section 39 in respect of inventions made by an employee after the date of the contract, so as to diminish the employee's rights.[215] However, it is possible for an employer and employee to agree to 'diminish the employee's rights' in respect of inventions made prior to the date of the contract. Moreover the statutory provisions do not apply to inventions made before commencement of that Act in 1978, and in such cases ownership will be governed by the contract of employment. In the case of copyright and designs generated by an employee, there is no statutory restriction on the parties agreeing a different position on ownership of such intellectual property to that contained in the statutory provisions.

Thus there are a number of situations in which it is lawful for an employer to agree with his or her employee that the employer will own intellectual property generated by the employee. In such cases, the only restriction on the terms of such an agreement is that it must not be an unreasonable restraint of trade. The following case gives some indication of the circumstances in which there would be an unreasonable restraint of trade.

In the case, arising under the law *prior* to the Patents Act 1977,[216] it was held that a clause in a contract of employment, giving the benefit of inventions made by the employee to his employer, was too wide to be enforceable since it was concerned with the discovery of any process, invention or improvement relating to articles not only manufactured by the employer but by any of its associated companies in the UK or elsewhere. It was doubtful whether such a provision was appropriate or reasonable even for a research worker employed by the plaintiffs. In this case the employee was a senior storekeeper, who was not employed to invent.

---

214 For a discussion of those rights please refer to in Ch 4.
215 See Patents Act 1977, ss 40–42.
216 *Electrolux Ltd v Hudson and others* [1977] FSR 313. This case is also authority for the propositions that an agreement calling for assignment of inventions made outside the field of the employer's operations will ordinarily be unreasonable, as may such an agreement relating to inventions within the employer's field if it extends to inventions made in the employee's own time and with his or her own materials.

General

An agreement to sell a patent or an interest in a patent need not be in writing[217] and may be enforced by an order for specific performance,[218] or in the case of an agreement for sale made before grant of the patent, by applying to the comptroller for a direction that the application proceed in the name of the purchaser.[219]

SELECTED CONTRACT LAW STATUTES AFFECTING INTELLECTUAL PROPERTY TRANSACTIONS

Introduction[220]

The following paragraphs consider statutes and regulations in the contract law field which either establish special rules for intellectual property transactions, or have features of particular relevance to such transactions. However, this section is not intended to be a comprehensive review of contract law statutes which may affect intellectual property transactions – in many areas of contract law, no special issues are raised by intellectual property transactions and the law which applies to 'ordinary' commercial agreements will also apply to intellectual property transactions.

The following Acts and regulations are considered in this section:

- Unfair Contract Terms Act 1977;

- Unfair Terms in Consumer Contracts Regulations 1999;

- Sale of Goods Act 1979 (as amended in particular by the Sale and Supply of Goods Act 1994);

- Supply of Goods and Services Act 1982;

- Contracts (Rights of Third Parties) Act 1999;

- Late Payment of Commercial Debts (Interest) Act 1998; and

- Provision of Services Regulations 2009.

---

217 *Smith v Neale* (1857) 26 LJCP 143.
218 *Bewley v Hancock* (1856) 6 De GM & G 391; *Printing and Numerical Registering Co v Sampson* (1875) 19 Eq 462; *Liardet v Hammond Electric Light and Power Co* (1883) 31 WR 710; as to enforcement of equitable rights in foreign patents, see *Worthington Pumping Engine Co v Moore* (1902) 20 RPC 41; *Rickmond & Co Ltd v Wrightson* (1904) 22 RPC 25.
219 Patents Act 1977, s 8.
220 The purpose of this section is to highlight areas of particular relevance to intellectual property transactions. For a fuller discussion, particularly in the important area of the use and acceptability of exclusion and limitation of liability clauses and the Unfair Contracts Terms Act 1977, see Anderson and Warner, *Drafting and Negotiating Commercial Contracts* (2nd edn, Tottel Publishing, 2007).

Unfair Contract Terms Act 1977 (as amended)

The Unfair Contract Terms Act 1977 (UCTA) is described in its preamble as:

'An Act to impose further[221] limits on the extent to which under the law of England and Wales and Northern Ireland civil liability for breach of contract, or for negligence or other breach of duty, can be avoided by means of contract terms and otherwise, and under the law of Scotland civil liability can be avoided by means of contract terms'.

In summary, the Act imposes limits on the extent to which one can exclude or limit liability, including certain limits in the following situations:

- *Negligence:* under section 2 of UCTA it is not permitted to exclude or restrict liability, by a contract term or notice, for death or personal injury caused by one's negligence. In the case of other loss or damage caused by negligence, any exclusion or restriction of liability will not be effective unless it 'satisfies the requirement of reasonableness'.[222]

- *Standard terms of business/consumer transactions:* under section 3 of UCTA, where a contract is made on a party's written standard terms of business, or where the other party 'deals as consumer',[223] that party may not, inter alia, exclude or restrict liability for breach of contract, unless the contract term satisfies the requirement of reasonableness.[224]

---

221 The impact of the common law (see *Boomsma v Clark and Rose Ltd* 1983 SLT (Sh Ct) 67) and other legislation upon exclusion clauses should not be overlooked, including the provisions of the Unfair Terms in Consumer Contracts Regulations 1999 and the Consumer Protection Act 1987.

222 As to which see Unfair Contract Terms Act 1977, s 11 and Sch 2. In many commercial agreements there is often standard wording which specifically addresses this point, such as 'Nothing in this Agreement excludes any person's liability to the extent that it may not be so excluded under applicable law, including any such liability for death or personal injury caused by that person's negligence, or liability for fraud'. Although, however, it is arguable that such wording is not necessary as it reflects no more than the default position as imposed by UCTA. But such wording is added as part of a range of provisions intended to limit or exclude liability, so that if there is any court action and a judge has to decide on the reasonableness of any exclusion or limitation of liability clauses then he or she will not find them unreasonable because they could potentially exclude or limit liability for death or personal injury.

223 Ie not in a business context – see definition in Unfair Contract Terms Act 1977, s 12.

224 This has been an area which has been subject to considerable judicial scrutiny and also the views of the judiciary have changed over time. Until fairly recently they took a more interventionist approach as to whether particular clauses which excluded or restricted liability were reasonable and whether they should apply. The position now appears to be, particularly in regard to commercial contracts, that there is a more 'hands-off' approach, perhaps best summarised in this passage from *Watford Electronics Ltd v Sanderson CFL Ltd* [2001] EWCA Civ 317: 'Where experienced businessmen representing substantial companies of equal power negotiated an agreement, they may be taken to have had regard to the matters known to them. They should, in my view, be taken to be the best judges of the commercial fairness of the agreement which they have made; including the fairness of each of the terms of the agreement'.

- *Unreasonable indemnity clauses:* under section 4 of UCTA a person dealing as consumer cannot by reference to any contract term be made to indemnify another person in respect of liability incurred by the other for negligence or breach of contract, except in so far as the contract term satisfies the requirement of reasonableness.

- *Terms implied by the Sale of Goods Act/Supply of Goods and Services Act:* under sections 6 and 7 of UCTA it is not possible to exclude liability for breach of the implied terms as to title nor (in the case of consumer sales) the other terms implied by these statutes.[225] In the case of non-consumer sales, any exclusion of the other implied terms must be reasonable in order to be effective.

UCTA also includes specific provisions concerning liability relating to consumer guarantees.[226]

Certain contracts for the international supply of goods are excluded from some of the provisions of UCTA (principally those provisions controlling exclusion and limitations of liability).[227] Where a technology-based agreement does involve the sale or transfer of ownership or possession of goods[228] then the provisions will not apply. Intellectual property transactions commonly involve parties which are based in different countries, but not all of them will be 'international supply contracts' for the purpose of UCTA.

A contract for the international supply of goods will be one where:

- there is a contract of sale of goods or it is a contract where the possession or ownership of goods passes; and

- the parties are based in different countries.[229]

In order for these conditions to be fulfilled:

- the goods involved must travel from one state to another; or

---

225 Such as Sale of Goods Act 1979, s 13 (implied term as to description), s 14 (implied terms about quality and fitness for a particular purpose) and s 15 (sale by sample).
226 Unfair Contract Terms Act 1977, s 5.
227 See Unfair Contract Terms Act 1977, s 26. The wording used in this section has come in for judicial criticism recently, both for the wording used and the purpose of the clause (see *Amiri Flight Authority v BAE Systems plc* [2003] EWCA Civ 1447, [2004] 1 All ER (Comm) 385; and *Trident Turboprop (Dublin) Ltd v First Flight Couriers Ltd* [2009] EWCA Civ 290, [2009] 2 All ER (Comm) 1050, [2009] 3 WLR 861).
228 For example, where an owner of a patent is licensing its use for manufacture together with a supply of materials, chemicals or machinery, or where a company testing the safety of medicines needs to licence software to assist in the testing, but the software comes, perhaps, with some equipment such as a specially adapted computer or with a USB key containing a password to run the computer. The issue of whether (particular forms of) intellectual property are goods is considered below.
229 Unfair Contract Terms Act 1977, s 26(3).

- the acts of making the offer and acceptance to create the contract have to be done in different states; or

- the goods need to be delivered to a third state.[230]

Where the conditions are met then the limits imposed by UCTA on the extent to which a person may exclude or restrict liability by reference to a contract term do not apply to liability arising under an international supply contract.[231] The terms of such a contract are also not subject to any requirement of reasonableness under section 3 or 4 of UCTA.[232]

For example, a contract between two English companies for the supply of goods to the manufacturing facility in France of one of the parties would not be an international supply contract for the purpose of UCTA. But if one of the parties was a French company and the other was an English company, and the order for the supply of goods was made in France and was accepted in England, the contract would be an international supply contract and it would not matter whether the goods moved from one country to another. However a contract between an English company and a French company signed in France but with the goods always present in England and their delivery also in England would not be an international supply contract.[233] However, if the contract had been made in England but the goods were delivered to France then the contract would be an international supply contract.

These highly narrow distinctions may appear to be hard to explain logically but could easily affect some commercial intellectual property transactions where goods are being sold or provided, as any limitations or exclusions of liability would not then be judged, by the English courts, as to their 'reasonableness' in the event of any dispute.[234] Also it seems that if any item of goods were provided then the whole contract would be an international supply contract and its exemption clauses etc would be excluded from scrutiny by a court for their reasonableness. For example, if the primary purpose of a contract is the licensing of a patent, but a small sample of chemical is being supplied as well and the licensing agreement refers to the provision of these chemicals, then

---

230 Unfair Contract Terms Act 1977, s 26(4).
231 However, it is still not permitted to exclude or restrict liability, by a contract term or notice, for death or personal injury caused by one's negligence.
232 The wording for Unfair Contract Terms Act 1977 is set out in the companion website to this book.
233 *Amiri Flight Authority v BAE Systems plc* [2003] EWCA Civ 1447, [2004] 1 All ER (Comm) 385, affirmed in *Trident Turboprop (Dublin) Ltd v First Flight Couriers Ltd* [2009] EWCA Civ 290, [2009] 2 All ER (Comm) 1050, [2009] 3 WLR 861.
234 The wording chosen in Unfair Contract Terms Act 1977, s 26 is to exclude all (international supply) contracts from the controls imposed by the UCTA in relation to exemption clauses (and the requirement for reasonableness) and can include leases (*Trident Turboprop (Dublin) Ltd v First Flight Couriers Ltd* [2009] EWCA Civ 290, [2009] 2 All ER (Comm) 1050, [2009] 3 WLR 861). The Court of Appeal was in effect saying that a restrictive approach as to the type of contract is not the approach to be taken.

the licensor would be able to include very unreasonable terms regarding the licensing of the patents which the licensor might have more difficulty justifying were the agreement only to be concerned with the licensing of a patent.

UCTA does not apply to certain contracts which are agreed to be made under the law of a part of the UK[235] if, in the absence of such agreement, the contract would not be subject to the law of any part of the UK.[236] On the other hand it is not possible to evade the operation of UCTA by agreeing to apply another country's laws.[237]

In general, the limits imposed by UCTA apply equally to contracts concerning or involving intellectual property as they do to other types of contract, but with one significant exception. Schedule 1, paragraph 1(c) to UCTA (as amended) provides[238] that sections 2 to 4 of the Act (summarised above) do not extend to:

> '... any contract so far as it relates to the creation or transfer of a right or interest in any patent, trade mark, copyright, design right, registered design, technical or commercial information or other intellectual property, or relates to the termination of any such right or interest ...'

The extent of this exception is not entirely clear. In a case concerning the development and supply of computer software it was held that these words only apply to the provisions of a contract concerning the creation of a right or interest in intellectual property (ie not those provisions relating to other matters).[239] In this case part of the contract related to the supply of services. Even before the case was decided, many lawyers were cautious about relying on the words quoted above when drafting intellectual property agreements. The reasons for such caution may include the following:

- The above exception only applies *'in so far as [the contract] relates to'* the creation or transfer of a right or interest in intellectual property. As the above-mentioned case confirmed, an agreement could relate to several matters.

  For example, an agreement might provide for the carrying out of research work and the provision of reports of the research work as well as the assignment, to the person commissioning the work, of any intellectual property generated in the course of performing the contract. It seems that the carrying out of the research work or the provision of a report would not come within the wording of the exception, but the assignment of intellectual property would.

---

235 Ie under the law of (a) England and Wales, or (b) Northern Ireland, or (c) Scotland.
236 Unfair Contract Terms Act 1977, s 27(1).
237 Unfair Contract Terms Act 1977, s 27(2).
238 See also Unfair Contract Terms Act 1977, s 1(2), which gives statutory effect to Sch 1; and s 1(3) which indicates that ss 2–4 apply only to business liability.
239 *The Salvage Association v CAP Financial Services Limited* [1995] FSR 654.

But the position may be less clear in relation to other clauses of an agreement. Would a warranty of title, contained in an agreement to assign a patent, be held to 'relate to' the transfer of the patent? Would a clause in a licence, providing that one party will defend any proceedings brought by a third party alleging breach of intellectual property rights, be held to relate to the transfer of an interest in the patent? In the light of the above-mentioned case, it seems likely that the wording of Schedule 1 to UCTA applies only to liabilities associated with the grant clause and termination clause[240] of an assignment or licence, and not to other provisions of the assignment or licence agreement.

It is also interesting to note decisions which relate to other parts of Schedule 1, paragraph 1, which are similarly worded to the part concerning intellectual property, in particular those relating to a decision[241] concerning Schedule 1 to UCTA and real property leases.[242] In a case involving the non-payment of rent [243] it was held that a covenant requiring the payment of rent without set-off was within the exception of Schedule 1 as the covenant was an integral part of the creation of the lease.

On the basis of the cases dealing with real property, provisions in an assignment of intellectual property such as the payment of money and other commercial issues (such as further assurances clauses etc) would all come within the exception to Schedule 1.

- The exception only applies to the creation or transfer of *a right or interest in* intellectual property. As was discussed earlier,[244] a licence is generally regarded as a right *under* the licensed intellectual property, rather than a right *in* the intellectual property.[245] Accordingly, a court might hold that Schedule 1 could apply to assignments but not to licences of intellectual property. However, such a narrow interpretation would seem to be inconsistent with the broad definition of intellectual property given later in the exception. The reference to 'technical or commercial

---

240 That is because of the last 11 words of para 1(c) quoted above.
241 *Electricity Supply Nominees Limited v IAF Group Limited* [1993] 1 WLR 1059. See also the cases referred to in this case.
242 The wording for real property is as follows: '... any contract so far as it relates to the creation or transfer of an interest in land, or the termination of such an interest, whether by extinction, merger, surrender, forfeiture or the like'. Assignments of intellectual property have been considered analogous to real property transactions by the courts (see Ch 9 under 'Does the LPA apply to intellectual property').
243 *Electricity Supply Nominees Limited v IAF Group Limited* [1993] 1 WLR 1059. This approach was also followed in *Start Rider Ltd v Inntrepreneur Pub Co* [1998] 1 EGLR 53 and *Unchained Growth III plc v Granby Village (Manchester) Management Co Ltd* (unreported, 8 October 1999, CA).
244 See 'Nature of a licence' above.
245 See *Insituform Technical Services Ltd v Inliner UK plc* [1992] RPC 83; *Crittall Windows Limited v Stormseal (UPVC) Window Systems Limited and another* [1991] RPC 265.

information'[246] as a type of intellectual property may suggest a broad, commercial approach to the drafting of Schedule 1, paragraph 1(c) to UCTA; if so that provision might be intended to encompass licences as well as assignments. Ultimately, it would be for a court to decide this issue.

In view of these uncertainties it may be unwise in practice to rely on Schedule 1, paragraph 1(c) to UCTA when drafting exclusion clauses for use in an intellectual property agreement.

Unfair Terms in Consumer Contracts Regulations 1999

These Regulations may be said to overlap with the provisions of UCTA, in that:

- contract terms which are 'unfair' as defined by the Regulations are void;

- the Regulations cover a wider range of contract clauses than UCTA – UCTA is only concerned with clauses which seek to limit or exclude liability and not with unfair terms generally (despite the title of UCTA) whilst the Regulations are also concerned, for example, with one-sided termination clauses and other clauses that are unduly favourable to one party; but

- the Regulations only apply to contracts with 'consumers' (as defined).[247]

This book does not focus on consumer transactions as such, and in any event there are no special provisions in the Regulations for intellectual property transactions. Accordingly, this chapter will not discuss the Regulations further.

Sale of Goods Act 1979

Supply of living materials and other materials, software and records

There are many situations in which the transfer of technology involves the supply of physical materials. For example:

---

246 Arguably information, as such, is not property – see Aplin, Bently and Malynicz, *Gurry on Breach of Confidence: The Protection of Confidential Information* (2nd edn, Oxford University Press, 2010).,

247 The definition of a consumer is different for UCTA and in the Regulations. Under UCTA it is possible for a business to be classified as a consumer for particular purposes, which is not possible under the Regulations. This point is explored in 7(2) *Encyclopaedia of Forms and Precedents* (5th edn, LexisNexis, 2005 reissue), 'Commercial Contracts and Other Documents', paras 123–126.3, [274]–[299].

- In the biotechnology field, it is common to provide samples of biological materials under a research collaboration or licence agreement. Sometimes those materials are living materials such as a cell line, which may be grown and used by the recipient to produce antibodies for research or commercial purposes.

- In the information technology field where as part of a software licence agreement the licensor may still provide the licensee with a CD/DVD on which the software is recorded together with printed manuals (or provided in electronic format).

- In many industries it is common to provide know-how under a licence agreement in the form of paper records or on computer disc (although this is less likely as such information might now be provided electronically, perhaps via a password-protected internet site).

- In the pharmaceutical research field, a research, development and licensing agreement might not only provide for the licensing of intellectual property but also for the licensor to supply some raw materials or chemicals to enable the licensee to carry out the research or to make products.

In such cases, the transaction could involve a sale of goods,[248] to which the Sale of Goods Act 1979 (SGA) applies.[249] In a case concerning the supply of a computer system[250] the court considered that the supply of software 'probably' was a supply of goods although these remarks were obiter dicta.

A contract for the sale of goods is defined in the SGA[251] as 'a contract by which the seller transfers or agrees to transfer the property in goods to the buyer for a money consideration, called the price'. If the SGA applies, the transaction becomes subject to an extensive set of rules, including a number of implied conditions and warranties. Liability for breach of those implied terms may not, in some cases, be limited or excluded.

---

248   Sale of Goods Act 1979, s 61(1) defines goods as including 'all personal chattels other than things in action and money, and in Scotland all corporeal moveables except money; and in particular "goods" includes emblements, industrial growing crops, and things attached to or forming part of the land which are agreed to be severed before sale or under the contract of sale [and includes an undivided share in goods]'. The meaning of 'personal chattels' is considered further below.

249   In the case of international sales of goods, the provisions of the Uniform Laws on International Sales Act 1967 should be considered.

250   *St Albans District Council v International Computers Limited* [1995] FSR 686. Chitty (see n 1), at para 43-006, cites this case and a number of other cases, including *Beta Computers (Europe) Ltd v Adobe Systems (Europe) Ltd* 1996 SLT 604, *Tob Constructions Products Pty Ltd v Computa Bar (Sales) Pty Ltd* [1983] 2 NSWLR 48, and *Watford Electronics Ltd v Sanderson CFL Ltd* [2001] EWCA Civ 317 in support for the proposition that a sale of both hardware and software is a sale of goods.

251   Sale of Goods Act 1979, s 2(1).

With a view to avoiding the operation of the SGA, it is common for the provider of materials etc under a licence agreement to state specifically that property in such materials remains with the provider, even when the materials are in the possession of the recipient. If property is not transferred, the transaction does not come within the definition of a sale of goods quoted above.

The terms implied into a sale of goods

Where the technology-related transaction does involve a sale of goods it will be governed by the SGA, which deals with many different aspects of such sales. It is not proposed to review that law in this chapter, except to summarise very briefly one area that the SGA covers, namely the terms implied into a sale of goods.[252] These are:

(1) *Implied terms about title etc:*[253] an implied condition that the seller has the right to sell the goods; an implied warranty that the goods are free from any charge or encumbrance not disclosed or known to the buyer before the contract is made; and an implied warranty that the buyer will enjoy quiet possession of the goods, except for disturbance by a person holding a charge or encumbrance over the goods which was disclosed or known to the buyer before the contract was made.

> However, the above terms are not implied where there appears from the contract or is to be inferred from its circumstances an intention that the seller should transfer only such title as he/she or a third person may have. Instead, there is an implied warranty that all charges or encumbrances known to the seller and not known to the buyer have been disclosed to the buyer before the contract is made; and an implied warranty that the seller or other person transferring title to the buyer, and anyone claiming through or under such person (other than a holder of a charge or encumbrance known to the buyer before the contract is made), will not disturb the buyer's quiet possession.

> It has been held that the implied term of quiet possession is breached if the product is subject to third-party patent rights[254] or trade-mark rights[255] (see further 'Rights of purchasers of licensed products; implied warranty by seller' above).

(2) *Implied terms about quality:*[256] where the goods are sold in the course of a business, an implied term that the goods are of satisfactory quality. Goods are of satisfactory quality for the purposes of the Act if 'they meet the standard that a reasonable person would regard as satisfactory, taking account of any description of the goods, the price (if relevant) and

---

252 See Sale of Goods Act 1979, ss 12–15.
253 Sale of Goods Act 1979, s 12.
254 *Microbeads v Vinhurst Road Markings Limited* [1975] 1 All ER 529, CA.
255 *Niblett Limited v Confectioners Materials Limited* [1921] 3 KB 387, CA.
256 Sale of Goods Act 1979, s 14, as substituted by Sale and Supply of Goods Act 1994, s 1.

all the other relevant circumstances'.[257] The meaning of what constitutes 'quality of goods' is further defined[258] as follows:

'(2B) For the purposes of this Act, the quality of goods includes their state and condition and the following (among others) are in appropriate cases aspects of the quality of goods–

(a) fitness for all the purposes for which goods of the kind in question are commonly supplied,

(b) appearance and finish,

(c) freedom from minor defects,

(d) safety, and

(e) durability'.

However, the implied term of satisfactory quality does not apply to any matter which is drawn to the buyer's attention before the contract is made or, where the buyer examined the goods before the contract was made, any matter which that examination ought to have revealed or, in the case of a sale by sample, any matter which would have been apparent on a reasonable examination of the sample.[259]

(3) *Implied terms about fitness for purpose:*[260] where the goods are sold in the course of a business, and the buyer expressly or by implication makes known any particular purpose for which the goods are being bought, an implied condition that the goods are reasonably fit for that purpose, except where the circumstances show that the buyer does not rely, or that it is unreasonable for him or her to rely, on the skill and judgement of the seller. It is interesting to note that in one case a court held that in a contract for the supply of software there was an implied term that the software would be fit for its purpose, although the court did not make clear whether this implied term arose by virtue of the SGA.[261]

(4) *Implied terms about sale by sample:*[262] an implied condition that (i) the bulk will comply with the sample in quality and (ii) the goods will be free from any defect making their quality unsatisfactory, which would not be apparent on reasonable examination of the sample.

(5) *Implied terms about sale by description:*[263] where there is a sale of goods by description, an implied condition that the goods will correspond with the description.

---

257 Sale of Goods Act 1979, s 14(2A).
258 Sale of Goods Act 1979, s 14(2B).
259 Sale of Goods Act 1979, s 14(2C).
260 Sale of Goods Act 1979, s 14.
261 *Saphena Computing Limited v Allied Collection Agencies Limited* [1995] FSR 616, CA, and Official Referees Court.
262 Sale of Goods Act 1979, s 15.
263 Sale of Goods Act 1979, s 13.

Under UCTA, it is not possible to contract out of liability for breach of the terms referred to in (1) above; nor, in the case of a consumer sale, to contract out of liability for breach of the terms referred to in (2)–(5) above. In the case of non-consumer sales, any exclusion or limitation of liability for breach of (2)–(5) above must be reasonable.[264] In the case of non-consumer sales, the buyer's right to reject the goods for breach of an implied condition is qualified by an amendment to the SGA.[265]

Is a sale (assignment) of patents a sale of 'goods'?

'Goods' are defined in the SGA as including:

'... all personal chattels other than things in action and money'.[266]

It is generally assumed that the SGA does not apply to the sale (ie assignment) of a patent or other intellectual property, because a patent is not 'goods'. It is worthwhile examining this point as the consequences would be great if the SGA did apply to intellectual property assignments.

The expression 'personal chattels' (see definition of 'goods' quoted above) is not defined in the SGA. The standard legal practitioner's work on contract law states[267] that the expression 'personal chattels':

- '[C]overs any tangible movable property except money ... [but] does not include things in action, such as ... industrial property'.

- As is discussed elsewhere,[268] the term 'industrial property' means approximately the same as intellectual property, and certainly includes patents. But a patent is expressly, by statute, not a thing in action.[269] This suggests that the definition provided immediately above is flawed. However, if the first part of the definition is accepted, a patent is not a personal chattel if it is not 'tangible movable property'.

- The term 'movable' in this context excludes 'immovables' (ie land).[270] Thus a patent is movable property. But is it tangible property? Unfortunately, this is not clear. The specification of a patent is published[271] and is tangible in the sense that it is recorded on paper; but

---

264 Unfair Contract Terms Act 1977, s 6.
265 Ie under Sale and Supply of Goods Act 1994, s 15.
266 Sale of Goods Act 1979, s 61(1).
267 2 *Chitty on Contracts* (30th edn, Sweet & Maxwell, 2009), para 43–005, n 23.
268 See Ch 3 under 'Meaning of the term "intellectual property"'.
269 Patents Act 1977, s 30(1) states that a patent is 'personal property (without being a thing in action)'; however, copyright, design right and registered designs might be things in action – see Copyright, Designs and Patents Act 1988, ss 90, 222 and the proviso to Registered Designs Act 1949, s 19(4) (the only place where the status of registered designs is addressed).
270 See Bell, *Modern Law of Personal Property in England and Ireland* (Butterworths, 1989) 19.
271 Patents Act 1977, s 24(3).

the specification may not be the same thing as the patent itself. It may be that a patent is that which is registered in the register of patents,[272] but again, the (tangible) register is not the patent itself. Common sense may suggest that a patent is intangible property.

Another phrase is that of 'chattels personal', which has been defined as follows:

> 'Chattels personal are, strictly speaking, things movable, but in modern times the expression is used to denote any kind of property other than real property and chattels real'.[273]

This definition suggests that a patent could be a personal chattel, as it is property[274] and is not 'real', ie relating to land or buildings.

The basic problem is that intellectual property is, or is becoming, a distinct class of property which is not encompassed by some of the traditional definitions.[275] The language of the SGA does not take account of this development.

In practice, it is generally assumed that the SGA does not apply to the sale of intellectual property and in the absence of a higher court decision to the contrary, this is likely to remain the general view.

The question of whether intellectual property should be classified as goods or services, or neither, also arises in relation to the Supply of Goods and Services Act 1982 and the Consumer Protection Act 1987.[276]

Supply of Goods and Services Act 1982

Similar questions arise under the Supply of Goods and Services Act 1982 (SGSA) as arise under the SGA: does the legislation apply to agreements for the exploitation (ie licensing) or transfer of technology?

To the authors' knowledge this issue has been raised by lawyers specialising in computer law, particularly in relation to the commercial supply of software (embodied in a disc and manual) under licence; it could equally have been raised in relation to any other form of intellectual property transaction in which physical materials are supplied (eg in the biotechnology field, where a cell line is provided as part of a licence to commercialise an antibody produced

---

272 Ie under Patents Act 1977, s 32.
273 35 *Halsbury's Laws of England* (5th edn, LexisNexis, 2008), 'Personal Property', para 1204.
274 Patents Act 1977, s 30(1).
275 Bell, *Modern Law of Personal Property in England and Ireland* (Butterworths, 1989) 23, s 3.
276 See 'Supply of Goods and Services Act 1982' below.

by that cell line). It is considered by some people that such transactions must either involve a supply of goods[277] (eg the disc on which the computer program is recorded) or a supply of services.

However, the real value of such a transaction may be in the supply of information (the computer program or, in other examples, know-how) together with the grant of rights to use the technology and/or intellectual property, and these items may form a distinct, third category (particularly if no disc is supplied and the program is downloaded), such that neither the implied terms under the SGA nor the implied terms under the SGSA would apply to the agreement. As was discussed earlier,[278] the common law does not generally imply warranties as to title etc into intellectual property licence agreements.[279]

In the authors' view, the supply of information as such should not be interpreted as a supply of goods or services. This issue has yet to be finally resolved by the courts. However, in one case the court considered that the supply of software 'probably' was a supply of goods and commented that if it was not, it was difficult to see what it was, other than something to which no statutory rules applied.[280] By contrast in another case,[281] a contract to supply software was characterised as a supply of services. In an earlier, unreported case, [282] the court refused to decide whether software constituted goods or services, and commented that the position appeared to be far more complex than had at first been realised.

Supply of materials etc

As was mentioned earlier, the SGA will not apply to the supply of materials or other physical items if the property in such items is not transferred. The SGSA is broader in its application, as it is concerned with:

- contracts for the transfer of property in goods;

---

277 It has been held in a criminal case that the offence of criminal damage to property under Criminal Damage Act 1971, s 10(1) was committed by a hacker in altering the contents of a computer disc (*R v Whiteley* [1993] FSR 168, CA).

278 See 'Warranties and implied terms' above.

279 For an unreported case in which an implied term of fitness for purpose was implied, even though the contract pre-dated the passing of the SGSA, see *Mackenzie Patten & Co v British Olivetti Ltd* (unreported, 11 January 1984, Michael Davies J).

280 *St Albans City and District Council v International Computers Ltd* [1995] FSR 686. The Court also referred to an Australian case where it was held that a sale of a computer system, including both hardware and software, is a sale of goods; the position where software alone is supplied is less clear. See *Toby Construction Products Pty Ltd v Computa Bar (Sales) Pty Ltd* [1983] 2 NSWLR 48.

281 *Salvage Association v CAP Financial Services Limited* [1995] FSR 654.

282 *Eurodynamic Systems plc v General Automation Ltd* (unreported, 6 September 1988) cited in 12 *Atkin's Court Forms* (2nd edn, LexisNexis, 1990), notes at p 124, which also cite some US decisions based on similar laws.

- contracts for the hire of goods; and

- contracts for the supply of services.

As is discussed in more detail below, the SGSA implies certain terms into such contracts, including conditions or warranties as to title, freedom from encumbrances, quiet possession, correspondence with description or sample, quality, fitness for purpose, right to transfer possession and, in relation to the supply of services, that the service will be carried out with reasonable care and skill, in a reasonable time and for a reasonable charge. As will be discussed below, there may well be situations in which some of these terms will be implied into a contract for the exploitation or transfer of technology.

Contracts for the transfer of property in goods

This category of contract is broader than a sale of goods,[283] and covers for example a contract where the consideration is something other than money. The same comment applies to such contracts as applies to the sale of goods, namely that if property in the goods is not transferred the relevant provisions of the SGSA will not operate. The terms implied into contracts for the transfer of property in goods are very similar to those implied into contracts for the sale of goods, as to which see 'The terms implied into a sale of goods' above.

Contracts for the hire of goods

Such contracts are defined for the purposes of the SGSA as follows:

> 'In this Act a "contract for the hire of goods" means a contract under which one person bails or agrees to bail goods to another by way of hire, other than ... (a) a hire purchase agreement; [or] ... (b) a contract under which goods are (or are to be) bailed in exchange for trading stamps on their redemption'.[284]

It may not be usual to regard the supply of, say, micro-organisms under a biotechnology research agreement, or a computer disc under a software licence agreement, as being (or including) a contract for the hire of goods. However, it is at least arguable that such an arrangement could be interpreted in this way, depending on the facts of the case. As is discussed elsewhere,[285] the supply of such materials may give rise to a bailment. If that is the case, the only remaining question is whether the bailment is 'by way of hire'. Chitty[286] describes hire in this way:

---

283 See Supply of Goods and Services Act 1982, s 1; excluded from the definition are certain categories, eg hire-purchase agreements and mortgages.
284 Supply of Goods and Services Act 1982, s 6.
285 See Ch 9.
286 2 *Chitty on Contracts* (29th edn, Sweet & Maxwell, 2009), para 33–063.

'In the bailment termed "hire" the bailee receives both possession of the chattel and the right to use it, in return for remuneration to be paid to the bailor. The bailee is under an obligation to return the chattel to the owner (or his nominee) at the expiration of the fixed period of the hiring and to pay the cost of returning it; but in a hiring or lease of livestock, the progeny of the livestock born during the hiring belongs to the hirer (unless the contract provides to the contrary)'.

This definition of 'hire' would seem to cover many typical arrangements in the biotechnology industry in which materials are supplied by one person to another, for example to enable research work to be carried out. Sometimes materials are supplied without 'remuneration', in which case (on Chitty's definition) the arrangement may not be a hire. It is interesting to note that the progeny of hired livestock does not belong to the hirer of the livestock unless the contract provides otherwise.[287] It may be arguable that the term 'livestock' would cover living biological materials, eg a cell line and its 'progeny', antibodies.

Where a supply of materials is a contract for the hire of goods as defined by the SGSA, a number of terms may be implied into the contract. These may be summarised as follows:

- *Implied terms about right to transfer possession, etc:* an implied condition that the bailor has the right to transfer possession of the goods; and an implied warranty that the bailee will enjoy quiet possession of the goods for the period of the bailment except for disturbance by the holder of charge or encumbrance which was disclosed or known to the bailee before the contract is made.

- *Implied terms about quality:* where the bailor bails goods in the course of a business, an implied condition that the goods supplied are of satisfactory quality, except for defects specifically drawn to the bailee's attention before the contract is made or, if the bailee examines the goods before the contract is made, except for defects which the examination ought to reveal.

- *Implied terms about fitness for purpose:* where the bailor bails goods in the course of a business and the bailee makes known, expressly or by implication, any particular purpose for which the goods are being bailed, an implied condition that the goods supplied are reasonably fit for that purpose, unless the bailee does not rely, or it is unreasonable for him or her to rely, on the skill and judgement of the bailor.

- *Implied terms where hire is by sample:* where the bailor bails goods by reference to a sample, an implied condition (i) that the bulk will correspond with the sample in quality, (ii) that the bailee will have a reasonable

---

287   Chitty cites *Tucker v Farm and General Investment Trust Ltd* [1966] 2 QB 421.

opportunity of comparing the bulk with the sample, and (iii) that the goods will be free from any defect rendering them unmerchantable, which would not be apparent on reasonable examination of the sample.

- *Implied terms where hire is by description:* where the bailor bails the goods 'by description', an implied condition that the goods will correspond with the description.

These terms may be 'negatived or varied by express agreement, or by the course of dealing between the parties, or by such usage as binds both parties to the contract' (unless this is prohibited under the Unfair Contract Terms Act 1977.[288] In addition to these statutory terms, terms may also be implied[289] under the common law of bailment.[290]

Contracts for the supply of services

Such contracts are defined[291] for the purposes of the SGSA as 'a contract under which a person ('the supplier') agrees to carry out a service'. This may or may not also involve a transfer or hire of goods. However, a contract of service (ie employment) or apprenticeship is excluded. The Secretary of State may by Statutory Instrument exclude categories of service from one or more of the implied terms under the Act.[292]

This definition will cover many activities carried out under agreements for the exploitation or transfer of technology. The examples that come immediately to mind are:

- the provision of assistance by a licensor to a licensee under a patent and know-how licence for such activities as providing or explaining the know-how supplied or providing ongoing technical assistance as the licensee works the patent;

- the provision of assistance by a licensor to a licensee under a manufacturing licence agreement in the setting up of manufacturing facilities;

- the provision of research work and reports under a research and development agreement;

- the provision of advice, assistance and reports under a consultancy agreement;

---

288 Supply of Goods and Services Act 1982, s 11.
289 Other than in relation to quality of fitness – see Supply of Goods and Services Act 1982, ss 11(3), 9(1).
290 See Ch 9 under 'Bailment'.
291 Supply of Goods and Services Act 1982, s 12.
292 A number of categories of service have been excluded by the Secretary of State in relation to the implied term of care and skill, eg the services of an advocate in court or before an arbitrator and the services of a company director to the company when acting in that capacity.

- the provision of computer programming under a software development agreement; and

- the provision of maintenance services in relation to licensed software.

Where such a contract for the supply of services exists, the SGSA provides that certain terms are implied into the contract. These may be summarised as follows:

- *Implied term about care and skill:* where the supplier is acting in the course of a business, an implied term that the supplier will carry out the service with reasonable care and skill.

- *Implied term about time for performance:* where the supplier is acting in the course of a business and the time for the service to be carried out is not (i) fixed by the contract, (ii) left to be fixed in a manner agreed by the contract or (iii) determined by the course of dealing between the parties, an implied term that the supplier will carry out the service within a reasonable time.

- *Implied term about reasonable charges:* where the consideration for the service is not (i) determined by the contract, (ii) left to be determined in a manner agreed by the contract, or (iii) determined by the course of dealing between the parties, an implied term that the party contracting with the supplier will pay a reasonable charge.

Such terms may be 'negatived or varied by express agreement, or by the course of dealing between the parties, or by such usage as binds both parties to the contract', unless this is prohibited by the UCTA.[293]

Contracts (Rights of Third Parties) Act 1999

Changes to doctrine of privity of contract

The Contracts (Rights of Third Parties) Act 1999 (referred to in this section as 'C(RTP)A') has made important changes to English contract law.[294] The C(RTP)A modifies the common law doctrine of privity of contract by granting rights to certain third parties to enforce certain terms of contracts to which the C(RTP)A applies. These changes have had a practical effect on the way in which contracts are drafted.

---

293 Supply of Goods and Services Act 1982, s 16.
294 The Contracts (Rights of Third Parties) Act 1999 applies to contracts governed by English law entered into on or after 11 May 2000 (there are some transitional provisions for contracts entered into before that date).

The C(RTP)A allows a third party[295] a right to enforce a term of a contract in two situations, namely where:

- the contract states explicitly that he or she may do so;[296] or

- a term of the contract purports to confer a benefit on him or her.[297]

This provision only applies if on the proper construction of the contract it appears that the parties intended that the term be enforceable by the third party.[298]

This right is in addition to any other right or remedy that the third party may have independently of the C(RTP)A.[299]

If a contract indicates that the third party can enforce a particular term then there is no further requirement necessary for the third party to do so (unless the contracting parties have specified some such requirement).

Exceptions to application of C(RTP)A

The C(RTP)A does not apply to all contracts. In particular:

- it does not apply to any contract made before 11 November 1999;[300] and

- it does not apply to a contract made between 11 November 1999 and 10 May 2000 unless the parties expressly agree to apply the 1999 Act;[301] and

- certain categories of contract are automatically excluded from the 1999 Act, eg contracts of employment; and

- the 1999 Act only grants rights to a third party who meets the criteria set out in the C(RTP)A,[302] and those rights are qualified by the other provisions of the 1999 Act.

---

295 A third party is 'a person who is not a party to a contract' (Contracts (Rights of Third Parties) Act 1999, s 1(1)).
296 Contracts (Rights of Third Parties) Act 1999, s 1(1)(a).
297 Contracts (Rights of Third Parties) Act 1999, s 1(1)(b).
298 Contracts (Rights of Third Parties) Act 1999, s 1(2). In *Nisshin Shipping Co Ltd v Cleaves & Company Ltd and others* [2003] EWHC 2602 (Comm), [2004] 1 All ER (Comm) 481 it was held that there would have to be an express clause in a contract which stated that the third party should not have the right to enforce benefit (ie to disapply C(RTP)A, s 1(1)(b)). Also it was held that if a contract is silent on how a person can enforce a provision which confers a benefit on him or her, such silence does not mean that there was no intention to grant any rights of enforcement. See also *Laemthong International Lines Co Ltd v Artis and others* [2005] EWCA Civ 519, [2005] 23 All ER (Comm) 167.
299 Contracts (Rights of Third Parties) Act 1999, s 7(1).
300 Contracts (Rights of Third Parties) Act 1999, s 10(1).
301 Contracts (Rights of Third Parties) Act 1999, s 10(3), (4).
302 In particular Contracts (Rights of Third Parties) Act 1999, s 1(1).

Who will benefit from the Act?

The C(RTP)A gives to persons who are not parties to a contract (described in the C(RTP)A as 'third parties') certain rights to enforce that contract and therefore alters the English common law doctrine of privity of contract. The common law doctrine of privity of contract will continue, unaltered, in situations where C(RTP)A does not apply. Moreover, C(RTP)A does not prevent a third party from relying on rights that exist apart from C(RTP)A, for example claims based in tort.[303]

This doctrine generally provides that only the parties to a contract (the 'contracting parties') can have enforceable rights and obligations under the contract. Put another way, only a contracting party may sue another contracting party for breach of contract. It is, in general, not enough that a person is referred to in the text of the contract; to be contracting parties persons must generally sign the contract or have their agent or representative do so on their behalf. English law in this area has been fairly strict, compared with some other countries' laws. The 1999 Act gives greater rights to third parties than they had under previous English law rules.

Third party beneficiary examples

Contract with contracting party that is part of international group of companies

The contracting party may wish the contract to benefit other companies in the same group as itself. An example might be a licence agreement covering several territories, in which the licensee is a major international company. It is not uncommon for such a licensee to seek to include in the contract a definition of 'affiliate' (eg its subsidiaries in particular territories covered by the licence) and provide that both it and its affiliates may exploit the licence. Under some countries' laws, such a provision may give the affiliates enforceable rights under the contract. By contrast, the English law rules in this area have been quite strict; prior to the coming into force of the C(RTP)A, the affiliates would not have had direct, enforceable rights against the licensor.

This assumes that the affiliates are not contracting parties. Sometimes, techniques are used to overcome this difficulty. For example, the licensee might expressly enter into the contract as the agent of its affiliates. However, such techniques have their own difficulties, eg how does the licensee obtain its agency authority? The C(RTP)A will make it much easier, in this example, for the affiliates to enforce the contract directly against the licensor.

---

303 Contracts (Rights of Third Parties) Act 1999, s 7(1).

Research contract between sponsoring company and university

Research contracts with universities will often provide for research work to be done by, or under the supervision of, a named academic scientist who will usually be an employee of the university. Sometimes that scientist is referred to in the research contract; and sometimes, but not always, he or she is asked to be a signatory to the research contract. Where he or she is not made a contracting party, he or she would (prior to the coming into force of the C(RTP)A) have had no enforceable rights or obligations vis-a-vis the sponsoring company. For example, the contract may provide that he or she will chair a steering committee that will review the progress of the research project, or that he or she will have confidentiality obligations to the sponsoring company. On occasion, such contracts have been drafted (generally by non-lawyers) without due attention being given to the rules on privity of contract, and have not given the scientist enforceable rights or obligations. With the coming into force of the C(RTP)A, enforceable rights (but not obligations) may be given to the scientist who is not a contracting party but is named in the contract as having certain rights.

Contract containing indemnity

A detailed indemnity clause in a contract to which only A and B are parties might include the following words:

> 'A shall indemnify and hold harmless B, its affiliates, and their respective officers, employees, consultants, agents and representatives ...'

Prior to the coming into force of the C(RTP)A, B's employees (for example) would not have had enforceable rights against A under the indemnity. B might have been able to enforce the indemnity on their behalf. Under the C(RTP)A, B's employees may well have directly enforceable rights.

Revenue sharing by academic employees

Many academic institutions have policies or schemes which allow their employees to share in the revenues generated by the institution from the commercial exploitation of inventions or discoveries made by those employees. If the academic institution enters into an agreement with a commercial party for the exploitation of an invention, and the agreements refer to the fact that there is such a scheme in place, a share of the payments made by the commercial company will be paid to the employee. An employee may wish, if payment is not made by the commercial company to the academic institution, to enforce the payment provisions directly where the academic institution does not wish to engage in litigation to enforce payment. Prior to the introduction of the C(RTP)A, the employee would not be able to consider such action.

How third party is to be identified

The C(RTP)A states that the third party must be expressly identified in the contract:

- by name; or

- as a member of a class; or

- as answering a particular description.[304]

The third party need not be in existence at the time the contract is entered into.[305] This could include allowing contracting parties to confer enforceable rights on, for example:

- a company that has not yet been incorporated; or

- a sub-licensee which has not yet been granted a sub-licence; or

- a named role, which is to carry a specific function under the contract, but from time to time may be changed, such as a project director in a hardware and software installation contract; or

- (*unlikely to occur in a commercial agreement*) an unborn child; or

- (*unlikely to occur in a commercial agreement*) a future spouse.

Where it is intended to give enforceable rights to a third party, the parties to an agreement should be careful not only to identify the third party but also to make it clear what term(s) is/are to be enforceable by the third party and the extent to which it/they can be enforced. Merely naming a third party would not necessarily make the latter point clear.

---

304 Contracts (Rights of Third Parties) Act 1999, s 1(3). In *Avraamides and another v Colwill and another* [2006] EWCA Civ 1533, [2006] All ER (D) 167 (Nov) the issue of whether the claimants were expressly identified in an agreement came under consideration by the court. The claimants contracted with a building company for two bathrooms to be built. The work was not carried out satisfactorily. The assets and goodwill of the company were transferred by an agreement to the defendants (the company being left with no assets) and there was nothing left to pay the claimants. The key wording from the agreement was: 'The purchasers (sic) undertakes to complete outstanding customer orders taking into account any deposits paid by customers as at 31 March 2003, and to pay in the normal course of time any liabilities properly incurred by the company as at 31 March 2003. The Colwill loan account after adjustment to be transferred on by the partnership'. The court relied on the word 'express' in C(RTP)A, s 1(3). The court held that the use of the word 'express' does not allow a process of construction or implication and that although 'customers' are identified in the first part of the quoted extract from the agreement as beneficiaries, as far as the second part of the extract is concerned, it held that there was not sufficient precision in the phrase 'to pay in the normal course of time any liabilities properly incurred by the company as at 31 March 2003' to identify the customers (claimants) and which could include a large number of unidentified classes (see in particular para 19 of the judgment).

305 Contracts (Rights of Third Parties) Act 1999, s 1(3).

Remedies given to third parties

A third party is provided with the same remedies as if he or she was one of the contracting parties. The third party can recover damages for loss of bargain and the principles of remoteness and mitigation which apply to the parties would also apply to the third party. Note that the C(RTP)A does not cause the third party to become a contracting party.[306] It merely gives the third party similar rights to those that it would have if it were a contracting party.

If a contract allows the third party to enforce a term of that contract by virtue of the C(RTP)A, s 1(1) then he will have available 'any remedy that would have been available to him in an action for breach of contract if he had been a party to the contract'.[307]

The C(RTP)A provides also that the rules regarding damages, injunctions, specific performance and other relief are to apply accordingly.[308]

Defences of contracting party (as promisor) to third-party action

The C(RTP)A provides for a number of separate defences:

(a) 'The promisor shall have available to him by way of defence or set-off any matter that:

    (i) arises from or in connection with the contract and is relevant to the term; and

    (ii) would have been available to him by way of defence or set-off if the proceedings had been brought by the promise'.[309]

This would allow the promisor to rely against the third party on, for example:

    (A) a valid exemption clause in the contract between the parties;

    (B) the fact that the contract was void for mistake or voidable for misrepresentation; or

    (C) the fact that the contract had been frustrated; or

    (D) the fact that the promisor was justified in refusing to perform it on account of the promisee's repudiatory breach.

(b) 'The promisor shall also have available to him by way of defence or set-off any matter if:

---

306 Contracts (Rights of Third Parties) Act 1999, s 7(4).
307 Contracts (Rights of Third Parties) Act 1999, s 1(5).
308 Contracts (Rights of Third Parties) Act 1999, s 1(5).
309 Contracts (Rights of Third Parties) Act 1999, s 3(2).

(i)   an express term of the contract provides for it to be available to him in proceedings brought by the third party, and

(ii)   it would have been available to him by way of defence or set-off if the proceedings had been brought by the promisee'.[310]

(c)   'The promisor shall also have available to him:

(i)   by way of defence or set-off any matter, and

(ii)   by way of counterclaim any matter not arising from the contract,

that would have been available to him by way of defence or set-off or, as the case may be, by way of counterclaim against the third party if the third party had been a party to the contract'.[311]

(d)   'Subsections (2) and (4) [of Section 3 of the C(RTP)A] are subject to any express term of the contract as to the matters that are not available to the promisor by way of defence, set-off or counterclaim'.[312]

(e)   'Where in any proceedings brought against him a third party seeks in reliance on Section 1 to enforce a term of a contract (including, in particular, a term purporting to exclude or limit liability), he may not do so if he could not have done so (whether by reason of any circumstance relating to him or otherwise) had he been a party to the contract'.[313]

> For example, this subsection would operate if the third party sought to rely on a clause that purported to exclude liability for death or personal injury caused by the third party's negligence: such a clause would be void under Unfair Contract Terms Act 1977, s 2(1).[314]

> Similarly, a complete exclusion of liability in standard contract terms would often be void under Unfair Contract Terms Act 1977, s 3. However, note that in the case of liability for other types of loss or damage resulting from negligence, C(RTP)A provides as follows:

> 'Section 2(2) of the Unfair Contract Terms Act 1977 (restriction on exclusion etc of liability for negligence) shall not apply where the negligence consists of the breach of an obligation arising from a term of a contract and the person seeking to enforce it is a third party acting in reliance on Section 1 of the Contracts (Rights of Third Parties Act) 1999'.[315]

> Thus, some of the prohibitions under the Unfair Contract Terms Act 1977 apply to third parties under C(RTP)A, and some do not.

---

310 Contracts (Rights of Third Parties) Act 1999, s 3(3).
311 Contracts (Rights of Third Parties) Act 1999, s 3(4).
312 Contracts (Rights of Third Parties) Act 1999, s 3(5).
313 Contracts (Rights of Third Parties) Act 1999, s 3(6).
314 Unfair Contract Terms Act 1977, s 2(1).
315 Contracts (Rights of Third Parties) Act 1999, s 7(2).

Exceptions to application of Act to third parties

C(RTP)A provides that no rights are conferred on a third party in certain situations, for example a third party acquires no rights to enforce a term of a 'contract of employment' against an employee.[316] Similar exclusions apply to 'workers' contracts' and contracts with 'agency workers'.[317] For example, if an employee is engaged as an account manager for a major customer of the employer, the customer would acquire no rights under C(RTP)A to enforce the contract of employment against the employee, eg to enforce confidentiality provisions of the contract of employment.

Arbitration

If a term of the contract provides that a dispute is to be settled by arbitration then the third party is also bound by that term. A third party is to be treated as a party to an arbitration agreement as regards 'disputes between himself and the promisor relating to the enforcement of the substantive term by the third party'.[318] This applies where (a) the right under the C(RTP)A, s 1 to enforce a term (the 'substantive term') is subject to a term providing for the submission of the dispute to arbitration (the 'arbitration agreement'), and (b) the arbitration agreement as defined by C(RTP)A is an agreement in writing for the purposes of the Arbitration Agreement Act 1996, Part I.[319]

Exclusion or variation of third party's rights

There are three situations where the contracting parties may not, without the third party's consent, rescind or vary rights previously given to a third party under a term of a contract.[320] Those situations are:

- where the third party has communicated his assent to the term of the contract to the promisor;[321] or

- where the promisor is aware that the third party has relied on the term;[322] or

- where the promisor can reasonably be expected to have foreseen that the third party would rely on the term and the third party has in fact relied on it.[323]

316 Contracts (Rights of Third Parties) Act 1999, s 6(3)(a).
317 Contracts (Rights of Third Parties) Act 1999, s 6(3)(b), (c).
318 Contracts (Rights of Third Parties) Act 1999, s 8(1).
319 Contracts (Rights of Third Parties) Act 1999, s 8(1).
320 Contracts (Rights of Third Parties) Act 1999, s 2(1).
321 Contracts (Rights of Third Parties) Act 1999, s 2(1)(a).
322 Contracts (Rights of Third Parties) Act 1999, s 2(1)(b).
323 Contracts (Rights of Third Parties) Act 1999, s 2(1)(c).

The parties may rescind or vary the contract term if:

- the third party signifies his or her consent to the variation in question;[324] or

- the contracting parties include an express term in the contract that they may by agreement rescind or vary the contract without the consent of the third party;[325]

- the consent of the third party is required in circumstances specified in the contract instead of those set out above;[326]

- the court or arbitral tribunal decides to dispense with the requirement for consent on the grounds that the third party's whereabouts cannot reasonably be obtained or that he or she is mentally incapable of giving his or her consent;[327]

- the court or arbitral tribunal decides to dispense with the requirement for consent on the grounds that it cannot reasonably be ascertained whether or not the third party has in fact relied on the term.

Where the court or arbitral tribunal dispenses with consent, it may impose such conditions as it thinks fit, including a condition requiring the payment of compensation to the third party.[328]

It seems that the restriction on variation of a third party's rights operates in both a negative and a positive way. For example, if the contracting parties wish to enhance a term of a contract which the third party has a right to enforce, such as increased payment, the third party would also need to provide his or her consent.

Issues for drafting

The C(RTP)A has been of major commercial significance in the drafting of contracts made under English law. Most commercial agreements which have been drafted since the introduction of C(RTP)A now include a provision explicitly excluding the application of it as well as the right of any third party being able to enforce any of the provisions of the agreement. This has become an (almost) invariable standard 'boilerplate' provisions of such agreements.

However, in some cases it may be relevant that a third party can enforce a benefit under an agreement. Where this is the case, the parties to an agreement

---

324 Contracts (Rights of Third Parties) Act 1999, s 2(1).
325 Contracts (Rights of Third Parties) Act 1999, s 2(3)(a).
326 Contracts (Rights of Third Parties) Act 1999, s 2(3)(b).
327 Contracts (Rights of Third Parties) Act 1999, s 2(8).
328 Contracts (Rights of Third Parties) Act 1999, s 2(6).

will need to clarify whether the whole agreement, or any of its terms, is intended to benefit any third parties, and if so:

- who are the third parties;

- which provisions of the contract are made for their benefit;

- whether the party accepting obligations to third parties wishes to make such obligations subject to conditions or obligations, and if so what are those conditions or obligations;

- whether the third parties' rights are assignable; and

- whether the contracting parties can agree to revoke a third party's rights without the consent of the third party.

Examples of when third parties may be able to or may not be able to enforce

Confidentiality agreements or confidentiality clauses

If a contracting party to an agreement agrees that certain information is to be kept confidential, and the obligation extends to confidential information received from a third party, then the third party may be able to enforce that obligation if the contracting party receiving the confidential information breaks the obligation.

Licensing of technology and software

Where an owner of intellectual property grants a licence to a licensee to work a patent, or distribute software, with the right to sub-license, the licence may include an obligation on the licensee to allow the licensor to audit his or her financial records to establish the amount of royalties due. The agreement may also include a clause requiring the licensee to include such an audit provision in any sub-licence that it may grant. The term of a sub-licence agreement, which states that the head licensor shall have this audit right, may be directly enforceable by the head licensor.

Indemnities

If one contracting party gives an indemnity in favour of another contracting party, and the indemnity extends to third parties, such third parties may enforce the indemnity directly against the indemnifying contracting party.

Payment to third party

In an agreement between two parties, there may be a provision that one of the parties will make a payment to a third party. In such a case the third party may be able to enforce the payment term directly against the paying party if the paying party fails to make payment.

Exclusion of liability

If a contract states that proceedings shall not be taken against third parties of a contracting party (such as officers or employees), then those third parties may be able to rely on such a term.

Settlement agreements

If a dispute between two contracting parties is compromised or settled, and as part of the settlement or compromise some benefit or right is conferred on a third party, the third party may be able to enforce that benefit or right directly.

Late Payment of Commercial Debts (Interest) Act 1998

If the parties to an agreement do not indicate in an agreement that interest is payable on payments which are made late, then the Late Payment of Commercial Debts (Interest) Act 1998 ('1998 Act') may apply when a payment is made late.

Before the 1998 Act was passed interest was not due on the late payment of a contractual debt, unless this had been expressly agreed or could be implied from a course of dealing or trade custom.[329] However, the 1998 Act now makes provision:

- for interest to be payable on qualifying debts[330] in contracts for the supply of goods or services where the purchaser and the supplier are each acting in the course of a business;[331] and

- for fixed sums to be paid in addition to the interest.[332]

---

329 In some limited statutory situations interest is payable, such as on a court judgment: see County Courts Act 1984, s 74, as amended. There is also old case law whereby if royalties are paid late then interest is payable.

330 A 'qualifying debt' is a debt created by virtue of an obligation to pay the whole or any part of the contract price where the contract is one to which Late Payment of Commercial Debts (Interest) Act 1998, s 3(1) applies.

331 Late Payment of Commercial Debts (Interest) Act 1998, ss 1, 2(1). The payment of interest is an implied term of such contracts. The Late Payment of Commercial Debts (Interest) Act 1998 was brought into effect in stages, each stage applying to certain categories of business (ie by size), mainly to protect small business. As from 7 August 2002 the 1998 Act applies to all sizes of organisations.

332 Late Payments of Commercial Debts (Interest) Act 1998, s 5A(1), as inserted by reg 2(4) of the Late Payment of Commercial Debts Regulations 2002 (SI 2002/1674) implementing Directive 2000/35/EC ([2000] OJ L200/35) on combating late payment in commercial transactions. The fixed sums are £40 for debts less than £1,000; £70 for debts of more than £1,000 but less than £10,000; and £100 for debts of £10,000 or more. This additional right comes into force on 7 August 2002, and does not affect contracts entered into before that date.

The 1998 Act implies a term into contracts that any qualifying debt created by the contract carries simple interest.[333] The parties to a contract cannot contract out of the 1998 Act except in accordance with the 1998 Act, which is only normally possible where there is a 'substantial contractual remedy' for late payment of the debt.[334]

The 1998 Act does not apply to an 'excepted contract', which will be a consumer credit agreement, a contract intended to operate by way of mortgage, pledge, charge or other security. Most of these are unlikely to be encountered in mainstream intellectual property transactions.[335]

Interest runs from the day after the date agreed for payment of the debt or, if no such date is agreed, the day after 30 days has elapsed since the obligation to pay arose.[336]

The Consumer Credit Act 1974 imposes limits on extortionate credit bargains (ie credit agreements which stipulate grossly exorbitant repayments or grossly contravene ordinary principles of fair dealing), which may affect a contractual obligation to pay interest on loans. In the case of most commercial contracts, the main restriction on interest provisions is that they should not amount to a penalty, as this would make them unenforceable. The rate of interest should therefore be made comparable to the likely cost of borrowing the money from a bank.

The Provision of Services Regulations 2009

General

From 28 December 2009 any provider of a service must provide certain details to a recipient of those services,[337] including:

- information about itself (contact details, legal status);
- the terms and conditions on which it provides those services as well as details of the services provided and how the price for them is calculated;

---

333 Late Payment of Commercial Debts (Interest) Act 1998, s 1(1). For the meaning of a qualifying debt, see n 322 above.

334 Late Payment of Commercial Debts (Interest) Act 1998, ss 7–10. This is of course a different issue as to whether a party entitled to interest under this Act would claim the interest or other 'substantial contractual remedy' if the party in default was in a (much) stronger bargaining position. For example, if a major drugs company wished to have a new drug tested by a small company which undertook such work, the small company is unlikely to wish to claim interest.

335 Late Payment of Commercial Debts (Interest) Act 1998, s 2(5). Also further types of contract can be specified following an order made by the Secretary of State.

336 Late Payment of Commercial Debts (Interest) Act 1998, s 4.

337 Provision of Services Regulations 2009 (SI 2009/2999), regs 7–12, implementing Directive 2006/123/EC ([2006] OJ L376/36) on services in the internal market.

- its professional or authorised status (if a member of a regulated professional or a trade which requires authorisation) and its (indemnity) insurance provision;

- how disputes can be resolved (including details of the disputes procedure).

The Regulations apply to all providers of services (except for a number of excluded categories, none of which are likely to be of much relevance where commercial agreements relating to intellectual property or technology transfer are involved).[338]

None of these requirements (and others in the Regulations) specify that these details have to be included as contractual provisions between a service provider and its customer/clients. The Regulations are also silent as to what is to happen if this information is not provided, ie whether the customer/client can take legal action and on what basis such action will be, eg whether there will be a claim for breach of contract, a claim based on tort, and what will be the remedies, although in some instances it seems clear that existing remedies under English law would apply in any case. For example, one requirement of the Regulations is that the service provider states the price for the service. Under English law, where this is not specified in the contract (nor the means of calculating it), the price would be what is reasonable.[339] But it is harder to see what loss would be suffered if a service provider failed to provide its fax number (but provided all the other required contact details). Perhaps the usual remedies will continue to apply, ie although a user of a service can establish a breach, however the user would not be entitled to any damages as he or she had not suffered any loss.

In addition, the Regulations are also silent as to whether any of the requirements for providing information are implied into a contract as a contractual term between a service provider and a recipient of services.

Information to be provided

1. Information to be provided following a request for information about the service or where recipients of the service can send a complaint: contact details for the service provider (postal address, fax number or email address; telephone number and the official address of the service provider (if it has one));[340]

---

338 See Provision of Services Regulations 2009 (SI 2009/2999), reg 2. For example, the providers of financial services, electronic communications services and networks, healthcare services, and transportation.
339 Supply of Goods and Services Act 1982. s 15.
340 Provision of Services Regulations 2009 (SI 2009/2999), reg 7. The official address of a service provider is that which it is required by law to register, notify or maintain for the purpose of receiving notices or other communications (Provision of Services Regulations 2009 (SI 2009/2999), reg 7(2)).

2. Information which the service provider to make available to a recipient of the service:[341]

- *information and contact details:* the name of the service provider, legal status, the place where the service provider is established, details where the service provider can be contacted rapidly and communicated with directly (including any electronic means);

- *information about any authorisation, regulation or registration:*

  — if the provider is registered in a trade or similar public register, the name of the register, the provider's registration number (or equivalent means of identification);

  — if the activity of the provider is subject to an authorisation scheme in the UK, the details of the competent authority (or electronic means of contacting and using the services provided by it);

  — if the provider is carrying on a regulated profession, the provider's professional title, in which EEA that title has been granted and the name of the professional with which the provider is registered;

- *information about the terms on which the service provides its services:*

  — the general terms and conditions used by the provider (if any);

  — the existence of contractual terms used by the provider regarding which law applies to the contract or which country's courts have jurisdiction (if any);

  — any after-sales guarantee (other than those that are imposed by law);

  — the price of the service, where the price is pre-determined by the provider for a given type of service;

  — the main features of the service to be provided (if not apparent from the context);

  — where the provider is required to hold professional liability insurance or provide a guarantee then information about the insurance or guarantee including contact details of the insurer or guarantor and the territorial coverage of the insurance or guarantee.

3. Information to be provided on request: where a recipient of a service asks, the following information must be provided by the provider to the recipient:

- if the price for the service is not pre-determined, then the price of the service or how the price for the service is calculated (so that the recipient can check the price or a detailed estimate);

341 Provision of Services Regulations 2009 (SI 2009/2999), reg 8(1).

- if the provider is carrying out a regulated profession, a reference to the professional rules in the EEA state in which the provider is established and how to access the rules;

- information on the other activities carried out by the service provider which are directly linked to the service provided to the recipient, and how any conflicts of interest are avoided;

- any codes of conduct that the service provider is subject to, along with how the codes can be accessed and the language(s) in which they are available.

4. Dispute resolution:[342] where there is a non-judicial dispute resolution procedure available as a result of a service provider being subject to a code of practice or as a member of a professional body or trade association, then the service provider:

- must let the recipient of the service know about the procedure; and

- must mention it in any information document provided by him or her which outlines a detailed description of the service (including specifying how to access detailed information about it).

Method of making information available

How information to be made available under '2. Information which the service provider to make available to a recipient of the service' above

The information is to be made available by the service provider to the recipient:[343]

- on the service provider's own initiative;

- by being easily accessible to the recipient at the place where the service is provided or the contract is concluded;

- by being easily accessible to the recipient by electronic means (via an address supplied by the service provider); or

- by being contained in a document supplied by the service provider to the recipient and which contains a detailed description of the service.

When (and the manner in which) the information is to be provided

The time at which the information that is to be supplied or made available by the service provider to the recipient will be:

---

342 Provision of Services Regulations 2009 (SI 2009/2999), reg 10.
343 Provision of Services Regulations 2009 (SI 2009/2999), reg 8(2).

- in good time before the conclusion of the contract; or

- if there is no written contract, before the service is provided.[344]

The manner in which the information has to be supplied or made available is to be clear and unambiguous.[345]

Complaints

If the service provider has received a complaint from a recipient of a service he or she must respond to it as quickly possible.[346] The service provider must also use its best efforts to find a satisfactory solution to the complaint.[347]

PROPOSALS TO CODIFY THE LAW REGARDING UNFAIR TERMS AND EXCLUSION AND LIMITATIONS OF LIABILITY

UCTA and UTCCR overlap in some areas and provide different rights and remedies in others. Although UCCR is not considered in any detail in this book, the Law Commission has published a Joint Consultation Paper[348] on replacing these two pieces of legislation with one unified legislative regime in this area.[349] The proposals and draft Bill may be implemented during the lifetime of this edition of the book. This section is merely to note the Law Commission's proposals, although much of it will be of little interest in terms of this book; however the new Act would 'cover the kinds of unfair term in a "business-to-business" contract that are presently outside the scope of UCTA but that, had they been in a consumer contract, would have been within UTCCR'.[350]

The conclusion of the Law Commission concerning 'business-to-business' contracts is that the 'wider range of terms that (for consumer contracts) are subject to UTCCR should equally be subject to control in business-to-business contracts. Terms that, for instance, make it hard for a business to cancel a long-term contract, or that commit it to paying price increases, have just as much potential for unfairness as many of the clauses already

---

344   Provision of Services Regulations 2009 (SI 2009/2999), reg 11(b). Unless the service provider is asked for the information specified in 'Information to be provided on request' above after the provision of the service.
345   Provision of Services Regulations 2009 (SI 2009/2999), reg 11(a).
346   Provision of Services Regulations 2009 (SI 2009/2999), reg 12(1)(a).
347   Provision of Services Regulations 2009 (SI 2009/2999), reg 12(1)(b). Unless the complaint is vexatious (Provision of Services Regulations 2009 (SI 2009/2999), reg 12(2)).
348   With the Scottish Law Commission.
349   *Unfair Terms in Contracts*, a Joint Consultation Paper (Law Commission Consultation Paper No 166, August 2002). A caveat should be entered – there are many Law Commission proposals produced, but only a small selection of them is translated into statute.
350   *Unfair Terms in Contracts* (see n 347), Executive Summary, para S.10, p iii.

covered by UCTA. Protection should not depend on the size of the business affected by the term, though relative size should be a factor in determining whether the term is fair and reasonable. Some of the stringent controls of UCTA should be maintained'.[351] Much of the proposed new Act would restate existing law found in UCTA, such as the inability to exclude liability for death and personal injury caused by negligence.

The Joint Consultation Paper does not make any specific proposals concerning whether the exception for intellectual property found under UCTA[352] will be retained under the proposed Act. Other than to note that the exception for intellectual property only affects business-to-business contracts,[353] and the Joint Consultation Paper notes that there are 'no calls for business-to-business contracts [concerning the areas excepted from UCTA] to be brought within the scope of the unfair terms legislation [of the new Act]'.[354]

---

351 As above, para S.16, pp v–vi.
352 See 'Unfair Terms in Consumer Contracts Regulations 1999' above.
353 Unlike other exceptions, eg contracts of insurance, which do affect consumers.
354 *Unfair Terms in Contracts* (see n 347), para 5.66.

CHAPTER 11

Regulatory Requirements

INTRODUCTION

There are numerous regulatory requirements relating to the transfer, exploitation or use of technology which impose obligations on individuals and organisations. This chapter deals with selected regulatory requirements as they relate to information technology, pharmaceutical or biotechnological research, and import and export regulations. Within these areas, particular attention is paid to data protection, freedom of information and the internet, and to research involving human gametes and embryos, human tissue and clinical trials.

There are a large number of regulations governing activities in the pharmaceutical and biotechnology industries. These affect various classes of people, including wholesalers, parallel importers, retail pharmacists, contractors, researchers and users. Many of these regulations concern environmental issues, the safety of those involved in the industry, the safety of the products developed (especially medicines and food) and the labelling and classification of products. Also important are what might be classed as moral issues, including genetic engineering, experiments using live animals, and research using human tissue, gametes and embryos. Clinical trials are subject to detailed regulation as a result of European Directives.

Data protection laws can affect a wide range of activities, including many types of technology transfer. For example, clinical trials, which involve generating data on individuals, will normally be subject to the requirements of data protection law, as will many e-commerce ventures. These requirements are strict and not always fully considered.

492

Many of the organisations that are involved in technology transfer are publicly owned bodies (such as educational institutions and research councils). Under freedom of information laws, such bodies have to release information that they hold, when requested to do so. However, when they enter into commercial transactions with third parties, both sides to the transaction may wish to avoid releasing information about the transaction, on the grounds of commercial confidentiality or for other practical reasons. Although there are many potential exemptions a public authority can rely on to avoid releasing commercial information, the general trend is towards greater disclosure by public authorities. In effect, the public body has to carry out an exercise, in response to a request, so that only information, which genuinely comes within a permitted exemption, is not released. Later sections of this chapter consider those exemptions which are of most relevance in making such an assessment.''

INFORMATION PROTECTION AND RELEASE AND COMPUTER TECHNOLOGY

Data protection

Most researchers who use data obtained from living persons will need to consider the requirements of both the Data Protection Act 1998[1] and the law of confidential information.[2] Further considerations come into play when medical data are involved.

A second area which is particularly relevant to research and the exploitation of technology concerns the export of data outside the European Economic Area. Many research projects involve, for example, several parties located in two or more EEA countries (especially where EU funding is involved).

This section focuses on some of the key issues involving data protection in relation to research in general and medical research and clinical trials in particular, and the special requirements required for transferring data outside the UK or the EU.[3]

The Data Protection Act 1998

The following are the basic principles behind the Data Protection Act 1998:

---

1   This Act implemented Directive 95/46/EC ([1995] OJ L281/31) on the protection of individuals with regard to the processing of personal data and on the free movement of such data.
2   See Ch 8.
3   This section is no more than a brief outline, and does not consider such matters as the regulatory and enforcement powers of the Information Commissioner, procedures and requirements for notification, etc. Detailed exposition of the requirements of the 1998 Act is outside the scope of this book.

- A person or organisation (a '*data controller*') who processes personal data is required to comply with *eight data protection principles.*[4]

- The 1998 Act applies to data whether recorded in a manual or electronic form.[5]

- The 1998 Act only applies to personal data, which are data which relate to a living individual who can be identified from those data, or from those data plus other information which is in the possession of, or is likely to come into the possession of, a data controller.[6]

- Sensitive personal data are personal data which refer to, for example, a person's physical or mental health or condition, sexual life, racial or ethnic origin or political opinions.[7] There are additional requirements relating to the processing of sensitive personal data.

- The first, second and eighth data protection principles are particularly important in research and development and technology transfer, and are briefly considered here.

- The first data protection principle provides:

  'Personal data shall be processed fairly and lawfully, and in particular, shall not be processed unless:

  (a) at least one of the conditions in Schedule 2 is met; and

  (b) in the case of sensitive personal data, at least one of the conditions in Schedule 3 is also met.'[8]

  Among the conditions set out in *Schedule 2*, at least one of which must be met, are the following:

  (a) a data subject has given his or her *consent* to the processing of the personal data;

  (b) the processing is necessary to protect the vital interests of the data subject;

  (c) the processing is necessary for the exercise of functions of a public nature exercised in the public interest; or

  (d) the processing is necessary for the purposes of legitimate interest pursued by the data controller or by the third party

---

4   Data Protection Act 1998, s 4(4). The eight principles are set out in Sch 1, and are to be interpreted in accordance with Pt II of Sch 1. The key definitions used in the Act and the eight data protection principles are set out at the end of this section.

5   This contrasts with the position under the Data Protection Act 1984, which applied only to electronically recorded data. There are exceptions for some manual data recorded before 1998, but in due course these will no longer be effective.

6   Data Protection Act 1998, s 1(1). See full definition at the end of this section.

7   Data Protection Act 1998, s 2.

8   Data Protection Act 1998, Sch 1, Pt I, para 1.

or parties to whom the data are disclosed, except where the processing is unwarranted in any particular case by reason of prejudice to the rights and freedoms of legitimate interests of the data subject.

Among the conditions set out in *Schedule 3*, at least one of which must be met for the processing of sensitive personal data (in addition to one of the conditions in Schedule 2), are the following:

(a)   a data subject has given his or her explicit consent to the processing of the personal data;

(b)   the processing is necessary in order to protect the vital interests of the data subject or another person, where the data controller cannot be reasonably expected to obtain consent from the data subject;[9]

(c)   the processing is necessary for the purpose of, or in connection with, any legal proceedings (including prospective legal proceedings), and is necessary for the purpose of obtaining legal advice, or is otherwise necessary for the purpose of establishing, exercising or defending legal rights; or

(d)   the processing is necessary for medical purposes and is undertaken by a health professional or a person who in the circumstances owes a duty of confidentiality which is equivalent to that which would arise if that person were a health professional.[10]

Schedule 3 has been supplemented (by statutory instrument) by further conditions. Satisfying one of these will also meet the requirement of satisfying a Schedule 3 condition for the purpose of processing sensitive personal data:

(a)   the processing is necessary for the purpose of identifying or keeping under review the existence or absence of equality of opportunity or treatment between persons (i) holding different beliefs, or (ii) of different states of physical or mental health or different physical or mental conditions, with a view to enabling such equality to be promoted or maintained; or

(b)   the processing is in the substantial public interest, and is necessary for the purpose of research whose object is not to support decisions with respect to any particular data subject otherwise than with the explicit consent of the data subject and which is unlikely to cause

---

9   The Information Commissioner considers 'vital interests' to mean matters of life or death: see p 4 of *Use and Disclosure of Health Data: Guidance on the Application of the Data Protection Act 1998, May 2002,* which can be found at http://www.ico.gov.uk/upload/documents/library/ data_protection/practical_application/health_data_-_use_and_disclosure001.pdf.

10   'Medical purposes' is defined as including the purposes of preventative medicine, medical diagnosis, medical research, the provision of care and treatment and the management of healthcare services (Data Protection Act 1998, Sch 3, para 8(2)).

substantial damage or substantial distress to the data subject or any other person.[11]

- The second data protection principle provides:

  'Personal data shall be obtained only for one or more specified and lawful purposes, and *shall not be further processed* in any manner incompatible with that purpose or those purposes'.[12]

- The eighth data protection principle provides:

  'Personal data *shall not be transferred to a country or territory outside the European Economic Area* unless that country or territory ensures an adequate level of protection for the rights and freedoms of data subjects in relation to the processing of personal data'.[13]

- A data subject normally has the right to know what personal data a data controller has on him, and for what purposes it is being used (the 'subject *access right*').[14]

- There are a number of *exemptions*, some which are exemptions to one or more of the data protection principles and some which are exemptions to the subject access right.

- A data controller is required to *notify the Information Commissioner* of certain details if they wish to process personal data.[15] The data controller is required to comply with the terms of the notification.

The requirement to process personal data fairly and lawfully

For data to be processed a data controller needs to comply with the following requirements:

- the requirement to satisfy a condition in Schedule 2 and Schedule 3 to the 1998 Act;

- the requirement to collect personal data fairly; and

- the requirement to process data lawfully.

The main conditions in Schedules 2 and 3 to the 1998 Act are set out above. Personal data are normally required to be processed with the consent (if sensitive personal data, explicit consent) of the data subject. Most medical or scientific research will normally require compliance with Schedule 3. If obtaining consent is not possible, the other provisions of Schedules 2 and 3

---

11   Data Protection (Processing of Sensitive Personal Data) Order 2000 (SI 2000/417), Sch, paras 7, 9.
12   Data Protection Act 1998, Sch 1, Pt I, para 2.
13   Data Protection Act 1998, Sch 1, Pt I, para 3.
14   Data Protection Act 1998, ss 7, 8.
15   Data Protection Act 1998, ss 17, 18.

can be used, but most are only available if the processing is 'necessary' for the purpose in question.

The Information Commissioner has provided the following guidance on this point:[16]

- In order for a data controller to satisfy one or more of the other conditions found in Schedules 2 and 3 (other than obtaining the consent of the data subject), the data controller needs to indicate that it is not possible for the data controller to achieve his or her purpose with a reasonable degree of ease without processing personal data.

- If the data controller can, with a reasonable degree of ease, achieve his or her purpose by removing personal identifiers from data, this is the approach he or she should take.

- The word 'necessary' needs to be considered objectively, ie can the purpose that the data controller wishes to achieve only be accomplished by the use of personal data, and is the processing proportionate to the aim to be achieved? In this regard the first data protection principle is reinforced by the third data protection principle.[17]

- There should be use of 'Privacy Enhancing Technologies' (PETs). The idea behind these is that data should be held securely through the use of encryption, password control and other appropriate measures; patient preferences should also be stored. More relevantly in this context, such systems are designed to protect patient identity by replacing details such as a name, address or National Insurance number with a pseudonym. PETs are not a replacement for data protection principles but an application of them. Therefore consent should always be obtained from patients but, if that is not possible, then data should be processed only if necessary and in accordance with the requirements of Schedules 2 and 3. If it is never necessary to know the identity of a person then the data should be anonymised, by removing all personal identifiers. The Information Commissioner indicates that *permanent* anonymisation is not always acceptable:

'For instance a researcher may have no need to know the identity of the patients suffering from a particular condition. He or she may, however, need to know that the patient who was diagnosed with the condition on a particular date is the same patient who was diagnosed with a different condition on another date. Pseudonymisation, sometimes described

---

16 The Information Commissioner's Office has regulatory powers under the Data Protection Act 1994, the Freedom of Information Act 2000, the Environmental Information Regulations 2004 (SI 2004/3391) and the Privacy and Electronic Communications (EC Directive) Regulations 2003 (SI 2003/2426). See www.ico.gov.uk.

17 *Use and Disclosure of Health Data: Guidance on the Application of the Data Protection Act 1998, May 2002*, p 4.

as "reversible anonymisation" provides a solution. In effect a computer system is used to substitute true patient identifiers with pseudonyms. The true identities are not, however, discarded but retained in a secure part of the computer system allowing the original data to be reconstituted as and when this is required. Typically those making day-to-day uses of pseudonymised data would not have the 'keys' allowing the data to be reconstituted'.[18]

As to whether personal data is processed fairly, the 1998 Act provides a list of criteria. In general terms regard is to be had to the method by which the personal data is obtained:

> '... in particular whether any person from whom the personal data is obtained is deceived as to the purpose or purposes for which they are to be processed'.[19]

More specifically, personal data is not considered to have been processed fairly unless the following information is provided to the data subject, or made readily available to the data subject:

- the identity of the data controller;[20]

- the identity of a representative nominated by the data controller for the purposes of the 1998 Act;

- the purpose or purposes for which the data are intended to be processed; and

- any further information which is necessary, having regard to the specific circumstances in which the data is to be processed, to enable processing in respect of the data subject to be fair.[21]

As to the requirement to process personal data lawfully, a data controller must generally comply with other legal requirements. For example, where there are specific provisions as to where personal data cannot be disclosed, he or she must comply with them.

18 As above, p 5.
19 Data Protection Act 1998, Sch 1, Pt II, para 1(1).
20 In academic and hospital settings it may not be clear (and the researchers conducting the research may not be clear) who legally is the data controller. For example, ABCXYZ hospital might be, as far as the data subject is concerned, the data controller. In fact, there could easily be three or more legal entities using the premises, eg an NHS Trust, a medical school, a university, plus one or more private contractors. To use the name of the ABCXYZ hospital as that of the data controller would be incorrect if it has no legal status. In this example, it would be eg the NHS Trust or the university.
21 Data Protection Act 1998, Sch 1, Pt II, para 2.

The research purposes exemption

The 1998 Act provides a limited exemption from some of the data protection principles and the subject access right where personal data is being processed for research purposes.[22] The phrase 'research purposes' is not further defined in the 1998 Act, other than to indicate that it includes statistical or historical purposes. Hence all types of legitimate research from purely academic research to commercial research, such as market research, would be covered.

The main elements in the research purpose exemption are as follows:

- The *further* processing of personal data only for research purposes is not incompatible with the purposes for which the data was obtained. This is a partial exemption from the second data protection principle. Data controllers are still required to obtain such personal data only for one or more lawful purposes, but the further processing of personal data for research purposes would not be incompatible with the principle that personal data only be obtained for one or more lawful purposes.[23]

- Personal data processed for research purposes can be kept indefinitely. This is an exemption to the fifth data protection principle.[24]

- The data controller does not need to comply with the subject access right,[25] as long as the results of any research (or any resulting statistics) are not made available in a form which identifies the data subject.

These three exemptions are subject to the following two conditions:

- The data should not be processed to support measures or decisions with respect to particular individuals.

- The data should not be processed in such a way that substantial damage or substantial distress is, or is likely to be, caused to any data subject.

If either condition is not met, the three exemptions will not be met. For example, a clinical trial involving human patients is undertaken for research purposes: its purpose is to evaluate the efficacy of a medicinal product. A clinical trial would involve the obtaining of personal data (including sensitive personal data) about a person; that data would be used in assessing whether the person would join the clinical trial and would influence the type of treatment he or she would receive, and would therefore be 'processed to support measures or decisions with respect to particular individuals'.[26]

---

22   Data Protection Act 1998, s 33.
23   Data Protection Act 1998, s 33(2).
24   'Personal data processed for any purpose or purposes shall not be kept for longer than is necessary for that purpose or those purposes.'
25   As provided by the Data Protection Act 1998, s 7.
26   Data Protection Act 1998, s 33(1).

The Information Commissioner indicates some useful points in relation to the research purposes exemption:[27]

- Even if the research purposes exemption applies, the data controller is still required to comply with the rest of the 1998 Act including the first and second data protection principles.

- At the time the data are collected the data controller should make the data subject fully aware of what the data controller is going to do with the data.

- If the data controller wishes to use the personal data for further research in a way which would not have been envisaged by the data subject at the time it was collected, this further processing would require the data controller, in regard to this further processing, to comply with the requirements of fair processing under the first data protection principle (ie to meet the requirements of Schedules 2 and 3 of the 1998 Act).

- Although one of the exemptions is that personal data processed for research purposes can be kept indefinitely, this is based on the assumption that there has to be a definite research programme to be carried out in the future which will use the personal data or there is a research programme in fact under way. If the personal data is kept only in the hope that a research programme will take place, then this research purposes exemption cannot be used.

Transference of data outside of the European Economic Area

The eighth data protection principle provides that personal data must not be transferred outside the European Economic Area to another country which does not have adequate levels of protection.[28]

It was realised that, if implemented strictly, this principle would bring certain aspects of international trade and e-commerce between the EU and the US to a standstill, and so high-level discussions and negotiations took place between the US Department of Commerce and the European Commission in 1998. The US Department of Commerce proposed a 'safe harbor' scheme that would allow firms to self-certify privacy practices. Without such a safe harbor, a UK subsidiary of a US company could not report back regularly to its US parent with a list of new customers' details, key accounts, major defaulters, etc. The safe harbor scheme has been operational since November 2000. US companies can join at any time once they have brought their policies and practices into line with the safe harbor requirements. The safe harbor principles apply solely to US–EU data transfers and compliance with them by US companies is entirely voluntary. By undertaking to comply with the principles, however, a US company may receive imports of personal data from the EU.

---

27 Some of these are no more than is required under the 1998 Act in any case.
28 The EU countries, plus Iceland, Liechtenstein and Norway.

The EC has provided a decision[29] to allow for the data controller and the organisation receiving the data in a country outside of the EEA to use standard contractual clauses in order to fulfil the requirements of the Directive underlying the 1998 Act. The standard contractual clauses can be used where a country is not recognised by the EU as providing adequate protection of data,[30] or one of the exceptions to the eighth data protection principle cannot be relied on.[31]

Key definitions used in the Data Protection Act 1998

Data controller	means ... a person who (either alone or jointly or in common with other persons) determines the purposes for which and the manner in which any personal data are, or are to be, processed.
Data processor	in relation to personal data, means any person (other than an employee of the data controller) who processes the data on behalf of the data controller.
Data subject	means an individual who is the subject of personal data.
Personal data	means data which relate to a living individual who can be identified–
	(a) from those data, or
	(b) from those data and other information which is in the possession of, or is likely to come into the possession of, the data controller,
	and includes any expression of opinion about the individual and any indication of the intentions of the data controller or any other person in respect of the individual.
Processing	in relation to information or data, means obtaining, recording or holding the information or data or carrying out any operation or set of operations on the information or data, including–
	(a) organisation, adaptation or alteration of the information or data,
	(b) retrieval, consultation or use of the information or data,
	(c) disclosure of the information or data by transmission, dissemination or otherwise making available, or
	(d) alignment, combination, blocking, erasure or destruction of the information or data.

29   Commission Decision 2001/497/EC ([2001] OJ L181/19) on standard contractual clauses for the transfer of personal data to third countries, under Directive 95/46/EC. The decision only applies to data controllers, and does not cover transference to data processors in third countries. There is a separate decision on transference to data processors in third countries: Commission Decision 2002/16/EC ([2002] OJ L6/52) on standard contractual clauses for the transfer of personal data to processors established in third countries, under Directive 95/46/EC.

30   For a list of countries which are currently considered acceptable (including Argentina, Canada and Switzerland), see http://ec.europa.eu/justice_home/fsj/privacy/thridcountries/index_en.htm. The US is acceptable in the case of companies adhering to the Safe Harbor Privacy Principles issued by the US Department of Commerce (see IP/00/865).

31   Data Protection Act 1998, Sch 4. It covers such matters as where the data subject has given his or her consent, or the transfer of data is necessary for the performance of a contract between the data subject and the data controller, for example.

Sensitive personal data	means personal data consisting of information as to–
	(a) the racial or ethnic origin of the data subject,
	(b) his political opinions,
	(c) his religious beliefs or other beliefs of a similar nature,
	(d) whether he is a member of a trade union (within the meaning of the Trade Union and Labour Relations (Consolidation) Act 1992),
	(e) his physical or mental health or condition,
	(f) his sexual life,
	(g) the commission or alleged commission by him of any offence, or
	(h) any proceedings for any offence committed or alleged to have been committed by him, the disposal of such proceedings or the sentence of any court in such proceedings.
Eight data protection principles	1. Personal data shall be processed fairly and lawfully and, in particular, shall not be processed unless–
	(a) at least one of the conditions in Schedule 2 is met, and
	(b) in the case of sensitive personal data, at least one of the conditions in Schedule 3 is also met.
	2. Personal data shall be obtained only for one or more specified and lawful purposes, and shall not be further processed in any manner incompatible with that purpose or those purposes.
	3. Personal data shall be adequate, relevant and not excessive in relation to the purpose or purposes for which they are processed.
	4. Personal data shall be accurate and, where necessary, kept up to date.
	5. Personal data processed for any purpose or purposes shall not be kept for longer than is necessary for that purpose or those purposes.
	6. Personal data shall be processed in accordance with the rights of data subjects under this Act.
	7. Appropriate technical and organisational measures shall be taken against unauthorised or unlawful processing of personal data and against accidental loss or destruction of, or damage to, personal data.
	8. Personal data shall not be transferred to a country or territory outside the European Economic Area unless that country or territory ensures an adequate level of protection for the rights and freedoms of data subjects in relation to the processing of personal data.

Freedom of information

Introduction

Many commercial transactions involving technology or intellectual property have as one of the parties a governmental, regulatory, academic or health service body or organisations. Any of these types of organisation is likely to be classed as a 'public authority'. In such a case any person will have the right to request the public authority to release information held by it. The

Freedom of Information Act 2000 (FOIA)[32] gives that right and applies to most types of information held by a public authority.

The right a person has to the information held by a public body is subject to a number of exemptions. The most relevant to technology transfer or intellectual property transactions are that the information is held subject to obligations of confidentiality, that it constitutes a trade secret or would prejudice the commercial interests of a person. Also relevant, but less likely to be of importance involving commercial transactions is information which constitutes personal information, or which the public body holding is intending to publish or which is subject to legal professional privilege.

This section does not cover all aspects of the FOIA,[33] but concentrates on those aspects which are most likely to be relevant to public authorities holding information which relates to commercial transactions involving intellectual property: whether an organisation is subject to FOIA, what type of information is caught by FOIA, and the circumstances when information need not be disclosed.

Following the implementation of the FOIA in 2005, many requests to public authorities were rejected because the public authorities frequently argued that exemptions such as the 'commercial interests of a person would be prejudiced' or there would be a 'breach of obligations of confidentiality' could apply to any situation where a transaction with a commercial party was involved.

Such a 'broad brush' approach is no longer in accordance with the recent approach taken by the Information Commissioner and the Information Tribunal. Also, the Information Commissioner has issued guidance to almost every section of, and issue raised by, the FOIA.[34]

The result of the cases before the Information Tribunal and the guidance is that if a public authority wishes to rely on exemptions then only that information which comes truly within an exemption will be caught. A blanket ban on the

---

32　In force since 1 January 2005.
33　This section does not consider the detail of making a request for the release of information, the grounds or procedures for internal reviews, the detailed procedures concerning where payment of fees are due, etc, or the enforcement powers of the Information Commissioner. Also not considered are some of the available exemptions which are relevant to the type of public authorities which are involved in the creation of intellectual property or technology transfer.
34　There is now guidance which covers virtually all aspects of the Freedom of Information Act 2000. This is available from http://www.ico.gov.uk. It is regularly revised. The relevant guidance is considered in this section but checks should be carried out from time to time on whether newer versions have been issued by the Information Commissioner.

release of any details of a commercial contract between a public authority and a commercial organisation is unlikely to be maintainable. The public authority will be required to sift out that information which is genuinely, for example, confidential from that which is not (just to take one of the possible exemptions available).

This approach has an implication for commercial organisations entering into agreements with public authorities: rather than assuming that a commercial agreement will be (automatically) exempt from disclosure, the commercial organisation will need to identify that information which it believes can harm it and try to isolate it.

Aim of the Freedom of Information Act 2000

The FOIA allows a person (applicant) to make a request to a public authority for the information that the public body holds. The right is twofold:

- a right to be told whether the public authority holds or does not hold the requested information;[35] or

- a right to be provided with the requested information.[36]

Making a request for information held by a public authority

How the request must be made

For an applicant to receive the information a public authority holds, the applicant has to:

- make a request a writing;[37]

- provide his or her name and an address for the correspondence;[38]

- describe what information he or she is seeking.[39]

---

35 Freedom of Information Act 2000, s 1(1)(a). Known as 'the duty to confirm or deny' (Freedom of Information Act 2000, s 1(6)). The confirmation from the public authority has to be in writing. The duty to confirm or deny is also met where the public body provides the requested information (Freedom of Information Act 2000, s 1(5)).

36 Freedom of Information Act 2000, s 1(1)(b).

37 Freedom of Information Act 2000, s 8(1)(a). The use of electronic means is permitted to transmit the request, but whatever method is used the request has to be in a legible form and capable of being used for subsequent reference (Freedom of Information Act 2000, s 8(2)).

38 Freedom of Information Act 2000, s 8(1)(b). It appears that the address does not have to be a physical address, but could only be an email address.

39 Freedom of Information Act 2000, s 8(1)(c).

Other than these points (and where any possible exemption applies or permissible reason for not providing the information requested, such as it is vexatious) the public authority cannot enquire further into the identity of the applicant or seek the motive of him or her in wishing to receive the information he or she requests.[40]

Who can make a request

There are no restrictions on who can make the request for information.[41] For example, there is nothing to prevent a commercial organisation making a request for information held by a public authority regarding the contracts the public authority has entered into with competitors of that commercial organisation.

How long does the public authority have to consider the request?

Once a public authority has received a request from an applicant for information it must comply with the request promptly and in any case no later than 20 working days following the date of receipt.[42] There are certain circumstances in which the period can be extended, including if the public authority needs further information from the applicant to help it to identify what information is in fact sought;[43] or where a fee is sought from the applicant and the public authority is awaiting the payment of the fee.[44]

Also, if the public authority wishes to rely on a qualified exemption, the time for compliance can also be extended in order to enable the public authority to consider the statutory public interest test in relation to that qualified exemption. In such a case the public authority must issue a refusal notice[45] and include with the notice an estimate of how long it will take to make a decision.[46]

---

40   This point is considered further in the Information Commissioner's Freedom of Information Good Practice Guidance No 6.

41   As long as applicant complies with the points made under 'How the request must be made' above.

42   Freedom of Information Act 2000, s 10(1).

43   Freedom of Information Act 2000, s 1(3).

44   Freedom of Information Act 2000, s 9.

45   Freedom of Information Act 2000, s 17(1).

46   Freedom of Information Act 2000, s 10(3). In the Information Commissioner's Freedom of Information Act Awareness Guidance No 4, *Time limits on considering the public interest following requests for information under the Freedom of Information Act 2000*, p 2, the Information Commissioner indicates that public authorities should deal with all requests where the public interest is being considered within 20 working days (ie the normal statutory requirement). However 'where the public interest considerations are exceptionally complex it may be reasonable to take longer but, in our view, in no case should the total time exceed 40 working days'.

How must the public authority provide the information requested?

The public authority can communicate the information requested by any means which are reasonable in the circumstances.[47] However the applicant can at the time he or she makes the request specify the means of communication of the information, including that it be provided in a permanent form (such as on paper, electronically, on a carrier etc), or inspect the records held by the public authority containing the information requested or ask the public authority to provide a digest or summary of the information requested in a permanent or other form acceptable to the applicant.[48]

Advice and assistance

A public authority is under a duty to provide advice and assistance to a person who is considering making a request under FOIA or has made one, as far as it would be reasonable to expect the public authority to do so.[49] The wording appears to mean that the duty on the public authority is not one-off, but continues for as long as the applicant needs the advice or assistance.

The guidance issued by the Information Commissioner indicates that the public authority should provide advice and assistance in the following areas:

- help the applicant to clarify unclear requests;

- if the public authority cannot provide the information in a format or method requested by the applicant, help the applicant by providing the information requested in an acceptable format;

- help the applicant to narrow his or her request so that it does not exceed the cost limit;

- inform the applicant that the request by an applicant is covered by exemptions for information which is accessible to the applicant by other means[50] or for information intended for future publication,[51] and in appropriate cases where the information can be found; and

---

47   Freedom of Information Act 2000, s 11(4). See also the Information Commissioner's Freedom of Information Act Awareness Guidance No 29, *Means of communication*. This guidance also deals with aspects of how the information must be communicated, as well as the public authority's right to make a reasonable charge for providing the information (eg photocopying and post costs).

48   Freedom of Information Act 2000, s 11(1).

49   Freedom of Information Act 2000, s 16(1). The duty includes complying with a relevant code of practice, namely the 'Access Code' issued by the Secretary of State under Freedom of Information Act 2000, s 45 (available from www.fco.gov.uk).

50   Under Freedom of Information Act 2000, s 21.

51   under Freedom of Information Act 2000, s 22.

- if the information requested is held by another public authority then transfer the request to another public authority and let the applicant know that this has happened.[52]

Refusing a request

If the public authority is refusing a request by an applicant, it is required to issue a refusal notice, which must be issued within the 20 working-day period. The refusal notice must:

- state that the public authority is relying on an exemption;

- specify which exemption it is relying on; and

- state the reason why the exemption applies (unless it is obvious why the exemption applies).[53]

The refusal also has to state the internal procedure that the public authority has for dealing with complaints about the handling of requests for information (or state that the authority does not provide such a procedure) and must also state that the applicant has the right to apply to the Information Commissioner concerning whether the public authority has dealt with the applicant's request in accordance with the Freedom of Information Act 2000.[54]

If a refusal is provided by a public authority and the applicant asks for an internal review of the refusal (a complaint), the public authority, according to the guidance issued by the Information Commissioner, should take no longer than 20 working days or, exceptionally, 40 working days to deal with the internal review.[55]

The content of the notices to be provided and the procedures to be followed where a public authority does not hold the information requested or where it considers the request to be vexatious or repetitious are different to those stated immediately above.[56] In addition, another possible form of refusal is

---

52   Information Commissioner's guidance on advice and assistance.
53   Freedom of Information Act 2000, s 17(1)(a)–(c). The public authority does not need to state the reason why the exemption applies if to do so would involve the disclosure of the information the applicant requested (Freedom of Information Act 2000, s 17(5)).
54   Freedom of Information Act 2000, s 17(7).
55   The Freedom of Information Act 2000 itself provides no time limit for dealing with complaints. The Code of Practice issued under Freedom of Information Act 2000, s 45 (see http://www.justice.gov.uk/guidance/foi-code-of-practice.htm) states that the complaint should be dealt with within a reasonable time. It appears that public authorities have, in some cases, taken a long time to deal with complaints made by applicants whose requests for information have been denied. In some cases the period has extended to several months or even more than a year. The guidance issued by the Information Commissioner states that the period should now be normally not more than 20 working days, or at worst 40 working days (Information Commissioner Freedom of Information Act Awareness Guidance, *Internal Reviews*, p 2).
56   Freedom of Information Act 2000, s 17(5).

where the public authority considers that the cost of compliance exceeds the applicable limit (see below).

Where the cost of compliance is exceeded

If an applicant's request means that the public authority, in order to comply with it, exceeds certain time limits, the public authority has to notify the applicant within the 20-working-day period for dealing with requests.[57] Currently the limits are £600 for central government and £450 for other types of public authorities, including the health service and education.[58] The duty to confirm or deny and the duty to communicate the information requested each have their own appropriate limit.[59]

In considering whether the time limit will be exceeded or not, the following are the only permissible activities that can be taken into account: (i) determining whether the public authority holds the information; (ii) locating the information, or a document containing it; (iii) retrieving the information, or a document containing it; and (iv) extracting the information from a document containing it.[60] And the time taken can only be charged at £25 per person per hour.[61]

Publication scheme

Public authorities are required to adopt and maintain a publication scheme. Essentially a public authority specifies which categories of information it will make available and then information which falls within those categories will be published.[62] The aim of a publication scheme is that if the public authority makes information available then there will be less of a need for persons to make requests for that information to be provided.

Any scheme must indicate what type of information is covered by the scheme, how the information will be made available (eg electronically or on paper) and whether there will be a charge for it or if it will be made available free of charge.[63]

---

57   See n 56.
58   Freedom of Information and Data Protection (Appropriate Limit and Fees) Regulations 2004 (SI 2004/3244), reg 3.
59   Freedom of Information Act 2000, s 12(1), (2).
60   Freedom of Information and Data Protection (Appropriate Limit and Fees) Regulations 2004 (SI 2004/3244), reg 4(3). Such tasks as reading time, time to consider and consult on whether the information should be disclosed or whether the information request exceeds the time limit cannot be taken into account.
61   Freedom of Information and Data Protection (Appropriate Limit and Fees) Regulations 2004 (SI 2004/3244), reg 4(4).
62   Freedom of Information Act 2000, s 19(1). The Information Commissioner must approve each scheme and any amendment to it.
63   Freedom of Information Act 2000, s 19(2).

Rather than creating its own publication scheme, a public authority may adopt a model scheme prepared by the Information Commissioner.[64] Model schemes are provided by the Information Commissioner for certain categories of public authorities, including higher and further education institutions and certain organisations involved in the provision of medical services (but not NHS Trusts, for example).[65]

What is a 'public authority'

Public authorities – those listed in FOIA

The right to obtain information only applies where the information is held by a public authority. The FOIA does not provide a definition for what constitutes a 'public authority' but rather adopts a list approach, that is, for an organisation to be a public authority it has to be included in a list of organisations set out in Schedule 1[66] to the FOIA or be designated a public authority by the Secretary of State.[67]

A 'public authority' includes the following types of organisations:

- government departments;

- local authorities (including county councils, the Greater London Authority, fire and rescue authorities, waste disposal authorities and so on);

- health-related organisations, such as a primary care trust, a special health authority, an NHS foundation trust, an NHS Trust, a person providing general medical or dental services;

- education-related organisations, such as universities, further education colleges, etc;

- research and other types of councils and advisory groups (such as the Engineering and Physical Sciences Research Council, Medical Research Council).

However a public authority may not be subject to the provisions of the Freedom of Information Act 2000 for all of its activities, and where this

---

64   Freedom of Information Act 2000, s 20(1).
65   Where a public authority adopts a model scheme without amendment, the public authority does not need to seek the approval of the Information Commissioner, but if it makes any amendments to the model scheme at any time, it does (Freedom of Information Act 2000, s 20(2)).
66   Freedom of Information Act 2000, s 3(1)(a). The list of organisations found in Sch 1 is continually added to. It is necessary to consult the list to check whether a particular organisation has been added.
67   Freedom of Information Act 2000, s 3(1)(b). The power is set out in further detail in Freedom of Information Act 2000, s 5 (see below).

exception applies it is listed in Schedule 1.[68] In practice this exception applies only to a few organisations.

Public authorities – those designated by the Secretary of State

Where the Secretary of State wishes to designate an organisation as a public authority, a number of conditions need to be fulfilled:

- the organisation is not listed in Schedule 1 and is not capable of being listed; and

- the organisation exercises functions of a public nature; or

- is providing a service under a contract made with a public authority and the service which is provided is a function of that public authority.[69]

Publicly owned companies

The meaning of a public authority will also include a company which is wholly owned by a public authority.[70] 'Wholly owned' means that ownership has to be vested:

- wholly in the owning public authority; or

- in a company which is itself wholly owned by a public authority; or

- in a person who is acting on behalf of the public authority or a wholly owned company.

For example:

- universities usually carry out their technology transfer activities through a separate (technology transfer) company, and if such a company is wholly owned by the university then the separate company would count as a public authority;

- to develop the example in the previous bullet point, if the technology transfer company creates a spin-out company to commercially exploit a piece of technology and it is the sole shareholder (initially, for example) then the spin-out company would be a public authority. However if the spin-out company is formed with some of the shareholding being held by others, then it would not be a public authority for the purposes of the FOIA;

---

68 Freedom of Information Act 2000, s 7(1). For example the BBC would not be required to provide information held for the purposes of journalism, art or literature, or the Competition Commission would not need to provide information held by it where it is acting as a tribunal.

69 Freedom of Information Act 2000, s 5(1).

70 Freedom of Information Act 2000, ss 3(1)(b), 5.

- but if the technology transfer company sold one share to a private finance company, then the technology transfer company would no longer be a public authority for the purposes of the FOIA. The motive for taking the company outside the remit of the FOIA appears not to be relevant;

- if the university wished to offer the services of its academics as consultants and experts in order to obtain income from the use of such expertise, and it created a separate company to undertake such activity which the university wholly owned, then that too would be a public authority for the purposes of the FOIA. The FOIA does not appear to make any distinction as to what activities the publicly owned company can or cannot carry out (ie the publicly owned company does not need to be restricted to non-commercial activities).

'Sharing of ownership' by public authorities: a publicly owned company if owned by more than one public authority will not be subject to the FOIA, that is the ownership cannot be shared between a number of public authorities, unless one of the public authorities is the Crown.[71]

For example the Russell Group of Universities' membership (ownership) is made up of the 20 universities who are part of that group. Each university on its own account would be a public authority, but since they jointly own the Russell Group of Universities, that organisation would not be a public authority under the Freedom of Information Act 2000. But if only one university owned the Russell Group of Universities then it would be a public authority.

What type of information can be obtained from a public authority?

In principle most types of information held by a public authority can be requested (subject to the available exemptions).[72] A public authority will hold information:

- either directly; or

- indirectly, ie information which is held by someone on behalf of the public authority.[73]

---

71 That is a government department, a minister of the Crown, a company wholly owned by the government department or a minister of the Crown or a person acting under the direction of one of these. This is recognised in the wording of the Freedom of Information Act 2000 where ownership of a publicly owned company by the Crown is stated in the plural while the section governing other public authorities is in the singular and refers to 'a company [which] is wholly owned by a public authority ... if it has no members except ... that public authority or companies wholly owned by that public authority...' (Freedom of Information Act 2000, s 6(2) (b)).

72 See 'Exemptions' below.

73 Freedom of Information Act 2000, s 3(2).

For example, a university's technology transfer company is involved in the obtaining of patents for the intellectual property created by one of the university's academics. It decides that the administration of applications, registration and maintaining of patents as well as accounting of royalties from licensing can be more efficiently carried out by a contractor. The contractor will hold all such records. Since the activities just listed are likely to be core activities of the technology transfer company, then if dealt with by the contractor they are being held on behalf of the technology transfer company.[74]

The main exceptions where information is not held by a public authority would be:

- the information is held on behalf of another person; or

- the information is not 'official' information, that is information which is not created by the public authority's employees as part of carrying out their duties or is not intended to be used by the authority for its own use or in the course of its functions.

For example,

- if there is a social club or trade union branch at the public authority and the members of the club or union need to exchange emails about its activities;[75] or

- if an employee sends or receives an email about a non-work matter using the public authority's email system;

then such information but would not count as being held by the public authority although the information contained in those emails will be stored by, and processed by, equipment owned or used by the public authority.

Where a request is made for information the public authority must provide the information as it was held at the time the request was made.[76]

---

74 A common example in a domestic situation would be when a local authority outsources an activity such as the administration of council tax or housing benefit to a private contractor.

75 To develop this example, if there is an exchange of emails between a trade union and the human resources department of the public authority concerning, eg the working conditions at the public authority, the information contained in the emails is likely to be information created as part of the function of the public authority.

76 Freedom of Information Act 2000, s 1(4). Although amendments to the information can be made if they occur in the period between the request and the supply of the information and if the amendments would have been made regardless of whether the request would have been made or not (Freedom of Information Act 2000, s 1(4)).

A public authority is not permitted to alter, deface, block, erase, destroy or conceal information which is requested by an applicant where the intention of carrying out any of these things is to prevent the provision of that information to the applicant.[77] The public authority will be guilty of an offence where these activities are carried out. An offence will also be committed by any employees or officers of the public authority, and any person acting under the direction of the public authority.[78]

Exemptions

While in principle all types of information held by a public authority are available for disclosure, there are, however, circumstances when disclosure does not apply, plus a number of exemptions.

Disclosure is not required where the public authority, in order to comply with a request, would exceed the appropriate cost limit set out in the relevant regulation[79] or where a request is vexatious or repetitious.[80]

There are a number of specific exemptions from the requirement to disclose information following a request. These exemptions fall into two categories, absolute and qualified. If the exemption is a qualified exemption then the public authority is required to apply a public interest test.

The exemptions which are set out below are only those which are most likely to be relevant to those organisations that are public authorities and that carry out technology transfer or other commercial intellectual property transactions.

Information provided in confidence

Information does not have to be disclosed by a public authority if:

- that information was obtained by the public authority from any other person; and

---

77 Freedom of Information Act 2000, s 77(1). The offence is only punishable by a fine (not exceeding level 5 (currently £5,000) on the standard scale) on summary conviction.
78 Freedom of Information Act 2000, s 77(2).
79 The limit is set out in the Freedom of Information and Data Protection (Appropriate Limit and Fees) Regulations 2004 (SI 2004/3244). Although if the limit is exceeded the public authority can continue to search beyond the limit. Of relevance is the Lord Chancellor's Code of Practice on Management of Records and the Information Commissioner's Freedom of Information Act Awareness Guidance No 8, *Records Management FAQs*.
80 Freedom of Information Act 2000, s 14. The Information Commissioner's Freedom of Information Act Awareness Guidance No 22, *Vexatious and Repeated Requests* should be considered for the detail of what might amount to a vexatious or repetitious request. This guidance provides some illustrative responses.

- the disclosure of that information to the public by the public authority holding it would constitute a breach of confidence actionable by the person who it was obtained from (or any other person).[81]

This exemption is absolute[82] (the public authority does not have to apply a public interest test).

Points to note:

- information held by a public authority will only be exempt where it is the confidential information of a third party. In addition the fact that it is marked confidential or was provided to the public authority subject to obligations of confidentiality is not enough, at the time when a request made for its disclosure, for it to still be confidential. The public authority has to make its own determination that such information still has the necessary 'quality of confidentiality' (although it can consult with the provider of the information, the decision has to be that of the public authority);[83]

- where the information is the public authority's own confidential information, the public authority cannot rely on this exemption. The fact that the public authority marks it as 'confidential' or any other such statement is irrelevant;

- there has to be an enforceable obligation of confidence for the exemption to apply;

- the FOIA does not displace the existing law of confidence;[84]

- the decision on whether information provided to a public authority is subject to actionable obligations of confidence is for the public authority, and not for a third party who is objecting to its disclosure.

---

81 Freedom of Information Act 2000, s 41. For this exemption to be engaged, the test the public authority must use where it is considering disclosing information and confidentiality is an issue is as follows: would the disclosure expose the public authority to a breach of confidence claim, which on the balance of probabilities, would succeed (as well as establishing whether the public authority would have a defence to such a claim). Establishing only that such a claim would be arguable would not be sufficient to bring the exemption into play. See para 30, Information Tribunal Appeal Number: EA/2009/0036, *The Higher Education Funding Council for England v The Information Commissioner* (*Guardian News and Media Ltd*, additional party), decision promulgated 13 January 2010.

82 Freedom of Information Act 2000, s 2(3).

83 See Information Commissioner Freedom of Information Act Awareness Guidance No 2, *Information provided in confidence*, version 4, 12 September 2008, at para F.

84 This is outlined in Ch 8. Much of the Information Commissioner Freedom of Information Act Awareness Guidance No 2, *Information Provided in Confidence*, version 4, 12 September 2008, is in effect a statement of the existing law of confidence.

Contracts entered into by a public authority with a commercial party

Contracts between some commercial parties and public authorities sometimes contain provisions where:

- the existence of the contract between the public authority and the commercial party is to be treated as confidential; and/or

- the identity of the commercial party is to be treated as confidential; and/or

- the provisions of the contract are to be treated as confidential; and/or

- certain provisions are to be treated as confidential.

It is unlikely that, based on the current guidance issued by the Information Commissioner and cases which have been before the Information Tribunal, that the first items in the above list would not be discloseable following an applicant's request for disclosure. The following appears to be the position:

- a concluded contract between a public authority and a commercial party would normally not be exempt from being disclosed. This is because it would not contain information obtained by the public authority from a third party (as the concluded contract would contain mutual obligations of the parties, and be the parties' document);[85]

- information regarding a pre-contractual negotiation position or technical information whether contained in the contract, in a schedule to the contract or elsewhere may still be characterised as confidential information obtained by a public authority from a third party.

Points to note:

- the fact information requested by an applicant is not exempt as confidential information does not necessarily mean that it will have to be disclosed. It may have the benefit of other exemptions available under FOIA. For example, that the information requested may prejudice the commercial interests of a third party or may be a trade secret;

- that technical or other particular information which is genuinely confidential could be placed in a separate schedule to the contract or provided in a redacted form.

- that a public authority, as a matter of good practice when entering into a contract:

---

85 This would most probably cover the position where a commercial party provides a draft contract and the public authority signs it, as after signature the document no longer has been provided by the commercial party as it will contain obligations on both parties.

— should inform the other party, before the contract is drawn up, that some or all of the contract may be disclosed following a freedom of information request; and

— can use confidentiality clauses to help identify information which would be exempt from a freedom of information request but must consider with care whether such clauses are compatible with their duty under the FOIA;

— be aware that any clauses in a contract dealing with the issue of confidentiality cannot prevent disclosure under the FOIA of information which is protected by the confidentiality clause if, in fact, the information itself is not confidential.

Commercial interests

Information held by a public authority does not need to be disclosed following a request where:

- the information is a trade secret; or
- the information if released is likely to prejudice the commercial interests of any person.[86]

This exemption is a qualified exemption under the FOIA[87] (that is the public authority will have to carry out a public interest test into whether or not to release the information requested).

Meaning of a trade secret

The FOIA does not define what amounts to a 'trade secret' but it appears to not displace what case law has considered to be trade secrets.[88]

Where a public authority has received a request for information which constitutes a trade secret the public authority has to confirm whether or not it has (although, as a trade secret, that information would not need to be disclosed).

Meaning of commercial interests

The concept of commercial interests could cover a wide range of factors or issues, but the Information Commissioner[89] considers 'commercial interests' to consist of the following:

---

86   Freedom of Information Act 2000, s 43.

87   Freedom of Information Act 2000, s 2(3).

88   See Ch 8 for a description of what can amount to a trade secret. See also Section B, a) of Information Commissioner's Freedom of Information Act Awareness Guidance No 5, *Commercial Interests*, 5 March 2008.

89   Information Commissioner's Freedom of Information Act Awareness Guidance No 5 (see n 88).

- 'a person's ability to participate competitively in a commercial activity, ie the purchase and sale of goods and services';

- profit does not have to be the motive for such activity, but can be simply a charge made to cover the cost of the provision of goods and services;

- while trading may be a key element of the meaning of 'commercial interests', information can still be caught by this exemption where it only indirectly relates to the activities of buying and selling;[90]

- the fact that the financial interests of a public authority are prejudiced by the release of information does not necessarily mean that the commercial interests of that public authority are prejudiced.[91]

The Information Commissioner has provided an indicative list of what type of information that can affect commercial interests, of which the most relevant are likely to be for public authorities involved in the commercial exploitation of intellectual property:

- the public authority's own commercial activities (this would cover information held in regard to trading and other similar activities);

- policy development;[92]

- policy implementation.

Other types of information which could fall within the commercial interest exemption are procurement, the public authority's purchasing position, regulation (ie where the public authority has regulatory functions), private finance initiative/public private partnerships. In addition to the guidance issued by the Information Commissioner, the Ministry of Justice has provided

---

90   For example, a company obtains a patent licence from a university. The company decides it no longer wishes to exploit that licence and writes to the university to terminate the licence. One consequence is that the company will have to make a large number of research staff redundant, and has informed the relevant government department that it is making staff redundant. While the fact that staff are being made redundant may not directly relate to the commercial activity of the company under the patent licence of making sales of a patented product, the fact that staff are being made redundant could affect the company, eg loss of potential sales, reduction in share price and so on.

91   For example, a university has been overpaying their administrative staff in the technology transfer department because they have failed to correctly calculate pay. This is likely to be embarrassing to the university if disclosed but could hardly be said to be related to the negotiating, entering into and servicing of contracts entered into with commercial parties regarding the commercial exploitation of the university's intellectual property.

92   For example, a university technology transfer company (or the university) may undertake research, surveys or analysis of various industry sectors (and technical developments within them) to determine where to undertake future research work and where not to carry out such work. Such work may influence the commercial strategy to be followed by the technology transfer company and could be valuable to those who invest in the work spun out of universities and other research organisations.

an indicative list of the types of specific business information which could particularly damage commercial interests:

- research and plans relating to a potential new product;

- product manufacturing cost information;

- product sales forecast information;

- strategic business plans, including for example, plans to enter, develop or withdraw from a product or geographical market sector;

- marketing plans, to promote a new or existing product;

- information relating to the preparation of a competitive bid;

- information about the financial and business viability of a company;

- information provided to a public authority in respect of an application for a licence or as a requirement of a licence condition or under a regulatory regime.[93]

The Information Commissioner's guidance provides an indicative list of factors which will assist in determining whether there is prejudice to the commercial interests of a person:

- *Does the information relate to, or could it impact on, a commercial activity?*

  Does the information relate directly to the *commercial* activities of the public authority? For example, if the technology transfer company of a university mis-spends funds on a photocopier (ie signing a very expensive long-term contract for use of a photocopier, when cheaper and shorter term options are available) is unlikely to affect its commercial activities. More difficult is where there might be an indirect relationship to its commercial activities. For example, if a licensee of a patent licensed by the technology transfer company is seeking to relocate all its research and administrative facilities to India this may affect employment relationships and perhaps the long-term commitment to working the licence and could be indirectly related to the commercial interest of the licensee.

- *Is the commercial activity conducted in a competitive environment?*

  If a company is a monopoly supplier to a public authority of particular goods or services, then the information the public authority holds is less likely to have a prejudicial impact on that supplier. However, if the public authority is the sole purchaser of a particular type of good or service, then companies who are suppliers could have their com-

93 Ministry of Justice, Freedom of Information Guidance, *Exemptions*, Section 43 ('Commercial interests'), 14 May 2008, p 5.

mercial interests adversely affected by the procurement plans of the public authority.

- *Would there be damage to reputation or business confidence?*

    If information is released by the public authority that can cause damage to the company's reputation or the standing in which the company is seen by its customers, suppliers or investors. In order for such information to amount to prejudice it has to have a significant impact on the company's revenue or pose a threat to it obtaining supplies or raising finance. Mere embarrassment will not suffice.

- *Whose commercial interests are affected?*

    In some cases it is obvious whose commercial interests are prejudiced where there is a disclosure of information. However it may be necessary to identify who, if anyone, is affected. It may be necessary to establish whether the public authority itself is prejudiced. For example, if a technology transfer company carries out an analysis of the average cost of transferring technology to a spin-out company, and the analysis includes the average costs of using external accountants, lawyers and other specialists, could the disclosure of this information lead to those providers of services setting their fees at a higher level? Or could it affect the technology transfer company being able to negotiate reasonable levels of fees for some types of spin-out transactions where the limited number of specialist suppliers to a technology transfer company are aware what the 'going rate' is? In addition the release of such information might also affect the commercial interests of suppliers, if the level of fees they charge that technology transfer company is substantially different to what they charge elsewhere.[94]

- *Is the information commercially sensitive?*

    Often the information which is provided to the public authority by a company can be commercially sensitive. For example, the price at which a company sells its goods to a public authority might be publicly available, but how it can offer the goods at the price, or its profit margins, may not be. Also, information as to how its goods or services are unique which may have been supplied to the public authority could also be commercially sensitive and would be of interest to competitors. Working practices which allow services to be delivered efficiently and which may be disclosed to the public authority during contract negotiations may also be valuable to others.

---

94 Eg, a firm of lawyers could charge a university technology transfer company a much lower hourly rate for work undertaken where a technology is being spun-out, in the expectation that when the spin-out company becomes successful, it will be able to charge its 'normal' rate. If this information was released then its other clients could start to demand that the fees they pay are also reduced for some or all work done by the lawyers. This could adversely affect the profitability of the firm of lawyers.

- *What is the likelihood of the prejudice being caused?*

  Judgement must be used to decide whether a particular disclosure would be likely to cause prejudice, and two factors need to be considered: (a) likelihood the prejudice will occur: it need not be certain to occur, but there must be a significant risk of the prejudice occurring rather than a remote possibility of it occurring; (b) the degree of prejudice caused: it need not be substantial but has to be more than trivial.

In other guidance issued by the Information Commissioner,[95] the issue of how a public authority is to assess what 'would, or would be likely to, prejudice the commercial interests of any person' is explored further:

- the public authority must explain why it considers the commercial interests of a third party are likely to be prejudiced,[96]

- it is not enough for the public authority to speculate why the interests of a third party will be prejudiced;

- if possible, the third party should be asked for their opinions as to whether their interests will be prejudiced;

- if it is not possible to obtain the opinion of the third party, a public authority can put forward arguments made by the third party if the public authority has knowledge of the third party's opinion based on prior knowledge;

- if the third party does not forward an opinion, the public authority should not speculate on behalf of the public authority; and

- the decision is the public authority's to make, ie just because a third party considers its interests are prejudiced, is not enough for the public authority to exempt the request from disclosure, although the public authority can take into account the third party's view.

Other potentially relevant exemptions

In addition to those listed above, other exemptions which can sometimes be relevant include:

Information intended for future publication:[97] a public authority need not provide information which is requested where it is held with a view to

---

95 Information Commissioner Freedom of Information Act Awareness Guidance, *Commercial Detriment of Third Parties.*

96 It is not enough that there is a mere assertion by an individual or company that its interests will be prejudiced. See Ministry of Justice, Freedom of Information Guidance, *Exemptions*, Section 43 ('Commercial interests'),14 May 2008, p 5, where *John Connor Press Associates Limited v The Information Commissioner* (EA/2005/0005), 25 January 2006 is cited in support of this point.

97 Freedom of Information Act 2000, s 22.

publication (whether by the public authority itself or any other person) at some future date (whether or not the date has yet been determined) if:

- the information was already held with a view to publication at the date the request for access was made; and

- it is reasonable in all the circumstances to withhold access until the date referred to above.[98]

The duty to confirm or deny does not apply if to do so would disclose any information covered by this exemption. This is an absolute exemption.[99]

Legal professional privilege: this exemption covers information in respect of which a claim to legal professional privilege could be maintained in legal proceedings;[100] this exemption would cover:

- communications between a solicitor or a barrister and his or her client for the purposes of giving legal advice; and

- any document which has been prepared by any person where the primary purpose of creating the document was for the purpose of litigation, whether actual or intended.

This is a qualified exemption.[101]

If the information requested comes within either of these categories then the public authority will need to apply the public interest test, ie whether the public interest in maintaining the exemption outweighs the public interest in disclosing the information.[102]

The duty to confirm or deny still applies to requests for information covered by the legal professional privilege, except where a response would disclose the information covered by the legal professional privilege.[103]

The underlying law concerning legal professional privilege is not affected or altered by the FOIA (just as with the law of confidentiality). The privilege will extend to whether the lawyer involved is external or an in-house lawyer

---

98 This exemption could, presumably, apply where a university is working on an invention with a view to applying for a patent. In such a case, when the application for the patent is published by the UK Intellectual Property Office, the information about the invention which is the subject of the patent would be publicly available.
99 Freedom of Information Act 2000, s 2(3).
100 Freedom of Information Act 2000, s 421.
101 Freedom of Information Act 2000, s 2(3).
102 Under Freedom of Information Act 2000, s 2(2).
103 Freedom of Information Act 2000, s 42(2).

and thus would cover communications between staff of a public authority and its in-house lawyer.[104]

The guidance issued by the ICO provides some of the circumstances where it is more likely that it will be in the public interest that information subject to legal professional privilege should be disclosed:

- although it may be more difficult to show the balance lies in favour of disclosure under the public interest test where legal professional privilege applies, there is no need for those factors to be exceptional; but the public interest in disclosure is not enough;

- the older the information which is subject to legal professional privilege, the less likely it is relevant to current decision-making or challenge and the more likely it has served its purpose;[105]

- a very large sum of public money is at stake;

- the legal advice or a decision resulting from the advice will influence a significant number of people;

- where it appears that the public authority is engaging in unlawful activity or misrepresentation;

- there is a lack of transparency in the way that the public authority carries out its action but there has to be more than mere curiosity in seeing the advice.

Personal information: the public authority is exempt from providing information following a request where the personal data:

- relates to the applicant himself or herself,[106] in which case the public authority must deal with the applicant's request as a request under the Data Protection Act 1999 in accordance with the time limit set out by that Act (40 rather than 20 working days) and check the identity of the applicant;[107]

---

104 Confirmed in *Calland v Information Commissioner and FSA* (EA/2007/0136, 8 August 2008), Information Tribunal.

105 The guidance cites two cases before the information tribunal where information that was six years old was considered still to be relatively recent while that which was over ten years old was considered not recent and which was one factor to take into account in favour of disclosure.

106 Freedom of Information Act 2000, s 41(1).

107 Information Commissioner's Freedom of Information Act Awareness Guidance No 1, *Personal Data*, p 1.

- relates to another person,[108] where it is normally exempt if it would breach the data protection principles under the Data Protection Act 1998, where the information sought relates to personal and private information (for example, the person's home, family life, personal finances or certain personnel information). But the information would not be exempt where the information sought is about someone acting in an official or work capacity unless there is some risk to that individual.[109]

This is an absolute exemption.[110]

Prohibition on disclosure: information is exempt where if disclosed by the public authority the disclosure:

- is prohibited by or under any existing enactment;

- is incompatible with any EU obligation;

- would constitute or be punishable as a contempt of court (such as where it would breach a court order).[111]

This is an absolute exemption.[112]

Health and safety: information is exempt if its disclosure would or would be likely to:

- endanger the physical or mental health of any individual;

- endanger the safety of any individual.[113]

This exemption is a qualified exemption.[114]

The public interest test

Where an exemption is qualified, the public authority has to establish whether it is in the public interest to disclose the information requested by an applicant. There is no requirement to apply the public interest test where the exemption is absolute.[115]

---

108 Freedom of Information Act 2000, s 40(2)–(5).
109 See Information Commissioner's Freedom of Information Act Awareness Guidance No 1, *Personal Data*, p 4.
110 Freedom of Information Act 2000, s 2(3).
111 Freedom of Information Act 2000, s 44.
112 Freedom of Information Act 2000, s 2(3).
113 Freedom of Information Act 2000, s 38.
114 Freedom of Information Act 2000, s 2(3).
115 Freedom of Information Act 2000, s 2(1)(a), (2)(b), (3).

The tests are for

- *the duty to confirm or deny:* in all the circumstances of the case, the public interest is in maintaining the exclusion of the duty to confirm or deny which outweighs the public interest in disclosing whether the public authority holds the information;[116] and

- *the information held:* in all the circumstances of the case, the public interest is in maintaining the exemption which outweighs the public interest in disclosing the information.[117]

The Information Commissioner's guidance[118] makes the following points:

- the 'public interest' is that which serves the interests of the public;

- openness is something which is in itself to be regarded as in the public interest;[119]

- where a qualified exemption applies (ie not an absolute exemption) to the information requested the starting point is that the information must be disclosed unless there is a public interest in maintaining the exemption and it is greater than the public interest in disclosing the information;

- the public interest test must be applied separately to each exemption;

- the public authority has to carry out a balancing exercise – consider the factors for releasing the information and for not doing so;

- the public interest cannot be used by itself, it has to be tied to a specific exemption, ie the first step a public authority should carry is whether the requested information engages a specific exemption;

- only the public interest considerations relevant to the particular exemption should be applied in considering whether that exemption should be maintained;[120]

- the public interest should be applied as it stood at the time of the request (or by the time when the public authority should respond to requests or refuse requests, eg the 20-working-day limit).

---

116 Freedom of Information Act 2000, s 2(1)(b).
117 Freedom of Information Act 2000, s 2(2)(b).
118 See Information Commissioner's Freedom of Information Act Awareness Guidance No 3, *The Public Interest Test*.
119 The Guidance cites an Information Tribunal decision that, although the Freedom of Information Act 2000 does not state this explicitly, there is an assumption in favour of disclosure: *Guardian Newspapers Limited and Heather Brooke v the Information Commissioner and the BBC* (EA 2006/0011, EA 2006/0013, 8 January 2007).
120 See *Bellamy v the Information Commissioner and the DTI* (EA/2005/0023, 4 April 2006).

Below are the factors which a public authority should take into account:[121]

Examples of arguments that could weigh in favour of disclosure	Examples of arguments that could weigh in favour of maintenance of the exemption – but only where relevant to the specific exemption being claimed	Irrelevant considerations in applying the public interest test
General arguments in favour of promoting transparency, accountability and participation.	The specific circumstances of the case and the content of the information requested in relation to those circumstances.	The identity of the person making the request.
Disclosure might enhance the quality of discussions and decision-making generally.	The age of the information might tip the balance in favour of maintaining the exemption or exception. The passage of time may impact upon the strength of the public-interest arguments.	The possibility that the information requested could be misunderstood or regarded as too technical or complex.
The balance might be tipped in favour of disclosure by financial issues. For instance, if the information requested involved a large amount of public money, this might favour disclosure.	The likelihood and severity of any harm or prejudice that disclosure could cause.	The 'status' of the information; for instance if it is classified, or if it relates to senior individuals.
The specific circumstances of the case and the content of the information requested in relation to those circumstances.	The significance or sensitivity of the information. For instance, is it 'live'?	The number of exemptions being claimed.
The age of the information might tip the balance in favour of disclosure. The passage of time may impact upon the strength of the public interest arguments.	The need for a 'safe space' for government and civil servants to formulate and debate issues away from public scrutiny.	In relation to maintenance of the exemption, factors concerning a different exemption to the one being used are irrelevant.
The timing of a request, in respect of information relating to an investigation, may be relevant. This would depend on the stage the investigation had reached and how much information was in the public domain.	The balance might lie in favour of maintaining the exemption or exception in view of the risk of disclosure inhibiting frankness and candour in debate and decision-making, especially within government. The strength of this argument depends on clear evidence that it will have this effect.	The accuracy of the information.

---

121 This wording appears on pp 6, 7 of the Guidance, but is reformatted here as a table for presentational purposes.

Examples of arguments that could weigh in favour of disclosure	Examples of arguments that could weigh in favour of maintenance of the exemption – but only where relevant to the specific exemption being claimed	Irrelevant considerations in applying the public interest test
The impact (beneficial or otherwise) of disclosure upon individuals and /or the wider public.	In respect of information relating to an investigation, the timing of the request may be relevant, depending on the stage the investigation had reached, and how much information was in the public domain. The impact (beneficial or otherwise) of disclosure upon individuals and /or the wider public.	Arguments that disclosure will lead to poorer record-keeping.

Environmental information

There is a separate statutory regime in place for environmental information held by public authorities. Although the law for environmental information is not contained in the Freedom of Information Act 2000, in essence there is not substantive difference in the legal regime governing environmental information and other information held by a public authority. Environmental information held by a public authority is governed by the Environmental Information Regulations 2004 ('the Regulations').[122] Accordingly the making of requests, the exemptions available, and what is a public authority etc are not considered separately. Below is an outline of any significant differences between the two regimes.

Information

The Regulations only apply to environmental information which is defined as meaning:

> 'namely any information in written, visual, aural, electronic or any other material form on–
>
> (a) the state of the elements of the environment, such as air and atmosphere, water, soil, land, landscape and natural sites including wetlands, coastal and marine areas, biological diversity and its components, including genetically modified organisms, and the interaction among these elements;

---

122 SI 2004/3391.

(b)   factors, such as substances, energy, noise, radiation or waste, including radioactive waste, emissions, discharges and other releases into the environment, affecting or likely to affect the elements of the environment referred to in (a);

(c)   measures (including administrative measures), such as policies, legislation, plans, programmes, environmental agreements, and activities affecting or likely to affect the elements and factors referred to in (a) and (b) as well as measures or activities designed to protect those elements;

(d)   reports on the implementation of environmental legislation;

(e)   cost-benefit and other economic analyses and assumptions used within the framework of the measures and activities referred to in (c); and

(f)   the state of human health and safety, including the contamination of the food chain, where relevant, conditions of human life, cultural sites and built structures inasmuch as they are or may be affected by the state of the elements of the environment referred to in (a) or, through those elements, by any of the matters referred to in (b) and (c)'.[123]

Any information held by a public authority which comes into the above categories will require an applicant to make an application under the Regulations rather than the Freedom of Information Act 2000.

Public authority

A public authority has essentially the same meaning under the Regulations as under the Act, but includes a greater range of persons and organisations which might come within the meaning of a public authority, and would include:

'(c)   any other body or other person, that carries out functions of public administration; or

(d)   any other body or other person, that is under the control of a [public authority and]–

(i)   has public responsibilities relating to the environment;

(ii)   exercises functions of a public nature relating to the environment; or

(iii)   provides public services relating to the environment'.[124]

---

123   Environmental Information Regulations 2004 (SI 2004/3391), reg 2(1).
124   Environmental Information Regulations 2004 (SI 2004/3391), reg 2(2).

This could mean that a company which was not wholly owned by a public authority could be a public authority,[125] but obviously only in relation to environmental information it held.

Information held by a public authority

Under the Act, a public authority will be required to only disclose its own information, where it is held directly or indirectly by it (ie by someone holding it on the behalf of the public authority). Under the Regulations information will be discloseable which is in the authority's possession, whether such information is produced by it or received by it, or the information is held by someone on the behalf of the public authority.[126]

The Regulations can require the public authority to provide information which belongs to another person if the public authority is holding it on the behalf of the other person (which is not possible under the Act).

Method in which a request can be made

Under the Regulations a request for environmental information does not have to be made in writing; it is possible to make a valid request verbally.[127]

Time in which a response can be provided by a public authority

The same 20-working-day period must normally be complied with in providing a response for environmental information, but unlike for information caught by the Act, a public authority can more easily extend the period (to 40 working days).[128]

Exceptions

The exemptions available under the Act are generally the same for environmental information, but there are some differences:

- they are called exceptions not exemptions;[129]

- where an exception requires prejudice under the Act, the term used for an exception is 'adversely affected';[130]

---

125 But the information the company held for purposes other than the Regulations would not be discloseable under the Freedom of Information Act 2000 as it would not be a public authority under the Act (as not being wholly owned by the ultimate public authority.

126 Environmental Information Regulations 2004 (SI 2004/3391), reg 3(2).

127 See Environmental Information Regulations 2004 (SI 2004/3391), reg 5(1).

128 See Environmental Information Regulations 2004 (SI 2004/3391), reg 7.

129 See Environmental Information Regulations 2004 (SI 2004/3391), reg 12.

130 See Environmental Information Regulations 2004 (SI 2004/3391), reg 12(5).

- there are less of them, but the Regulations include a specific exception for intellectual property rights; and

- all of them are subject to the public interest test. There is not a category of exceptions which are 'absolute', ie not subject to the public interest test (such as exemption for information provided in confidence under the Act).[131]

Exceeding a stated cost

Unlike under the Act, where if a certain limit is reached then there is no longer a requirement on the public authority to release the information requested, under the Regulations there is no such limit, but the public authority can charge a reasonable amount.[132]

Law and the Internet

Operating a website

Required information

The operator of a website must by law provide certain information to the website's users. This includes the following:[133]

- in the case of *an individual*, his or her name; in the case of *a partnership*, the names of all the partners; and in the case of *a company*, the name, place of registration, registered number and physical address of the company;

- the name of the *contracting entity* to any transaction, if different from the above;

- *contact details* allowing rapid and direct communication;

- *membership* of a professional body and details of any *supervising authority*;

- the VAT number;

- any information required under the *Distance Selling Regulations*;

- in the case of any prices mentioned, whether they include *tax and delivery charges*.

---

131 See Environmental Information Regulations 2004 (SI 2004/3391), reg 12.
132 See Environmental Information Regulations 2004 (SI 2004/3391), reg 8.
133 See the Companies Act 2006, the Consumer Protection (Distance Selling) Regulations 2000 (SI 2000/2334) and the Electronic Commerce (EC Directive) Regulations 2002 (SI 2002/2013).

Disabled users

It is unlawful for the provider of a service to discriminate against a disabled person by making it impossible or unreasonably difficult for the disabled person to make use of that service.[134] This applies to the provision of a website, since the Disability Discrimination Act 1995 defines the provision of services as including providing access to communication and information services.[135] Relevant guidelines have been produced by the World Wide Web Consortium and the British Standards Institute,[136] which is in the process of producing a new code of practice for building accessible websites.[137]

Data protection

Any collection of personal data by a website must comply with the data protection principles set out in the Data Protection Act 1998.[138] If any personal data are to be collected, the operator of the website will need to register as a data controller with the Information Commissioner's Office.[139] Since no personal data may be exported outside the EU without the data subject's consent, this point should be addressed in the website's terms and conditions if any such export is likely.[140]

Liability

The website operator or internet service provider is potentially liable to a claim if, for example, content on a website infringes someone's intellectual property or is defamatory. However, the Electronic Commerce Regulations provide three exemptions that may protect from liability the provider of an information society service, defined as 'any service normally provided for remuneration, at a distance, by means of electronic equipment for the processing (including digital compression) and storage of data, and at the individual request of a recipient of a service'.[141] These three exemptions are as follows.

---

134 Disability Discrimination Act 1995, s 19(1)(b).
135 Disability Discrimination Act 1995, s 19(3)(b), (c).
136 See www.w3.org/wai/intro/wcag.php and www.bsi-globa.com/net.
137 *Web Accessibility: Building Accessible Experiences for Disabled People: Code of Practice* (BS 8878): a draft version is currently available on the BSI website. This will replace the current guidelines, set out in *Guide to Good Practice in Commissioning Accessible Websites* (PAS 78, 2006).
138 See above under 'Data protection'.
139 See www.ico.gov.uk
140 See 'Transferrence of data outside of the European Economic Area'.
141 Electronic Commerce (EC Directive) Regulations 2002, reg 2(1). There are similar exemptions relating to liability in relation to terrorism in the Electronic Commerce Directive (Terrorism Act 2006) Regulations 2007 (SI 2007/1550), and in relation to racial and religious hatred in the Electronic Commerce Directive (Racial and Religious Hatred Act 2006) Regulations 2007 (SI 2007/2497). Where none of the exemptions apply, it should be noted that legislation such as the Obscene Publications Acts 1959 and 1964, the Protection of Children Act 1978 and the Sex Offences Act 2003 apply to online content.

- The *mere conduit exemption* exempts a person who provides a service that consists of the transmission of information across a communications network from civil or criminal liability arising as a result of such transmission provided that he or she (a) did not initiate the transmission; (b) did not select the receiver of the transmission; and (c) did not select or modify the information contained in the transmission.[142]

- The *caching exemption* exempts a service provider from civil or criminal liability where the information is subject to automatic, intermediate and temporary storage for the sole purpose of transmitting the information more efficiently. The service provider must, however, act expeditiously to remove or disable access to information once he or she becomes aware that, at the initial source of the transmission, the information has been removed, or access has been disabled, or that a court has ordered such removal or disablement.[143]

- The *hosting exemption* exempts a service provider from civil or criminal liability when the service consists of information provided by the recipient of the service where the service provider (a) did not know about the unlawful activity or information, or of any facts or circumstances from which the unlawful activity or information would have been apparent, and (b) acts expeditiously to remove or disable access to the information once he or she becomes aware of it.[144]

Using a website to do business

The Distance Selling Regulations

Those using a website to do business must comply with the Distance Selling Regulations, which apply to contracts for the supply of goods and/or services where the parties make exclusive use of one or more means of distance communication up to and including the moment at which the contract is concluded.[145] The Distance Selling Regulations apply only to consumer contracts; among other exceptions, they do not apply to contracts relating to financial services.[146]

Among the provisions of the Distance Selling Regulations are the following:

- Certain information must be provided to the consumer before the conclusion of the contract, and further information must be provided on the conclusion of the contract.[147]

---

142 Electronic Commerce (EC Directive) Regulations 2002, reg 17.
143 Electronic Commerce (EC Directive) Regulations 2002, reg 18.
144 Electronic Commerce (EC Directive) Regulations 2002, reg 19.
145 Consumer Protection (Distance Selling) Regulations 2000, reg 3(1).
146 Consumer Protection (Distance Selling) Regulations 2000, reg 5(1).
147 Consumer Protection (Distance Selling) Regulations 2000, regs 7(1), 8.

- With certain exceptions,[148] the consumer must have a cooling-off period of seven working days from the day after the goods ordered are received or from the day when the consumer agrees to a contract for services. During this period the consumer may cancel the contract.[149]

- If the information required under the first bullet point has not been provided, the cooling-off period may be extended up to three months and seven working days.[150]

The Office of Fair Trading enforces the Regulations, and may seek an injunction against a non-compliant supplier.[151]

The E-Commerce Regulations

As already mentioned in the section on liability, the E-Commerce Regulations apply to suppliers of information society services, and hence any website used to sell or market a product or service.[152] The E-Commerce Regulations require the following.

- Where a contract is to be concluded by electronic means, a supplier must, before accepting an order:

  — define the technical steps needed to conclude the contract;

  — state whether or not the contract will be kept by the supplier;

  — provide the purchaser with the opportunity to identify and correct errors before placing an order; and

  — state the languages offered for the conclusion of the contract.[153]

- The consumer must be able to store and reproduce the terms and conditions.[154]

- The supplier must acknowledge receipt of an order without delay and provide a further opportunity for the consumer to identify and correct any errors in the order.[155]

- Non-compliance by the supplier can entitle the consumer to rescind the contract.[156]

---

148 Consumer Protection (Distance Selling) Regulations 2000, reg 13.
149 Consumer Protection (Distance Selling) Regulations 2000, regs 11(2), 12(2).
150 Consumer Protection (Distance Selling) Regulations 2000, regs 11(4), 12(4).
151 Consumer Protection (Distance Selling) Regulations 2000, regs 26, 27; see www.oft.gov.uk.
152 Electronic Commerce (EC Directive) Regulations 2002, reg 2(1).
153 Electronic Commerce (EC Directive) Regulations 2002, reg 9.
154 Electronic Commerce (EC Directive) Regulations 2002, reg 9(3).
155 Electronic Commerce (EC Directive) Regulations 2002, reg 11(1).
156 Electronic Commerce (EC Directive) Regulations 2002, reg 15.

The Regulations also regulate commercial communications by email. They include the following requirements:

- Any commercial email must:

  — be clearly identifiable as a commercial communication;

  — clearly identify the person on whose behalf the commercial communication is made;

  — clearly identify any promotional offer, competition or game and present any conditions for participation accessibly, clearly and unambiguously.[157]

- Any unsolicited commercial email must clearly identify itself as such on receipt.[158]

Administration of the internet

All websites are named according to the domain name system (DNS), which is co-ordinated by the Internet Corporation for Assigned Names and Numbers (*ICANN*), a not-for-profit public-benefit corporation formed in 1998.[159] ICANN is responsible for setting the procedures used for resolving disputes about domain names, known as the Uniform Dispute for Domain Names Resolution Policy (UDRP).[160] Entities registering a generic top-level domain (ending in .com, .org, .info or .net, for example) must usually agree to the UDRP when they register. ICANN does not itself participate in the resolution of domain-name disputes, but it maintains a list of authorised dispute-resolution providers.[161] Agreement to the UDRP does not preclude action through the courts if a party considers it necessary.

Administration of the UK's country-code top-level domain (.uk) lies with *Nominet UK*, a not-for profit organisation established as a company limited by guarantee.[162] Entities registering a .uk address must agree to Nominet's dispute-resolution procedure (DRS) and accept its terms and conditions.[163] As with the UDRP, however, this does not preclude court action: if a party goes to court, the dispute-resolution procedure is suspended.

The *Internet Watch Foundation* (IWF), a charitable company limited by guarantee, is an independent self-regulatory body set up by the UK internet

---

157 Electronic Commerce (EC Directive) Regulations 2002, reg 7.
158 Electronic Commerce (EC Directive) Regulations 2002, reg 8. The Privacy and Electronic Communications (EC Directive) Regulations 2003 (SI 2003/2426) also apply to unsolicited emails.
159 See www.icann.org.
160 See www.icann.org/en/udrp/udrp.htm.
161 See www.icann.org/en/dndr/udrp/approved-providers.htm.
162 See www.nominet.org.uk.
163 See www.nominet.org.uk/disputes/drs.

industry in 1996.[164] Its aim is to restrict access to illegal content on the internet. If a user reports illegal material to the IWF, and the site in question is hosted in the UK, the IWF can require the internet service provider hosting the site to remove the content in question. If the site is hosted abroad, its URL can be placed on a backlist enabling access to it to be blocked by UK internet service providers.

The *World Wide Web Consortium* (W3C) is an international consortium that develops standards for the internet, with the aim of improving its operation by ensuring the compatibility of web-based technologies.[165] It is administered by the Massachusetts Institute of Technology, the European Research Consortium for Informatics and Mathematics, and Keio University. As already mentioned, among its guidelines are the *Website Content Accessibility Guidelines*, which aim to ensure accessibility to the internet for disabled users.[166]

Computer-related crime

In addition to criminal provisions concerning infringement of copyright, the Computer Misuse Act 1990 sets out the following criminal offences:

- unauthorised access to computer material (hacking);[167]

- unauthorised access to computer material with intent to commit or facilitate the commission of further offences;[168]

- unauthorised acts with intent to impair, or with recklessness as to impairing, operation of a computer;[169] and

- making, supplying or obtaining articles for use in any of the above offences.[170]

Telecommunications

The most important legislation concerning telecommunications is the Communications Act 2003, which replaced the Telecommunications Act 1984. Under the Communications Act, the Office of Communications (Ofcom) is responsible for licensing the provision of telecommunications systems.[171] Ofcom is responsible for the duties previously carried out by the Broadcasting Standards Commission, the Independent Television Commission, the Office of Telecommunications, the Radio Authority and the Radiocommunications Agency.

---

164 See www.iwf.org.uk.
165 See www.w3.org.
166 See http://www.w3.org/tr/wcag20.
167 Computer Misuse Act 1990, s 1.
168 Computer Misuse Act 1990, s 2.
169 Computer Misuse Act 1990 (as amended), s 3.
170 Computer Misuse Act 1990 (as amended), s 3A.
171 See www.ofcom.org.uk.

THE BIOTECHNOLOGY AND PHARMACEUTICAL INDUSTRIES

This section aims to introduce some of the main regulatory requirements relevant to the biotechnology and pharmaceutical industries. The focus is on the requirements relating to the various stages in the development of a new drug, from initial scientific research into possible compounds through clinical trials to gaining authorisation to place the new drug on the market.[172]

Outline of the process of developing a new drug

The process of discovering and developing a new drug may be divided into pre-clinical and clinical phases, each of which has several stages.[173]

Pre-clinical phase: identification and validation of target

The pre-clinical stage typically begins with the identification of a potential target, connected with the disease which is being researched, on which a new drug might act. A target could be a gene or protein associated with the disease in question. The scientist aims to find a target molecule which, when affected by a compound, will change its activity in such a way as to have a positive therapeutic effect. The target's activity in normal and diseased conditions will be studied in order to understand as well as possible how its activity is related to the disease under investigation: this is known as validating the target. Research of this kind is typically carried out in universities and, if successful, may result in an application for a patent for the discovery.

Identification of compounds that may act on the target

Once a target has been validated, the next stage is to identify compounds that will act on the target in such a way as to have a therapeutically beneficial effect. It may be necessary to assess many such potential compounds, using assay techniques to measure their effect on the target in question. High throughput screening can be used to test a large number of compounds efficiently. Pharmaceutical companies typically carry out this work, the results of which is the selection of a number of compounds that act beneficially on the target and have the potential for development into a drug.

---

172 A major legal resource for the pharmaceutical sector is Eudralex, which collects European legislation and guidance on medicinal products for human and veterinary use in 10 volumes. See http://ec.europa.eu/enterprise/sectors/pharmaceuticals/documents/eudralex/index_en.htm.

173 For a more detailed account, see Anderson, *Drafting Agreements in the Biotechnology and Pharmaceutical Industries* (Oxford University Press, 2009), Ch 10.

Identification of lead compounds

The compounds selected for development are then studied in greater detail. Work is done on their pharmacokinetics – how the body absorbs, distributes, metabolises and excretes them. Particular attention is paid to the way in which they are transmitted to the target. The compounds which appear from this study that show the greatest potential to form a new drug are identified as lead compounds.

Optimisation of lead compounds

The lead compounds selected then undergo further work, in order to assess whether there are any modifications that can be made to them that it will optimise their effects. The modified derivatives of the lead compounds are tested again for their effect on the target, and work is done on how selected optimised compounds can be made into a medicinal product that can be tested on animals and human beings.

Tests on animals

The final pre-clinical stage in the development of a new drug is to test it for safety by administering it to animals. This is to test the toxicity of the optimised compounds in order to determine whether they will be safe when administered to humans, and to ascertain what an appropriate dose would be. The potential new drug must meet an appropriate standard of safety in these tests before it can be given to human beings.

Clinical phase: clinical trials

If the results of the tests on animals are satisfactory, the potential new drug now proceeds to the clinical stage of development. It will undergo a series of clinical trials, in order to ascertain that it is both safe, when administered to humans, and therapeutically effective. Clinical trials are traditionally divided into three phases, using increasingly greater numbers of participants.

Phase I trials

Phase I clinical trials are focused on safety. The drug is given to a small number of healthy volunteers, usually between 10 and 200, in order to check that it is safe and ascertain what an appropriate dosage would be. This is sometimes known as the 'first into man' study. About 70 per cent of experimental drugs pass this phase.

Phase II trials

In Phase II clinical trials, the drug is given to between 100 and 400 patients suffering from the disease in question. Phase II trials are typically divided into two stages, known as Phase IIa and Phase IIb. In a Phase IIa trial, a single dose of the new drug is given to a small number of patients under controlled conditions in order to assess whether it has a beneficial effect; this is known as a 'proof of principle' study. A Phase IIb trial is conducted with a larger group of patients: it aims to identify whether the drug has any side-effects and to refine the conclusions already reached about appropriate dosage. Phase II trials may last several months or longer. About one-third of experimental drugs successfully complete both Phase I and Phase II trials.

Phase III trials

If the Phase II trials show that the drug is effective and has no unacceptable side-effects, a Phase III trial will be undertaken. This will check the safety and efficacy of the new drug among a larger sample of patients in several locations – typically between 500 and 5,000 patients, depending partly on the rarity of the disease under investigation. A Phase III trial is usually a randomised control trial, with the effect of the drug on the patients it is administered to compared to what happens to a control group, who may be given a placebo or, increasingly, a drug that is already in use to treat the same disease. Phase III trials are often conducted blind, so that the patient and, in some cases, the doctor do not know whether it is the trial drug that is being administered. Information about side-effects is carefully recorded. Phase III trials may last several years and take place in several different hospitals. Of drugs that enter Phase III trials, between 70 and 90 per cent complete them successfully.

Launch of the new drug and Phase IV trials

Once a Phase III trial has been successfully completed, the drug company can apply for authorisation to put its new medicinal product on the market. Even after a drug has been brought into regular clinical use, further studies may be undertaken in the shape of Phase IV clinical trials. These aim to find out what the long-term effects of the drug are, to identify any rare side-effects that may not have become apparent in the earlier trials, and to note how the drug interacts with other medication that patients may be taking.

Regulatory bodies

There are many regulatory bodies potentially relevant to the drug development process in the UK, including:

- the Home Office (for animal research);
- the Human Tissue Authority; and
- the Human Fertilisation and Embryology Authority;

all of which are considered in further detail below. The two principal bodies in the field, however, are:

- the European Medicines Agency; and
- the UK's Medical and Healthcare Products Regulatory Agency.

The European Medicines Agency

The European Medicines Agency (EMEA) is the EU's agency responsible for the evaluation and supervision of medicinal products for human and veterinary use.[174] On the basis of EMEA's opinion, the European Commission authorises the marketing of innovative products and arbitrates between Member States for other medicinal products in case of disagreement. It also has a role in maintaining the EU database on clinical trials and is to be notified, for example, of certain details regarding clinical trials.[175]

The Medical and Healthcare Products Regulatory Agency

The Medical and Healthcare Products Regulatory Agency (MHRA) is an executive agency of the Department of Health.[176] It was formed in 2003 by amalgamation of the former Medicines Control Agency and Medical Devices Agency, and is responsible for issuing marketing authorisations for medicinal products in the UK. The MHRA's Inspection and Standards Division comprises inspectorates for Good Clinical Practice, Good Laboratory Practice, Good Manufacturing and Distribution Practice and Good Pharmacovigilance Practice.

Good laboratory practice

Good laboratory practice (GLP) is concerned with the organisational processes and conditions under which certain laboratory studies are carried out.[177] These studies may be concerned with health and the environment, or the testing of human and veterinary pharmaceuticals, agrochemicals, cosmetics, food and feed additives and industrial chemicals. The entities under study

---

174 The Agency was set up as the European Medicines Evaluation Agency by Regulation 2309/93/ EEC. That Regulation has now been replaced by Regulation 726/2004/EC ([2004] OJ L136/1), which renamed the agency as the European Medicines Agency; the abbreviation EMEA is still used, however, as the initials EMA had already been appropriated by the European Medical Association. See also Regulation 658/2007/EC ([2007] OJ L155/10). The Agency's website is at www.emea.europa.eu.
175 See 'The Clinical Trials Directive below.
176 See www.mhra.gov.uk.
177 See the *Guide to UK GLP Regulations 1999* (Department of Health, 2000), available at www. mhra.gov.uk/howweregulate/medicines/inspectionandstandards/goodlaboratorypractice/ publicationsandapplicationform/index.htm.

are frequently synthetic chemicals but may also be of natural or biological origin; in some circumstances, they may be living organisms.[178]

The principles of good laboratory practice originated in the US and were established internationally by the Organisation for Economic Co-operation and Development (OECD) in 1981. They are intended to prevent fraud upon the registration authorities dealing with the receipt of data for the evaluation of chemical products. These principles have been adopted by the EU in the Good Laboratory Practice Directive,[179] which has been transposed into UK legislation in the form of the Good Laboratory Practice Regulations 1999.[180]

Schedule 1 to the Good Laboratory Practice Regulations sets out the following principles of good laboratory practice, as derived from the Good Laboratory Practice Directive:

- the test facility organisation and personnel, including the responsibilities of the study director, principal investigator and study personnel;

- the quality assurance programme, including the responsibilities of the quality assurance personnel;

- facilities, including test system facilities, facilities for handling test and reference items, archive facilities and waste disposal;

- apparatus, materials and reagents;

- test systems (physical/chemical and biological);

- test and reference items, including receipt, handling, sampling, storage and characterisation;

- standard operating procedures;

- the performance of the regulatory study, including the study plan, its content and the conduct of the regulatory study;

- reporting the regulatory study results, including the content of the final report; and

- storage and retention of records and materials.

---

178 Also relevant is the joint statement issued in 1998 by the Director General of the Research Councils and the chief executives of research councils entitled 'Safeguarding Good Scientific Practice'. This statement provides information for research councils and organisations funded by them on how to comply with good scientific conduct and to prevent scientific misconduct. It sets out the following principles of good scientific practice: (i) fundamentals of scientific work such as maintaining professional standards, documenting results, questioning one's own findings, attributing honestly the contribution of others; (ii) leadership and co-operation in research groups; (iii) taking special account of the needs of young researchers; (iv) securing and storing primary data. See www.ukoln.ac.uk/projects/ebank-uk/docs/scientific-practice.doc; for Research Councils UK, see www.rcuk.ac.uk.
179 Directive 2004/10/EC ([2004] OJ L50/44) on the harmonisation of laws, regulations and administrative provisions relating to the application of the principles of good laboratory practice and the verification of their applications for tests on chemical substances.
180 SI 1999/3106, as amended: for the principles of good laboratory practice, see Sch 1.

Any place that undertakes a regulatory study – that is, a study whose results are to be submitted to a regulatory authority – must adhere to good laboratory practice. This applies both to the organisational structure surrounding the study and to the conditions under which it is planned, performed, monitored, recorded, archived and reported.[181]

The Good Laboratory Practice Monitoring Authority (GLPMA) at the MHRA is responsible for inspecting laboratories to ensure compliance with good laboratory practice,[182] and has powers of entry, inspection and seizure in pursuit of its functions.[183] The Authority may serve a warning notice on an operator whom it believes not to be compliant.[184] It is an offence not to comply with a warning notice,[185] although an operator served with such a notice has the right of appeal to a magistrates court.[186]

The Good Laboratory Practice Regulations also provide that any regulatory study must be carried out at a test facility operated by either a member or a prospective member of the UK good laboratory practice compliance programme.[187] The GLP Monitoring Authority may refuse to admit an operator to membership of the programme, but must explain their reasons for doing so and give him or her a specified period in which to make representations to them.[188] The Authority may also deprive an existing member of his or her membership if, for example, he or she is incapable of ensuring adherence to the principles of good laboratory practice; again, it must offer a period in which representations can be made.[189]

It is an offence to obstruct an officer of the GLPMA,[190] or to make a false good laboratory practice instrument (such as a statement attesting that good laboratory practice has been complied with).[191] Where a body corporate commits such an offence, any director, manager, secretary or partner also commits it,[192] although there is a defence of due diligence.[193] Penalties include

181 Good Laboratory Practice Regulations (SI 1999/3106), reg 7(1).
182 Good Laboratory Practice Regulations, reg 3. The GLPMA is part of the Inspectorate Group of the MHRA's Inspection and Standards Division. See www.mhra.gov.uk/howweregulate/medicines/inspectionandstandards/goodlaboratorypractice/index.htm.
183 Good Laboratory Practice Regulations, reg 9. Guidance for the conduct of inspections is set out in Sch 2. Provision is made for the protection of confidential information (reg 10).
184 Good Laboratory Practice Regulations, reg 7(2).
185 Good Laboratory Practice Regulations, reg 7(3).
186 Good Laboratory Practice Regulations, reg 8.
187 Good Laboratory Practice Regulations, reg 4.
188 Good Laboratory Practice Regulations, reg 5.
189 Good Laboratory Practice Regulations, reg 6.
190 Good Laboratory Practice Regulations, reg 11.
191 Good Laboratory Practice Regulations, reg 12.
192 Good Laboratory Practice Regulations, reg 13.
193 Good Laboratory Practice Regulations, reg 14.

fines and imprisonment.[194] The GLPMA may charge fees for its inspections and services.[195]

Environmental issues and health and safety

The Environmental Protection Act 1990

The most important legislation relating to environmental issues is the Environmental Protection Act 1990, and regulations made under it.[196] The Environmental Protection Act covers planning control, pollution control, disposal of waste and control of dangerous substances as well as the escape or release of genetically modified organisms (GMOs), an area which is also covered by secondary legislation.[197] It creates a number of criminal offences, some of which relate to failure to comply with regulatory procedure and carry a maximum penalty of five years' imprisonment and/or an unlimited fine.

The Health and Safety at Work Act 1974

In addition to provisions under the Environmental Protection Act 1990, the health and safety of employees is governed by the Health and Safety at Work Act 1974 which includes, among other things, controls on dangerous substances.[198] There is also separate legislation dealing with radioactive substances[199] and flammable substances.[200] UK and EU regulations often impose duties which have particular application to those working in the pharmaceutical and chemical industries. The REACH Regulation, relating to the registration, evaluation, authorisation and restriction of chemicals, is of particular importance.[201]

---

194 Good Laboratory Practice Regulations, reg 15.
195 Good Laboratory Practice Regulations, reg 16.
196 For further information on the range of issues involved, see the website of the Department of Environment, Food and Rural Affairs (DEFRA) at www.defra.gov.uk/environment/policy/index.htm.
197 See the Management of Health and Safety at Work Regulations 1999 (SI 1999/3242).
198 See the Control of Substances Hazardous to Health Regulations 2002 (SI 2002/2677); also the Carriage of Dangerous Goods and Use of Transportable Pressure Equipment Regulations 2009 (SI 2009/1348).
199 See the Radioactive Substances Act 1993.
200 See the Regulatory Reform (Fire Safety) Order 2005 (SI 2005/1541, replacing the Fire Precautions Act 1971), and the Manufacture and Storage of Explosives Regulations (SI 2005/1082, largely replacing the Explosives Act 1875).
201 See Regulation 1907/2006/EC ([2006] OJ L396/1) concerning the Registration, Evaluation, Authorisation and Restriction of Chemicals. There is useful guidance on the European Chemicals Agency's website: www.echa.europa.eu/doc/reach/reach_faq.pdf. Enforcement in the UK is governed by the REACH Enforcement Regulations 2008 (SI 2008/2852).

Genetically modified organisms

Special legislation applies to the use of genetically modified organisms (GMOs) in the workplace. The Genetically Modified Organisms (Contained Use) Regulations 2000 gave effect in the UK to the Contained Use Directive.[202] The Contained Use Regulations are enforced by the Health and Safety Executive (HSE).[203] Other aspects of the use of genetically modified organisms are governed by further legislation.[204]

Legislation affecting the use of animals in research

Animals are used in many of the stages in the drug development process outlined above. In the initial work on targets and compounds, genetically modified animals such as mice and rats are often used to identify targets and to study the pharmacokinetics of selected compounds. Once a lead compound has been optimised, it is necessary to test its safety and efficacy on animals before any clinical trials on human beings can be carried out.[205] Studies using animals may continue during human clinical trials, and even after the new drug has been launched on the market.

The Animals (Scientific Procedures) Act 1986

The principal legislation governing the use of animals for medical research in the UK is the Animals (Scientific Procedures) Act 1986, which transposed the Experimental Animals Directive into UK law.[206] The 1986 Act regulates

---

202 SI 2000/2831, implementing Council Directive 90/219/EEC ([1990] OJ L117/1) on the contained use of genetically modified micro-organisms (the Contained Use Directive), as amended by Directives 94/51/EC ([1994] OJ L297/29) and 98/81/EC ([1998] OJ L330/13).

203 See www.hse.gov.uk/biosafety/gmo/index.htm.

204 The deliberate release of genetically modified organisms into the environment is governed by the Genetically Modified Organisms (Deliberate Release) Regulations 2002 (SI 2002/2443), implementing Council Directive 2001/18/EC ([2001] OJ L106/1) on the deliberate release into the environment of genetically modified organisms (the Deliberate Release Directive); see also the Genetically Modified Organisms (Deliberate Release and Risk Assessment) (Amendment) Regulations 1997 (SI 1997/1900). The deliberate release of GMOs is regulated by the Department for Environment, Food and Rural Affairs (DEFRA): see www.defra.gov.uk/environment/quality/gm/index.htm. Genetically modified food is regulated by the Food Standards Agency: see www.food.gov.uk/gmfoods. The Plant Health Act 1967, the Public Health (Control of Disease) Act 1984 and the Food and Environment Protection Act 1985 may also be relevant.

205 This is a European requirement under the Medicinal Products Directive (2001/83/EC) ([2001] OJ L311/67).

206 Council Directive 86/609/EEC ([1986] OJ L358/1) on the approximation of laws, regulations and administrative provisions of the Member States regarding the protection of animals used for experimental and other scientific purposes. See also the Council of Europe Convention for the Protection of Vertebrate Animals Used for Experimental and other Scientific Purposes (ETS 123, 1986), which may be found at http://conventions.coe.int/treaty/en/treaties/html/123.htm. The 1986 Act goes beyond the requirements of the Directive, and in certain respects corresponding legislation in some other member states is less stringent.

experiments using live vertebrates other than man, described as 'protected animals',[207] and controls 'any experimental procedure applied to a protected animal which may have the effect of causing that animal pain, suffering, distress or lasting harm' (a 'regulated procedure').[208] It also controls animal breeding, production of blood products and maintenance of tumours and parasites.

Personal licences

In order to carry out a regulated procedure on a protected animal, it is necessary for two types of licence to be in place: a personal licence and a project licence.[209] A personal licence qualifies the holder 'to apply specified regulated procedures to animals of specified descriptions at a specified place or specified places'.[210] The holder of a personal licence must have received appropriate education and training in handling animals for the research to be undertaken.[211] A personal licence must be renewed every five years.[212]

Project licences

A project licence authorises 'specified regulated procedures to animals of specified descriptions at a specified place or specified places' as part of a specified programme of work,[213] for which an individual must take overall responsibility.[214] The decision whether or not to grant a licence is taken by weighing 'the likely adverse affects on the animals concerned against the benefit likely to accrue as a result of the programme';[215] this is known as the cost-benefit analysis. A project licence will be granted only if the desired purpose cannot be achieved without the use of animals, and the procedures to be used cause as little suffering to the animals as possible.[216] A project licence lasts for a maximum of five years.[217]

Designated establishments

Research using animals can only be carried out at a place certified by the Home Office as a scientific procedure establishment,[218] unless special dispensation

207 Animals (Scientific Procedures) Act 1986, s 1. The common octopus is also included by the Animals (Scientific Procedures) Act Amendment Order 1993 (SI 1993/2103).
208 Animals (Scientific Procedures) Act 1986, s 2.
209 Animals (Scientific Procedures) Act 1986, s 3.
210 Animals (Scientific Procedures) Act 1986, s 4(1).
211 Animals (Scientific Procedures) Act 1986, s 4(4A).
212 Animals (Scientific Procedures) Act 1986, s 4(5).
213 Animals (Scientific Procedures) Act 1986, s 5(1).
214 Animals (Scientific Procedures) Act 1986, s 5(2).
215 Animals (Scientific Procedures) Act 1986, s 5(4).
216 Animals (Scientific Procedures) Act 1986, s 5(5).
217 Animals (Scientific Procedures) Act 1986, s 5(7).
218 Animals (Scientific Procedures) Act 1986, s 6(1).

is granted.[219] There must be nominated a person to be responsible for the day-to-day care of the animals and a vet to provide advice on their health and welfare.[220] Places where animals are bred for scientific research, or where they are kept in order to be supplied for use in scientific research, must also be certified as breeding or supplying establishments.[221]

Conditions and licences

Various conditions which personal and project licences and designation certificates must include are set out in the Act.[222] The applicant for a licence has the right to make representations if his or her application is refused.[223] A licence may be suspended if necessary for the welfare of any protected animals.[224] There are additional controls relating to the re-use of animals which have already suffered severe pain or distress,[225] and express authorisation is needed for the use of any neuromuscular blocking agent.[226]

Enforcement

The provisions of the Act are enforced by the Animals (Scientific Procedures) Division of the Home Office (ASPD), which comprises a policy team, a licensing team and an inspectorate.[227] Inspectors visit places where regulated procedures are carried out to determine whether the licence conditions are being complied with.[228] Breach of the terms of a licence may amount to a criminal offence carrying a maximum penalty of two years' imprisonment and/or unlimited fines.[229]

Other legislation and guidance

Other legislation may also be relevant to the use of animals in research.[230] As well as the three-fold requirement for a personal licence, project licence and designated establishment, it is also necessary for any experimental protocol involving the use of animals to be approved by a local ethics committee. The Home Office publishes codes of practice regulating various aspects of animal use and handling,[231] and the Medical Research Council

---

219 Animals (Scientific Procedures) Act 1986, s 6(2).
220 Animals (Scientific Procedures) Act 1986, s 6(5).
221 Animals (Scientific Procedures) Act 1986, s 7.
222 Animals (Scientific Procedures) Act 1986, s 10.
223 Animals (Scientific Procedures) Act 1986, s 12.
224 Animals (Scientific Procedures) Act 1986, s 13.
225 Animals (Scientific Procedures) Act 1986, s 14.
226 Animals (Scientific Procedures) Act 1986, s 17.
227 See www.scienceandresearch.homeoffice.gov.uk/animal-research.
228 Animals (Scientific Procedures) Act 1986, s 18.
229 Animals (Scientific Procedures) Act 1986, s 22.
230 For example, the Animal Health and Welfare Act 1984 and the Animal Health Act 2002.
231 See www.scienceandresearch.homeoffice.gov.uk/animal-research/publications-and-reference/
     publications/guidance.

also publishes useful booklets addressing various ethical issues relating to medical research.[232]

The use of human tissue in research

The Human Tissue Act 2004

The Human Tissue Act 2004 governs the use of human tissue for scientific research in England, Wales and Northern Ireland.[233] The Scottish equivalent is the Human Tissue (Scotland) Act 2006.

Replacing earlier legislation, the 2004 Act has established a consistent regulatory regime for the use of human tissue, including organs and other body parts taken from a donor (whether living or deceased), for research and other purposes based on the donor's consent. It was passed as a result of public concern following the use without consent of organs taken from deceased children at Bristol Children's Hospital and Alder Hey Children's Hospital in Liverpool.

The following paragraphs summarise the provisions of the three parts of the Act (defined terms are explained at the end of this section).

Removal, storage and use of human organs and other tissue for scheduled purposes

Schedule 1 to the Act lists certain purposes for which activities specified in the Act require consent. These are referred to as the 'scheduled purposes' and are listed in two parts.

Part 1 of Schedule 1 sets out the following purposes as requiring consent:

- anatomical examination;

- determining the cause of death;

- establishing after a person's death the efficacy of any drug or other treatment administered to him or her;

- obtaining scientific or medical information about a living or deceased person which may be relevant to any other person (including a future person);

- public display;

---

232 See www.mrc.ac.uk.
233 See also the Tissues and Cells Directive 2004/23/EC ([2004] OJ L102/48), and the Council of Europe Convention on Human Rights and Biomedicine (ETS 164, 1997), which may be found at http://conventions.coe.int/treaty/en/treaties/html/164.htm.

- research in connection with disorders, or the functioning, of the human body; and

- transplantation.

Part 2 of Schedule 1 sets out the following purposes as requiring consent if the activity relates to deceased persons:

- clinical audit;

- education or training relating to human health;

- performance assessment;

- public health monitoring; and

- quality assurance.

Under the Act, the following activities are lawful if done for a scheduled purpose with appropriate consent:[234]

- the storage of the body of a deceased person (other than for anatomical examination);

- the use of the body of a deceased person (other than for anatomical examination);

- the removal from the body of a deceased person of any relevant material of which the body consists or which it contains;

- the storage for use of any relevant material which has come from a human body; and

- the use of any relevant material which has come from a human body.

The following activity is lawful if done with appropriate consent and after a certificate of the cause of death has been signed:

- the use or storage of the body of a deceased person for anatomical examination.[235]

It is an offence for a person to carry out any of these activities without appropriate consent unless he or she reasonably believes that such consent is in place or that what he or she is doing does not constitute such an activity. The maximum penalty is imprisonment for up to three years and/ or a fine.[236]

---

234 Human Tissue Act 2004, s 1(1).
235 Human Tissue Act 2004, s 1(2)–(3).
236 Human Tissue Act 2004, s 5.

It is also an offence to use or store donated material otherwise than for a scheduled purpose, medical diagnosis or treatment, decent disposal, or a purpose specified in regulations.[237]

Consent is not needed for the storage or use of material from the body of a living person for medical research where the research is ethically approved in accordance with regulations and the researcher is not able to identify the person from whom the material has come.[238] Nor is it needed for the storage or use of material from the body of a living person for a purpose specified in Part 2 of Schedule 1 (see above).[239]

In the case of a child, the person who has parental responsibility for the child may give appropriate consent.[240] In the case of an adult who has died, a person who stood in a qualifying relationship to the adult immediately before the adult died may give appropriate consent,[241] or this may be given by one or more persons appointed by the adult for the purpose of giving consent before he or she died ('nominated representatives').[242] Such an appointment may be made orally or in writing, but in either case must be witnessed.[243] In the case of adults lacking the capacity to give consent, consent may be deemed to be given in certain circumstances.[244]

For storage or use of material for public display or anatomical examination, however, the person concerned (whether an adult or a child) must himself or herself have given consent in writing (which must be witnessed) before they died.[245]

---

237 Human Tissue Act 2004, s 8.
238 Human Tissue Act 2004, s 1(7)–(9); s 1(10)(c). The Human Tissue Act 2004 (Ethical Approval, Exceptions from Licensing and Supply of Information about Transplants) Regulations 2006 (SI 2006/1260) state that research is ethically approved for this purpose where it is approved by a research ethics authority (reg 2), defined as an ethics committee established or recognised in accordance with Pt 2 of the Medicines for Human Use (Clinical Trials) Regulations 2004 (SI 2004/1031), or other committee or person established or appointed for the purpose and recognised by the Secretary of State (reg 1(2)).
239 Human Tissue Act 2004, s 1(10)(a), (b).
240 Human Tissue Act 2004, s 2. Parental responsibility has the same meaning as in the Children Act 1989.
241 Human Tissue Act 2004, s 3. The qualifying relationships are set out in s 27(4), and are ranked in the following order: (a) spouse, civil partner or partner; (b) parent or child; (c) brother or sister; (d) grandparent or grandchild; (e) child of a person falling within para (c); (f) stepfather or stepmother; (g) half-brother or half-sister; (h) friend of longstanding. Consent should be obtained from the person whose relationship to the person concerned is accorded the highest ranking (s 27(6)), provided that he or she is willing and able to deal with the issue of consent and it is reasonably practicable to communicate with him or her within the time available (s 27(8)).
242 Human Tissue Act 2004, s 4.
243 Human Tissue Act 2004, s 4(3)–(5).
244 Human Tissue Act 2004, s 6 and the Human Tissue Act (Persons who Lack Capacity to Consent and Transplants) Regulations 2006 (SI 2006/1659).
245 Human Tissue Act 2004, ss 2(4–6), 3(3)–(5). Public display does not include display for the purpose of enabling people to pay their final respects to the deceased or display incidental to the deceased's funeral (s 54(5)).

Where it is desirable in the interests of another person to use relevant material from a living person in order to obtain scientific or medical information about the donor, the Human Tissue Authority may dispense with the need for consent if the donor cannot be traced or does not respond to reasonable efforts to get him or her to decide whether to consent.[246]

None of the above provisions applies to anything done for purposes of the functions of a coroner or under the authority of a coroner.[247]

Regulation of activities involving human tissue

Activities involving human tissue are regulated by the Human Tissue Authority (HTA), which issues codes of practice relating to activities within its remit.[248] The following activities require a licence from the HTA (unless relating to the body of a person who has been dead for 100 years or longer):[249]

- anatomical examination;

- post-mortem examination;

- removal of relevant material from the body of a deceased person for use other than transplantation;

- storage of an anatomical specimen;

- storage of the body of a deceased person or relevant material from a human body for a scheduled purpose; and

- public display of the body of a deceased person or relevant material from the body of a deceased person.

It is an offence for a person to carry out any of these activities without a licence unless he or she reasonably believes that no licence is required or that a licence is in place. The maximum penalty is imprisonment for up to three years and/or a fine.[250]

A licence applies to the individual designated in that licence, other persons notified to the HTA by that individual, and anyone acting under his, her or their direction.[251] The designated individual has a duty to secure that the persons to whom the licence applies and the practices used to carry out the

---

246 Human Tissue Act 2004, s 8.
247 Human Tissue Act 2004, s 11.
248 Human Tissue Act 2004, ss 13–15 and Sch 2. Current codes of practice relate to (1) consent; (2) donation of solid organs for transplantation; (3) post-mortem examination; (4) anatomical examination; (5) disposal of human tissue; (6) donation of allogeneic bone marrow and peripheral blood stem cells for transplantation; (7) public display; (8) import and export of human bodies, body parts and tissue; (9) research.
249 Human Tissue Act 2004, s 16.
250 Human Tissue Act 2004, s 25.
251 Human Tissue Act 2004, s 17.

activity are suitable, and that the conditions of the licence are complied with.[252] The HTA may issue directions in relation to the conduct of an activity authorised by licences generally, licences of a particular description or a particular licence.[253] In carrying out a licensed activity, a person must comply with any applicable requirements imposed by directions.[254]

There is a procedure for appeal if an application for the grant, revocation or variation of a licence is refused.[255]

The Act prohibits the possession of an anatomical specimen away from licensed premises without authorisation,[256] and commercial dealings in human material for transplantation.[257] Removal of transplantable material from the body of a living person for transplantation and using any such material for transplantation are forbidden unless the HTA is satisfied that no reward has been or is to be given and the conditions specified in regulations are satisfied.[258] The requirement to hold a licence does not apply to anything done for purposes relating to the prevention or detection of crime or the conduct of a prosecution,[259] nor to the public display of religious relics at a place of public worship.[260]

Miscellaneous and general

There are provisions enabling a person managing a hospital, nursing home or other institution to preserve part of a body that may be suitable for use for transplantation, to retain the body for that purpose,[261] and to treat as waste surplus material coming from a person's body in the course of his or her receiving medical treatment, undergoing diagnostic testing or participating in research.[262]

It is an offence to have any bodily material with the intention of analysing any human DNA in it without qualifying consent and otherwise than for an excepted purpose; this does not apply to material from a person who has been dead for more than 100 years or from an embryo outside the human

---

252 Human Tissue Act 2004, s 18.
253 Human Tissue Act 2004, s 23(1), (2).
254 Human Tissue Act 2004, s 23(3).
255 Human Tissue Act 2004, ss 19–22.
256 Human Tissue Act 2004, ss 30–31.
257 Human Tissue Act 2004, s 32.
258 Human Tissue Act 2004, ss 33–34. See also the Human Tissue Act 2004 (Persons who Lack Capacity to Consent and Transplants) Regulations 2006 (SI 2006/1659), and the Human Tissue Act 2004 (Ethical Approval, Exceptions from Licensing and Supply of Information about Transplants) Regulations 2006 (SI 2006/1260).
259 Human Tissue Act 2004, s 39.
260 Human Tissue Act 2004, s 40.
261 Human Tissue Act 2004, s 43.
262 Human Tissue Act 2004, s 44.

body.[263] As well as the medical diagnosis or treatment of the person whose body manufactured the DNA,[264] the excepted purposes include research in connection with disorders or functioning of the human body if the bodily material concerned is the subject of an order of the High Court;[265] in the case of existing holdings, such research is an excepted purpose if the material is from a living person, the research is ethically approved in accordance with regulations, and the analyst cannot identify the individual from whose body the material has come.[266]

The trustees of certain national museums may, if they consider it appropriate, transfer from their collections any human remains of a person who they believe died less than 1,000 years before 3 October 2005.[267]

A person duly authorised by the HTA may inspect records kept under the Act and enter and inspect licensed premises.[268] The HTA can apply to a justice of the peace for a warrant to enter and search any premises if there are reasonable grounds for believing that an offence under the Act is being or has been committed there.[269] A duly authorised person can seize anything found in the course of an inspection or search which may be required for the HTA's functions relating to licensing or to use as evidence.[270]

When an offence under the Act is committed by a body corporate with the consent or connivance of any director, manager, secretary or similar officer, or is attributable to any neglect on the part of such a person, that person, as well as the body corporate, is liable for the offence and may be proceeded against and punished accordingly.[271]

Data protection

The Data Protection Act 1998 is also relevant to the use of human tissue for research, as scientists will need to have access to the patient data associated with the tissue they are using.[272] Also relevant are the Human Rights Act 1998 and the law of confidentiality, as well as the tort of the misuse of private information.

---

263 Human Tissue Act 2004, s 45 and Sch 4.
264 Human Tissue Act 2004, Sch 4, para 5(1)(a).
265 Human Tissue Act 2004, Sch 4, para 6.
266 Human Tissue Act 2004, Sch 4, para 10. Other excepted purposes include the functions of a coroner or procurator fiscal; the prevention or detection of crime; the conduct of a prosecution; national security; and implementing an order or direction of a court or tribunal (Sch 4, para 5(1)); see Sch 4 generally.
267 Human Tissue Act 2004, s 47.
268 Human Tissue Act 2004, s 48 and Sch 5, paras 1, 2.
269 Human Tissue Act 2004, Sch 5, paras 3, 4.
270 Human Tissue Act 2004, Sch 5, para 5.
271 Human Tissue Act 2004, s 49.
272 See 'Data protection' above.

Some defined terms used in the Human Tissue Act 2004

Adult	A person who has attained the age of 18 years
Anatomical examination	Macroscopic examination by dissection for anatomical purposes, which are purposes of teaching or studying, or researching into, the gross structure of the human body.
Child	A person who has not attained the age of 18 years.
Donated material	The donated body of a deceased person, or donated relevant material that has come from a human body.
Material from the body of a deceased person	Material from the body of a person not alive at the point of separation (s 54(2)(a)).
Material from the body of a living person	Material from the body of a person alive at the point of separation.
Relevant material	Material, other than gametes, which consists of or includes human cells, but not embryos outside the human body or hair and nail from the body of a living person.

Human reproductive technology

Human reproductive technologies are regulated by the Human Fertilisation and Embryology Act 1990, as amended by the Human Fertilisation and Embryology Act 2008. The 2008 Act, which followed a review of the 1990 Act, updated the 1990 Act to reflect scientific developments, in particular new ways of creating embryos, and social developments, in particular same-sex partnerships.[273]

As amended, the 1990 Act now regulates all live human embryos outside the body, however created, and all live human gametes; it also regulates embryos created for research purposes from a combination of human and animal genetic material ('human admixed embryos').

The amended Act makes the sex selection of offspring illegal, except for medical reasons; enables same-sex couples to be recognised as the legal parents of children conceived by means of donated sperm, eggs or embryos; replaces the reference to 'the need for a father' in the 1990 Act as originally enacted with 'the need for supportive parenting'; and facilitates follow-up research of infertility treatment by opening up the register of information relating to such treatment.

The main provisions of the amended Act as they affect scientific research are as follows (defined terms are explained at the end of this section).

---

273 The provisions amending the 1990 Act came into force on 1 October 2009.

Activities governed by the Act

The following activities are forbidden by the Act:

- placing in a woman an embryo other than a permitted embryo, or any gametes other than permitted eggs or permitted sperm;[274]

- using female germ cells (ie cells of the female germ line at any stage of maturity, including eggs) taken or derived from a foetus for the purpose of providing fertility services;[275] and

- placing in a woman a human admixed embryo, any other embryo that is not a human embryo or any gametes other than human gametes.[276]

Under the Act, the following activities may be carried out only in pursuance of a licence:

- bringing about the creation of an embryo;[277]

- keeping or using any embryo;[278]

- storing any gametes;[279]

- placing sperm and eggs in any woman in any circumstances specified in regulations;[280] and

- mixing human gametes with animal gametes, bringing about the creation of a new human admixed embryo, or keeping or using a human admixed embryo.[281]

The following activities may be carried out only in pursuance of a licence or a third-party agreement:[282]

- keeping or using, without storage, an embryo intended for human application;[283]

- procuring or distributing an embryo intended for human application;[284] and

---

274 Human Fertilisation and Embryology Act 1990, ss 3(2), 3(ZA). See below for the definition of what is permitted.
275 Human Fertilisation and Embryology Act 1990, s 3A.
276 Human Fertilisation and Embryology Act 1990, s 4A(1).
277 Human Fertilisation and Embryology Act 1990, s 3(1).
278 Human Fertilisation and Embryology Act 1990, s 3(1A)(a).
279 Human Fertilisation and Embryology Act 1990, s 4(1)(a).
280 Human Fertilisation and Embryology Act 1990, s 4(3).
281 Human Fertilisation and Embryology Act 1990, s 4A(2).
282 A third-party agreement is defined in s 2A: it refers to an agreement between the holder of a licence under the Act and another person who '(a) procures, tests or processes gametes or embryos (or both), on behalf of the holder of the licence, or (b) supplies to the holder of the licence any goods or services (including distribution services) which may affect the quality or safety of gametes or embryos'.
283 Human Fertilisation and Embryology Act 1990, s 3(1A)(b).
284 Human Fertilisation and Embryology Act 1990, s 3(1), (1A), (1B).

- procuring, testing, processing or distributing any gametes intended for human application.[285]

The Human Fertilisation and Embryology Authority and licences

Licences are issued by the Human Fertilisation and Embryology Authority (HFEA).[286] The HFEA grants separate licences in respect of treatment, fertility, storage and research activities, each of which is subject to various conditions, including consent requirements.[287] All parties concerned share control of gametes and embryos. The HFEA may also issue directions and must maintain a code of practice giving guidance about the proper conduct of activities carried on in pursuance of a licence.[288]

Storage licences are subject to conditions prohibiting storage of gametes and embryos beyond the statutory storage period, although the terms of a donor's consent may shorten such period.[289]

Research licences may not authorise any activity unless the HFEA believes it is necessary or desirable for one of a number of principal purposes, as follows:

- increasing knowledge about serious disease or other serious medical conditions;

- developing treatments for serious disease or other serious medical conditions;

- increasing knowledge about the causes of any congenital disease or congenital medical condition that does not fall within the first bullet point above;

- promoting advances in the treatment of infertility;

- increasing knowledge about the causes of miscarriage;

- developing more effective techniques of contraception;

- developing methods for detecting the presence of gene, chromosome or mitochondrion abnormalities in embryos before implantation; or

- increasing knowledge about the development of embryos.[290]

285 Human Fertilisation and Embryology Act 1990, s 4(1), (1A).
286 Human Fertilisation and Embryology Act 1990, ss 5–9 and Sch 1. See www.hfea.gov.uk.
287 Human Fertilisation and Embryology Act 1990, ss 11–21 and Sch 2. On consent, see Sch 3.
288 Human Fertilisation and Embryology Act 1990, ss 23–26. The current code of practice is the eighth edition (2009): see www.hfea.gov.uk/code.html.
289 Human Fertilisation and Embryology Act 1990, s 14. The statutory storage period for gametes and embryos is ten years (s 14(3)–(4A)).
290 Human Fertilisation and Embryology Act 1990, Sch 2, para 3A.

Information

The HFEA keeps a register containing information relating to treatment services to an identifiable individual, the procurement or distribution of sperm other than that donated by a partner, and the keeping of gametes and embryos and their use.[291] It also keeps a register of licences and a register of serious adverse events and serious adverse reactions.[292] There are restrictions on disclosure of protected information, but such information may be disclosed for the purposes of medical or other research, where so permitted by regulations, or in the interests of justice.[293]

Offences

It is an offence punishable by a fine and/or imprisonment for up to ten years to keep or use an embryo in any circumstances prohibited by regulations.[294] Keeping or using gametes in contravention of the 1990 Act is an offence punishable by a fine and/or imprisonment for up to two years.[295] There is a defence of due diligence.[296] The HFEA has powers of inspection, entry, search and seizure.[297]

No money or other benefit may be given or received for the supply of gametes or embryos unless authorised by directions issued by the HFEA.[298]

Some defined terms used in the 1990 Act as amended[299]

Permitted egg	A permitted egg is one (a) which has been produced by or extracted from the ovaries of a woman, and (b) whose nuclear or mitochondrial DNA has not been altered.
Permitted sperm	Permitted sperm are sperm (a) which have been produced by or extracted from the testes of a man, and (b) whose nuclear or mitochondrial DNA has not been altered.
Permitted embryo	An embryo is a permitted embryo if (a) it has been created by the fertilisation of a permitted egg by permitted sperm, (b) no nuclear or mitochondrial DNA of any cell of the embryo has been altered, and (c) no cell has been added to it other than by division of the embryo's own cells.

291 Human Fertilisation and Embryology Act 1990, ss 31–31ZG.
292 Human Fertilisation and Embryology Act 1990, ss 31A, 31B.
293 Human Fertilisation and Embryology Act 1990, ss 33–35.
294 Human Fertilisation and Embryology Act 1990, s 41(1).
295 Human Fertilisation and Embryology Act 1990, ss 41(2)–(4).
296 Human Fertilisation and Embryology Act 1990, s 41(11).
297 Human Fertilisation and Embryology Act 1990, Sch 3B.
298 Human Fertilisation and Embryology Act 1990, ss 12(1)(e), 23.
299 For the definition of permitted eggs, sperm and embryos, see the Human Fertilisation and Embryology Act 1990, s 3ZA; for the definition of human admixed embryo, see s 4A(6).

Human admixed embryo

(a) An embryo created by replacing the nucleus of an animal egg or of an animal cell, or two animal pronuclei, with:

    (i) two human pronuclei,

    (ii) one nucleus of a human gamete or of any other human cell; or

    (iii) one human gamete or other human cell.

(b) Any other embryo created by using:

    (i) human gametes and animal gametes; or

    (ii) one human pronucleus and one animal pronucleus.

(c) A human embryo that has been altered by the introduction of any sequence of nuclear or mitochondrial DNA of an animal into one or more cells of the embryo.

(d) A human embryo that has been altered by the introduction of one or more animal cells. Or:

(e) Any embryo not falling within paragraphs (a)–(d) which contains both nuclear or mitochondrial DNA of a human and nuclear or mitochondrial DNA of an animal ('animal DNA') but in which the animal DNA is not predominant.

Clinical trials

The Declaration of Helsinki

The most widely accepted ethical guidance concerning medical research involving human subjects is found in the Declaration of Helsinki, originally issued by the World Medical Association (WMA) in 1964.[300] The Declaration has been subject to numerous revisions; the current version is that adopted in 2008.[301] Some of the fundamental principles enshrined in the Declaration are as follows:

- It is the duty of the physician to promote and safeguard the health of patients, including those who are involved in medical research. The physician's knowledge and conscience are dedicated to the fulfilment of this duty. (Paragraph 3)

- In medical research involving human subjects, the well-being of the individual research subject must take precedence over all other interests. (Paragraph 6)

- Physicians should consider the ethical, legal and regulatory norms and standards for research involving human subjects in their own countries

---

300 See www.wma.net.
301 *World Medical Association Declaration of Helsinki: Ethical Principles for Medical Research Involving Human Subjects*, last amended by the 59th WMA General Assembly, Seoul, 22 October 2008. See www.wma.net/en/30publications/10policies/b3/index.html.

as well as applicable international norms and standards. No national or international ethical, legal or regulatory requirement should reduce or eliminate any of the protections for research subjects set forth in the Declaration. (Paragraph 10)

- The design and performance of each research study involving human subjects must be clearly described in a research protocol. The protocol should contain a statement of the ethical considerations involved and should indicate how the principles in this Declaration have been addressed. (Paragraph 14)

- The research protocol must be submitted for consideration, comment, guidance and approval to a research ethics committee before the study begins. This committee must be independent of the researcher, the sponsor and any other undue influence. (Paragraph 15)

- Every medical research study involving human subjects must be preceded by careful assessment of predictable risks and burdens to the individuals and communities involved in the research in comparison with foreseeable benefits to them and to other individuals or communities affected by the condition under investigation. (Paragraph 18)

- Medical research involving human subjects may only be conducted if the importance of the objective outweighs the inherent risks and burdens to the research subjects. (Paragraph 21)

- Participation by competent individuals as subjects in medical research must be voluntary. Although it may be appropriate to consult family members or community leaders, no competent individual may be enrolled in a research study unless he or she freely agrees. (Paragraph 22)

- In medical research involving competent human subjects, each potential subject must be adequately informed of the aims, methods, sources of funding, any possible conflicts of interest, institutional affiliations of the researcher, the anticipated benefits and potential risks of the study and the discomfort it may entail, and any other relevant aspects of the study. The potential subject must be informed of the right to refuse to participate in the study or to withdraw consent to participate at any time without reprisal. Special attention should be given to the specific information needs of individual potential subjects as well as to the methods used to deliver the information. After ensuring that the potential subject has understood the information, the physician or another appropriately qualified individual must then seek the potential subject's freely given informed consent, preferably in writing. If the consent cannot be expressed in writing, the non-written consent must be formally documented and witnessed. (Paragraph 24)

Although the Declaration does not itself have legal force, its principles are widely accepted. In Europe, those principles are reflected in the Clinical Trials

556

Directive,[302] and the Good Clinical Practice Directive requires that clinical trials should be carried out in accordance with the Declaration.[303] These Directives and the legislation transposing them into UK law are considered in more detail below.

It should be noted, however, that one principle set out in the current version of the Declaration has not been universally accepted. Paragraph 32 states that the benefits, risks, burdens and effectiveness of a new intervention must be tested against those of the best current proven intervention, except where no current proven intervention exists or where necessary for compelling and scientifically sound methodological reasons and the patients receiving the placebo are not subject to any risk of serious or irreversible harm. Earlier versions of the Declaration, before 2000, did not limit the use of placebos to studies where no current proven intervention exists. Both the Clinical Trials Directive and national legislation in the UK, among other countries, refer expressly to the Declaration of Helsinki as amended up to 1996, in which the use of placebo-controlled trials is less restricted.[304]

The Clinical Trials Directive

The Clinical Trials Directive harmonised the law among member states on the conduct of clinical trials and ensured that all such trials follow good clinical practice.[305] It requires that all clinical trials are designed, conducted and reported in accordance with the principles of good clinical practice,[306] and that all medicines used in a clinical trial should be subject to the principles of good manufacturing practice.[307] Many clinical trials take place not only

---

302 Directive 2001/20/EC ([2001] OJ L121/34) on the approximation of the laws, regulations and administrative provisions of the member states relating to the implementing of good clinical practice in the conduct of clinical trials on medicinal products for human use; see also Directive 2001/83/EC ([2001] OJ L311/67) on the Community code relating to medicinal products for human use (the Medicinal Products Directive).

303 Commission Directive 2005/28 EC ([2005] OJ L91/13) laying down principles and detailed guidelines for good clinical practice as regards investigational medicinal products for human use, as well as the requirements for authorisation of the manufacturing or importation of such products.

304 Medicines for Human Use (Clinical Trials) Regulations 2004 (SI 2004/1031), Sch 1, Pt 1, para 2.

305 The Clinical Trials Directive contains a significant number of definitions of terms which are also employed in the Clinical Trials Regulations. These are reproduced at the end of this section so as not to burden the outline of the provisions with excessive footnotes.

The MHRA has produced a *Description of the Medicines for Human Use (Clinical Trials) Regulations 2004*, which (along with other guidance) can be downloaded from www.mhra.gov.uk/howweregulate/medicines/licensingofmedicines/clinicaltrials/legislation andguidancedocuments/index.htm.

306 Clinical Trials Directive, Art 1(4); see the Good Clinical Practice Directive, which was transposed into English law by way of amendment of the Clinical Trials Regulations by the Medicines for Human Use (Clinical Trials) Amendment Regulations 2006 (SI 2006/1928).

307 Clinical Trials Directive, Recital 12. Medicines used in clinical trials are described as 'investigational medicinal products': see definition at the end of this section.

at several trial sites but also across several countries: the Clinical Trials Directive makes uniform the requirements relating to such multi-centre and multi-territory clinical trials, and enables the EC to co-ordinate information relating to such trials and to control them.

The Clinical Trials Regulations

The Clinical Trials Directive was transposed into UK law by the Medicines for Human Use (Clinical Trials) Regulations 2004 ('Clinical Trials Regulations'). This brought about a significant change in the regulation of clinical trials in the UK from what had previously been in place. The old regime, governed by the Medicines Act 1968, did not apply to Phase I clinical trials and did not require approval of a proposed trial by an ethics committee. The Clinical Trials Regulations, on the other hand, apply to all clinical trials involving 'medicinal products',[308] whether sponsored by industry, government, research council, charity or university and whether commercial or non-commercial.[309] This section outlines the main provisions of the Regulations.

Before a clinical trial can take place, two conditions must be fulfilled. First, the foreseeable risks and inconveniences of the trial must be weighed against the anticipated benefit for the individual trial subject and other present and future patients.[310] Secondly, both an ethics committee and the MHRA must come to a conclusion that the anticipated therapeutic and public health benefits justify the risks – a requirement that must be permanently monitored during the continuance of the trial.[311]

Ethics committees and opinions

The United Kingdom Ethics Committees Authority (UKECA) is responsible for establishing and recognising ethics committees.[312] Provisions relating to the membership, chairmen, sub-committees, meetings, procedures, deputies, co-opted members, staff, premises, facilities, expenses, annual report and transfer of functions of ethics committees are set out in Schedule 2 to the Clinical Trials Regulations.

---

308 See definition at the end of this section.
309 Non-commercial clinical trials are those conducted by academics without the participation of the pharmaceutical industry.
310 Clinical Trials Regulations, Sch 1, Pt 2, para 10. For minors and adults not able to give informed consent there are additional requirements and restrictions set out in Pts 4, 5 of Sch 1.
311 Clinical Trials Regulations, Sch 1, Pt 2, para 12.
312 Clinical Trials Regulations, regs 5–10. Its members are the Secretary of State for Health, the National Assembly for Wales, the Scottish Ministers and the Department of Health, Social Services and Public Safety for Northern Ireland; its functions may, by agreement, be performed by only one of them.

The work of ethics committees is co-ordinated by the National Research Ethics Service, which, among other functions, provides ethical guidance and management support to ethics committees.[313] It publishes Standard Operating Procedures which ethics committees must follow.[314] Ethics committees are divided into three categories, according to the type of clinical trial for which they are recognised to give an opinion:

- *Type 1 ethics committees* deal with Phase 1 clinical trials in healthy volunteers taking place anywhere in the UK;

- *Type 2 ethics committees* deal with clinical trials in patients taking place in one NHS domain only; and

- *Type 3 ethics committees* deal with clinical trials in patients taking place anywhere in the UK.[315]

As well as their statutory functions under the Clinical Trials Regulations, ethics committees also fulfil the Department of Health's policy that all research (not just clinical trials of investigational medicinal products) involving NHS patients, service users, care professionals or volunteers, or their organs, tissue, or data, is reviewed independently to ensure it meets ethical standards.[316] While only an ethics committee that has been recognised by the UKECA may review a clinical trial, however, research that does not constitute a clinical trial may be reviewed by any ethics committee that has been authorised to do so.[317]

An application for an ethics committee opinion must be made by the chief investigator of the trial in question.[318] The particulars and documents that must accompany the application are set out in Part 1 of Schedule 3 to the Clinical Trials Regulations. The ethics committee must give its opinion in relation to the trial within a specified period (see below).[319] If so requested, the ethics committee must give an opinion on any relevant issue relating to the trial.[320]

313 The NRES is a division of the National Patient Safety Agency, an agency of the Department of Health.

314 See www.nres.npsa.nhs.uk/news-and-publications/publications/standard-operating-procedures.

315 *Standard Operating Procedures for Research Ethics Committees*, version 4.0 (NRES, April 2009), p 29.

316 *Research Governance Framework for Health and Social Care* (2nd edn, Department of Health, 2005), p 7: see www.dh.gov.uk/en/publicationsandstatistics/publications/publicationspolicy andguidance/dh_4108962. See also *Governance Arrangements for Research Ethics Committees* (Department of Health, 2001): see www.dh.gov.uk/en/publicationsandstatistics/ publications/publicationspolicyandguidance/dh_4005727.

317 *Standard Operating Procedures for Research Ethics Committees*, p 6.

318 Clinical Trial Regulations, reg 14(1).

319 Clinical Trials Regulations, reg 15(1).

320 Clinical Trials Regulations, reg 15(8).

In preparing its opinion, the ethics committee must consider, in particular, the following matters:[321]

- the relevance of the trial and its design;

- whether the evaluation of the anticipated benefits and risks is satisfactory and whether the conclusions are justified;[322]

- the protocol;

- the suitability of the investigator and the supporting staff;

- the investigator's brochure or, where the investigational medicinal product has a marketing authorisation and the product is to be used in accordance with the terms of that authorisation, the summary of product characteristics relating to that product;

- the quality of the facilities for the trial;

- the adequacy and completeness of the written information to be given, and the procedure to be followed, for the purpose of obtaining informed consent to the subject's participation in the trial;

- if the subjects are to include minors or persons incapable of giving informed consent, whether the research is justified and the justification for the research on persons incapable of giving informed consent;[323]

- provision for indemnity or compensation in the event of injury or death attributable to a clinical trial;

- any insurance or indemnity to cover the liability of the investigator and sponsor;

- the amounts, and, where appropriate, the arrangements for rewarding or compensating investigators and trial subjects;

- the terms of any agreement between the sponsor and the owner or occupier of the trial site which are relevant to those arrangements;[324] and

- the arrangements for the recruitment of subjects.

---

321 Clinical Trials Regulations, reg 15(5).
322 As required under the Regulations, Sch 1, Pt 2, para 10: see above [*paragraph on requirements to be met before a clinical trial commences*].
323 Having regard to the conditions specified in Pt 4 and Pt 5 respectively of Sch 1: see 'Pre-clinical phase: identification and validation of target' above.
324 In the UK, pharmaceutical companies normally offer compensation via the Association of the British Pharmaceutical Industry's standard form of indemnity for clinical studies. Universities may take up clinical trials insurance. The NHS may make an ex-gratia payment where harm is caused without its negligence.

The ethics committee has 60 days to give a reasoned opinion from the date it receives a valid application from an applicant.[325] This period can be modified, extended or disregarded in the following circumstances:

- The ethics committee can make one request for further information to that received from the applicant. The 60-day limit is suspended until it receives the further information.[326]

- If the clinical trial involves a medicinal product for gene therapy or somatic therapy, or a medicinal product containing a genetically modified organism, the ethics committee has 90 days to give its opinion, or 180 days if it is necessary to consult a specialist group or committee.[327]

- For xenogenic cell therapy there is no time limit for authorisation.[328]

If a clinical trial is to be carried out at several trial sites in one country, then only one ethics committee opinion need be given.[329] If a clinical trial is to be carried out simultaneously in several member states, each member state should provide one opinion for that trial.[330] There is a procedure for appeal against an unfavourable decision by an ethics committee.[331]

Authorisation by the MHRA

As well as receiving a favourable opinion from an ethics committee, a proposed trial must also be authorised by the MHRA.[332]

Responsibility for making a request for authorisation to the MHRA to conduct a clinical trial lies with the sponsor.[333] Among the information that must be included in a request for authorisation are the following:[334]

- the name and address of the sponsor and any other person fulfilling any of the sponsor's responsibilities;

---

325 Longer periods are allowed in the case of clinical trials involving a medicinal product for gene therapy or somatic therapy or a medicinal product containing a genetically modified organism (reg 15(10)).
326 Clinical Trials Regulations, reg 15(2), (3).
327 Clinical Trials Regulations, reg 15(10).
328 Clinical Trials Regulations, reg 19(9); Clinical Trials Directive, Art 6(7).
329 Clinical Trials Regulations, reg 14(2).
330 Clinical Trials Directive, Art 7.
331 Clinical Trials Regulations, reg 16 and Sch 4.
332 The MHRA is the 'competent authority' for the purposes of the Clinical Trials Directive and the Good Clinical Practice Directive (reg 4). The MHRA and ethics committee may disclose to each other any information acquired in carrying out their functions under the Clinical Trials Regulations (reg 27A).
333 Clinical Trials Regulations, reg 17. The sponsor is the person who takes responsibility for the initiation, management and financing of the trial (reg 3); the sponsor is also responsible for the investigator's brochure (reg 3A).
334 Clinical Trials Regulations, Sch 3, Pt 2.

- the address of each trial site and the name and address of the investigator responsible for the conduct of the trial at each site;

- a copy of the ethics committee opinion in relation to that trial, if available;

- a description of any investigational medicinal product to be used in the trial;

- the name and address of the person responsible for the manufacture or importation of any finished investigational medicinal product to be used in the trial and the details of their authorisation;

- the address where any batch of finished investigational medicinal products to be used in the trial has been, or is to be, checked for conformity with GMP;

- a description of the proposed trial;

- the protocol for the proposed trial;

- a dossier on each investigational medicinal product to be used in the trial containing the particulars set out in the Clinical Trials Regulations, Sch 3, Pt 2, para 11; and

- a description or sample of the labelling which is to appear on each investigational medicinal product when supplied to a subject in the trial.

The number assigned to the trial by the European clinical trials database (EudraCT) should also be included.[335]

If the MHRA establishes grounds for non-acceptance of the application, the sponsor gets one chance to amend his or her application. If the sponsor does not do so, then the application will be rejected and the sponsor will not be able to start the clinical trial.[336] The sponsor has the right of appeal to the Commission on Human Medicines or other appropriate committee.[337]

General medicinal products: 60-day applications. The MHRA has up to 30 days to consider applications from sponsors. If within that period the MHRA gives notice to the sponsor that it accepts the application, or gives no notice to the sponsor, the trial is to be treated as authorised. Alternatively, the MHRA may reject the application (setting out its grounds for so doing), or accept it subject to specified conditions.[338]

If the application is refused, or accepted subject to conditions, the sponsor may submit an amended request for further consideration within 14 days. The

---

335 See 'EudraCT: a European database of clinical trials' below.
336 Clinical Trials Regulations, reg 18.
337 Clinical Trials Regulations, reg 26 and Sch 5.
338 Clinical Trials Regulations, reg 18(2)–(4).

MHRA must determine the amended request within 60 days of the original application.[339]

Medicinal products for gene or somatic cell therapy: 90-day applications. If the clinical trial involves medicinal products for gene therapy or somatic cell therapy, or medicinal products containing genetically modified organisms, the 60-day period is extended to 90 days.[340]

Medicinal products for xenogenic cell therapy: no-time-limit applications. There is no time limit for the MHRA's authorisation of a trial involving a medicinal product for xenogenic cell therapy.[341]

Notification to the sponsor. If the sponsor has not heard from the MHRA by the end of the 30-day period, then the sponsor can begin the trial except as provided in the following paragraphs.

The MHRA may, within seven days of receiving an application for a trial, inform the sponsor that written authorisation for that trial is required, if the proposed trial involves medicinal products which do not have a marketing authorisation, or which have an active ingredient that is a biological product of human or animal origin, or contain biological components of human or animal origin, or the manufacturing of which requires such components.[342]

Written authorisation from the MHRA is always required before the commencement of a clinical trial involving medicinal products for gene therapy and somatic cell therapy, including xenogenic cell therapy, or medicinal products containing genetically modified organisms.[343]

If the clinical trial is to be conducted partly in a non-EEA country as well as in the UK, the MHRA may require an undertaking by the sponsor or the owner of the premises where the trial is to be conducted permitting inspection by the MHRA to establish that the conditions and principles of good clinical practice are adhered to.[344]

Amendment of the conduct of the clinical trial

Either the sponsor or the MHRA may amend the trial authorisation after the commencement of the trial.[345] The MHRA may amend the authorisation by giving at least 14 days' notice to the sponsor, if it believes such amendment to

---

339 Clinical Trials Regulations, reg 18(5)–(8).
340 Clinical Trials Regulations, reg 19. The period can also be extended for a further 90 days if it is necessary to consult a relevant committee.
341 Clinical Trials Regulations, reg 19(9).
342 Clinical Trials Regulations, reg 20.
343 Clinical Trials Regulations, reg 19.
344 Clinical Trials Regulations, reg 21.
345 Clinical Trials Regulations, reg 22.

be necessary to ensure the safety or scientific validity of the trial or adherence to the conditions and principles of good clinical practice.[346] The sponsor may make representations to the MHRA within the 14-day notice period.[347]

The sponsor may make a non-substantial amendment to the trial authorisation at any time, but the procedure set down in the Regulations must be followed if the amendment is substantial.[348] A substantial amendment is one which is likely to affect to a significant degree:

- the safety or physical or mental integrity of the subjects of the trial;

- the scientific value of the trial;

- the conduct or management of the trial;

- the quality or safety of any investigational medicinal product used in the trial.[349]

If the amendment consists of or includes an amendment to the request for authorisation of the trial, or to the particulars or documents that accompanied that request, the sponsor must notify the MHRA. If it consists of or includes an amendment to the terms of an application for an ethics committee opinion, the sponsor must notify the ethics committee.[350]

The sponsor must notify the MHRA and/or the ethics committee of the reasons for, and the content of, the amendment.[351] The MHRA may, within 35 days of receiving the notice of amendment, notify the sponsor of its grounds for not accepting the proposed amendment or of its acceptance of the amendment subject to any specified conditions. Hence if the sponsor has received no response within 35 days the sponsor may make the amendment.[352]

In the case of a notice of amendment to an ethics committee, the ethics committee must give its opinion of the amendment to the sponsor within 35 days of receiving the notice of amendment. Hence the sponsor may make the amendment only if the ethics committee has given a favourable opinion.[353]

If there are grounds for non-acceptance the sponsor has the choice of either amending the proposed amendment to take account of the grounds for non-acceptance or withdrawing the proposed amendment.[354] There is provision

---

346 Clinical Trials Regulations, reg 23(1), (2).
347 Clinical Trials Regulations, reg 23(3).
348 Clinical Trials Regulations, reg 24(1).
349 Clinical Trials Regulations, reg 11.
350 Clinical Trials Regulations, reg 24.
351 Clinical Trials Regulations, Sch 3, Pt 3.
352 Clinical Trials Regulations, reg 24 (5), (7).
353 Clinical Trials Regulations, reg 24(6), (9).
354 Clinical Trials Regulations, reg 25.

of appeal by the sponsor to the Commission for Human Medicines or other appropriate committee if the MHRA declines to accept an amendment proposed by the sponsor or imposes an amendment that the sponsor does not accept.[355]

The end of a clinical trial

The sponsor is required to inform the competent authority and the ethics committee within 90 days of the end of the clinical trial. If the clinical trial has ended early for any reason, the period for notification is reduced to 15 days. The reasons for the early termination must be stated.[356]

EudraCT: a European database of clinical trials

Each member state is to enter certain details of clinical trials taking place in its territory into a European database known as EudraCT. The details required to be entered are as follows:[357]

- extracts from the request for authorisation;

- any amendments made to the request for authorisation;

- any amendments made to the protocol (after the start of the clinical trial);

- the favourable opinion of the ethics committee; and

- the declaration at the end of the clinical trial.

The database is accessible only to the competent authorities in each member state, the European Commission and the EMEA.

The MHRA may be requested by the UK government, the EC or the EMEA to provide further information on a clinical trial in addition to the items described immediately above.[358]

Good clinical practice

The ICH guidelines and their implementation

Good clinical practice (GCP) is an international ethical and scientific quality standard for designing, conducting, recording and reporting clinical trials that involve the participation of human subjects. Compliance with this standard provides public assurance that the rights, safety and well-being

---

355 Clinical Trials Regulations, reg 26 and Sch 5.
356 Clinical Trials Regulations, reg 27 and Sch 3, Pt 4.
357 Clinical Trials Directive, Arts 11(1)(a)–(e).
358 Clinical Trials Directive, Art 11(2).

of trial subjects are protected, consistent with the principles that have their origin in the Declaration of Helsinki, and that the trial data collected are credible.

The International Conference on Harmonisation of Technical Requirements for Registration of Pharmaceuticals for Human Use (ICH) introduced guidelines for good clinical practice in 1996 for the registration of pharmaceuticals for human use.[359] Regulatory authorities and industry experts from the United States, Europe and Japan produced these guidelines in order to harmonise the way in which these three regions conduct testing procedures and determine technical requirements for new products.

Good clinical practice for the EU has been interpreted in the Good Clinical Practice Directive,[360] which is broadly in line with the ICH guidelines, and the Clinical Trials Directive. It has been implemented in the UK by the Clinical Trials Regulations.[361]

The Good Clinical Practice Directive

The current standard for good clinical practice in the EU is the Good Clinical Practice Directive. Article 2 of the Directive summarises the principles of good clinical practice as follows:[362]

- The rights, safety and well-being of the trial subjects shall prevail over the interests of science and society.

- Each individual involved in conducting a trial shall be qualified by education, training, and experience to perform his or her tasks.

- Clinical trials shall be scientifically sound and guided by ethical principles in all their aspects.

- The necessary procedures to secure the quality of every aspect of the trials shall be complied with.

The Directive requires that clinical trials be conducted in accordance with the 1996 version of the Declaration of Helsinki,[363] and that:

---

359 The ICH's website is at www.ich.org. For the *ICH Harmonised Tripartite Guideline for Good Clinical Practice* (ICH, 1996), see www.ich.org/lob/media/media482.pdf.

360 Commission Directive 2005/28/EC ([2005] OJ L91/13) laying down principles and detailed guidelines for good clinical practice as regards investigational medicinal products for human use, as well as the requirements for authorisation of the manufacturing or importation of such products.

361 SI 2004/1031, as amended by the Medicines for Human Use (Clinical Trials) Amendment Regulations 2006 (SI 2006/1928).

362 These principles are also rehearsed in Pt 2 of Sch 1 to the Clinical Trials Regulations.

363 Good Clinical Practice Directive, Art 3.

'[A]ll clinical trial information shall be recorded, handled and stored in such a way that it can be accurately reported, interpreted and verified, while the confidentiality of records of the trial subjects remains protected'.[364]

Authorisation is needed for the manufacture or import of an investigational medicinal product.[365] The applicant for authorisation must specify the types of medicinal products to be manufactured or imported, the relevant manufacture or import operations, the manufacturing process and the place of manufacture, and provide evidence that he or she complies with the requirements of the Directive.[366] The competent authority must verify the information provided by the applicant before granting authorisation.[367]

The holder of an authorisation must have at his or her disposal the services of staff that comply with relevant legal requirements relating to manufacture and controls, must inform the competent authority of any changes he or she wishes to make to this application for authorisation, must allow inspectors access to his or her premises and must comply with the principles of good manufacturing practice (see below).[368] The competent authority may suspend the authorisation if the holder fails to comply with the relevant requirements.[369]

The essential documents allowing the conduct of the trial and the quality of the data produced to be evaluated must be collected in a trial master file, which must be retained by the sponsor and investigator for at least five years after completion of the trial and be available for inspection.[370]

Inspectors must be appropriately qualified and trained and work to standard operating procedures.[371] They may make inspections before, during or after the conduct of clinical trials, as part of the verification of applications for marketing authorisation and/or as a follow-up to the granting of authorisation.[372]

Good clinical practice in the UK

The Good Clinical Practice Directive was transposed into UK law by the Medicinal Products for Human Use (Clinical Trials) Amendment Regulations 2005, which incorporated the requirements of the Directive into the Clinical

---

364 Good Clinical Practice Directive, Art 5.
365 Good Clinical Practice Directive, Art 9.
366 Good Clinical Practice Directive, Art 10.
367 Good Clinical Practice Directive, Art 11.
368 Good Clinical Practice Directive, Art 12.
369 Good Clinical Practice Directive, Art 15.
370 Good Clinical Practice Directive, Arts 16–20.
371 Good Clinical Practice Directive, Arts 21, 22.
372 Good Clinical Practice Directive, Art 23.

Trials Regulations and the Medicines Act 1968. As amended, therefore, the Clinical Trials Regulations implement the provisions of both the Clinical Trials Directive and the Good Clinical Practice Directive.

Schedule 1 to the Clinical Trials Directive sets out the conditions and principles of good clinical practice and for the protection of clinical trial subjects. Part 3 provides that a trial subject must:

- in a prior interview with the investigator or another member of the investigating team, be given an opportunity to understand the objectives, risks and inconveniences of the trial, and the conditions under which it is to be conducted;[373]

- have been informed of his or her right to withdraw from the trial at any time;[374]

- have given his or her informed consent to taking part in the trial;[375]

- be able to withdraw from the trial at any time by revoking his or her informed consent without being subject to any resulting detriment;[376] and

- have been provided with a contact point where he or she may obtain further information about the trial.[377]

There are special conditions relating to minors,[378] and to incapacitated adults.[379]

More generally, the trial subject's physical and mental integrity, his or her privacy, and the protection of the data concerning him or her in accordance with the Data Protection Act 1998 must be safeguarded.[380] Provision must be made for insurance and indemnity to cover the liability of the investigator and the sponsor.[381] An appropriately qualified doctor (or dentist, where appropriate) must be responsible for the medical care given to, and the medical decisions made on behalf of, a subject.[382]

Part 4 of the Clinical Trials Regulations provides that all clinical trials must comply with good clinical practice,[383] and that no trial may be conducted otherwise than in accordance with the trial protocol, the documents submitted

---

373 Clinical Trials Regulations, Sch 1, Pt 3, para 1.
374 Clinical Trials Regulations, Sch 1, Pt 3, para 2.
375 Clinical Trials Regulations, Sch 1, Pt 3, para 3.
376 Clinical Trials Regulations, Sch 1, Pt 3, para 4.
377 Clinical Trials Regulations, Sch 1, Pt 3, para 5.
378 Clinical Trials Regulations, Sch 1, Pt 4.
379 Clinical Trials Regulations, Sch 1, Pt 5.
380 Clinical Trials Regulations, Sch 1, Pt 2, para 13.
381 Clinical Trials Regulations, Sch 1, Pt 2, para 14.
382 Clinical Trials Regulations, Sch 1, Pt 2, para 11.
383 Clinical Trials Regulations, reg 28. See also Sch 1.

to the MHRA and ethics committee and any conditions imposed by the MHRA.[384] The sponsor must notify the MHRA of any serious breach of good clinical practice or the protocol within seven days of becoming aware of the breach.[385] A serious breach is one likely to affect to a significant degree the safety or physical or mental integrity of the subjects of the trial or its scientific value.[386]

The sponsor and investigator may take appropriate urgent safety measures to protect the subjects of a trial against any immediate hazard to their health or safety, and must notify the MHRA and ethics committee within three days.[387] The MHRA may suspend or terminate a trial if it considers that a condition of its authorisation is not being complied with or it has doubts about the safety or scientific validity of the trial, by serving notice on the sponsor or investigator.[388] Unless there is imminent risk to the health and safety of a trial subject, the MHRA must inform the sponsor or investigator of the reasons for their concern at least a week before the notice is issued, and advise them that they may make representations in response within the week.[389]

The sponsor must keep a trial master file containing the essential documents for the trial and ensure that it is readily available for inspection by the MHRA.[390] The essential documents are those which enable the conduct of the trial and the quality of the data produced to be evaluated, and show whether the conduct of the trial is in accordance with applicable Directives.[391] Any alteration to a document in the trial master file must be traceable,[392] and both the trial master file and the medical files of trial subjects must be retained for at least five years after the end of the trial.[393] The sponsor must appoint named individuals to be responsible for the trial master archive, and access to it is to be restricted to them.[394]

Powers of enforcement are given to the MHRA by the Medicines Act 1968, and are exercised by its Good Clinical Practice Inspectorate (part of the Inspection and Standards Division).[395] The Good Clinical Practice

---

384 Clinical Trials Regulations, reg 29.
385 Clinical Trials Regulations, reg 29A(1).
386 Clinical Trials Regulations, reg 29A(2).
387 Clinical Trials Regulations, reg 30.
388 Clinical Trials Regulations, reg 31(1)–(3).
389 Clinical Trials Regulations, reg 31(5), (6).
390 Clinical Trials Directive, reg 31A(1)–(3).
391 Clinical Trials Regulations, reg 31A(4). The applicable Directives are the Medicinal Products Directive 2001/83/EC ([2001] OJ L311/67), the Clinical Trials Directive 2001/20/EC ([2001] OJ L121/34), the Good Clinical Practice Directive 2005/28/EC ([2005] OJ L91/13) and the Good Manufacturing Practice Directive 2003/94/EC ([2003] OJ L262/22).
392 Clinical Trials Regulations, reg 31A(6).
393 Clinical Trials Regulations, reg 31A(7), (8).
394 Clinical Trials Regulations, reg 31A(9).
395 Clinical Trials Regulations, reg 47. See http://mhra.gov.uk/howweregulate/medicines/inspectionandstandards/goodclinicalpractice/index.htm

Inspectorate can inspect the premises of sponsors and organisations that provide services to them, including pharmaceutical companies, contract research organisations, NHS Trusts, trial sites, clinical laboratories and GCP archives.[396] Its powers include carrying out inspections, taking samples and seizing goods and documents.[397]

It is an offence to conduct a clinical trial otherwise than in accordance with good clinical practice,[398] and to provide false or misleading information to the MHRA or an ethics committee in connection with a clinical trial.[399] In either case, it is a defence if the person concerned took all reasonable precautions and exercised all due diligence to avoid committing the offence.[400] The maximum penalty is imprisonment for two years and/or a fine.[401] It is also an offence to obstruct an inspector during an inspection.[402]

Pharmacovigilance: notification of adverse events

Matters related to pharmacovigilance are treated in Part 5 of the Clinical Trials Regulations.

The investigator is required to report all *serious adverse events* immediately to the sponsor, orally or in writing.[403] After the immediate report, a detailed written report must be made.

Adverse events and/or laboratory abnormalities which are identified in the protocol as critical to evaluations of safety of the trial are to be reported according to the timetable set out in the protocol.[404]

If a subject dies, the investigator is to supply to the sponsor and ethics committee any additional information requested by them.[405]

The sponsor must keep detailed records of all adverse events reported to him or her by the investigators, and the MHRA may ask to be sent those records.[406]

---

396 Medicines Act 1968, s 111.
397 Medicines Act 1968, s 112.
398 Clinical Trials Regulations, regs 28, 49.
399 Clinical Trials Regulations, reg 50.
400 Clinical Trials Regulations, reg 51.
401 Clinical Trials Regulations, reg 52.
402 Medicines Act 1968, s 114.
403 Clinical Trials Regulations, reg 32(1)–(4). This requirement does not apply to those serious adverse events that are specified in the protocol or investigator's brochure as not requiring immediate reporting. Subjects are to be identified by a unique code number in both reports (reg 32(6), (7)).
404 Clinical Trials Regulations, reg 32(5).
405 Clinical Trials Regulations, reg 32(8).
406 Clinical Trials Regulations, reg 32(9), (10).

Notification of serious adverse reactions

The sponsor must ensure that all relevant information about *suspected serious unexpected adverse reactions that are fatal or life-threatening* is recorded and reported as soon as possible, and in any event no later than 7 days after the sponsor was first aware of the reaction, to the MHRA, the competent authorities of any other EEA state in which the trial is being conducted and the ethics committee. Any additional relevant information must be provided within 8 days of such a report. The report to the competent authorities may be made via EudraCT.[407] All suspected unexpected serious adverse reactions occurring at a trial site in a third country must be entered onto EudraCT.[408]

Other suspected unexpected adverse reactions are to be reported to the same bodies as soon as possible and in any event no later than 15 days after the sponsor is first aware of the reaction.[409]

The sponsor is required to notify all investigators concerned of all suspected unexpected serious adverse reactions.[410] A sponsor is required to provide to the MHRA and the ethics committee once a year a list of all suspected serious adverse reactions which have occurred during the year and a report on the safety of the subjects of those trials.[411]

The MHRA must keep a record of all suspected unexpected serious adverse reactions and ensure that details are entered on EudraCT, the European database.[412]

Clinical trials may be inspected by the MHRA's Good Pharmacovigilance Inspectorate, which may serve an infringement notice on any person considered to have contravened the Clinical Trials Regulations.[413]

Good manufacturing practice

The Good Manufacturing Practice Directive

As well as conforming to good clinical practice, the Clinical Trials Directive and Clinical Trials Regulations also require conformity with

---

407 Clinical Trials Regulations, reg 33(1), (2), (4).
408 Clinical Trials Regulations, reg 34.
409 Clinical Trials Regulations, reg 33(3).
410 Clinical Trials Regulations, reg 33(5).
411 Clinical Trials Regulations, reg 35.
412 Clinical Trials Regulations, reg 35(6).
413 Clinical Trials Regulations, reg 48.

good manufacturing practice (GMP) for investigational medicinal products.[414] The current EU standard for good manufacturing practice is set out in the Good Manufacturing Practice Directive, which applies both to medicinal products in general and to investigational medicinal products in particular.[415]

The Good Manufacturing Practice Directive requires that manufacturers of medicinal products ensure that manufacturing operations are carried out in accordance with good manufacturing practice, and that importers of medicinal products ensure that the products have been manufactured in accordance with standards which are at least equivalent to good manufacturing practice.[416] In the case of investigational medicinal products, compliance with a marketing authorisation is not necessary, but the manufacturer must ensure that all manufacturing operations are carried out in accordance with the information provided by the sponsor in the application for authorisation for the trial.[417]

Manufacturers must have in place an effective pharmaceutical assurance system,[418] a sufficient number of competent and appropriately qualified personnel to achieve the pharmaceutical quality assurance objective,[419] and suitably located, designed, constructed, adapted and maintained premises.[420] The manufacturer must establish and maintain a documentation system covering the various manufacturing operations performed, that will enable the history of each batch and the changes introduced during the development of an investigational medicinal product to be traced; batch documentation for an investigational medicinal product must be kept for five years from the end of the trial.[421] The manufacturing process for investigational medicinal products must be validated in its entirety as appropriate for a product at that stage in development, and all steps in the design and development of the manufacturing process must be fully documented.[422]

The manufacturer must have a quality control system, and sufficient samples of each batch of bulk formulated product and key packaging components

---

414 Clinical Trials Directive, Recital 12 and Art 13; Clinical Trials Regulations, reg 42.

415 Commission Directive 2003/94/EC ([2003] OJ L262/22) laying down the principles and guidelines of good manufacturing practice in respect of medicinal products for human use and investigational medicinal products for human use. This replaced Directive 91/356/EEC; by Art 16 of Directive 2003/94/EC, references to the repealed Directive 91/356/EEC shall be construed as references to Directive 2003/94/EC.

416 Good Manufacturing Practice Directive, Art 4.

417 Good Manufacturing Practice Directive, Art 5.

418 Good Manufacturing Practice Directive, Art 6.

419 Good Manufacturing Practice Directive, Art 7.

420 Good Manufacturing Practice Directive, Art 8.

421 Good Manufacturing Practice Directive, Art 9.

422 Good Manufacturing Practice Directive, Art 10.

must be kept for at least two years after the end of the trial.[423] There must also be a system for recording and reviewing complaints and recalling promptly investigational medicinal products.[424] The manufacturer must conduct repeated self-inspections, which must be recorded, to monitor the implementation of good manufacturing practice.[425] Investigational medicinal products must be labelled so as to ensure protection of the subject, traceability, identification of the product and trial, and proper use.[426]

Good manufacturing practice in the UK: medicinal products which have a marketing authorisation

For medicinal products which have a marketing authorisation, the requirements of the Good Manufacturing Practice Directive have been implemented in the UK by the Medicines (Standard Provisions for Licences and Certificates) Amendment Regulations 2004.[427] These Regulations changed the then-current definition of 'good manufacturing practice' in paragraph (1) of regulation 2 of the Medicines (Standard Provisions for Licences and Certificates) Regulations 1971 to the following:[428]

> 'Good manufacturing practice means the part of quality assurance which ensures that products are consistently produced and controlled in accordance with the quality standards appropriate to their intended use, the principles and guidelines of which are specified in Commission Directive 2003/94/EC'.[429]

The 1971 Regulations require that the holder of a licence to manufacture medicinal products for human use, which have a marketing authorisation, must conduct all manufacture and assembly operations in accordance with the principles and guidelines of good manufacturing practice as defined above.[430]

Good manufacturing practice in the UK: investigational medicinal products

In the case of investigational medicinal products, provisions relating to good manufacturing practice are to be found in Part 6 of the Clinical Trials Regulations. Those Regulations require the holder of a manufacturing authorisation for an investigational medicinal product to comply with the

---

423 Good Manufacturing Practice Directive, Art 11.
424 Good Manufacturing Practice Directive, Art 13.
425 Good Manufacturing Practice Directive, Art 14.
426 Good Manufacturing Practice Directive, Art 15.
427 SI 2004/1678.
428 SI 1971/972.
429 That is, the Good Clinical Practice Directive.
430 Clinical Trials Regulations, reg 3 and para 3 of Sch 2 to the 1971 Regulations.

principles and guidelines of good manufacturing practice set out in the Good Manufacturing Practice Directive.[431]

Other provisions relating to the manufacture of investigational medicinal products are set out in Part 6 of the Clinical Trials Regulations. Importantly, these include the requirement that anyone who manufactures, assembles or imports any investigational medicinal product must hold a manufacturing authorisation from the MHRA, unless the manufacture or assembly is in accordance with a marketing authorisation for that product.[432]

Applications for a manufacturing authorisation must be accompanied by the particulars set out in Schedule 6 to the Clinical Trials Regulations;[433] the MHRA must respond to an application within 90 days.[434] Manufacturing authorisation will be granted only if the applicant has at his or her disposal the services of staff and suitable and sufficient premises, technical equipment and facilities to comply with the requirements of the Good Manufacturing Practice Directive,[435] and at least one qualified person (see below).[436] The MHRA will not grant a manufacturing authorisation unless it has established that the particulars set out in the application are accurate.[437] A manufacturing authorisation applies only in relation to the products, operations and premises specified in the application in respect of which the authorisation is granted.[438]

---

431 Clinical Trials Regulations, reg 42.
432 Clinical Trials Regulations, reg 36. This does not apply to the assembly of an investigational medicinal product in a hospital or health centre by a doctor or pharmacist for use in that hospital or health centre or another trial site (reg 37).
433 Clinical Trials Regulations, reg 38. The particulars set out in Sch 6 include details of (i) the applicant's name and address; (ii) the types of investigational medicinal product for which authorisation is required; (iii) the manufacturing, assembling or importation operations to which the authorisation is to relate; (iv) the premises where the manufacture, assembly or import are to be carried out and where the investigational medicinal products are to be stored; (v) any other manufacturing operations carried on at those premises; (vi) the qualified person, production manager and person responsible for quality control; (vii) arrangements for identification and storage of materials, ingredients and finished products; (viii) arrangements for satisfactory turnover of stocks; (ix) record-keeping and reference samples.
434 Clinical Trials Regulations, reg 39.
435 Clinical Trials Regulations, reg 40(1)(a)(ii).
436 Clinical Trials Regulations, reg 40(1)(a)(iii). A qualified person is a person who as respects qualifications and experience satisfies the requirements of Art 49 or 50 of the Medicinal Products Directive (reg 2); see also reg 43. A qualified person may be a member of the Institute of Biology, Pharmaceutical Society or Royal Society of Chemistry who is regarded by that body as satisfying those requirements.
437 Clinical Trials Regulations, reg 40(1)(b).
438 Clinical Trials Regulations, reg 41.

In addition to complying with good manufacturing practice, the applicant must also comply with any provisions of the manufacturing authorisation,[439] allow the MHRA access to his or her premises at any reasonable time, and put and keep in place arrangements which enable the qualified person to carry out his or her duties, including all necessary facilities.[440] The qualified person is the person responsible for performing the functions set out in Article 13(3) and (4) of the Clinical Trials Directive, namely:

- ensuring that each batch of medicinal products has been manufactured and checked in compliance with the requirements of the Good Manufacturing Practice Directive,[441] the product specification file and the application for manufacturing authorisation;[442] and

- certifying in a register, which must be available to the MHRA and kept for at least five years, that each production batch satisfies these requirements.[443]

There are provisions for varying,[444] suspending or revoking a manufacturing authorisation.[445]

If these requirements are complied with, then investigational medicinal products do not have to undergo further checks if they are imported into another member state and have been checked and certified by a qualified person.[446]

---

439 Standard provisions for manufacturing authorisations are set out in Pt 2 of Sch 7 of the Clinical Trials Regulations. Among them are provisions that the holder of the authorisation must (i) provide and maintain the necessary staff, premises and plant for the manufacture and storage of the investigational medicinal product and use only the premises specified in the authorisation; (ii) place the quality-control system under one of the persons notified to the MHRA as responsible for it; (iii) use a contract laboratory only if operated by a person approved by the MHRA; (iv) provide such information as the MHRA may request; (v) inform the MHRA before making any material alteration in premises, plant or operations and of any change in personnel responsible for supervision or quality control; (vi) keep batch records and samples available for inspection by the MHRA; (vii) withhold any non-conforming batches; (viii) ensure that products are tested as appropriate; (ix) permit inspection by the MHRA; and (x) provide and maintain such staff, premises, equipment and facilities as will enable the qualified person to carry out his or her duties.
440 Clinical Trials Regulations, reg 43.
441 Or, in the case of investigational medicinal products manufactured in a third country, in accordance with equivalent standards of good manufacturing practice.
442 Clinical Trials Directive, Art 13(3). For the meaning of 'product specification', see Pt 1 of Sch 7 to the Regulations.
443 Clinical Trials Directive, Art 13(4). In carrying out these functions, the qualified person must comply with the *Code of Practice for Qualified Persons in the Pharmaceutical Industry*, published jointly by the Institute of Biology, the Royal Pharmaceutical Society of Great Britain and the Royal Society of Chemistry in March 2004.
444 Clinical Trials Regulations, reg 44.
445 Clinical Trials Regulations, reg 45. Procedural provisions relating to proposals to grant, refuse to grant, vary, suspend or revoke manufacturing authorisations are set out in Sch 8.
446 Clinical Trials Regulations, reg 13(2).

Part 7 of the Clinical Trials Regulations requires that investigational medicinal products must be labelled in accordance with Article 15 of the Good Manufacturing Practice Directive, namely in such a way as to ensure protection of the subject and traceability, to enable identification of the product and trial, and to facilitate proper use of the investigational medicinal product.[447]

Compliance with manufacturing authorisations is monitored by the MHRA's Good Manufacturing Practice Inspectorate, which is part of its Inspection and Standards Division. It may inspect the trial sites, the manufacturing site of the investigational medicinal product, any laboratory used for analysis in the trial and the sponsor's premises, and has the right to take samples and seize articles and documents.[448]

The Clinical Trials Regulations create the following offences related to manufacturing authorisations:[449]

- manufacturing, assembling or importing any investigational medicinal product except in accordance with a manufacturing authorisation;

- failing to comply with the principles and guidelines of good manufacturing practice;

- failing to comply with any provisions in a manufacturing authorisation;

- failing to allow the MHRA access to the holder's premises at any reasonable time;

- failing to put and keep in place arrangements which enable the qualified person to carry out his or her duties, including placing at his or her disposal all necessary facilities;

- failing to have at his or her disposal the services of at least one qualified person who is responsible for carrying out the duties specified in the Clinical Trials Directive (see above); and

- permitting a person to act as a qualified person after having been notified by the MHRA that that person does not satisfy the requirements to be a qualified person or is failing to carry out his or her duties adequately or at all.

---

447 Clinical Trials Regulations, reg 46.
448 Clinical Trials Regulations, reg 47 and Schs 7 and 9, modifying the enforcement provisions of the Medicines Act 1968. See MHRA's publication *Rules and Guidance for Pharmaceutical Manufacturers and Distributors 2007*, known as 'the Orange Guide', available at www.mhra. gov.uk/publications/regulatoryguidance/medicines/con2030291.
449 Clinical Trials Regulations, reg 49(1)(k), (l), (m), referring to regs 36(1), 42 and 43(1), (6).

Definitions used in the Clinical Trials Regulations (where stated taken from the Clinical Trials Directive)

Adverse event	Any untoward medical occurrence in a subject to whom a medicinal product has been administered, including occurrences which are not necessarily caused by or related to that product.
Adverse reaction	Any untoward and unintended response in a subject to an investigational medicinal product which is related to any dose administered to that subject.
Ethics committee (definition from Clinical Trials Directive)	An independent body in a member state, consisting of healthcare professionals and non-medical members, whose responsibility it is to protect the rights, safety and well-being of human subjects involved in a trial and to provide public assurance of that protection, by, among other things, expressing an opinion on the trial protocol, the suitability of the investigators and the adequacy of facilities, and on the methods and documents to be used to inform trial subjects and obtain their informed consent.
Informed consent (definition from Clinical Trials Directive)	The decision, which must be written, dated and signed, to take part in a clinical trial, taken freely after being duly informed of its nature, significance, implications and risks and appropriately documented, by any person capable of giving consent or, where the person is not capable of giving consent, by his or her legal representative; if the person concerned is unable to write, oral consent in the presence of at least one witness may be given in exceptional cases, as provided for in national legislation.
Inspection (definition from Clinical Trials Directive)	The act by a competent authority of conducting an official review of documents, facilities, records, quality assurance arrangements, and any other resources that are deemed by the competent authority to be related to the clinical trial and that may be located at the site of the trial, at the sponsor's and/or contract research organisation's facilities, or at other establishments which the competent authority sees fit to inspect.
Investigational medicinal product	A pharmaceutical form of an active substance or placebo being tested, or to be tested, or used, or to be used, as a reference in a clinical trial, and includes a medicinal product which already has a marketing authorisation but is, for the purpose of the trial (a) used or assembled (formulated or packaged) in a way different from the form of the product authorised under the authorisation, (b) used for an indication not included in the summary of product characteristics under the authorisation for that product, or (c) used to gain further information about the form of the product as authorised under the authorisation.
Investigator	The authorised health professional responsible for the conduct of a trial at a trial site, and if the trial is being conducted by a team of authorised health professionals at a trial site, the investigator is the leader responsible for that team.
Investigator's brochure	A document containing a summary of the clinical and non-clinical data relating to an investigational medicinal product which are relevant to the study of the product in human subjects.
Multi-centre clinical trial (definition from Clinical Trials Directive)	A clinical trial conducted according to a single protocol but at more than one site, and therefore by more than one investigator, in which the trial sites may be located in a single member state, in a number of member states and/or in member states and third countries.

577

Non-interventional trial	A study of one or more medicinal products which have a marketing authorisation, where the following conditions are met:

(a) the products are prescribed in the usual manner in accordance with the terms of that authorisation;

(b) the assignment of any patient involved in the study to a particular therapeutic strategy is not decided in advance by a protocol but falls within current practice;

(c) the decision to prescribe a particular medicinal product is clearly separated from the decision to include the patient in the study;

(d) no diagnostic or monitoring procedures are applied to the patients included in the study, other than those which are ordinarily applied in the course of the particular therapeutic strategy in question; and

(e) epidemiological methods are to be used for the analysis of the data arising from the study.

Protocol	A document that describes the objectives, design, methodology, statistical considerations and organisation of a clinical trial.
Serious adverse event, serious adverse reaction or unexpected serious adverse reaction	Any adverse event, adverse reaction or unexpected adverse reaction, respectively, that:

(a) results in death;

(b) is life-threatening;

(c) requires hospitalisation or prolongation of existing hospitalisation;

(d) results in persistent or significant disability or incapacity; or

(e) consists of a congenital anomaly or birth defect.

Sponsor (definition from Clinical Trials Directive)	An individual, company, institution or organisation which takes responsibility for the initiation, management and/or financing of a clinical trial.
Subject	An individual who participates in a clinical trial (a) as a recipient of an investigational medicinal product or of some other treatment or product, or (b) without receiving any treatment or product, as a control.
Unexpected adverse reaction	An adverse reaction the nature or severity of which is not consistent with the information about the medicinal product in question set out (a) in the case of a product with a marketing authorisation, in the summary of product characteristics for that product, (b) in the case of any other investigational medicinal product, in the investigator's brochure relating to the trial in question.

Definitions used in the Medicinal Products Directive

Medicinal product	• Any substance or combination of substances presented for treating or preventing disease in human beings.
	• Any substance or combination which may be administered to human beings with a view to making a medical diagnosis or to restoring, correcting or modifying physiological functions in human beings is likewise considered a medicinal product.

Substance	Any matter irrespective of origin which may be:
	• human, eg human blood and human blood products;
	• animal, eg micro-organisms, whole animals, parts of organs, animal secretions, toxins, extracts, blood products;
	• vegetable, eg micro-organisms, plants, parts of plants, vegetable secretions, extracts;
	• chemical, eg elements, naturally occurring chemical materials and chemical products obtained by chemical change or synthesis.

Marketing authorisations

Once a Phase III trial has been successfully carried out, the sponsor can apply for a marketing authorisation for the new drug which will enable the sponsor to launch it on the market.

The Medicinal Products Directive

The principles underlying marketing authorisation in the EU are to be found in the Medicinal Products Directive, which sets out the Community code relating to medicinal products for human use.[450] Among the provisions of that Directive are the following:

- No medicinal product may be placed on the market of a member state unless a marketing authorisation has been issued by the competent authorities of that member state in accordance with the Directive.[451] An application for marketing authorisation must be accompanied by specified particulars and documents,[452] though the requirement for certain

---

450 Directive 2001/83/EC ([2001] OJ L311/67) on the Community code relating to medicinal products for human use. This Directive has been amended numerous times, and the current version (at the time of writing, that incorporating amendments made up to 20 July 2009) should be consulted. This Directive does not apply to medicinal products intended for research and development trials (Art 3(3)).

451 Or an authorisation has been granted in accordance with Regulation 2004/726/EC ([2004] OJ L136/34) (Medicinal Products Directive, Art 6).

452 Medicinal Products Directive, Art 8(3). The applicant must supply details of (i) his or her name and address; (ii) the name of the medicinal product; (iii) the constituents of the medicinal product; (iv) evaluation of the medicinal product's potential environmental risks; (iv) the manufacturing method; (iv) therapeutic indications, contra-indications and adverse reactions; (v) posology, pharmaceutical form, method and route of administration and expected shelf life; (vi) any precautionary and safety measures for storage, administration and disposal; (vii) manufacturer's control methods; (viii) results of tests, including clinical trials; (x) the pharmacovigilance and, where appropriate, risk-management system; (xi) how the clinical trials met the ethical requirements of the Clinical Trials Directive; (ix) a summary of product characteristics (see further Art 11) and specimens of packaging; (x) his or her authorisation to produce medicinal products; (xi) any marketing authorisation for another member state or third country; (xii) any designation of the medicinal product as an orphan medicinal product; (xiii) proof that he or she has the services of a qualified person responsible for pharmacovigilance and the means for notification of any suspected adverse reaction. This information must be updated on a regular basis.

particulars is waived if the medicinal product is essentially similar to one already authorised in the EU.[453] There are tests which have to be carried out by appropriately qualified experts. Detailed summaries must accompany the application.[454] There are special provisions applicable to homoeopathic medicinal products,[455] traditional herbal medicinal products,[456] and medicinal products derived from human blood and plasma.[457]

- Applications for a marketing authorisation should be determined within 210 days of submission.[458] The competent authority must verify whether the particulars submitted with the application comply with the Directive and whether the conditions for issuing an authorisation are complied with;[459] it may carry out its own tests and require the submission of further information.[460]

- A marketing authorisation is initially valid for five years and may then be renewed for an indefinite period after an evaluation of the risk-benefit balance by the competent authority, unless a further five-year period is deemed necessary on pharmacovigilance grounds.[461] Marketing authorisation may be refused if the risk-benefit balance is not favourable, the medicinal product's therapeutic efficiency is insufficiently substantiated, its qualitative and quantitative composition is not as declared, or if any particulars or documents do not comply with the Directive.[462] There are special procedures relating to mutual recognition of authorisations between member states.[463]

- It is also necessary for the manufacturer of the medicinal products concerned to hold a manufacturing authorisation, as set out above.[464] There are detailed provisions relating to the labelling of medicinal products and the provision of a package leaflet.[465] The competent authority must determine whether the medicinal product is subject to medical prescription.[466] The holder of a manufacturing authorisation

---

453 Medicinal Products Directive, Art 10.
454 Medicinal Products Directive, Art 12.
455 Medicinal Products Directive, Arts 13–16.
456 Medicinal Products Directive, Arts 16a–16i.
457 Medicinal Products Directive, Arts 109, 110.
458 Medicinal Products Directive, Art 17(1).
459 Medicinal Products Directive, Art 19(1).
460 Medicinal Products Directive, Art 19(2), (3).
461 Medicinal Products Directive, Art 24. On the risk-benefit balance, see Art 1, as amended by Directive 2004/27/EC ([2004] OJ L136/34): it is defined as 'an evaluation of the positive therapeutic effects of the medicinal product in relation to the risks', where the risks include 'any risk relating to the quality, safety or efficacy of the medicinal product as regards patients' health or public health'.
462 Medicinal Products Directive, Art 26.
463 Medicinal Products Directive, Arts 27–39.
464 Medicinal Products Directive, Arts 40–53.
465 Medicinal Products Directive, Arts 54–69.
466 Medicinal Products Directive, Arts 70–75.

may also distribute by wholesale the medicinal products covered by that authorisation,[467] but those authorised to supply medicinal products to the public need a separate distribution authorisation,[468] and must meet specified minimum requirements.[469]

- Provisions are set out with regard to the advertising of medicinal products,[470] and no medicinal product may be advertised that does not have a marketing authorisation.[471] Advertising must encourage rational use of the medicinal product and must not be misleading.[472] Medicinal products available on medical prescription only may not be advertised.[473]

- Member states must establish a pharmacovigilance system,[474] and the marketing authorisation holder must have permanently and continuously at his or her disposal an appropriately qualified person for pharmacovigilance, with responsibility for establishing and maintaining a system for collecting and collating information about suspected adverse reactions and reporting it to the competent authority.[475] The marketing authorisation holder must maintain detailed records of all suspected adverse reactions and report them to the competent authority periodically.[476] The EMEA must set up a data-processing network to facilitate the exchange of pharmacovigilance information.[477]

- Member states are to ensure, by means of repeated inspections, that the legal requirements governing medicinal products are complied with.[478] A competent authority must suspend or revoke a marketing authorisation if the product proves to be harmful in the normal conditions of use, where its therapeutic efficacy is lacking, or where its qualitative or quantitative composition is not as declared.[479]

Analytical, pharmacotoxicological and clinical standards and protocols in respect of the testing of medicinal products are set out in Annex I to the Directive.

---

467 Medicinal Products Directive, Art 77(3).
468 Medicinal Products Directive, Art 77 (1), (2).
469 Medicinal Products Directive, Arts 76–85. The Commission has published guidelines on good distribution practice.
470 Medicinal Products Directive, Arts 86–100.
471 Medicinal Products Directive, Art 87(1).
472 Medicinal Products Directive, Art 87(3).
473 Medicinal Products Directive, Art 88(1).
474 Medicinal Products Directive, Arts 101–108.
475 Medicinal Products Directive, Art 103.
476 Medicinal Products Directive, Art 104.
477 Medicinal Products Directive, Art 105.
478 Medicinal Products Directive, Arts 111–19.
479 Medicinal Products Directive, Art 116.

Getting marketing authorisation in the EU: the three procedures

It is possible to get marketing authorisation for a medicinal product in the EU by using one of three procedures: the centralised procedure, the decentralised procedure and the mutual recognition procedure:

- *The centralised procedure* entails making an application for marketing authorisation to the EMEA according to the procedure set down in Regulation 726/2004.[480] If the application is successful, the EMEA will issue a marketing authorisation which is valid throughout the EU. The centralised procedure is mandatory for (i) medicinal products developed by means of certain biotechnological processes, (ii) advanced therapy medicinal products,[481] (iii) medicinal products containing a new active substance for the treatment of Aids, cancer, neurodegenerative disorders, diabetes, auto-immune diseases and vial diseases,[482] and (iv) orphan medicinal products.[483] The centralised procedure may also be used, but is not mandatory, for medicinal products (i) containing a new active substance or (ii) constituting a significant therapeutic, scientific or technical innovation, or where use of the centralised procedure is in the interests of patients at Community level. In practice, the centralised procedure is generally used for medicinal products which incorporate a new chemical entity.

- *The mutual recognition procedure* is set out in the Medicinal Products Directive.[484] Once a medicinal product has been granted a marketing authorisation by the competent authority in one member state, the holder can apply to the competent authority in other member states for recognition of the marketing authorisation there. The holder requests the competent authority in the member state which granted the authorisation, known as the reference member state, to prepare an assessment report on the medicinal product and send it to the other member states in which marketing authorisation is sought. The other member states are to approve the assessment report within 90 days of receiving it.[485] If, on the grounds of potential serious risk to public health, a member state cannot approve the assessment report, the application is to be referred to the Co-ordination Group for Mutual Recognition and Decentralised

---

480 Regulation 726/2004/EC ([2004] OJ L136/1) laying down Community procedures for the authorisation and supervision of medicinal products for human and veterinary use and establishing a European Medicines Agency. This Regulation has been amended several times.

481 As defined in Regulation 1394/2007/EC ([2007] OJ L324/121), Art 2.

482 'New' here means not authorised at the date when the Regulation came into force, 20 May 2004.

483 Regulation 726/2004/EC ([2004] OJ L136/1), Annex. For the definition of 'orphan medicinal product', see below.

484 Arts 27–39.

485 Medicinal Products Directive, Art 28.

Procedure – Human (CMD(h)), which must resolve the disagreement within 60 days.[486] If the matter cannot be resolved within the CMD(h), it is reported to EMEA's Committee for Medicinal Products for Human Use, which issues an opinion to guide the Commission in making a final decision. This is binding on the member states.[487]

- *The decentralised procedure* is a variant of the mutual recognition procedure, and applies when a medicinal product does not yet have marketing authorisation in any member state. In this case, the applicant must nominate one member state to be the reference member state, which will prepare a draft assessment report, summary of product characteristics, and draft of labelling and package leaflet within 120 days after receiving an application and send them to the other member states.[488] The other member states are to approve the assessment report within 90 days, and the procedures set out in the previous paragraph apply if there is disagreement.[489]

Getting marketing authorisation in the UK: the Marketing Authorisations Regulations

The Medicinal Products Directive was implemented in the UK by way of amendments to the Medicines for Human Use (Marketing Authorisations Etc) Regulations 1994,[490] cited here as the Marketing Authorisations Regulations. The Marketing Authorisations Regulations provide that no medicinal product can be placed on the market or distributed by way of wholesale dealing unless it has been granted marketing authorisation in accordance with the relevant Community provisions.[491] Applications are made to the MHRA,[492] which will consider the application in accordance with the relevant Community provisions.[493] There is provision for revoking, suspending or varying a UK marketing authorisation.[494]

The holder of a marketing authorisation must comply with all obligations which relate to him or her by virtue of the relevant Community provisions, especially those relating to providing or updating information, making changes, applying to vary the authorisation, pharmacovigilance, and labels

---

486 Medicinal Products Directive, Art 29.
487 Medicinal Products Directive, Arts 30–34.
488 Medicinal Products Directive, Art 28(3).
489 Medicinal Products Directive, Arts 28–34.
490 SI 1994/3144; see also the Medicines (Homoeopathic Medicinal Products for Human Use) (Amendment) Regulations 2005 (SI 2005/2753), the Medicines (Marketing Authorisations etc) (Amendment) Regulations 2005 (SI 2005/2759), the Medicines (Advertising Amendments) Regulations 2005 (SI 2005/2787) and the Medicines for Human Use (Manufacturing, Wholesale Dealing and Miscellaneous Amendments) Regulations 2005 (SI 2005/2789).
491 Marketing Authorisations Regulations, reg 3.
492 Marketing Authorisations Regulations, reg 4.
493 Marketing Authorisations Regulations, reg 5.
494 Marketing Authorisations Regulations, reg 6.

and package leaflets.[495] He or she must maintain a record of suspected adverse reactions, open to inspection by the MHRA,[496] and keep documents enabling the withdrawal or recall from sale of any medicinal product as necessary.[497]

Procedural provisions relating to the grant, renewal, variation, revocation and suspension of marketing authorisations are set out in Schedule 2 to the Regulations; see also sections 6–50 of the Medicines Act 1968 (where marketing authorisation in the UK is referred to as a product licence). The MHRA will assess the safety, quality and efficacy of the medicinal product for which authorisation is sought. It may refer to the Commission on Human Medicines, which is supported by various Expert Advisory Groups, and in certain circumstances must do so. The applicant has the right to make representations and be heard by a person appointed by the MHRA if refusal of marketing authorisation is recommended.

Offences, including placing a medicinal product on the market without holding a Community or UK marketing authorisation for it and not complying with Community provisions for pharmacovigilance, are set out in Schedule 3.

Once a licence has been granted there are additional provisions relating to post-approval regulation of medicinal products. Conditions are often attached to the grant of product licences; these may cover such matters as packaging, manufacturing practice, manufacturer and dealer licences, retail outlets, advertising, pricing and promotion.[498]

There are further EC-wide provisions regulating the advertising and marketing of medicinal products.[499]

---

495 Marketing Authorisations Regulations, reg 7(1).

496 Marketing Authorisations Regulations, reg 7(2).

497 Marketing Authorisations Regulations, reg 7(3).

498 The manufacture, distribution and import of medicinal products is governed by the Medicines for Human Use (Manufacturing, Wholesale Dealing and Miscellaneous Amendments) Regulations 2005 (SI 2005/2789), which transposed into English law the relevant provisions of the Medicinal Products Directive (2001/83/EC ([2001] OJ L311/67), as amended by Directive 2004/27/EC ([2004] OJ L136/34)). It is necessary to hold a licence from the MHRA in order to manufacture or distribute medicinal products. See MHRA's publication *Rules and Guidance for Pharmaceutical Manufacturers and Distributors 2007*, known as 'the Orange Guide', available at www.mhra.gov.uk/publications/regulatoryguidance/medicines/con2030291. On distribution, see Directive 92/25/EEC ([1992] OJ L113/1) and the *Guidelines on Good Distribution Practice of Medicinal Products for Human Use* (94/C 63/03), available at http://ec.europa.eu/enterprise/pharmaceuticals/pharmacos/docs/doc2001/may/gdpguidelines1.pdf.

499 In order to market a medicinal product, it is necessary to comply with the Medicines for Human Use (Marketing Authorisations etc) Regulations 1994 (SI 1994/3144), the Medicines (Advertising) Regulations 1994 (SI 1994/1932) and the Medicines (Monitoring of Advertising) Regulations 1994 (SI 1994/1933). Marketing authorisation must be sought from either the MHRA or the EMEA. See the MHRA's *Advertising and Promotion of Medicines in the UK* (2005), known as 'the Blue Guide'. See http://www.mhra.gov.uk/home/groups/pl-a/documents/websiteresources/con007552.pdf. If the medicinal product is to be used in the NHS, it is also necessary to apply to the National Institute of Health and Clinical Excellence (NICE), which will assess the product's efficacy and cost-effectiveness (see www.nice.org.uk).

Medical devices are licensed in a similar fashion to medicinal products. The primary provisions relating to the licensing of medical devices are to be found in the Medical Devices Regulations 2002.[500] There are provisions for post-approval regulation of medical devices equivalent to those for medicinal products.

Pharmacovigilance of medicinal products with marketing authorisation

The Medicinal Products Directive requires member states to take all appropriate measures to encourage doctors and other healthcare professionals to report suspected reactions to the competent authorities.[501] A European database has been set up to collect information about adverse reactions centrally.[502] It is a requirement of the Directive that a marketing authorisation holder should have permanently and continuously at his or her disposal an appropriately qualified person for pharmacovigilance, who must ensure that information about all suspected adverse reactions is collected and reported to the competent authority and provide any additional information requested.[503] A marketing authorisation holder must maintain detailed records of all suspected adverse reactions, recording them and reporting them promptly to the competent authority; other adverse reactions should be reported in a periodic safety report, including a scientific evaluation of the risk-benefit balance of the medicinal product.[504] A member state may suspend, revoke or vary a marketing authorisation in the light of pharmacovigilance data; if it does so, it must inform the EMEA, the other member states and the marketing authorisation holder.[505]

A competent authority (the MHRA in the UK) may also suspend, revoke or withdraw a marketing authorisation if it believes that the medicinal product is harmful or lacks therapeutic efficacy, that the risk-benefit balance is not positive, or that qualitative and quantitative composition is not as declared.[506]

---

500 SI 2002/618, implementing the Medical Devices Directives 90/385/EEC ([1990] OJ L189/17), 93/42/EEC ([1993] OJ L169/1) and 98/79/EEC ([1998] OJ L331/1).
501 Medicinal Products Directive, Art 101.
502 Medicinal Products Directive, Arts 102, 105.
503 Medicinal Products Directive, Art 103.
504 Medicinal Products Directive, Art 104.
505 Medicinal Products Directive, Art 107.
506 Medicinal Products Directive, Art 116. See also Regulation 658/2007/EC ([2007] OJ L115/10), which imposes financial penalties for certain infringements of marketing authorisations granted under the centralised procedure.

Incentives for drug development

Orphan drugs

There is a special regime relating to the development of drugs for the treatment of rare diseases, where, because of their rarity, the costs of developing a new drug are unlikely to be recovered by its expected sales. These are known as 'orphan' drugs: the EU defines an orphan medicinal product as one 'intended for the diagnosis, prevention or treatment of a life-threatening or chronically debilitating condition affecting not more than five in ten thousand persons in the Community when the application is made', where no satisfactory treatment is already available.[507] A sponsor can apply to the EMEA to have a medicinal product designated as an orphan medicinal product at any stage of its development before application for marketing authorisation.[508] The EMEA's Committee for Orphan Medicinal Products will examine the application.[509]

Designation as an orphan medicinal product confers the following advantages:

- advice from the EMEA on the conduct of clinical trials;[510]

- access to the centralised procedure for marketing authorisation and remission of fees;[511]

- market exclusivity for ten years after the grant of marketing authorisation;[512] and

- eligibility for incentives to support research into orphan medicinal products.[513]

Supplementary Protection Certificates[514]

Because the process of developing a drug is a lengthy one, the standard patent term of 20 years may not provide enough protection to enable a pharmaceutical company to recover its costs. The EU has therefore provided that, in the case of a medicinal product which has been granted marketing authorisation, the patent holder can apply for a Supplementary Protection

---

507 Regulation 141/2000/EC ([2000] OJ L018/1) on orphan medicinal products (here cited as the Orphan Medicinal Products Regulation), Art 3(1). See also Regulation 847/2000/EC ([2000] OJ L103/5).
508 Orphan Medicinal Products Regulation, Art 5(1).
509 Orphan Medicinal Products Regulation, Art 4.
510 Orphan Medicinal Products Regulation, Art 6.
511 Orphan Medicinal Products Regulation, Art 7.
512 Orphan Medicinal Products Regulation, Art 8.
513 Orphan Medicinal Products Regulation, Art 9.
514 See Ch 4 under 'Supplementary protection certificates' for an outline of the law and its application in the UK.

Certificate, which effectively extends the patent for a period not exceeding a further five years. An application should be made to the intellectual property office of the member state concerned within six months of the grant of marketing authorisation or patent, whichever is the later.[515]

Data exclusivity

The holder of a marketing authorisation for a drug (the reference medicinal product) has a data exclusivity period of ten years during which a competitor may not obtain marketing authorisation for a competing generic drug based on the data submitted for the reference medicinal product. During that period, the competitor would have to sponsor fresh clinical trials for the generic medicinal product (taking care not to infringe any rights held by the holder of marketing authorisation of the reference medicinal product). During the first eight years, the holder of the marketing authorisation may apply for one further year's protection if it obtains an authorisation for one or more new therapeutic indications which bring a significant clinical benefit. This is known as the '8 + 2 + 1' formula.[516]

IMPORT AND EXPORT REGULATIONS

Export regulations

Strategic export controls

The export of certain goods is subject to strategic export controls. Goods that are controlled in this way include:

- military items;
- items that have both military and civilian uses (dual-use items);
- items that may be used for torture; and
- items that are radioactive sources.

Strategic export controls may apply to an export because of the nature of the goods in question, their destination, or their ultimate end-use. Certain activities, such as arranging a contract between overseas companies, are subject to strategic controls in the same way.

---

515 Regulation 1768/92/EEC ([1992] OJ L182/1) concerning the creation of a supplementary protection certificate for medicinal products.
516 See Directive 2004/27/EC ([2004] OJ L136/34) amending Directive 2001/83/EC on the Community code relating to medicinal products for human use.

Licences

The Export Control Organisation, part of the Department for Business, Innovation and Skills (BIS)[517] issues licences enabling controlled goods to be exported and controlled activities to be carried out.[518] Licences are free and are normally issued between 20 and 60 working days after an application has been made.

Three types of export licences can be granted:

- An *open general export licence* (OGL) requires no application and is available for any exporter meeting its requirements, although an exporter must first register with BIS.[519] See BIS's website for a list of currently available open general export licences.[520]

- A *standard individual export licence* (SIEL) covers a specific supply from the applicant to a named recipient.

- An *open individual export licence* (OIEL) covers multiple supplies of specific goods from the applicant to either a named recipient or a named destination. Such licences are normally issued to those who have made, or will need to make, repeated applications for standard individual open licences. They do not cover items used for nuclear, biological or chemical weapons, dual-use items intended for military use, or items intended for re-export to a destination not covered by the licence.

Goods

The UK Strategic Export Control Lists, published on BIS's website, comprise the military, explosive-related, dual-use control, radioactive sources, security and paramilitary, EU dual-use and EU human rights lists.[521]

The category of *military goods* includes goods, software and technology designed for military use. Technology is defined as 'information (including but not limited to information comprised in software and documents such as blueprints, manuals, diagrams and designs) that is capable of use in connection with the development, production or use of any goods',[522] but information

---

517 Formerly the Department for Business, Enterprise and Regulatory Reform.
518 See www.berr.gov.uk/whatwedo/europeandtrade/strategic-export-control/index.html/strategic-export-control/index.html.
519 Registration is by means of the SPIRE system: see www.spire.bis.gov.uk.
520 See www.berr.gov.uk/whatwedo/europeandtrade/strategic-export-control/licences/ogels/index.html.
521 See www.berr.gov.uk/whatwedo/europeandtrade/strategic-export-control/control-lists/page 40521.html. The legislation from which the lists are derived is the Export Control Order 2008 (SI 2008/3231), the Export of Radioactive Sources (Control) Order 2006 (SI 2006/1846), as amended, Sch 1A; and Regulations 1334/2000/EC ([2000] OJ L159/1) (as amended), Annex I and 1236/2005/EC ([2005] OJ L200/1), Annexes II and III.
522 Export Control Order 2008, art 2(1).

that is already in the public domain or relates to basic scientific research is not controlled.[523] 'In the public domain' means 'available without restriction upon further dissemination (no account being taken of restrictions arising solely from copyright)';[524] and 'basic scientific research' means 'experimental or theoretical work undertaken principally to acquire new knowledge of the fundamental principles of phenomena or observable facts and not primarily directed towards a specific practical aim or objective'.[525]

Dual-use goods are covered by the Dual Use Regulation, which lists, in Annex I, goods in the following ten categories for which a licence is required for export outside the Community:

- nuclear materials, facilities and equipment;

- materials, chemicals, micro-organisms and toxins;

- materials processing;

- electronics;

- computers;

- telecommunications and information security;

- sensors and lasers;

- navigation and avionics;

- marine; and

- aerospace and propulsion.

Annex IV lists particularly sensitive items for which a licence is required for transfer even between Community countries.

Embargoes for particular destination

Some countries are affected by embargoes imposed by the United Nations or other sanctions restricting trade. A current list may be found on the BIS and Foreign and Commonwealth Office websites.[526] Export to these countries may require a licence for any type of goods.

End use: weapons of mass destruction

A special restriction applies to the export of goods, software or technology whose likely end use is in connection with weapons of mass destruction.

523 Export Control Order 2008, art 18.
524 Export Control Order 2008, art 2(1).
525 Export Control Order 2008, art 18.
526 www.berr.gov.uk/whatwedo/europeandtrade/strategic-export-control/sanctions-embargoes/
     by-country/index.html.

Export outside the Community of dual-use goods software or technology, other than those specified in Annex I to the Dual-Use Regulation, is forbidden without a licence where there are grounds for suspecting that they are or may be intended, in their entirety or in part, for purposes connected with weapons of mass destruction.[527] The restriction also applies to the electronic transfer of software or technology.[528] It does not apply if the exporter has made all reasonable enquiries as to the proposed use of the goods, software or technology in question and is satisfied that they will not be used for such purposes.[529] If the exporter is not so satisfied, a licence for export is required; in case of doubt, guidance should be sought from BIS by way of a rating enquiry.[530]

Activities

Certain brokering and trafficking activities are also subject to strategic export controls, as set out in the Export Control Order 2008.[531] This divides controlled goods into three categories, A, B and C:

- *Category A goods* (the highest risk): include certain security and para-military police equipment and cluster munitions, explosive submunitions and explosive bomblets.[532] No person may supply or deliver, agree to supply or deliver, or do any act calculated to promote the supply or delivery of any such goods where that person knows or has reason to believe that such action may result in the removal of those goods from one third country to another. This applies both to persons carrying out activities in the UK and UK persons operating abroad.[533]

- *Category B goods* (lower risk than Category A but higher than Category C): include certain small arms and light weapons, including their accessories and ammunition, hand grenades, man-portable air defence systems, long-range missiles, and the components for any of these.[534] Such goods are subject to the same restriction as applies to goods in category A, except that the provision of financing or financial services, insurance or reinsurance services or general advertising or promotion

---

527 Export Control Order 2008, art 6(1). The restriction covers intended 'use in connection with the development, production, handling, operation, maintenance, storage, detection, identification or dissemination of chemical, biological or nuclear weapons or other nuclear explosive devices, or the development, production, maintenance or storage of missiles capable of delivering such weapons' (art 2(1)).
528 Export Control Order 2008, art 6(2)(b).
529 Export Control Order 2008, art 6(2).
530 See www.berr.gov.uk/whatwedo/europeandtrade/strategic-export-control/rating/index.html.
531 The Order was made under the Export Control Act 2002.
532 Export Control Order 2008, Sch 1, Pt 1.
533 Export Control Order 2008, art 21.
534 Export Control Order 2008, Sch 1, Pt 2.

services by a person whose only involvement is to provide such services is not prohibited.[535] Contract promotion activities, that is activities to promote the arrangement or negotiation of a contract for the acquisition, disposal or movement of goods, are also permitted provided that no payment is received.

- *Category C goods* (lowest risk): include all other military goods, portable devices for the purpose of riot control or self-protection by the administration or dissemination of an incapacitating chemical substance, and certain substances.[536] Such goods are subject to the same restriction as applies to goods in category A, with the same exemption as applies to goods in category B, and with the additional exemption that the provision of transportation services is not prohibited by a person whose only involvement is to provide such services. Furthermore, the prohibition in relation to goods in category C does not apply to UK persons operating abroad. Contract promotion activities carried out without payment are also permitted.

Controlled activities are subject to a licensing system similar to that which applies to controlled goods:[537]

- An *open general trade control licence* (OGTCL) allows a trader to carry out certain activities in respect of category C goods and small arms to and from specified countries. Such a licence requires no application, although an exporter must first register with BIS.[538] See BIS's website for a list of currently available open general export licences.[539]

- A *standard individual trade control export licence* (SITCL) is specific to a named trader and covers a single deal where a specific quantity of specified goods passes from a specified supplier to a specified recipient for a specified end-user.

An *open individual trade control licence* (OITCL) is also specific to a named trader, but allows a range of activities connected with trade in specific goods between specified overseas sources and destination countries.

Other export controls

Certain other goods are also subject to export controls, as set out below.

---

535 Export Control Order 2008, art 22.
536 Export Control Order 2008, art 1(2).
537 See www.berr.gov.uk/whatwedo/europeandtrade/strategic-export-control/licences/trade-control-individual.
538 Registration is by means of the SPIRE system: see www.spire.bis.gov.uk.
539 See www.berr.gov.uk/whatwedo/europeandtrade/strategic-export-control/licences/ogels/trade-controls.

Chemicals and pesticides

These are regulated by the EU by means of the Dangerous Chemicals Regulation, which implemented the Rotterdam Convention.[540] The chemicals to which the Regulation applies are listed in Annex I. If such chemicals are exported outside the Community, they must be packaged in the same way as if they were to be sold within the Community. If a chemical is listed as hazardous, the exporter must submit a prior informed consent form (PIC) to the competent authority of the member state from which it is to be exported (in the UK, the Health and Safety Executive), which must give its consent before the export can take place.[541]

Drugs

It is usually necessary to obtain an export certificate for a medicinal product in order to meet the requirements of the country to which the product in question is to be exported. In the UK, export certificates are issued by the MHRA, and there are four different types:[542]

- A *certificate of a pharmaceutical product* (CPP) can apply to a licensed or unlicensed medicinal product and provides certain details about the product, its manufacture and its marketing authorisation.

- A *certificate of leaving status* (CLS) can also apply to a licensed or unlicensed medicinal product, but is less detailed; it is used by importing agents for bids made in response to an international tender.

- A *certificate of manufacturing status* (CMS) does not contain any information specific to the product in question, but confirms that the place where it was manufactured meets the requirements of good manufacturing practice.

- A *certificate for the importation of a pharmaceutical constituent* (CPC) is used where a particular ingredient of a medicinal product is to be exported.

A special licence is needed for the export of controlled drugs.[543] The Drug Licensing and Compliance Unit of the Home Office issues such a licence.[544]

---

540 Regulation 689/2008/EC ([2008] OJ L204/1) concerning the export and import of dangerous chemicals. On the Rotterdam Convention, see www.pic.int.

541 See www.hse.gov.uk/pic.

542 See www.mhra.gov.uk/howweregulate/medicines/importingandexportingmedicines/exporting medicines.

543 That is, drugs that are controlled under the Misuse of Drugs Act 1971 and the Misuse of Drugs Regulations 2001 (SI 2001/3998).

544 See http://drugs.homeoffice.gov.uk/drugs-laws.

Seeds and plants

There is usually no restriction on exports of seeds and plants to other member states in the Community. If the seed or plant is susceptible to serious pests or diseases, however, a plant passport may be required. The grower issues his or her own passport, and the grower needs to be authorised for the purpose by the Food and Environment Research Agency (FERA, an executive agency of the Department for the Environment, Food and Rural Affairs).[545]

If seeds or plants are to be exported outside the Community, the importing country will normally require a phytosanitary certificate, issued by FERA, to prove that the seeds or plants in question have been produced in accordance with the relevant standards.

Import regulations

Goods generally

Goods can generally be imported into the UK without a licence. No duty is payable on goods imported from another member state, but goods imported from outside the Community will be subject to the European Community Common Customs Tariff (CCT), and may also be subject to import quotas. Further details of applicable tariffs, and the rare cases where a licence is required, may be obtained from HMRC.[546] If a quota applies, it is possible to import the goods in question even when the quota has been reached, but at a full, rather than reduced, tariff. The following are among the categories of goods that require an import licence.

Military equipment, nuclear material and chemicals

The import of certain *military equipment* requires a licence from the Import Licensing Branch (ILB) of the Department for Business, Innovation and Skills.[547] The ILB's Notices to Importers should be consulted.[548]

Nuclear material

Nuclear material cannot be imported without a licence issued by the Office for Civil Nuclear Safety (OCNS), a division of the Health and Safety Executive.[549]

---

545 See www.fera.defra.gov.uk/plants/planthealth/plantpassporting.cfm.
546 See www.hmrc.gov.uk.
547 See www.berr.gov.uk/whatwedo/europeandtrade/importing-into-uk/import-licensing/page9780.html.
548 See www.berr.gov.uk/whatwedo/europeandtrade/importing-into-uk/import-licensing/notices-to-importers/page22864.html.
549 See www.hse.gov.uk/nuclear/ocns.

Chemicals

Certain *chemicals* require a licence from the ILB for import, including chemicals that can be used to produce controlled drugs. Under the Reach Regulation,[550] those who import more than one tonne of chemicals per year must register with the European Chemicals Agency in Helsinki.[551]

Pharmaceutical products, seeds, plants and animals

It is necessary to hold a wholesale dealer's licence from the MHRA to import *pharmaceutical products* from another member state, and an import licence to import them from outside the EEA.[552] The import licence can apply to medicinal products without a marketing authorisation provided that they are for use by a named patient only.

A licence is necessary to import certain *seeds, plants and animals* that are endangered species: see the Convention on International Trade in Endangered Species of Flora and Fauna (CITES).[553] The CITES Regulation divides plants and animals into four categories: an import licence is required for those listed in Annexes A and B; an import notification form, to be stamped by HMRC at the port of entry, is required for those listed in Annexes C and D.[554]

---

550 Regulation 1907/2006/EC ([2006] OJ L396/1) concerning the Registration, Evaluation, Authorisation and Restriction of Chemicals (REACH).
551 See http://echa.europa.eu.
552 See www.mhra.gov.uk
553 See www.cites.org.
554 Regulation 318/2008/EC ([2008] OJ L95/3) amending Regulation 338/97/EEC ([1997] OJ L61/1) on the protection of species of wild fauna and flora by regulating trade therein.

CHAPTER 12

Introduction to EC Competition Laws Affecting Technology Transfer Agreements

INTRODUCTION[1]

Impact of EC competition law upon commercial agreements

Under English law there are relatively few legal constraints upon the terms that may be included in a technology transfer agreement, whether it be an R&D agreement, intellectual property licence or assignment, or other technology-related agreement. Unlike the position in some countries, the commercial terms do not generally have to be approved by a government authority. Nor is there any problem over the export of royalties from the UK, as exchange controls were abolished here many years ago.

There are, of course, laws and regulations affecting certain technology transfer *activities,* including activities performed under agreements. Two obvious examples are tax laws (in respect of payments arising under technology transfer agreements),[2] and regulations on the conduct of clinical trials of drugs, use of human and animal issue and the export of technology.[3]

But as to laws constraining the terms of commercial agreements themselves, competition laws are most likely to feature prominently and affect the provisions of a commercial agreement. There are two kinds of competition law:

- domestic UK competition law; and
- EC competition law.

The latter applies in the UK due to its membership of the European Union.[4] UK competition law is considered in Chapter 15. In recent years UK competition law has steadily been brought into line with EC competition law and is now largely the equivalent of its EC counterpart.

EC competition law is complex and addresses the detailed terms of technology transfer agreements. For those advising on legal aspects of such agreements, EC competition law is often the area which requires the most analysis – in

---

1   Following the acceptance of the Lisbon Treaty (see 'EC Treaties' and n 6 below) and its coming into force in December 2009, the Articles of the EC Treaty are to be renumbered. This chapter adopts the following method: the existing numbering is retained with the new numbers in parenthesis (as most people are likely to be still familiar with the existing numbering). The EC Treaty will be renamed the 'Treaty on the Functioning of the European Union', but for ease of reference it will continue to be called the EC Treaty in this edition of the book.

2   See Ch 17.

3   See Ch 11.

4   That is pursuant to the European Communities Act 1972 and subsequent legislation.

order to decide whether the law applies at all to the agreement and, if it does, whether the terms proposed would be acceptable to the EC competition authorities. The prudent and most cost-effective course is to assume that often the law does apply, and to tailor the agreement to meet the requirements of a block exemption Regulation, where this is possible. The main block exemption Regulations in this field will be considered in some detail later in this chapter.

SOURCES OF EC COMPETITION LAW: ARTICLES 81 (101), 82 (102) AND 28–30 (34–36]) OF THE EC TREATY; EUROPEAN ECONOMIC AREA AGREEMENT

EC Treaties

The 1957 Treaty, which established the European Economic Community, known as the Treaty of Rome or the EEC Treaty, is the primary source of EC competition law. The Treaty became part of English law when the UK joined the Community on 1 January 1973.[5] It has subsequently been amended and supplemented, in particular by the Single European Act (in 1982), the Treaty on European Union (signed at Maastricht in 1992, and commonly known as the Maastricht Treaty) and the Treaty of Amsterdam (signed in 1997). The Treaty of Nice was signed in 2001. The Maastricht Treaty renamed the EEC Treaty as the European Community (EC) Treaty and also established the European Union by a separate Treaty. The latter Treaty is concerned mainly with political and defence matters, and not with legislation. Thus, there is the rather confusing position that for some purposes it is correct to refer to the European Community (eg in relation to competition laws) whilst for certain other purposes (eg citizenship) it is appropriate to refer to the European Union. Consistent with this approach, this chapter generally uses the abbreviation 'EC' in respect of European competition laws, but 'EU' when referring to the geographical and political entity known as the European Union.

At the time material was prepared for this edition the Lisbon Treaty[6] had finally received approval and came into force on 1 December 2009. Most of the provisions of the Lisbon Treaty are beyond the scope of this book, but the following are a few brief points:

---

5   That is under the European Communities Act 1972.
6   Treaty of Lisbon amending the Treaty on European Union and the Treaty establishing the European Community, signed at Lisbon, 13 December 2007 ([2007] OJ C306/01).

- the European Union will replace and succeed the European Community;

- the EC Treaty will become the 'Treaty on the Functioning of the European Union'; and

- the Articles of the EC treaty will be renumbered with additional Articles.

Currently the membership of the EU consists of the following 27 countries: Austria, Belgium, Bulgaria, Cyprus, Czech Republic, Denmark, Estonia, Finland, France, Germany, Greece, Hungary, Ireland, Italy, Latvia, Lithuania, Luxembourg, Malta, Netherlands, Poland, Portugal, Romania, Slovakia, Slovenia, Spain, Sweden, and the United Kingdom. Turkey, Croatia and the Former Yugoslav Republic of Macedonia have applied to join the EU.

The provisions of the EC Treaty[7] that most closely affect intellectual property rights and their exploitation are Articles 81 (101), 82 (102) and 28–30 (34–36). These Articles are concerned with prohibiting particular kinds of anti-competitive behaviour. It is now long-established under EC law that the exercising of intellectual property rights (eg through licensing or litigation) can amount to a breach of one or more of these Articles[8].

Article 81 (101)

Article 81 (101), with which this chapter is mainly concerned, prohibits certain agreements and concerted practices that have anti-competitive effects

---

7   To become the Treaty on the Functioning of the European Union.
8   At first sight, two Articles of the EC Treaty would appear to exclude intellectual property rights from the provisions of the Treaty:
     (1) Art 295 (345) states: 'This Treaty shall in no way prejudice the rules of member states governing the system of property ownership'. This Article applies to intellectual property, which is a national system of property ownership (although some limited international rights also exist).
     (2) Art 30 (36) provides that Art 28 (34) shall not apply, inter alia, to restrictions concerning: 'the protection of industrial and commercial property'. However, Art 30 (36) goes on to provide that such restrictions: 'shall not ... constitute a means of arbitrary discrimination or a disguised restriction on trade between member states'.
     In practice, decisions on the anti-competitive effects of exercising intellectual property rights have formed a significant part of the European Court's and European Commission's workload. Two lines of reasoning have been developed by the Court which have enabled it to apply the competition rules to intellectual property rights despite the constraints imposed by the above-quoted Articles. First, in a series of cases under Art 81 (101), commencing in 1966 with *Establisssements Consten SA & Grundig-Verkaufs-GmbH v Commission* [1966] ECR 299, [1966] CMLR 418 the Court has distinguished between the 'existence' of an intellectual property right, which is covered by Art 295 (345), and the 'exercise' of that right, which may infringe Art 81 (101). Secondly, in a series of cases concerning Arts 28–30 (34–36), beginning in 1974 with *Centrafarm BV and Adnaan de Peijpper v Sterling Drug Inc* [1974] ECR 1183, [1974] 2 CMLR 480, [1976] FSR 164, the Court distinguished between the 'specific subject matter' of a patent (or other intellectual property) which gave the owner of the patent the exclusive right to manufacture a patented product and be the first to supply it, and other, less central, rights which could not be exercised in an anti-competitive way, for example the bringing of infringement proceedings against parallel importers of products which were originally put on the market in the EEC by the patent owner or with his or her consent.

or objectives within the EU. The text of Article 81 (101) is reproduced below.[9]

Article 82 (102)[10] prohibits undertakings, which have a dominant position within the EU, from abusing their dominant position. 'Dominant position' is a flexible concept, but would normally apply to a company with a high market share. A market share of 40 per cent is sometimes mentioned in this context but there is really no set figure – a company with a smaller market share than 40 per cent could be dominant, particularly if the rest of the relevant market was supplied by a large number of companies, each with a very small market share.[11] Abuse of a dominant position might arise, for example, from a company's pricing activities or where the company restricted access to certain types of technical information. The same anti-competitive activity could be a breach of Article 81 if carried out by more than one party under an agreement or concerted practice, or a breach of Article 82 if carried out by one party alone where that party is in a dominant position. In some situations a contractual obligation may also amount to a breach of Article 82 (102).

Articles 28–30 (34–36)

Articles 28–30 (34–36)[12] are concerned with activities that restrict the free movement of goods between different countries of the EU, such as import restrictions. Such restrictions are considered to be contrary to the objective of creating a single European market, and are prohibited under Article 28 (34). In certain situations these Articles will prohibit the owner or licensee of rights in technology from taking action to enforce his or her rights, where this would restrict the free movement of goods from one EU country to another. For example, the bringing of a patent infringement action against a parallel importer of patented goods from another EU country may in certain situations amount to such a breach.

Thus, there are several ways in which EC competition laws can constrain an individual or organisation from exploiting its intellectual property rights. Where an agreement is entered into in respect of the intellectual property, the terms may breach Article 81 (101). Where the party exploiting the rights is in a dominant position, its actions in relation to those rights may breach

9   See 'Text of Article 81(101) and author's summary' below.
10 See the companion website to this book and also see http://eur-lex.europa.eu/en/treaties/index. htm under 'Consolidated versions of the Treaty on European Union and the Treaty on the Functioning of the European Union'.
11 In different contexts, it is interesting to note that the European Commission has focused on the dangers of a 20 per cent or 30 per cent market share (eg in Technology Transfer Agreements Regulation, Art 3(1), (2)) and of a 10 per cent or 15 per cent market share (eg in 2001 Notice on agreements of minor importance, para 7).
12 See the companion website to this book and also see http://eur-lex.europa.eu/en/treaties/index. htm under 'Consolidated versions of the Treaty on European Union and the Treaty on the Functioning of the European Union'.

Article 82 (102). Where the rights are exercised in such a way as to restrict the movement of goods within the EU, there may be a breach of Articles 28–30 (34–36).

European Economic Area Agreement

The Agreement on a European Economic Area ('EEA Agreement') should be mentioned.[13] The EEA Agreement, which came into effect on 1 January 1994, created a free-trade zone, now comprising the 27 members of the EU plus 3 of the 4 members of the EFTA (European Free Trade Association), Iceland, Lichtenstein and Norway (only Switzerland as a member of EFTA is not part of the EEA Agreement). The EEA extended EC competition rules to these non-EU European countries. For example, Article 53 of the EEA Agreement uses language very similar to Article 81 (101). Similarly the block exemption Regulations described later in this chapter apply in these countries as well as in member states of the EU. In effect there is a parallel set of rules for these non-EU countries, with parallel enforcement authorities – for example the so-called 'Surveillance Authority' is equivalent to the European Commission. Switzerland remains outside the EEA (although it is a member of the European Patent Convention).

Where an agreement has anti-competitive effects in EU countries only, it should be notified to the European Commission. Where it has anti-competitive effects only in the non-EU countries that are party to the EEA Agreement, then it should be notified to the Surveillance Authority. Where it has anti-competitive effects in both areas, and the effects in the EU are 'appreciable', the European Commission will have jurisdiction. There are detailed rules on the overlap between the two jurisdictions, as well as transitional provisions in respect of agreements in force prior to 1 January 1994.

Association Agreements with Central and Eastern European countries

EC and EEA countries have entered into agreements, known as Association Agreements, with certain East European countries that are candidates to become members of the EC/EU; whilst these agreements include provisions concerning the protection of intellectual property, they don't provide for equivalent competition laws to those operating in EC and EEA countries.

Thus, the competition rules are very similar in all countries in the EEA, although the legal basis will differ, depending on whether the agreement is concerned with activities or effects in EU countries. The remainder of this

---

13   In the UK, see the European Economic Area Act 1993.

chapter will consider agreements within the jurisdiction of the European Commission (and references to member states will include these further countries, where applicable), and will refer to the EC legislation.

SCOPE AND PURPOSE OF THIS CHAPTER

This chapter considers Article 81 (101). It is designed to give practical assistance to anyone who wishes to take account of Article 81 (101) when drafting or reviewing a technology-related agreement. The following subjects are discussed:

- First, there is a general explanation of the provisions of Article 81 (101), and of the types of situation in which it may apply, the consequences of infringing Article 81(1) (101(1)) and the procedure for applying for an individual exemption under Article 81(3) (101(3)). The main advantages and disadvantages of applying for such an exemption are considered.

- Next, there is an overview of the main steps involved in analysing whether a technology transfer agreement (particularly R&D agreements and intellectual property licences) may breach Article 81(1) (101(1)) and, if so, whether it may receive block exemption under Article 81(3) (101(3)).

- The main part of this chapter then considers the detailed provisions of certain Commission Notices and Regulations that are most relevant in practice to technology-related agreements, namely:

De minimis

- Notice on agreements of minor importance which do not appreciably restrict competition under Article 81(1) of the Treaty establishing the European Community.[14]

Horizontal agreements (including R&D agreements)

- Guidelines on horizontal cooperation agreements;[15]

- R&D Agreements Regulation;[16]

- Specialisation Agreements Regulation.[17]

---

14 [2001] OJ C368/7.
15 [2001] OJ C3/2.
16 Commission Regulation (EC) 2659/2000 ([2000] OJ L304/7) on the application of Article 81(3) of the Treaty to categories of research and development agreements.
17 Regulation 2658/2000 ([2000] OJ L304/3).

Vertical agreements (including intellectual property licences)

- Guidelines on vertical restraints[18] (considered only in outline);

- Regulation on Vertical Agreements[19] (considered only in outline);

- Notice on subcontracting agreements;[20]

- Technology Transfer Agreements Regulation.[21]

This chapter does not provide a general description of EC competition laws and the institutions that enforce them.[22] Nor does it provide a general analysis of the very extensive case law (including Commission decisions) under Article 81 (101), although particularly relevant case law is discussed at various points to clarify particular provisions of the block exemption Regulations, or to give a flavour of the interpretation that has been placed on Article 81(1) (101(1)) by the European Commission and European Court, respectively. A comprehensive review of Article 81 (101) and EC competition law is felt to be outside the scope of this book. Instead, this chapter focuses on the practical aspects of compliance with Article 81 (101) and on how to bring an agreement within the scope of relevant Commission Notices and block exemption Regulations.

Clearly, an understanding of the omitted areas is highly desirable for anyone involved in drafting or advising on agreements of this kind, particularly where the agreement cannot be made to fit within a block exemption Regulation or Commission Notice, or where particularly unusual provisions are contemplated and it is not clear whether they would be in breach of Article

---

18 [2000] OJ C291/1.
19 Regulation 2790/99 ([1999] OJ L336/21). Due to be replaced from 1 June 2010 by Commission Regulation 330/2010 on the application of Article 101(3) of the Treaty of the Functioning of the European Union to categories of vertical agreements and concerted [2010] OJ L 102/1. There are transitional arrangements for agreements covered by Regulation 2790/99. As proofs were being returned to the publisher, the new Regulation was due to come into force, and appears to have provisions broadly similar to Regulation 2790/1999 with modifications (such as taking account of internet sales and for sales taking place across borders). An outline of the new Regulation will appear on the website which accompanies this book.
20 [1979] OJ C1/2.
21 Regulation 772/2004 ([2004] OJ L123/11).
22 In very brief summary, the Council of the European Communities (the Council) is the highest level of authority in respect of the passing of legislation; in some cases the Council has delegated authority to the Commission of the European Communities (the Commission). Thus, the block exemption Regulations are Commission Regulations implemented pursuant to powers originally granted to the Commission by the Council under Council Regulation 19/65/EEC OJ [1965] 36.

In respect of the interpretation of legislation, certain decisions of the Commission (eg on whether Art 81(1) applies to an agreement) can be appealed to the European Court (which nowadays comprises two levels: the Court itself and a lower level 'Court of First Instance' to which competition cases are referred). National courts also have authority to decide whether Art 81(1) applies to an agreement (but have no power to grant exemptions under Art 81(3) – only the Commission may do this).

81 (101). A list of specialist books on EC competition law is included in the bibliography at p xi.

Many technology-related agreements are concerned with activities in more than one country, as in the case of a pan-European licence agreement. As was mentioned earlier, the laws described in this chapter apply equally in most European countries. However, the separate requirements of national competition laws may also need to be taken into account. Non-UK 'domestic' competition laws are beyond the scope of this book.[23] UK domestic competition law is considered in Chapter 15.

If the agreement extends beyond Europe, competition laws in non-European countries may also be relevant, and local advice should be obtained.[24]

At various points in this section, the text of European legislation will be quoted, mainly that of Article 81 (101), several Commission Notices and three block exemption Regulations. The format of European legislation, particularly the older legislation, can be complex, with long, unbroken sentences that deal with several issues in the same sentence. To assist comprehension, some quotations will appear with additional headings and spacing that do not appear in the original text, and in some cases additional numbering which will be in square brackets.[25] Care has been taken not to change the sense, so far as this can be gleaned from the legislation.

ARTICLE 81 (101) AND COMMERCIAL AGREEMENTS

Text of Article 81(101) and author's summary

The text of Article 81 (101) follows. The drafting style of the original can be difficult to follow in places, particularly where it incorporates several concepts and examples into a single sentence. To assist analysis of the Article, italicised comments (which are not part of the original text) and additional spacing have been incorporated into the following text.[26]

---

23 A (short) summary can be found in Anderson (ed), *Drafting Agreements in the Biotechnology and Pharmaceutical Industries* (looseleaf, Oxford University Press).

24 For example, if the agreement involves the acquisition of US assets worth $50m or more, the agreement may have to be notified to the US authorities under the Hart-Scott-Rodino Antitrust Improvements Act of 1976, as amended, and rules promulgated by the US Federal Trade Commission thereunder. Thus, an IP licence agreement that includes the US as part of the licensed territory might be notifiable if the value of the US element of the deal is sufficiently large. Where the acquisition price of the US assets is wholly or partly contingent (eg royalties based on sales), the fair market value of the assets may have to be determined (similar to a net present value calculation). Further information on the Act is available on the Federal Trade Commission website (http://www.ftc.gov/).

25 See the companion website to this book and also see http://eur-lex.europa.eu/en/treaties/index. htm under 'Consolidated versions of the Treaty on European Union and the Treaty on the Functioning of the European Union'.

26 For Article 81(101) in its original form, see previous footnote.

Author's summary	Text of Article 81 (101)
81(1)(101(1)) – certain activities are incompatible with the Common Market:	81(1) (101(1)). The following shall be prohibited as incompatible with the common market:
agreements *etc*	all agreements between undertakings, decisions by associations of undertakings and concerted practices
*which may **affect trade between member states***	which may affect trade between member states
	And
*and have **anti-competitive objectives or effects in the EC***	which have as their object or effect the prevention, restriction or distortion of competition within the common market,
for example – price fixing, market rigging, discrimination between customers	and in particular those which:
	(a) directly or indirectly fix purchase or selling prices or any other trading conditions;
	(b) limit or control production, markets, technical development, or investment;
	(c) share markets or sources of supply;
	(d) apply dissimilar conditions to equivalent transactions with other trading parties, thereby placing them at a competitive disadvantage;
	(e) make the conclusion of contracts subject to acceptance by the other parties of supplementary obligations which, by their nature or according to commercial usage, have no connection with the subject of such contracts.
*81(2)(101(2)) – agreements which breach 81(1) (101(1)) are **automatically void***	(2). Any agreements or decisions prohibited pursuant to this Article shall be automatically void.
*81(3)(101(1)) – but **exemptions** from 81(1) (101(1)) may be available if:*	(3). The provisions of paragraph (1) may, however, be declared inapplicable in the case of:
the agreement	— any agreement or category of agreements between undertakings;
	— any decision or category of decisions by associations of undertakings;
	— any concerted practice or category of concerted practices;
has certain public benefits	which contributes to improving the production or distribution of goods or to promoting technical or economic progress, while allowing consumers a fair share of the resulting benefit,
and the anti-competitive aspects are not too bad	and which does not:
	(a) impose on the undertakings concerned restrictions which are not indispensable to the attainment of these objectives;
	(b) afford such undertakings the possibility of eliminating competition in respect of a substantial part of the products in question.

When does Article 81(1) (101(1)) apply?

Broad scope of Article 81(1) (101(1))

The language of Article 81(1) (101(1)) has been interpreted broadly by the European Commission and European Court. In particular:

Undertakings

An undertaking is not defined in the EC Treaty but has been considered in many ECJ cases, and in one case it has been held that:

> 'the concept of an undertaking, encompasses every entity engaged in an economic activity, regardless of the legal status of the entity or the way in which it is financed'.[27]

This term therefore can cover any company (a group of companies being treated as a single undertaking), and any other organisation or individual engaged in commercial activities; it is suggested that it will normally include inventors and research institutes who take steps to exploit their inventions commercially.[28]

Agreements, decisions and concerted practices

These terms cover not only formal agreements but any form of collusion including, for example, recommendations by a trade association to its members, and informal arrangements[29] (eg where a patent owner agrees to bring infringement proceedings for the benefit of its exclusive licensee) and including direct or indirect contact, attending meetings, co-operation on a limited basis, information exchanges etc.[30] Agreements between a parent and subsidiary company are generally outside Article 81 (101), as they are normally treated as one undertaking.[31]

---

27 In Case C-41/90, *Höfner and Elser v Macroton GmbH* [1991] ECR I-1979, [1993] 4 CMLR 306, para 21. This definition has been used in a number of succeeding ECJ cases.
28 *AOPI/Beyrard* [1976] 1 CMLR D14; *Vaesen/Moris* [1979] 1 CMLR 511; *Theal/Watts* [1977] 1 CMLR D44; *Tepea v Commission* [1978] ECR 1391.
29 See eg Case C-238/05, *Anserf-Equifax, Servicios de Información sobre Solvenica y Crédito, SL v Associación de Usuarios de Servicios Bancarios (Ausbanc)* [2006] ECR I-11125, where the Court held that the use of the different terms (agreements, decisions, concerted practices) was aimed to catch the different forms of collusion and co-ordination between undertakings and 'Accordingly ... a precise characterization of the nature of the cooperation at issue in the main proceedings is not liable to alter the legal analysis to be carried out under Article 81 ...'
30 Eg Cases 40–8, 50, 54–6, 111 and 113–4/73, *Re the European Sugar Cartel; Cooperatiёve Vereniging 'Suiker Unie' UA v Commission* [1975] ECR 1663, [1976] 1 CMLR 295; *Polypropylene* [1986] OJ L230/1, [1988] 4 CMLR 347; *Interbrew and Alken-Maes (Belgian Beer)* [2003] OJ L200/1.
31 See *Christiani v Nelson* [1969] CMLR D36; *Hydrotherm v Andreoli* [1984] ECR 299.

Which may affect trade between member states

The European Court and the European Commission have interpreted these words broadly. A major objective behind them is to bring about a single European market with no national or other barriers to trade within the EU. In order to be caught by this provision, the agreement need not be between parties in different member states. Moreover, the agreement need not be concerned with activities in more than one member state,[32] although the agreement is far more likely to affect trade between member states if it is. If an agreement, which is concerned only with activities in one member state, could distort the pattern of trade coming from another member state, it will be caught by Article 81 (101) (subject to the other requirements of the Article being met). Article 81 (101) could even apply to an agreement concerned with only part of the territory of a member state, if it (or, more likely, a network of such agreements) could have an effect on inter-state trade.[33]

Having said this, many agreements with no international element will clearly not infringe Article 81 (101). For example, an agreement between an inventor and a manufacturer, under which the latter is contracted by the former to build a prototype of an invention, is unlikely by itself to be subject to Article 81 (101).[34] If the agreement also includes an exclusive licence to the manufacturer to manufacture and sell in the UK, it may affect trade between member states, although in many cases it is unlikely to do so. If the product becomes successful, and a network of exclusive licensees is appointed throughout the EU, the chances of an effect on trade between member states increase significantly.[35]

With the coming into force of the EEA Agreement in 1994 (see 'European Economic Area Agreement' above), the list of countries to which the European competition rules apply was expanded to include Iceland, Lichtenstein and Norway. At the date of writing, Switzerland remains outside both the EU and the EEA and is therefore not bound by Article 81 (101). However, as was mentioned earlier, an agreement may be caught by Article 81 (101) even if it concerns a territory outside the EU/EEA, if the agreement could affect the

---

32 Eg see *Michelin v Commission* [1983] ECR 3461.
33 See, for example, *Vereenging van Cementhandelaren v Commission* [1972] ECR 977. In that case, the recommendations of a trade association to its members, all of whom were cement dealers based in the Netherlands, were considered by the European Court. The recommendations were as to the prices at which members should sell in the Netherlands and the parties to whom they should sell in the Netherlands. The European Court held that such recommendations could affect trade between member states, even though the recommendations did not apply to sales outside the Netherlands. In the words of the Court (at para 30):
   '... the provisions of the agreement which are mutually binding on the members of the ... association, and the prohibition by the association on all sales to resellers who are not authorised by it, make it more difficult for producers or sellers from other member states to be active in or penetrate the Netherlands market'.
34 See para 1 of the Commission Notice on subcontracting agreements (referred to below).
35 Eg see *Boussois v Interpane* [1988] 4 CMLR 124.

pattern of trade within the EU/EEA. Given the close proximity of Switzerland to several EU countries, it is likely that there will be many cases in which an agreement relating to Switzerland is caught by Article 81 (101).

Which have as their object or effect the prevention, restriction or distortion of competition

This requirement is central to Article 81 (101). Two questions arise: namely, does the agreement have anti-competitive objects/effects, and if so, are they significant?

Anti-competitive

The European Commission considers that many kinds of provision that are commonly included in technology-related agreements have such objects or effects. The European Court has held that the grant of an exclusive licence, by itself, does not amount to an infringement of Article 81(1) (101(1)) where it is concerned with new technology and is only an 'open' exclusive licence, that is to say it does not grant absolute territorial protection against parallel importers and other licensees.[36] However, this type of non-restrictive licence is relatively rarely encountered in practice, as most exclusive licensees will require protection against other licensees. Moreover, the practice of the Commission has been to interpret this ruling narrowly.

The most commonly encountered types of restriction, which the Commission considers will infringe Article 81(1) (101(1)), are those listed in the block exemption Regulations, which are either hardcore (ie the most severe) restrictions or are exempt, but only in the circumstances described in the relevant Regulation. Where the Regulation does not apply, for example because the type of agreement in question is excluded from the scope of the Regulation, the attitude of the Commission to the provision in question *may* be similar to that indicated in the Regulation, but this cannot be automatically assumed – much will depend on the economic effects of the agreement in question, as determined by the Commission. In such cases, the previous method of seeking clarity by way of obtaining an individual exemption for such agreements by notifcation to the Commission is no longer available.[37] The main types of provision that the Commission considers will infringe Article 81(1) (101(1)) will be discussed further in the sections dealing with block exemption Regulations and in the special sections on software licences and joint ventures.

Significant

If the effects are minimal, for example because the market shares of the parties to the agreement are very small, Article 81 will not be infringed (even if it

36 See *Nungesser v Commission* [1982] ECR 2015.
37 Following the implementation of Regulation 1/2003 ([2003] OJ L1/1).

contains, potentially, hardcore-type restrictions, such as price fixing or absolute territorial protection).[38] However, it is not easy to determine from the case law when the effects would be considered to be minimal in any particular case. Moreover, the position may change throughout the life of an agreement, for example if the products which are the subject matter of the agreement turn out to be very commercially successful several years into the life of the agreement.

In order to remove some of this uncertainty, in 1977 the European Commission issued its Notice on agreements of minor importance; the latest version dates from 2001.[39] The Notice describes circumstances in which the Commission considers that an agreement would not be sufficiently significant to be subject to Article 81 (101). It will be considered further under 'Notice on agreements of minor importance' below.

Within the common market

Most agreements which are caught by this requirement will be between European parties and concern activities within the EC. However, the Commission considers that an agreement can be contrary to Article 81(1) (101(1)) even where the parties to it have no direct connection with the EC, and do not carry on activities within the EC, if their agreement has anti-competitive effects within the EC.[40]

Difficulties of determining whether Article 81(1) (101(1)) applies

From the foregoing it can be seen that there are a considerable number of 'grey areas' when it comes to determining whether or not an agreement infringes Article 81(1) (101(1)). In part these result from the following issues:-

- The difficulty of assessing the impact of an agreement, or rather the impact of activities carried out under the agreement, upon the market in which it operates. This issue raises questions of economics as well as law, and is particularly problematic in the case of agreements concerning unproven technology, where the likely market shares may be difficult or impossible to predict.

- The approach of the European Commission, which until 2004 had been to decide that many types of contract clause, particularly those restraining a party's conduct, infringe Article 81(1)(101(1)), and to

---

38   See *Volk v Vervaecke* [1969] ECR 295, [1969] ECR 273 where the Court considered an agreement for the distribution of washing machines. The parties had only a 0.2 per cent share of the market and the Court held that the agreement was not within Art 81. See also *Cadillon v Hoss* [1971] ECR 351, and *Miller v Commission* [1978] ECR 131 (where a 5 per cent share was held *not* to be minimal, ie Art 81 could apply).

39   [2001] OJ C368/13.

40   See the wood pulp case – *Ahlstrom v Commission* [1988] ECR 5193.

grant individual exemptions under Article 81(3) (101(3)) to the less harmful infringements. This contrasts with, for example, the US anti-trust authorities, who have tended to declare less harmful restrictions on conduct not to be subject to their competition laws at all. Although this approach has changed following adoption of Regulation 1/2003, where the Commission no longer grants individual exemptions, but leaves it to the parties to decide whether an agreement or contract clause comes within the exemptions available under the block exemption Regulations or a Commission Notice.

- The non-literal approach that is required for EU legislation – ie it is necessary to comply with the spirit of the legislation, as well as its letter, to a greater extent than is the case with domestic UK legislation.

One consequence of these uncertainties is that the prudent course, particularly when considering an exclusive licence agreement, is often to assume that Article 81(1) (101(1)) does apply in principle, and to try to ensure that the agreement falls within one of the Commission Notices (in particular the Notice on agreements of minor importance[41] and the Notice on sub-contracting agreements) or one of the block exemption Regulations.

Consequences if Article 81(1) applies

Provisions are void; possibility of fines

Article 81(2) (101(2)) provides that agreements etc which infringe Article 81(1) (101(1)) are 'automatically void'. They may, however, be given an exemption under Article 81(3) (101(3)) (discussed below). The wording of Article 81(2) (101(2)) may appear misleading, particularly to someone who is familiar with the English law distinction between:

- an agreement being *void* in its entirety; and
- particular provisions of an agreement being *unenforceable*.

The European Court has held that it is only the provisions which infringe Article 81(1) (101(1)) which are void. The remainder of the agreement may be enforceable if, after removing the offending provisions, the nature of the contract is not fundamentally altered.[42]

The European Commission also has the power to fine the parties to an agreement for deliberate or negligent infringement of Article 81 (101), the maximum fine being €1 million or 10 per cent of the party's (including any group companies') worldwide turnover in the preceding year, whichever is higher.

---

41 Although strictly speaking these Notices describe when Art 81(1) does *not* apply, it is convenient to consider the Notices and block exemption Regulations together.

42 See *Societe Technique Miniere v Maschinenbau Ulm* [1966] ECR 235 at 250 ; *Societe de Vente de Ciments et Betons v Kerpen & Kerpen* [1983] ECR 4173 at 4184 ; *Chemidus Wavin v TERI* [1978] 3 CMLR 514.

Exemption under Article 81(3) (101(3)) – only the European Commission may exempt

Article 81(3) (101(3)) provides that in certain situations, the provisions of Article 81(1) (101(1)) may be 'declared inapplicable', ie the agreement may be exempted. Until 1 May 2004 there was a mechanism for granting (individual) exemptions, established in 1962, when the Council of the European Communities (the Council) implemented Regulation 17. Regulation 17 (and Regulation 3385/94, which supplemented it in 1994) provided that only the European Commission may grant an exemption under Article 81(3).[43]

In 1965, the Council implemented Regulation 19 which enabled the Commission to introduce regulations giving 'block exemption' to agreements under Article 81(3) without the need for the parties to make an individual notification to the Commission.

It is now no longer possible to apply for an individual exemption through notification to the Commission, or other methods which were available such as 'negative clearance' or obtain a 'letter of comfort' from the Commission. This significant change in approach follows the introduction of Regulation 1/2003 from 1 May 2004.[44] Besides forcing the parties to an agreement to carry out their own assessment as to whether the agreement is in accordance with EU competition law, Regulation 1/2003 also indicates that if an agreement is exempt under Article 81(3) (101(3)) then there is no need for the parties concerned to carry out any action or make any application for the exemption to apply.

This new regime has the benefit of being simpler (to some extent) than the previous one in the sense that the parties do not need to spend their time and money on making applications to the Commission. On the other hand the parties can be left in doubt as to whether in fact their agreement is considered, or will be considered at some (indeterminable) time in the future compliant with EU competition law. The parties to an agreement will face uncertainty as to whether the Commission (and now national competition authorities and national courts) will not choose to take action against the parties after an agreement has been operating for some time.

---

43 Under this former law, except where a block exemption Regulation applied, the agreement must be notified to the Commission, in order for an individual exemption to be given to it under Art 81(3).

44 Council Regulation (EC) 1/2003 ([2003] OJ L1/1) on the implementation of the rules on competition laid down in Articles 81 and 82 of the Treaty (Text with EEA relevance). This Regulation is considered below under 'Modernisation Regulation'.

In consequence, the parties have to try, as far as it is possible to do so, that their agreement is within the scope of one of the Commission Notices or block exemption Regulations.[45]

OVERVIEW OF HOW TO DETERMINE WHETHER ARTICLE 81(1) (101(1)) APPLIES, AND WHETHER A BLOCK EXEMPTION APPLIES, TO A TECHNOLOGY-RELATED AGREEMENT

This section will briefly address the following questions, some of which are dealt with in more detail in subsequent sections:

- Does the agreement have a Community dimension?

- Does the Notice on agreements of minor importance apply?

- Is it a horizontal or vertical agreement?

- If the agreement is horizontal, is it a full-function joint venture with a Community dimension to which the Merger Regulation[46] applies, or is it subject to the Article 81 regime?

- If the Article 81 regime applies, does it seem from the Guidelines on horizontal agreements that the agreement may breach Article 81(1)?

- Does either the R&D Agreements Regulation, or the Specialisation Agreements Regulation, apply, and if so does the agreement receive block exemption under the relevant Regulation?

- If the agreement is vertical, does it seem from the Guidelines on vertical restraints that it may breach Article 81(1) (101(1))?

- Does the Vertical Agreements block exemption Regulation apply? If so, does the agreement meet the requirements of that Regulation?

- Does the Notice on subcontracting apply? If so, does the agreement meet the requirements of that Notice?

- Does the Technology Transfer Agreements block exemption Regulation apply? Does the agreement fit within or receive block exemption under that Regulation?

---

45 See Regulation 1/2003, Recital 10 which indicates the power of the Commission to provide for further block exemptions, but also to withdraw them in particular cases where an agreement is incompatible with Art 81(3) (101(3)).

46 Council Regulation (EC) 139/2004 ([2004] OJ L24/1) on the control of concentrations between undertakings (the EC Merger Regulation) from 1 May 2004.

Does the agreement have a Community dimension?

The term 'Community dimension' has a specific meaning when considering whether the EC Merger Regulation applies to a merger or joint venture, as to which see relevant paragraph below.

The term is also useable as convenient shorthand for the tests under Article 81 (101), referred to above, as to whether an agreement (a) affects trade between member states of the EU, and (b) has anti-competitive objects or effects within the EU. Agreements that do not meet these tests, because the scale of activities is too small and localised, are sometimes known as 'de minimis'. A number of sources of information may help a person to determine whether an agreement potentially breaches Article 81 (101) or can be dismissed at the outset as de minimis (and, perhaps just as important, whether the European Commission will determine it to be de minimis), including:

- case law of the European Court and Commission decisions;

- the Notice on agreements of minor importance;

- Guidelines on horizontal agreements;

- Guidelines on vertical restraints;

In practice, a good starting point is to consider whether the Notice on agreements of minor importance applies. For particular types of agreement, eg an early-stage research agreement with a university, comments in the Guidelines can also be helpful.

Does the Notice on agreements of minor importance apply?

As discussed later in this chapter in detail, the latest version of the Notice indicates that the Commission considers that an agreement will not breach Article 81 (101) if the parties' combined market shares, in the relevant goods or services that are the subject of the agreement, does not exceed certain percentage levels and the agreement does not include any 'hardcore' restrictions. Oversimplified, these market-share thresholds are:

- 10 per cent where the parties are competitors;

- 15 per cent where the parties are not competitors[47].

---

47   Commission Notice on agreements of minor importance, para 7.

And the hardcore restrictions are:

(1) price-fixing terms;

(2) sales/output limits;

(3) market/customer allocation;

(4) some territory restrictions;

(5) some restrictions on sales where the parties are in a distribution network.[48]

The first, second and fifth of these restrictions will rarely be encountered in technology transfer agreements. The Notice also gives some guidance, although this guidance is stated not to form part of the Notice, to the effect that the Commission considers that agreements between small- and medium-sized undertakings[49] are 'rarely capable of appreciably affecting trade between member states'. The use of the word 'rarely' and the fact that this statement is not officially part of the Notice, should make advisers cautious about placing reliance on what seems to be in the nature of a *sotto voce* comment by the Commission. For example, if the parties to an agreement have a large market share in an essential new technology, the fact that they are both medium-sized companies is unlikely to result in their agreement being treated as de minimis. The Notice does not, however, provide guidance as to when an agreement will be unlikely to be capable of appreciably affecting trade between member states – this is available in a separate Commission Notice.[50]

Is it a horizontal or vertical agreement?

The distinction between horizontal and vertical agreements can seem rather theoretical to the non-economist, particularly when dealing with technology-related agreements. In a traditional industry, there may be a clear distinction between people at different levels of production, eg manufacturers, distributors, wholesalers and retailers. In such cases it may be relatively easy to distinguish between a horizontal agreement (eg a co-operation agreement between two manufacturers or between two distributors) and a vertical agreement (eg a supply agreement between a manufacturer or a licensor of IP and a distributor).

---

48   Commission Notice on Agreements of minor importance, para 11.
49   See Commission Notice on Agreements of minor importance, para 3, which makes reference to Annex to Commission Recommendation 96/280/EC ([1996] OJ L107). At the date of the Notice, these limits were 250 employees and an annual turnover not exceeding 40m Euros or an annual balance sheet not exceeding 27m Euros.
50   Commission Notice *Guidelines on the effect on trade concept contained in Articles 81 and 82 of the Treaty* ([2004] OJ C101/07).

In theory, the same distinction can be made in technology-related agreements. Thus, an R&D agreement is considered to be a horizontal agreement, whilst a patent licence agreement is considered to be vertical. In the latter case, the owner of IP is considered to be at a different level in the chain of production and supply to the licensee, who may be a manufacturer or supplier. But there are a number of practical problems with this type of analysis in the high-tech field, including:

- Agreements often incorporate both horizontal and vertical elements, as in the case of an agreement between a biotech company that owns rights to a drug, and a large pharmaceutical company that is to acquire rights to commercialise the drug. Such agreements often involve a joint programme of R&D, combined with a licence to the biotech company's underlying IP that protects the drug. It may be difficult to determine the 'centre of gravity' of the agreement for the purposes of EC competition law, ie is it principally an R&D agreement or a licence agreement?

- Companies in the high-tech sector can have different roles and ambitions, depending on the particular project. For one project, a company may be a simple owner of technology, intending to license it out at an early stage. For the next project, it may intend to develop it to, or near to, the market, and enter into joint-marketing activities with another company. Its position in the supply chain may therefore be different for each project. Its marketing partner may be a competitor in respect of one project, and a non-competitor in respect of the next project.

It may, therefore, be necessary to consider some of the provisions of the agreement by reference to the rules on horizontal agreements, and other provisions by reference to the vertical agreements regime. Despite the difficulties, it is an important step in the competition analysis to decide whether the agreement is vertical or horizontal.

If the agreement is horizontal, is it a full-function joint venture with a Community dimension to which the Merger Regulation applies, or is it subject to the Article 81 regime?

A further complication, in the case of horizontal agreements such as R&D collaboration agreements, is to determine whether the agreement amounts to a 'full-function' joint venture with a 'Community dimension'. If so, then the EC Merger Regulation will apply, and Article 81 (101) will usually not apply.[51] The law and practice of corporate mergers is considered to be outside

---

51   However, the Commission has confirmed that in future ancillary agreements that form part of a merger may need to be considered under Art 81 – see Box 7, p 54 of the Commission's 31st *Report on Competition Policy* (2001).

the main scope of this book, and will therefore be treated briefly. First, a little background to the current EC competition law on mergers may be of assistance.

The term 'joint venture' has no precise meaning under English law. Sometimes the term is used in a narrow sense to mean a company that is formed by two or more other companies for the purposes of a joint-business activity; on other occasions the term is used more broadly to mean any type of (contractual) business collaboration between companies. Many R&D collaboration agreements could be regarded as joint ventures in the latter sense.

Prior to 1998, EC competition law distinguished between 'concentrative' joint ventures, treated as a merger of the joint venture owners' interests, and 'co-operative' joint ventures, that did not amount to a merger. Mergers were dealt with under the EC Merger Regulation. With effect from 1 March 1998, the Merger Regulation was amended[52] to cover a larger category of joint ventures known as 'full-function' joint ventures.[53] In effect, part of the category of co-operative joint ventures was moved into the Merger Regulation regime.

The Merger Regulation now applies to *full-function* joint ventures that have a *Community dimension*. Thus, if the joint venture is not full-function, or is full-function but does not have a Community dimension, the Merger Regulation will not apply, and the agreement will fall to be analysed under Article 81 (101).[54]

Full-function joint ventures are defined as autonomous economic entities that operate on a lasting basis, and perform all the functions of such entities.[55] Examples of joint ventures that are not 'full-function' might include joint ventures that have no employees (the parents providing their employees for any work that is required), or are set up for a limited period of time, or rely on the services of the parents.

'Community dimension' for the purposes of the Merger Regulation means, in practice, large-scale mergers spread across several Member States and where at least some of the participants are large-scale companies. Two main tests, plus a 'two-thirds rule', are defined by the Regulation.[56] If either test is satisfied, and the two-thirds rule is also satisfied, the Merger Regulation applies.

---

52 Regulation 1310/97, now replaced by Council Regulation (EC) 139/2004 ([2004] OJ L24/1) on the control of concentrations between undertakings (the EC Merger Regulation) from 1 May 2004.
53 See Regulation 139/2004, Art 3(4).
54 See further on this issue Commission Consolidated Jurisdictional Notice ([2008] OJ C95/01) under Council Regulation (EC)139/2004 on the control of concentrations between undertakings,para 91 ff and in particular para 94.
55 Regulation 139/2004, Art 3(4).
56 Regulation 139/2004, Art 1(1)–(3).

Test 1

- the aggregate worldwide turnover of all the undertakings concerned exceeds 5,000 million euros; and

- the aggregate Community-wide turnover of each of at least two of the undertakings concerned exceeds 250 million euros.

Test 2

- the aggregate worldwide turnover of all the undertakings concerned exceeds 2,500 million euros; and

- in each of at least 3 member states, the combined aggregate turnover of all the undertakings concerned is more than 100 million euros; and

- in each of at least 3 member states identified above, any 2 of the undertakings concerned each have a turnover in excess of 25 million euros; and

- the aggregate Community-wide turnover of each of at least two of the undertakings concerned exceeds 100 million euros.

Two-thirds rule

- there must be no single member state in which all the undertakings concerned achieve at least two-thirds of their aggregate Community-wide turnover.

It will be seen that most R&D collaborations are not full-function joint ventures with a Community dimension. Further treatment of the Merger Regulation is considered to be outside the scope of this book. Readers are referred to books which focus on competition law.[57]

If the Article 81 regime applies, does it seem from the Guidelines on horizontal agreements that the agreement may breach Article 81(1)?

The Guidelines consider different types of horizontal agreement, and include a chapter dealing specifically with R&D collaborations. The Guidelines are helpful in clarifying that certain types of R&D collaboration are unlikely to be in breach of Article 81. The detailed provisions of the Guidelines are discussed in more detail in a later section of this chapter,[58] but it may be helpful to give here a flavour of the topics discussed. Examples of agreements that are unlikely to breach Article 81 include:

---

57   A list of standard works that deal with legal issues that may be relevant to technology transfer is set out in the Bibliography at p xi.

58   As well as in Ch 14.

- agreements concerning co-operation in R&D at an early ('rather theoretical') stage far removed from the marketing of a resulting new product or technology;

- R&D co-operation between non-competitors, although there may be a breach of Article 81(1) if there is exclusive exploitation of results, and one of the parties has significant market power with respect to key technology;

- outsourcing to specialised companies (which probably doesn't mean the typical small, high-tech company), research institutes or academic bodies that are not active in the exploitation of the results. Article 81(1) does not apply because of the complementary nature of the co-operating parties in these scenarios;

- if the parties are unable to carry out the necessary R&D independently, there is no competition to be restricted.

Issues that might cause the above types of agreement to be caught by EC Treaty, Article 81 include:

- *Market share:* a significant market share in terms of competing products or competing technologies.

- *Foreclosure effects:* if one of the parties has significant market power with respect to key technology and there are 'foreclosure effects' in relation to an exclusive exploitation of the results of the R&D.

(In relation to R&D co-operation to improve existing products, the risk of these effects may be higher if there is joint production and/or marketing of the resulting products, rather than just joint exploitation by licensing. In relation to R&D of entirely new products, the risk of anti-competitive effects is lower, as such co-operation is generally considered to be pro-competitive.)

- *Reduced competition for innovation:* if effective competition with respect to innovation is significantly reduced.

- *Close to market:* if the R&D co-operation takes place shortly before the product reaches the market.

The Guidelines explain how the relevant market should be identified when assessing the effects on competition of the agreement. The Commission considers three main types of market:

- existing product markets;

- existing technology markets;

- the impact of the agreement on innovation.

When assessing a new technology, for which there is no existing market, the Commission will look at the impact of the agreement on innovation, and in particular whether there are credible, alternative, 'poles' of research. For example, if an R&D collaboration agreement is directed to finding a new cure for cancer, are there alternative lines of research, perhaps based on unrelated scientific concepts, that might lead to the same end result, ie an effective cure for a particular type of cancer? If there are, then the Commission's concerns about restrictions in the R&D agreement might be reduced if not removed altogether.

The Guidelines also give some helpful case examples of horizontal agreements that would either (a) not breach Article 81(1) (101(1)), or (b) breach Article 81(1) (101(1)) but receive exemption under Article 81(3) (101(3)), or (c) breach Article 81(1) (101(1)) and not receive exemption under Article 81(3) (101(3)).

Does the R&D Agreements Regulation apply, and if so does the agreement receive block exemption under that Regulation?

The main issues to consider, when analysing whether an R&D agreement would receive block exemption under the R&D Agreements Regulation, can be summarised as follows. These issues are considered in detail later in this chapter.

Is it a 'research and development agreement'?

R&D agreements are defined, for the purposes of the R&D Agreements Regulation, as agreements that provide for joint R&D of products or processes, and/or for joint exploitation of the results of R&D. Where the agreement is only concerned with joint exploitation of results, the results must have been jointly developed by the parties pursuant to a prior agreement between them. Thus, most R&D agreements are, in principle, covered.

Does it meet the conditions for exemption?

The main conditions are:

- *Access rights for research and exploitation:* all the parties must have access to the results of the work for the purposes of further research or exploitation. Research institutes, academic bodies and 'contract R&D organisations' can be restricted as to their rights to exploit the results. In some circumstances a party's rights of exploitation can be restricted to a specific technical field.

- *Freedom to exploit:* subject to the above, if there is no joint exploitation, each party must be free to exploit results and any necessary pre-existing know-how. Exploitation rights can be limited to technical fields where the parties are not competing undertakings.

- *Joint exploitation and IP protection:* joint exploitation qualifies for exemption only where the results of the R&D are protected by intellectual property rights or constitute know-how, and are 'decisive' for the manufacture of the contract products or application of the contract processes.

- *Specialisation:* there is a condition regarding specialised manufacture by one party.

- *Combined market share of competitors:* if parties are competitors, combined market share must not exceed 25 per cent.

Duration of the exemption; is the market share below 25 per cent?

The R&D Agreements Regulation includes complex conditions relating to market share which affect the duration of the exemption:

- *Non-competitors' initial period of exemption:* where the parties to the agreement are not competitors, the initial period of the exemption is the duration of the joint R&D and, if there is joint exploitation, for seven years from the date the contract products are first put on the EC market.

- *Competitors' initial period:* where the parties are competitors, the initial period of exemption described above only applies if, at the time the agreement is made, the parties and their group companies do not have a combined market share of more than 25 per cent.

- *Continuation of exemption:* after the initial period described above, the exemption continues as long as the parties and their group companies do not have a combined market share of more than 25 per cent.

Does the agreement include any blacklisted provisions?

The main provisions on the blacklist are:

- *Non-compete clauses*: either restrictions on R&D in an unconnected field, or on R&D in the same field after a term of R&D co-operation.

- *No challenge clauses*: prohibitions on challenging validity of relevant IP (in certain circumstances).

- *Output or sales limits.*

- *Price-fixing.*

- *Customer restrictions*: after seven years from putting products on the EU market.

- *Passive sales restrictions*: in other parties' territories.

- *Active sales restrictions*: in other parties' EU territories, after seven years from putting products on the EU market.

- *Restrictions on third-party licences to manufacture*: where not all the parties exploit the results.

- *Ban on sales to resellers*: who would market in other EU territories.

- *Obligations to take steps against parallel importers.*

Does the Specialisation Agreements Regulation apply, and if so does the agreement receive block exemption under that Regulation?

Parties collaborating on a technology venture sometimes apportion responsibility between themselves for commercial activities in different territories. For example, they may agree that one will have marketing rights in Europe, and the other will have marketing rights in North America. Or they might apportion responsibility for particular activities. For example, in a biotechnology collaboration that combined antibodies with gene technology, one of them might produce the antibodies, and the other might produce the DNA required.

In the authors' experience, very few technology agreements amount to a specialisation agreement that would receive block exemption under the Specialisation Agreements Regulation. Often, this is either because the main focus of the agreement is not specialisation but is something else (eg R&D collaboration or IP licensing), or because the parties do not include any restrictive provisions relating to specialisation that would breach Article 81 (101). However, the Regulation should not be entirely overlooked. The main features of a specialisation agreement that would benefit from block exemption (to be discussed in greater detail in a later section of this chapter) are:

- The Regulation provides block exemption to agreements that relate to the conditions under which the parties specialise in the production of goods or services. Three types of specialisation agreement are identified: unilateral specialisation agreements, reciprocal specialisation agreements and joint production agreements. With the first two types, one or more parties agree to cease or refrain from producing certain products and to purchase them from another party or parties. In the case of joint production agreements, the parties agree to produce certain products jointly.

- The exemption also applies to ancillary provisions in specialisation agreements, eg provisions under which IP rights are assigned or licensed, as long as those ancillary provisions are necessary for the implementation of the specialisation agreement.

- The exemption will not be available if the parties' combined market share is greater than 20 per cent of the relevant market.

- The exemption will not be available if the agreement includes any hardcore restrictions such as price-fixing, output/sales limitations, or market/ customer allocation, although in certain circumstances it is permissible to agree the amount of production, or to set sales targets and prices to immediate customers (in the case of a production joint venture).

If the agreement is vertical, does it seem from the Guidelines on vertical restraints that it may breach Article 81(1)?[59]

The Guidelines on vertical restraints:

> '... set out the principles for the assessment of vertical agreements under Article 81 of the EC Treaty. What are considered vertical agreements is defined in Article 2(1) of [the Vertical Agreements Block Exemption Regulation]'.

Article 2(1) of the Regulation defines vertical agreements as:

> '... agreements or concerted practices entered into between two or more undertakings each of which operates, for the purposes of the agreement, at a different level of the production or distribution chain, and relating to the conditions under which the parties may purchase, sell or resell certain goods or services'.

As is discussed under "Does the Vertical Agreements block exemption Regulation apply? If so, does the agreement meet the requirements of that Regulation?" heading below, the Regulation exempts vertical agreements containing IP provisions, provided that those provisions do not constitute the primary object of such agreements. Thus, agreements that are primarily IP licence agreements are not covered by the Regulation.

Much of the Guidelines consists of comments on the application of the Vertical Agreements Regulation, and on Commission policy for different types of distribution agreement. Although they discuss the circumstances in which IP provisions may be included in distribution agreements under the Vertical Agreements Regulation (including separate discussion of trade mark, copyright and know-how provisions, eg in franchising agreements or software distribution agreements), there is effectively no separate analysis of IP agreements per se.

The Guidelines on vertical restraints are therefore of limited assistance in determining whether a technology agreement would infringe Article 81.

---

59 Regulation 2790/1999. Due to be replaced from 1 June 2010 by Commission Regulation 330/2010 on the application of Article 101(3) of the Treaty of the Functioning of the European Union to categories of vertical agreements and concerted [2010] OJ L 102/1. There are transitional arrangements for agreements covered by Regulation 2790/99. As proofs were being returned to the publisher, the new Regulation was due to come into force, and appears to have provisions broadly similar to Regulation 2790/1999 with modifications (such as taking account of internet sales and for sales taking place across borders). An outline of the new Regulation will appear on the website which accompanies this book.

Does the Vertical Agreements block exemption Regulation apply? If so, does the agreement meet the requirements of that Regulation?[60]

The Regulation is most likely to apply if the agreement is a distribution, agency or franchise agreement. Relatively few technology agreements will qualify for block exemption under the Regulation, although in some areas (eg software distribution) the distinction between a distribution agreement and licence agreement may not always be easy to establish. Software agreements are discussed separately later in this chapter. The main provisions of the Regulation can be briefly summarised as follows:

- *Vertical agreements:* as was discussed in the previous section, the Regulation applies to 'agreements or concerted practices entered into between two or more undertakings each of which operates, for the purposes of the agreement, at a different level of the production or distribution chain, and relating to the conditions under which the parties may purchase, sell or resell certain goods or services'.[61]

- *Intellectual property provisions in vertical agreements:* the exemption applies to vertical agreements that include 'provisions which relate to the assignment to the buyer or use by the buyer of intellectual property rights, provided that those provisions do not constitute the primary object of such agreements and are directly related to the use, sale or resale of goods or services by the buyer or its customers. The exemption applies on condition that, in relation to the contract goods or services, those provisions do not contain restrictions of competition having the same object or effect as vertical restraints which are not exempted under this Regulation'.;

- *Agreements between competitors:* the exemption does not apply to agreements between competitors, although non-reciprocal vertical agreements between competitors are exempted if certain detailed conditions are met.

- *Market-share limits:* for the exemption to apply, the market share of the supplier must not exceed 30 per cent. In the case of agreements containing exclusive supply obligations, the market share of the buyer must not exceed 30 per cent.

- *Blacklist:* the exemption will not apply if the agreement contains certain types of restriction, described in detail in Article 4 of the Regulation, concerning:

---

60 Regulation 2790/1999. Due to be replaced from 1 June 2010 by Commission Regulation 330/2010 on the application of Article 101(3) of the Treaty of the Functioning of the European Union to categories of vertical agreements and concerted [2010] OJ L 102/1. There are transitional arrangements for agreements covered by Regulation 2790/99. As proofs were being returned to the publisher, the new Regulation was due to come into force, and appears to have provisions broadly similar to Regulation 2790/1999 with modifications (such as taking account of internet sales and for sales taking place across borders). An outline of the new Regulation will appear on the website which accompanies this book.

61 Art 2(1).

— the resale price of the buyer (other than maximum sales prices, and recommended prices);

— certain territory restrictions;

— certain restrictions on sales within distribution networks;

— non-compete obligations of greater than five years (other than on the supplier's land);

— post-termination restrictions on the buyer (other than certain one-year restrictions at the contract premises and where indispensable to protect the seller's know-how).

Does the Notice on subcontracting apply? If so, does the agreement meet the requirements of that Notice?

The Notice on subcontracting may sometimes be relevant to technology-related agreements. Take the example of an R&D programme to develop a pharmaceutical drug. Specialist companies are often engaged as subcontractors, for example to manufacture quantities of the drug for trials, to apply their own technology to the principal's drug for experimental purposes, or to conduct tests and trials of the drug. Another area in which subcontracting agreements are encountered is in the information technology field, where a company might be engaged to write software for a client in the expectation that the client will incorporate or use that software in another marketed product. Agreements with such subcontractors often include provisions dealing with ownership and use of intellectual property, which could in principle breach Article 81. The Notice is therefore helpful in describing a set of circumstances in which the Commission considers that such provisions will not breach Article 81(101).

Although it continues in force, this Notice has been in existence for some time and it may no longer reflect the current view of the Commission as to the application of competition law.

The main provisions of the Notice can be summarised as follows, and are considered in more detail later in this chapter.

- *Meaning of subcontracting agreements:* section 1 of the Notice provides: 'The Commission considers that agreements under which one firm, called "the contractor", whether or not in consequence of a prior order from a third party, entrusts to another, called "the subcontractor", the manufacture of goods, the supply of services or the performance of work under the contractor's instructions, to be provided to the contractor or performed on his behalf, are not of themselves caught by the prohibition in Article 81(1) [(101(1))]'.

- *Restrictive provisions:* the Notice acknowledges that the contractor may need to provide the subcontractor with technology or equipment to enable him or her to perform the contract. And that the contractor may wish to impose restrictions on the subcontractor as to the use that may be made of these items. The Notice considers whether such restrictions infringe Article 81(1) (101(1)).

- *Permitted restrictions:* the Notice permits certain restrictions on the subcontractor's use of the contractor's technology and equipment, and of items produced using the contractor's technology and equipment.

  — subject to certain conditions, referred to below, the subcontractor may be limited to using such technology, equipment and items only for the purposes of performing work for the contractor;

  — the Commission also confirms that confidentiality obligations on the subcontractor in respect of the contractor's confidential information will not normally infringe Article 81(1);

  — similarly, where the contractor permits the subcontractor to use the contractor's trade marks or get up, the subcontractor can be limited to using them solely in relation to the contract goods or services;

  — where the subcontractor makes improvements to the contractor's technology, and those improvements are 'incapable of being used independently of the contractor's secret know-how or patent', the agreement can include an undertaking by the subcontractor 'to pass on to the contractor' those improvements on an exclusive basis;

  — however, where such improvements 'are capable of being used independently' of the contractor's technology, the subcontractor must be able to exploit the improvements independently. The most that can be granted to the contractor are non-exclusive rights to use the improvements.

- *Conditions of permission:* the Commission's sanguine view of such restrictions is subject to a number of conditions:

  — the contractor's technology and equipment must be 'necessary' to perform the contract work;

  — the subcontractor does not already have, and could not obtain the technology and equipment from another source on 'reasonable conditions'.

Does the Technology Transfer Agreements block exemption Regulation apply? Does the agreement fit receive block exemption under that Regulation?

The latest version of the Technology Transfer Agreements Regulation applies from 1 May 2004 and reflects practice in more recent block exemptions and Notices, where the Commission has been moving away from a 'list' or form-based approach towards what is described as a more economics-based approach. The practical effect of the economics-based approach is fewer lists, and more general criteria, eg defining a maximum market share, below which many types of provision will be regarded as permissible. Therefore the Technology Transfer Agreements Regulation as currently formulated no longer describes in great detail the types of provision that respectively may, and may not, be included in patent and know-how licence agreements, if they are to receive block exemption from Article 81(1) (101(1)). The current Technology Transfer Agreements Regulation takes a radically different and (deceptively) simpler method of providing a block exemption to technology transfer agreements than its immediate predecessor.

The availability of the block exemption in the Technology Transfer Agreements Regulation will depend on a number of factors;

- whether there is the 'right' type of technology transfer agreement;

- whether there are only two parties to the technology transfer agreement;

- whether the agreement's primary purpose is the transfer of technology and whether the technology which will be used to produce goods and services;

- whether the parties do not have a market share exceeding particular percentages (the calculation depending on whether they are competing or non-competing undertakings);

- whether the parties' agreement contains restrictions which contain severe or less severe anti-competitive restraints (which will either make either the whole agreement or just the infringing provision in an agreement ineligible for benefiting from the block exemption).

The following paragraphs will provide a brief summary of the main provisions of the Regulation, including summary lists of:

- primary purpose of the Regulation;

- period the block exemption lasts;

- types of agreement that qualify for block exemption under the Regulation;

- excluded types of agreement;

- market-share thresholds;

- impermissible (hardcore) restrictions making a whole agreement ineligible for protection (and exemptions);

- impermissible (softcore) restrictions making a provision in an agreement ineligible for protection.

For a more detailed discussion of these matters, see Chapter 13.

Primary purpose of the Regulation

A technology transfer agreement, in order to benefit from an exemption to Article 81(1) (101(1)), must concern the licensing (transfer) of technology where the production of goods and services are permitted (ie not an agreement where the primary purpose is the sale and purchase of goods and services).[62]

Period of time that the block exemption lasts

A block exemption will apply only for so long as the intellectual property right in the licensed technology has not expired, lapsed or been declared invalid.[63] Where know-how is involved there is a different formulation: the exemption will last for so long as the know-how remains secret.[64]

Summary list of qualifying agreements

(a) pure patent[65] licence agreements;

(b) pure know-how[66] licence agreements;

(c) software copyright licensing agreement;

(d) mixed patent, know-how or software copyright licensing agreement;

(e) an agreement in categories (a)–(d) but which contains provisions for:

   (i)   the sale and purchase of products; or

   (ii) the licensing of other intellectual property rights; or

   (iii) the assignment of intellectual property rights;

   as long as the provisions in (i)–(iii) do not constitute the primary object of the agreement and those provisions are related directly to the production of contract products;[67]

---

62 Regulation 772/2004, Art 2(1) and Recital 17.

63 Regulation 772/2004, Art 2, para 2. This formulation is considerably simplified compared to that of the previous Technology Transfer Agreements Regulation, where specific time periods were available for the different exemptions available.

64 But where the know-how becomes publicly known other than through the fault of the licensee, the exemption shall last for the period of the agreement.

65 Patent applications, utility models, utility model applications, supplementary protection certificates, plant breeders' certificates and semiconductor topographies are deemed to be patents for the purposes of the Regulation (Regulation 772/2004, Art 1(h)).

66 Know-how is described in the Regulation as 'a package of non-patented practical information, resulting from experience and testing, which is: (i) secret, that is to say, not generally known or easily accessible, (ii) substantial, that is to say, significant and useful for the production of the contract products, and (iii) identified, that is to say, described in a sufficiently comprehensive manner so as to make it possible to verify that it fulfils the criteria of secrecy and substantiality' (Council Regulation 772/2004, Art 1(i)).

67 Contract products are defined as those products which are produced with the licensed technology, while a 'product' means a good or service (including intermediate and final goods and services). See Regulation 772/2004, Art 1(1)(e), (f)).

● assignments of patents, know-how or software (or any combination of these) as long as the risk associated with exploitation remains with the assignor, eg if the assignor receives royalty on sales.

Summary list of excluded agreements

● *multi-party agreements:* agreements to which more than two undertakings are party (group companies being treated as one undertaking);

● *technology pools with territory restrictions:* licence agreements which set up technology pools;

● *sub-licensing:* agreements whose primary purpose is sub-licensing;

● *subcontracts:* agreements where the primary purpose is not the licensing of technology;

● *research and development:* agreements whose primary purpose is carrying out research and development;

● *trade marks;*

● *involving rights in performances and other rights related to copyright.*

Market-share thresholds

The block exemption available under the Technology Transfer Agreements Regulation depends on the market share held by parties to an agreement; the method of calculating the market share depends on whether the parties are competing or non-competing undertakings.[68]

Competing undertakings[66]	Non-competing undertakings[67]
The block exemption is available if the combined market share of all the parties does not exceed 20 per cent on the affected relevant technology and product market.	The block exemption is available if the market share of each party does not exceed 30 per cent on the affecte d relevant technology and product market.

---

68 A competing undertaking is defined as one 'which competes on the relevant technology market and/or the relevant product market ...'. The relevant technology market being 'undertakings which license out competing technologies without infringing each others' intellectual property rights (actual competitors on the technology market); the relevant technology market includes technologies which are regarded by the licensees as interchangeable with or substitutable for the licensed technology, by reason of the technologies' characteristics, their royalties and their intended use'. Product market essentially means that the competitive undertakings are present in the relevant product/geographical markets where the contract products are sold. See Regulation 772/2004, Art 1(1)(j)).

69 Regulation 772/2004, Art 3(1).

70 Regulation 772/2004, Art 3(2).

Summary of impermissible (hardcore) restrictions making a whole agreement ineligible for protection[71]

Where parties to a technology transfer agreement are competitors or non-competitors and their agreement has as its object 'severely anti-competitive restraints', the whole agreement will be ineligible to benefit from the block exemption provided by the Technology Transfer Agreements Regulation.

Competing undertakings	Non-competing undertakings
Price fixing: restricting a party's ability to determine its prices when selling products to third parties	*Price fixing:* restricting a party's ability to determine its prices when selling products to third parties.
	But a maximum or recommended sale price is possible (as long as it is not treated as a fixed or minimum sale price resulting from pressure or incentives).
Limiting output: limiting the amount of products that can be produced or sold.	No equivalent
But such a restriction is permissible where imposed:	
1. on *the* licensee in a reciprocal[69] agreement; or	
2. on *only one* licensee in a non-reciprocal[70] agreement.	
Allocation of customers or markets: this restriction is not further defined or limited *by itself* and could include almost any restriction as to the type of exclusivity imposed by a licensor (territory, customer, type of product). But there are a number of exceptions where this type of restriction is permissible:	No direct equivalent
• *Field of use restriction on licensee.* Obligation on licensee not to produce with the licensed technology in one or more technical fields of use or one or more product markets.	

71 Not all of the restrictions or exceptions to the restrictions are listed here, only those most relevant to technology transfer agreements.

72 A reciprocal agreement means 'a technology transfer agreement where two undertakings grant each other, in the same or separate contracts, a patent licence, a know-how licence, a software copyright licence or a mixed patent, know-how or software copyright licence and where these licences concern competing technologies or can be used for the production of competing products' (Reg 772/2004, Art 1(c)).

73 A non-reciprocal agreement means 'a technology transfer agreement where one undertaking grants another undertaking a patent licence, a know-how licence, a software copyright licence or a mixed patent, know-how or software copyright licence, or where two undertakings grant each other such a licence but where these licences do not concern competing technologies and cannot be used for the production of competing products' (Regulation 772/2004, Art 1(d)).

Competing undertakings	Non-competing undertakings
• *Field of use or exclusive territory restriction on either party.* Obligation on either party, in a non-reciprocal agreement, not to produce with the licensed technology in one or more technical fields or one or more product markets or one or more exclusive territories reserved for the other party.	
• *Licensor not to license technology to another licensee in a territory.*	
• *Restriction on active/passive sales into the territory of the other party.* In a non-reciprocal agreement a restriction can be imposed concerning making active and/or passive sales in the exclusive territory or to the exclusive customer group of the other party.	
• *Restriction on making active sales in another licensee's territory.* In a non-reciprocal agreement a restriction can be imposed by the licensor stopping *one* licensee making active sales in the exclusive territory of another licensee (as long as the other licensee is not a competing undertaking of the licensor when the other licensee and the licensor enter into their licence).	
• *Own-use restriction.* A licensee can be restricted so that it can only make contract products for its own use as long as it sells them as spare parts (actively or passively) for its own products	
Restricting a licensee's ability to exploit its own technology or any party to carry out research and development. The latter restriction is only permissible if it is 'indispensable' to prevent the disclosure of licensed know-how to third parties.	No equivalent
	Restriction on licensee making passive sales into a territory or to customers. A licensee cannot be restricted from making passive sales outside a particular territory or group of customers. But there are a number of exceptions where this type of restriction is permissible:
	• *Restriction on making passive sales to exclusive territory/customer group of licensor.*
	• *Restriction on making active sales in another licensee's exclusive territory for first two years of other licensee's sales.*

Competing undertakings	Non-competing undertakings
	• *Own-use restriction.* A licensee can be restricted so that it can only make contract products for its own use as long as it can sell them as spare parts (actively or passively) for its own products. • *Restricting sales to end-users (where licensee is a wholesaler).*

Summary of impermissible (softcore) restrictions making an individual provision ineligible for protection[74]

Where a technology transfer agreement includes a provision such as the following then *that provision* will not have the benefit of the block exemption provided by the Technology Transfer Agreements Regulation (ie the rest of the agreement could still be eligible):[75]

- *Requiring the licensee to grant exclusive license to its improvements:* a licensee cannot be required to grant an exclusive license to the licensor or a third party designated by the licensor for its severable improvements[76] to or its own new application of the licensed technology.

- *Requiring the licensee to assign its improvements:* a licensee cannot be required to assign to the licensor or a third party designated by the licensor for its severable improvements to or its own new application of the licensed technology. This captures the principal other way a licensor can control use of a severable improvement made by a licensee.

- *Requiring a licensee not to challenge validity of licensor IP:* this restriction is subject to one proviso: a licensor can terminate a technology transfer agreement where the licensee does challenge the validity of one or more of the licensed intellectual property rights.

- *Restricting a licensee's ability to exploit its own technology or any party to carry out research and development (where parties are not competing undertakings):* the latter restriction is only permissible if it is 'indispensable' to prevent the disclosure of licensed know-how to third parties.[77]

74　Regulation 772/2004, Art 5.
75　Unlike the 'hardcore' restrictions, these are not differentiated (except for one) on whether the parties are competing or non-competing undertakings.
76　A severable improvement is defined as 'an improvement that can be exploited without infringing the licensed technology' (Regulation 772/2004, Art 1(1)(n)).
77　This is the mirror of the hardcore restriction, which applies only to competing parties, and which would take the whole agreement outside the block exemption.

SOFTWARE LICENCES

Until 2004 software licences were generally not covered by any of the then existing block exemption Regulations concerned with technology transfer. With the introduction of the most recent Technology Transfer Agreements Regulation[78] a software copyright licensing agreement is specifically recognised as qualifying for block exemption under the Technology Transfer Agreements Regulation.

In addition to the Technology Transfer Agreements Regulation, in limited circumstances, as is discussed below, software distribution agreements may benefit from block exemption under the Vertical Agreements Regulation.

The following paragraphs explain in more detail the relevance or otherwise of existing block exemption Regulations to software licences, and provide some comments on which terms in a typical software licence are thought likely to infringe Article 81(1) of the EC Treaty.

Technology Transfer Agreements Regulation

In the previous edition of this book there was considerable discussion as to whether the then existing block exemption for technology transfer agreements could be construed to apply to software licences. Such an approach is no longer necessary, and as noted above, the current Technology Transfer Agreements Regulation specifically recognises software licences. It is striking that the Regulation itself, its Recitals and the accompanying Guidelines[79] do not discuss any issues or points arising from the inclusion of software copyright licences or as to whether this type of licensing leads to any issues or points which are distinct from the other types of licensing and assignments covered by the Technology Transfer Agreements Regulation.

Accordingly it is no longer necessary to consider software copyright licences as such in this section as they are one of the forms of licences considered above under 'Does the Technology Transfer Agreements block exemption Regulation apply? Does the agreement receive block exemption under that Regulation?'. However the following brief points can be added. The Technology Transfer Agreements Regulation will only cover those software copyright licences which:

- are between two undertakings;

- permit the production of contract products (goods and services); and

---

78 Regulation 772/2004.

79 Commission Notice *Guidelines on the application of Article 81 of the EC Treaty to technology transfer agreements* ([2004] OJ C1010/02).

- contain restrictions which are in breach of Article 81(1) (101(1)) but those restrictions are not hardcore or excluded restrictions.

Therefore a software copyright licence is unlikely to fall to be considered by the Technology Transfer Agreements Regulation if it does not permit the production of contract products. This might mean, for example:

- the licensing of software to enable another company to carry out further development of other software (which ultimately might be licensed so as to permit the production products); or

- the licensing of software to end users (eg a word-processing program to be installed on a person's home computer);

would not be covered by the Technology Transfer Agreements Regulation. Needless to say, a software copyright licence which does not contain restrictions which do not breach Article 81(1) (101(1)) would not need to be considered by the Technology Transfer Agreements Regulation.

Vertical Agreements Regulation and Guidelines on vertical restraints

The Vertical Agreements Regulation is concerned with:

> '... agreements ... between two or more undertakings each of which operates, for the purposes of the agreement, at a different level of the production or distribution chain, and relating to the conditions under which the parties may purchase, sell or resell certain goods or services ("vertical agreements")'.[80]

The block exemption given by the Regulation extends to intellectual property licensing provisions (and assignments):

> '... provided that those provisions do not constitute the primary object of such agreements and are directly related to the use, sale or resale of goods or services by the buyer or its customers. The exemption applies on condition that ... those provisions do not contain restrictions of competition having the same object or effect as vertical restraints which are not exempted under this Regulation'.[81]

Thus, where an agreement is principally concerned with the grant of an IP licence, it will not receive block exemption under the Regulation. The Guidelines on vertical restraints provide some guidance on when the sale of copies of software will qualify for exemption under the Regulation:

---

80   Art 2.1.
81   Art 2.3.

'(40) Agreements under which hard copies of software are supplied for resale and where the reseller does not acquire a licence to any rights over the software but only has the right to resell the hard copies, are to be regarded as agreements for the supply of goods for resale for the purposes of the Block Exemption Regulation. Under this form of distribution the licence of the software only takes place between the copyright owner and the use of the software. This may take the form of a 'shrink wrap' licence, i.e. a set of conditions included in the package of the hard copy which the end user is deemed to accept by opening the package.

(41) Buyers of hardware incorporating the software protected by copyright may be obliged by the copyright holder not to infringe the copyright, for example not to make copies and resell the software or not to make copies and use the software in combination with other hardware. Such use-restrictions, to the extent that they fall within Article 81(1) at all, are covered by the Block Exemption Regulation.'

The EC Software Directive

Arguably the most significant item of competition law that has emerged from the EU in the area of software licensing is the EC Software Directive.[82] Although this Directive is mainly concerned with establishing a uniform regime of copyright protection for computer programs throughout the EU, it includes some provisions which, in effect, are competition law provisions rather than intellectual property measures. Most significantly, it gives a licensee of a computer program certain rights to 'decompile' the computer code, to make back-up copies, or make copies or adapt the program where necessary for the licensee's lawful use of the program. These rights are subject to certain detailed conditions and exceptions.[83] Contractual provisions which conflict with the decompilation right and right to make necessary back-up copies are declared to be void. The decompilation right is only for the purpose of interoperability and includes the right to obtain information from the copyright owner of the program, and the refusal to provide such information by a 'dominant supplier' can lead to the application of Articles 81 (101) and 82 (102).[84] The Directive also provides that the first sale of a program in the

---

82 Council Directive 91/250/EEC ([1991] OJ L122/42). The Directive has been implemented in the UK by the Copyright (Computer Programs) Regulations 1992, discussed in Ch 9 under 'Computers and computer programs'.

83 The provision in the Directive (Art 6(1)) permits decompilation to 'achieve interoperability of an independently created computer program with other programs' but does not state that the other programs cannot compete with the program which is decompiled. Art 82 (102) has been applied by the Commission where Microsoft has refused to reveal certain interface information. See eg Commission Decision ComP/C-3.792 and the case law which has followed.

84 See Directive 91/250/EEC, Recital 27: 'Whereas the provisions of this Directive are without prejudice to the application of the competition rules under Articles 85 [81 (101)] and 86 [82 (102)] of the Treaty if a dominant supplier refuses to make information available which is necessary for interoperability as defined in this Directive'.

EU by the copyright owner 'exhausts' his or her rights in the program.

The Directive was implemented in the UK by the Copyright (Computer Programs) Regulations 1992.[85] These Regulations amended the Copyright, Designs and Patents Act 1988 in relation to computer programs only; the amendments are discussed in Chapter 9. Perhaps the most notable change of a competition law nature was the introduction of a new section to the Copyright, Designs and Patents Act 1988, which reads as follows:

> '296A. – (1) Where a person has the use of a computer program under an agreement, any term or condition in the agreement shall be void in so far as it purports to prohibit or restrict–
>
> (a) the making of any back up copy of the program which it is necessary for him to have for the purposes of the agreed use;
>
> (b) where the conditions in section 50B(2) are met, the decompiling of the program; or
>
> (c) the use of any device or means to observe, study or test the functioning of the program in order to understand the ideas and principles which underlie any element of the program.
>
> (2) In this section, decompile, in relation to a computer program, has the same meaning as in section 50B'.

Except for the provisions mentioned above, the Directive does not state whether typical provisions in software licence agreements are contrary to Article 81 (101). The provisions of typical software licences that are most likely to be contrary to Article 81 (101) (assuming that the agreement is sufficiently significant to have an effect on trade between member states) are discussed briefly in the following paragraphs.

Applying the block exemption Regulations and Guidelines by analogy: which terms of a typical software licence are likely to infringe Article 81(1) (101)?

The following discussion assumes:

- that the software licence under consideration does not escape from Article 81(1) under the Notice on agreements of minor importance, or the de minimis rules generally;

---

85   SI 1992/3233. There has been criticism from the Commission that the Directive has not been correctly implemented into UK law (see *Report from the Commission on the implementation and effects of Directive 91/250/EEC on the legal protection of computer programs*, COM(2000) 199 final. See the website accompanying this book for the text of the statutory instrument.

- the licence does not come within the block exemption provided by the Technology Transfer Agreements Regulation because it is between more than two parties;

- that the licensing provisions are not 'ancillary' to some other type of agreement that receives block exemption or benefits from a Commission Notice, eg an R&D collaboration agreement, a distribution agreement that qualifies under the Vertical Agreements Regulation (which, as discussed above, might include software sold via a shrink-wrap licence), or a subcontracting agreement that meets the terms of the Notice on subcontracting agreements (see further the discussion of these subjects, above);

- that the licence does not contain any provisions that are void under the Software Directive (and national implementing legislation), as discussed above (eg in relation to back-up copies and de-compilation).

Terms unique to software licences

Some of the typical provisions in software licence agreements are unique to software licences, whilst others are similar to those found in other types of intellectual property licence. Some of the former provisions include:

- designated machine clauses (ie the licence permits use of the software only on a designated machine or an agreed number of machines);

- designated site licences (in the sense of a licence to use the software at a particular site; the concept of site licences in patent licences tends to be rather different, and to refer to licensing a manufacturing facility at a particular site);

- own-use licences (ie the licensee may use the software for its own internal purposes only).

The above provisions are not commonly found in patent licences, and it is therefore not surprising that they are not referred to in the Technology Transfer Agreements Regulation. Some industry commentators have argued that the above provisions are pro-competitive and do not breach Article 81(1) (101(1)).[86] A central argument is that such provisions are merely a means of establishing a fair pricing regime for the software and are not designed to prevent competition. In the absence of authoritative guidance on the subject from the Commission or the European Court, any comment must be speculative. However, the above provisions are very often seen in software licences, and have been for many years now. It would be an extraordinary

---

86 See, for example, the June 2002 response of the Business Software Alliance to the Commission's Evaluation Report on the Technology Transfer Agreements Regulation, which is included on the Commission's website. That response includes, for example, the following comments on designated machine clauses: 'Designated machine clauses do not restrict competition within the meaning of Article 81(1) [(101(1))] because they are a reasonable way for licensors to link the payment of royalties to use of the licensed software'.

measure if the Commission decided that what has become a conventional business model is illegal. A distinction should perhaps be drawn between three categories of agreement that might include such provisions:

- agreements that are too minor to infringe Article 81(1) (101(1));

- agreements that potentially infringe Article 81(1) (101(1)) but do not involve an infringement of Article 82 (102) (abuse of a dominant position); and

- agreements that potentially infringe both Article 81 (101) and Article 82 (102).

The authors' view is that if the Commission decides to attack clauses of the kind referred to above, it is more likely to do so in situations where the licensor is a major supplier of software and Article 82 (102) issues arise. For run-of-the-mill agreements in the second category above, it seems less likely that the Commission would be interested in holding provisions such as those described above in breach of Article 81(1) (101(1)).

However, these comments are speculative. Clarification from the Commission would be welcomed, as the current Technology Transfer Agreements Regulation and even its Guidance do not address these provisions (given that the Guidance on vertical restraints does not really address this subject, except where IP provisions are ancillary to distribution).

Hardcore restrictions (and their exceptions) and the Technology Transfer Agreements Regulation

None of the hardcore or excluded restrictions expressly deal with the above type of provisions commonly found in software licences as stated above. Also none of the permitted exceptions to certain hardcore restrictions come close to the above provisions.

Some of the other, typical provisions in software licences are closer to those found in patent licences, and in these cases the provisions of the current Technology Transfer Agreements Regulation may provide some pointers. In particular, it would be prudent to avoid any provision that is a hardcore or an excluded restriction under that Regulation (as to which see the discussion of the Regulation elsewhere in this chapter under 'Does the Technology Transfer Agreements block exemption Regulation apply? Does the agreement receive block exemption under that Regulation?' above).

AGREEMENTS THAT PROVIDE FOR BOTH R&D WORK AND THE LICENSING OF TECHNOLOGY OR KNOW-HOW

The overview sections, above, describe a sequence of steps that lead to reviewing the agreement as either a vertical or horizontal agreement. Different

Notices and Regulations are relevant depending on which of these categories is applicable to the agreement in question.

In practice, though, agreements sometimes have elements of both a horizontal R&D agreement and a vertical IP licence. In such situations, it is appropriate to consider whether the 'centre of gravity' of the agreement is an R&D agreement or a licence agreement. Sometimes, this is not easy to decide.

In such situations, the parties may occasionally be tempted to consider whether their agreement stands a better chance of receiving block exemption under the R&D Agreements Regulation, the Specialisation Agreements Regulation, or the Technology Transfer Agreements Regulation, and whether the terms of the agreement could be modified to fit within one or other category (although the provisions in the current Technology Transfer Agreements Regulation concerning R&D are much more limited). This is a high-risk strategy: the Commission may have a different view of the centre of gravity of the agreement to that of the parties. Nevertheless, it is an area that it may, occasionally, be useful to explore. In any case the current Technology Transfer Agreements Regulation contains some guidance as to the current thinking of the Commission: an R&D agreement will be covered by the Technology Transfer Agreements Regulation as long as the focus of the agreement is the production 'of an identified contract product'.[87]

In this context, it may be useful to compare briefly the main features of these three Regulations.

---

87 Commission Notice *Guidelines on the application of Article 81 of the EC Treaty to technology transfer agreements* ([2004] OJ C1010/02), para 45. The whole paragraph is worth quoting in full as it states in a fairly practical way the distinction between whether an agreement would be covered by a Technology Transfer Agreements Regulation or not (although most of it is not surprising): 'The TTBER also applies to agreements whereby the licensee must carry out development work before obtaining a product or a process that is ready for commercial exploitation, provided that a contract product has been identified. Even if such further work and investment is required, the object of the agreement is the production of an identified contract product. On the other hand, the TTBER and the guidelines do not cover agreements whereby a technology is licensed for the purpose of enabling the licensee to carry out further research and development in various fields. For instance, the TTBER and the guidelines do not cover the licensing of a technological research tool used in the process of further research activity. The framework of the TTBER and the guidelines is based on the premise that there is a direct link between the licensed technology and an identified contract product. In cases where no such link exists the main object of the agreement is research and development as opposed to bringing a particular product to the market; in that case the analytical framework of the TTBER and the guidelines may not be appropriate. For the same reasons the TTBER and the guidelines do not cover research and development sub-contracting whereby the licensee undertakes to carry out research and development in the field of the licensed technology and to hand back the improved technology package to the licensor. The main object of such agreements is the provision of research and development services aimed at improving the technology as opposed to the production of goods and services on the basis of the licensed technology'.

What does each Regulation exempt?

The following is a very brief summary of the types of agreement covered by each of the three Regulations, to enable a comparison to be made. More detailed and comprehensive descriptions of the types of agreement covered by each Regulation appear in subsequent sections. The main types of agreement covered are as follows.

(1) The Technology Transfer Agreements Regulation covers:

- pure patent licensing agreements;

- pure know-how licensing agreements;

- software copyright licensing agreements;

- mixed know-how, patent and copyright software licensing agreements;

- any of the above agreements which contain provisions which relate to the sale and purchase of products or which relate to the licensing of other intellectual property rights, provided that those provisions do not constitute the primary object of the agreement and are directly related to the production of contract products;

- assignments of patents, know-how or copyright software (or a combination) as long as the risk of exploitation is retained by the assignor.

To benefit from the exemption the agreements covered by the Technology Transfer Agreements Regulation must permit the production of contract products, and where know-how is involved it must be secret, substantial and identified.

This Regulation will not apply if the agreement restricts any party from carrying out R&D unless such a restriction is indispensable to prevent the disclosure of licensed know-how to third parties.[88]

The Technology Transfer Agreements Regulation provides that the exemption it provides to Article 81(1) (101(1)) shall apply for only so long as the intellectual property right in the licensed technology has not expired, lapsed or been declared invalid. For know-how, the exemption lasts as long as the know-how remains secret.

---

88 See Regulation 772/2004, Art 4(1)(d), a hardcore restriction between competing parties only and which would take a whole agreement outside the benefit of the Technology Transfer Agreements Regulation; and Regulation 772/2004, Art 5(2), an excluded restriction which applies between non-competing parties and which would take the offending obligation outside the benefit of the Technology Transfer Agreements Regulation.

(2) The Research and Development Agreements Regulation covers:

- joint R&D and joint exploitation of the results;

- joint exploitation of the results of R&D which was previously carried out by agreement of the same parties; and

- joint R&D excluding joint exploitation of the results (in so far as this infringes Article 81 at all).

The period of the exemption is likely to be shorter than that available under the Technology Transfer Agreements Regulation (where patents are involved, and is likely always to be the case where copyright is involved); eg where the parties are engaged in joint exploitation or are involved in active or passive sales, there is a basic period of seven years from the time the contract products are first put on the market in the EU, if the parties are not competitors; thereafter, or if the parties do compete, the period of exemption depends on the parties' market shares.

It has been argued that the R&D Regulation may not apply where the parties agree that each will have the exclusive right to exploit the results in separate, defined territories, and they agree not to manufacture and sell in each other's territory. In this case there may not be 'joint exploitation', as this term is defined in the Regulation. So far as the authors are aware, this question remains unresolved[89] If this is not joint exploitation, the parties may need to consider whether the Technology Transfer Agreements Regulation would be applicable.

(3) The Specialisation Agreements Regulation exempts:

- unilateral specialisation agreements;

- reciprocal specialisation agreements;

- joint-production agreements.

With the first two types of agreement, one or more parties agree to cease or refrain from producing certain products and to purchase them from another party or parties. In the case of joint-production agreements, the parties agree to produce certain products jointly.

The exemption also applies to ancillary provisions in specialisation agreements, eg provisions under which IP rights are assigned or licensed, as long as those ancillary provisions are necessary for the implementation of the specialisation agreement.

---

89   See Korah, *Research and Development and the EEC Competition Rules: Regulation 418/81* (Sweet & Maxwell, 1986) at 24, where this question is discussed in relation to an earlier version of the R&D Regulation – Korah supports the view that such activities are covered by the Regulation.

The exemption will not be available if the parties' combined market share is greater than 20 per cent of the relevant market. Nor will it be available if the agreement includes any hardcore restrictions such as price-fixing, output/sales limitations, or market/customer allocation, although in certain circumstances it is permissible to agree the amount of production, or to set sales targets and prices to immediate customers (in the case of a production joint venture).

Such agreements may well involve the licensing of intellectual property rights; this Regulation should not be overlooked, particularly in relation to agreements under which parties are engaged in collaborative activities which include the manufacture of technology-based products.

Which Regulation is to be preferred – Technology Transfer Regulation or R&D Regulation?

Use of the licensing Regulation may enable a longer period of territorial protection to be included in the licence. However, the licensing Regulations will not be available if there are some particular restrictions on the carrying out of R&D.[90] Depending on the commercial priorities of the parties, it may be desirable to remove the restrictions on R&D (to enable one to argue that the Technology Transfer Agreements Regulation applies) or accept a reduced period of territorial protection for licences (ie relying on the permitted periods of joint exploitation under the R&D Regulation).

DETAILED CONSIDERATION OF NOTICES, GUIDELINES AND BLOCK EXEMPTION REGULATIONS

The remainder of this chapter will consider the detailed provisions of the main Commission Notices (including the Guidelines on horizontal agreements, and the Guidelines on vertical restraints, respectively) that are likely to be useful when considering whether a technology agreement infringes Article 81 (101).

Status of Commission Notices

From time to time the European Commission has published Notices which set out its views on the relevance of Article 81(1) (101(1)) to particular kinds of commercial arrangement. Such Notices are merely an expression of opinion, and are not legally binding. Thus, an agreement that comes within the scope of a Notice and therefore, apparently, does not infringe Article 81(1) (101(1)), may in exceptional cases be held to infringe Article 81(1) (101(1)). In such

---

90 See Ch 14 under 'Blacklisted provisions under provisions which prevent application of exemption.'

a case, the offending provisions will be void. In practice, this is unlikely to happen very often. However, Notices can also become out of date, in that subsequent decisions by the Commission in particular cases may indicate a change of attitude on its part.

Nevertheless, the Notices do provide a useful service, particularly since:

(a) Fines are extremely unlikely to be imposed on parties who rely on the Notice. The Notice on agreements of minor importance states that fines will not be imposed where:

  (i)   the agreement complies with the Notice but nevertheless is found to infringe Article 81(1); or

  (ii) the parties mistakenly believe they come within the Notice (unless the mistake was due to negligence).[91]

Although the Notice is not legislation and therefore not legally binding on the Commission, this statement on fines may create some kind of estoppel against the Commission, which would make it unlawful to act contrary to this statement. It is likely that the Commission would take a similar approach when applying the Notice on subcontracting.

(b) Given the general uncertainty as to whether Article 81(1) (101(1)) applies to many types of agreement, as discussed earlier, the guidance provided by a Notice is useful, even if it is not legally binding. By complying with a Notice, the parties may reduce the risk of infringement of Article 81(1) (101(1)) to a level at which they are prepared to proceed with the agreement. Alternatively, they may notify the agreement to the Commission if they wish to be certain that the agreement's provisions are enforceable.

Relevant Commission Notices

The following list excludes any Notices in special market sectors such as motor vehicle distribution, transport, agriculture, insurance, coal and steel. It also excludes Notices on procedural and definitional matters, eg those concerned with defining the market and with the meaning of 'small and medium-sized enterprises'.[92] There are also one or two old Notices that have not been formally repealed, eg one covering Japanese trade practices in the 1970s. The following general published Notices have not been superseded, and are the most relevant to technology transfer agreements:

---

91   See para 5 of the Notice.
92   A set of Commission Notices, block exemption Regulations, etc can be found in the Appendices to Bellamy and Child (Roth and Rose ed), *European Community Law of Competition* (6th edn, Oxford University Press, 2008).

- Agreements of minor importance, 2001;

- Subcontracting agreements, 1978;[93]

- Guidelines on horizontal agreements, 2001;[94]

- Guidelines on vertical restraints, 2000.[95]

As was discussed earlier,[96] the Guidelines on vertical restraints are concerned mostly with distribution agreements and like matters (eg agency and franchise agreements) and are not primarily concerned with technology transfer agreements such as intellectual property licences and assignments. Accordingly, it is not proposed to consider those Guidelines in close detail. A summary of the Guidelines appears earlier in this chapter.[97]

Relevant block exemption Regulations

The block exemption Regulations that may be relevant to a technology agreement are:

- Technology Transfer Agreements Regulation, 2004;[98]

- Research and Development Agreements Regulation, 2000;[99]

- Specialisation Agreements Regulation, 2000;[100]

- Vertical Agreements Regulation, 1999.[101]

In practice, the first two of these Regulations are most likely to be relevant. For the reasons outlined above,[102] the Vertical Agreements Regulation will only rarely be of relevance to intellectual property-based agreements, whilst the Specialisation Agreements Regulation will occasionally be relevant. For this reason the detailed discussion of the block exemption Regulations that follows will concentrate on those for technology transfer and R&D, will deal

---

93   [1979] OJ CI/2.
94   [2001] OJ /C3/2.
95   [2000] OJ C291/1.
96   See above under 'Does the Vertical Agreements block exemption Regulation apply? If so, does the agreement meet the requirements of that Regulation?'
97   See n 95.
98   Regulation 772/2004 ([2004] OJ L123/11).
99   Regulation 2659/2000 ([2000] OJ L304/7).
100 Regulation 2658/2000 ([2000] OJ L304/3).
101 Regulation 2790/99 ([1999] OJ L336/21). Due to be replaced from 1 June 2010 by Commission Regulation 330/2010 on the application of Article 101(3) of the Treaty of the Functioning of the European Union to categories of vertical agreements and concerted [2010] OJ L 102/1. There are transitional arrangements for agreements covered by Regulation 2790/99. As proofs were being returned to the publisher, the new Regulation was due to come into force, and appears to have provisions broadly similar to Regulation 2790/1999 with modifications (such as taking account of internet sales and for sales taking place across borders). An outline of the new Regulation will appear on the website which accompanies this book.
102 See n 93.

more briefly with specialisation agreements, and will omit detailed discussion of the Vertical Agreements Regulation.[103]

Horizontal and vertical agreements

As has previously been mentioned, an early step in the EC-competition-law-analysis of a commercial agreement is to decide whether the agreement is principally a vertical agreement or a horizontal agreement. It makes sense, therefore, to consider the vertical Notices and Regulations as a group, and their horizontal siblings as a separate group. The remainder of this chapter and the following chapters will therefore consider the above-mentioned Notices and Regulations in the following order:

This Chapter

● Notice on agreements of minor importance;

● Notice on subcontracting agreements;

Chapter 13

● Technology Transfer Agreements Regulation;

Chapter 14

● Guidelines on horizontal agreements;

● Research and Development Agreements Regulation;

● Specialisation Agreements Regulation.

For a general overview of how these Notices and Regulations relate to one another, and of how to decide which of them may be most relevant to the particular agreement under consideration, the reader is referred to earlier sections of this chapter.

NOTICE ON AGREEMENTS OF MINOR IMPORTANCE[104]

Background and summary of provisions

The Commission first published this Notice in 1970; at the time of writing, the most recent version was published in December 2001. Its purpose is to describe certain categories of agreement that the Commission considers to be so insignificant that they do not come within the scope of Article 81(1). In essence, if the parties have a combined market share of less than 10 per cent (if they are competitors) or 15 per cent (if they are not competitors), the Commission considers that their agreement will generally not infringe Article 81 (101), provided it does not include any of the 'hardcore' restrictions referred to in the Notice (eg price-fixing) – discussed further below.

103 As above.
104 [2001] OJ C368/7.

These thresholds reflect a gradual relaxation in the views of the Commission; earlier versions of the Notice referred to 5 per cent and 10 per cent market shares and excluded the operation of the Notice where the parties' turnover exceeded a certain level. The latest Notice does not include any turnover exclusion; instead, it comments that agreements between small- and medium-sized undertakings[105] will rarely affect trade between member states.

Compared with the block exemption Regulations,[106] the format of the Notice is relatively simple. It first describes the purpose of the Notice, then sets out the market-share thresholds, below which agreements are not considered restrictive of competition. Next, there is a list of hardcore restrictions which, if included in an agreement, would prevent the Notice from applying. Finally, there are some definitions of terms used in the Notice.

The paragraphs of the Notice can be summarised as follows:

Background and purpose

Article 81 (101) does not apply if effects are not appreciable: by way of background, the Commission refers to clarification given by the European Court, that an agreement will not be in breach of Article 81(1) (101(1)) if its impact on:

(a)   intra-Community trade; or

(b)   competition

is not appreciable.

The distinction between (a) and (b) may seem rather a subtle one, but it is important in this latest version of the Notice, for reasons which become clear in the next few paragraphs. Thus, an agreement might have anti-competitive effects, but (to take an example) these might be limited to a small part of Oxfordshire, and therefore Article 81 (101) would not apply because trade between member states was not affected. An example of this might be an agreement between an Oxfordshire solicitor and an Oxfordshire biotech company, under which the latter agreed to purchase legal services exclusively from the former. Conversely, an agreement might affect intra-Community trade, for example if it is an agreement between an English firm of solicitors and a French client, but its effects on competition might not be appreciable (eg because the parties each have a small market share) and therefore no breach of Article 81 (101) would arise.

Notice is concerned with effects on competition: the Commission explains that the Notice is concerned with (b) above, ie agreements whose effect on

---

105   For a definition of SMEs, see [1996] OJ L107/4, at 8; according to the Notice, the definition is due to be revised upwards.

106   Perhaps with the exception of the Technology Transfer Agreements Regulation, which is a relatively short document (certainly compared to its predecessor).

competition is not appreciable because they fall below the market-share thresholds set out in the Notice. The Commission acknowledges that even above these thresholds, an agreement may still not have an appreciable effect on competition.

Notice is not concerned with effects on intra-Community trade: the Commission further explains that the Notice is not concerned with (a) above, ie whether an agreement will have an effect on intra-Community trade. The Commission acknowledges, though, that agreements between small- and medium-sized undertakings[107] are 'rarely capable of appreciably affecting trade between member states'. This may give some comfort, but this statement is not strictly part of the Notice and arguably would not be binding on the Commission.

Consequences of meeting requirements of Notice: where an agreement meets the requirements of the Notice for being of minor importance, the Notice states that the Commission will not institute proceedings against the parties. Where the parties assume in good faith that their agreement meets the requirements of the Notice, the Commission will not impose fines. Thus although the Notice does not amount to legislation, the Commission has declared its intention to be bound by it, subject to any differing interpretation given by the European Court. Although the Notice is not binding on member states, the Commission intends that the Notice will give guidance to member states in their application of Article 81 (101).

Agreements covered by the Notice – market-share thresholds

The Commission considers that an agreement will not 'appreciably' restrict competition and therefore will not be in breach of Article 81 if the following market-share thresholds are not exceeded and the agreement does not include any 'hardcore' restrictions, as summarised below.

Competitors: where the parties are actual or potential competitors, their aggregate market share must not exceed 10 per cent in any of the relevant markets affected by the agreement.

Non-competitors: where the parties are not actual or potential competitors in any of the relevant markets affected by the agreement, the market share of each of them in those markets does not exceed 15 per cent.

---

107 As defined in Commission Recommendation 96/289/EC [1996] OJ L107/4, referred to in Commission Notice on agreements of minor importance, para 3. At the date of the Notice, these limits were 250 employees and an annual turnover not exceeding €40m or an annual balance sheet not exceeding €27m. The footnote to para 3 notes that the figures will be revised upwards, from €40m to €50m and from €27m to €43m. However this does not appear to have taken place yet.

Difficult to classify as competitors or non-competitors: where it is difficult to classify the agreement as being between competitors or non-competitors, the 10 per cent threshold referred to above will apply.

Cumulative foreclosure effects: where competition is restricted by the cumulative foreclosure effect of parallel networks of agreement, the market-share thresholds above (ie 10 per cent and 15 per cent) are reduced to 5 per cent. The Commission states that a cumulative foreclosure effect is unlikely to exist if less than 30 per cent of the relevant market is covered by parallel networks of agreements.

Temporary exceeding of threshold: where the above thresholds are exceeded by not more than 2 percentage points during two successive calendar years, the agreement will still fall within the requirements of the Notice.

Calculating market share: the Commission refers the reader to the Notice on the definition of the relevant market[108] and gives some further information on how to calculate market share.

Notice doesn't apply if hardcore restrictions included: the Notice will not apply to agreements that include any of the following 'hardcore' restrictions. Many (but not all) of these restrictions are concerned with the supply of goods within distribution networks and are unlikely to be of direct relevance to most technology transfer agreements.

Hardcore restrictions between competitors:

- the fixing of prices to third parties;
- limitation of output or sales;
- allocation of markets or customers.

Hardcore restrictions between non-competitors (and between competitors operating at a different level of production or distribution):

- restriction of the buyer's ability to determine its sale price (maximum or recommended sales prices are acceptable, with some conditions);
- restriction of the territories into which the buyer may sell contract goods or services, except that the following are *not* considered to be hardcore restrictions:
  — restrictions on active sales to another territory, provided this doesn't limit sales by customers of the buyer;

108 [1997] OJ C372/5.

—   restrictions on sales to end-users by buyers operating at a wholesale level of trade;

—   restrictions on sales to unauthorised distributors by members of a selective distribution system;

—   restrictions on the buyer's ability to sell components for the purposes of manufacture of competing goods.

● restrictions on active or passive sales to end-users by members of a selective distribution system at a retail level of trade;

● restrictions on cross-supplies between distributors within a selective distribution system;

● restrictions between a supplier of components and a buyer who incorporates those components, which limits the supplier's ability to supply spare parts to end-users or repairers.

Comments

The Notice provides guidance on the types of minor agreements that the Commission considers not to infringe Article 81 (101); this is clearly useful. Reliance on the Notice should protect the parties from fines, unless the parties negligently miscalculate their market-share figures. The agreement may still be held to infringe Article 81 (101) even though it complies with the Notice, but this is highly unlikely to happen in practice.

When applying the Notice, parties will need to calculate their market share in accordance with the Notice. This will be particularly difficult when the agreement concerns unproven technology, not least because the Commission's guidance document[109] on defining relevant markets, referred to in this Notice, focuses on product markets and not technology markets some further guidance on technology markets is given in the Commission's Guidelines on horizontal cooperation agreements – see for example, paragraphs 44–54 of the Guidelines[110]). At the time the agreement is entered into, the (product) market-share may be zero. If the agreement (for example a licence agreement) continues for several years, and the technology proves to be successful, the (product) market share may increase beyond the 10 or 15 per cent limit during the life of the agreement. Similarly, the market share may increase if the parties acquire other product lines within the same market sector after the agreement is made. The parties should periodically review their market-share figures throughout the life of the agreement to ensure they still come within the Notice.

109   [1997] OJ C372/5.
110   [2001] OJ C3/2.

It should be noted that the maximum permitted market share set out in the Notice relates to the combined figures of both parties together with their group companies (as defined).

COMMISSION NOTICE ON SUBCONTRACTING AGREEMENTS[111]

Background and summary

The Notice was issued in 1978. Unlike the Notice on agreements of minor importance, it has not been amended or reissued; the text is now very old. It is no longer known whether it reflects the current thinking of the Commission; however it does remain in force.[112]

The Notice describes certain provisions in subcontracting agreements which, in the Commission's opinion and subject to conditions, do not infringe Article 81(1) (101(1)). The main focus of the Notice is restrictions imposed by the contractor on the subcontractor, particularly in the areas of intellectual property and exclusivity.

The Notice is more complex than the Notice on agreements of minor importance, and reflects an old-style, form-based Commission approach, with a detailed description of permissible clauses and various conditions that must be met. Like an embryonic 1980s block exemption Regulation, it almost, but not quite, sets out a list of exempted clauses, a whitelist and a blacklist. It is, in the authors' view, one of the worst-drafted pieces of Commission (quasi-) legislation still in use. The types of permitted provision are:

- restrictions on the use, and supply to, third parties by the subcontractor of the contractor's technology and equipment;

- restrictions on the use by the subcontractor of goods, services and work which result from the use of such technology and equipment;

- confidentiality obligations;

- obligations on the subcontractor to communicate and license to the contractor any improvements made by the subcontractor; and

- restrictions on the use of the contractor's trade marks.

---

111 [1979] OJ C1/2. The full title is 'Commission Notice of 18 December 1978 concerning its assessment of certain subcontracting agreements in relation to Article 81(1) of the EEC Treaty'.

112 There have been very few published decisions by the Commission on subcontracting agreements.

The following paragraphs will discuss in turn the permitted restrictions, the conditions for acceptability, and the 'whitelist', as well as the definitions of certain terms used in the Notice.

Meaning of subcontracting agreements; purpose of Notice

Section 1 of the Notice, inter alia, describes what is meant by a subcontracting agreement and states the Commission's view that subcontracting agreements are not of themselves caught by Article 81(1)(101(1)):

> 'The Commission considers that agreements under which one firm, called "the contractor", whether or not in consequence of a prior order from a third party, entrusts to another, called "the subcontractor", the manufacture of goods, the supply of services or the performance of work under the contractor's instructions, to be provided to the contractor or performed on his behalf, are not themselves caught by the prohibition in Article 81(1)[(101(1))]'.

However, where the contractor provides the subcontractor with technology or equipment to enable him or her to perform the contract, the Notice recognises that the contractor may wish to impose restrictions on the subcontractor as to the use that may be made of such items. The Notice considers whether restrictions of this kind infringe Article 81(1)(101(1)).

Permitted restrictions: use of contractor's technology and equipment; use of items produced using such technology and equipment

Section 2 describes three types of restriction which, in the Commission's view, do not infringe Article 81(1)(101(1)). This favourable view is qualified by two statements which appear later in the Notice, which will be referred to below. The permitted restrictions are clauses whereby:

> '[1] technology or equipment provided by the contractor may not be used except for the purposes of the subcontracting agreement,
>
> [2] technology or equipment provided by the contractor may not be made available to third parties,
>
> [3] the goods, services or work resulting from the use of such technology or equipment may be supplied only to the contractor or performed on his behalf'.

Examples of contractor's technology and equipment

The Notice gives examples, albeit in a convoluted way,[113] of what is meant by the phrase 'technology or equipment provided by the contractor'. These are:

- **Contractor's intellectual property:** 'industrial property rights of the contractor or at his disposal, in the form of patents, utility models, designs protected by copyright, registered designs or other rights'.

- **Contractor's secret know-how:** 'secret knowledge or manufacturing processes (know-how) of the contractor or at his disposal'.

- **Contractor's documentation:** 'studies, plans or documents accompanying the information given which have been prepared by or for the contractor ... which, even though not covered by industrial property rights nor containing any element of secrecy, permit the manufacture of goods which differ in form, function or composition from other goods manufactured or supplied on the market'.[114]

- **Contractor's equipment:** 'dies, patterns or tools, and accessory equipment that are distinctively the contractor's which, even though not covered by industrial property rights nor containing any element of secrecy, permit the manufacture of goods which differ in form, function or composition from other goods manufactured or supplied on the market'.

Two qualifications to the Commission's favourable view of these restrictions

The Commission's favourable view of the three types of restriction mentioned above is qualified by two statements. The first is expressed as a proviso to the Commission's favourable view of these restrictions, and appears towards the beginning of section 2; the second is a statement of circumstances in which the Commission would regard the restrictions as not justifiable, and appears as a separate paragraph at the end of section 2. It is thought that both

---

113 The examples are given in a section of the Notice which describes instances of where the 'above proviso is satisfied'. This proviso (to be discussed in the next section of this chapter) states that the restrictions are only acceptable to the Commission where the contractor's technology and equipment are 'necessary' to enable the work to be carried out.

  The examples are introduced with the phrase: 'The above proviso is satisfied where performance of the subcontracting agreement makes necessary the use by the subcontractor of ...'.

  Thus, to take one of the stated examples, the contractor's manufacturing know-how: the proviso (ie that the contractor's technology should be necessary) is satisfied where performance of the agreement makes necessary the use of the contractor's know-how.

  This is a highly complex construction; it appears to be circular. The only way this writer can find to understand it is to assume that the four examples given are simply examples of what is meant by the expression 'technology or equipment provided by the contractor'. If this is the case, the drafting leaves much to be desired. If something more is meant, it is not clear to this writer – any suggestions as to what it does mean will be gratefully received!

114 The writer assumes that this qualification applies to the third and fourth examples given, but not the first two; this appears to be the most sensible construction.

qualifications are intended to apply equally to the three permitted restrictions. The qualifications are expressed as follows:

Contractor's technology or equipment must be necessary to perform the work

'[Article 81(1) (101(1)) does not apply to the three types of restriction described earlier] provided that and in so far as this technology or equipment is necessary to enable the subcontractor, under reasonable conditions to manufacture the goods, to supply the services or to carry out the work in accordance with the contractor's instructions. To that extent the subcontractor is providing goods, services or work in respect of which he is not an independent supplier in the market.'

Subcontractor has no reasonable access to alternative technology or equipment to perform the work

'... the restrictions mentioned above are not justifiable where the subcontractor has at his disposal or could under reasonable conditions obtain access to the technology and equipment needed to produce the goods, provide the services or carry out the work. In such circumstances the restrictions could deprive the subcontractor of the possibility of developing his own business in the fields covered by the agreement.'

The Notice gives an example of the second situation:

'... this is the case when the contractor provides no more than general information which merely describes the work to be done'.

Both of these qualifications appear to be concerned with the same basic theme. The technology and equipment provided by the contractor should be significant and proprietary, and should not be available from another source. The imposition of restrictions in these circumstances is justified to protect the contractor's proprietary technology. In any other circumstances, the restrictions may or may not be anti-competitive, but in any event the Notice would not be applicable.

Other permitted restrictions: confidentiality, improvements and trade marks

Section 3 of the Notice describes some further provisions which, if included in a subcontracting agreement, the Commission considers would not infringe Article 81(1) (101(1)). These are:

Non-disclosure of confidential information

'An undertaking by either of the parties not to reveal manufacturing processes or other know-how of a secret character, or confidential information given by the other party during the negotiation and performance of the agreement,

as long as the know-how or information in question has not become public knowledge'.

Such provisions have long been accepted by the Commission as necessary to protect confidential information.

Non-use of confidential information

'An undertaking by the subcontractor not to make use, even after expiry of the agreement, of manufacturing processes or other know-how of a secret character received by him during the currency of the agreement, as long as they have not become public knowledge'.

Note that this paragraph refers to an undertaking by the subcontractor, unlike the previous paragraph which referred to either of the parties. This may reflect a cautious approach by the Commission on whether restrictions on use by the contractor of the subcontractor's know-how would infringe Article 81(1) (101(1)). Restrictions of this kind on the contractor should be avoided, if parties intend to rely on the Notice.

Subcontractor's improvements and inventions

The Notice distinguishes between:

(1) improvements (including patentable inventions) made by the subcontractor to the contractor's technology, which are either

(a) capable of being used independently of the contractor's patented or secret technology; or

(b) not capable of being used independently of the contractor's patented or secret technology; and

(2) the results of the subcontractor's own research and development, where such results are capable of being used independently.

The Notice provides that in the case of improvements which can be used independently, the subcontractor may be required to license such improvements non-exclusively to the contractor, whilst in the case of improvements which cannot be used independently, the licence may be exclusive in favour of the contractor. The implication is that assignment of the improvements to the contractor would not be permitted under the Notice. However, for the Notice to apply, the subcontractor must not be restricted at all in relation to his or her disposal[115] of the results of his or her own research and development, *where such results are capable of being used independently,*[116] that is to say not even a non-exclusive licence may be required to be granted to the contractor, if the Notice is to apply. The relevant paragraphs of the Notice read as follows:

Improvements to the contractor's technology

'An undertaking by the subcontractor

[a]   to pass on to the contractor on a non-exclusive basis any technical improvements which he has made during the currency of the agreement or

[b]   where a patentable invention has been discovered by the subcontractor, to grant non-exclusive licences in respect of inventions relating to improvements and new applications of the original invention to the contractor for the term of the patent held by the latter.

This undertaking by the subcontractor may be exclusive in favour of the contractor in so far as improvements and inventions made by the subcontractor during the currency of the agreement are incapable of being used independently of the contractor's secret know-how or patent, since this does not constitute an appreciable restriction of competition.'

Results of subcontractor's research and development

'However, any undertaking by the subcontractor regarding the right to dispose of the results of his own research and development work may restrain competition, where such results are capable of being used independently. In such circumstances, the subcontracting relationship is not sufficient to displace the ordinary competition rules on the disposal of industrial property rights or secret know-how.'

Contractor's trade marks

'Where the subcontractor is authorized by a subcontracting agreement to use a specified trade mark, trade name or get-up, the contractor may at the same time forbid such use by the subcontractor in the case of goods, services or work which are not to be supplied to the contractor.'

This paragraph seems uncontroversial. It is difficult to see how such a restriction could be regarded as anti-competitive.

---

115 Presumably this includes both requirements to license or assign the results to the contractor and restrictions on licensing or assigning the results to third parties. In view of the quality of the drafting generally, it is recommended that parties should not assume that 'dispose' means merely providing, assigning or granting rights to third parties.

116 Presumably, where the results cannot be used independently of the contractor's patented or secret technology, they may be licensed exclusively to the contractor.

Comments

The Notice is helpful as far as it goes. Many simple subcontracting agreements are unlikely to affect trade between member states or infringe Article 81 (101). Of particular interest is the question of whether the Notice can be applied to an agreement between a licensor and licensee. For example, consider the situation where a licensee/distributor of computer software is commissioned by his or her licensor/principal to make modifications to the software to make it suitable for use on a new type of computer system, and so as to operate in a different computer language to the one in which it was originally written. On completing the modifications, he or she is licensed to distribute the modified software. The agreement provides that the principal will be exclusively licensed to use the modifications outside the distributor's territory.

Would the subcontracting Notice apply, such that the exclusive licence granted to the principal could fall outside Article 81(1) (101(1))?[117] If not, it may be that Article 81(1) (101(1)) would be infringed; by analogy[118] with the Technology Transfer Agreements Regulation in a licensing agreement, anything more than a non-exclusive licence back of improvements is likely to infringe Article 81(1) (101(1)). The Notice seems to suggest that subcontracting agreements are less likely to infringe Article 81(1) (101(1)) than 'ordinary' licence agreements.[119]

MODERNISATION REGULATION

Introduction

The Modernisation Regulation[120] is part of the approach of the European Commission to modernise the regulation and enforcement of competition law and practice. This Regulation includes provisions that:

---

117 Assume that the modifications cannot be used independently of the principal's technology, on the basis that the modifications would be an adaptation or translation of the original software, and accordingly an infringement of the copyright in that software.

118 Since there is as yet no block exemption Regulation for software licences.

119 The Notice states that restrictions are assessed in the Notice: '... with due regard to the purpose of such agreements, which distinguishes them from ordinary patent and know-how licensing agreements'.

120 Council Regulation (EC) 1/2003 ([2003] OJ L1/1) on the implementation of the rules on competition laid down in Articles 81 and 82 of the Treaty. This Regulation has been accompanied by other another Regulation, Notices and Guidelines which add further details to the working of the Modernisation Regulation: (i) Commission Regulation (EC) 773/2004 [2004] OJ L123/18 relating to the conduct of proceedings by the Commission pursuant to Articles 81 and 82 of the EC Treaty; (ii) Commission Notice on co-operation within the network of competition authorities [2004] OJ L123/18; (iii) Commission Notice on co-operation between the Commission and the courts of the EU Member States in the application of Articles 81 and 82 [2004] OJ C101/54; (iv) Commission Notice on the handling of complaints by the Commission under Articles 81 and 82 of the EC Treaty [2004] OJ C101/65; (v) Guidelines on the effect of trade concept contained in Articles 81 and 82 [2004] OJ C101; (vi) Guidelines on the application of Article 81(3) and (vii) Commission Notice on informal guidance relating to novel questions concerning Articles 81 and 82 that arise in individual cases (guidance letters) [2004] OJ C101/78.

- the enforcement of competition law should be decentralised to local competition authorities (while the Commission retains, and extends, its own powers);

- parties to an agreement should make their own assessment as to whether the agreement is compatible with competition law;[121] and

- the Commission will move from assessing an agreement, practice etc before it occurs (ie by the parties notifying the Commission, getting clearance, receiving a comfort letter, applying for an exemption, etc) to analysing the effect an agreement has on competition after it has entered into force.

Summary of provisions

The Modernisation Regulation, which came into force on 1 May 2004,[122] in summary provides for the following:

- Articles 81(1) (101(1)), 81(3) (101(2)) and 82 (102) can be directly applied by national competition authorities and courts.[123]

- The Modernisation Regulation replaces Regulation 17/1962 (which contained similar provisions to the Modernisation Regulation),[124] but has extensively increased and recast the powers of the Commission.

- There is no longer a need to notify the Commission if an individual exemption is sought under Article 81(3) (101(3)) (ie it is simply not possible to do this any longer).[125]

- The Commission has wide powers to carry out investigations, require the provision of information, take statements and carry out inspections of premises (of parties thought to be in breach of competition law as well as of those of other persons).[126] A national competition authority can carry out inspections in its territory on behalf of another member state or as required by the Commission.[127]

- The Commission and national competition authorities are required to co-operate and exchange information.[128] This will be done through a

---

121 White Paper on modernisation of the rules implementing Articles 85 and 86 of the EC Treaty [1999] OJ C132/1.
122 Regulation 1/2003, Art 45.
123 Regulation 1/2003, Art 3(1), 6.
124 Regulation 1/2003, Art 43.
125 Regulation 1/2003, Art 1(2).
126 Regulation 1/2003, Arts 17–21.
127 Regulation 1/2003, Art 22.
128 Where information is provided by a competition authority to another or to the Commission (or from the Commission) the information can be used as 'evidence [in] any matter of fact or of law, including confidential information (Regulation 1/2003, Art 12(1)).

network of competition authorities (European Competition Network).[129] For example, a national competition authority will have to inform the Commission, in writing, when it commences investigative measures, will be adopting a decision on infringement, accepting a commitment or will be withdrawing a block exemption, etc.[130]

- A national competition authority or court cannot rule on an agreement, decision or practice under Articles 81 (101) or 82 (102) which is counter to a Commission decision on the same subject.[131]

- A national competition authority can apply Article 81(101) or 82(102) to individual cases, whether on their own initiative or by following a complaint, and the national competition authority can:

  — require an infringement to stop;

  — order interim measures;

  — accept commitments;

  — impose a range of financial measures (fines, periodic penalty payments etc).[132]

- The Commission has more far-reaching powers than set out in the previous bullet points, including making findings of inapplicability.[133]

Although the Commission will no longer receive notifications etc, in particular cases it will issue informal guidance letters.[134] Although the thrust of the new regime is that the rules in force provide greater certainty and help the promotion of innovation and investment, it is recognised that as there can be 'genuine uncertainty because they present novel or unresolved questions for the application of the rules, individual undertakings may wish

---

129 See http://ec.europa.eu/competition/ecn/index_en.html for further details.

130 Regulation 1/2003, Arts 11–16. There are also provisions dealing with exchange of information and what is to happen, for example, where the Commission or another member state commences investigations.

131 Regulation 1/2003, Art 16. In the case of courts, they must avoid giving decisions which would conflict with a decision which is contemplated by the Commission in proceedings that the Commission has initiated. The correct approach is likely to be for a court to stay proceedings.

132 Regulation 1/2003, Art 5.

133 Regulation 1/2003, Arts 7–10. Where the Commission requires an undertaking or associations of undertakings to bring an infringement to an end the Commission can 'impose any behavioural or structural remedies which are proportionate to the infringement committed and necessary to bring the infringement effectively to an end. Structural remedies can only be imposed either where there is no equally effective behavioural remedy or where any equally effective behavioural remedy would be more burdensome for the undertaking concerned than the structural remedy. If the Commission has a legitimate interest in doing so, it may also find that an infringement has been committed in the past' (from Regulation 1/2003, Art 7(1)).

134 Commission Notice on informal guidance relating to novel questions concerning Articles 81 and 82 that arise in individual cases (guidance letters) [2004] C101/78.

to seek informal guidance from the Commission'.[135] The guidance will be available despite the strong emphasis that the parties are best placed to deal (being close to the facts) with whether the provisions of an agreement are in accordance with competition law, and have available to them a large number of documents concerning the block exemptions, rules, guidance, guidelines etc. The Commission has set out when it will not provide this informal guidance, as follows:

> 'The Commission will consider whether it is appropriate to process a request for informal guidance by looking at:
>
> * whether the question really is a novel one concerning Article 81 or 82;
>
> * the economic importance from the point of view of the consumer of the goods or services concerned by the agreement or practice, and/or the extent to which the agreement or practice corresponds to more widely spread economic usage in the marketplace and/or the extent of the investments linked to the transaction in relation to the size of the companies concerned;
>
> * whether any further fact-finding is required and whether all the information is available.
>
> The Commission will not consider hypothetical questions and will not issue guidance letters on agreements or practices:
>
> * that are no longer being implemented by the parties;
>
> * that have been raised in a case pending before the European Court of First Instance or the European Court of Justice;
>
> * that are subject to proceedings pending with the Commission, a Member State court or Member State competition authority'.[136]

Any letters issued will be posted on the Commission website and may prove useful in providing a view as to particular competition law issues which may arise in future (to parties or to an agreement or national competition authority).

UK law following the bringing into force of the Modernisation Regulation

The Modernisation Regulation has resulted in changes to UK competition law, including:[137]

---

135 See Regulation 1/2003, Recital 38.
136 See http://europa.eu/legislation_summaries/competition/firms/l26112_en.htm.
137 Enterprise Act 2002, s 209 provides powers to change the competition regime in the UK to match that of European Community competition law.

- the Office of Fair Trading (OFT) being designated as the national competition authority for the UK[138] and it can exercise all the powers and functions of a competition authority of a member state under the relevant provisions of the Modernisation Regulation;[139]

- the Competition Act 1998 is amended so that the granting or cancellation of individual exemptions shall cease to have effect for agreements falling within the scope of Chapter I (section 2) of the Competition Act 1998 but which satisfy the conditions set out in section 9 of the Competition Act 1998.[140] It is also not possible to make notifications to the OFT etc;

- the OFT to have the same powers as the Commission to carry out investigations under Article 81 of the EC Treaty and Chapter I of the Competition Act 1998;[141]

- block exemption orders may continue to be made;[142]

- the OFT can provide guidance on novel or unresolved questions of law, as the Commission is able to.[143]

---

138 Competition Act 1998 and Other Enactments (Amendment) Regulations 2004 (SI 2004/1261), para 3(1).
139 Competition Act 1998 and Other Enactments (Amendment) Regulations 2004 (SI 2004/1261), para 3(2).
140 Competition Act 1998 and Other Enactments (Amendment) Regulations 2004 (SI 2004/1261), para 4 and Sch 1. Although any individual exemptions, etc will continue in effect.
141 Competition Act 1998 and Other Enactments (Amendment) Regulations 2004 (SI 2004/1261), para 4 and Sch 1, substituting Competition Act 1998, s 25 and amending other following sections.
142 Competition Act 1998 and Other Enactments (Amendment) Regulations 2004 (SI 2004/1261), para 4 and Sch 1, amending Competition Act 1998, s 7.
143 See OFT Competition Law Guideline on *Agreements and concerted practices* (OFT 401). The Guideline gives guidance on novel or unresolved questions about the application of Art 81, EC Treaty as well as the Competition Act 1998, Ch 1 prohibition. In OFT 442, more detail is given as to when the OFT will not consider a request for an opinion.

CHAPTER 13

EU Guidelines and Regulation on Technology Transfer Agreements[1]

---

[1] Following the passing of the acceptance of the Lisbon Treaty and its coming into force in December 2009, the Articles of the EC Treaty are renumbered. This chapter adopts the following method: the existing numbering is retained with the new numbers in parenthesis. The EC Treaty is renamed the 'Treaty on the Functioning of the European Union', but for ease of reference it will continue to be called the EC Treaty in this edition of the book.

INTRODUCTION

The latest Technology Transfer Agreements Regulation[2] ('TTR') came into force on 1 May 2004 and is due to continue in force until 30 April 2014. It is the latest in a long line of block exemption regulations for patent and know-how licensing, including, most recently, the 1996 Technology Transfer Agreements Regulation.[3]

From an industry standpoint, much of the original thinking of the European Commission, when it started to draft the 2004 Regulation, was sound. In particular, the Commission's approach seemed to be that:

- it now has greater experience of technology licences, and has been persuaded that in many cases they do not present major competition problems, as long as they don't include 'hardcore', or very anti-competitive, provisions;

- it is appropriate to move away from the previous approach of block exemption regulations, which set out long lists of acceptable or unacceptable clauses. Instead, the Regulation should provide a general framework within which technology transfer agreements are regarded as acceptable from a competition standpoint.

Less attractive, from an industry standpoint, was the Commission's view that certain categories of agreements raised major competition concerns, namely:

- agreements between parties who are competitors; and

- agreements between parties with significant market shares.

As the new Regulation went through a number of drafts, it was these last two areas that proved to be most problematic. The Commission had moved from a regime where many types of agreements could qualify for block exemption, as long as their terms fitted within detailed lists of acceptable or unacceptable clauses, to one where fewer agreements qualified.

The early drafts seemed likely to result in a more restrictive regime than that under the 1996 Regulation, such that many apparently harmless technology transfer agreements either would not qualify for block exemption, or there was uncertainty and risk that they might not qualify. Extensive lobbying of Commission officials by industry representatives and their advisers resulted in

---

2   Commission Regulation (EC) 772/2004 ([2004] OJ L123/11) on the application of Article 81(3) of the Treaty to categories of technology transfer agreements.
3   Commission Regulation (EC) 240/96 [1996] OJ L31/2. This Regulation ceased to apply on 31 March 2006. It is discussed in depth in the second edition of this book (see Ch 5, Pt 2, pp 220–273).

some changes of the original draft text. In general, these changes removed or relaxed some of the most restrictive provisions.[4] The criticisms concerned the uncertainty of whether an agreement will come within market shares limits and required parties (and their advisers) having to analyse agreements in new ways, such as not only identifying whether an agreement or a provision in an agreement comes within a list of restraints but also carry out an economic evaluation as to whether the agreement comes within or without the exemption to Art 81 (101).

The provisions of the TTR are significantly different from the 1996 Technology Transfer Agreements Regulations, particularly in that:

• a wider range of agreements are within the provisions of the exemption provided under the TTR – not only patent and know-how licences, but also computer software and design licences;

• the exemption under the TTR will only apply where a certain market share[5] is not exceeded (the TTR sets a different level of market share depending on whether the parties to a licence are competing or non-competing);

• as indicated in the previous bullet point, the TTR differentiates between competing and non-competing parties to a licence agreement, including differentiating between market share and a list of severe ('hardcore') restrictions which would take an agreement outside of the exemption provided by the TTR.

The EC has also issued guidance to accompany the TTR ('Guidelines' in this chapter).[6] The Guidelines have the following purposes:

• to set out how Art 81(101) will apply to technology transfer agreements which do not come within the TTR;[7]

• to explain what the principles are for the assessment of technology transfer agreements under Art 81(101);[8] and

• to give guidance on how the TTR will be applied.[9]

---

4   See the response of the Commission to the submissions and criticisms made to the draft TTR in the speech of the European Commissioner for Competition Policy, Mario Monti, in a speech on 16 January 2004 (http://ec.europa.eu/competition/speeches/index_speeches_by_the_commissioner.html).

5   The speech by Commissioner Monti (see n 3) indicates that the TTR applies to all sectors, not just 'high-tech' sectors.

6   Commission Notice – Guidelines on the application of Article 81 of the EC Treaty to technology transfer agreements (Text with EEA relevance) ([2004] OJ C101/02).

7   As n 6, para 2.

8   As n 6, para 2.

9   As n 6, para 2.

The TTR cannot be properly understood without consulting the Guidelines.[10] They also give detailed guidance as to the application of the TTR, giving in some places detailed examples as well as information on the application of Art 81 (101) to technology transfer agreements which fall outside the scope of the TTR.

CRITICISMS OF THE PREVIOUS TECHNOLOGY TRANSFER REGULATION

The previous Technology Transfer Regulation (Reg 240/96) came in for considerable criticism. The EC also found deficiencies in this Regulation (which were reflected in an evaluation report[11] concerning it), including:

- it was too complex and too narrow in scope;

- it did not cover licensing agreements which posed no risk to competition;[12] and

- the model chosen to disapply Art 81(1) (101(1)) did not accord with the reforms introduced concerning horizontal and vertical agreements.

GENERAL APPROACH OF THE COMMISSION TO TECHNOLOGY TRANSFER AGREEMENTS

It should be noted that not all technology transfer agreements will be caught by the TTR. For example, a technology transfer agreement may not contain any provisions that restrict competition at all. Or if it does contain provisions which restrict competition then the restrictions are not appreciable. But in any case the approach of the Commission generally, in the latest TTR, is to take a more favourable view of such agreements, as it considers that such agreements usually:

- improve economic efficiency; and

- are pro-competitive.[13]

---

10 See n 6.
11 Evaluation Report on the Transfer Technology Block Exemption Regulation 240/96.
12 As n 11; see para 175, where the restricted number of agreements which could benefit from the exemption provided by Reg 240/96 'in some cases, [imposed] on companies an unnecessary compliance burden and forcing industry into a legal straight-jacket ... [Reg 240/96] ... may skew enforcement toward over deterrence, which may have negative impact on dynamic efficiency'.
13 TTR, Recital 5.

Four reasons are stated for taking this more favourable approach towards providing a block exemption for technology transfer agreements:

- there is a reduction in the duplication of research and development;

- the incentive for carrying out early stage research and development is strengthened;

- it helps to spread the results of the research and development;

- it helps to create a market for products to compete in.[14]

The Commission now considers most licence agreements as being pro-competitive, leading to efficiencies by combining the licensor's technologies together with the assets and technologies of the licensee (either leading to (lower) cost and/or (higher) output that would not be otherwise available).[15]

Also of note is that the Commission will not presume that, just because the market share of the parties to an agreement is higher than that stated in the TTR, the agreement will infringe Art 81(1) (101(1)).[16]

Where an agreement fulfils the conditions set out by the TTR it is block exempted from the prohibitions contained in Art 81(1) (101(1)) and such an agreement is legally enforceable and valid. One implication of such a result is that a national court or national competition authority cannot prohibit such an agreement under Art 81(1) (101(1)) by private litigation.[17]

STRUCTURE OF THE TTR

The TTR is structured with 20 Recitals and 11 Articles,[18] as follows:

---

14 TTR, Recital 5.
15 Guidelines, para 17.
16 TTR, Recital 12. Also Guidelines, para 37. Only if the agreement contains 'hardcore' restrictions can the it be presumed to be prohibited by Art 81(101).
17 See TTR, para 34.
18 As a comparison, the previous Technology Transfer Regulation (240/96) consisted of 27 Recitals and 13 Articles. Although this type of count seems to indicate that the two Regulations are of similar length, a wordcount will show that the newer Regulation is almost half the length of the former.

20 Recitals	Provide details as to:
	• the statutory basis for the (previous) TTR (Recitals 1–2);
	• the review carried out of the previous TTR (Recital 3);
	• the economic and pro-competitive effects of having the TTR (Recitals 4–6);
	• that the TTR only deals with agreements designed to exploit licensed technology which lead to the production of goods and services (and not other types of agreements) (Recital 7);
	• how agreements which fall within Art 81(3) (101(3)) are to be dealt with (Recitals 8–9);
	• how issues of market thresholds are to be dealt with (Recitals 10–12);
	• what is to happen with agreements which contain anti-competitive restrictions etc (Recitals 13–15);
	• remaining recitals deal with withdrawing the block exemption in particular cases (the Modernisation Regulation etc)[19].
Article 1	This Article provides the meaning of certain words and phrases which are used in the TTR.
Article 2	This Article provides for (and the meaning of) the block exemption pursuant to Art 81(3) (101(3)), from Art 81(1) (101) for technology transfer agreements (ie a technology transfer agreement entered into between two undertakings where the licensed technology is to be used for the production of goods and services).
Article 3	This Article indicates the market share thresholds that the parties to an agreement must not exceed in order to have the benefit of the exemption provided by Art 2. The threshold is lower where the parties are competing (horizontal agreement) than where the parties are not competing (vertical agreement).
Article 4	This Article provides 'hardcore' restrictions where if one or more are present will take the whole agreement outside the benefit of the exemption provided by Art 2. The restrictions for competing undertakings are stricter than for non-competing undertakings:
	(a) *competing undertakings*: price fixing, limiting output, allocation of markets or customer*; restricting a licensee using own technology;
	(b) *non-competing* undertakings: price fixing, restricting licensee making passive sales in a territory or to certain customers.*
	* there are exceptions to these restrictions (ie where a provision contains this restriction, and it is within the specified exception, it will not take the agreement outside the benefit of the exemption provided by Art 2).
Article 5	This Article specifies that a provision in an agreement which contains one of the following restrictions will take only that provision (and not the whole agreement) outside the exemption provided by Art 2:
	(a) licensee being required to grant an exclusive licence or assign its own (severable) improvements to licensor/third party;
	(b) stopping a licensee challenging validity of licensor's IP;
	(c) where parties are non-competing, stopping a licensee exploiting its own technology.
Article 6	This Article allows the Commission to withdraw benefit of the exemption provided in Art 2 in specified circumstances.
Article 7	This Article prevents the TTR applying to parallel networks of similar technology transfer agreements which cover more than 50% of a relevant market.
Article 8	This Article sets out how the market share thresholds in Art 3 are calculated.
Article 9	Repeals the previous TTR (240/96).
Article 10	Provided a transitional period (until 31 March 2006) for agreements which were covered by the earlier TTR (240/96).

---

19   This regulation (Council Regulation (EC) 1/2003 ([2003] OJ L1/1) on the implementation of the rules on competition laid down in Articles 81 and 82 of the Treaty is discussed in Chapter 12 under 'Modernisation Regulation'.

THE PURPOSE OF THE TTR

The TTR disapplies Art 81(1) (101(1))[20] of the EC Treaty to a technology transfer agreement, as long as:

- the agreement is entered into between two undertakings; and

- the agreement permits the production of contract products;[21]

subject to the other provisions of the TTR.

The exemption from Art 81(1) (101(1)) will apply to a technology transfer agreement that contains restrictions of competition falling within the scope of Art 81(1) (101(1))[22] and is between a licensor and a licensee.[23] In regard to the later point, the TTR will cover an agreement whereby:[24]

- conditions are stipulated for more than one level of trade;[25] and

- the licensor can specify the obligations on the licensee which the licensee must or may impose on resellers of the products produced under the licence.

HOW LONG WILL AN EXEMPTION LAST FOR?

The exemption will last for:[26]

- so long as the intellectual property rights in the licensed technology are in force, namely they have:

  — not expired;

  — not lapsed;

  — not been declared invalid.

Where know-how is involved, that the know-how remains secret. If the know-how becomes publicly known because of the actions of the licensee, the exemption will continue for the duration of the agreement.

---

20   See Ch 12 under 'Article 81(101)'.
21   TTR, Art 2.
22   TTR, Art 2, para 2.
23   TTR, Recital 19.
24   TTR, Recital 19. But any conditions and obligations should comply with competition rules which apply to supply and distribution agreements. A supply and distribution agreement between a licensee and its buyers will not be exempted by the TTR.
25   Such as requiring the licensee to set-up a particular distribution system.
26   Commission Regulation (EC) 772/2004 ([2004] OJ L123/11) on the application of Article 81(3) of the Treaty to categories of technology transfer agreements, Art 2, para 2.

An agreement may contain a number of different types of intellectual property or several of the same kind and in such a case the block exemption will last until the last of the items of intellectual property remains in force.[27] For example, if an agreement licences several patents all of which expire on different dates, then the block exemption will come to an end on the date when the patent with the last expiry date expires.

The shortly stated exemption is dependant on a number of definitions, particularly the meaning of technology transfer agreement, contract products, undertakings, know-how, and competing and non-competing undertakings.

Also, the application of the exemption will depend on whether:

● the undertakings have a certain market share;[28] and

● a technology transfer agreement contains certain 'hardcore' (more severe) or 'softcore' (less severe) restrictions.

DURATION OF THE TTR

The TTR is valid from 1 May 2004 to 30 April 2014.

It is likely that after its expiry date agreements which have benefited from the exemption of the TTR will continue to do so for a limited period after the expiry date.[29]

TYPES OF AGREEMENT COVERED BY THE TTR

The exemption provided by the TTR will apply to technology transfer agreements. The TTR defines a technology transfer agreement[30] as:

(a) a patent licence;

(b) a know-how licensing agreement;

---

27 See Guidelines, para 55; the wording used in the Guidelines is not absolutely clear on this point, as it states: 'The block exemption applies to each licensed property right covered by the agreement and ceases to apply on the date of expiry, invalidity or the coming into the public domain of the last intellectual property right which constitutes 'technology' within the meaning of the [TTR]'. The wording used here could, from one point of view, mean that there is a block exemption for each form of intellectual property licensed in an agreement and comes to an end as each expires.

28 The market share depending on whether they are competitors or not: see below under 'Market Share' for further details.

29 The TTR provides that agreements in force at 30 April 2004 and which satisfy the conditions for exemption under Reg 240/96 (but not under the TTR) would continue to do so until 31 March 2006 (Art 10).

30 TTR, Art 1.1(b).

(c)   a software copyright licensing agreement;

(d)   a mixed patent, know-how or software copyright licensing agreement;

(e)   an agreement in categories (a) to (d) but which has provisions for:

   (i)   the sale and purchase of products; or

   (ii)   the licensing of other intellectual property rights; or

   (iii)   the assignment of intellectual property rights;

   provided the provisions in (i) to (iii) do not constitute the primary object of the agreement and those provisions are related directly to the production of contract goods;

(f)   assignment of patents, know-how, software (or a combination of these intellectual property) as long as part of the risk remains with the assignor. The risk, as the definition explains, would include the sum paid to the assignor in consideration of the assignment being dependent on the turnover obtained by the assignee from production of goods using the assigned technology.

A sub-contract will not be excluded from the TTR 'whereby the licensor licenses technology to the licensee who undertakes to produce certain products on the basis thereof exclusively for the licensor'.[31] The primarily focus must be on the licensing of the technology (and not on other purposes, eg where a sub-contracting agreement includes the provision of equipment from the licensor to the licensee).

TYPES OF AGREEMENT TO WHICH THE TTR DOES NOT APPLY

The TTR is not intended to deal with licensing agreements:

- which have more than two undertakings to them;[32]

- that set up technology pools;[33]

---

31   Guidelines, para 44.
32   TTR, Art 2, para 1. But an 'undertaking' can include more than one company or one organisation as an undertaking can include 'connected undertakings', which essentially means group companies (see TTR, Art 1(2)). Presumably, the technology transfer company (which if a wholly owned subsidiary of a university), when entering into a patent and know-how licence, could include the university as a party as it most probably comes within the definition of being a connected undertaking.
33   TTR, Recital 7. Technology pools being 'agreements for the pooling of technologies with the purpose of licensing the created package of intellectual property rights to third parties'. Technology pools are considered in the Guidelines at paras 210–235.

- whose primarily purpose is sub-licensing;[34]

- which are sub-contract agreements whose primarily purpose is not the licensing of technology;

- where the primarily purpose of the licensed technology is to carry out further research and development;[35]

- whose purpose is to sub-contract research and development work;[36]

- that concern a trade mark;[37]

- involving rights in performances and other rights related to copyright.[38]

TYPES OF PARTY WHO BENEFIT FROM THE TTR

The exemption provided by the TTR only applies where the technology transfer agreement is between two parties.[39] Therefore, a multi-party agreement would not have the benefit of the exemption provided by the TTR.[40]

'Undertaking' is itself not defined in the TTR, but an undertaking will include their respective 'connected undertakings'.

---

34 Guidelines, para 42.
35 Guidelines, para 45. But a licensing agreement which permits the licensee to exploit the licensed technology, possibly after carrying out further research and development, is permitted as long as the licence is concerned with the production of goods or services (see TTR, Recital 7); ie there must be a direct link between the technology which is licensed and the contract product.
36 Ie where the licensee is only responsible for carrying out research and development work in the field of the technology which is licensed to it, and on completing the research and development work provides to the licensor a package of improved technology (see Guidelines, para 45). The Guidelines state that the main purpose of an agreement of this type is 'the provision of research and development services aimed at improving the technology as opposed to the production of goods and services on the basis of the licensed technology'.
37 Guidelines, para 53.
38 Guidelines, para 52.
39 Art 2, para 1.
40 See Guidelines, para 38. What appears determinative is whether the 'agreement is concluded between more than two undertakings'. An agreement which is concluded between two undertakings but covers more than one level of trade will still have the benefit of the exemption provided by the TTR to Art 81 (101). The Guidelines note that the TTR would apply to a licensor providing a licence which would cover a licensee who manufactures and then distributes a product, and the licence could include a requirement on the licensee imposing obligations on resellers concerning the manufactured products (see para 39). Even if there is an agreement is between more than two undertakings it is likely that the principles contained in the TTR will be applied by the Commission if the agreement is of the 'same nature' as of the type of agreement explicitly covered by the TTR (see para 40).

However if an agreement is concluded between more than two undertakings and where the EC conducts an individual assessment of the agreement which is of the same nature as those covered by the TTR, the EC will apply the principles set out in the TTR by analogy to such agreements.[41]

TYPES OF INTELLECTUAL PROPERTY COVERED BY THE TTR

The TTR covers, principally, the following types of intellectual property:

- patents;

- applications for patents;

- designs;

- other 'lesser' forms of intellectual property, such as:

  — utility models;

  — applications for registration of utility models;

  — topographies of semiconductor products;

  — supplementary protection certificates for medicinal products (or other products for which supplementary protection certificates are available); and

  — plant breeders' certificates;[42]

- copyright (as far as it relates to software);

- know-how, as long as it is 'a package of non-patented practical information, resulting from experience and testing, which is:

  (a) secret, that is to say, not generally known or easily accessible;

  (b) substantial, that is to say, significant and useful for the production of the contract products; and

  (c) identified, that is to say, described in a sufficiently comprehensive manner so as to make it possible to verify that it fulfils the criteria of secrecy and substantiality';[43]

- other forms of intellectual property (such as copyright generally or trade marks) as long as such intellectual property is related directly to the

---

41   Guidelines, para 40.
42   TTR, Art 1(h).
43   TTR, Art 1(i). Also see the next, heading concerning know-how.

exploitation of the licensed technology and such intellectual property is not the primarily purpose of the technology transfer agreement.[44]

Know-how

Know-how calls for further elaboration, particularly as the EC has had reservations concerning agreements which involve the licensing of know-how where in fact such an agreement is a method of introducing an anti-competitive restriction but the know-how does not protect licensed products or does not exist. The definition of know-how (as set out above under 'Types of intellectual property covered by the TTR') has a specific meaning. The definition indicates that know-how has to be practical and of use in the production of contract products. In addition to the definition, the EC has also set out guidance regarding know-how,[45] in particular:

Concerning 'substantial':

- for know-how to be 'substantial' it must significantly contribute to or facilitate the production of contract products;

- know-how will not be substantial where the contract product can be produced with freely available technology;

- where contract products are concerned, substantial will mean the know-how is useful for the production of contract products but does not mean that the contract product is of a higher value than one produced with freely available technology;

- where process technologies are concerned, substantial will mean that the know-how is useful in that it will improve the competitive position of the licensee at the date of conclusion of the agreement. This can reduce the licensee's production costs

Concerning 'identified':

- for know-how to be identified means that it is possible to verify that it is secret and substantial;

---

44 Guidelines, para 50. This paragraph of the guidance provides an illustrative example of where associated intellectual property would be covered: 'The licensor may for instance authorise the licensee to use his trademark on the products incorporating the licensed technology. The trademark licence may allow the licensee to better exploit the licensed technology by allowing consumers to make an immediate link between the product and the characteristics imputed to it by the licensed technology. An obligation on the licensee to use the licensor's trademark may also promote the dissemination of technology by allowing the licensor to identify himself as the source of the underlying technology. However, where the value of the licensed technology to the licensee is limited because he already employs an identical or very similar technology and the main object of the agreement is the trademark, the [TTR] does not apply'.

45 Guidelines, para 47.

- know-how can also be identified if it is described in a written form or in manuals;

- if the know-how cannot reasonably be in a permanent form it can still meet the criteria of being 'identified' if it consists of practical knowledge which is possessed by the employees of the licensor,[46] as long as:

  — the know-how is described in a general way; and

  — a list of employees will be provided who will be or have been involved in passing the know-how on to the licensee.

MARKET SHARE

Market share levels before exemption is lost

In addition to the other conditions the parties to a technology transfer agreement must not exceed certain market shares.[47] It should be noted that the mere fact that the parties exceed the market share specified in the TTR will not by itself mean that their technology transfer agreement will infringe Art 81(1) (101(1)).[48] Such an agreement could still satisfy the conditions for exemption.

The particular market share depends on whether the parties are competing or non-competing undertakings:[49]

- if the parties to a technology transfer agreement are competing undertakings, the combined market share of the parties must not exceed 20 per cent of the affected relevant technology and product market;

- if the parties to a technology transfer agreement are not competing undertakings, then the market of each of the parties must not exceed 30 per cent of the affected relevant technology and product market.

To determine the market share of a party on the relevant technology market it is necessary to look at the presence of the licensed technology on the relevant product market.[50] For a licensor, a slightly different method is used for determining the licensor's market share on the relevant technology market. It

---

46   The example given in the Guidelines is that the employees may possess secret and substantial knowledge about a particular production process which is supplied to the licensee by training the licensee's employees.

47   The EC has set out its approach on how a market is defined: see para 19 of the Guidelines.

48   See TTR, Recital 12.

49   See 'Meaning of "competing" and "non-competing" undertakings' below for a description of the meaning of competing and non-competing undertakings.

50   TTR, Art 3(3).

is the combined market share on the relevant product market of the contract products that are produced by the licensor and also its licensees.[51]

If the market share is not exceeded at time agreement entered into, but is subsequently exceeded

If the market shares are not initially more then those stated above but subsequently exceed those levels, the block exemption provided by the TTR shall continue for a period of two consecutive calendar years following the year when the relevant market share is exceeded.[52]

Meaning of 'competing' and 'non-competing' undertakings[53]

TTR provides two ways in which undertakings can compete; either:

- on the relevant technology market;[54] and/or
- on the relevant product market.

Meaning of relevant technology market

For competing undertakings that are competing on the relevant technology market, this will mean that:

- they are licensing out competing technologies which do not infringe the other undertaking's intellectual property rights ('actual competitors on the technology market');
- the market includes technologies which the licensees consider interchangeable or substitutable for the licensed technology.

Meaning of relevant product market

For competing undertakings that are competing on the relevant product market, this will mean that they are:

---

51 TTR, Art 3(3).
52 TTR, Art 8(2).
53 TTR, Art 1(1)(j). See also Guidelines, paras 26–33.
54 See Guidelines, paras 20–23 for explanation of the way the Commission considers a technology market can be defined in practice.

- actually active on the product and geographic market where contract products are sold;

- potentially active on the product and geographic market if there was a small and permanent increase in relative prices if they realistically undertake any necessary additional investment to enter that market (by reason of the technologies' characteristics, royalties or their intended use);

- competing where such activity does not infringe the other undertaking's intellectual property rights;

- competing where the relevant product market consists of products which are considered as interchangeable by their buyers (by reason of their characteristics, price or intended use).

'HARDCORE' RESTRICTIONS

The exemption from Art 81(1) (101(1)) is also not available where a technology transfer agreement contains restrictive provisions which are considered particularly anti-competitive. An agreement which contains restrictions which are not 'indispensable to the improvement of production or distribution', and such restrictions are 'severely anti-competitive restraints' (such as fixing the price to be charged to third parties) cannot enjoy the benefit of the block exemption regardless of the market share of the parties, and the whole agreement is to be excluded from the benefit of the block exemption provided by the TTR.[55]

There are different 'hardcore' restrictions depending on whether the undertakings to an agreement are competing or non-competing undertakings. In addition, the restrictions on reciprocal agreements (essentially cross-licensing agreements)[56] are stricter than on non-reciprocal agreements.[57] If an agreement contains a 'hardcore' restriction then the whole of the agreement will not benefit from the exemption from Art 81(1).[58]

---

55 TTR, Recital 13. Such hardcore restrictions are considered to be almost always anti-competitive and cannot be severed from an agreement (Guidelines, paras 74, 75). It is highly unlikely that an agreement which contains such a restriction can, where an individual assessment is carried, fulfil the four conditions of Art 81(3) (101(3)).

56 A reciprocal agreement is a cross-licensing agreement where the 'licensed technologies are competing technologies or can be used for the production of competing products' (from Guidelines, para 78). An agreement will not be reciprocal merely because there is a grant back obligation or there is obligation on the licensee to grant back improvements to the licensed technology.

57 A non-reciprocal agreement is one where either: (a) only one party is licensing its technology to another; or (b) if cross-licensing is taking place then the licensed technologies are not competing technologies and cannot be used to produce competing products.

58 TTR, Art 4(1) and Recital 13; and Guidelines, para 75.

Hardcore restrictions and competing undertakings

The exemption from Art 81(1) (101(1)) will not apply to an agreement where the parties are *competing undertakings* and where the agreement contains one of the restrictions detailed below. If the agreement contains one of the restrictions, the whole agreement will not benefit from the exemption.

The agreement which has as its object, which directly or indirectly, in isolation or in combination with other factors under the control of the parties, one of the following restrictions:

- *Price restrictions.* The block exemption is not available where an agreement restricts the price that a party can charge for products it sells to a third party[59] which may include agreements where royalties are calculated on the basis of all product sales irrespective of whether licensed products are sold.[60] However, this restriction, in itself, will not cover an obligation on a licensee to pay a minimum royalty.[61]

- *Limit on output.* The block exemption is not available where an agreement limits the output of contract productions. However it is possible to impose limits on the output of contract products on:

    — the licensee in a non-reciprocal agreement; or

---

59   TTR, Art 4(1)(a). The Guidelines, at para 79, indicate that both direct and indirect price fixing is caught by this restriction. Direct agreement would include an agreement to fix the exact price to be charged or a pricelist with certain allowed maximum rebates. It does not matter whether the price fixing is for fixed, minimum, maximum or recommended prices, they all would be caught. Indirect price fixing would include disincentives to deviate from an agreed price level whereby royalties would be increased if the price for the product was reduced below a certain level.

60   See Guidelines, para 81. The Guidelines indicate that this approach to royalties restricts competition because it 'restrict[s] competition since the agreement raises the cost of using the licensee's own competing technology and restricts competition that existed in the absence of the agreement'. The Guidelines go on to note that such an approach to royalties may not restrict competition where it can be objectively justified so that it is 'indispensable for pro-competitive licensing to occur. This may be the case where in the absence of the restraint it would be impossible or unduly difficult to calculate and monitor the royalty payable by the licensee, for instance because the licensor's technology leaves no visible trace on the final product and practicable alternative monitoring methods are unavailable'.

61   Guidelines, para 79. The Guidelines go on to note, at para 80, that royalties payable on individual product sales have '... a direct impact on the marginal cost of the product and thus a direct impact on product prices ... Competitors can therefore use cross licensing with reciprocal running royalties as a means of co-ordinating prices on downstream product markets. However, the Commission will only treat cross licences with reciprocal running royalties as price fixing where the agreement is devoid of any pro-competitive purpose and therefore does not constitute a bona fide licensing arrangement. In such cases where the agreement does not create any value and therefore has no valid business justification, the arrangement is a sham and amounts to a cartel'.

— only one of the licensees in a reciprocal agreement.[62]

- *The allocation of markets and customers.*[63] The block exemption is not available where an agreement allocates markets or customers.[64] This exclusion from the block exemption is potentially vast. For example it could stop any attempt by a licensor to control the territory into which a licensee could sell products. However, it is possible for the parties to an agreement to allocate markets or customers in the following seven circumstances (and thus come within the benefit of the block exemption of the TTR):

  — *field of use or product market restrictions on licensee* – it is permissible to have a restriction which limits the licensee to produce the licensed technology within one or more technical fields of use or one or more product markets;[65]

  — *field of use, product market or exclusive territory restrictions on either party* – it is permissible to have an '… obligation on the licensor and/or licensee, in a non-reciprocal agreement, not to

---

62   TTR, Art 4(1)(b). Ie this restriction targets reciprocal output restrictions on the parties to an agreement and output restrictions on the licensor of the technology: 'when competitors agree to impose reciprocal output limitations, the object and likely effect of the agreement is to reduce output in the market. The same is true of agreements that reduce the incentive of the parties to expand output, for example by obliging each other to make payments if a certain level of output is exceeded' (from Guidelines, para 82). This restriction does not deal with a limitation on output placed on the licensee where a non-reciprocal agreement is involved. Nor is the restriction concerned on a limitation on output on one of the licensees in a reciprocal agreement, so long as the limitation only concerns the production of contract products produced with the licensed technology.

63   TTR, Art 4(1)(c). The exceptions to this restriction use defined phrases: 'exclusive territories' means 'a territory in which only one undertaking is allowed to produce the contract products with the licensed technology, without prejudice to the possibility of allowing within that territory another licensee to produce the contract products only for a particular customer where this second licence was granted in order to create an alternative source of supply for that customer' (Art 1(1)(l)); and 'exclusive customer' group means 'a group of customers to which only one undertaking is allowed actively to sell the contract products produced with the licensed technology' (Art 1(1)(m)).

64   Where the parties are competing undertakings and have entered into a cross-licensing (reciprocal) agreement it will be a hardcore restriction for them to agree not to (i) produce contract products in certain territories; or (ii) sell actively and/or passively into certain territories; or (iii) sell to customers which are reserved to the other party (Guidelines, para 84). Also, the Guidelines (at para 85) indicate that this restriction applies whether or not the licensee remains free to use its own technology, and the reasoning is as follows: 'Once the licensee has tooled up to use the licensor's technology to produce a given product, it may be costly to maintain a separate production line using another technology in order to serve customers covered by the restrictions. Moreover, given the anti-competitive potential of the restraint the licensee may have little incentive to produce under his own technology. Such restrictions are also highly unlikely to be indispensable for pro-competitive licensing to occur'.

65   TTR, Art 4(1)(c)(I). The Guidelines indicate (at para 90) that such a restriction is block exempted up to a market share of 20% regardless of whether the agreement is reciprocal or not, but the field of use restriction cannot go beyond the scope of the licensed technology and the licensee is not restricted in the use of its own technology.

produce the licensed technology within one or more technical fields of use or one or more product markets or one or more exclusive territories reserved for the other party';[66]

— *sole licence* – it is permissible to have a restriction on the licensor so that it is not able to license its technology to another licensee in a particular territory (ie this exemption does not state that the licensor cannot work the technology itself);[67]

— *active and/or passive sales restriction* – it is permissible to have a restriction, in a non-reciprocal agreement, on making active or allowing passive sales in the exclusive territory of the other party or to the exclusive customer group of the other party;[68]

— *active sales restriction into another licensee's territory (or customer group)* – it is permissible to have a restriction, in a non-reciprocal agreement, on one licensee making active sales into the exclusive territory or to the exclusive customer group of another licensee. This restriction is worded so that:

   o   the exclusive territory or exclusive customer is allocated by the licensor; and

   o   the other licensee was not a competing undertaking of the licensor at the time the other licensee entered into its licence with the licensor;[69]

— *own use restriction* – it is permissible to have a restriction on the licensee so that it can only produce contract products for its own use. This permissible restriction is subject to there being no

---

66   TTR, Art 4(1)(c)(ii). The Guidelines (at para 86) indicate that an exclusive agreement with this restriction is block exempted irrespective of the scope of the territory, if the licence is worldwide, it would mean, as the Guidelines note, that the licensor is not able to enter the market. The purpose of this exemption, according to the Guidelines, is to give the licensee an incentive to invest in and develop the licensed technology.

67   TTR, Art 4(1)(c)(iii). This block exemption applies whether the agreement is reciprocal or not, for the reason, the Guidelines note (at para 88), that the agreement will not affect the 'ability of the parties to fully exploit their own technology in the respective territories'.

68   TTR, Art 4(1)(c)(iv). This restriction is limited to either the licensor's or the licensee's territory. It does not allow for a restriction in another licensee's territory or to another licensee's customer group.

69   TTR, Art 4(1)(c)(v). The Guidelines indicate (at para 89) that this block exemption applies up to the market share threshold restrictions. The Guidelines provide the rationale for this exemption: 'By allowing the licensor to grant a licensee, who was not already on the market, protection against active sales by licensees which are competitors of the licensor and which for that reason are already established on the market, such restrictions are likely to induce the licensee to exploit the licensed technology more efficiently'. However, if the licensees get together to restrict active or passive sales in certain territories or to certain customers, the licensees will be seen as a cartel. But such activity would not involve the transfer of technology and thus it would not be subject to the TTR, although it could infringe other EU competition law provisions.

restriction on it selling the contract products as spare parts for its own products;[70]

— *particular customer restriction* – it is permissible to have a restriction on a licensee, in a non-reciprocal agreement, to produce contract products only for a particular customer. A condition for this restriction is that the licensor granted the license in order to create an alternative source of supply for the customer;[71]

- *licensee's freedom to use own technology.* The block exemption is not available where an agreement restricts the licensee's ability to exploit its own technology.[72] This is effectively a restriction on the licensor inserting 'non-compete' clauses into an agreement.[73] Also covered is a restriction on any of the parties to an agreement being able to carry out research and development, unless such a restriction is 'indispensable to prevent the disclosure of the licensed know-how to third parties'.[74]

Hardcore restrictions and non-competing undertakings

The exemption from Art 81(1) (101(1)) will not apply to an agreement where the parties are *non-competing undertakings* and it contains one of the restrictions detailed below. If it contains one of the restrictions the whole agreement will not benefit from the exemption.

The agreement has as its object, which directly or indirectly, in isolation or in combination with other factors under the control of the parties one of the following restrictions:

---

70 TTR, Art 4(1)(c)(vi).
71 TTR, Art 4(1)(c)(vii). The Guidelines note (at para 93) that the licensor is not limited to only granting one such licence, and thus more than one undertaking could supply a specified customer.
72 TTR, Art 4(d).
73 The Guidelines give examples (at para 95) of what is not permitted in relation to the licensee's own technology: (i) no restriction on where the licensee produces or sells; (ii) no restriction on how much the licensee produces or sells; (iii) the price the licensee can charge; (iv) no payment of royalties on products produced with the licensee's own technology; (v) no restriction on licensing the licensee's own technology to third parties.
74 TTR, Art 4(d). The Guidelines note (at para 94) that such a restriction is not permitted 'irrespective of whether the restriction applies to a field covered by the licence or to other fields'. A provision which indicates that the parties agree to provide each other with improvements created in the future will not come within this restriction on independent research and development. However a restriction on a party carrying out research and development with a third party is permissible where the restriction is for the purpose of stopping disclosure of the licensor's know-how. Such a restriction must be 'necessary and proportionate' to protect the licensor's know-how. The Guidelines provide an example of where such a restriction would be acceptable: 'where the agreement designates particular employees of the licensee to be trained in and responsible for the use of the licensed know-how, it may be sufficient to oblige the licensee not to allow those employees to be involved in research and development with third parties'.

- *Price restrictions.*[75] The block exemption is not available where an agreement restricts the price that a party can charge for products it sells to a third party.[76] The restriction would not cover where a maximum or recommended sales price is imposed, as long as this price does not become a maximum or minimum price caused by pressure from any party (or caused by any incentive by a party).

- *Passive sales restrictions.* The block exemption is not available where an agreement restricts the licensee's freedom in making passive sales of contract products into a territory or to customers.[77] There are six exceptions to this restriction:

  — *passive sales restriction into exclusive territory/customer group* – it is permissible to have a restriction on the licensee from making passive sales into an exclusive territory or to an exclusive customer group of the licensor;[78]

  — *time-limited passive sales restrictions into another licensee's territory (or customer group)* – it is permissible to have a restriction on a licensee from making passive sales for two years into an exclusive territory or to an exclusive customer group of another licensee.[79] The two years start from the date that the other

---

75   TTR, Art 4(2)(a).

76   TTR, Art 4(2)(a). The Guidelines indicate (at para 97) that both direct and indirect price fixing is caught by this restriction. Direct agreement would include fixing on the exact price to be charged. Examples of indirect price fixing are: (i) fixing the margin; (ii) fixing the maximum level of discounts; (iii) linking the sales price of a product to the prices of competitors' products; (iv) threats; (v) intimidation; (vi) warnings; (vii) penalties; or (viii) contract terminations in relation to whether the price level is observed. The Guidelines go on to note that the price fixing can be 'more effective when combined with measures that reduce the licensee's incentive to lower his selling price, such as the licensor obliging the licensee to apply a most-favoured-customer clause, ie an obligation to grant to a customer any more favourable terms granted to any other customer'.

77   TTR, Art 4(2)(b). The Guidelines give examples (at para 98) of what is not permitted: (i) direct or indirect obligations, such as not selling to certain customers or to customers in certain territories or a requirement to refer orders to another licensee; (ii) indirect obligations, such as inducing the licensee to make sales by providing financial incentives or implementing a monitoring system to determine where licensed products end up or a quantity limitation. The Guidelines also note (at para 99) that this restriction does not cover sales restrictions on the licensor and that all sales restrictions are exempted up to a market share threshold of 30 per cent.

78   TTR, Article 4(2)(b)(i). The Guidelines also note (at para 100) that a territory or customer group may be reserved for the licensor, and the licensor does not need to actually produce with the licensed technology any contract products for the specified territory or customer group. For example, such a reservation could be made by the licensor for later exploitation.

79   TTR, Art 4(2)(b)(ii).

licensee commences selling contract products in that territory or to that customer group;[80]

— *own use restriction* – it is permissible to have a restriction on a licensee so that it can only produce contract products for its own use. This is only possible if the licensee is not prevented, whether actively or passively, from selling the contract products as spare parts for its own products;[81]

— *particular customer restriction* – it is permissible to have a restriction on the licensee so that it produces contract products only for a particular customer.[82] A condition for this restriction is that the licensor granted the license in order to create an alternative source of supply for the customer;

— *end-user restriction for a wholesale level licensee* – it is permissible to have a restriction on a licensee so that it cannot make sales to end-users (but only to retailers) where the licensee is operating at the wholesale level of trade;[83]

— *unauthorised distributors restriction* – it is permissible to have a restriction on a licensee so that it does not sell to unauthorised distributors, ie the licensee is a member of a selective distribution system.[84]

• *Restriction on licensee making active/passive sales to end-users.* The block exemption is not available where an agreement restricts a licensee in making passive or active sales to end-users where the licensee is a member of a 'selective distribution system'.[85]

Less serious restrictions

If a licence agreement contains a provision with one of the following restrictions only that provision will not have the benefit of the exemption provided by Art 81(1) (101(1)); the rest of the agreement can have the benefit

---

80 The Guidelines provide (at para 101) the rationale for this exception, that a licensee will need to make substantial investment in facilities (eg manufacturing plant) and in engaging in promotional and marketing effort. Such expenditure/investment cannot be recovered on the licensee exiting a market. After the expiry of the first two years, such a restriction as this exception will constitute a hardcore restriction and will generally be caught by Art 81(1) (101(1)) and is unlikely to fulfil the requirements of Art 81(3) (101(3)): 'In particular, passive sales restrictions are unlikely to be indispensable for the attainment of efficiencies'.

81 TTR, Art 4(2)(b)(iii).

82 TTR, Art 4(2)(b)(iv).

83 TTR, Art 4(2)(b)(v). See Guidelines, para 104.

84 TTR, Art 4(2)(b)(vi). A 'selective distribution system' is defined as 'a distribution system where the licensor undertakes to license the production of the contract products only to licensees selected on the basis of specified criteria and where these licensees undertake not to sell the contract products to unauthorised distributors' (TTR, Art 1(1)(k)).

85 TTR, Art 4(2)(c).

of the block exemption.[86] The reason stated for these restrictions not being able to benefit from the block exemption is that there is a need to 'protect incentives and to innovate and the appropriate application of intellectual property rights'.[87]

The restrictions are:

- *Restriction on licensee being forced to grant exclusive licences to improvements.* The block exemption is not available where an agreement requires the licensee to grant (back) an exclusive licence to the licensor or a designated third party for the licensee's 'severable improvements to its own new applications of the licensed technology'.[88] The restriction applies whether there is a direct or indirect obligation on the licensee to grant such a licence.

- *Restriction on licensee being forced to assign improvements.* The block exemption is not available where an agreement requires the licensee to assign rights to its 'severable improvements to its own new applications of the licensed technology' to the licensor or a designated third party.[89] The restriction applies whether there is a direct or indirect obligation on the licensee to assign.

- *Restriction on licensee challenging validity of licensor intellectual property.* The block exemption is not available where an agreement stops the licensee challenging the validity of the intellectual property

---

86 TTR, Art 5. See also the Guidelines (at para 107), which note that the restrictions set out in this Article will require individual assessment as to their anti- or pro-competitive effect and if they are anti-competitive would be severed from the agreement in which they are contained.

87 From TTR, Recital 14. The Recital goes on to note that exclusive grant back obligations for severable improvements should be excluded from the block exemption.

88 TTR, Art 5(1)(a). A severable improvement being one that can be exploited without infringing the licensed technology, as defined by TTR, Art 1(1)(n). The Guidelines note (at para 109) that a grant back on a non-exclusive basis for severable improvements is permitted, even if such obligation is only placed on the licensee and the licensor can provide (feed-on) such severable improvements to other licensees. The restriction will not depend on whether the licensor pays consideration for the grant back of the severable improvement or for acquiring it on an exclusive basis. However the existence and level of consideration may be relevant when an individual assessment is carried out under Art 81 (101). Where consideration is paid then the incentive of the licensee to innovate is unlikely to be lessened according to the Guidelines (see para 110). The Guidelines also mention a possible negative effect on innovation where cross-licensing is taking place where there is a grant back obligation on both parties and obligation to share improvements. The effect may be that competitors cannot gain a competitive lead over each other, unless the purpose of the licence is to allow the parties to develop their respective technologies 'and where the licence does not lead to use of the same technological base in the design of their products'. This is the case where the purpose of the licence is to create design freedom rather than improve the technological base of the licensee' (from Guidelines, para 111).

89 TTR, Art 5(1)(b). See n 85, which equally applies to this restriction.

rights held by the licensor in the common market.[90] However, a licensor can include a provision in a technology transfer agreement which allows the licensor to terminate the agreement if its intellectual property is challenged.[91]

- *Restriction on non-competition.* The block exemption is not available where an agreement restricts, whether directly or indirectly:

  — a licensee's ability to exploit its own technology; or

  — any party's ability to carry out research and development (unless such a restriction is 'indispensable to prevent the disclosure of the licensed know-how to third parties').[92]

    Such an obligation on a licensee to not compete with the licensor is often seen as a reasonable method of controlling the activities of the licensee (at least by a licensor) in an exclusive licence agreement. If a clause is included which forbids competition by itself this is likely to be in breach of Art 81 (101) and therefore will not have the benefit provided by the TTR. An alternative method is for a licensee to provide a series of warranties, including:

    — that it is not developing, marketing and commercialising a competing product;

    — that it has not entered into an agreement with a third party in connection with any of the activities listed above; and

    — that it will notify the licensor if it starts any such activities or enters in an agreement with a third party regarding such activities;

---

90   TTR, Art 5(1)(c). The reasoning given in the Guidelines (at para 112) for forbidding no challenge clauses is that the licensee is in the best position to determine the validity of the intellectual property rights. The Guidelines also indicate (also at para 112) that the Commission will not be opposed to no-challenge clauses which relate to know-how 'where once disclosed it is likely to be impossible or very difficult to recover the licensed know-how. In such cases, an obligation on the licensee not to challenge the licensed know-how promotes dissemination of new technology, in particular by allowing weaker licensors to license stronger licensees without fear of a challenge once the know-how has been absorbed by the licensee'.

91   TTR, Art 5(1)(c). The Guidelines note (at para 113) that the licensor is not forced to continue dealing with a licensee who is in effect challenging the whole basis of the agreement between the parties and 'implying that any further use by the licensee of the challenged technology is at the challenger's own risk. Article 5(1)(c) ensures, however, that the [TTR] does not cover contractual obligations obliging the licensee not to challenge the licensed technology, which would permit the licensor to sue the licensee for breach of contract and thereby create a further disincentive for the licensee to challenge the validity of the licensor's technology. The provision thereby ensures that the licensee is in the same position as third parties'.

92   TTR, Art 5(2). This restriction is the same as the hardcore restriction in Art 4(1)(d) (which concerns competitors rather than non-competitors here). The Guidelines (at para 114) note that for agreements between non-competitors, restrictions such as the one dealt with here generally do not have negative effects on competition or that the conditions of Art 81(3) (101(3)) are generally not satisfied and therefore an individual assessment is required.

(none of these specifically state that it cannot exploit its own technology to compete with the licensor);

and for a separate clause to provide that the licensor to have the right to terminate the agreement if the licensee develops or acquires the rights to a competing product.

WITHDRAWAL OF BENEFIT OF THE TTR IN AN INDIVIDUAL CASE

The Commission has the power to withdraw the benefit of the TTR[93] in an individual case. This can be where a technology transfer agreement, to which the block exemption under the TTR applies, is nevertheless incompatible with Art 81(3) (101(3)).[94] Three instances are specified 'in particular':

- access of third parties' technologies to the market is restricted;[95]

- access of the potential licensees to the market is restricted;[96]

- the parties do not exploit the licensed technology and there is no objectively valid reason for this failure.[97]

In addition, a competent authority (such as the Office of Fair Trading in the UK) in a particular member state can also withdraw the benefit of the TTR where the technology transfer agreement is incompatible with Art 81(3) (101(3)) in that member state.[98]

NON-APPLICATION OF TTR FOR PARALLEL NETWORKS

The Commission can, by regulation, disapply the TTR in the case of parallel networks of similar technology transfer agreements that cover more than

---

93 The Commission has power to do this under Regulation (EC) 1/2003 [2003] OJ L1/1, Art 29(1).

94 TTR, Art 6(1).

95 TTR, Art 6(1)(a).

96 TTR, Art 6(1)(b).

97 TTR, Art 6(1)(c).

98 TTR, Art 6(2). A competition authority has this power under Regulation (EC) 1/2003 [2003] OJ L1/1, Art 29(2). The Guidelines note (at para 119) that where a block exemption is to be withdrawn then the burden is on the competition authority to prove that the agreement falls within Art 81(1), EC Treaty and that it does not satisfy all the four conditions of Art 81(3), EC Treaty. The Guidelines indicate that the four conditions stated in Art 81(3) are cumulative and all must be fulfilled for the exception rule to be applicable, and accordingly the block exemption can be withdrawn where an agreement fails to fulfil one or more of the four conditions in Art 81(3) (see Guidelines, para 118).

50 per cent[99] of a relevant market in respect of specific restraints in such agreements.[100] Where the Commission makes an exclusion from the scope of the TTR, then it would affect all undertakings involved (ie it will not apply to one undertaking only).[101]

Where a Regulation is made it cannot come into force until six months after its adoption.[102]

RELATIONSHIP BETWEEN TTR AND OTHER BLOCK EXEMPTIONS

The Commission, in the Guidelines, provides limited guidance as to where the TTR and other block exemptions relevant to this book interact. The following are the relevant points from the Guidelines:

R&D Regulation[103]

The Guidelines note that the purpose of the R&D Regulation covers:

- *two or more* undertakings;

- who agree to carry out research and development;

- who agree to *jointly* exploit the results of the research and development.

This can be done by a joint team of the undertakings, a separate organisation or the undertakings themselves, or given to a third party, or as allocated between parties depending on the specialisation of the undertakings as to research, development, production and distribution as well as licensing. A research and development agreement can deal with the question of licensing of the results of the research and development and come within the R&D Regulation. However, any actual licence entered into with a third party would not come within the R&D Regulation. The Guidelines indicate that this is because the third party would not be party to the research and development

---

99 To establish the 50% market coverage ratio, each individual network of licence agreements which contain restraints (or combinations of restraints) will be taken into account (see Guidelines, para 125).
100 TTR, Art 7(1).
101 See Guidelines, para 123. Where the Commission adopts a Regulation as provided for under TTR, Art 7, they will then provide guidance on the Application of Art 81 to individual agreements and where 'appropriate, the Commission will take a decision in an individual case, which can provide guidance to all the undertakings operating in the market concerned (Guidelines, para 124).
102 TTR, Art 7(2).
103 Commission Regulation (EC) 2659/2000 [2001] OJ L304/7 on the application of Article 81(3) of the Treaty to categories of research and development agreements (see Guidelines, paras 59–60).

agreement. However it would be block exempted by the TTR, if they fulfilled the conditions of the TTR.

Vertical Agreements Regulation[104]

The Vertical Agreements Regulation covers:

- an agreement between two or more undertakings;
- where the undertakings are operating at different levels of the production or distribution chain for the purposes of the agreement; and
- the agreement deals with the conditions under which the parties may purchase, sell or resell goods or services.

The Guidelines note that the TTR will only cover two undertakings and also only where a licensee sells products which incorporate licensed technology. A licensee will be a supplier for the purposes of the Vertical Agreements Regulation. Although there is a close link between the TTR and the Vertical Agreements Regulation, the TTR will cover the licensor and the licensee, while the Vertical Agreements Regulations (and the Guidelines on Vertical Restrains) will cover the licensee and its buyers.

The Guidelines also note here that the TTR can block exempt an agreement between a licensor and a licensee which requires the licensee to sell the products which incorporate the licensed technology in a particular way, such as obliging the licensee to establish a certain type of distribution system (eg an exclusive or selective distribution system). Any distribution agreements concluded by the licensee would be covered by the Vertical Agreements Regulation and not the TTR. The Guidelines provide an example of the link between the two regulations:

- a licensor can require the licensee to establish a system based on exclusive distribution in accordance with specified rules;
- but in accordance with the Vertical Agreements Regulation one distributor must be free to make passive sales into the territories of other exclusive distributors.[105]

---

104 Commission Regulation (EC) 2790/1999 [1999] OJ L336/21 on the application of Article 81(3) of the Treaty to categories of vertical agreements and concerted practices (see Guidelines, paras 61–64). Due to be replaced from 1 June 2010 by Commission Regulation 330/2010 on the application of Article 101(3) of the Treaty of the Functioning of the European Union to categories of vertical agreements [2010] OJ L 102/1. There are transitional arrangements for agreements covered by Regulation 2790/99. As proofs were being returned to the publisher, the new Regulation was due to come into force, and appears to have provisions broadly similar to Regulation 2790/1999 with modifications (such as taking account of internet sales and for sales taking place across borders). An outline of the new Regulation will appear on the website which accompanies this book.

105 This point is further developed in para 64 of the Guidelines.

CHAPTER 14

Guidelines and Regulation on R&D Agreements[1]

---

1   Following the acceptance of the Lisbon Treaty and its coming into force in December 2009, the Articles of the EC Treaty is renumbered. This chapters adopts the following method: the existing numbering is retained, with the new numbers in parenthesis. The EC Treaty is renamed the 'Treaty on the Functioning of the European Union', but for ease of reference it will continue to be called the EC Treaty in this edition of the book.

SCOPE OF THIS CHAPTER

This chapter provides detailed descriptions of two Regulations and the Guidelines concerning research and development described in summary in Chapter 12. The following are covered:

- Research and development agreements block exemption Regulation ('R&D Regulation').[2]

- Specialisation agreements Regulation ('Specialisation Regulation').[3]

- Guidelines on horizontal agreements (the 'Guidelines' or 'Commission Guidelines').[4]

PROPOSALS

The R&D and Specialisation Regulations are due to expire on 31 December 2010. The Commission has carried out an initial public consultation to receive feedback on the working of the current Guidelines, particularly in

---

2　Commission Regulation (EC) 2659/2000 ([2000] OJ L304/7) on the application of Article 81(3) of the Treaty to categories of research and development agreements.

3　Commission Regulation (EC) 2658/2000 ([2000] OJ L304/3) on the application of Article 81(3) of the Treaty to categories of specialisation agreements.

4　*Guidelines on the applicability of Article 81 of the EC Treaty to horizontal cooperation agreements* ([2001] OJ C3/02).

relation to the R&D and Specialisation Regulations.[5] At the date material was prepared for this edition of the book no drafts of the new Regulations or the new Guidelines were available, although they are due sometime in 2010. However, it appears that there will not be any radical change from the current approach.[6]

GUIDELINES ON HORIZONTAL AGREEMENTS

The Guidelines were published in 2001[7] and represent a major advance on the information that was previously available from the Commission on whether horizontal agreements infringe Article 81(1) (101(1)) of the EC Treaty. They are particularly helpful on the subject of smaller-scale R&D agreements.

The Guidelines include both a general discussion of horizontal agreements and a discussion of certain, specific types of horizontal agreement, namely:

- agreements on research and development;

- production agreements, including:

  — joint production agreements, whereby the parties agree to produce certain products jointly, and

  — specialisation agreements, whereby the parties agree unilaterally or reciprocally to cease production of a product and to purchase it from the other party;

  — sub-contracting agreements (which the Commission considers to be sometimes vertical agreements and sometimes horizontal agreements; only horizontal aspects are dealt with in this Notice);

- purchasing agreements (ie agreements for the joint buying of products);

- commercialisation agreements (ie co-operation between competitors in the selling, distribution or promotion of their products);

---

5   See   http://ec.europa.eu/competition/consultations/2009_horizontal_agreements/index.html for details on the consultation and feedback. The consultation lasted from 4 December 2008 to 30 January 2009. The object of the consultation was: 'To receive input from stakeholders on the functioning of the current regime for the assessment of horizontal cooperation agreements under EU antitrust rules, in particular, the Specialisation and Research & Development Block Exemption Regulations and the Horizontal Guidelines. The purpose of the review is to evaluate how these rules have worked in practice and to facilitate the preparation of the regime to be applied after these two Block Exemption Regulations have expired at the end of 2010'.

6   See the speech of Neelie Kroes, European Commissioner for Competition Policy, on 15 October 2009.

7   *Guidelines on the applicability of Article 81 of the EC Treaty to horizontal cooperation agreements* ([2001] OJ C3/02).

- agreements on standards (ie agreements which have as their primary objective the definition of technical or quality requirements with which current or future products, production processes or methods may comply);

- environmental agreements (ie agreements by which the parties undertake to achieve pollution abatement, as defined in environmental law, or environmental objectives, in particular those set out in Article 174 (191) of the EC Treaty).

The following paragraphs will summarise relevant parts of the Commission Guidelines. They will focus mainly on R&D agreements, but will also mention production agreements, particularly specialisation agreements, as these may occasionally be relevant to technology transfer. The other types of agreement described in the Notice will not be discussed here.

Background

Whilst the Guidelines are not strictly binding on the Commission, they provide useful guidance on when the Commission considers that an R&D agreement will breach Article 81(1) (101(1)) and whether an R&D agreement is likely to qualify for exemption under EC Treaty, Article 81(3) (101(3)). Before the introduction of the Guidelines, it was difficult to advise with confidence on whether many R&D agreements infringed Article 81 of the EC Treaty. Many R&D agreements appeared to be either too 'early-stage' or insignificant to be caught by Article 81.

Over the years, the Commission has indicated that certain categories of agreement, including certain types of R&D agreements, do not breach Article 81. However, this has not always helped, as many R&D agreements have not fitted into these categories. An example of this is the Commission's often-repeated statement[8] that R&D agreements which are purely concerned with R&D and do not include any restrictions in relation to commercialisation, do not generally breach Article 81. However, agreements of this kind are rarely encountered in practice: many R&D agreements include provisions under which the parties have different commercialisation rights, for example one party has exclusive rights, or each party has rights in a different field or territory.

---

8   Eg see Commission Notice (EEC) ([1968] OJ C84/14) on cooperation agreements, replaced by the EC Commission Guidelines (see n 4), and Commission Regulation (EEC) 418/85 ([1985]) OJ L53/5) on the application of Article 85(3) of the Treaty to categories of research and development agreements, replaced by Commission Regulation (EC) 2659/2000 (see n 2).

At the other end of the scale, the Commission's views on R&D agreements that have major effects on the European market are better known.[9]

Most R&D agreements have fallen between these two extremes and there has been relatively little helpful guidance from the Commission in respect of such agreements. Many relatively small-scale R&D agreements have been neither clearly outside the scope of Article 81, nor clearly within the scope of the 1985 R&D block exemption Regulation. Parties to such agreements have therefore faced the dilemma of whether (a) to do nothing, hoping that the agreement falls outside Article 81 but running the risk that it does not, or (b) to incur the expense of an individual notification to the Commission. In practice, the Commission has not been interested in giving formal decisions in relation to such agreements.[10]

In this context, the Guidelines are a major step forward. They provide a detailed analysis of when certain types of agreement, including R&D agreements, are likely to present EC competition law problems.

Purpose of the Guidelines

The Guidelines[11] replaced two EC Notices on co-operative agreements[12] and complement the R&D and Specialisation Regulations. The purpose of the Guidelines is to provide an analytical framework for the most common types of horizontal co-operation. The framework is primarily based on criteria intended to help the analysis of the economic context of a co-operation agreement by the parties involved. However, being only guidelines, they are without prejudice to any interpretation that may be given by the Court of First Instance and the Court of Justice of the European Communities in relation to the application of Article 81 to horizontal co-operation agreements.

Scope of the Guidelines

The Commission's Guidelines[13] cover agreements or concerted practices entered into between two or more companies operating at the same level(s)

---

9   There are published decisions of the Commission on R&D agreements involving major companies and major products, eg milk cartons, tyres or chemical production plants.

10 Very often, in return for conducting an expensive notification exercise, the Commission has issued comfort letters stating that it is closing its file on the agreement and taking no further action.

11 See n 4.

12 Commission Notice (EEC) ([1968] OJ C84/14)on co-operation agreements, and Commission Notice (EEC) ([1992] OJ C43/2) concerning the assessment of co-operative joint ventures pursuant to Article 85 of the EC Treaty.

13 See n 4.

in the market, for example at the same level of production or distribution.[14] The focus is on co-operation between competitors, but the term 'competitors' is used to include both actual and potential competitors.[15] The Guidelines are concerned only with certain types of co-operation which, in the Commission's view, potentially generate efficiency gains, namely agreements on R&D, production, purchasing, commercialisation, standardisation, and environmental matters.[16]

The Guidelines are divided into chapters dealing with each category of horizontal co-operation. Each chapter contains:

- a definition of the category of horizontal co-operation to which it refers;
- a discussion of the relevant market;
- criteria for assessment under EC Treaty, Article 81(1) (101(1));
- criteria for assessment under Article 81(3) (101(3));
- 'case study'-type examples.

These case studies are worth reading as they indicate situations in which an agreement (eg an R&D agreement) will either not infringe Article 81(1) (101(1)), qualify for exemption under Article 81(3) (101(3)), or be regarded as anti-competitive and not qualify for exemption.

Vertical agreements, ie agreements that are entered into between companies operating at a different level of the production or distribution chain are, in principle, excluded from these Guidelines.[17] However, if a vertical agreement contains horizontal elements, they must be considered under the Guidelines. Agreements may combine different levels of co-operation, for example R&D and the production of its results.[18] Unless they fall under the Merger Control Regulation,[19] these agreements are covered by the Guidelines.

---

14 Commission Guidelines (see n 4), para 9.
15 See n 15.
16 Commission Guidelines (see n 4), para 10.
17 Commission Guidelines (see n 4), para 11. See Commission Regulation (EC) 2790/1999 ([1999] OJ L336/21) and EC Commission *Guidelines on vertical restraints* ([2000] OJ C291/1).Due to be replaced from 1 June 2010 by Commission Regulation 330/2010 on the application of Article 101(3) of the Treaty of the Functioning of the European Union to categories of vertical agreements [2010] OJ L 102/1. There are transitional arrangements for agreements covered by Regulation 2790/99. As proofs were being returned to the publisher, the new Regulation was due to come into force, and appears to have provisions broadly similar to Regulation 2790/1999 with modifications (such as taking account of internet sales and for sales taking place across borders). An outline of the new Regulation will appear on the website which accompanies this book.
18 Commission Guidelines (see n 4), para 12.
19 Council Regulation 4064/89 (EEC) ([1989] OJ L395/1) as amended by Council Regulation 1310/97 (EC) ([1997] OJ L180/1).

Chapter on R&D agreements

The chapter of the Commission's Guidelines which deals with R&D agreements applies to all forms of R&D agreements including related agreements concerning the production or commercialisation of the R&D results, provided that the co-operation's centre of gravity lies in the R&D.[20] The Guidelines include encouraging comments about R&D co-operation in general, and the needs and pro-competitive activities of small and medium-sized companies and 'start-up' companies in R&D intensive sectors, in particular.[21]

Relevant markets

According to the Commission's Guidelines, the key to defining the relevant market when assessing the effects of an R&D agreement is 'to identify those products, technologies or R&D efforts that will act as a competitive constraint on the parties'.[22] The Commission recognises that R&D may result in:[23]

- a product or technology which competes in an existing product or technology market (for example a new model of an existing product);
- an entirely new product that creates its own new market (for example a new vaccine for a previously incurable disease); or
- a combination of the above, for example a new product that over time replaces existing products (for example CDs replacing records).

Any analysis of the competitive effect of an R&D agreement may, therefore, have to include:[24]

- existing product markets;
- existing technology markets; and
- the impact of the agreement on innovation.

These different types of market make the analysis rather complicated compared with the analysis of, say, a product distribution agreement, where only product markets may need to be considered. The Guidelines discuss how to identify existing markets, how to consider competition in innovation and the calculation of market shares.[25] The concepts of technology markets and competition in innovation may appear nebulous and difficult to assess, and it is therefore useful to consider the Commission's guidance on these areas. The Commission considers that 'technology markets consist of the intellectual property that is licensed and its close substitutes, ie other technologies which customers could use as a substitute'.[26]

---

20   Commission Guidelines (see n 4), Ch 2.
21   Commission Guidelines (see n 4), paras 40, 41.
22   Commission Guidelines (see n 4), para 43.
23   See n 23.
24   See n 23.
25   Commission Guidelines (see n 4), paras 44–54.
26   Commission Guidelines (see n 4), para 47.

With regard to competition in innovation (R&D efforts), the Commission distinguishes between situations in industries on the basis of whether it is possible to identify 'R&D poles'. These poles occur where different types of R&D activity may be directed towards the same or similar products.[27] For example, in the pharmaceutical sector, many different types of research are being directed towards finding a cure for particular types of cancer, eg research into monoclonal antibodies, natural products, apoptosis (planned cell death), and gene therapy. Thus, even if an R&D agreement significantly reduces competition in one pole of research, this may not be regarded as causing major competition law issues, if there are alternatives. When assessing the relevant market, the Commission considers any credible, alternative R&D poles.[28] In industries where there are no alternative R&D poles, the Commission does not usually assess competition in innovation, but confines its analysis to product or technology markets.[29]

The Guidelines also outline the Commission's method of calculating market shares and refer to the provisions of the R&D Regulation on this subject.[30]

R&D agreements that do not fall under Article 81(1) (101(1))

According to the Commission's Guidelines, most R&D agreements do not fall under EC Treaty, Article 81(1) (101(1)).[31] Examples of such agreements include:

- agreements concerning co-operation in R&D at an early ('rather theoretical') stage far removed from the marketing of a resulting new product or technology;[32]

- R&D co-operation between non-competitors, although there may be a breach of Article 81(1) (101(1)) if there is exclusive exploitation of results, and one of the parties has significant market power with respect to key technology;[33]

- outsourcing to specialised companies, research institutes or academic bodies that are not active in the exploitation of the results. Article 81(1) (101(1)) does not apply because of the complementary nature of the co-operating parties in these scenarios.[34]

With respect to the last category, it should be noted that 'specialised companies' probably do not include young, technology-based companies

---

27 Commission Guidelines (see n 4), para 51.
28 See n 28.
29 Commission Guidelines (see n 4), para 52.
30 Commission Guidelines (see n 4), paras 53, 54.
31 Commission Guidelines (see n 4), para 55.
32 See n 32.
33 Commission Guidelines (see n 4), para 56.
34 Commission Guidelines (see n 4), para 57.

that intend to commercialise their technologies, for example by licensing. The term 'outsourcing' suggests a particular type of R&D co-operation, and it remains to be seen whether all R&D agreements with universities would fall within this category.

If the parties are unable to carry out the necessary R&D independently, there is no competition to be restricted.

Agreements that almost always fall under Article 81(1) (101(1))

Agreements that are really vehicles for disguised cartels fall under EC Treaty, Article 81(1) (101(1)). The Guidelines state that these may include agreements concerned with price-fixing, output limitation and market allocation. However, R&D agreements that provide for joint marketing of results are not necessarily restrictive of competition.[35]

Agreements that may fall under Article 81(1) (101(1))

The Guidelines provide that R&D agreements that cannot be assessed from the outset as clearly non-restrictive may fall under EC Treaty, Article 81(1) (101(1)) and have to be analysed in their economic context. This applies to agreements between competitors which are 'set up at a stage rather close to the market launch'.[36]

Market share

The Guidelines discuss the circumstances in which the market power of one or both parties may cause R&D co-operation to have anti-competitive effects. Most R&D agreements involving less than a 25 per cent market share are exempted under the R&D Regulation, therefore only if the market share is greater than 25 per cent will restrictive effects need to be considered. A market share of more than 25 per cent does not necessarily mean that there is a breach of Article 81(1) (101(1)), but the stronger the combined market position of the parties, the more likely that it will be necessary to conduct a detailed analysis of the agreement under Article 81(1) (101(1)).[37]

A key issue to be considered is whether negative market effects such as foreclosure problems result where an agreement involves at least one player with significant market power for a key technology and the exclusive exploitation of results.[38]

---

35 Commission Guidelines (see n 4), para 59.
36 Commission Guidelines (see n 4), para 60.
37 Commission Guidelines (see n 4), para 63.
38 Commission Guidelines (see n 4), para 64.

Nature of co-operation[39]

Pure R&D agreements rarely breach EC Treaty, Article 81(1) (101(1)). Where the R&D co-operation also concerns exploitation, but only by means of licensing, restrictive effects such as foreclosure problems are unlikely, particularly if the co-operation concerns only a limited improvement of existing products and technology. Where joint production and/or marketing of the slightly improved products/technology are included, the co-operation has to be examined more closely.

Innovation[40]

If the R&D concerns an entirely new product or technology which creates its own new market, the analysis has to focus on possible restrictions of innovation, for example the quality and variety of new products or technology or the speed of innovation. If the parties co-operate when they are independently near to the launch of the product, there may be restrictive effects, even in pure R&D agreements. Generally, though, R&D co-operation concerning new products is pro-competitive, even where there is joint exploitation or joint marketing, unless there is foreclosure from key technologies. These problems would not arise where the parties grant licences to third parties.

In some cases there can be restrictive effects on existing markets and a negative effect on innovation by means of slowing down the speed of development. Examples would be if significant competitors with substantial market power in an existing technology market, and significant R&D, co-operate to develop a new technology that may one day replace existing products, or if a major player in an existing market co-operates with a much smaller or even potential competitor who is just about to emerge with a new product/technology that may endanger the incumbent's position.

Access

Even where the market share is small, R&D agreements may fall outside the block exemption, for example because they restrict a party's access to the results of the work. Agreements containing exclusive access rights may breach EC Treaty, Article 81(1) (101(1)) but meet the criteria for exemption under Article 81(3) (101(3)) where exclusive access rights are economically indispensable in view of the market, risks and scale of investment required to exploit the results of the R&D.[41] It is therefore dangerous to restrict the parties' rights of access to the results, particularly if the agreement does not meet the requirements for block exemption.

---

39 See n 40.
40 Commission Guidelines (see n 4), paras 65, 66.
41 Commission Guidelines (see n 4), para 67.

Although the Commission holds out the possibility that such provisions may be individually exempted, it may be unlikely that it will reach a formal decision under Article 81(3) (101(3)) unless the agreement is of major importance. Instead, the Commission may simply issue a comfort letter which will not formally exempt the offending provision.

Assessment under Article 81(3) (101(3))

The Guidelines indicate some of the criteria that the Commission follows when considering whether to grant an individual exemption under EC Treaty, Article 81(3) (101(3)).[42] Given the limited resources and manpower of the Commission, these criteria are rather academic unless the agreement is of such significance that the Commission can be persuaded to give it a detailed assessment and grant, or otherwise, an individual exemption under Article 81(3) (101(3)). The Guidelines recite the usual tests applied by the Commission under Article 81(3) (101(3)), and give some limited examples in the R&D field of how these tests might be applied.

Case study examples

The Guidelines conclude with a number of examples: a set of facts concerning a fictitious R&D agreement is followed in each case by an analysis of whether the agreement breaches EC Treaty, Article 81:[43]

- The first example describes a situation where an individual exemption might be refused, involving two major companies having significant market share who pool their R&D efforts.

- The second describes a situation where the agreement is unlikely to restrict competition, involving R&D co-operation between a small biotech company and a large pharmaceutical company.

    In this example, there are several alternative poles of research and a number of other features that the Commission views with approval.

- The final example describes a situation where the agreement is likely to benefit from an individual exemption, involving parties with high market share but many competing technologies.

It is worth reading these examples in detail when assessing whether an R&D agreement breaches EC Treaty, Article 81.

---

42   Commission Guidelines (see n 4), paras 68–74.
43   Commission Guidelines (see n 4), paras 75–77.

Chapter on production (including specialisation) agreements

Introduction

The term 'specialisation agreement' may be unfamiliar, but the concept is simple enough: typically two competing manufacturers agree that only one of them will manufacture certain products and the other will manufacture other products, thus saving costs of building factories, and achieving economies of scale. They also agree to supply one another with these products. In a number of reported decisions, the European Commission has held that such arrangements were contrary to Article 81(1) (101(1)) but were individually exempted under Article 81(3) (101(3)).

As had been previously mentioned, this chapter focuses on block exemption Regulations and Commission Notices that are relevant to the exploitation of technology, rather than on case law. However, it may be helpful to mention one of the leading cases where the Commission exempted a specialisation agreement, if only as an example of where a specialisation agreement is concerned with technology-based products.

In the Bayer/Gist-Brocades case[44] both Bayer and Gist were manufacturers of raw penicillin and a related product known as 6-APA. Bayer lent Gist money to finance the expansion of Gist's penicillin plant, whilst Gist lent Bayer money to finance the expansion of Bayer's 6-APA plant. Gist agreed to supply Bayer with its requirements for penicillin, and Bayer agreed to supply Gist with its requirements for 6-APA, in both cases at favourable prices and on a long-term basis. They also agreed to exchange certain research results and to licensed improvements relating to these products to one another.

After the parties had made certain changes to the agreement at the request of the Commission, the Commission exempted the agreement. The Commission identified certain pro-competitive aspects to the arrangement, including increased production of the products, which led to increased competition.

Thus, agreements for the production of goods may involve elements of technology transfer. In some cases the distinction between production agreements and technology transfer agreements may not be great, as in the case of agreements for the distribution of software to the retail market under 'shrink-wrap' licences, particularly if the distributor has the task of making copies of the software. However, in most cases it will be clear where the centre of gravity (to coin a phrase) of the agreement lies – production or technology transfer.

---

44   [1976] 1 CMLR D98.

The Notice on sub-contracting agreements has already been discussed[45]. That Notice is concerned, among other things, with agreements for the production of goods or services where the sub-contractor uses technology supplied by the contractor. Thus, a type of production agreement also becomes a type of technology transfer agreement. Because that Notice is so closely concerned with technology transfer issues, it is appropriate to mention it in a discussion of EC competition aspects of technology transfer.

For similar reasons, as was mentioned at the beginning of this chapter, the EC rules on specialisation agreements may occasionally be of help when assessing whether a technology agreement infringes Article 81 (101)). Specialisation agreements are another type of production agreement, but may form part of a larger technology-based relationship. An example of this is where a collaboration agreement covers all stages of research, development, production and sale, and where the parties to the collaboration divide up between them responsibility for all these different elements.

It is therefore appropriate to mention, at least briefly, those paragraphs of the Guidelines on horizontal agreements that refer to production agreements.

What are production agreements?

The Guidelines acknowledge that production agreements can come in different guises, including both joint-venture companies and contractual arrangements between parties. The Commission distinguishes three categories:

- joint-production agreements;

- specialisation agreements;

- sub-contracting agreements.

The Commission considers that sub-contracting agreements are vertical agreements covered by the Vertical Agreements Regulation and the Guidelines on vertical restraints, but identifies two exceptions:

- sub-contracting agreements between competitors; and

- sub-contracting agreements between non-competitors involving the transfer of know-how to the sub-contractor.

The Commission points out that the latter exceptional category is addressed in the Notice on sub-contracting agreements (discussed earlier in this chapter). The Guidelines on horizontal agreements consider the former category, ie sub-contracting agreements between competitors.

---

45   See Chapter 12 under 'Commission Notice on subcontracting agreements'.

Detailed treatment of production agreements

The Guidelines consider in detail the competitive effects of production agreements. Much of the detailed discussion seems far removed from technology-transfer agreements. For example, the chapter includes several case studies, most of which are not obviously relevant to technology transfer.

One paragraph that does stand out is paragraph 89, which reads as follows:

'Thirdly, subcontracting agreements between competitors do not fall under Article 81(1) [(101(1))] if they are limited to individual sales and purchases on the merchant market without any further obligations and without forming part of a wider commercial relationship between the parties'.

A footnote to this paragraph reads as follows:

'As [with] any subcontracting agreement such an agreement can however fall under Article 81(1) [(101(1))] if it contains vertical restraints, such as restrictions on passive sales, resale price maintenance, etc'.

These paragraphs may be of assistance, together with the Notice on sub-contracting agreements, when assessing one-off sub-contracting relationships that form part of a technology development programme.

None of the other paragraphs in the chapter on production agreements would seem to merit highlighting here. Clearly the chapter should be read in its entirety when assessing a production agreement.

R&D AGREEMENTS BLOCK EXEMPTION REGULATION

Introduction

An agreement may be automatically exempted under EC Treaty, Article 81(3) (101(3)) if it meets the criteria specified in one of the Commission's block exemption Regulations. The EC Regulations that are most likely to be relevant to R&D agreements, or agreements that include obligations to conduct R&D, are the block exemption Regulations on:

- *R&D agreements:* EC Commission Regulation 2659/2000.[46]

- *Technology transfer agreements:* EC Commission Regulation 772/2004 ([2004] OJ L123/11) which is mostly concerned with patent, know-

---

46   Commission Regulation (EC) 2659/2000 ([2000] OJ L304/7) replaces Commission Regulation (EC) 418/85 ([1985]) OJ L53/5).

how and software licensing agreements (or combinations thereof) and where there is a focus on the production of products or services, but may occasionally be relevant to licensing agreements that also involve R&D. If, however, the centre of gravity of the agreement is R&D, it is very unlikely that the technology transfer Regulation will be relevant.

- Specialisation agreements: EC Commission Regulation 2658/2000.[47] This block exemption is concerned with 'specialisation' in production, for example one party manufactures one product and the other party manufactures another product. Although of marginal relevance to most R&D agreements, it may occasionally be relevant.

Introduction to the R&D Regulation

The current R&D Regulation has provided greater flexibility in the terms of R&D agreements than its predecessor.[48]

The Commission's traditional view has been that R&D agreements are generally not anti-competitive if they are concerned only with the conduct of R&D itself, and do not contain restrictive provisions such as non-compete clauses and exclusive licences.[49] Even this very cautious view is qualified in situations where the parties have market power, for example a high market share. However, most R&D agreements do not conform to this simple model, as most contain provisions as to the commercialisation of the results of the work done under the agreement. In practice, it is often agreed that one of the parties will have exclusive rights to commercialise those results, in some or all territories or fields of application. Provisions of this kind have been viewed by the Commission as, potentially, in breach of EC Treaty, Article 81(1) (101(1)).

The general approach of the Commission has developed significantly with the publication of the new Guidelines[50] and the R&D Regulation. The Commission now recognises that many R&D agreements do not infringe Article 81(1) (101(1)), or if they do they should be considered as pro-competitive overall

---

47   Commission Regulation (EC) 2658/2000 ([2000] OJ L304/3) replaces Commission Regulation (EC) 417/85 ([1985]) OJ L53/5).

48   Commission Regulation (EC) 2659/2000 ([2000] OJ L304/7) came into force on 1 January 2001 and expires on 31 December 2010. Art 8 includes transitional provisions for agreements in existence on 31 December 2000 which do not comply with Regulation 2659/2000 but meet the requirements of the previous Regulation, Regulation 418/85. Such agreements continued to receive block exemption for an 18-month grace period, which expired on 30 June 2002.

49   See eg Commission Notice (EEC) ([1968] OJ C84/14) on co-operation agreements, and Commission Notice (EEC) ([1993] OJ C43/2) concerning the assessment of co-operative joint ventures.

50   Commission Guidelines (see n 4), and see below.

and should be exempted. The following comments assume that one wishes to bring an R&D agreement within the scope of the R&D Regulation on the basis that there is at least a risk that it would be regarded as breaching Article 81(1) (101(1)).

Comparison with 1985 R&D block exemption Regulation; structure of R&D Regulation

The earlier R&D block exemption Regulation (418/85) permitted some restrictions on commercialisation, but that block exemption was widely regarded as being rather narrow and difficult to apply to many R&D agreements that were encountered in practice. The R&D Regulation is more liberal in approach, but some problems of interpretation remain, as is discussed below. Some of the Commission's traditional approach continues to be found in the R&D Regulation. For example, Recital 3 remains virtually unchanged from Regulation 418/85:

> 'Agreements on the joint execution of research work or the joint development of the results of the research, up to but not including the stage of industrial application, generally do not fall within the scope of Article 81(1) [(101(1))] of the Treaty. In certain circumstances, however, such as where the parties agree not to carry out other research and development in the same field, thereby foregoing the opportunity of gaining competitive advantages over the other parties, such agreements may fall within Article 81(1) [(101(1))] and should therefore be included within the scope of this Regulation'.

Other Recitals in the R&D Regulation are completely new, and suggest an enthusiasm for R&D agreements that was missing from Regulation 418/85. They include the following, none of which may be thought particularly controversial, but their inclusion indicates a significant change of emphasis by the Commission:

- a reference to EC Treaty, Article 163(2) (179(2)) which calls upon the Community to encourage undertakings, including small and medium-sized enterprises, in R&D activities;[51]

- a reference to the Fifth (now Seventh) Framework Programme of EC funding for research projects, which promotes the conduct of co-operative research;[52]

- the statement: 'below a certain level of market power it can for the application of Article 81(3) (101(3)), in general, be presumed that the

---

51 Commission Regulation 2659/2000 (see n 2), Recital 2.
52 See n 52. As to EC funding of R&D, see Ch 1. Since the publication of the Guidelines (see n 4), Framework 5 has been replaced by Framework 7.

positive effects of research and development agreements will outweigh any negative effects upon competition';[53]

- the statement:

  'Agreements between undertakings which are not competing manufacturers of products capable of being improved or replaced by the results of the research and development will only eliminate effective competition in research and development in exceptional circumstances. It is therefore appropriate to enable such agreements to benefit from the block exemption irrespective of market share and to address such exceptional cases by way of withdrawal of the benefit of this Regulation'.[54]

The R&D Regulation began the approach, closely followed in the Technology Transfer Regulation and the Implementation Regulation, requiring an economic analysis (through market share) to be undertaken to establish whether a particular agreement or provision would have the benefit of the block exemption. Also there is a move away from including provisions which are permissible (a 'white list') which has also been followed in the Technology Transfer Regulation. And since the introduction of Regulation 1/2003[55] and where a party has doubts about whether a particular agreement comes within a block exemption or wishes to seek clarification from the Commission, it is no longer possible for the party to notify the agreement to the Commission, or apply for 'negative clearance', an individual exemption or a comfort letter. The party will have to carry out their own assessment and hope, if challenged, that the Commission, a national competition authority or court agrees with their assessment that the agreement has the benefit of a block exemption.

The structure of the R&D Regulation has both similarities to, and differences from, that of the existing block exemption Regulations from the Commission. The familiar features include:

- lengthy Recitals which should be considered carefully in order to understand the scope and meaning of the operative provisions;

- a description of the types of R&D agreements that qualify for exemption under the Regulation (Art 1);

- detailed definitions of terms used in the R&D Regulation (Art 2) and rules for calculating market share (Art 6);

- a list of conditions which must be satisfied in order for the exemption to apply (Art 3);

---

53   Commission Regulation 2659/2000 (see n 2), Recital 5.
54   Commission Regulation 2659/2000 (see n 2), Recital 20.
55   Council Regulation (EC) 1/2003 ([2003] OJ L1/1) on the implementation of the rules on competition laid down in Articles 81 and 82 of the Treaty.

- provisions as to the duration of the exemption, including some special conditions for agreements involving a high market share or between competitors (Art 4);

- a 'blacklist' of terms that may not be included in an agreement, if it is to benefit from the block exemption (Art 5);

- a provision allowing withdrawal of the benefit of the block exemption by the Commission in cases where competition is being stifled (Art 7);

- transitional and procedural provisions (Arts 8–10).

The main difference from many of the earlier Regulations, including Regulation 418/85, is the absence of a list of the type of terms that would be allowable if included in R&D agreements. Traditionally, there were two such lists:

- a list of exempted provisions, ie provisions that are potentially anti-competitive, but are nevertheless permitted under the block exemption Regulations; and

- a so-called whitelist of provisions that are not considered anti-competitive.

Recital 7 of the R&D Regulation explains the absence of these lists:

'It is appropriate to move away from the approach of listing exempted clauses and to place greater emphasis on defining the categories of agreements which are exempted up to a certain level of market power and on specifying the restrictions or clauses which are not to be contained in such agreements. This is consistent with an economics based approach which assesses the impact of agreements on the relevant market'.

This is one of a number of statements in the R&D Regulation that indicates a more relaxed approach by the Commission to R&D agreements. In general, this new approach by the Commission has been refreshing and is to be welcomed; taken together with other changes to EC competition law and practice,[56] it is becoming easier to advise with confidence that many smaller-scale R&D agreements do not breach EC competition law.

The main structural difference between the R&D Regulation and the earlier R&D block exemption Regulation is the absence in the R&D Regulation of an 'opposition procedure' or fast-track notification procedure for agreements that contain terms that are not exempted, whitelisted or blacklisted. This procedure enabled agreements to be notified to the Commission on the basis that if the Commission did not object to the agreements within a defined time-period, they would be automatically exempted. Such a procedure is

---

56   Commission Notice on agreements of minor importance ([1997] OJ C372/13).

inappropriate where the block exemption does not contain lists of exempted and whitelisted clauses, and in any case the Commission has tended not to provide for such a procedure in recent block exemption Regulations. It is understood that very few notifications under the opposition procedures (of several block exemption Regulations) have been made. In any case such an approach would not be available following the introduction of Regulation 1/2003.

Although there are significant differences between the texts of the new and old R&D block exemption Regulations, most notably the absence of the lists referred to above, the changes are not as great as might have been expected from reading the Recitals to the R&D Regulation and the Commission's Guidelines.[57] The Guidelines in particular suggest a much more friendly attitude to R&D agreements than had existed previously. Regrettably, a number of key provisions of the R&D Regulation are as they were in the earlier Regulation and remain unclear and confusing.[58] Nevertheless, as is discussed below, it may be possible to take a more relaxed view of some of these provisions in the light of some of the helpful commentary in the Guidelines.

Qualifying R&D agreements

In order to determine whether an R&D agreement benefits from the block exemption under the R&D Regulation, it is necessary to consider in detail the terms of both the Regulation and the agreement.

The R&D Regulation applies to certain types of agreement between undertakings[59] which are concerned with joint R&D and/or joint exploitation of the results of joint R&D. Clearly, a first step in determining whether an agreement benefits from the block exemption is to decide whether it is one of the types of R&D agreement that are exempted.

- The R&D Regulation exempts three main types of agreement, which can be summarised as agreements which govern:[60] joint R&D and joint exploitation: joint R&D of products or processes ('joint R&D') *and* joint exploitation of the results of that R&D ('joint exploitation'); or

- *joint exploitation only*: joint exploitation of the results of joint R&D which was carried out pursuant to a prior agreement between the same undertakings; or

---

57 Commission Guidelines (see n 4).
58 Eg provisions relating to joint exploitation (see 'Joint exploitation' below).
59 The question of what amounts to an undertaking has been considered by the Commission. It seems that it can include an individual or a research institution.
60 Commission Regulation 2659/2000 (see n 2), Art 1, para 1.

- *joint R&D only*: joint R&D *excluding* joint exploitation, in so far as such agreements fall within Article 85(1).

Joint exploitation

R&D, or exploitation of the results, is carried out 'jointly' where the work involved is carried out by a joint team, organisation or undertaking; jointly entrusted to a third party; or allocated between the parties by way of specialisation in research, development, or exploitation.[61]

This definition leaves a number of questions unanswered, particularly in relation to the issue of what amounts to joint exploitation. For example, it is unclear whether an R&D collaboration agreement which provides that one of the parties to the agreement will have exclusive, worldwide rights to commercialise the results of the joint R&D programme, amounts to joint exploitation.

It might be argued that the parties have allocated commercialisation rights between them, 100 per cent to one party, and 0 per cent to the other, and therefore they fall under Article 11 of the Regulation which provides that joint R&D or exploitation occurs where the work is 'allocated between the parties by way of specialisation in research, development, production or distribution'.[62] Perhaps a better example would be where the contracting parties agree that one of them will have exclusive exploitation rights to the results of the joint R&D in one technical field or territory, and the other party will have exclusive exploitation rights in another field or territory. This would seem to amount to an allocation by way of specialisation in production or distribution.

However, Article 3 of the Regulation, which sets out conditions for exemption may suggest, by inference, that the parties' terms would not amount to joint exploitation. Where the R&D agreement covers joint R&D but not joint exploitation, Article 3 of the Regulation indicates that the parties may limit their respective exploitation rights to one or more technical fields of application.[63] Thus, party A may have exploitation rights in one field, whilst party B has exploitation rights in another field. It would seem illogical for this to amount to joint exploitation, because the premise of Article 3 is that the agreement provides only for joint R&D. That the R&D Regulation is unclear on this point is a serious shortcoming, as many R&D agreements include similar terms on exploitation.

---

61 Commission Regulation 2659/2000 (see n 2), Art 2, para 11.
62 Commission Regulation 2659/2000 (see n 2), Art 2, para 11(c).
63 Commission Regulation 2659/2000 (see n 2), Art 3, para 3.

Conditions for exemption

The exemption of certain R&D agreements from Article 81(1) (101(1)) is subject to certain conditions, set out in Article 3, on the following topics:

- access by parties to the results;

- freedom of parties to exploit results;

- joint exploitation must be in respect of 'decisive' intellectual property; and

- specialisation in production.

These are now discussed in turn. The Regulation does not include the previous requirement that 'the joint research and development work is carried out within the framework of a programme defining the objectives of the work and the field in which it is to be carried out'. The omission of this condition, and of Recitals from Regulation 418/85, suggests a less suspicious attitude on the part of the Commission to R&D agreements.

Access by parties to the results

The Regulation provides that:

> 'all the parties must have access to the results of the work for the purposes of further research or exploitation. However, research institutes, academic bodies, or undertakings which supply research and development as a commercial service without normally being active in the exploitation of results may agree to confine their use of the results for the purposes of further research'.[64]

Contract terms that would cause an R&D agreement not to meet this condition may include the following:

- in an agreement between two commercial companies that are active in intellectual property exploitation, an exclusive licence to one party to use the results for the purposes of further research or exploitation, or (having the same effect) a prohibition on the other party from using the results for these purposes;

- in an agreement between a university and a company active in intellectual property exploitation, an exclusive licence to the company to use the results for further research, or (having the same effect) a prohibition on the university doing so.

---

64   Art 3(2).

A licence to one of the contracting parties drafted in terms such as:

> 'an exclusive, worldwide licence under the Foreground Intellectual Property[65] to research, develop, manufacture, use and sell [products that incorporate the results of the joint research and development conducted under this agreement]'

may well fall foul of this condition.

The Regulation is not specific as to what 'further research or exploitation' in the above-quoted provision means. Take the example of a joint R&D programme that is funded by one of the parties. The results of the programme are focussed on the development of particular products. The funding party wishes to acquire exclusive rights to commercialise those products, perhaps by means of an exclusive licence under any intellectual property that forms part of or protects the results, and perhaps limited to a particular field. The authors assume that it would be permissible for the non-funding party to grant exclusive rights to the funding party in that field, whilst reserving the right to use the results to conduct research in a different field or for different products and to commercialise the fruits of that further research.

A stricter interpretation of the above-quoted words would be that the non-funding party must be allowed to use the results of the joint R&D to conduct further research directly in the field of interest of the funding party and which might lead to the development of a product that competes with any products that are exclusively licensed to the funding party. Presumably, even if this interpretation is correct, it would still be permissible for the funding party to be granted an exclusive option on commercial terms, to acquire exclusive commercialisation rights to the fruits of the further research.

The overall policy objective behind this condition is presumably to ensure that block exemption is not given in a situation where promising lines of research are blocked off by restrictive contract terms. A contract drafter may be well-advised to enquire of the parties' scientists whether any proposed terms would have this effect, and to modify the wording where appropriate.

The relationship between the above provisions, set out in Article 3(2), and the provisions of Article 3(3), discussed below, is not entirely clear. They appear to overlap, in that both Articles are concerned with giving each party the freedom to exploit. The authors' surmise is that where Article 3(2) refers to 'further research or exploitation', it is concerned with use of the results of the joint R&D to conduct further (independent) research, and to exploit the fruits of that independent research. This can be distinguished from Article 3(3), which is concerned with exploitation of the results of the joint R&D.

---

65   As to the use of the term Foreground Intellectual Property, see Ch 2 under 'Definition of Foreground Intellectual Property'.

As has already been mentioned, it seems likely that a fairly narrow interpretation should be put on the words:

> 'undertakings which supply research and development as a commercial service without normally being active in the exploitation of the results.'

This probably refers to organisations such as (in the biotechnology industry) companies providing testing or trials services, and not to companies that are developing their own products, such as drugs, with a view to licensing them to large pharmaceutical companies.

Freedom of parties to exploit results

The Regulation states that without prejudice to the parties' rights of access to the results:[66]

> 'where the agreement provides only for joint research and development, each party must be free independently to exploit the results of the joint research and development and any pre-existing know-how necessary for the purpose of such exploitation. Such right to exploitation may be limited to one or more technical fields of application, where the parties are not competing undertakings at the time the research and development agreement is entered into'.[67]

The condition only applies to agreements that do *not* provide for joint exploitation. This begs the question of what is 'joint exploitation', as discussed above.[68] In effect, this condition seems to require each party (party A) to permit the other party (party B) to use any intellectual property generated by party A in the course of the R&D programme. Parties may limit each other's rights to exploit such results to one or more technical fields of application.[69] The concept of a technical field of application is a familiar one in block exemption Regulations, for example the EC Commission Technology Transfer Regulation.[70] The restriction should be a genuine field restriction and not a customer restriction. Certain customer restrictions are blacklisted,[71] but even if a restriction is not blacklisted it may not qualify as a technical field restriction.[72]

---

66 Commission Regulation 2659/2000 (see n 2), Art 3, para 2.
67 See n 64.
68 See 'Joint exploitation' above.
69 See n 64.
70 Commission Regulation (EC) 240/96 ([1996] OJ L31/2) on technology transfer agreements.
71 Under Commission Regulation 2659/2000 (see n 2), Art 5, para 1(e).
72 For the purposes of Commission Regulation 2659/2000 (see n 2), Art 3, para 3. See further the distinction drawn between field and customer restrictions in, for example, Commission Regulation 240/96 (see n 71) and in reported Commission decisions on the application of EC Treaty Article 81 (101).

One of the Recitals to the R&D Regulation gives some guidance on the intention of the wording on joint exploitation. It states:

'... non-competitors may agree to limit their right to exploitation to one or more technical fields of application to facilitate cooperation between parties with complementary skills'.[73]

It remains to be seen whether it will be permissible to grant one party a very narrow field of application, and the other party all remaining fields of application, such that for practical purposes one party will have exclusive exploitation rights for all commercially valuable fields of application. This would seem to be a potential loophole in the wording of this condition.

Joint exploitation must be in respect of 'decisive' intellectual property

The Regulation provides that any joint exploitation must relate to results which are protected by intellectual property rights or constitute know-how, which substantially[74] contribute to technical or economic progress, and the results must be decisive for the manufacture of the contract products or the application of the contract processes.[75]

This condition remains virtually unaltered from the earlier R&D block exemption Regulation (418/85) and seems to reflect a concern by the Commission that the block exemption should not be used for agreements that are not genuinely concerned with the exploitation of joint R&D.[76] Whilst

73 Commission Regulation 2659/2000 (see n 2), Recital 14.
74 The word 'substantially' in this condition echoes the requirement in Commission Regulation 240/96 on technology transfer agreements (see n 71) that know-how must be 'secret, substantial and identified'. It is noteworthy that Regulation 2659/2000 (see n 2) has removed a condition for exemption that appeared in Regulation 418/85 (see n 9) that required the research programme to be conducted under a 'defined framework' – similar in intent to a requirement that know-how be identified – but has not chosen to drop the requirement of substantiality.
75 Commission Regulation 2659/2000 (see n 2), Art 3, para 4.
76 Commission Regulation 2659/2000 (see n 2), Recital 14 states: 'In order to justify the exemption, the joint exploitation should relate to products or processes for which the use of the results of the research and development is decisive ...'. This virtually repeats the second part of the condition quoted above and adds little. It is interesting that in Commission Regulation 418/85 (see n 9) similar words were used in Recital 7, but were followed by the following phrase, which has been omitted from Commission Regulation 2659/2000:
    'Joint exploitation is not therefore justified where it relates to improvements which were not made within the framework of a joint research and development programme but under an agreement having some other principal objective, such as the licensing of intellectual property rights, joint manufacture or specialisation, and merely containing ancillary provisions on joint research and development'.
This additional wording helps to explain the rationale for requiring the results to be 'decisive'. But these words were probably thought too restrictive under the more liberal approach now being taken by the Commission.

this condition is one to watch out for, it will probably not cause problems in relation to many joint R&D agreements.

Specialisation in production

'Undertakings charged with manufacture by way of specialisation in production must be required to fulfil orders for supplies from all the parties, except where the R&D agreement also provides for joint distribution.'[77]

The condition addresses a situation that is not often encountered in early-stage R&D agreements, and is unlikely to cause a problem in most such agreements.

The phrase 'except where the R&D agreement also provides for joint distribution' was not included in EC Commission Regulation 418/85.

For further guidance on what is acceptable in specialisation agreements, see EC Commission Regulation 2658/2000 on specialisation agreements and the Guidelines.[78]

Duration of exemption and market share criteria

Non-competitors

The duration of the block exemption under EC Commission Regulation 2659/2000 depends, in part, upon whether the parties to the agreement are competitors and upon their combined share of the relevant market.

For non-competitors, the exemption applies for the duration of the R&D.[79] Where the results are jointly exploited, the exemption continues to apply for seven years from the time the contract products are first put on the market within the common market.[80]

Competitors with less than 25 per cent market share – initial period of exemption

For competitors with less than 25 per cent market share of the relevant market for the contract products,[81] the exemption applies for the duration of the

---

77   Art 3(5).
78   See n 4.
79   Commission Regulation 2659/2000 (see n 2), Art 4, para 1.
80   See n 80.
81   'Relevant market for the contract products' means the relevant product and geographic market(s) to which the contract products belong (Commission Regulation 2659/2000 (see n 2), Art 2, para 13.

R&D. Where the results are jointly exploited, the exemption continues to apply for seven years from the time the contract products are first put on the market within the common market.[82]

Competitors with less than 25 per cent market share – subsequent period of exemption

After the end of the initial period,[83] the exemption shall continue to apply as long as the combined market share of the participating undertakings does not exceed 25 per cent of the relevant market for the contract products.[84]

Market share above 25 per cent

If the parties wish to continue their joint exploitation arrangements after the initial period[85] has expired, and both (a) their combined market share exceeds 25 per cent, and (b) the arrangements include provisions that breach EC Treaty, Article 81(1) (101(1)), they will need to seek an individual exemption from the Commission.

Definition of market share

The provisions dealing with market share in the new Regulation are, in some respects, simpler than the equivalent provisions in EC Commission Regulation 418/85, and more liberal, not least because the equivalent market share limit in the earlier Regulation was 20 per cent.[86] However, unlike Regulation 418/85, they do not make clear that it is market share in the EU that is relevant. Article 6 of Regulation 2659/2000, which includes a definition of market share, does not make this clear although it does clarify other aspects of market share, including provisions allowing the exemption to continue where market share exceeds the 25 per cent figure for a defined temporary period.

---

82 Commission Regulation 2659/2000 (see n 2), Art 4, para 2.
83 Commission Regulation 2659/2000 (see n 2), Art 4, para 1.
84 'Relevant market for the contract products' means the relevant product and geographic market(s) to which the contract products belong: Commission Regulation 2659/2000 (see n 2), Art 2, para 13.
85 Commission Regulation 2659/2000 (see n 2), Art 4, para 1.
86 The general flavour of these provisions is given in Regulation 2659/2000 (see n 2), Recitals 5, 20. These include the following sentences which were not in Regulation 418/85 (see n 9):
    'Below a certain level of market power it can for the application of Article 81(3) [(101(3))], in general, be presumed that the positive effects of research and development agreements will outweigh any negative effects on competition'.

    'Agreements between undertakings which are not competing manufacturers ... will only eliminate effective competition in research and development in exceptional circumstances. It is therefore appropriate to enable such agreements to benefit from the block exemption irrespective of market share and to address such exceptional cases by way of withdrawal of the benefit of this Regulation'.

Provisions which prevent application of exemption

Blacklisted provisions

The inclusion of blacklisted provisions in an R&D agreement will prevent the block exemption from applying to the agreement. Such provisions are highly likely to be contrary to EC Treaty, Article 81(1) (101(1)) and their inclusion in an agreement might increase the probability of fines being imposed, unless the agreement is individually notified to the Commission. It may be difficult to persuade the Commission to give an individual exemption to an agreement containing such provisions. They should therefore normally be avoided.

The blacklisted provisions are as follows. The exemption does not apply to R&D agreements which have, 'directly or indirectly in isolation or in combination with other factors under the control of the parties',[87] as their object any of the following:

- *Unnecessary restrictions on R&D:* the restriction of the participating undertakings' freedom to carry out R&D independently or in co-operation with third parties:

    — in a field unconnected with that to which the programme relates, or

    — after its completion, in the field to which the programme relates or in a connected field.[88]

- *No-challenge clauses – intellectual property rights:* the prohibition of any challenge, after completion of the R&D or the expiry of the R&D agreement, to the validity of intellectual property rights which:

    — are relevant to the R&D programme (after completion);

    — protect the results of the R&D (after expiry of the agreement);

    without prejudice to the possibility to provide for termination of the agreement in the event of one of the parties challenging the validity of such intellectual property rights.[89]

    The R&D Regulation does not include an opposition procedure, so it is perhaps inevitable that no-challenge clauses continue to be blacklisted. It should be noted that no-challenge clauses are perhaps not considered by the Commission to be so irredeemably bad as some other types of blacklisted clauses, and it may be possible to make a case for their retention in an individual notification of an agreement to the Commission.

---

87 Commission Regulation 2659/2000 (see n 2), Art 5, para 1.
88 Commission Regulation 2659/2000 (see n 2), Art 5, para 1(a). See also Art 5.1(h) which blacklists a restriction on granting certain third-party manufacturing licences.
89 Commission Regulation 2659/2000 (see n 2), Art 5, para 1(b).

- *Output and sales restrictions:* the limitation of output or sales.[90]

- *Price restrictions:* the fixing of prices when selling the contract product to third parties.[91]

  Price restrictions are generally regarded as anti-competitive, and are mentioned specifically in Article 81 (101)). They are also specifically provided for under domestic UK competition law, in the Competition Act 1998, and should generally be avoided in most types of commercial agreement.

- *Customer restrictions:* restriction of the customers which participating undertakings may serve seven years after the contract products are first put on the market within the common market.[92]

  The equivalent term in the previous Regulation (418/85) was stated to be without prejudice to a provision in the list of exempted clauses in that Regulation that permitted certain restrictions as to technical fields of application. There is no list of exempted clauses in the R&D Regulation, but it is likely that the Commission intends this distinction between customer restrictions (prohibited) and field restrictions (acceptable) to continue. The distinction is not, however, always easy to apply.[93] Although there has been some case law on these types of issue, it is not always easy to determine whether the parties' split of markets is a permitted 'field' or prohibited 'customer' split.

- *Restrictions on passive sales:* prohibition of passive sales of the contract products in territories reserved for other parties.[94]

  An example of a passive sale is where the supplier does not advertise or have a presence in the relevant territory but a sophisticated customer finds the supplier nevertheless. The purchase of cars on the Continent by UK buyers or the purchase of software from the website of an online retailer based in Europe by UK buyers are examples of passive sales.

  It is not specifically stated that the reference to 'territories reserved

---

90 Commission Regulation 2659/2000 (see n 2), Art 5, para 1(c).
91 Commission Regulation 2659/2000 (see n 2), Art 5, para 1(d).
92 Commission Regulation 2659/2000 (see n 2), Art 5, para 1(e).This provision is similar in effect to provisions in Commission Regulation 418/85 (see n 9) although the seven-year grace period was not specifically included.
93 Eg in a joint R&D programme which leads to a pharmaceutical drug being developed, where one party is licensed to exploit the market for drugs prescribed by medical general practitioners and the other to sell to hospitals, the following questions arise: Is this a customer allocation? What if hospitals require the drug in a different formulation, eg pills with different quantities of the active ingredient, or require the drug in injectable form rather than pill form? Would this amount to a different technical field of use?
94 Commission Regulation 2659/2000 (see n 2), Art 5, para 1(f). It is puzzling that there is no seven-year grace period as in the provision on customer restrictions (Commission Regulation 2659/2000, Art 5, para 1(e)). Presumably, in that period one could nominate all customers in other parties' territories as being 'out of bounds' and achieve the same effect as a ban on passive sales.
      This black-listed provision was not specifically included in Commission Regulation 418/85 (see n 9) although other black-listed clauses may have had a similar effect.

for other parties' means other territories of the EU (and other European countries with whom the EU has common competition arrangements). This may be implicit, but it is unfortunate that the point is not made clear.

- *Restrictions on active sales in other parties' territories:* prohibition on putting the contract products on the market or pursuing an active sales policy for them in territories within the common market that are reserved for other parties seven years after the products are first put on the market within the common market.[95]

  If one party has exclusive sales rights in the whole of the common market, and the other party has exclusive sales rights outside the common market, and such exclusive sales rights are agreed to continue for more than seven years, such a provision would not appear to be blacklisted, provided that it is not, in effect, a ban on passive sales, which is separately blacklisted as mentioned above.[96]

- *Restrictions on third-party manufacture:* the 'requirement not to grant licences to third parties to manufacture the contract products or to apply the contract processes where the exploitation by at least one of the parties of the results of the joint R&D is not provided for or does not take place'.[97]

  The Commission is concerned to ensure that the results of R&D are not completely blocked from exploitation, as this would be regarded as anti-competitive.

- *Restrictions on grey sales:* the 'requirement to refuse to meet demand from users or resellers in their respective territories who would market the contract products in other territories within the common market, or to make it difficult for users or resellers to obtain the contract products from other resellers within the common market, and in particular to exercise intellectual property rights or take measures so as to prevent users or resellers from obtaining, or from putting on the market within the common market, products which have been lawfully put on the market within the Community by another party or with its consent'.[98]

  This provision blacklists, among other things, obligations to take action against parallel importers of products that have previously been put on the common market. The ban on restricting parallel imports is broadly consistent with EC competition law under EC Treaty, Articles 28–30 (34–36); in certain circumstances an intellectual-property-owner is not permitted to enforce his intellectual property rights against an un-

---

95 Commission Regulation 2659/2000 (see n 2), Art 5, para 1(g).
96 See 'Black-listed provisions' above.
97 Commission Regulation 2659/2000 (see n 2), Art 5, para 1(h). This provision (or one like it) first appeared in Commission Regulation (EEC) 151/93 ([1993] OJ L021/8) which amended Commission Regulation 418/85 (see n 9).
98 Commission Regulation 2659/2000 (see n 2), Art 5, para 1(i), (j).

authorised importer of goods where the goods were originally put on the market in another EU member state by the intellectual-property-owner or with his or her consent.

Exceptions to blacklist

EC Commission Regulation 2659/2000 provides that the black-list does not apply to:[99]

- 'the setting of production targets where the exploitation of the results includes the joint production of the contract products;

- the setting of sales targets and the fixing of prices charged to immediate customers where the exploitation of the results includes the joint distribution of the contract products'.

Risk list

The EC Commission is entitled to withdraw the block exemption for an agreement if it considers that the agreement has effects which are incompatible with EC Treaty, Article 81(3) (101(3)).[100] It may do so where the existence of the R&D agreement:

- substantially restricts the scope for third parties to carry out R&D in the relevant field because of the limited research capacity available elsewhere;

- substantially restricts the access of third parties to the market for the contract products because of the particular structure of supply;

- would eliminate effective competition in R&D in a particular market;[101]

Or where:

— the parties do not exploit the results of the joint R&D without any validly objective reason;

— the contract products are not subject in the whole or a substantial part of the common market to effective competition from identical products or products considered by users as equivalent in view of their characteristics, price and intended use.

---

99   Commission Regulation 2659/2000 (see n 2), Art 5, para 2. These exceptions, which were not included in Commission Regulation 418/85 (see n 9), have presumably been introduced in response to specific concerns raised by companies about the black-list.
100   Commission Regulation 2659/2000 (see n 2), Art 7.
101   This effect was not included in Commission Regulation 418/85 (see n 9) and may be thought of as a 'catch-all' provision. The other four provisions are identical in wording to Regulation 418/85.

Although this power is thought to have been exercised very rarely, if ever, it would be prudent for parties to bear these examples in mind (especially the last two of these items) when structuring their R&D collaboration agreement, particularly if the agreement is likely to have a 'high profile' or otherwise come to the attention of the Commission.

SPECIALISATION AGREEMENTS REGULATION

The relevance of the rules on specialisation agreements to technology-based agreements has already been discussed.[102] The following paragraphs will provide a brief summary of the detailed provisions of the Specialisation Regulation.[103]

The Regulation has a similar, but not identical, format to the R&D Regulation.[104] The main provisions can be summarised as follows:

- *Qualifying agreements:* after some lengthy Recitals, the Specialisation Regulation begins with a description of the types of agreement that are exempted by the Regulation. Three types of specialisation agreement are identified:

  — *unilateral specialisation agreements,* where one party agrees not to produce certain products and to buy them from a competing undertaking, and the competing undertaking agrees to supply them;

  — *reciprocal specialisation agreements,* where each party accepts the obligations described in the previous paragraph, ie each party accepts such obligations in respect of different products; and

  — *joint-production agreements,* where the parties agree to produce certain products jointly.

- *Agreements with ancillary IP provisions:* the block exemption also applies where the specialisation agreement includes ancillary provisions that:

  'do not constitute the primary object of such agreements, but are directly related to and necessary for their implementation, such as those concerning the assignment or use of intellectual property rights'.[105]

- *Definitions:* detailed definitions of certain terms used in the Specialisation Regulation.

---

102 See Ch 12 under 'Does the Specialisation Agreements Regulation apply, and if so does the agreement receive block exemption under that Regulation?'.
103 Regulation 2658/2000 (see n 3).
104 Regulation 2659/2000 (see n 2).
105 Art 1(2).

- *Exempted terms on purchasing and marketing:* a provision that clarifies that certain exclusive purchasing and supply obligations, and certain joint distribution arrangements, may be included in qualifying agreements.

- *Market-share threshold:* the block exemption applies on condition that the combined market share of the parties does not exceed 20 per cent. Detailed rules for calculating market share are set out later in the Regulation.

- *Hardcore restrictions:* the inclusion of certain hardcore restrictions in a specialisation agreement will cause it not to receive block exemption. Those restrictions, which are familiar from other competition legislation, including Article 81 itself, are:

  — the fixing of prices to third parties;

  — limitation of output or sales;

  — allocation of markets or customers.

- *Non-hardcore restrictions:* however, the following provisions are not treated as hardcore restrictions:

  — agreements on the amounts of products covered by unilateral or reciprocal specialisation agreements;

  — the setting of capacity and production volumes in a joint-production agreement;

  — the setting of sales targets and the fixing of prices that a production joint venture charges to its immediate customers.

- *Other provisions:* the Specialisation Regulation includes some other provisions, familiar to readers of block exemption regulations, including a right for the Commission to withdraw the block exemption in individual cases.

- *Expiry:* the Regulation is stated to expire on 31 December 2010.

CHAPTER 15

UK Competition Law[1]

INTRODUCTION

The impact of EC competition law upon commercial agreements, particularly those concerned with the development or exploitation of technology, has been considerable and has continued to strengthen since the previous edition of this book.[2] Anyone drafting such an agreement must consider whether Article 81 (101) applies to the agreement and, if it does, whether the proposed terms meet the detailed requirements of the European Commission. The requirements of several block exemption regulations and Commission Notices in this field are considered in detail in earlier chapters.

With such extensive regulation of technology-related agreements under EC competition laws, it is easy to overlook the separate requirements of domestic UK competition laws. The latter are just as important, as breach of their

---

1   Following the passing of the Lisbon Treaty and its coming into force in December 2009, the Articles of the EC Treaty is renumbered. This chapter adopts the following method: the existing numbering is retained with the new numbers in parenthesis (as most people are likely to be familiar with the existing numbering). The EC Treaty will be renamed the 'Treaty on the Functioning of the European Union', but for ease of reference it will continue to be called the EC Treaty in this edition of the book.

2   Particularly following the introduction of Council Regulation (EC) 1/2003 ([2003] OJ L001/1) on the implementation of the rules on competition laid down in Articles 81 and 82 of the Treaty which is summarised below under 'Consistency and harmonisation between UK and EC competition law' and in Ch 14.

requirements can lead to an agreement being void or may result in fines.[3]

Before proceeding further, it may be useful to distinguish between four types of 'competition' laws:

(a) *European competition laws,* which protect the European markets from larger scale economic abuses, particularly under Articles 81 (101), 82 (102) and 28–30 (34–36) of the EC Treaty, in respect of European Union countries, and extending to most other western European countries (with the notable exception of Switzerland) under the European Economic Area Agreement.[4] Article 81 (101) forms the main subject matter of Chapter 12.

(b) *The application of European law directly by relevant UK national bodies* (the Office of Fair Trading, 'OFT' in this chapter) and the UK courts under Regulation 1/2003.

(c) *UK domestic competition laws, particularly through the Competition Act 1998 (the 'Act' in this chapter),* which protect the UK markets from economic abuses which are considered not to be in the public interest.

(d) *So-called 'unfair competition' laws,* which seek to prevent a person from trading in a way which is 'unfair' with respect to competitors. This category of laws, which should not be confused with the above-mentioned types of competition law, is more highly developed in some countries than others. It is not generally recognised as a separate category in English law, unlike the position in some continental European countries.

However, there are areas of English law that are analogous to continental unfair competition laws. For example:

● there is the common law (case-based) English law of 'passing off' which prevents a person from deliberately trading off another's reputation in certain situations; and

● there are also some statutory provisions in UK intellectual property law which might be classified as 'unfair competition' laws, most notably under the law relating to registered trade marks.

This book does not consider the subject of 'passing off', nor registered trade marks, as these areas of law do not protect technology as such.

In a broader sense of the term, 'UK competition laws' are now concerned with (b), (c) and (d) in the list above. Item (b) provides the (relatively) new

---

3　See 'Competition Act 1998' below.
4　See further Ch 12.

powers to the OFT (and the UK courts) to apply EC competition law directly and like item (c) is policy-based and inquisitorial in nature – the competition authorities may require parties to justify their conduct in relation to the public interest. Item (d) tends to be more concerned with the protection of individual interests and is adversarial in nature – for example where a party makes use of such laws in a private dispute with another party.[5]

This chapter is principally concerned with item (c), that is UK competition laws. Since 1998, this area consists principally of the Competition Act 1998 (as amended by the Enterprise Act 2002), but also includes the common law on agreements in restraint of trade. This chapter also includes consideration of item (b) above.

UK STATUTORY (AND OTHER LEGISLATIVE) PROVISIONS CONCERNING COMPETITION

Introductory points

The relevant statutory rules governing UK competition in relation to technology transfer agreements are now contained in the Competition Act 1998 ('the Act' in this chapter), which came into force on 1 March 2000.[6] From 1 May 2004, following the bringing into force of Regulation 1/2003 (the 'Modernisation Regulation'),[7] the UK now also has the power to apply EU competition law directly (primarily through the OFT). Therefore, the OFT can apply, in any particular situation, either UK competition law, EU competition law or both to an agreement. UK competition law has been changed principally as follows:

- the Act has been amended so that the OFT's investigative powers (such as obtaining evidence, powers regarding searching premises, etc) now

---

5   Eg in the case of *Chiron v Organon* [1993] FSR 567, where (the now repealed) Patents Act 1977, s 44 was used as a defence in patent infringement proceedings.

6   As extensively amended by the Enterprise Act 2002 (including changes which are largely outside the scope of this book, such as introducing a system of market investigations, providing for controlling mergers, providing for criminal sanctions where a person is involved in a cartel, and the disqualification of a director of a company where the director infringes competition law).

7   Council Regulation (EC) 1/2003 ([2003] OJ L 001/1) on the implementation of the rules on competition laid down in Articles 81 and 82 of the Treaty. The changes are summarised in Ch 14 under 'Modernisation Regulation'; Enterprise Act 2009, s 209 gives the Secretary of State the power to amend the Competition Act 1998 as 'he considers appropriate for the purpose of eliminating or reducing any differences between (a) the domestic provisions of the 1998 Act, and (b) European Community competition law which result (or would otherwise result) from a relevant Community instrument made after the passing of this Act'.

equally apply (as well as being strengthened) to an infringement of UK or EU competition law;[8]

- the authority for the OFT to apply EU competition law is not contained directly in the Act, but is contained in a statutory instrument which:

  — designates the Office of Fair Trading as the national competition authority;

  — allows the OFT to apply the powers provided in the Implementation Regulations;[9]

- the OFT is no longer able to grant individual exemptions;[10]

- agreements can no longer be notified to the OFT;[11]

- in particular cases where novel or unresolved questions of law arise guidance may be provided by the OFT (in the form of an 'opinion').[12]

The OFT is under a duty to publish 'general' advice and information about the OFT's application and enforcement of Article 81 (101) and Article 82 (102).[13] A large amount of documentation was issued in 2004; much of it appears to that indicate that the OFT will take the same approach whether UK or EU competition law is involved. For the purposes of this chapter the following are the two most relevant documents:

- *Agreements and concerted practices – Understanding competition law* (OFT 401);

- *Modernisation – Understanding competition law* (OFT 442).

---

8   Competition Act 1998 and Other Enactments (Amendment) Regulations 2004 (SI 2004/1261), reg 4 and Sch 1.
9   Competition Act 1998 and Other Enactments (Amendment) Regulations 2004 (SI 2004/1261), reg 3.
10 Competition Act 1998 and Other Enactments (Amendment) Regulations 2004 (SI 2004/1261), reg 4 and Sch 1, paras 2, 3, repealing Competition Act 1998, ss 4, 5. There are transitional measures for individual exemptions already in place.
11 Competition Act 1998 and Other Enactments (Amendment) Regulations 2004 (SI 2004/1261), reg 4 and Sch 1, para 9, repealing Competition Act 1998, ss 12–16, 20–24.
12 This is the equivalent of the approach of the Commission: see Commission Notice on informal guidance relating to novel questions concerning Articles 81 and 82 of the EC Treaty that arise in individual cases (guidance letters) ([2004] OJ C101/78). The OFT's approach as to when and the conditions on which it will issue such an opinion can be found in Section 7 of their guideline *Modernisation* (OFT 442).
13 Competition Act 1998, s 52. The available publications relevant to competition law can be found at http://www.oft.gov.uk/advice_and_resources/publications/guidance/competition-act/, none of which address intellectual property directly. In the second edition of this book there was discussed a draft guideline on intellectual property rights which was issued by the OFT (OFT 418). This has not been published, no doubt because EU Regulations and block exemptions can now be applied directly to intellectual property-type agreements where only UK competition law is in issue. Therefore it is perhaps no longer thought necessary to publish a specific guideline on how UK competition law would operate in relation to agreements and conduct which concern intellectual property rights.

Relevant parts are referred to in this chapter, but much of what they contain closely reflects the application of EU competition law, with at appropriate points, adaptations to reflect the situation in the UK.

Competition Act 1998

The Act led to the repeal of much existing legislation.[14] The old regime was more preoccupied with the form of an agreement rather than its objective.

The Act introduces two prohibitions:

- of agreements (whether written or not) which prevent, restrict or distort competition and which may affect trade within the UK (known as the 'Chapter I prohibition'); and

- of conduct by undertakings which amounts to an abuse of a dominant position in a market and which may affect trade within the UK (the 'Chapter II prohibition').

It is the Chapter I prohibition which is of concern in drafting and advising on technology-related agreements and which will be discussed in this section.

The elements of the Chapter I prohibition correspond with provisions of Article 81 (101) of the EC Treaty. Indeed section 60 of the Act requires that the UK authorities in handling cases must act in such a way as to ensure consistency with Community law. However, it should be noted that the UK regime was not introduced in order to comply with a specific European law as such. Whilst it has adopted virtually all of the same way of thinking as the European competition regime, and this facilitates the UK as a member state in upholding its treaty obligations, nevertheless the UK regime is more of a parallel scheme as opposed to a subservient one.

When will an agreement breach Chapter I of the Competition Act?

Section 2(1) of the Act provides that:

> 'Subject to section 3, agreements between undertakings, decisions by associations of undertakings or concerted practices which–
>
> (a)   may affect trade within the United Kingdom; and

---

14   Including the Restrictive Trade Practices Act 1976, the Resale Prices Act 1976, the Restrictive Trade Practices Act 1977 and the anti-competitive practice provisions of the Competition Act 1980.

(b)   have as their object of effect the prevention, restriction or distortion of competition within the United Kingdom,

are prohibited unless they are exempt in accordance with [this part of the Act]'.[15]

It will be seen that the wording of section 2(1) is very similar to that of Article 81(1) (101(1)) of the EC Treaty, the main difference being the substitution of 'within the United Kingdom' for 'between member states'. The prohibition only applies if the agreement, decision or practice is, or is intended to be, implemented in the UK.

It is not proposed to discuss all the different requirements for a breach of section 2(1) as most of these are the same as under EC competition law and have already been dealt with.[16] Instead, the main differences from EC competition law will be discussed and some practical points arising highlighted, namely:

- 'within the United Kingdom';
- 'beween undertakings';
- whether the effects 'appreciable'; immunity for 'small agreements';
- agreements;
- void agreements;
- excluded and exempted agreements; and
- consistency and harmonisation between UK and EC competition law.

Within the United Kingdom

UK competition law will apply if 'the agreement, decision or practice is, or is intended to be, implemented in the United Kingdom'.[17] The 'United Kingdom' means England and Wales, Scotland and Northern Ireland and there is no requirement in the Act that it should be a significant part of the country.

Between undertakings

As with the EC Treaty, the Act does not provide a definition of the meaning of 'undertaking' but the following explanation of an undertaking is used by the OFT:

---

15   While Competition Act 1998, s 2(2) lists the types of agreements, decisions or practices which are prohibited. These are the same as those listed in Art 81 (101).

16   See Ch 12.

17   Competition Act 1998, s 2(3). In this context the meaning of the United Kingdom will include the situation where an agreement operates or is intended to operate in only a part of the UK (Competition Act 1998, s 2(7)).

'the concept of an undertaking, encompasses every entity engaged in an economic activity, regardless of the legal status of the entity or the way in which it is financed'.[18]

An undertaking would cover:[19]

- companies;
- firms;
- businesses;
- partnerships;
- individuals operating as sole traders;
- associations of undertakings (trade associations);
- non profit-making organisations (presumably such as (research) charities, universities);
- public entities offering goods and services on a given market.[20]

According to the OFT guidance the key point for consideration is whether the undertaking is engaged in economic activity (although the economic activity does not have to be in all its functions). Presumably, an organisation such as a university could fulfil this criteria, as the provision of education (as long as this is not seen as economic activity) would take the university outside of the definition of an 'undertaking', but where it engages in research work in the hope of future financial gain, such as assigning intellectual property rights to a spin-out company or to an existing commercial organisation, then such activity could bring the university within the definition of an 'undertaking'.

Whether the effects 'appreciable'; is it a 'small agreement'?

It is well-established under EC competition law that for there to be a breach of Article 81 (101), the effects on competition must be 'appreciable'. The

18 In Case C-41/90, *Höfner and Elser v Macroton GmbH* [1991] ECR I-1979, [1993] 4 CMLR 306, para 21. This definition has been used in a number of succeeding ECJ cases (such as Case T-319/99, *Fenin v Commission* [2003] ECR IT-357. *Agreements and concerted practices* (OFT 401), para 2.5.
19 Drawn from OFT 401, para 2.5 (see n 18).
20 Whether a public body is subject to competition law should be seen in the light of OFT Policy note 1/2004, *The Competition Act 1998 and public bodies* (OFT 443). In Case No 1006/2/1/01 *BetterCare Group Ltd v Director General of Fair Trading* [2002] CAT 7, [2002] Com AR 299, a health trust purchasing social care from the private sector (ie contracting out some of the trust's activities) amounted to an economic activity. But a decision by the ECJ has taken a different view, that where there is the purchase of such a service in order to provide a public service by a public body then the public body will not do so as an undertaking (Case C-205/03 *Fenin v Commission* [2006] ECR I-695, [2006] 5 CMLR 559), although the facts between the cases are different.

same principle would be applied under UK law, by virtue of section 60 of the Act, particularly following the coming into force of the Modernisation Regulation.

The OFT guidelines indicate, as a general proposition, that an agreement will not fall within an Article 81 (101) or a Chapter I prohibition if it is covered by the Commission Notice on Agreements of Minor Importance.[21]

The Commission Notice is set out in detail in Chapter 12, but the key is that the Commission considers that agreements between undertakings which affect trade between member states do not appreciably restrict competition (within the meaning of Article 81 (101)) if:

- the *combined* market share of the parties to an agreement does not exceed 10 per cent and the parties *are* actual or potential competitors;

- the market share of *each* party to an agreement does not exceed 15 per cent and the parties are *not* actual or potential competitors.

In addition the agreement must not contain 'hardcore' restrictions set out in the Commission Notice.[22]

Furthermore, where the parties have used good faith in relying on the terms of the Commission Notice the OFT will not impose a financial penalty where in fact there is an infringement of an Article 81 (101) and/or Chapter I[23].

Although the OFT's view on what is 'appreciable' is not legally binding, it is likely to influence the UK courts.

Under section 39 of the Act, there is a limited immunity from fines for 'small agreements', provided they are not price-fixing agreements.[24] This immunity does not affect the question of whether the agreement breaches Part I of

---

21 Commission Notice on agreements of minor importance which do not appreciably restrict competition under Article 81(1) of the Treaty establishing the European Community (de minimis) (2001/C368/07) (OFT 401, para 2.19). In the second edition of this book the OFT guidance, at the time, indicated that the combined market threshold of the parties was set at 25 per cent where it was considered there was no appreciable effect on competition. Therefore the speculation made in that edition about situations where parties to an agreement have a greater market share in the UK than the EU, and deciding whether EU competition law had to be considered, is no longer relevant now that the UK and EU law are more closely aligned since the adoption of Regulation 1/2003 ([2003] OJ L 001/1) in 2004 and the amendments to UK competition law.

22 These are set out in Ch 12 at 'Notice on agreements of minor importance'.

23 See OFT 401, para 2.19.

24 A price fixing agreement is one 'which has as its object or effect, or one of its objects or effects, restricting the freedom of a party to the agreement to determine the price to be charged (otherwise than as between that party and another party to the agreement) for the product, service or other matter to which the agreement relates'.

the Act;[25] thus an agreement could be immune from fines but still void. Under the Competition Act 1998 (Small Agreements and Conduct of Minor Significance) Regulations 2000,[26] small agreements are defined as:

> 'all agreements between undertakings the combined applicable turnover of which for the business year ending in the calendar year preceding one in which the infringement occurred does not exceed £20 million'.

Agreements

Although there is no difference in the approach between UK and EU competition law as to the meaning of an 'agreement' the OFT has provided some practical pointers as to what is meant by an 'agreement', including:

- that the word 'agreement' has a wide meaning;

- agreements which are legally enforceable;

- agreements which are not legally enforceable;

- so-called 'gentlemen's agreements';

- an agreement which reached without there being any physical meeting of the parties;

- an exchange of letters or telephone calls.[27]

A party to an agreement will include:

- a party who played only a limited part in setting up of the agreement;

- a party who is not fully committed to its implementation;

- a party who only participated due to pressure from other parties.[28]

Although a person may be a party to an agreement, these three circumstances may be taken into account when the OFT decides on the level of financial penalty.

Void agreements

As with Article 81(2) (101(2)), an agreement or decision which is prohibited by Chapter I is void.[29] In one case it has been held by the UK courts that

---

25 Even after the amendments made as a result of the implementation of Regulation 1/2003 ([2003] OJ L 001/1), this section still only applies to UK competition law.
26 SI 2000/262.
27 See para 2.7, *Agreements and concerted practices* (OFT 401).
28 See para 2.8 of guidance above. See also *Decision of the Director General of Fair Trading, No CA98/9/2002, Market sharing by Arriva plc and FirstGroup plc*, 30 January 2002 (Case CP/1163-00) at paras 29–33.
29 Competition Act 1998, s 2(4).

an agreement which infringes Article 81(1) (101(1)) is not only void and unenforceable but also illegal.[30] It could make certain restitutionary measures which are available, at least under English law, unavailable to a party who has paid money under an agreement.

Such an all-encompassing approach has not been followed in European case law. In one case it has been held that national law can stop a party who is responsible for restricting competition in an agreement from obtaining damages from another party to the agreement.[31] Presumably this reasoning would be followed where a Chapter I infringement occurred (ie in pursuance of section 60 of the Act).

Exclusions and exemptions under UK law

The main types of excluded or exempted agreement which are not subject to Chapter I of the Act are the following:

(a) exclusions under Schedules 1 to 3 to the Act:

(i) mergers and concentrations:

— agreements which would result in two enterprises ceasing to be distinct enterprises for the purposes of Enterprise Act 2002, Pt 3;

— agreements which are subject to the exclusive jurisdiction of the Merger Regulation;[32]

(ii) agreements that are subject to other competition scrutiny, including under financial services, and broadcasting, legislation;[33]

(iii) some planning agreements;[34]

(iv) EEA regulated financial markets;[35]

(v) services of general economic interest;[36]

(vi) compliance with legal requirements;[37]

(vii) avoidance of conflict with international obligations;[38]

---

30   *Gibbs Mews plc v Gemmell* [1999] 1 EGLR 43, CA.
31   *Crehan v Courage Ltd*, Case C-453/99, [2001] ECR I-6297, [2001] 5 CMLR 1058. However, Art 81 (101) would prevent national law forbidding a party to an agreement (which restricts or distorts competition) being totally barred from claiming damages for loss of performance of that contract on the sole ground that it is a party to the agreement.
32   Competition Act 1998, s 3(1)(a) and Sch 1.
33   Competition Act 1998, s 3(1)(b) and Sch 2.
34   Competition Act 1998, s 3(1)(c) and Sch 3.
35   See n 33.
36   See n 33.
37   See n 33.
38   See n 33.

(viii) public policy;[39]

(ix) coal and steel;[40]

(x) agricultural product;[41]

(xi) recognised professional bodies and their guidance or rules relating to the carrying on of investment business;[42]

(b) a land agreement to the extent that it is a land agreement as defined in a statutory instrument under section 50 of the Act.[43] Under section 50, vertical agreements could also be exempt but it appears that after the adoption of the Modernisation Regulation, the way vertical agreements are treated under UK law should be aligned with EU law, and thus, where appropriate, could benefit from the EU block exemption for vertical agreements;[44]

(c) agreements covered by a UK block exemption order made by the Secretary of State.[45] To date no such orders have been made in relation to R&D agreements or IP licence agreements and it is understood that there is unlikely to be any such order in the foreseeable future. Apparently, the OFT takes the view that given the EC block exemption regulations for R&D agreements and technology transfer agreements (as to which see (d) below), there is no need for a separate UK block exemption;

(d) agreements which meet the requirements of an EC block exemption regulation, under the parallel exemptions provisions of the Act, will also be exempt from the Chapter I prohibition.[46] Therefore an individual block exemption under Chapter I will not be necessary for an agreement which is restricted to the UK but otherwise contains a Chapter I prohibition to benefit from an EU block exemption.

---

39   See n 33.
40   See n 33.
41   See n 33.
42   Competition Act 1998, s 3(1)(b) and Sch 2.
43   Competition Act 1998, s 50 and Competition Act 1998 (Land Agreements and Revocation) Order 2004 (SI 2004/1260). The Order replaces the Competition Act 1998 (Land and Vertical Agreements Exclusion) Order 2000 (SI 2000/310). The main difference between the two orders is that only land agreements are excluded from the Chapter I prohibition (unless a vertical agreement also happens to be a land agreement).
44   The view of Whish in *Competition Law* (6th edn, Oxford University Press, 2009) at p 348 (his comments carry extra weight as he is currently a non-executive director of the OFT).
45   Competition Act 1998, s 6. To date only one block exemption order has been made under the Competition Act 1998, concerning public ticketing (allowing purchases to buy one ticket which can be used on more than one transport operator's services): Competition Act 1998 (Public Transport Ticketing Schemes Block Exemption) Order 2001 (SI 2001/319).
46   Competition Act 1998, s 10.

Consistency and harmonisation between UK and EC competition law

The Act (under section 60) strives[47] for consistency and harmony with EU competition law, although it does not implement Article 81 (101) as such. However, following the adoption of the Modernisation Regulation, the differences (real, and of the method of handling) have to some extent narrowed or been removed. For example, some agreements will be subject to both UK and EU competition law, and since the need to make notification is no longer available, the effort and the cost of making a notification is removed. Also, it is still possible for the EU and the UK to come to conflicting views of an agreement. However, again Regulation 1/2003 has lessened the chances of this:

- where the Commission has come to a decision on an agreement, decision or practice under Article 81 (101) or Article 82 (102) the OFT cannot take a decision which runs counter to the Commission's decision;[48]

- similarly, the UK courts cannot hand down a judgment which runs counter to a Commission decision on an agreement, decision or practice under Article 81 (101) or Article 82 (102).[49]

In addition, where the OFT or a UK court wishes to apply national competition law to an agreement which may affect trade between member states (within the meaning of Article 81(1) (101(1))) the OFT or UK court no longer has the choice but now must apply Article 81 (101)). Specifically the OFT or a UK court in applying UK competition law cannot prohibit an agreement which may affect trade between member states:

- where competition is not restricted within the meaning of Article 81(1) (101(1)); or

- which fulfils the conditions of Article 81(3) (101(3)); or

- which is covered by a EC block exemption.[50]

The requirement to achieve consistency[51] is only to be achieved as far as it is possible do so. However, it appears now that only where the OFT (or the

---

47 Eg see Competition Act 1998, s 60, which requires that questions arising under UK competition law are dealt with in a manner that is consistent with EC competition law.
48 Regulation 1/2003 ([2003] OJ L 001/1), Art 16(2).
49 Regulation 1/2003 ([2003] OJ L 001/1), Art 16(1). Where the Commission has initiated proceedings the court cannot make a decision which would run counter to a decision which is contemplated by the Commission.
50 Regulation 1/2003 ([2003] OJ L 001/1), Art 3(2).
51 The relevant wording from Competition Act 1998, s 60 is 'so that questions arising under Part I of the Act in relation to competition within the UK are dealt with in a manner which is consistent with the treatment of corresponding questions arising in Community law in relation to competition within the Community'.

courts) are driven to do so (such as the Act clearly providing differently to EU law) will a different approach be taken under UK competition law to that of EU competition law.[52]

The remaining significant differences are not directly relevant to mainstream issues relating to advising on and drafting agreements concerning technology transfer or intellectual property matters.[53] To illustrate the effect of the changes made in recent years:

- in-house lawyers' advice on competition law issues can be withheld from an OFT investigation on the basis that it is subject to legal professional privilege. Under EU law, in-house lawyers' advice is not privileged and, following the bringing into force of the Modernisation Regulation, would in any case not be available to the OFT where it is acting on a request from the Commission or another member state (under Articles 21 and 22 of the Modernisation Regulation);[54] and

- fines may not exceed 10 per cent of the parties' turnover. The former restriction (before the adoption of the Modernisation Regulation to limit the amount to turnover in the UK is removed.[55]

COMMON LAW RULES ON RESTRAINT OF TRADE

Under the common law, all restrictions contained in contracts are potentially unenforceable if they are in restraint of trade.[56] It should be emphasised at the outset that in practice this doctrine is unlikely to affect most commercial transactions involving technology, such as licences, assignments, distribution agreements and so on, which are freely entered into between commercial parties. Nevertheless, the doctrine should not be entirely overlooked, particularly if unusual or very onerous contract terms are included in the agreement.

---

52 This is the view of Whish in *Competition Law* (6th edn, Oxford University Press, 2009) atp 363 (his comment carries extra weight as he is currently a non-executive director of the OFT). As he notes: 'Where there is some doubt in a particular case, these words [about the Government and the Competition Appeals Tribunal views on this point] indicate that there is a policy preference towards maintaining consistency with EC law'.

53 These are usefully summarised in Whish, n 51, at p 364.

54 Competition Act 1998, s 30.

55 Competition Act 1998, s 36. Calculated in accordance with the Competition Act 1998 (Determination of Turnover for Penalties) Order 2000 (SI 2000/309) (as amended). See also 'Are the effects "appreciable"; is it a "small agreement"?' above concerning the limited availability of immunity from fines. For further information on the OFT's position concerning the imposition of penalties, see *Guidance as to the appropriate amount of a penalty* (OFT423) and in particular where an undertaking has committed an infringement of both Article 81 and Chapter I the undertaking will not be fined twice (see para 1.15).

56 See *Chitty on Contracts* (30th edn, Sweet & Maxwell, 2008), Vol 1 at para 16–075.

The doctrine has been applied in case law dating back as far as the 16th century; it is probably fair to say that there is no single court judgment which states definitively the scope of the doctrine. As Lord Wilberforce commented in one of the leading modern cases:[57]

'... the common law has often ... thrived on ambiguity and it would be mistaken, even if it were possible, to try to crystallise the rules of this or any aspect of public policy into neat propositions. The doctrine of restraint of trade is one to be applied to factual situations with a broad and flexible rule of reason'.

There have been a number of attempts to describe the scope of the doctrine in different situations. It seems the doctrine will affect certain types of contract more frequently than others. For example, there have been many cases concerned with employment contracts where, for example, restrictions on the employee's activities after his or her employment is terminated have been held to be unenforceable for being in restraint of trade. It is generally regarded as difficult to draft such restrictions in employment contracts in such a way as to be confident that they will be upheld by the court.

Rather different approaches have been taken to restrictive terms in, respectively, contracts for the sale of a business (including goodwill),[58] partnership and joint venture agreements, contracts for the supply of goods, and contracts concerning the use of land and other property. There would seem to be no separate version of the doctrine for intellectual property transactions such as licences and assignments, and the lack of case law in this field makes it difficult to draw strong conclusions as to the application of the doctrine to such agreements; the cases concerning sale of goods and use of land and other property probably provide the best guidance.[59] However, the common law doctrine and at least European competition law appear incompatible, as

---

57 *Esso Petroleum Co Ltd v Harper's Garage (Stourport) Ltd* [1968] AC 269.
58 An illustration of the flexibility of the doctrine of restraint of trade is illustrated in *Buchanan v Alba Diagnostics Ltd* [2004] UKHL 5, [2004] SC (HL) 9, [2004] All ER (D) 73 (Feb), where the doctrine of restraint of trade was applied to an assignment of patents (and improvements) as security for a loan to the patent. It was held that a perpetual restraint in an assignment of a patent entitling the assignee to the rights of any improvements in the patent (even those made after the assignment) was valid. Lord Hoffman held it was in the public interest for any of the inventors to be able to borrow money on the security of future rights as well as lenders to protect the value of the patent.
59 A series of cases earlier this century involving leases of shoe manufacturing machinery may provide the closest factual analogy to intellectual property licences. These cases are thought to have led to the introduction of the (now-repealed) Patents Act 1977, s 44, which made unenforceable certain types of 'tying' clause in contracts concerned with patented inventions and patented articles. See eg *United Shoe Machinery Co of Canada v Brunet* [1909] AC 330. However, Chitty (see n 55) comments (at para 16–106) that the reasons given in that case are unsatisfactory. See also the leading case of *Tool Metal Manufacturing Co Ltd v Tungsten Electric Co Ltd* [1955] 1 WLR 761; that case concerned a manufacturing licence under a patent.

in a case involving restraints in a vertical agreement, where it was held that an agreement to which European competition law applies, such as Article 81 (101), could not be subject to the common law of restraint.[60] Recent cases concerned with contracts between musicians and record companies are also of interest.[61]

If a contract term is found unenforceable at common law for restraint of trade, it is likely to have some or all of the following features:

- it restricts the trading activity of one of the parties to the contract, eg in the case of a tying clause which prohibits a party from purchasing goods from a third party;

- it goes further than is necessary to protect a legitimate business interest of the party who benefits from the term, eg in scope, territory or duration;

- it is unreasonable, unfair or oppressive;

- it is against the public interest;

- it is not a term that has gained general commercial acceptance in the past;

- it forms part of a contract entered into between parties of unequal bargaining power.

A full discussion of the doctrine of restraint of trade, including analysis of the many court judgments in which the doctrine has been applied and developed, is beyond the scope of this section. Such a discussion can be found in the specialist texts.[62] The following general observations may be of assistance when considering whether the doctrine applies to a technology-related agreement:

- *Restrictive covenants:* the doctrine is most frequently encountered in relation to restrictive covenants, such as non-compete and non-solicitation clauses, in employment contracts and contracts for the sale of a business. Very broadly speaking, it is more difficult to impose enforceable restrictions on an employee than on the seller of a business, as the courts are reluctant to prevent an individual from earning a living. The case law for employment contracts may also be relevant to some contracts that have similar features to employment contracts,

---

60   *Days Medical Aids Ltd v Pihsiang Machinery Co Ltd* [2004] EWHC 44 (Comm). This case involved the distributorship of mobility scooters. The judgment is long and complex and runs to over 260 paragraphs, but the relevant paragraphs concerning this point are to be found at 258 to 266.

61   Eg the case of *Panayiotou v Sony Music Entertainment (UK) Ltd* [1994] EMLR 229 and other cases, discussed in Copinger and Skone, *James on Copyright* (15th edn, Sweet & Maxwell, 2009) at, Vol 1, para 29–305, p 1754ff.

62   Eg *Chitty on Contracts* (30th edn, Sweet & Maxwell, 2008), Vol 1, Ch 16.

eg a consultancy or agency agreement with an individual. An example of such an agreement would be an agreement between a company and an inventor, under which the latter is contracted to carry out research activities for the former, but is not an employee of the company. The doctrine seems to be less frequently encountered in relation to commercial agreements concerning ongoing trading activities.

- *Contracts involving individuals:* contracts involving individuals may be affected by the doctrine more than contracts where both parties are companies, particularly if the individual has less bargaining power than the company or is not properly advised. See for example the line of cases concerning contracts between young pop stars and their record companies. It should be pointed out, though, that it is rare, under English law, for a contract to be found unenforceable simply because of the unequal bargaining power of the parties.

- *Very unusual or onerous terms:* very unusual or onerous contract terms should be considered with particular care – eg if an exclusive licence agreement is stated to continue for 50 years without the opportunity for earlier termination, this would be highly unusual and might well be unenforceable, depending on the circumstances.

- *Giving up a pre-existing freedom:* restrictions on the exercise of intellectual property rights by a licensee or assignee seem to be regarded as less anti-competitive under domestic English competition laws than under EC laws. An example of such a restriction would be a term preventing a licensee from selling outside his licensed territory. Arguably such a term is not in restraint of trade since the licensee or assignee is not giving up a pre-existing freedom – in the absence of the agreement he would have no rights to use the intellectual property.[63]

In practice, the requirements of the Act and Article 81 (101) are more likely to affect most technology-related agreements than the common law of restraint of trade. Where the terms of an agreement meet the detailed requirements of Article 81 (101), eg by coming within the scope of a block exemption regulation, it is unlikely that they will then be found to be unenforceable under the English common law. It seems that an agreement that operates in restraint of trade only outside the jurisdiction of the English courts may not be in breach of English law.[64]

---

63   This point was addressed, in the context of the Restrictive Trade Practices Act 1976, in *Ravenseft Properties v Director General of Fair Trading* [1977] 1 All ER 47. To take another example, in *Tool Metal Manufacturing Co Ltd v Tungsten Electric Co Ltd*, HL 72 RPC 209 (1955) it was held that an agreement to pay compensation for exceeding an agreed level of production is not void for being in restraint of trade.

64   *Fyffes v Chiquita Brands* [1993] FSR 83, per Vinelott J in interlocutory proceedings relating to a trade mark agreement.

CHAPTER 16

Valuation of Technology and Products

INTRODUCTION

Much has been written on the subject of valuing technology and technology-based products.[1] Typically, articles and books on this topic will describe a number of different theories or techniques for valuation. Some of these techniques provide a method for calculating the value of a high-tech company

---

1   See for example the many articles in *Les Nouvelles*, the Journal of the Licensing Executives Society. See also articles in the *European Intellectual Property Review*, eg Romary, 'Patents for Sale: Evaluating the Value of US Patent Licences' [1995] 8 EIPR 385.

or its technology or product portfolio. The same techniques can also be used to calculate the 'correct' price that should be paid for the grant of rights to develop and exploit a company's technology or product.

At the outset, it should be mentioned that a distinction is often made between 'technology' and technology-based 'products'. In general, it is easier to value a product than an area of technology as the latter may have different fields of application which are more difficult to quantify in terms of market, size etc.

Calculation of value

Many of the valuation techniques use a financial model or algorithm for calculating value, for example those used by financial analysts working in the high-tech sector. Usually, the model depends upon 'net present value' ('NPV') calculations, which are discussed further below. Unfortunately, different valuation models can result in widely differing valuation figures for the same product. Even where a single model or technique is used, it is possible to establish different valuations for the same product. Often the model requires assumptions or predictions to be made as to future market size, market share, cost of production, strength of patents, etc. Different people make different assumptions. Changing each of the assumptions, even by a small amount, can substantially affect the overall valuation.

One reason for these uncertainties in valuation is that technology is often licensed or assigned at a time when its market potential has yet to be realised. Sometimes, parties will agree licensing terms even before the technology has been developed, for example as part of a research collaboration agreement. At such an early stage, it may be very difficult or impossible to predict such matters as the market size and share of an undeveloped product.

Some other methods of calculating the value of a technology, which do not depend on NPV calculations, are discussed later in this chapter.

Going rate or benchmarking

Another approach to valuation and pricing is to look to the going rate for licensing a particular type of technology, based on general experience in the relevant industry. Another term that is sometimes used for this approach is 'benchmarking'. Some writers have prepared tables of so-called standard financial terms, including royalty rates, for particular technologies. Use of such tables may be the best solution available in a particular case, but will not take account of any special facts in that case (eg particularly high or low profit levels for the product in question), which arguably should affect the royalty level. Some published information on royalty rates is included later in this chapter.

Ball-park figures

Sometimes, parties may decide a ball-park total figure for the value of the technology (perhaps, but not necessarily, using a NPV calculation), and then propose different elements – research payments, licence fees, royalties etc – which add up to the ball-park sum.

In the authors' experience, parties do not always engage in detailed analysis when determining the price to be paid for technology, particularly early-stage technology. Instead they may rely on their intuition, and an assessment of what the other party in the negotiations is likely to accept. They may also have ball-park figures in their minds, particularly on possible royalty rates. This is understandable, given the limitations of investment theories in this field. Nevertheless, it is surprising how little preparatory work is sometimes done before setting a price, and equally surprising how large is the initial gap between the expectations of each party as to the financial terms.

Factors affecting valuation and pricing

A large number of factors can affect the price for acquiring rights to technology and products.[2] Some of these factors are discussed further below.[3] They can include matters that are difficult to quantify or put a value on, such as how badly a party wants to do the deal and how effective the licensed intellectual property will be to deter potential infringers.

Despite the presence of these and other variable factors, a number of 'standard' methods for establishing a value have emerged, some of which have already been mentioned. The methods most frequently suggested are the following:

- calculation of value, including NPV calculations;
- going rate/benchmarking;
- 25 per cent rule;
- past court decisions.

Each of these methods will now be discussed in more detail.

---

2   For a list of 15 factors identified by the court in a leading US decision, see *Georgia-Pacific Corporation v United States Plywood Corporation* 318 F Supp 1116 (SDNY 1970), affirmed in principle on appeal 446 F 2d (2nd Cir 1971).
3   See 'Factors affecting valuation and pricing'.

METHODS OF CALCULATING VALUE

The assessment of the value of products or technologies is paramount not only in licensing but also in mergers and acquisitions of businesses, including technology-based businesses. There are a number of approaches to determine such value; however, in general, a truthful absolute figure cannot be obtained, whichever method is used. It will always be an estimation, the accuracy of which depends largely on the data available, which in turn depends on the product/technology itself and on the stage of development. There are two main methods of calculation, which are fundamentally different from one another: calculations based on costs, and calculations based on projected income.

Calculations based on costs

Calculations can be based on either:

- the costs that have been incurred to date to develop the product or technology; or

- the replacement cost, which takes into account any increase/decrease in cost that would be incurred if the product or technology was developed today.

The cost incurred in developing a technology often does not reflect the present or future value of the technology. For example, the development could be very expensive in relation to future income from sales, but the contrary could also apply. In addition, the costs are to some extent subjective when replacement costs are concerned; for example, a different company could theoretically develop the product or technology at lower cost or in less time. Therefore costs may not be a realistic assessment of future value. Nevertheless, this is a method that is sometimes used.

Calculations based on net present value

Calculation based on income from future sales is a commonly used method to evaluate the present value of a product or technology. This can be the most complex of the standard methods for determining value but it may also lead to the most equitable result. The term 'net present value' is a shorthand expression for a valuation method that makes use of NPV calculations. These are based on the concept that payment of a sum today is always worth more to the recipient than payment of the same sum to the recipient at a future date. If paid today, the sum can increase, for example by paying it into an interest-bearing bank account. By performing certain calculations (including making assumptions on appropriate interest rates) it is possible to work out the present value of a future sum.

The following paragraph aims is intended to provide an introduction to the subject for non-specialist readers (together with two examples).

Greatly simplified example

A very simple example of a net present value calculation follows:

Assumptions that the available interest rate is 5% per annum. Thus, if £100 is banked, it will earn £5 in one year, making a total after one year of £105. In other words the present value of £105 payable in one year's time is £100. Equally, the present value of £100 payable in one year's time is £95.24 (£95.24 × 1.05 = £100).

The discount factor, to convert a sum due in one year's time to its NPV, is therefore 0.9524. Multiply the sum due in one year's time by this figure and you arrive at the present value.

If a sum is due in two years' time, the calculation is slightly more complicated: £100 invested today will be worth £105 in one year (£100 × 1.05), and £110.25 in two years (£105 × 1.05), assuming interest rates remain constant and assuming annual compound interest. The initial £100 will have increased to 1.1025 times its original value.

The present value of £110.25 due in two years' time is therefore £100.00. Equally, the present value of £100 due in two years' time is £90.70 (£90.70 × 1.1025 = £100.00).

The discount factor is the amount by which future sums must be multiplied to arrive at the present value. In arithmetical terms, the discount factor may be calculated as follows:

$$DF = 1/(1 + IR)^n$$

where DF is the discount factor; IR is the annual interest rate expressed as a fraction (ie in the present case 0.05); and n is the number of years until the sum is due.

Thus, for the next five years, if interest rates remained at 5%, the discount factors for each year would be:

Year 1	0.9524
Year 2	0.9070
Year 3	0.8639
Year 4	0.8227
Year 5	0.7835

To calculate the present value of a stream of royalties, on the assumption in a particular case that: (i) there will be sales of licensed products for a period of five years; (ii) royalties of £10,000 per year will be earned at the end of the first year; and (iii) the royalties will increase each year by £2,000 as the business becomes more successful. Consequently the sale of licensed products will generate (a total of £70,000 in royalties over the five-year period). Assuming a constant interest rate of 5% per annum as above, the present value of this royalty stream will be:

$$
\begin{array}{rcl}
0.9524 \times £10,000 & = & £9,524.00 \\
+\ 0.9070 \times £12,000 & = & £10,844.00 \\
+\ 0.8639 \times £14,000 & = & £12,094.60 \\
+\ 0.8227 \times £16,000 & = & £13,163.20 \\
+\ 0.7835 \times £18,000 & = & £14,103.00 \\
\text{PRESENT VALUE} & = & £59,728.80
\end{array}
$$

It can be seen that the present value figure is considerably less than the total amount of royalties payable, ie £70,000. In practice, a person would not only calculate the royalty stream of a product but would also calculate the net present value of the whole project. This is the difference between the present value of projected revenues (eg up-front payments as well as royalties) and the present value of costs (including capital investment, operating costs, etc as well as any payments to be made to third parties, eg under other licences).

Discount rate

A further complication when calculating a NPV, not referred to in the above example, is deciding on an appropriate rate of interest at which to discount the cash flows, ie the discount rate. Selecting the appropriate discount rate is an important factor. High-tech projects are usually regarded as high risk, and therefore investors will expect a higher rate of return than bank interest rates. The discount rate will usually reflect the higher level of risk and may take account of both the company's cost of debt (ie the interest rate it is charged on borrowings) and its cost of capital (ie the rate of return that investors expect from investing in the company).[4]

The calculation of the discount rate is a complicated process, which is often carried out by specialist groups and cannot be explained here in further detail.[5] For illustration of the range of percentages, discount rates of 11 per cent[6] and 30 per cent[7] have been used for biotech companies in analyst reports.

4   The combination of these costs is known as the company's weighted average cost of capital (WACC).
5   For further reading, see Pratt and Grabowski, *Cost of Capital* (3rd edn, John Wiley & Sons Inc, 2008).
6   Altium Capital, *Sector Review*, January 2002.
7   Credit Suisse First Boston, *Xenova*, November 2001.

More detailed description of NPV calculations – biotechnology industry

The following paragraphs provide a description of how a biotechnology product or technology might be valued. Although more detailed than the greatly simplified example given above, the following description is still in a simplified form.

For the calculation of the NPV of a product or a technology, a number of inputs need inclusion, which are further detailed below. However, in many cases, data for these inputs are not available and assumptions have to be made, in particular where technologies or products at an early stage of development are the subject of the valuation. For example, as the properties and benefits of a product are not finally established, the ultimate population which is targeted to use the product cannot be defined. Similarly, the cost of the product or technology at a commercial scale of production will often be different from the cost of production at a small scale for development purposes.

In contrast, it is easier to value products that are developed into a marketable form and therefore are closer to market, although assumptions would also have to be made, albeit with greater confidence.

Probability of successful development to market

A further critical factor, especially in the valuation of pharmaceutical products, is the probability factor, which is dependent on the stage of development of a product. Each stage of development has a specific attrition rate, which reflects the risk of failure or, in other words, the probability of success intrinsic to that stage. The attrition rates of the current and all future stages of development are multiplied to give the probability of success of the product considered. This implies that a product close to market has a higher probability of success compared to an early-stage product. Attrition rates for pharmaceutical products are based on historically determined rates of success for the various stages of the clinical trials process.

In practice, a probability factor relevant to the stage is applied to each cost or revenue in a NPV calculation. For example, a milestone payment, due when a product enters Phase III of development, will have a probability factor which is the product of the probabilities of Phase III and regulatory submission.

Example of NPV calculation in biotech industry

The following is a simplified illustration of a calculation of a NPV (excluding a probability weighting), with the following assumptions:

- Product A is licensed today, and today is the beginning of year one.

- Royalty payments to the licensor are 18 per cent of sales price.

- Launch is expected in two years.

- The patent expires seven years from launch, and no sales are made thereafter.

- Peak sales (at maximum penetration rate) are reached four years from launch and build up in a linear fashion.

- The target population which would buy Product A is theoretically 100,000 in every year.

- There are two other competing products which take up 60 per cent of the total market share, which gives a penetration rate of 40 per cent for Product A.

- The product has a fixed price of £50.

The first step in a NPV calculation is the calculation of present and future annual cash flows, such as for example revenues from sales. The calculation of such revenue requires first the calculation of total sales, which are calculated by multiplying the price of the product or technology with the target population. A proportion of these total sales will represent the revenues and this proportion depends on which route to market is taken, where principally three options exist: direct sales, joint ventures with shared profits, or licence with royalty obligations. The annual cash flow of revenues, which are in the example a licence with royalties, can then be calculated in a simple spreadsheet as illustrated in Table 1:

Table 1

Year (all figures in UK £)		1	2	3	4	5	6	7	8	9	10
Target population		100,000	100,000	100,000	100,000	100,000	100,000	100,000	100,000	100,000	100,000
Price of product		50	50	50	50	50	50	50	50	50	50
Penetration rate	40%			10%	20%	30%	40%	40%	40%	40%	40%
Total sales				500,000	1,000,000	1,500,000	2,000,000	2,000,000	2,000,000	2,000,000	
Royalties	18%			90,000	180,000	270,000	360,000	360,000	360,000	360,000	0
Cash flow of revenue from sales for licensor				90,000	180,000	270,000	360,000	360,000	360,000	360,000	0
Discount rate	12%										
Discount factor		0.89286	0.79719	0.71178	0.63552	0.56743	0.50663	0.45235	0.40388	0.36061	0.32197
Discounted cash flow of revenue from sales for licensor		0	0	64,060	114,393	153,205	182,387	162,846	145,398	129,820	0
NPV of revenue from sales for licensor	952,109										

The second step in a NPV calculation is applying a discount factor to the annual cash flow, whereby the discount factor for each year is calculated by the following formula:

$$\text{Present value} = \frac{CF_n}{(1+r)^n}$$

where: CF = Cash flow
n = period (year)
r = discount rate)

Assuming the Present Value = 1, the number of periods is 10, and the discount rate is 12 per cent, it is possible to calculate the following discount factors for each of the ten years:

Year	Discount factor (12% discount rate)
1	0.892857
2	0.797194
3	0.711780
4	0.635518
5	0.567427
6	0.506631
7	0.452349
8	0.403883
9	0.360610
10	0.321973

Applying the calculated discount factors to the annual cash flows, in the example revenues from sales, discounted cash flows are obtained.

Finally, the NPV is obtained by adding up the values of all periods considered. In the example in Table 1, the NPV for revenue from sales would be £952,109 for the licensor (for reasons of keeping the example simple, neither financial terms of the licence agreement nor any costs are included).

Input data for the NPV calculation

It is possible to calculate the NPVs in a very simple manner, or in a more sophisticated model, depending on the accuracy required, the availability of data, the complexity of the commercialisation of the product/technology and on the degree of flexibility which would be necessary to assess different scenarios of commercialisation.

Regardless of the simplicity of the model, it is possible to base NPV calculations on a specific market or on specific population data. If a market is well defined by existing products, historic data can be used, for example sales figures or prescriptions. New products or technologies are more difficult to forecast, and here a population-based market calculation can be used, built up from a particular population such as a specific age group, patients, or end users in general.

In a more refined model, a growth or decline factor can be applied to the population over time, and also another factor, which narrows a population down further to a more realistic sub-population, for example only patients with early-stage disease or a population with a certain income. With both factors, a target population can be estimated, which is necessary to calculate the total sales and cost of goods.

Using NPV calculations to help decide on the best deal structure

An important consideration, particularly for a small company, is to have options for selecting the route to market as mentioned earlier (direct sales, licence arrangements or joint ventures with profit share). As cash flows of cost and expenses vary between each route to market, it is therefore important to select the most appropriate one for the company concerned. Alternatively, different scenarios could be evaluated, such as the route to market which would identify the most profitable or rewarding, and also the most or least expensive, route. For that reason it would make sense to split the NPV calculation into costs and revenues, possibly also into pre- and post-launch costs and revenues. By doing so, cash flows will become more apparent and it would be easier to influence them by modifying certain inputs such as the route to market, which could be helpful in the short- and longer-term financial strategy of a company. For instance, where a company may not have the funds or infrastructure to sell a product directly, or needs a cash injection to survive until other revenues start to happen, an NPV model can help in laying out alternative options whilst retaining a comparable NPV of the product.

- *Pre-launch costs:* these consist typically of R&D costs, which can be split into internal costs and external costs, for example costs to contractors. Pre-launch costs can also include payments to third parties either for licensing of the product/technology in the first place or for licensing additional IP to protect the product or technology. These third-party payments can include a licence fee and milestone payments upon achievement of specified development milestones. If a joint-venture-type arrangement is selected, R&D costs and third party payments would have to be proportioned according to the anticipated profit share.

- *Pre-launch revenues:* these are normally not anticipated prior to launch, except when the product is licensed, where in most cases an up-front payment and development milestones are paid by the licensee. Up-

745

front payments can be in the form of an option fee, an option extension fee, a licence fee or a deferred licence fee, either as a cash or equity component or a mixture of both. In addition, in a licence arrangement, further revenues could be realised in some cases in the form of payments towards the R&D costs, or even total funding.

- *Post-launch costs:* these include, in the case of direct sales or a joint-venture-type arrangement, the cost of goods (COGs), launch costs and sales and marketing costs, whereby in the joint venture costs would have to be proportioned as described under pre-launch costs. In a licence arrangement, cost of goods, launch costs and sales and marketing costs are borne by the licensee and therefore would not be calculated. Sales and marketing costs are often assumed to be a certain percentage of sales, except for products that are close to market and where more accurately estimated forecasts will be available. 'Cost of goods' is calculated by multiplying the production cost per unit by the number of applications per individual of the target population. Irrespective of the route to market, any third party payments would have to be indicated here, whether they are royalty rates from sales or a percentage of the licensor's net income or in-market milestones. Tax on net income would be another parameter to consider.

- *Post-launch revenues:* for these, a factor for a certain market share is added in practice, which is defined as the maximum market penetration and which value largely depends on the number of competing products or alternative approaches intended for the same target population and their combined share of the market. Maximum sales are reached typically after a number of years of sales, which is achieved in the calculation by increasing the market penetration factor in a linear mode or any other type of curve over the period from launch of product to peak sales, which, by definition, have the maximum penetration rate. For example, the time to peak sales is generally assumed to be five to six years for pharmaceutical products. It is important that assumptions about the price are carefully made, giving consideration to factors such as the acceptance of a particular price by end-users, competition in the market and, in the case of pharmaceutical products, reimbursement practices in the respective territories of sale. Further post-launch revenues include in-market milestones, which might be paid by a licensee to the licensor once specified annual sales levels are reached.

An essential input, for both post-launch costs and post-launch revenues, is the year in which the patent for a product or technology expires. It is possible to make assumptions as to whether sales reduce to zero, or whether residual sales remain and decline over time as generic products take up some market share. As patents are granted on a territorial basis, it would make sense to include options for different territories in the NPV calculation, particularly when patents expire on different dates in different territories. Again, the case for having the NPV calculations performed on a territorial basis has the advantage that it is possible to assume different prices for different territories, which might be necessary due to differences in the market configuration and dynamics. Similarly, it might be necessary to take into account differences in sales and marketing costs and target population, for example age structure.

GOING RATE/BENCHMARKING

Value assessment by benchmarking

In contrast to calculating a value, benchmarking is comparing a product or technology with similar products or technologies which already exist and where a value has been assigned and is 'accepted', eg verified by a published licence agreement. However, this approach is not as straightforward as it seems. It might often be quite difficult to identify similar products, which are comparable in stage of development, which have a comparable field and frequency of application, similar cost of goods and similar costs of sales and marketing, IP protection etc. Even if there are comparable products, data might not be available. Another complicating factor is that technology-related agreements often include several financial elements as well as royalties, including lump-sum payments, milestone payments, minimum royalties, payments for research work, and even the issue of shares by one of the parties to the other party. This can make it very difficult to compare past transactions to the one under review, even where the past agreements are in the same area of technology.

Moreover, it is rare for public announcements on technology deals to mention all the financial elements of the transaction. For example, press releases on such transactions often mention up-front payments but not royalty rates. Companies that are listed on US stock exchanges will generally need to file copies of agreements that are 'material' to their business with the Securities and Exchange Commission, and those copies are publicly available. However, the financial details of such agreements tend to be redacted (ie deleted) with the consent of the SEC in the publicly available version.

If sufficient data are available, benchmarking can be a useful tool in licensing negotiations, to justify for example up-front and milestone payments or certain royalty rates, or to support assumptions in an NPV model. Whether a NPV calculation, benchmarking, or a combination of both is used, is in the end a matter of judgement on the individual technology or product concerned.

Headline figures

When companies disclose financial details of product or technology licences, frequently so-called headline values are given. Again, these figures need careful evaluation as they may include every theoretically possible payment by the licensor, which may be a very ambitious judgement of the success of a technology or product. In comparing technology alliances, attention should also be paid to the overall timeframe of the alliance, which is correlated to the overall headline value. In most cases royalty rates are not published, whereas up-front payments are more readily available and on some occasions also development milestones and R&D funding.

Use of benchmarking in determining royalties

Royalty rates (as distinct from up-front and milestone payments) are often not disclosed in public announcements of the headline value of technology deals. Nevertheless, some going rates have emerged and are commonly used as a reference point when negotiating the terms of licence agreements.

A typical licensing deal may include other financial elements as well as a royalty, so that using the going rate method for royalties only really makes sense if the other financial components of the deal, eg up-front payments, are comparable.

A number of writers have made following suggestions on typical royalty rates.[8] Except where otherwise stated, these rates are based on the sales price of the licensed product.

Pharmaceuticals/biotechnology

'In general, life sciences products, and in particular pharmaceuticals, once they are proven or once well on the way to being so, are able to secure a much higher royalty than is available in other industries as the gross margins that are available on a successful product are so large that they will support a substantial royalty.'[9]

'The average fixed rate for preclinical products was 4.3%, with the average rates for biological products being slightly higher than small molecules. The ranges of tiered rates by stage of development were 5–8% for preclinical, 7–10% for pre-proof of concept and 14–18% for post-proof of concept.'[10]

---

8 Most of these suggestions have appeared in articles in *Les Nouvelles*, the journal of the Licensing Executives Society, on the dates indicated in later footnotes. Other sources include analyses of filings with the US Securities and Exchange Commission (www.sec.gov), and commercial providers such as www.royaltysource.com, www.royaltystat.com and Morningstar Document Research (www.10kwizard.com). A major annual publication is Battersby and Grimes, *Licensing Royalty Rates* (Aspen Publishers).

9 Cook, *Pharmaceuticals, Biotechnology and the Law* (2nd edn, LexisNexis, 2009) 55.

10 As above, at 56, drawing on a survey carried out by the Licensing Executives Society (USA and Canada) of over 150 deals in 2006 and 2007.

'In a typical alliance for development of a drug with significant preclinical data, royalties will range between 8% and 12% [of the sales price], with an outside range of 5% to 15%.'[11]

'[One pharmaceutical industry] respondent indicated that his or her company typically pays 0–2% royalties for process, formulation or software technology, 2–5% for preclinical compounds, 5–10% for early-stage clinical compounds, and 10–15% for late-stage clinical compounds.'[12]

'The average royalty rates on sales by R&D stage at signing of agreements were reported by Mark G. Edwards of Recombinant Capital at the 1995 LES (USA and Canada) Annual Meeting in Orlando. These figures are averaged rates of many deals and are shown [below].'[13]

R&D stage	Biotech company to university	Major pharmaceutical company to biotech company
Discovery	3%	7%
Lead molecule	4–5%	9%
Pre-clinical	6–7%	10%
Phase II–III clinical	–	15%

McKinsey and Medius associates have reported the following average up-front and milestone payments and royalty percentages (monetary values are $M).[14] The 'improved' average figures are those suggested by McKinsey as what would be expected if the deal terms generate a high enough rate of return. The Medius numbers are based on a larger survey of 68 pharmaceutical companies.

Development Phase	Up-front current	Up-front improved	McKinsey Milestones current	McKinsey Milestones improved	Royalty % current	Royalty % improved	Medius Royalty % low	Medius Royalty % high
Preclinical	2	5	15	37	7	17	0	5
Phase I	5	10	25	50	10	20	5	10
Phase II	10	12	35	42	20	25	8	15
Phase III	15	15	50	50	25	25	10	20

11 Clark and Sharron, 'State of the Art in Biotechnology Alliances', *Les Nouvelles*, June 1994.
12 Reported by McGavock and others in 'Factors Affecting Royalty Rates', *Les Nouvelles*, June 1992, an interesting survey of licensing professionals across a range of industries.
13 Yamasaki, *Les Nouvelles*, September 1996.
14 Jousma, 'Considering Pharmaceutical Royalties', *Les Nouvelles*, June 2005, 65–77, at 73.

A survey of publicly available royalty rates in the period from 1984 to 2006 produced the following results. The authors of the survey also found a gradual increase over that period.[15]

Industry		95% Confidence interval			
	Number of observations	Average royalty rate	(+)/(−)	Lower bound	Upper bound
Medical device	77	4.35%	0.64%	3.71%	5.00%
Pharmaceutical	90	5.66%	0.91%	4.75%	6.57%
Chemical	21	3.70%	0.88%	2.82%	4.57%

Chemical industry

'Dr Khoury, with the help of Arthur D Little, developed the value grid for the chemical industry [shown below].'[16]

Economic impact	Process	Product	Application/composition of matter
Compact	0.1%–1%	1–2%	1–3%
Speciality	1–3%	2–5%	3–7%
High performance	3–5%	5–7%	7–10%

Computer industry

'[In the computer hardware industry] the percentage rate is the most difficult to obtain. Nevertheless there is virtually unanimous agreement that this figure is found between 1% and 5% [of the price of the licensee's manufactured unit].'[17]

'After two years of experimentation … licensing experience with actual licensed software, and price comparisons with market products, it was found empirically that taking 5% of the modified replacement cost yielded a reasonable first estimate of a nonexclusive selling price … It is a one-time purchase price for a single user, nonexclusive, executable code, license, with no right to sublicense.'[18]

15   Porter, Mills and Weinstein, 'Industry Norms and Reasonable Royalty Rate Determination', *Les Nouvelles*, March 2008, 47–64, at 50.
16   Presentation at LES Annual Meeting 1998, reported by Khoury, Daniele and Germeraad in *Les Nouvelles*, September 2001.
17   Sullivan, *Les Nouvelles*, September 1994.
18   Betton, *Les Nouvelles*, September 1999.

Miscellaneous manufacturing

'A 5% royalty level is commonplace for many manufactured products.'[19]

'Typical percentage royalties based on ex-factory price:'[20]

Type of product	Volume	Margin	Royalties
General consumer	High	Low	0.5–4%
Specialist consumer/general industrial	Medium	Medium	4–10%
Specialist industrial	Low	High	10–15%

'[In typical franchising agreements] the price paid by the franchisee is principally by a royalty equal to 5% of the turnover tax free ... [Some] franchising agreements of computer equipment [include] a royalty that is equal to about 8% of the turnover tax free. In license agreements between [organisations] of similar technical standard and the purpose of which is the manufacturing of measuring apparatus ... protected by a few patents and a little know-how, the royalties are close to 5% of the tax free selling price of the apparatus.'[21]

Industries generally

The following royalty rates have been stated to have been 'published as industry averages' in the US.[22] These figures are for a non-exclusive licence. The author of the article in which these figures appeared quotes other authors who suggest an average 20–50 per cent premium for an exclusive licence, and in the case of the pharmaceutical field up to a 300 per cent premium for exclusivity:

Overall average	5–6%	(1984)
	3–10%	(1988)
	3–5%	(1979)
	3–5.9%	(1993)
	5%	(1975)
Chemical	2–5%	(1984)
	2–5%	(1975)
	1–3%	(1991)
Petroleum	1%	(1975)
Wood products equipment	4–5%	(1975)

19 Erlich (Chief Patent Adviser, US Air Force), *Les Nouvelles*, June 1994.
20 Comerford, *How to Find and License New Products* (Gower Publishing Company, 1990).
21 Collette, 'Assessing Technology Values', *Les Nouvelles*, June 1989.
22 See Romary, 'Patents for Sale: Evaluating the Value of US Patent Licences' [1995] 8 EIPR 385. This article quotes the sources of these suggested rates, mostly from US books and articles published between 1975 and 1993.

Folding cartons	1–1.5%	(1975)
Electronics	<1%	(1984)
	5%	(1975)
Computers	3–5%	(1984)
	3–5%	(1991)
Semiconductors	1.75–3%	(1991)
Automobiles	5%	(1975)
Consumer products	2%	(1975)
Pharmaceuticals	8–15%	(1991)
	4–7%	(1984)

Another source gives the following figures, for the period from the late 1980s to 2000:[23]

Industry	No of licensees	Minimum royalty rate	Maximum royalty rate	Median royalty rate
Automotive	35	1.0%	15.0%	4.0%
Chemicals	72	0.5%	25.0%	3.6%
Computers	68	0.2%	15.0%	4.0%
Consumer goods	90	0.0%	17.0%	5.0%
Electronics	132	0.5%	15.0%	4.0%
Energy and environment	86	0.5%	20.0%	5.0%
Food	32	0.3%	7.0%	2.8%
Healthcare products	280	0.1%	77.0%	4.8%
Internet	47	0.3%	40.0%	7.5%
Machine/Tools	84	0.5%	25.0%	4.5%
Media and entertainment	19	2.0%	50.0%	8.0%
Pharma and biotech	328	0.1%	40.0%	5.1%
Semiconductors	78	0.0%	30.0%	3.2%
Software	119	0.0%	70.0%	6.8%
Telecom	63	0.4%	25.0%	4.7%
Total	1,533	0.0%	77.0%	[4.5% median]

Given the wide variation in these 'average' figures, and the lack of specific detail as to the transactions to which they relate, they may be of limited value when determining the 'correct' royalty rate for a particular transaction. Ultimately, as one writer has commented, 'when all is said and done, the evaluation of intangible intellectual property rights such as patent rights is for the most part a seat-of-the-pants, non-scientific undertaking'.[24] It is hoped that readers of this book will find it helpful to have these figures, for all their limitations, collated and included in this chapter.

---

23 Goldscheider, Jarosz and Mulhern, 'Use of the 25 Per Cent Rule in Valuing IP', *Les Nouvelles*, December 2002, 123–33, at 128.
24 Evans, 'Turning Patents and Technology into Money', *First Annual Licensing Law and Business Institute*, E-5 (1979), quoted in Romary's article cited above, n 22.

FACTORS THAT MAY AFFECT VALUATION

Occasionally, a licence can also include valuable components to which it is not possible to assign a defined value but which can influence the figures of any other component of a licence agreement. Frequently, equity payments are included in a product or technology licence, where the value is defined only at the moment of the transaction, but which may change drastically over time. In addition, components of a licence could also have been negotiated to accommodate the specific, sometimes desperate, needs of the licensor or licensee and reasons could include:

For the licensee:

- need for up-front cash to reduce the cash burn;

- freeing up resources for further development of other products;

- lack of expertise and know-how if the technology/product in question has spun off from other technologies or products;

- benefit from the development expertise of licensor;

- reduction of development cost in favour of other products;

- avoidance of patent litigation if the licensee could potentially block the commercialisation of the product or technology.

For the licensor:

- fill in gaps in the product pipeline;

- access technology rather than building expertise in-house;

- expansion into new areas;

- gain earlier access to market compared with in-house developed products;

- build or strengthen a franchise in a particular territory;

- total amount available for licensing a technology or product.

Obviously the product or technology itself is crucial for the overall value of a licence. Aspects that may be relevant to a particular product or technology include: patent life, arising benefits from applying the product or technology, proof of concept or proof of efficacy, cost of production, ease of use, and timing.

For example, with respect to pharmaceutical products, the optimal timing for a licence is considered to be the point when efficacy data have been obtained, these normally being available at the end of Phase II clinical trial. Here, the risk is considerably reduced compared with earlier stages of the development process, and the majority of costs are yet to be incurred, namely in Phase III. Furthermore, the value of a licence could be driven by the market needs, particularly where no product or technology is available at all or only in an inadequate form. Finally, the general perception of the product or technology, which often depends on publicity campaigns, can affect the value by making the product or technology desirable or fashionable.

Other factors include:

- how badly each party wants to do the deal;

- how well-proven is the technology; how new is the technology; the anticipated life of the technology; and how great a contribution the technology makes to improving the product;

- how much capital investment is required to make use of the technology;

- to what extent the licensor will assist the licensee to make use of the technology;

- how profitable the sale of products which make use of the technology will be, and volume of sales; and to what extent the technology increases those profits/volume;

- how strong any patents or other intellectual property owned by the licensor in relation to the technology are, and whether either party has the resources to enforce these rights, by litigation or otherwise;

- to what extent third parties own rights which may impede the use of the technology;

- whether the licensed products can be sold through existing outlets or as part of an existing product range, or if a new sales network will be required;

- the nature of the right granted, including the degree of exclusivity, territory, field; likelihood of improvements and whether these are covered by the agreement;

- the cost and timescale for acquiring or developing alternative technologies which do not infringe the licensor's intellectual property.

25 per cent rule

This method of pricing or valuation is also known as the 'profits available' method. It is sometimes regarded as appropriate that a licensor should receive around 25 per cent (or, some would say, 25–33 per cent) of the profit achieved by the licensee from use of the licensed technology. Thus if the licensee makes a 20 per cent profit from the sale of licensed products, the 25 per cent rule would result in a 5 per cent royalty. This is indeed a typical figure: the survey across 15 industries mentioned below found a median royalty rate of 4.5 per cent,[25] and another recent survey across 23 industries found that 'the most frequently negotiated royalty rate is 5 per cent of net sales'.[26] Commonly, this method is used as a method of calculating a fixed percentage royalty which will be specified in the licence agreement. Clearly, it is necessary to calculate what those profit levels are likely to be, and this may be far from easy. It may involve carrying out some of the steps referred to above under the heading 'net present value'.

It is less common for profit-sharing mechanisms to be included in the licence agreement itself, although this does sometimes happen (for example, it has become fashionable recently in collaborative agreements in the biotechnology sector). The difficulty with profit-sharing provisions it is possible to manipulate profit figures, no matter how detailed the contractual term. It is less easy to manipulate a sales price, although this is sometimes encountered (eg if several products are sold as a package).

The 25 per cent rule may be a relatively crude method of calculating royalties, particularly where the licensed product is not yet on the market and it may be difficult to assess what the licensee's profits will be. There is criticism that the 25 per cent rule fails to take account of the cash flow needs of the licensee.[27] Nevertheless, it would seem to be commonly used by licensing managers as a guide when calculating royalty levels. A recent survey across 15 industries found that median royalty rate as percentage of average licensee operating profit margins was 26.7 per cent.[28] One suggested rationale for the rule is that, of the four stages in bringing a new product to market (developing the technology, making the product manufacturable, manufacturing it, and selling it), the licensor is typically responsible only for the first.

Of course, it is possible to adjust the percentage to the parties' relative contributions to the development of the product in question. Concerning pharmaceuticals, the following percentages are suggested as appropriate: 25 per cent has been suggested as appropriate for a start-of-Phase I deal; 33 per cent for a deal at the start of Phase II; 40 per cent for the start of Phase III; and 50 per cent for a deal at the end of the clinical development process; profit distributions for this last stage have been reported as ranging from 40 to 70 per cent.[29]

A variation on the 25 per cent rule is sometimes used in licences where sub-

---

25   See p 132 of the article by Goldscheider, Jarosz and Mulhern cited above, n 23.
26   Parr, 'Royalty Rates and License Fees for Technology', *Les Nouvelles*, March 2009, 15–17, at 15.
27   See, for example, Parr's article in *Managing Intellectual Property*, April 1991, and his books in this area, including *Valuation of Intellectual Property and Intangible Assets*, (3rd edn, John Wiley and Sons Inc, 2004).
28   See p 133 of the article by Goldscheider, Jarosz and Mulhern cited above, n 23.
29   See p 73 of the article by Jousma cited above, n 14, based on research published by Finch, 'Royalty Rates: Current Issues and Trends', 7 *Journal of Commercial Biotechnology* (2001).

licensing is permitted. In such cases, the parties may wish to base the licensee's royalty payments to the licensor on the amount the licensee receives from his sub-licensee, rather than the ultimate selling price of the licensed products, over which the licensee will generally have no control. Other factors may also be relevant, eg the value the licensee has added to the technology, but parties not infrequently agree that the licensee will pay the licensor 20–30 per cent of the amount the licensee receives from his sub-licensee.

Past court decisions

Past court decisions provide some guidance on royalty rates, but they need to be treated with caution. It is relatively rare, at least in the UK, for a court to be asked to fix a royalty level in a freely negotiated licence agreement. The decisions in this area tend to have arisen in very specific situations, such as when applying compulsory licensing laws. For example, in the UK there are cases where a court has had to fix a royalty for use of inventions claimed in pharmaceutical patents, under 'licence of right' provisions in UK patent law. Looking at these decisions, one might imagine that a standard royalty for a licence under such a patent would be as high as 35–45 per cent of the sales price of the patented product. Yet fixing the royalty at such levels has arisen in situations where the patent owner has already brought a product successfully to the market and incurred very significant development costs. Many pharmaceutical patent licences are negotiated at an earlier stage than this, or in different circumstances, and the level of royalties is generally much lower.

Nevertheless, court decisions do provide some guidance on the methods used by the courts to calculate royalty levels, and these methods may be applicable in other situations.

Summaries of reported US decisions on royalty rates are available in a regularly updated US publication.[30]

---

30   Chisum, *Chisum on Patents* (LexisNexis), section 20.03[3][d], cited in McGavock et al, 'Determining Reasonable Royalty Rate', *Les Nouvelles*, June 1992, 107).

CHAPTER 17

Taxation Aspects

A: OVERVIEW

Introduction

Taking account of tax issues in technology-related transactions

'Nothing is certain in this world except death and taxes.' (Benjamin Franklin, inventor of the lightning conductor.)

Most legal issues affecting technology-related transactions can be briefly summarised in simple terms for the busy business manager or contract negotiator, but this is not realistic with tax. One reason for this is the complexity of the UK tax system. A basic level of knowledge of the entire system is necessary simply to understand specialist tax advice. Another reason is that the tax treatment of a transaction may depend on a large number of different factors, including the current tax status of both parties and their other business activities; and these factors may make it difficult to give instant advice.

The general problem – that tax legislation is too complex in its structure and content – is recognised by the UK government. Specific measures to end anomalies and simplify the system have been a consistent feature of recent Budgets and ensuing Finance Acts. In 1995 the Chancellor of the Exchequer announced a five-year plan 'to simplify tax legislation for the benefit of business and taxpayers generally',[1] but despite reforms the basic problem remains.[2]

Indeed, one 'side-effect' of the reforms (especially the Tax Law Rewrite Project) has been to 'write-off' much day-to-day working knowledge of experienced accountants and tax practitioners. As a result they now have to spend hours tracking down previously familiar legislation to new destinations[3]

---

1   See Budget Press Release, REV 3, of 28 November 1995 following the Chancellor's Budget Statement and the Inland Revenue's Report, *The Path to Tax Simplification*, December 1995, which reviewed the scope for simplifying the UK tax system. This report, which launched the Tax Law Rewrite Project, concluded '... that the language of existing tax law can be simplified; that the benefits should substantially outweigh the costs; and that a rewrite of most of the existing tax code could be accomplished over a period of five years'.

2   The Tax Law Rewrite Project, introduced in Parliament on 10 January 2001, has produced results, and primary tax legislation has been simplified; but even the simplifications cannot be described as 'user friendly' to the layman. Furthermore, the sheer volume of new tax legislation which accompanies almost every Budget proposal (there have been over 9,000 pages of new tax legislation since *Technology: the Law of Exploitation and Transfer* was published in 1996, including 2,000 pages since the last update) means that even tax practitioners have lobbied the Government to simplify the system for their own benefit – the opposite of what the cynical layman would predict. Details on the Tax Law Rewrite Project can be found at http://www.hmrc.gov.uk/rewrite/.

3   In the Capital Allowances Act 2001 ('CAA 2001'), Income Tax (Earnings and Pensions) Act 2003 ('ITEPA 2003'), Income Tax (Trading and Other Income) Act 2005 ('ITTOIA 2005'), Income Tax Act 2007 ('ITA 2007') and Corporation Tax Act 2009 ('CTA 2009') et al.

and then laboriously compare the new wording with the previous wording to see if the 'rewrite' has made any change of substance. One particular area where this has caused difficulties is deduction of tax at source from royalties (see section H under 'Payments for intellectual property rights' below). At a time when consumer legislation requires contracts to be drafted in 'clear, intelligible language',[4] and when lawyers are rightly encouraged to write in modern English and avoid jargon,[5] the structure and language of tax legislation are anything but 'user friendly'. The latest initiative to combat this problem, in the Finance Act 2009, is to provide simple 'Explanatory Notes' – but the notes themselves are 422 pages long!

Despite recent reforms, the tax treatment of intellectual property transactions can be complex. Furthermore, the best tax structure for an agreement, ie the structure which makes the most 'tax sense', may not produce the best 'bottom-line' commercial result; but the commercial negotiator cannot know this without some understanding of the tax issues.

A valuable skill for business managers, charity administrators and contract negotiators is knowing when to seek professional tax advice. Many transactions do not justify seeking expensive tax advice, as the amount of tax at stake is too small to cover the costs and risks involved. Yet, even in relatively small transactions, tax planning can be cost effective if it reduces management time spent on tracking down and trying to understand the rules and, at a later date, tax compliance costs (and, possibly, interest and penalties). Furthermore, there are special tax incentives for expenditure on R&D which may not be available for grant-aided projects (see section E under 'Special relief for R&D income expenditure – small and medium-sized companies' below). This means that in any R&D project or agreement tax is a factor which needs to be taken into account at the outset to ensure that valuable reliefs (which affect the 'bottom line' of a transaction) can be obtained.

Aims of this chapter

This chapter aims to explain to business and technology transfer managers, contract negotiators and general legal advisers the main tax issues in R&D collaboration and other technology transfer agreements (referred to as 'technology agreements'), so that they can assimilate the 'tax picture' quickly and decide whether to involve tax specialists at the outset of a transaction. It

---

4   See Unfair Terms in Consumer Contracts Regulations 1999 (SI 1999/2083). There is an ancient rule of law that every charge upon the subject must be imposed by clear and unambiguous language (see *Denn d Manifold v Diamond* (1825) 2 B&C 243), but tax legislation is virtually incomprehensible to the layman.

5   As evidenced by the content of many legal drafting courses and by the lobbying of Clarity – the Plain English Campaign (http://www.plainenglish.co.uk/) who have produced, in association with the Law Society: Alder, *Clarity For Lawyers – Effective Legal Writing* (2nd edn, Law Society, 2006).

also aims to update legal advisers and accountants who are already familiar with the basic rules on important recent changes.

The chapter is confined to UK tax issues. Overseas tax is beyond the scope of this title, although it is briefly addressed in the context of double taxation and the use of offshore tax havens. UK taxation of oil and gas exploration,[6] film production, finance leasing and transactions in land and property (which may overlap with R&D tax issues) are also outside the scope of this title, as is a detailed consideration of capital gains tax.

Recent developments

The tax rules for R&D expenditure and intellectual property have, since 2000, been radically changed to encourage growth of UK enterprises,[7] especially new technology-based enterprises, and to simplify and update the tax system generally.

Since the last update of this title in 2002 there have been improvements to the R&D tax credits for both SME and large companies but also stricter time limits for claiming the reliefs (see section E under 'Special relief for R&D income expenditure – small and medium-sized companies' and 'Special relief for R&D income expenditure – large companies' below). In addition, there have been changes to tax rates generally, reform of capital gains tax (including the introduction of a standard 18 per cent rate on chargeable gains and an 'entrepreneur's relief' but the abolition of taper relief), new reliefs for investment in plant and machinery (see section C under 'Capital allowances for intellectual property or R&D incorporated into an intellectual property right or package: position for individuals (and companies before

---

6   Locating and exploiting oil, gas and mineral deposits is not normally within the Institute of Chartered Accountants' definition of R&D in SSAP 13, para 18, generally relied on for tax purposes; but this definition has been extended to include these activities for the purposes of claiming R&D capital allowances (see HMRC REV BN 6: *Improvements to Research and Development Tax Credits*, para 6).

7   The changes (see section E under 'Special relief for R&D income expenditure – small and medium-sized companies' and 'Special relief for R&D income expenditure – large companies' below) were part of a government initiative to boost innovation and encourage investment in the UK to bridge the 'productivity gap' with leading industrial competitors such as the US, Japan and Germany following the recommendations of Lord Trotman's report, 'Review of Government Measures for Enterprise Growth', March 2000. There has since been a shift in emphasis following the recommendations of the review by Lord Sainsbury ('The Race to the Top, A Review of Government's Science and Innovation Policies (October 2007))' to 'support the restructuring of British companies into high-value goods, services and industries' to survive in a global economy where emerging economies such as China can produce goods at only 5 per cent of the UK labour cost.

1 April 2002)' below)[8] and the announcement in the Chancellor's Pre-Budget Report of 9 December 2009 ('the 2009 Pre-Budget Report') that the rate of corporation tax on income from UK patents will be reduced to 10 per cent (see section H under 'Payments for intellectual property rights' at (a) below).

Furthermore, there have been some significant changes to the tax treatment of charities and universities which their administrators and business managers need to take into account before carrying out business activities (see section A under 'Publication rights in university research agreements' and section G under 'Exemptions for charities' below). There have also been two fundamental changes to the administration of the UK tax system which are summarised below.

First, in 2005 the Inland Revenue merged with Customs and Excise to form the Commissioners for Revenue and Customs ('HMRC').[9] One objective of the merger, according to the Chancellor, is 'minimising the burden of compliance by providing joined-up systems so that business needs to provide information only once, when possible through a single form'. Another objective is increasing the tax yield through pooling information about taxpayers, reducing errors and prosecuting evaders. It is no coincidence that HMRC now has an independent prosecutions office – the Revenue and Customs Prosecutions Office – to prosecute cases in England and Wales.

Secondly, the General and Special Commissioners,[10] the VAT & Duties Tribunal and the Section 706/704 ICTA 1988 Tribunal have all been replaced by a new tribunal system and this has dramatically changed the appeal process. It should be noted that in addition to purely administrative changes the new tribunals have a wider jurisdiction. Put simply, as from 1 April 2009 a taxpayer can appeal against a ruling by HMRC to the Tax Chamber of the First-tier Tribunal (a new generic tribunal established under the Tribunals, Courts and Enforcement Act 2007) and the appeal will be allocated to a tribunal of legally qualified judges and expert lay members according to the complexity of the case.[11] Either party can appeal against the decision to the Upper Tribunal, but only on a point of law. Any further appeal is then to the Court of Appeal. The tribunals have wide-ranging case-management

---

8   The new rules for the taxation of intellectual property are part of a post-1 April 2002 regime for the taxation of intangible fixed assets for companies introduced by FA 2002, s 84 and Schs 29, 30 and now contained in Corporation Tax Act 2009, Pts 8, 9.

9   The Commissioners for Revenue and Customs Act 2005 came into effect on 7 April 2005. References before that date, however, are to the 'Inland Revenue' and/or 'Her Majesty's Customs and Excise' ('HMCE'), as appropriate.

10   The General Commissioners for Income Tax were the UK's oldest tribunal, established by William Pitt the Younger's Income Tax Act (a temporary measure to finance the Napoleonic Wars), and the Special Commissioners were created in 1805 to assist them.

11   There are four levels of complexity – 'default paper', 'basic', 'standard' and 'complex' – and all three levels above 'default paper' will usually be determined at a hearing.

powers.[12] Administration is carried out by the Tribunals Service.[13] The new system[14] is designed to improve the quality, consistency and speed of the appeals process and has generally been welcomed by tax practitioners.

Finally, in addition to numerous new measures to counter tax avoidance and tax evasion (especially regarding offshore investments) there has been a general drive towards a tougher penalty regime for errors, delays and defaults in submitting tax returns and making tax payments to back-up self-assessment. This has significantly added to the burden of tax compliance, especially for the small business proprietor and the self-employed (see section F under 'Income tax, national insurance contributions (NICs) and returns' below). As a result there is now a more compelling case than ever for seeking tax advice at the outset of a transaction with a view to minimising the burden of tax compliance at a later date.

At a time of continuing change in the UK tax treatment of R&D and intellectual property, this chapter focuses on issues in technology agreements – to help to produce an agreement which makes 'tax sense' for the client. An agreement which takes account of the client's tax position is likely to be much more valuable than one which leaves tax to chance. Where potentially significant amounts of tax are at stake, the drafter should always seek specialist tax advice at the outset. Where there is only limited scope for tax planning, however, a clear and well-structured agreement will inevitably save the client compliance costs at a later date; and for small businesses the cost of UK tax compliance is generally a greater burden than the actual rates of tax.

Capital or income?

The remainder of the Overview will highlight some tax issues that commonly arise in technology agreements. A more detailed consideration of the issues is given later in the chapter.

One recurrent issue is whether payments under an agreement are treated for tax purposes as 'income' as opposed to 'capital'. Capital expenditure cannot generally be offset against income so as to reduce taxable profits; instead, there is usually more limited relief in the form of a writing down allowance ('WDA'). This allows a percentage (usually 20 per cent) of capital expenditure (calculated on a reducing-balance basis) to be offset against income annually. For example, initial lump sum payments under an exclusive licence agreement are usually treated as capital, whereas continuing royalties

---

12 See Tribunal Procedure (First-tier Tribunal) (Tax Chamber) Rules 2009 (SI 2009/273).

13 See www.tribunals.gov.uk/tax.

14 Following a review of the tribunals system by the Department for Constitutional Affairs and recommendations by the Tax Appeals Modernisation Stakeholder Group chaired by Sir Stephen Oliver QC, Acting President of the Tax Chamber of the First-tier Tribunal.

are usually treated as income. Licensees, therefore, typically try to describe the initial payments in terms that improve their chances of having them treated as income payments.

Both the scope for, and benefit of, describing initial payments for intellectual property as income has become more limited since the introduction of the new rules for the taxation of intellectual property.[15] The availability of R&D corporation tax credits for current expenditure on R&D generally creates an incentive for UK companies to have R&D expenditure treated as income or current expenditure (if possible) but this will depend on the particular circumstances of the case.[16]

Description of lump sum payments

Historically, another recurrent issue was whether initial payments under licence agreements were payments for the use of intellectual property or payments for research services. Again, the wording of the agreement will influence the accounting treatment and the tax treatment of the payments made under it (see section A under 'General guidance for the draftsman', para 2 below).

The following example (before the UK/Japanese Double Taxation Convention of 2 February 2006 came into effect) illustrates the consequences of ambiguous wording. Under a collaborative research and licence agreement between a UK licensor and a Japanese licensee, the licensor was required to perform certain research activities, and the licensee was granted an exclusive licence in respect of certain intellectual property generated under the agreement. The licensee was required to make lump sum payments, including an up-front payment and later stage payments, known as milestone payments. There was, however, some ambiguity in the wording of the clause under which the up-front lump sum was due. The Japanese tax authorities considered that the payment was for the use of intellectual property and required the Japanese licensee to deduct Japanese withholding tax at 20 per cent before making the payment (net of tax). Under the then double taxation agreement between Japan and the UK, there was only partial relief from double taxation: withholding tax was reduced from 20 per cent to 10 per cent. The licensee was therefore required to deduct 10 per cent of the lump sum payment before paying the net amount to the UK licensor. As the licensor did not carry on business in Japan, and could not recover any of the tax deducted from the Japanese tax authorities, it could merely claim credit relief in the UK against any UK corporation tax liability. The parties, however, managed to persuade the Japanese tax authorities that the payment was really a contribution to the costs of the research in which the intellectual property was generated.

---

15 See n 8 above.
16 See section A under 'Type of tax', 'Type of activity' and 'Type of taxpayer' below.

The amount of those costs exceeded the amount of the lump sum payment. Payments made to a UK company for research conducted in the UK were not subject to Japanese withholding tax. The parties made a written amendment to the wording of the agreement and the Japanese tax authorities allowed the payment to be made gross.

In this example the outcome was satisfactory, but it involved time and expense, which could have been avoided if the payment had originally been described as a contribution to research costs instead of a payment for the use of intellectual property. Sometimes such payments are described in agreements as 'technology access fees'. The UK and other national tax authorities are well aware of this particular drafting technique (known as 'bundling') and want to change the rules to subject any royalty element to deduction of tax at source.[17] Bundling can still benefit UK licensors notwithstanding the rules for the taxation of intellectual property and cross-border royalty payments introduced in 2002.[18] This is because these rules do not change the relief available in the UK for any overseas tax on UK licensors' income from overseas licensees.[19] Some licensors, however, will prefer royalty income if the payments can be made gross under the new optional scheme for cross-border payments within the EU or 100 per cent relief is available under a double tax treaty (see section A under 'Type of tax' and section H: 'International technology agreements' below).

The benefits of any creative tax solution must always be weighed against the commercial imperatives of having an understandable and conventional payment structure. This is often an issue with R&D agreements where there is no guarantee that the R&D will lead to any marketable product. It may, therefore, be difficult to justify expensive tax planning advice at the time an agreement is made, even if the parties hope that it will lead to major 'blockbuster' products.

Publication rights in university research agreements

A recurrent issue for a university or Higher Education Institution ('HEI') is whether payments received under a research collaboration agreement with a commercial sponsor are exempt from tax because of the institution's charitable status. Until recently HMRC and the Charity Commission considered that such payments were charitable and exempt from tax provided that the results

---

17 For the Inland Revenue's view on 'bundling' see their Technical Note, *Reform of the taxation of intellectual property*, March 1999, paras 226–230.
18 See n 8 above and n 23 below.
19 If there is no relief for overseas tax under a double tax treaty unilateral relief may be available under ICTA 1988, s 790. See SP7/91, *Double taxation: business profits: unilateral relief* as amended following *Yates v GCA International Limited*, 64 TC 37.

of the research were published and not retained exclusively for the sponsor.[20] A delay in publication for up to six months to allow patent applications to be made was considered acceptable.

Both HMRC and the Charity Commission have, however, recently reviewed their positions following the Charities Act 2006 and issued new guidelines.[21] It is important to understand the recent changes (see section G under 'Exemptions for charities' below) as failure to take them into account could have drastic consequences. At best, sponsorship income (which previously would have been exempt) may be liable to income or corporation tax; and, at worst, it could jeopardise the institution's charitable status. Sometimes, commercial sponsors seek a right of veto over publications if they contain information which they would prefer to remain a commercial secret. If so, the detailed wording of the publications clause of the research contract should be scrutinised to check that the sponsor's rights to preview publications are suitably limited so that the risk of such drastic consequences is minimised.

Type of tax

UK taxes have developed along separate 'evolutionary paths' or 'branches'. The branches most relevant to technology agreements are: (1) income and capital taxes; (2) VAT; and (to a lesser extent) (3) stamp duty. The most complex of these, the income and capital taxes system, consists of two sets of rules, one for income payments and the other for capital payments. Personal taxpayers are chargeable to income tax on income, and capital gains tax ('CGT') on capital gains. Corporate taxpayers are only chargeable to corporation tax; but there are still two sets of rules, one for income and the other for capital payments. The capital/income issue is the one most likely to concern the draftsman of a technology agreement.

In international transactions (ie between parties based in different countries) an agreement may need to be drafted to take account of the possibility of double taxation of a party, ie taxation in both countries of the same payments under the agreement. As double taxation may be removed or significantly reduced by a double tax treaty between the two countries, the draftsman should examine the terms of any such treaty before drafting the agreement.

---

20   See Ch 1 under 'University research and charitable status' for a further discussion of the Charity Commission's views on this point and, for a quick overview, see *University research contracts: are they charitable?* in the Legal Updates section of the Anderson and Company website, www.andlaw.eu.

21   See the Charity Commission's June 2009 guidance, *Research by Higher Education Institutions* (www.charity-commission.gov.uk) and HMRC's guidance, *Charities – Trading and business activities* (www.hmrc.gov.uk).

Type of activity

Tax liability also varies according to the type of activity for which payments are being made: the two main types of activity that are discussed in this section are:

- the provision of R&D services (including research collaborations involving payment); and

- the grant of intellectual property rights (eg for assignments, licences and options).

The provision of R&D services raises relatively straightforward tax issues. As, however, R&D agreements often include provisions dealing with the parties' rights to commercialise any intellectual property generated by an R&D project, more complicated tax issues also need to be considered. As there are different tax treatments for different types of intellectual property (eg patents, copyright and trade marks) these are considered separately below.

Type of taxpayer

Tax issues need to be considered by reference to the type and circumstances of the taxpayer. Identical payments may receive a different tax treatment depending on whether the parties to the agreement are (1) companies, individuals, charities or government departments; and (2) UK or overseas residents, and in which country they are resident.

For example, if a university is paid to conduct research for a commercial sponsor, the payments may be exempt from corporation tax by virtue of the university's charitable status whereas the same payments received by a trading company would be taxable. Conversely, the same payment can be treated as a capital or revenue expense according to the status of the taxpayer. The point is aptly illustrated by a decision of the Privy Council which shows just how inconsistent and artificial tax 'logic' can be.[22]

The tax treatment may also differ depending on whether a party is considered to be trading in intellectual property (where royalties are treated as 'pure investment income') or merely using it in the course of (another) business.

---

22   *IRC v New Zealand Forest Research Institute Ltd* [2000] 1 WLR 1755, [2000] STC 522, PC. The Privy Council decided that payments made by the taxpayer company (which had taken over the assets and liabilities of a former government research department) to employees for accrued unpaid leave deemed by statute to be a liability of the taxpayer was a capital expense, even though the payments were taxable as income of the employees and the department could have deducted them as a revenue expense had it been a trading entity. The 'logic' of the decision was that the acquisition price was reduced to allow for the liability and that was a capital expense.

Once the category of taxpayer has been determined, it is then necessary to consider his or her individual circumstances, for example ability to offset previous losses or expenditure against income arising under the agreement.

Income and corporation tax: bullet points

The main tax issues to consider when drafting a technology agreement are as follows:

- Whether payments under the agreement are treated as capital or income and tax implications for payer or payee.

- Special tax rules for patents (and certain other types of intellectual property) and for R&D payments.

- The benefits of incorporation.

- Special reliefs for expenditure on R&D.

- Withholding tax rules for intellectual property payments under UK law.[23]

- Taxation of payments in international transactions and double taxation relief.

- Optional schemes for making royalty payments gross.

- Transfer pricing rules.

- Tax-avoidance schemes, including use of offshore jurisdictions.

- Special tax incentives for investment in R&D-based businesses.

- Whether small start-up companies seeking funding would benefit more from grants or, alternatively, R&D tax reliefs.

These issues lead to a variety of different payment structures in agreements which cannot be reduced to a few, simple guidance points for the draftsman. A more detailed treatment of these issues is therefore given below.

VAT issues

Value Added Tax ('VAT') is a European Union ('EU') Tax. EU member states are required to charge VAT in accordance with the requirements of European Law so that supplies of goods and services are treated similarly

---

23 The rules for withholding tax on royalty payments to UK companies (and UK branches of overseas companies) and to exempt bodies and cross-border royalty payments were changed in 2007 and are now set out in ITA 2007, ss 903, 906–917. The changes are more fully considered in section H under 'Withholding tax' and 'Optional scheme for payment of royalties gross: cross-border payments' below.

for VAT purposes throughout the EU. Most of the detailed requirements are now contained in Council Directive 2006/112/EC ([2006] OJ L347/1) ('the Principal VAT Directive'). The principal UK rules are contained in the Value Added Tax Act 1994 ('VATA 1994') and the Value Added Tax Regulations 1995 (SI 1995/2518) ('the Principal Regulations').

The main VAT issue is whether VAT should be charged on payments to be made under a technology agreement. Normally (the major exceptions are described later in this chapter), VAT is chargeable on consideration for the supply of goods or services, including the provision of research services and consultancy services. The grant of intellectual property rights is treated as the supply of services for VAT purposes. Typically, in the case of a technology agreement (and assuming the supplier is a taxable person for VAT purposes):

● If both parties to the agreement are based in the UK, VAT is chargeable.

● If the supplier of the services is based in the UK, and the recipient of the services is based outside the EU, VAT is not chargeable.

● If the supplier of the services is based in the UK and the recipient of the services is in another EU country (eg France), VAT is chargeable in the 'place of supply' of the services. The 'place of supply' rules are complicated and there is an exception to the normal rules for 'services which are intellectual in character'. This exception includes:[24]

— research and development services, and some product testing, consultancy and other services;[25]

— telecommunications services, radio and television broadcasting services and electronically supplied services;[26] and

— licences and assignments of intellectual property.

The place of supply of 'services which are intellectual in character' is the EU member state in which the recipient of the services is based (in our example, France) provided he or she is in business, and VAT will be levied on the recipient of the services (ie the French company), not the UK supplier. In other words, the UK supplier does not charge VAT on his or her invoice. This, however, is subject to certain conditions and changes from 1 January 2010 (see section J under 'Place of supply of services – post-1 January 2010' below).

---

24 VATA 1994, s 5(2)(b).
25 VATA 1994, Sch5, paras 1–8, and VAT (Place of Supply of Services) Order 1992 (SI 1992/3121) and *VAT: Place of Supply of Services* (HMRC Notice 741, March 2008).
26 These categories were added by the VAT (Reverse Charge) (Anti-avoidance) Order 2003 (SI 2003/863), art 2(1)–(3) with effect for any services performed after 30 June 2003. See section J under 'Schedule 5, paragraph 7C' below.

Stamp duty issues

Stamp duty is no longer chargeable on intellectual property transactions.[27] From 28 March 2000 instruments transferring patents, trade marks, registered designs, copyrights, plant breeders' rights or agreements licensing them have all been exempt from stamp duty. The only exceptions relevant to technology agreements, ie where stamp duty is payable, are instruments which consist partly of intellectual property and partly of other chargeable property. Any composite agreements will need to be presented to the Stamp Office with an apportionment of the sale price for determination of the duty chargeable. From 23 April 2002, however, transfers of goodwill have also been exempt from stamp duty.[28] For instruments which remain so chargeable stamp duty is payable on an ad valorem basis.[29]

General guidance for the draftsman

Most technology agreements offer some scope for tax planning, either to cut tax or to reduce the mushrooming cost of tax compliance. This is especially true for transactions involving the transfer of intellectual property because the very anomalies and inconsistencies in the rules create tax planning opportunities.

The radical changes to the taxation of R&D and intellectual property for companies since 2000 mean that a new approach to drafting technology agreements is required if companies are to optimise their tax positions. The parties to more complex R&D agreements (especially universities and HEIs) will need to give their legal advisers more financial information (such as recent accounts) at an early stage of negotiations so that valuable tax reliefs will not be prejudiced by 'last-minute' drafting. The tax treatment of intellectual property will follow its accounting treatment; but the accounting treatment of a commercial transaction will follow the legal effect of the agreement. The company's internal accountants should therefore work with the company's legal and tax advisers to agree the best structure of the agreement. Companies concerned about the cost of external advice should consider instructing advisers with specialist knowledge of both intellectual property and taxation at the outset of a project as this approach is more likely to be cost effective than instructing legal advisers to draft and negotiate the agreement and then, after the agreement is signed, separate advisers on tax.

---

27 FA 2000, s 129. The change is designed to boost the small and medium-sized high-tech business enterprises perceived by the Government as vital to promote UK economic growth.
28 See Inland Revenue Budget Note, *Stamp Duty Exemption For Transfers Of Goodwill* (REV BN 9) and FA 2002, s 116.
29 Note that conveyances, transfers, and leases of (otherwise chargeable) property to charities are exempt from stamp duties. Where VAT is payable, stamp duty is calculated on the VAT-inclusive amount (see section K under 'Stamp duty and VAT' below).

The new rules for the taxation of intellectual property and R&D tax credits for companies, and the lower corporation tax rates, also mean that any individual intending to carry out R&D activity should seriously consider forming a company as a vehicle for the enterprise. Unlike individuals, companies have to incur expenses in complying with company law (and may have to file audited accounts with their annual returns to Companies House[30]) but the potential tax advantages, especially where profits can be retained in the company so that it is not simply a fiscally transparent intermediary, can easily outweigh these extra costs.[31] With the introduction of a new 50 per cent top rate of personal income tax on annual taxable income over £150,000 from 6 April 2010 the advantages could be significant if this threshold is exceeded (as the small companies rate of corporation tax until April 2011 – for companies with taxable profits below £300,000 pa – is only 21 per cent).[32] Changes announced in the 2009 Pre-Budget Report – including the freeze on income tax thresholds and allowances, abolition of personal allowances for incomes over £112,950 and Class 4 NIC increases for the self-employed from 2011–12 (ie to a new 9 per cent main rate and 2 per cent additional rate) – create other tax advantages in using a company as a vehicle for a new enterprise.

There is, however, no 'magic formula' to produce the optimum tax solution in every case. The best general guidance that can be given to the drafter is to identify clients' commercial priorities and liaise with their accountants and, if necessary, seek specialist tax advice at the earliest possible stage of the transaction.

Tax avoidance under UK law

The cardinal principle for UK tax planning is that everyone has the right to organise his or her affairs so as to pay less, rather than more, tax (*IRC v Duke of Westminster*);[33] but this principle has been severely eroded since 1981 following the landmark decision of the House of Lords in *WT Ramsay Ltd v IRC*.[34] New anti-avoidance rules (largely aimed at circular transactions involving associated or connected persons, offshore companies and non-

---

30   Although, following Budget 2004, companies can now submit online corporation tax returns and small companies can submit a short-form CT600 return to HMRC.
31   The Institute of Fiscal Studies have calculated that 1.2m self-employed people could gain over £500 per annum, with those earning £15,000 per annum achieving a total tax saving of £3,827 per annum, by incorporating: see Mr Edward Davey MP's contribution on the Finance Bill 2002 in Standing Committee F of 16 May 2002 at cols 110, 111 of the Official Report. See Inland Revenue guidance IR 175 *Supplying services through a limited company or partnership* (and their supplementary Tax Bulletin No 51, February 2001) for a summary of the tax (and NIC) treatment of intermediary companies, and n 35 below.
32   See FA 2008, s 6 , Sch 2 and FA 2009, s 8, and the 2009 Pre-Budget Report announcement to 'freeze' the rate.
33   *IRC v Duke of Westminster* [1936] AC 1, HL.
34   *WT Ramsay Ltd v IRC* (1978) 54 TC 101, HL.

residents) follow almost every Budget with the result that many schemes designed to avoid tax can easily *increase* the net tax burden when additional compliance costs and professional fees are taken into account. These anti-avoidance rules are not confined to tax exiles or multinational corporations. Recent measures to combat NIC-avoidance by using service companies and (from 6 April 2007) Managed Service Companies[35] aptly illustrate the point.

Furthermore, there is a 'live' proposal for a general anti-avoidance rule for direct taxes which, if fully enacted, will have very wide-reaching implications for tax planning generally. Indeed, such a proposal has already been partially embodied in the UK controlled foreign company ('CFC') rules. In a nutshell, and subject to certain exemptions, the CFC rules apply to a company resident overseas (in a jurisdiction where it is subject to less than 75 per cent of the tax it would pay if in the UK), but the company is controlled by UK residents (individuals or companies). Where a UK resident has an interest of 25 per cent or more in a CFC, HMRC can apportion chargeable profits to the UK-resident owner (ie profits, but not chargeable gains, computed according to UK rules) and assess the owner to tax but with an effective credit for any overseas tax paid.[36] The CFC rules are one reason why offshore tax havens (see section H under 'Offshore tax havens' below) have become much less viable in tax planning for UK residents in recent years.

A commentary on these anti-avoidance rules is beyond the scope of this title, but the draftsman of any technology agreement should be aware that they exist and seek specialist advice where appropriate.

B: INCOME AND CAPITAL TAXES

Are payments under a technology agreement income or capital?

This is usually the first tax issue for payments under a technology agreement, but it is not always an easy question to answer.[37] This is because the origins of the UK tax system date back to the Industrial Revolution when the

---

35 See FA 2000, Sch12 and IR 35 *Personal services provided through intermediaries*, February 2000. See also HMRC guidance notes at www.hmrc.gov.uk/emploment-status/info.htm.

36 See FA 2002, ss 89, 90 and Inland Revenue Budget 2002 Note, REV BN 26 *Chargeable Gains: Location of Assets etc*. The CFC legislation was, however, modified from 6 December 2006 following successful challenges under Art 43 of the EC Treaty, as an infringement of the freedom of establishment within the EU, in *Cadbury Schweppes plc v CIR*, CJEC Case C-196/04 and *Vodafone 2 v HMRC* [2008] EWHC 1569 (Ch), [2008] STC 2391.This decision, however, was reversed by the Court of Appeal: [2009] EWCA Civ 446, [2010] 2 WLR 288, [2009] STC 1480, (2009) Times, 26 June, [2009] SWTI 1795, [2009] All ER (D) 209 (May).

37 'No part of our law of taxation presents such almost insoluble conundrums as the decision whether a receipt or outgoing is capital or income for tax purposes' (Lord Upjohn in *Strick v Regent Oil Company Limited* (1965) 43 TC 1, HL). See HMRC *Business Income Manual* (BIM35000-35910) for HMRC's guidance on the issue.

fundamental distinction between income and capital made sound business sense, and much of the current case follows decisions made in the 19th century. A factory producing goods could easily distinguish between capital expenditure (for example, on plant and machinery) and income expenditure (for example raw materials). In an economy which has fundamentally changed with the decline in traditional manufacturing and the growth of service and new technology-based industries, this distinction is increasingly obsolete.[38] The most valuable assets of many businesses today are intangible items such as intellectual property rights or commercial 'know-how', or market research and product development programmes. Classifying such assets as either 'income' or 'capital' for tax purposes is an artificial exercise. Nevertheless, it is an important distinction for tax purposes. The remainder of Part B will summarise how the distinction is made in the case of payments arising under technology agreements.

Statutory definition of R&D

One recent measure to update the tax system in this respect is the introduction of a new statutory definition of 'research and development' ('R&D') for tax purposes. R&D is now defined as 'activities that fall to be treated as research and development in accordance with generally accepted accounting practice' except as specifically modified by Treasury regulations.[39]

The Institute of Chartered Accountants set out their guidance in SSAP 13: *Accounting for Research and Development (Revised)*.[40] SSAP 13 distinguishes R&D activity from non-research activity by the presence or absence of an appreciable element of innovation. The key test is whether the activity in question departs from routine and breaks new ground, in which case it should normally be included within the definition, or whether it follows an established pattern, in which case it should be excluded. There is an additional test set out in the Secretary of State for Trade and Industry's *Guidelines on the Meaning of Research and Development for Tax Purposes, 5 March 2004* ('the BIS Guidelines')[41] which also has to be satisfied. Essentially, an R&D project is one which seeks to 'achieve an advance in science or technology' and the 'activities which directly contribute to achieving this advance ... through the resolution of scientific or technological uncertainty are R&D'.[42]

---

38   See n 7 above.
39   ITA 2007, s 1006 and CTA 2009, s 814(5).
40   The Department for Business Innovation and Skills ('BIS') has renamed the guidelines of its predecessor, the Department of Business Enterprise and Regulatory Reform ('BERR'), known as 'the BERR guidelines'. SSAP 13, and for international companies the wider International Accounting Standard IAS 38, follow the OECD 'Frascati' definition of R&D, which excludes the humanities because they are not science or technology. Reference to the OECD model may be useful in borderline cases.
41   See http://www.dius.gov.uk/innovation/business_support/research_and_development.
42   See paras 3 and 4 of the BIS Guidelines.

Certain indirect activities also qualify.[43] However, 'an advance in science or technology means an advance in overall knowledge or capability in a field of science or technology (not a company's own state of knowledge or capability alone)'.[44] Specific examples are given to assist in borderline cases. Thus, 'operational research not tied to specific R&D activity' or 'market research' are both excluded; whereas 'experimental development' is included (but 'commercial development' including 'product development' is excluded).

UK businesses get tax relief for any R&D expenditure properly accounted for under the above definition. The amount of relief available, however, still depends on whether the relevant expenditure is 'income' or 'capital'. The definition leaves the draftsman of an R&D agreement real scope for tax planning, but he or she will have to liaise with accountants and tax advisers to ensure that any opportunities are maximised.

Payments for R&D or consultancy services

Payments for services are invariably treated as income.[45] Thus, regular payments for research services under a research or clinical trial agreement or a consultancy agreement are treated as income. Usually, the agreement includes a schedule specifying the amount, or a formula for calculating the amount of payments due and when they are payable. The more detailed the schedule, the more HMRC will rely on it to identify the true nature of the payment and thus its correct tax treatment. The same applies to invoices issued pursuant to the terms of the agreement. If, however, payments for services are 'bundled' with intellectual property rights or other property or the wording is unclear, HMRC are entitled to 'see through' the agreement to identify the true nature (ie the 'substance' as opposed to 'form') of the underlying bargain.[46]

Payments for acquisition of intellectual property rights: position for individuals (and companies before 1 April 2002)

Payments for the acquisition of rights in intellectual property (under an R&D agreement or otherwise) can be difficult to classify as income or capital.

---

43   See para 5 of the BIS Guidelines.
44   See para 6 of the BIS Guidelines.
45   A right of action for damages arising under an agreement for services, however, will be treated as an asset for CGT purposes and taxed accordingly following *Zim Properties Limited v Proctor*, [1985] 58 TC 371. See also ESC D33 *Capital Gains Tax on Compensation and Damages: Zim Properties Limited – Compensation and Damages* and CG13013 *Zim concession ESC D33: concession and other rights* on HMRC's website.
46   See n 17 above.

This is partly because intellectual property is intangible, and partly because ownership of intellectual property tends to give negative, rather than positive, rights. For example, a patent owner has the right to prevent others from manufacturing and selling goods which are within the claims of the patent, but does not have positive rights to use the invention: third parties may own rights which prevent the patent owner from doing so. In contrast, ownership of a machine for producing goods gives positive rights to the owner, ie the goods.

At one end of the spectrum, a single, fixed amount payable for an outright assignment of a patent is usually classified as a capital payment. At the opposite end of the spectrum, a royalty payable under a non-exclusive patent licence agreement, calculated as a percentage of the sales price of goods manufactured under the licence, is usually treated as an income payment. The former situation is regarded as a disposal of an asset; the latter is regarded as an income-generating transaction.

In between these two extremes, there are many situations in which the tax classification is not always clear. For example, the position is less clear if a lump sum is paid by instalments; or if an exclusive, irrevocable licence is granted, amounting virtually to a disposal of the patent; or if a payment under an assignment is calculated by reference to the amount of sales by the assignee of relevant products. Some general guidance is given by past court decisions (summarised below) but these are sometimes difficult to reconcile with one another.

A further complication is that in some situations tax law overrides the general principles and deems payments to fall into a particular category. For example, capital payments for the sale (or grant of an exclusive licence) of a UK patent, and for the sale (or grant of an exclusive licence) of a non-UK patent held by a UK resident, are deemed to be income payments.[47] Lump sum payments to a creative artist for licensing or assigning copyright are also taxed as income, but averaging relief may be available to spread the tax liability over more than one year.[48]

Although the general guidance given by past court decisions is not always clear, the main criteria for determining whether a payment is income or capital are as follows:

- Description of the payments in the agreement, invoices and accounts of the parties to the agreement: this may influence the tax treatment but will not be conclusive.[49]

---

47   ITTOIA 2005, s 587 (they were previously taxable under Schedule D, Case VI). ITTOIA 2005, s 590 allows a lump sum receipt to be spread over a maximum of six years.
48   ITTOIA 2005, ss 221–225. See also section D under 'Individuals' below.
49   See Lord Greene in *Rustproof Metal Windows v IRC* (1947) 29 TC 243, CA at 271.

- Basis or formula for calculating the payments: a lump sum suggests, but does not automatically imply, a capital payment. Similarly, a royalty based on sales suggests an income payment. However, a lump sum payment is not treated as income merely because a significant proportion is payable by instalments.[50]

- Where there is an outright disposal of intellectual property the payment is likely to be capital.[51] An assignment does not, however, necessarily involve an outright disposal of intellectual property (for example, it may be limited in time). If, as in the case of a licence, title to the intellectual property is retained, the payment is likely to be income; but, an exclusive, irrevocable intellectual property licence is virtually a disposal of the relevant intellectual property and is likely to be regarded as a capital disposal.

- Regardless of the above, if the disposal is by an intellectual property trader it is usually regarded as an income payment.

- Underlying economic reality: the courts are increasingly prepared to 'see through' the form of the transaction and look at the substance.[52]

- The practical scope of these decisions will, inevitably, be reduced by the introduction of the new rules for taxing intellectual property for companies as from 1 April 2002 (see section B under 'Payments for acquisition of intellectual property rights: position for companies after 31 March 2002' below).

Payments for acquisition of intellectual property rights: position for companies after 31 March 2002

Following extensive consultation with business and taxation lobbies a new taxation regime for the corporate tax treatment of 'intangible fixed assets'[53] came into effect on 1 April 2002.[54] The position for individuals, however, remains the same as before (see section B under 'Payments for acquisition of intellectual property rights: position for individuals (and companies before 1 April 2002)' above).

Intangible assets (ie items treated as intangible assets in a company's accounts according to generally accepted accounting practice) specifically include

---

50 *IRC v British Salmson Aero Engines* (1938) 22 TC 29, CA.
51 *Haig's (Earl) Trustees v IRC* (1939) 22 TC 725; *Nethersole v Withers* (1948) 28 TC 501, HL.
52 See n 17 above.
53 An 'intangible fixed asset' is defined as an 'intangible asset acquired or created by the company for use on a continuing basis in the course of the company's activities' and includes an option to acquire or dispose of intangible fixed assets (CTA 2009, s 713).
54 Originally contained in FA 2002, Schs 29, 30, the rules were rewritten to Pts 8 , 9 of CTA 2009.

intellectual property and similar rights.[55] It is submitted that the new database right and pan-European design rights should also be included.[56] Goodwill is included but interests in land, movable property, financial assets, shares and rights under a trust or in a partnership are excluded.[57]

The rules on the tax treatment of computer software are particularly intricate. The following summary provides guidance on the basic rules for those who are not familiar with them. Computer software treated (in a company's accounts) as part of the cost of related hardware is specifically excluded except to the extent that it relates to royalties.[58] A company can elect to exclude capital expenditure on computer software (which has not been treated as part of the cost of related hardware). Small companies can therefore preserve any existing 100 per cent First Year Allowance ('FYA') already claimed under the Capital Allowances Act 2001 ('CAA 2001'), or since 2008 the Annual Investment Allowance ('AIA') (see note 86), but any election is irrevocable.[59] Any expenditure on R&D per se, however, is also excluded.[60] Again, this preserves computer software's already favourable tax treatment with R&D allowances (see section C under 'Capital allowances for other capital expenditure on R&D' below).

The new regime is designed to modernise the corporate tax base and provide relief for the cost of acquiring intangible fixed assets (in accordance with their amortisation in company accounts) where no relief was previously available. The new rules, which include extensive transitional and anti-avoidance provisions, are intricate and are now contained in Parts 8 and 9 of the Corporation Tax Act 2009 ('CTA 2009'). Since their introduction in 2002 they have been amended but are still largely untested in the courts. In synopsis, the new regime means that as from 1 April 2002 the cost of an intellectual property right, or R&D incorporated into an intellectual property right or package, is deductible for corporation tax purposes.[61]

---

55 CTA 2009, s 712(3).
56 This would logically follow from the wording of CTA 2009, s 712(3)(b), the recent decision of *Crowson Fabrics v Rider and Others* [2007] EWHC 2942 (Ch), [2008] FSR 424, [2008] IRLR 288, [2007] All ER (D) 338 (Dec) and the fact that HMRC will treat certain database rights like copyright (see para 7 of CG68250 at www.hmrc.gov.uk/manuals/GC4manual/CG68250.htm).
57 A full list of exclusions (including partially excluded assets) is set out in CTA 2009, ss 800–816.
58 CTA 2009, s 813.
59 CTA 2009, s 816. Elections must be made in writing to HMRC within two years of the accounting period in which the expenditure was incurred.
60 CTA 2009, s 814.
61 Special rules apply to the acquisition of assets created before 1 April 2002 (CTA 2009, ss 880–900).

As the reforms only apply to companies, albeit with the prospect of being extended to individuals in the future,[62] any individual (or any other entity) planning substantial investment in intellectual property assets after 31 March 2002 should seek specialist advice on the 'pros' and 'cons' of forming a company to benefit from the new rules (see section A under 'General guidance for the draftsman' above and section H under 'Structuring agreements' below).

Key features of the new regime can be summarised as follows:

- *Relief for the cost of intellectual property and goodwill:* companies generally get relief against corporation tax based on their accounting treatment.[63] In addition, whether or not an asset has been written down in the profit and loss accounts, companies can make an irrevocable election to write down the cost of an intangible fixed asset at a fixed rate of relief of 4 per cent per annum, and have two years from the end of the accounting period in which the asset was created or acquired by the company in which to make the election.[64] Purchases of goodwill, however, no longer qualify for CGT 'roll-over' relief (except where reinvestment under the CGT tax rules took place before 1 April 2002 and within 12 months of disposal).

- *Eligible expenditure:* this includes expenditure on the creation, acquisition and enhancement of the asset (including abortive expenditure) and their preservation and maintenance. Relief is therefore available for the cost of internal development as well as acquiring outside intellectual property.

- *Intra-group transfers:* transfers of intellectual property between members of the same UK group of companies are tax neutral[65] but there are special anti-avoidance provisions when companies leave a group within six years of a transfer which deem it to be at market value and allow the tax charge to be 'clawed back' from another group company or a controlling director.[66]

---

62 The Government is keeping the income tax treatment of intangible assets under review, but one reason for confining the reforms to companies was the perceived difficulty in applying a reform which included goodwill to income tax (see the Inland Revenue's Technical Note, *Reform of the Taxation of Intellectual Property, Goodwill and Intangible Assets: the Next Stage*, 8 November 2000, paras 2.23, 2.24).
63 The scheme of the legislation assumes that 'generally accepted accounting practice' is adopted and, if not, the provisions will apply as if they had been so drawn up (CTA 2009, s 717).
64 CTA 2009, ss 730, 731.
65 CTA 2009, ss 774–799.
66 CTA 2009, ss 795.

Tax treatment of income and capital payments – summary

Establishing whether a payment is classified as income or capital is an important first step in understanding the tax treatment of the payment; but further, more detailed tax issues need to be considered before determining whether the ultimate tax treatment is optimal or can be improved by structuring or drafting the technology agreement in a different way. Some of those detailed issues will now be considered in outline. They include:

- The availability of tax relief for income and capital expenditure, respectively.

- The taxation of any capital gains on the disposal of intellectual property.

- The taxation of income in the hands of individuals and companies.

C: RELIEF FOR CAPITAL EXPENDITURE ON R&D

Depreciation per se not allowed

R&D expenditure of a capital nature qualifies for relief under the capital allowances system.

The basic principle is that capital expenditure (as opposed to income expenditure) is written-off against income over a period of time for tax purposes to reflect the economic life of the asset. Instead of allowing depreciation (as charged to the profit and loss account) the system allows a taxpayer to claim an annual capital or writing-down allowance. For plant and machinery, this is usually 20 per cent of the asset's acquisition cost calculated on a reducing-balance basis. However, following Budget 2009, from 1 April 2009 to 31 March 2010 only all businesses can claim a First Year Allowance ('FYA') for most investments in plant and machinery at a rate of 40 per cent. Furthermore, the Finance Act 2008 introduced an Annual Investment Allowance ('AIA') which provides a 100 per cent FYA for the first £50,000 in most plant and machinery (apart from cars). In contrast, the amortisation or write-down shown in a company's profit and loss accounts will be based on accepted accounting practices and guidelines.[67] Expenditure which has been financed by a government or local authority grant, however, is excluded from capital allowances.[68]

---

67 For guidance on the accounting treatment of intangible assets and goodwill see Accountancy Standards Board's FRS 10 as from 23 December 1998 (for large and medium-sized companies) and the Financial Reporting Standards for Smaller Entities ('FRSSE') as from January 2007.
68 CAA 2001, ss 532–536. By concession where grants are later repaid the amount of repayment may be treated as qualifying expenditure for capital allowances purposes (see Inland Revenue ESC B49, as amended, in IR1 Supp (November 2001)).

Capital allowances for intellectual property or R&D incorporated into an intellectual property right or package: position for individuals (and companies before 1 April 2002)

The rules for capital allowances, which are largely contained in the Capital Allowances Act 2001 ('CAA 2001'), are extremely complicated[69] and a detailed explanation of them is beyond the scope of this title. Different reliefs are available for capital expenditure on different types of intellectual property. The relief available for capital expenditure on R&D also varies according to the R&D 'product' acquired. If the R&D is incorporated into an intellectual property asset (eg a patent) acquired from another party then the main reliefs (and the mechanics for claiming them), in synopsis, are as follows:

- *Patents:* a person who incurs capital expenditure on the purchase of patent rights for the purposes of a UK trade ('qualifying trade expenditure'[70]), or is chargeable to tax on the receipts from their exploitation ('qualifying non-trade expenditure'[71]), can claim a patent allowance (at the rate of 25 per cent per annum calculated on a reducing-balance basis).[72] If the patent rights cease or he or she sells his or her interest or part of it then the allowances given may be 'clawed back' by a balancing charge.[73] Qualifying expenditure is pooled and a separate pool applies for each separate trade and for all qualifying non-trade expenditure. For each pool a writing-down allowance is available for each chargeable period (except the final chargeable period where a balancing allowance is available for any excess) which allows 25 per cent of the amount (if any) by which 'available qualifying expenditure' exceeds the total of any disposal values. If the reverse position arises, ie the total disposal value exceeds available qualifying expenditure, then a balancing charge on the excess arises. The acquisition of a licence in respect of a patent is regarded as a purchase of patent rights[74] as is the right to acquire future patents.[75]

---

69   The complexity of the system is mainly due to extensive anti-avoidance provisions, especially for transactions between 'connected persons' within ICTA 1988, s 839 and, in the context of R&D agreements with companies, its interaction with the new regime for the taxation of intellectual property. CAA 2001 is the first Act from the Tax Law Rewrite Project, but simplifications in codifying the legislation have not changed the fundamental complexity of the rules. Where significant amounts of tax are at stake it is worth noting that, in practice, accountants specialising in this area are likely to have a more detailed knowledge of the rules than lawyers.

70   CAA 2001, s 468.
71   CAA 2001, s 469.
72   CAA 2001, ss 470–472.
73   CAA 2001, ss 471–476.
74   CAA 2001, s 466.
75   CAA 2001, s 465.

- *Know-how:* capital expenditure on know-how is eligible for know-how allowances (at the rate of 25 per cent per annum on a reducing-balance basis), but only in so far as relief is not otherwise available.[76] Expenditure is pooled and relief is granted in the same way as it is for patents. Know-how for this purpose is defined by statute as 'any industrial information or techniques likely to assist in the manufacture or processing of goods or materials'.[77] HMRC, however, interpret this definition narrowly. In their view,[78] commercial know-how (for example 'industrial information or techniques' or 'market research, customer lists and sales techniques') is excluded because it does not directly assist the manufacture or processing of that product.

- *Computer software:* computer software is not defined in the capital allowances legislation but HMRC regard computer programs and data of any kind as computer software. Expenditure incurred for the purposes of a trade on (1) a right to use or otherwise deal with computer software *or* (2) the acquisition (and ownership) of computer software (for example by outright purchase or as the result of commissioned research) is treated as expenditure on plant and machinery. Capital allowances are generally available at 25 per cent per annum (on a reducing-balance basis) but small companies may be entitled to a 100 per cent FYA (see section B under 'Payments for acquisition of intellectual property rights: position for companies after 31 March 2002', para 3 above). Relief is granted in the same way as it is for patents and know-how but with special rules for bringing disposal values into account where the claimant grants rights to use or deal in the software to others. Where, however, computer software is expected to have a useful life of less than two years, HMRC will accept that the expenditure is revenue (ie income).[79]

- *Designs:* it is uncertain whether the purchase of designs would qualify for capital allowances as plant. It has been held that it does not,[80] but it is submitted that this case should now be decided differently (for registered designs at least).

---

76   CAA 2001, ss 452–463.
77   CAA 2001, s 452(2)(a).
78   See Manual CA 70030 *Know-how: General* on HMRC's website. Commercial know-how and franchise agreements do not qualify for capital allowances.
79   CAA 2001, ss 71, 72. See also HMRC Manuals CA23410 and BIM35815 (at para 6) for guidance on what, in practice, is regarded as 'computer software'.
80   *McVeigh v Arthur Sanderson & Sons Ltd* (1968) 45 TC 273.

Relief for capital expenditure by companies on intellectual property or R&D incorporated into an intellectual property right or package after 31 March 2002

Since 1 April 2002 the new rules for the taxation of intellectual property have applied. For companies the above rules for claiming capital allowances for capital expenditure on intellectual property or R&D incorporated into an intellectual property right or package were replaced (subject to transitional provisions and elections to continue existing capital allowances where applicable) by the new rules explained in section B under 'Payments for acquisition of intellectual property rights: position for companies after 31 March 2002' above. For individuals and other trading entities, however, capital allowances still apply.

Capital allowances for other capital expenditure on R&D

Where capital expenditure on R&D does not fall into any of the above categories, R&D allowances at a special rate of 100 per cent are available to a person carrying on a trade for the chargeable period in which the relevant expenditure was incurred. The relevant rules are contained in CAA 2001.[81] R&D allowances (which must be claimed[82]) are not available for expenditure which does not relate to a trading activity, although expenditure can be apportioned (on a just and reasonable basis) between qualifying and non-qualifying expenditure.[83]

For this purpose R&D is defined as 'activities that fall to be treated as research and development in accordance with generally accepted accounting practice' (except as specifically modified by Treasury regulations)'.[84] Expenditure on R&D includes expenditure incurred for 'providing facilities for carrying out R&D' but excludes expenditure on land and buildings except insofar as it relates to plant and machinery which become fixtures.[85] Again, there are provisions[86] for apportioning expenditure on land and buildings between qualifying and non-qualifying expenditure on a 'just and reasonable' basis. Dwellings are excluded except insofar as they are attached to R&D facilities and 25 per cent or less of the expenditure relates to the building, in which case the whole building is treated as qualifying. Expenditure incurred in the

---

81   CAA 2001, ss 437–451.
82   CAA 2001, s 441(3).
83   CAA 2001, Sch 3, Pt 8.
84   ICTA 1988, s 837A. See section B under 'Statutory definition of R&D', para 2 above for the extended definition of 'R&D'.
85   CAA 2001, s 440.
86   CAA 2001, s 440 and Sch 3, Pt 4.

acquisition of (1) rights in R&D, or (2) rights arising out of R&D is also excluded.[87]

Pre-trading expenditure on R&D is also allowable if the activity subsequently leads to the commencement of a trade connected with it.[88] The allowable expenditure includes any net VAT liability thereon.[89] The subsequent disposal of an asset for which a capital allowance has been made is a 'relevant event' which triggers an adjustment for tax purposes. The mechanism for making this adjustment is set out in detail in the legislation[90] but, put simply, the allowance is recalculated to bring the disposal value into charge as a trading receipt.

D: CAPITAL GAINS ON DISPOSAL OF INTELLECTUAL PROPERTY

Capital gains tax (CGT) – introduction

A detailed commentary on CGT is beyond the scope of this title. The rules, however, include a 'roll-over' relief for re-investment of the proceeds of sale of business assets, 'group relief' to make intra-group transfers by companies tax-neutral and a de-grouping charge when a company with an asset on which a chargeable gain has been deferred leaves the group, an exemption for disposals of 'substantial shareholdings' by a trading company, special rules for company reconstructions, 'taper relief' (before 6 April 2008), new rules for business and non-business assets and 'entrepreneur's relief' (after 5 April 2008), use of trading losses to offset chargeable gains and special rules to substitute market value for the actual consideration in transactions between 'connected persons'.[91] Notwithstanding recent simplification measures the CGT rules[92] are complex because they are replete with anti-avoidance provisions and were fundamentally changed in 2008. In practice, specialist tax planning advice should be sought where significant amounts of tax are at stake on a particular transaction.

To summarise the basic principles, if a capital asset is disposed of for more than the price at which it is acquired (after allowable expenditure is taken into account), a chargeable gain may arise and CGT (or, in the case of companies, corporation tax) may be payable thereon. The disposal will also be a relevant

---

87 CAA 2001, s 438.
88 CAA 2001, s 439.
89 CAA 2001, s 447.
90 CAA 2001, ss 442–444.
91 See n 69 for the meaning of this phrase.
92 The main rules are set out in the Taxation of Chargeable Gains Act 1992 ('TCGA 1992'), CTA 2009 and HMRC Interpretations (RIs), Statements of Practice (SPs) and Extra-Statutory Concessions (ESCs).

event for capital allowances purposes and a separate adjustment may be necessary to recapture capital allowances made.

Individuals

UK-resident individuals or persons carrying on a trade in the UK for which the asset is used are, in principle, within the CGT net. Special rules apply to professional self-employed writers and artists which may mean that disposals of copyright or royalty rights may be taxable as income (see section F under 'General' below). Non-residents who are not carrying on a UK trade (via an agent or otherwise) may be able to escape CGT. Separate (more intricate rules) govern assets held in trust and disposals by trustees.

Before 6 April 2008 the rate of CGT chargeable was the taxpayer's marginal rate of income tax (ie the chargeable gain was added to income and taxed according to the relevant tax band up to a top rate of 40 per cent).There were, however, tax planning opportunities. These included timing the transaction to make best use of annual exemptions and loss relief. In addition, there were other reliefs for business assets, such as 'roll-over' relief and taper relief (which reduced the chargeable gain to just 25 per cent for business assets held for 2 years or more giving a higher rate taxpayer an effective CGT rate of just 10 per cent[93]).

After 5 April 2008 chargeable gains are subject to a new 18 per cent flat rate of CGT.[94] As before, there is an annual exemption (£10,100 for 2009–2010) and deferment reliefs, including 'roll-over' relief which allows chargeable gains from the sale of certain assets to be deferred to the extent that the proceeds of sale are reinvested in other qualifying assets within a certain time period. In addition, a new 'entrepreneur's relief' (which has to be claimed[95]) is available for certain 'qualifying business disposals'.[96] Entrepreneur's relief is available where an individual (including, in certain situations, a trustee) sells certain businesses or business interests, company shares or assets used in a business. There are a number of qualifying conditions – with regard to the ownership of the business, use of the assets in the business and time limits – which need to be considered in detail to determine if the relief is available (and, if so, to what extent) on a case-by-case basis. Where the relief is available it is calculated by aggregating all relevant gains and deducting all relevant losses and reducing the net gain (up to a limit of £1m) by 4/9ths. It is this £1m limit which has hit the headlines because it makes the relief much less valuable than taper relief.

---

93   FA 2002, s 46 and Sch 10.
94   FA 2009, s 8(1).
95   TCGA 1992, s 169M.
96   FA 2008, s 9 and Sch 3; and TCGA 1992, ss 169H–169K.

The 2008 CGT reforms, especially the withdrawal of taper relief, have been widely criticised as discouraging entrepreneurs of successful new businesses from staying with them for the long-term to expand and develop them to the next stage (eg a flotation).This remains to be seen but, meanwhile, many successful business entrepreneurs will now have to plan a different exit strategy to minimise the CGT 'hit'.

Companies

In contrast to individuals, UK-resident companies or unincorporated associations are, in principle, liable to corporation tax on any chargeable gain. A separate CGT computation is, however, required. Any chargeable gain may be offset by allowances, capital and trading losses, and deferment relief for reinvestment may be available; however a more detailed commentary on CGT is beyond the scope of this title.

After 31 March 2002 the new regime for the taxation of intangible fixed assets (including intellectual property)[97] has governed disposals of any intellectual property or R&D incorporated into an intellectual property right or package. Such disposals are taxed on an income basis, but a new 'roll-over' relief applies where disposal proceeds are reinvested in new intellectual property (or any other intangible fixed asset) within the regime.[98]

Assets held at 1 April 2002 will generally be taxed under previous law. Capital gains on the disposal of intangible fixed assets (including intellectual property) will qualify for CGT 'roll-over' relief, but goodwill is specifically excluded from the relief except where reinvestment has taken place before 1 April 2002 and within 12 months of disposal.

Transfers of intangible fixed assets between companies in the same group are, in principle, tax neutral.[99] There are, however, special anti-avoidance provisions where a company leaves the group immediately after a transfer (which can 'claw back' the tax charge from another group company or a controlling director).[100]

---

97 FA 2002, Sch 29.
98 FA 2002, Sch 29, Pt 7.
99 FA 2002, Sch 29, Pts 8, 9 for definition of 'group' for this purpose and mechanics for claiming the relief on intra-group transfers.
100 FA 2002, Sch 29, paras 69, 70.

E: RELIEF FOR INCOME EXPENDITURE ON INTELLECTUAL PROPERTY AND R&D

The schedular system and recent reforms

Historically, the UK system has taxed income according to the Schedule (Schedules A–F) and (within a Schedule) the Case into which it falls. These schedules required separate tax computations and determined the amount of tax actually payable.[101] This commentary is confined to Schedule D which is divided into six cases of which, in technology agreements, only four are relevant: Case I (income from a trade), Case II (income from a profession or vocation), Case III (annual payments etc) and Case VI (a residual 'mop-up' category).

As from 6 April 2006 for income tax purposes the rules previously in Cases I and II of Schedule D have been rewritten to Part 2 of the Income Tax (Trading and Other Income) Act 2005 ('ITTOIA 2005'); and, for accounting periods ending after 1 April 2009, for corporation tax purposes they have been rewritten to Part 3 of CTA 2009 as part of the Tax Law Rewrite Project. The 'rewrite' rules are, however, essentially the same.

Relief for R&D income expenditure – general rule

The fundamental rule for computing the chargeable profits of a trade or profession under Schedule D, Case I or II and under Part 2 of ITTOIA 2005 is that current (or income) expenditure which is incurred 'wholly and exclusively' for the purposes of a trade or profession is deductible against the profits of that trade or profession (or, as appropriate, other trading profits or income).[102] Capital expenditure is therefore disallowed,[103] but capital allowances may be available. Some expenditure, in reality, may be incurred for business and non-business purposes. This is ultimately a question of fact on which there is very extensive case law. HMRC will, in practice, agree a just and reasonable apportionment of any such expenditure between business and non-business uses (and allow the former) where appropriate. The special rules for R&D expenditure set out below are therefore subject to this overriding qualification.

---

101 Schedules A–F were set out in ICTA 1988, ss 15–20 before their repeal, and pre-repeal cases obviously refer to these sections, not the 'rewrite' provisions in ITEPA 2003, ITTOIA 2005, ITA 2007 and CTA 2009.
102 ICTA 1988, s 74(1)(a) and ITTOIA 2005, ss 32, 34.
103 ITTOIA 2005, s 33.

Special relief for R&D income expenditure – small and medium-sized companies

Trading companies can deduct income expenditure on R&D related to a trade and directly undertaken by or on behalf of the company against the profits of the trade.[104] In addition, the Finance Act 2000[105] introduced a special relief for any company that qualifies as a small and medium-sized enterprise ('SME') and incurs income expenditure on R&D. The relief can now be claimed where an SME incurs expenditure on R&D of £10,000 or more in an accounting period.[106] The limit applies pro-rata for accounting periods shorter than one year. Following changes made by the Finance Act 2006, however, for accounting periods ending on or after 31 March 2006 all claims for R&D tax credits must now be made in a tax return and are subject to the normal corporation tax self-assessment ('CTSA') time limits for making, amending and withdrawing claims. Expenditure on R&D after 1 August 2008 attracts tax relief of 175 per cent.[107] The relief effectively reduces the cost of R&D by 36.75 per cent for companies paying the small companies' rate of corporation tax.[108]

The UK definition of an 'SME' adopts European Commission Recommendation 2003/361/EC ([2003] OJ L124/36), which sets three limits: a workforce of less than 250 employees; an annual turnover of 50m euros or less; and a balance sheet of 43m euros or less. It doubles these limits for expenditure incurred on or after 1 August 2008 to extend the relief to 'larger SMEs' (and large companies which became a larger SME for part of the accounting period 2008/09 will effectively make separate claims for expenditure on R&D before and after 1 August 2008). The tests, however, are applied differently according to whether an enterprise is an 'autonomous', 'partner' or 'linked' enterprise.

An autonomous enterprise must stay below the staff ceiling *and* one of the other (turnover and balance sheet) tests. An enterprise is an autonomous enterprise if other enterprises do not have a stake of 25 per cent or more of its capital or voting rights but this threshold can be exceeded in the case of public investment corporations and venture capital companies, 'business angels', universities or non-profit research centres and certain institutional investors and local authorities.[109] The autonomous enterprise itself must not have a holding of 25 per cent or more in another enterprise.

---

104 CTA 2009, s 87.
105 The rules in FA 2000, Sch 20 have been rewritten to CTA 2009, Pt 13.
106 CTA 2009, s 1050.
107 CTA 2009, s 1044(8) ; SI 2008/1880, art 1.
108 ICTA 1988, s 13.
109 See HMRC Manuals CIRD91500, CIRD92100 and CIRD92200 for detailed guidance.

A linked enterprise is, broadly, one which is connected to another (ie it controls the other or is controlled by it). For linked enterprises the ceiling tests (ie the staff ceiling *and* one of the other tests) are applied to the aggregate figures in the accounts of all linked enterprises.

A partnership enterprise is not linked but one which holds (either on its own or in combination with other enterprises with which it is linked) 25 per cent or more of the capital or voting rights of the other. For partnership enterprises the ceiling tests (ie the staff ceiling and one of the other tests) are applied to the figures in the accounts of the enterprise and a proportion of any other partner.

Relief is available for R&D carried on outside the UK provided that the R&D leads to a UK trade. Companies which have not started trading can benefit because they can elect to treat 175 per cent of their R&D expenditure as a trading loss.[110] Furthermore, a company with an unrelieved loss can surrender that loss (so far as attributable to R&D expenditure) in return for payment of an R&D tax credit at 14 per cent provided that it is a going concern.[111] However, this cash payment is limited to the total of the company's PAYE and NIC liabilities for the period.[112]

Before the change announced in the 2009 Pre-Budget Report SME companies carrying out R&D had to retain some intellectual property rights in their R&D to retain the tax credit.[113] The rules will, however, be changed to abolish this requirement and the changes (in the Finance Act 2010) will have effect for any expenditure incurred by an SME company on R&D in an accounting period ending on or after 9 December 2009.[114] An R&D tax credit can be lost if the company claiming it ceases to carry on a trade. If a company's only activity is to exploit intellectual property then a reorganisation resulting in a transfer of the intellectual property to an associated company could result in a loss of the R&D tax credit claimed by the transferor company.

For tax purposes 'R&D' is defined as 'activities that fall to be treated as research and development in accordance with generally accepted accounting practice'. This definition (the UK 'GAAP' definition) is narrower than the International Accounting Standard definition ('IAS 38').[115] It can, however, be extended or restricted by Treasury regulations and has now been extended by the BIS Guidelines.[116]

---

110 CTA 2009, s 1045(7).
111 CTA 2009, ss 1054–1058.
112 CTA 2009, s 1059.
113 CTA 2009, ss 1052, 1053.
114 See HMRC 2009 Pre-Budget Report PBRN06, *R&D Tax Relief*, 9 December 2009.
115 ICTA 1988, s 837A.
116 For guidance on 'GAAP' see the Financial Reporting Standards for Smaller Entities (January 2007) and the Institute of Chartered Accountants' *SSAP 13: Accounting for Research and Development* (Revised). See also HMRC's interpretation of the BIS Guidelines in Manual CIRD 81900 and n 41 above.

Finally, to comply with EU rules on notifiable State Aid, companies which receive grants for R&D projects cannot also receive R&D tax credits for the same project (which, in practice, is a serious disadvantage for small bio-tech start-up companies) and there is now a 'global cap' on any claim by a company for R&D and VRR reliefs (see section E under 'Tax relief for expenditure on vaccine research' below) of 7.5m euros for any one project.[117] These limits mean that companies, especially small start-up companies, embarking on R&D projects, are likely to benefit from some strategic tax planning before planning the projects and funding arrangements.

Special relief for R&D income expenditure – large companies

On 1 April 2002 a new R&D tax credit of 25 per cent, in addition to relief for the actual cost of the expenditure, became available for qualifying expenditure (see section E under 'Special relief for R&D income expenditure – small and medium-sized companies' above) by 'large' companies, ie companies not already entitled to the SME R&D tax credit. On 1 April 2008 the tax credit was increased to 30 per cent and total relief of 130 per cent will be given for such expenditure.[118] For a company paying the main rate of corporation tax at 28 per cent the credit will reduce the cost of the expenditure by 8.4 per cent.

The 30 per cent credit for large companies operates in basically the same way as the SME R&D tax credit[119] but (unlike SME companies before the changes announced in the 2009 Pre-Budget Report come into effect) large companies do not have to retain any intellectual property rights in their R&D to claim the tax credit. Like SME companies, however, they have to incur income expenditure on R&D of £10,000 or more in an accounting period.[120] The R&D tax credit is available for three different arrangements:

- First, for in-house R&D projects carried out by the company, including contract research (ie work contracted to it by another large company or a non-trading individual), on all qualifying expenditure on staff costs (including externally provided workers), software or consumable items and payments to subjects of a clinical trial.[121]

- Secondly, for contracted-out R&D where qualifying R&D activity is undertaken on the company's behalf but sub-contracted to a 'qualifying

---

117 SI 2008/1928 ; CTA 2009, s 1113.
118 CTA 2009, s 1074.
119 The rules for large companies are contained in CTA 2009, ss 1074–1080.
120 CTA 2009, s 1075. As with SME companies, the £10,000 requirement is reduced pro rata for shorter accounting periods.
121 CTA 2009, ss 1076, 1077.

body' (such as a university or HEI, charity, scientific research organisation[122] or NHS body) and individuals or partnerships.[123]

- Thirdly, for contributions towards qualifying R&D activity carried out by an independent organisation (ie qualifying body, individual or partnership) from which the company will not necessarily gain direct benefit.[124]

The new R&D tax credit will, therefore, benefit organisations which cannot themselves claim R&D tax credits under either scheme because, for example, they are not companies or have charitable status and are exempt from tax. Furthermore, where qualifying R&D activity is sub-contracted to SME companies,[125] they will be able to claim the new credit (at a rate of 30 per cent). Where, conversely, an SME company sub-contracts work to a large company, the SME company will continue to be entitled to a 75 per cent credit under the existing scheme (see section E under 'Special relief for R&D income expenditure – small and medium-sized companies' above).

Staff training and development

If R&D projects involve expenditure on staff training and/or development, it will usually be allowed as income expenditure even if it benefits staff personally (for example foreign language tuition for a business project) or has such an enduring benefit that it is, arguably, capital expenditure and therefore disallowable. HMRC, however, have indicated that where the expenditure is on a course for a business proprietor the test is whether it updates existing knowledge (in which case it will usually be allowable provided it satisfies the 'wholly and exclusively' test) or is intended to give new expertise, knowledge or skills and creates a new intangible asset (in which case it will be regarded as of a capital nature and disallowed).[126]

Tax relief for expenditure on vaccine research

Budget 2002[127] introduced a new relief ('VRR') for qualifying expenditure by SME companies on research into TB, malaria, HIV and AIDS.[128] The relief, which was extended to large companies in 2008, basically operates in

---

122 For tax purposes (including ICTA 1988, s 508) a 'scientific research organisation' is defined by the Scientific Research Organisation Regulations (SI 2007/3426), with effect for accounting periods beginning on or after 1 January 2008.
123 CTA 2009, ss 1076, 1078.
124 CTA 2009, ss 1076, 1079.
125 CTA 2009, s 1065.
126 ICTA 1988, s 74(1)(a), (f) and HMRC Manual BIM35660.
127 The rules are now contained in CTA 2009, ss 1085–1112. See also HMRC Press Release of 1 August 2008 on the new rules.
128 CTA 2009, s 1091(5).

the same way as R&D tax credits and can now be claimed by all companies within the same time limits as R&D tax credits (see section E under 'Special relief for R&D income expenditure – small and medium-sized companies' above). As from 1 August 2008 VRR was extended to larger SMEs[129] and improved. It now covers certain staff costs and clinical trial payments which previously did not qualify.[130] The rate of relief, however, was reduced to 40 per cent[131] and an overall cap of 7.5m euros on R&D and VRR for any one project was introduced.[132] VRR is available for the company's own expenditure on R&D, and the cost of sub-contracting it to other companies, charities, universities and scientific research organisations;[133] but, as from 1 August 2008, contributions to independent research by universities, charities or scientific research organisations will not qualify.[134]

F: TAXATION OF INCOME FROM R&D AND OTHER TECHNOLOGY-TRANSFER ACTIVITIES

Taxation of individuals providing R&D services

General

Before 6 April 2006 nearly all income received by an individual (including a member of a partnership) providing R&D services with a view to making a profit were taxable under Cases I or II of Schedule D (as income of a trade or a profession) and are now taxable under ITTOIA 2005[135] (see section E under 'The schedular system and recent reforms' above). In either case, the basic rules for computing taxable profits or losses (ie adjusting trading profits or losses for tax purposes) are the same. In particular, only business expenses which are 'wholly and exclusively' incurred for the purposes of the trade or profession are deductible.[136]

Professional researchers or R&D consultants will be familiar with the basic rules, but an employee who carries out R&D as a business activity for the first time may require guidance. Where the work is carried out for his or her existing employer, it is likely to be treated as earned income subject to PAYE, ie income tax and Class 1 NICs (at the rates of 11 per cent for 2010–11 and 12 per cent for 2011–12) will be deducted at source by the employer. It should,

---

129 SI 2008/1880.
130 SI 2008/1878 and SI 2008/1930.
131 SI 2008/1933. The rate was reduced from 50 per cent to meet EU State Aid requirements.
132 SI 2008/1928 ; CTA 2009, s 1113. See also section E under 'Special relief for R&D income expenditure – small and medium-sized companies', para 9 above.
133 See n 122 above.
134 SI 2008/1930.
135 This well-established test is enacted in ICTA 1988, s 74.
136 The relevant provisions are in ITTOIA 2005, Pt 2; ITA 2007, s 64; and Social Security Benefits Act 1992, s 15(1)(a).

however, be noted that even a 'one-off' payment for a project to another person or company could amount to the commencement of a business.

Special rules apply to professional self-employed writers and artists who may be able to treat royalties as earned income and therefore relieve losses against other income and get tax relief on pension contributions, but Class 4 NICs will be payable (see section D under 'Individuals' above).

In practice, the issue most likely to concern an individual providing R&D services is what expenses are allowable against his or her income for tax purposes. Only expenses which are 'wholly and exclusively' incurred for the purpose of a business or profession are allowable. This test can create problems where a project is pursued for personal or career objectives as well as a business one or if a personal project leads to commencement of a business at a later date. It can also create problems where there is business and personal use of, for example, a house or a car or laptop. In practice, inspectors will resolve these issues by judging each case on its facts with a view to agreeing a 'just and reasonable' apportionment between the two uses, and allow a percentage for business use.[137]

Income tax, national insurance contributions (NICs) and returns

An individual is liable to pay income tax only if his or her income exceeds the standard personal allowance for the year of assessment or tax year.[138]

In addition to flat-rate Class 2 NICs, an individual who is self-employed or a partner in a business will be liable to pay Class 4 NICs on his or her relevant earnings. For 2010–11 Class 4 NICs are payable at a rate of 8 per cent on profits between £5,715 and £43,875 plus 1 per cent on any profit above that amount. For 2011–12 they will increase to 9 per cent and 2 per cent respectively. Unearned or investment income escapes this NIC liability and there is a starting rate of 10 per cent for savings (on taxable income up to £2,440 for 2010–11) – two advantages of investment income.

Subject to certain de minimis limits or agreement with HMRC to extend payment deadlines, payments on account of both income tax and NIC are due on 31 January in the year of assessment and on 31 July in the following tax year. The balance due is payable on 31 January following the end of the year of assessment. Interest (chargeable at the official statutory rate published

---

137 The relevant provisions are in ITTOIA 2005, Pt 2; ITA 2007, s 64; and Social Security Benefits Act 1992, s 15(1)(a).The best practical guidance for anyone in this situation is to keep detailed records of all expenses.

138 For 2009–10 the personal allowance for an individual aged under 65 is £6,475. Income above that level is taxable at the basic rate of 20 per cent up to £37,400 and then at the higher rate of 40 per cent. For 2010–11 there is an additional rate of 50 per cent on annual earnings over £150,000 (42.5 per cent on dividends). See FA 2009, ss 3, 6 and Sch 2.

from time to time) is payable on any unpaid tax or NIC due from the due date to the payment date. Late payment attracts a 5 per cent surcharge after 28 days, an additional 5 per cent surcharge after 6 months and a further 5 per cent surcharge after 12 months.[139]

In 2007 a tougher penalty regime[140] was introduced to combat errors and delays in returns of income tax (including PAYE) and NICs and late payment of any amount due to HMRC. Under the new regime penalties of up to 100 per cent of the tax due can be imposed where there is an error, as follows: 30 per cent where there is an error and the taxpayer has no reasonable excuse; 70 per cent where there is deliberate understatement; and 100 per cent where there is deliberate understatement with concealment. However, where a taxpayer makes a disclosure (ie takes active steps to remedy the error) and acts promptly, these penalties can be substantially reduced. There is also an automatic £100 penalty for late filing of returns with an additional £10 per day for every day of delay in excess of 3 months.

Losses

Following Tax Law Rewrite the rules for loss relief are now contained in ITA 2007, Pt 4; and, in a nutshell, they can be summarised as follows. An individual can make a claim to relieve allowable losses (which are computed on the same basis as taxable profits) by set-off against other income in the same year of assessment (and the preceding tax year).[141] He or she can also carry them forward indefinitely to offset subsequent profits from the same trade.[142] He or she can also carry back losses against profits of the preceding year and (for losses incurred in accounting periods ending between 6 April 2008 and 5 April 2009) a further £50,000 of losses against profits of the two years prior to the preceding year. In each case there is a proviso that the trade is carried out on a commercial basis (ie with a view to making a profit).[143] If the trade ceases he or she can make a claim to carry back terminal losses.[144] Finally, the individual can offset surplus trading losses not otherwise relieved against chargeable gains[145] for the tax year in question (although this will only save CGT at 18 per cent). There are strict time limits for making any claim for loss relief.[146] There are special rules for trustees and members of a partnership but these are outside the scope of this title.

---

139 Taxes Management Act 1970, ss 59A–59C and FA 2009, s 101 and Sch 53.
140 The regime introduced by FA 2007, Sch 24 also applied to CT, CGT and VAT and was extended by FA 2009, Sch 53 to all taxes.
141 ITA 2007, s 64.
142 ITA 2007, s 83.
143 ITA 2007, ss 72–74.
144 ITA 2007, ss 89–94.
145 ITA 2007, s 72.
146 An individual has one year from the normal self-assessment filing date for the loss-making year in which to make the claim (ITA 2007, s 64(5)).

Taxation of companies providing R&D services

Introduction

This brief commentary is simply aimed at giving the drafter of technology agreements and business mangers some very basic guidance on the tax implications of using a company as a vehicle for an R&D contract.

Corporation tax net

A UK company, which is UK-resident,[147] is chargeable to corporation tax on its worldwide profits and gains. A non-resident company trading in the UK through a branch or agency will be chargeable to corporation tax on its worldwide profits and gains attributable to the branch or agency.[148] UK-registered companies will be required to file annual returns to Companies House and, unless the small company exemption applies, file audited accounts. The exemption,[149] which means that a company can file abbreviated accounts, is available to companies with an annual turnover of £6.5m or less and assets of £3.26m or less and 50 or fewer employees. In either case, profits from the provision of R&D services in the UK will be chargeable to corporation tax.

Computation of chargeable profits

The basis for calculating taxable profits (and allowable losses) is essentially the same as for individuals, but as from 1 April 2002 receipts from the exploitation of intellectual property have been taxed as income for companies under the new rules for intangible fixed assets (see section B under 'Payments for acquisition of intellectual property rights: position for companies after 31 March 2002' above) and the rules are now contained in the Corporation Tax Act 2009 ('CTA 2009'). There are, however, some other basic differences. These include the fact that companies are charged on profits not of tax years or years of assessment (ie 6 April to 5 April) but of financial years (ie 1 April to 31 March). A financial year is calculated by reference to its accounting periods (which may have to be time apportioned). In the case of companies, capital gains are also chargeable to corporation tax.

The nature of a receipt has important implications for offsetting expenses and losses as well as deducting tax at source. The important point for the draftsman

---

147 A company incorporated in the UK (ie a UK-registered company) is UK resident and is required to notify HMRC of its chargeability whether or not it has filed an annual return to Companies House. Companies incorporated overseas are treated as UK resident if their 'central management and control' is in the UK. This test is a factual one and there is extensive case law on it.
148 CTA 2009, ss 2, 5.
149 For further guidance see the Companies House guidance booklet, *Life of a Company* (October 2009, version 2).

of an R&D agreement to note is that the tax bill may be significantly different depending on the category into which the receipt falls.

Rates of corporation tax

There are two standard rates of corporation tax, the small companies rate and the main rate.[150] A corporation tax computation can, however, be tricky because of the mechanics for calculating marginal relief.[151] As, in practice, the mechanics of the actual calculation of the marginal rate applicable is best explained by examples, it is advisable to consult textbooks which set out specific detailed examples.[152] In addition, following the announcement in the 2009 Pre-Budget Report, a new 10 per cent rate of corporation tax on income from UK patents will be introduced with effect from 2013.

The rules for payment of corporation tax are similar for income tax except that the basic rule is that corporation tax is due 9 months and 1 day after the end of the relevant accounting period. Interest and penalties apply in the event of late payment, but instalment options are available.

Withholding tax on royalties for intellectual property

If, as part of a technology agreement, royalties are payable for the use of intellectual property, then the payer may be required to deduct income tax at source from the royalty payment and account for it to HMRC. Put simply, the UK withholding tax rules (which are more fully considered in the context of international technology agreements at section H 'International technology agreements' below) are designed to ensure collection of tax where it would be more difficult for HMRC to collect it from the recipient. The drafter of any technology agreement under which royalties are payable should establish whether withholding tax will apply and, if so, make this clear in the agreement.

The UK rules were simplified in 2001 and modified in 2004 to implement Council Directive 2003/49/EC ([2003] OJ L157/49).The Directive seeks to introduce a common system of taxation of interest and royalty payments between associated companies of different EU member states. The rules[153] allow a UK company or 'qualifying partnership' (ie a partnership with a UK company member) to make payments to other UK companies (or UK branches of overseas companies) or partnerships where all partners are UK residents without withholding tax from the payment provided that the

---

150 For tax years 2009–10 and 2010–11 the small companies rate is 21 per cent on profits up to £300,000; the main rate is 28 per cent on profits above £1,500,000.
151 For tax years 2009–10 and 2010–11 marginal relief applies on profits of £300,000–£1,500,000.
152 Eg Hyland, *Tolley's Corporation Tax 2009–10 (LexisNexis)*.
153 The rules are now contained in ITA 2007, Pt 15, chs 6 and 11.

company reasonably believes that the person *beneficially entitled* to the payment is UK resident (and therefore within the UK tax net).[154]

This optional scheme also applies to royalty payments to UK bodies which are exempt from tax (and would simply reclaim the tax deducted at a later date) including local authorities, NHS bodies, universities, charities and government research organisations.[155] In all cases, if it subsequently transpires that the beneficial owner was not UK resident (or an exempt body) then the paying company will be liable for the tax with interest thereon even if it can show that it held a reasonable belief to the contrary. Furthermore, if the company had no reasonable belief[156] that it was entitled to make the payments gross then it could be liable to penalties.[157] The payer must therefore look behind an intermediary or agent to establish the identity of the intellectual property being licensed. Similarly, a non-resident payer cannot come within the rules by simply using a UK company as an intermediary, agent or trustee. However, an officer of HMRC can make a direction that any payment can be made gross (ie without deduction of tax) if he or she has reasonable grounds for believing that the payment will be excepted (from the duty to deduct) at the time it is made.[158]

To minimise exposure to a liability to back tax, interest and penalties any company making gross royalty payments under the optional scheme should make prudent enquiries as to the tax residence or status of the beneficial owner, preferably through independent advisers, before finalising the agreement. If there is any doubt on the point the payer company should consider including an appropriately drafted tax indemnity from the recipient in the agreement.

Relief for losses

Companies carrying on a trade can claim to set off losses incurred in that trade against other profits of the same accounting period. Losses are computed on the same basis as chargeable profits[159] (and can include capital allowances) but capital losses cannot generally be set off against trading profits. Companies can additionally claim to carry back unrelieved trading losses[160] one year (three years for losses incurred in accounting periods ending between 24 November 2008 and 23 November 2010). Companies can also carry forward

---

154 ITA 2007, s 933.
155 ITA 2007, s 936 and ICTA 1988, ss 507, 508. See n 122 above.
156 ITA 2007, s 938.
157 TMA 1970, s 98(4A) prescribes a penalty of up to £3,000 for an incorrect return which fails to record a payment (or the amount of a payment) from which tax should have been deducted *and* there was no reasonable belief that it could be made gross.
158 ITA 2007, ss 930, 931.
159 CTA 2009, s 47.
160 Excess charges on income are excluded from losses available for carry back (unless the company has ceased to trade, in which case they may be carried back 36 months).

any unrelieved losses to offset any trading income from the same trade in succeeding accounting periods.

General guidance for the drafter

In practice, describing a payment as 'income' as opposed to 'capital' is an oversimplification. The drafter of an agreement should work in conjunction with the client's accountants and/or tax advisers to ensure the optimum tax treatment of any income under a technology agreement. Even if the amount of tax at stake is small, dispensing with any up-front tax advice is usually a 'false economy'. The cost saving can, if the agreement ignores the tax rules, easily be outweighed by greater compliance costs at a later date.

G: CHARITIES

Exemptions for charities

Most registered charities carrying out business activities on any scale will do so via a subsidiary company to avoid losing their charitable status and the valuable tax advantages which result from it. The company is then treated as any other business entity for tax purposes, but its profits are paid by Gift Aid to the charity. There are, however, some charitable institutions such as universities and higher education institutions ('HEIs') which receive payments for small-scale R&D activity without having set out to commercialise the operation. This section highlights some specific tax issues which could result from such activity.

Charities (whether unincorporated bodies of persons, trusts or charitable companies) are exempt from tax on most types of income (including royalties, trading income and all capital gains) if they are applicable *and in fact applied* for charitable purposes only.[161] For trading income to be covered by the exemption a further condition applies. The trade must be 'exercised in the course of the actual carrying out of a primary purpose of the charity' or 'the work in connection with the trade is mainly carried out by the beneficiaries of the charity'.[162]

There are other exemptions. Income from 'ancillary trading', ie income which contributes to the primary purposes of the charity (such as the sale of food and drink in a restaurant) is treated as part of 'primary purpose trading' for both charity law and tax purposes. There is another exemption for small-scale trading profits which applies if the charity's annual turnover is less than £5,000 or, if it exceeds this figure, 25 per cent or less of the charity's gross

---

161 ICTA 1988, ss 505, 506 and Sch 20; TCGA 1992, s 256; and ITA 2007, ss 518–563.
162 ICTA 1988, s 505(1).

income (ie total income from all sources including investment income and donations) or £50,000, whichever is lower. Charities also enjoy exemptions for lotteries and fund-raising events (but any consideration of these is beyond the scope of this title).[163]

More significantly, charity law also allows charities to carry on non-primary purpose trading to raise funds without losing their charitable status provided that the trading involves no 'significant risk' to the assets of the charity. This risk is that the turnover is insufficient to meet the costs of carrying on the trade and the deficit has to be financed out of the assets of the charity. If there is such a risk they must carry on non-primary purpose trading through a subsidiary company. There is, however, no exemption for the profits of non-primary purpose trading.

The Finance Act 2006[164] introduced a series of anti-avoidance measures to restrict exemptions and reliefs where charities engage in 'circular' transactions (ie transactions in which a donor gets tax relief, but the charity then directs funds or assets back to the donor) with a substantial donor and incur non-charitable expenditure or receive donations from companies in return for certain benefits. At the same time, the rules relating to trading by charities were relaxed so that tax relief is available where a charity carries on a trade only part of which is a primary purpose of the charity. These changes, however, created real uncertainty for universities in some trading transactions, such as research collaboration agreements.

HMRC responded by setting up a working group with universities and the CBI to discuss the issue, and on 1 June 2009 agreed guidelines, *The Corporation Tax Treatment of UK Universities Guidance Note*, were published.[165] No significant corporation tax liabilities should arise where appropriate action is taken to operate the guidelines, but universities may need to implement new procedures in their financial planning and reporting. In particular, it is now much more critical to identify non-primary purpose activity and non-charitable expenditure on a case-by-case basis; and, if necessary, to take appropriate action to avoid corporation tax liabilities.[166]

---

163 For further details see HMRC guidance note *Fund-raising events: Exemption for charities and other qualifying bodies* and the Charity Commission's advisory publication, CC35 *Trustees, trading and tax* (April 2007).

164 FA 2006, ss 54–58 amended ICTA 1988, ss 505, 506 (and related provisions) with effect from 22 March 2006, and certain provisions have been rewritten to ITA 2007, ss 518–523.

165 These guidelines, agreed by the British University Finance Directors Group and Ernst & Young LLP in consultation with HMRC to assist universities in planning for and meeting their corporation tax obligations, are not mandatory (universities can negotiate separate arrangements with HMRC). They supersede the tax guidelines agreed between the Committee of Vice-Chancellors and Principals and the Inland Revenue in 1994 (the 'CVCP Guidelines').

166 See article at www.andlaw.eu for further practical guidance.

In summary, trading activity which comes within both categories, ie primary purpose and non-primary purpose or 'mixed purpose' trading (eg a shop in a public art gallery which sells exhibition catalogues and promotional pens) can still cause problems for universities and HEIs. For tax purposes any 'mixed purpose' trading activity must be treated as two separate trades, and there must be a reasonable apportionment of expenses and receipts between them.

The tax treatment of income from business sponsorship of an R&D project will depend on the wording of any commercial participator agreement (required by the Charity Commission under Charities Act 1992, s 59) or the particular details of the arrangement. Subject to any Finance Act 2006 provisions which may apply, donations to R&D activity per se will be exempt even if the donation results in marketing opportunities for the sponsor, but where R&D services are provided for the 'donation' under a sponsorship agreement the payments are more likely to be treated as trading income. Other specific exemptions or concessions may be available, but a more detailed commentary on these is beyond the scope of this title.

Any charity embarking on R&D activity should carefully consider the tax provisions (and the impact of VAT discussed below) and, if appropriate, seek specialist tax advice from advisers with experience of charities for a cost-benefit analysis of hiving-off the R&D activity into a separate company.

Some scientific research organisations (see note 122) can apply for similar tax exemptions as charities (under ICTA 1988, s 508) and, as similar considerations apply, they should also seek specialist tax advice before embarking on certain R&D projects.

H: INTERNATIONAL TECHNOLOGY AGREEMENTS

Overview

There are, in practice, two main issues which affect any international technology agreement: withholding tax, where tax is deducted before making a payment to a person not resident in the UK for tax purposes ('a non-resident'); and double taxation, where the same payment is taxed in two countries. These issues are considered in some detail below and the topic of offshore tax planning is briefly addressed as a sequel.

Withholding tax

Introduction

Withholding tax is tax which a payer of money under an agreement is required to deduct from that money, and account for to HMRC, before paying the money (net of tax) to the payee. The tax is charged on the payee's income but is deducted by the payer who, in effect, acts as a free tax-collection agent for HMRC. Tax is withheld at the basic rate (currently 20 per cent), irrespective of the payee's tax liability. The payee may subsequently be entitled to a refund from HMRC of all or part of the tax deducted, depending on his or her tax situation. Even where he or she is ultimately liable for the tax, however, deduction in advance is a cashflow disadvantage.

The UK requirement to deduct tax at source applies to certain annual payments and royalties. It is essentially a mechanism designed to ensure collection of the tax in situations where it is difficult to collect it from the recipient. It therefore usually applies where a UK party to an agreement makes a payment to a person whose habitual place of abode is overseas (but see section F under 'Withholding tax on royalties for intellectual property' above for the special rules which apply to royalty payments between associated companies of different EU member states).

Many other countries operate similar withholding tax systems to the UK and this means that a UK party to an international technology agreement (for example, a UK institution carrying out work in the UK under an international collaboration agreement for an overseas party) may suffer a deduction on payments from overseas parties. This is an overseas tax issue which is beyond the scope of this title, and advice from overseas advisers should be sought.

It is critical to establish whether there is an obligation on the payer to withhold tax from a payment due under a technology agreement. If there is, but the payer fails to do so, he or she is liable to pay the tax to HMRC, whether or not he or she can recover it from the payee.

Criteria for deducting tax

Tax is only required to be withheld from particular types of payment such as certain royalties and annual payments. The rules, however, are complex and impose a considerable compliance burden on the payee.[167] Assuming that a payment is made under a legal obligation, however, the criteria established by UK case law for determining whether tax may or must be deducted can be summarised as follows:

- whether the payment relates to UK or overseas intellectual property and the type of intellectual property (eg patents, copyright etc);

- whether the parties to the transaction are individuals or companies;

- whether the payment is made to a non-resident individual or company;

---

167 Royalty payments between members of an international group are subject to transfer pricing rules (see section I 'Transfer pricing' below) and anti-avoidance provisions.

- whether the payee receives the payment as 'pure income profit', for example if the intellectual property was bought as an investment.

Given the large number of variable factors above, if potentially large amounts of tax are at stake, and sufficient time is available, the payer should seek a ruling from HMRC before making any payment. The payer can then avoid personal liability to pay tax which he or she has failed to withhold and a dispute with the payee for wrongly withholding tax. In the context of R&D collaboration agreements, payments for R&D services are generally outside the rules.

Payments for intellectual property rights

The rules have been rewritten as part of the Tax Law Rewrite Project. The project was not designed to change the substantive law, but this may be the effect in some situations (see note 173). Furthermore, there are special rules regarding royalty payments between associated companies of different EU member states (see section F under 'Withholding tax on royalties for intellectual property' above). Payments for intellectual property rights can be subject to withholding tax and these can be summarised as follows:

(a) *UK patents:* the payer will almost always have to deduct basic rate income tax (or presumably, if applicable, the new 10 per cent rate of corporation tax for UK patent income announced in the 2009 Pre-Budget Report as from 2013) at source from UK patent royalties,[168] even where the payment is of a capital nature.[169] There are exemptions (for UK source non-commercial payments etc) but, in practice, the scope of these exemptions is very limited.[170] A non-resident is still liable to UK tax in respect of income arising from a UK patent. This is because registration of the letters patent in the UK creates a UK source of income. It is HMRC's view that this source of income remains in the UK even if the licensing agreement is executed overseas and is governed by foreign law.[171] Tax must be deducted by the payer (unless the payee has obtained an exemption from HMRC pursuant to a double taxation agreement).

(b) *Trade marks:* basic rate income tax will also normally be deductible at source from pure-profit royalties paid for use of a trade mark.[172] If, however, services are performed and the payment is essentially for those

---

168 ITTOIA 2005, s 579 imposes the income tax charge, and ITA 2007, ss 903, 946 impose the duty on the payer to deduct basic rate income tax at source. See also ITA 2007, Annex 1, Changes 138–140 for HMRC's 'approach adopted in rewriting the provisions' on annual payments which constitute charges on income and patent royalties.

169 ITTOIA 2005, ss 587–591, ITA 2007, s 910 and CTA 2009, ss 912, 919.

170 ITTOIA 2005, s 727 and Pt 6.

171 HMRC stated this view in their letter to Anderson & Company of 10 June 1996.

172 ITTOIA, s 579 and ITA 2007, ss 900, 901.

services, the provisions requiring deduction of tax at source may not apply. In practice, some technology agreements are for packages of intellectual property rights and services, and these offer some scope for tax planning.

(c)   *Know-how and show-how:* royalties for know-how were usually taxed in the same way as royalties for trade marks and design rights, and this appears to remain the position post-Tax Law Rewrite.[173] In contrast to know-how, show-how essentially means technical assistance and training. This being the case, payments for show-how are usually taxed as trading income of the recipient and deduction of tax at source does not apply. Again, technology agreements for packages of know-how and show-how offer scope for tax planning.

(d)   *Copyright:* copyright royalties to UK residents were normally paid gross, but could be subject to deduction of basic rate income tax if they were received as 'pure income profit' under Schedule D, Case III. If, however, they were paid to an overseas owner they were subject to deduction of basic rate income tax at source unless the payment is to a professional author following the decisions in *Carson v Cheyney's Executors* (38 TC 240) and *Hume v Asquith* (45 TC 251). This appears to remain the position for copyright royalties post-Tax Law Rewrite (copyrights in films, videos or their soundtracks, however, are excluded insofar as they are 'separately exploited').[174]

(e)   *A right in a design or the public lending right in respect of a book:* royalties for the design right or in a design or the right in a registered design or the public lending right in respect of a book are treated in the same way as copyright royalties.[175]

(f)   *Foreign patents and intellectual property:* in the case of UK-resident licensors, tax was normally not deductible unless the royalties are received as 'pure income profit'. If the licensor was non-resident, basic rate income tax had to be deducted by the payer (unless the payee obtained an exemption from HMRC, pursuant to a double taxation agreement). This appears to remain the position for foreign patents and other intellectual property royalties post-Tax Law Rewrite.[176]

(g)   *Royalty payments between group companies:* royalty payments between group companies may normally be made gross, ie without deduction

---

173   ITTOIA 2005, s 192. ITTOIA 2005, s 579(2) omits any express reference to 'know-how', but s 583 imposes a charge on income from disposals of know-how. ITA 2007, ss 906, 907, which impose a duty to deduct income tax from other intellectual property payments, also omit any reference to know-how, but annual payments of a pure-profit nature appear to be caught by, ss 900, 901. Anderson & Company have written to HMRC for clarification on (e) and (f).

174   ITA 2007, ss 900, 901, 906, 907, 946; but see n 173 above.

175   ITA 2007, ss 900–901, 906–907; but see n 173 above.

176   Under ITA 2007, s 903(3) the duty to deduct income tax from patent royalties is limited to payments which 'arise in the UK', but ITA 2007, ss 900, 901 appear to cover annual payments of a pure-profit nature; but see n 173 above.

of tax subject to certain anti-avoidance provisions, provided that an election is made to the group's inspector of taxes.

Relief from double taxation

Many countries, including the UK, require the payer to withhold tax on making royalty and similar payments. In international transactions this can have the effect of taxing the same income twice, once by the payer's country, and a second time by the payee's country. The UK has an extensive network[177] of double taxation agreements with most other countries of the world to provide relief. These either remove or reduce the requirement to withhold tax in the country of the payer.

Most UK double taxation agreements have provisions dealing with royalties (based on an OECD Model Treaty[178]) which allow payments to be made gross (ie without deduction of UK income tax at the basic rate) or, alternatively, with a reduced rate of tax.[179] For example, the agreement with Germany allows payments by a UK licensee to a German licensor to be made gross. Tables showing these rates for each country of the world are readily available.[180] It should, however, be noted that most agreements contain provisions on transfer pricing (see section H under 'Liability of intermediaries' below) to counter tax avoidance on payments between companies with 'a special relationship'.

HMRC clearance

An application for exemption from withholding UK tax is made to the Financial Intermediaries and Claims Office (FICO) (International). They will need to obtain a report from the payer's local UK tax office before granting the exemption, and in practice, that local tax office will need to see a copy of the licence or other agreement. If the payee has any branch or place of business in the UK (for example a subsidiary company), HMRC will also need to be satisfied that the payment is attributable to the overseas company and not to the UK branch. There may be a delay of several months before any

---

177 There are more than 1,300 double tax treaties worldwide and the UK has the largest network, covering over 100 countries according to an Inland Revenue Press Release of 2 May 2000.
178 See art 12 of the OECD Model 2003 (the model double taxation convention agreed by the OECD's Fiscal Affairs Committee in 2003) which defines royalties as 'payments of any kind received as a consideration for the use of, or the right to use, any copyright of literary, artistic or scientific work including cinematograph films, any patent, trade mark, design or model, plan, secret formula or process, or for information concerning industrial, commercial or scientific experience'.
179 Each double taxation agreement is made part of UK domestic law by a statutory instrument; general administrative provisions are in the Double Taxation Relief (Taxes on Income) (General) Regulations 1970 (SI 1970/488) (as amended by SI 1996/783).
180 See *Simon's Direct Tax Service* (LexisNexis) for full text of agreements.

exemption is given. Meanwhile, tax must be deducted from any payments that are made, even if it is ultimately recoverable when the exemption is granted.

Liability of intermediaries

Where tax must be deducted from a payment,[181] it must be deducted by the person 'by or through whom the payment is made'.[182] This wording has been interpreted as requiring a firm of solicitors, which received a payment on behalf of its client, to account to HMRC for the tax.[183] In the case of copyright, a publisher can be treated as the agent of a non-resident author for this purpose, although the agent's commission can be deducted before calculating the amount on which tax should be withheld.[184] UK agents of a non-resident should be aware of their potential liability to pay the clients' tax if they transmit such payments without deducting tax where appropriate, and irrespective of whether they are reimbursed by their client.

Agreements not to withhold tax

Parties should generally avoid making agreements which try to circumvent the tax rules. In the specific areas of withholding taxes, the Taxes Management Act 1970, s 106(2) should not be overlooked. It imposes a penalty of £50 on a person who refuses to allow a deduction authorised by the Tax Acts and provides that:

> 'Every agreement for payment of interest, rent or other annual payment in full without allowing any such deduction shall be void'.

It is uncertain whether this provision applies to patent royalties. If it does, the inclusion in a licence agreement, for example, of a provision that royalties shall be paid gross, notwithstanding any requirement of tax law to deduct withholding tax, might in some situations cause the agreement to be void.

---

181 ITA 2007, ss 946, 963, 964.
182 The main rules are set out in ITA 2007, ss 900, 910, but this is a technical issue on which specialist tax advice should be sought if it cannot be answered without considering pre-Tax Law Rewrite cases regarding the correct tax treatment of the income by the recipient (ie whether it is trading or investment income).
183 See *Rye and Eyre v IRC* [1935] AC 274, HL where the House of Lords held that a firm of solicitors which had accounted for royalties on behalf of, and with funds from, its client was liable to account for the tax due.
184 ITA 2007, ss 906–909.

Structuring agreements

Withholding tax and the possibility of double taxation create a number of drafting issues which need to be addressed, including the following:

- Is the payer required to withhold tax, and if so is he or she required to provide the payee with a statement that tax has been deducted and paid to HMRC,[185] to enable relief from double taxation to be obtained? Where a payment is to be paid gross, it may be desirable to include a provision under which the payee indemnifies the payer against any liability the latter may incur to HMRC through failure to deduct tax.

- Does the agreement cover the transfer or licensing of intellectual property as well as the provision of research or other services? If so, payments may (unless the rules for the taxation of intellectual property considered in section B under 'Payments for acquisition of intellectual property rights: position for companies after 31 March 2002' and section D under 'Companies' above apply to both parties) need to be apportioned between these services and the intellectual property elements.

- In agreements concerning more than one type of intellectual property, should any express apportionment of payments be made, between the different types of intellectual property?

The growth of international business generally in response to the increasing globalisation of markets, and high-tech business involving intellectual property rights in particular, means that increasing amounts of tax are at stake in applying the deduction at source provisions. HMRC recognise this[186] and have become more sophisticated in their understanding of international business agreements. This means that any drafting technique designed to avoid or minimise the impact of these rules must stand up to close examination.

As the ultimate tax consequences of any payment structure may depend on the tax status of the parties to the agreement, knowledge of their accounts and commercial activities during the course of the agreement is needed to give effective tax-planning advice.

Where different intellectual property rights are licensed or transferred in a single transaction, it may be desirable to apportion the payments between the different types of intellectual property to take advantage of the different tax rules for each type of property. HMRC may challenge an apportionment but are unlikely to do so where the parties are at arm's length and the apportionment is not obviously artificial.[187] Where, however, the parties are 'connected'[188],

---

185 ITA 2007, s 975.
186 See the Inland Revenue's Technical Note *Reform of the taxation of intellectual property*, March 1999, paras 201, 208, 209.
187 See *Paterson Engineering Co Ltd v Duff* (1943) 25 TC 43.
188 See n 70 above.

the greater the precision with which a payment clause is drafted and the more it is seen to be based on underlying commercial reality, the more likely it is to be accepted by HMRC.

Apportionment is a less important issue in transactions between companies involving intellectual property assets created or acquired after 1 April 2002, and taxable under the new rules for intangible fixed assets (see section B under 'Payments for acquisition of intellectual property rights: position for companies after 31 March 2002' and section D under 'Companies' above), but should still be on the draftsman's checklist as the deduction of tax at source rules may still apply to the royalty element of the payments.

Optional scheme for payment of royalties gross: cross-border payments

From 1 October 2002 companies have had the option of paying royalties to non-residents gross or to withhold tax at the reduced rate allowed by double tax treaties without seeking prior clearance from HMRC where the company has a *reasonable belief* (see section F under 'Withholding tax on royalties for intellectual property' above and note 189 on the meaning of this phrase) that the beneficial owner of the royalties is entitled to relief from UK tax on those royalties under a double tax treaty.

The rules, which are designed to reduce tax compliance costs which would otherwise arise from the recipient's prior application for clearance, are contained in ITA 2007, ss 911–913. Under the scheme companies are required to include details of the royalties in their Corporation Tax Self Assessment (CTSA) return. If, at a later date, it transpires that the relief was not in fact due then *irrespective of any reasonable belief that relief was due* the company will be liable to the tax (with interest and, where the company could not hold such a belief, penalties) which should have been deducted when making the payment.[189]

To minimise their exposure to back-tax liabilities with interest and penalties companies using the new scheme should ascertain the availability of double tax treaty relief, preferably through independent tax advisers, before making royalty payments.

Offshore tax havens

One obvious tax avoidance device is to carry out commercial activities in a jurisdiction with low rates of tax. Further tax savings can be achieved

---

189 The test as to whether or not there was a 'reasonable belief' appears to be objective: see para 7 of the Inland Revenue's Budget 2002 Note, *Cross Border Royalties* (REV BN 24).

by exploiting anomalies in double taxation treaties between countries. Offshore tax planning is a rapidly changing growth industry in which tax-haven countries continually change the rules to attract investors in an increasingly competitive market, and countries such as the UK and the US produce anti-avoidance rules to close loopholes and protect their internal tax revenue.

Offshore tax planning is a specialist area which is beyond the scope of this title. It is, however, worth noting that, unlike agreements for pure exploitation of intellectual property rights, R&D agreements will be more difficult to incorporate into offshore tax plans if research staff, premises and equipment are located in the UK. Any R&D agreement which does involve a tax haven will therefore require specialist offshore tax-planning advice and this is likely to be expensive. It is likely to be uneconomic to set up offshore arrangements for transactions with less than £500,000 at stake. Furthermore, the recent 'blitz' of measures against offshore tax evasion culminating in the new measures announced in the 2009 Pre-Budget Report makes offshore tax planning an almost 'no go' area for UK residents.

I: TRANSFER PRICING

Transfer pricing is the term used to describe the pricing structure for transactions between associated enterprises. For multinational companies, tax planning is one of the chief considerations in transfer pricing as it creates an opportunity to 'transfer' income from a company in a high-tax country to an associated company in a low-tax country. In the context of technology agreements, the issue of transfer pricing usually arises in the pricing of intellectual property generated under the agreement between associated companies. It can, however, equally apply to supplies of services between associated companies or an individual and an offshore company controlled by him.

A typical example is where a subsidiary company located in a high-tax country, such as the UK, pays licence fees to its parent company, located in a tax haven, for the use of intellectual property owned by the parent company. Such an arrangement may be a tax-efficient way of diverting profits from the UK company to the offshore parent company (eg by charging an inflated royalty or by creating artificial licences).

In recent years the tax authorities in many jurisdictions, especially the US and the UK, have tightened the rules to counter tax avoidance through such arrangements. HMRC will examine any transfer pricing policy closely with a view to countering tax avoidance under ICTA 1988, s 770A and Sch 28AA or disallowing double taxation relief for royalties where there is a 'special relationship' between the parties (even if the royalty is not excessive) under the anti-avoidance provisions.[190] Indeed, HMRC consider that further measures are necessary to counter avoidance.[191]

The net effect of the current rules is as follows. In a transaction between a UK-resident enterprise and an associated non-resident, where:

- the buyer has control over the seller; or

- the seller has control over the buyer; or

- the same person has control over both buyer and seller;

HMRC can adjust the consideration to an 'arm's length price' to prevent loss of tax to the UK. An example is where a Bahamas company licenses its UK subsidiary company to manufacture and sell certain products under patents owned by the parent company. Under the licence agreement, the UK company is required to pay the parent company a royalty of 50 per cent of the sales price of the licensed products. HMRC can challenge the level of royalties, substituting a lower royalty rate for tax purposes and attributing a different tax treatment to the 'excess' amount of royalties.

It should be emphasised that section 770A applies not only where income or property is *actually transferred*, but also where that is the substantial effect of the transaction. For example, a UK intellectual property owner might permit its overseas subsidiary to make use of the intellectual property. If that permission arises from a formal licence agreement, HMRC can challenge the amount of the consideration under the licence. Even where there is no formal licence but merely a tacit acceptance of the subsidiary's activities, a challenge can still be made to substitute an 'arm's length price' for the 'licence' being assessed for tax purposes. Similarly, a policy decision by a UK company not to sue an associated overseas company for infringement of intellectual property (but without an agreement on the payment of licence fees) can be assessed in the same way by HMRC.

If a transfer pricing adjustment is made, the taxpayer may attract a double tax liability if the relevant overseas tax authorities do not accept the substituted price. Transfer pricing disputes involving separate tax authorities can be very costly and protracted. In practice, therefore, transfer pricing policies should be justified on commercial principles, and payment provisions in agreements for intellectual property or R&D services in cross-border transactions between associated entities should be seen to be arm's length. Where large amounts

---

190 ICTA 1988, ss 808A, 808B.
191 See Technical note *Reform of the taxation of intellectual property, goodwill and intangible assets: the next stage*, 8 November 2000, paras 3.38–3.44.

of tax are at stake on this issue, pricing policies should, if possible, be agreed with the relevant tax authorities in advance.[192]

J: VAT

Introduction

Value Added Tax ('VAT') is chargeable on a 'taxable supply' of goods or services in the course or furtherance of a business in the UK[193] by persons who are either registered or required to be registered for VAT.[194] A 'taxable supply' is a supply of goods or services which is not specifically exempt (or outside the scope of the tax). Most supplies of goods and services are taxable. There are currently 3 main rates of tax: 17.5 per cent (the standard rate);[195] 5 per cent (the reduced rate), which is charged on certain goods and services such as domestic fuel and power; and 0 per cent (known as the 'zero rate').

VAT is designed to be a tax on 'value added' (or 'added value') to goods and services, but is chargeable on a taxable supply whether or not it makes a profit.[196] The ultimate burden of the tax is borne by the final consumer of the goods or services supplied. VAT-registered businesses charge VAT on their taxable supplies (respectively known as 'output tax' and 'outputs') and reclaim VAT on expenditure attributable to those supplies (respectively known as 'input tax' and 'inputs'). The impact of VAT on a business is therefore neutral except insofar as:

- it creates an administrative burden, and (although businesses with an annual turnover of up to £150,000 exclusive of VAT can use an optional flat-rate accounting scheme[197]) this can be onerous on a small

---

192 Since 1999 there have been procedures for advance pricing agreements (ACAs), which are binding agreements between HMRC and the taxpayer designed to resolve complex transfer pricing issues in advance without a dispute. See Statement of Practice SP3/99 setting out their interpretation of the rules.

193 VATA 1994, s 4(1).

194 Registration is compulsory for any person carrying on business in the UK if the annual turnover exceeds £68,000 (from 1 May 2009), and is optional if the annual turnover is less than this threshold. See VATA 1994, Sch 1, para 1.

195 Which was temporarily reduced to 15 per cent up to 1 January 2010 when it reverted to 17.5 per cent (see VAT (Change of Rate) Order 2008 (SI 2008/3020) and FA 2009, s 9). The reduction was announced by the Chancellor in his 2008 Pre-Budget Report to help the economy during the 'credit crunch'.

196 This means that supplies where R&D costs are reimbursed will still be subject to VAT.

197 The scheme allows traders to calculate VAT liability as a percentage of total turnover instead of individual sales and purchases (see VATA 1994, s 26B and HMRC Notice No 733 *Flat rate schemes for businesses*, March 2007). VAT compliance was identified by respondents to the Government's March 2001 Technical Note as one of the main burdens of the UK tax system on small businesses (see *A Review of Small Business Taxation*, 27 November 2001).

business, especially as there are penalties[198] for late registration and misdeclaration;

- it affects cashflow;

- a business which makes (and to the extent that it makes) exempt supplies cannot recover attributable input VAT;[199] and

- charging VAT on supplies to the final (unregistered) consumer gives a competitive edge to an unregistered supplier.

The main VAT issue with technology agreements is whether VAT is chargeable on payments for research services or intellectual property rights; and, if so, whether the VAT paid is recoverable. If VAT is chargeable, the relevant payment clause should expressly state that it is VAT-exclusive and any VAT chargeable is payable by the recipient of the supply. In the absence of any such express provision, the payment may be deemed to be VAT-inclusive as an implied term of the contract and this means that the supplier will have to account for VAT out of the payment received.

The general VAT rules and accounting procedures are contained in the Value Added Tax Act 1994 ('VATA 1994'), the Principal Regulations[200] and a series of supplementary regulations, and are explained in a series of HMRC Notices (some of which are legally binding). The rules are, in practice, extremely difficult to assimilate for the first time. The following commentary therefore provides a simplified explanation of the system and addresses specific VAT issues in technology agreements.

VAT and charities

Special VAT rules apply to charities, giving them favourable treatment. For example, donations to charities are outside the scope of VAT, and special reliefs mean that charities do not have to pay VAT on certain purchases whereas other purchasers of the same goods and services would have to pay VAT.

A charity which supplies goods or services for a consideration, however, is in the same position as a business, and the supplies will generally be subject to VAT at the standard rate.[201] In practice, most charities will want to conduct

---

198 Of up to 15 per cent of the amount of VAT due (see HMRC Notice No 700/41 *Late Registration Penalty*, April 2009, for details).
199 The VAT Regulations 1995 (SI 1995/2518), reg 106 specify de minimis limits under which a partially exempt business can recover exempt input tax of up to £625 per month on average (£7,500 per annum) provided it is 50 per cent or less of total input tax in the relevant period. See HMRC Notice No 706 *Partial Exemption*, December 2006, for further details.
200 VAT Regulations 1995 (SI 1995/2518). See HMRC Notice No 700 *The VAT Guide*, April 2002, for a simplified guide to the detailed rules.
201 See HMRC guidance notes *Charities – Trading and business activities* and V1-9 *Charities*.

any commercial R&D activity through a separate company to preserve their charitable status and the income tax and CGT exemptions. Such companies will, in principle, be treated like any other business for VAT purposes. Consideration of the special rules is, accordingly, excluded from this section (but see section G under 'Exemptions for charities' above).

VAT on research and consultancy services

Charges for research or consultancy services, or the supply of staff, will usually be subject to VAT at the standard rate. Even if the provider of the services has not previously been engaged in any business activity and the supply is a 'one-off', for example a single consultancy fee for an academic's first item of private work, the supply can nevertheless be vatable if it exceeds the registration threshold.[202] This is because the definition of 'business' for VAT purposes is far-reaching; it embraces any 'economic activity, whatever the purpose of that activity'.[203]

Even if the value of the supply is below the threshold, the supplier will probably still wish to apply for voluntary registration in order to recover his input tax, ie the VAT incurred on any costs or overheads attributable to the supply. The only circumstances in which it will generally be to the supplier's advantage *not* to apply for voluntary registration are where the recipient is exempt and cannot recover the VAT (for example a bank or financial institution) and the supplier risks losing the contract to an unregistered competitor *or* where the supplier's input tax is minimal and outweighed by the administrative burden of being VAT registered. From 1 April 2010 all businesses with an annual turnover of £100,000 or more (excluding VAT) and all new businesses registering for the first time must file returns electronically and pay any VAT due electronically.

VAT on intellectual property rights

If a technology agreement between UK parties involves a supply of an intellectual property right (eg where a licence is granted by a UK licensor to a UK licensee) it is a taxable supply and will be chargeable to VAT at the standard rate. If, however, the supply is to an overseas party different rules apply (see section J under 'International transactions' et seq). In practice, the

---

202 £68,000 per year from 1 May 2009. See also HMRC Notice No 700 *The VAT Guide*, April 2002, for a general explanation of the system and, in particular, the registration and compliance requirements. See also HMRC Notice No 725 *The Single Market*, January 2007, regarding UK registration requirements on 'distance selling' to the UK and acquisitions from suppliers in EC countries.
203 Council Directive 2006/112/EC ([2006] OJ L347/1) on the common system of value added tax, Art 9.

main problem with international transactions is trying to persuade parties outside the EU[204] who are not familiar with VAT that it is reasonable to include a clause in the agreement stating that payments are *exclusive* of VAT which, if chargeable, is payable in addition.

The following paragraphs address common VAT issues that may arise in connection with the supply of services and/or grant of intellectual property rights in technology agreements and, in particular, agreements with an international dimension.

Is an intellectual property transaction a 'chargeable supply'?

The Principal VAT Directive defines 'economic activity' as including 'the exploitation of tangible or intangible property for the purposes of obtaining income therefrom on a continuing basis'.[205] This definition encompasses licensing by a person who exploits intellectual property (eg in non-licensed territories) and a passive investor who receives continuing payments (eg royalties).

The assignment or licensing of intellectual property in return for payment will normally be a taxable supply of services. VATA 1994, s 5(2)(b) includes a 'sweep-up' provision which provides that:

> 'anything which is not a supply of goods but is done for a consideration (including, if so done, the granting, assignment or surrender of any right) is a supply of services'.

International transactions

VAT is generally chargeable on the supply of goods and services by a UK supplier to customers in the UK. Many technology agreements, however, are international and provide for the grant of a licence in several countries or one where the parties are incorporated in different countries. For international agreements, different rules apply. In most cases, VAT will not be chargeable on supplies by a UK supplier to customers in non-EU countries (as they will be outside the scope of VAT). The rules for supplies to customers in other EU countries, however, are more complicated.

In many technology transactions, VAT will not be chargeable by the UK supplier to his or her customer in another EU country; instead customers will have to account for the VAT to their own country's tax authorities (at the rate chargeable in that country) under the 'reverse charge' procedure.

---

204   From 1 January 2007 the VAT territory of the EC (now referred to as the 'EU' – see section J under 'Overview' below) is the 27 member states listed in para 19 of HMRC Notice No 741 *Place of Supply of Services*, May 2008.
205   See n 203.

This procedure (also referred to as 'tax shift') effectively imposes liability for VAT (and the accounting for the same to the relevant tax authority) on the recipient of the intellectual property or service, rather than the supplier as would normally be the case.

The 'place of supply' and 'reverse charge' rules, which respectively determine the country in which VAT is payable and the mechanism for payment, are highly technical. They must, however, be considered to determine the correct VAT treatment of international agreements and, in particular, whether VAT should be charged on payments made under them. For this reason, they are considered in some detail below.

Place of supply of goods

General

Although most technology agreements involve the supply of services, it is useful to explain the 'place of supply' rules with reference to goods, as the rules appear to have been drafted with goods in mind and then modified for supplies of services.

VAT is normally payable at the 'place of supply'. For goods, the place of supply is the location of the goods when allocated to a customer's order. If they are in the UK when so allocated, the supply is in the UK, even if they are going to be exported.[206] If they are not in the UK when so allocated, the supply is normally outside the UK and outside the scope of UK VAT.[207] In practice, the rules for determining the place of supply of intellectual property classed as 'goods', for example off-the-shelf software packages (as opposed to tailor-made software which is treated as 'services'), are relatively straightforward.

The main point to be aware of is that international supply rules for goods differ according to whether goods are imported from outside the EU or supplied from one EU member state to another.

Importation of goods from outside the EU

VAT is chargeable (in addition to customs duty) on the importation of goods from countries outside the EU as if the goods had been supplied in the UK.[208]

---

206 The goods will usually be zero rated on despatch to VAT-registered persons in other EU member states as an 'acquisition' or 'arrival' (for VAT purposes the terms 'export' and 'import' only apply to non-EU member states) or exported to persons outside the EU. See HMRC Notice No 725 *The Single Market*, September 2008, paras 2.1–2.13.

207 Although relevant input VAT is still recoverable.

208 See HMRC Notice No 702 *Imports*, October 2006.

With limited exceptions,[209] the importer, whether registered or not, makes a declaration on importation and accounts for VAT to HMRC unless the goods are imported for non-business purposes. Where VAT is paid by registered persons on the value of goods imported for business purposes, they can reclaim VAT as input tax in the normal way.[210] The valuation of imported goods excludes any 'royalties and licence fees' as they are taxable under the reverse charge international service arrangements.

Intra-EU supplies of goods

Goods supplied by a UK supplier to a VAT-registered trader in another EU member state may be zero rated on despatch and any VAT due is payable on acquisition of the goods by the customer, who must account for it on their VAT return at the rate in force in the country of destination of the goods.[211] When, however, VAT-registered traders despatch goods to unregistered traders or private individuals in another EU member state, VAT is usually charged by the supplier at the rate in force in the country of despatch.

A UK supplier of goods to a customer registered for VAT in another EU member state can zero rate the supply provided he or she obtains the customer's VAT number[212] and shows it on his or her VAT invoice and has documentary evidence that the goods have in fact been removed to another member state. He or she must, however, charge and account for VAT on goods supplied to customers in other EU member states who are not registered, as if the goods were supplied in the UK, subject to certain limited exceptions.[213] In addition, he or she must complete a European Sales List ('ESL') with information about the cross-border supplies and return it to HMRC on a periodic basis. There are also special rules for intermediaries who arrange supplies of goods via third parties within the EU.

A UK-registered person receiving (in the UK) goods from a registered supplier in another EU member state must account for VAT in the UK on the acquisition of the goods at the rate of tax due for the supply of the same goods in the UK.[214] Where a business is not registered for VAT in the UK, any goods purchased from a supplier in another EU country will bear VAT at the place of origin of the goods. An unregistered person is liable to register in the UK if the value of 'acquisitions' from registered suppliers in other member states

---

209 Eg imports by charities claiming special relief. See HMRC Notices 701/1 *Charities*, May 2004 and 701/6 *Charity funded equipment for medical, veterinary etc uses*, September 2003, for further details.
210 See VAT Regulations 1995 (SI 1995/2518), Pts XIV, XV, XVI and HMRC Notices No 702 *Imports*, October 2006, and 725 *The Single Market*, September 2008.
211 VATA 1994, s 25 and HMRC Notice No 703 *Export of goods from the UK*, November 2006.
212 Local VAT offices can usually verify an EU customer's overseas registration number.
213 The main exceptions for intellectual property transactions are international organisations and bodies entitled to special relief.
214 See HMRC Notice No 725 *The Single Market*, September 2008, para 8.

exceeds the registration threshold. This is intended to avoid distortions of tax in the EU single market.

In summary, supplies of goods from a business in one EU member state to a business in another EU member state will normally attract VAT in the customer's member state, which will be accounted for by the customer to his or her local VAT collection authority.

Place of supply of services – pre-1 January 2010

Most technology transactions (including licences and assignments of intellectual property) involve supplies of services as opposed to goods. The 'place of supply' rules for services were changed with the 'completion' of the EC single market on 1 January 1993 and again on 1 January 2010 to implement Council Directive 2008/8/EC (see section J under 'Place of supply of services – post-1 January 2010' below). Before then most intellectual property transactions came within a special set of exceptions to the general rule for services. As these rules are still largely untested in the UK courts, the following commentary is only a simplified explanation of the rules and HMRC guidelines.[215]

If the place of supply of a service is in the UK, VAT is chargeable in the UK wherever the customer belongs. If the place of supply is outside the EU (including the UK), the supply will be outside the scope of VAT altogether.[216] If, however, the place of supply of a service is in another EU member state, the supply will be taxable in that country only; the UK supplier or his customer will be liable to account for the VAT to the tax authorities of that country.

The 'place of supply' is therefore the key issue in determining whether, by whom and at what rate VAT should be charged. Identifying the place of supply, however, is not always straightforward because the rules are far from being 'user friendly'. The 'basic rule' is that the place of supply of services is where the supplier belongs.[217] Most intellectual property transactions, however, come within exceptions or 'special rules'. These are explained below.[218]

---

215 VATA 1994, ss 7–9, Sch 5 and the VAT (Place of Supply of Services) Order 1992 (SI 1992/3121). See also HMRC Notice No 741 'Place of Supply of Services, May 2008.

216 Although related input tax is still recoverable if the supply would be taxable if made in the UK.

217 A supplier of services 'belongs' in the country where he or she (or it) has a business establishment (or, if there are business establishments in more than one country, in the country 'most directly connected with the supply') or his or her 'usual place of residence'; and a company's residence is in its country of registration.

218 See 'Services supplied where received' et seq below.

Services involving physical performance

The place of supply of 'cultural, artistic ... scientific, educational or entertainment services' is where they are carried out.[219] The HMRC guidance notes[220] give examples which could be relevant to an R&D collaboration agreement:

- 'Scientific services of technicians carrying out tests or experiments in order to obtain data. The final compilation of your record of results, carried out in the UK, will not make the supply liable to UK VAT provided your services were otherwise performed outside the UK'. If, however, the scientific services 'include a recommendation or conclusion' based on those results they will be treated as consultancy services or provision of information.[221]

- Educational and training services. Such services when made in the UK may be exempt or, if provided to an overseas government for sovereign (ie non-business) activities, zero-rated.[222]

Services supplied where received

Most intellectual property transactions come within the exceptions listed in Value Added Tax Act 1994, Sch 5. These exceptions include the grant of intellectual property rights and the 'acceptance of any obligation to refrain from pursuing or exercising' any such right. Consultancy services, data processing and the provision of information (but excluding any services relating to land) are also included. They also include the supply of telecommunications services, radio and television broadcasting and 'electronically supplied services' (including website supply, web-hosting and distance maintenance of programmes and equipment, the supply and updating of software and supply of information or data).[223] The 'place of supply' of such services is where the recipient of the services belongs, provided he or she is in business.

If an EU customer is not in business (if, for example, he or she is a private consumer) – or if he or she is in business but the services are to be used outside the EU – the place of supply is where the *supplier* belongs. Most recipients of 'intellectual services' are in business. In practice, the supplier must obtain evidence that the customer is in business before making the supply to ensure the correct VAT treatment is applied, ie the recipient's VAT number or some other acceptable evidence. For a non-EU customer, it is not necessary to establish that he or she is in business in order for the special 'place of supply' rules to operate.

---

219   VAT (Place of Supply of Services) Order 1992 (SI 1992/3121), art 15(a).
220   HMRC Notice No 741 *Place of Supply of Services*, May 2008, para 5.2.
221   HMRC Notice No 741 above, para 5.3.
222   HMRC Notice No 701/30 *Educational and vocational training*, January 2002.
223   VATA 1994, Sch 5, paras 7A–7C.

The test applied to identify where the recipient 'belongs' is the same as that for the supplier,[224] except that it obviously has to distinguish between services received for a business purpose and those which are not. If, therefore, such services are received by a person in another EU member state for a non-business purpose, the recipient 'belongs' to the country in which he or she has his or her 'usual place of residence'.

Value Added Tax Act 1994, Schedule 5 – supplies made where received

Schedule 5, paragraph 1

'Transfers and assignments of copyright, patents, licences, trademarks and similar rights.'

This wording covers licences, transfers and assignments of intellectual property and computer software. It also covers some rights in franchise agreements, the transfer of or permission to use a logo and publication rights but does not, however, include the sale of goodwill.[225]

Schedule 5, paragraph 3

'Services of consultants, engineers, consultancy bureaux, lawyers, accountants and other similar services; data processing and provision of information ...'

Paragraph 13.5 of Notice 741 gives examples of the services included in paragraph 3, including:

(a) research and development;

(b) market research;

(c) testing and analysis of goods (for example drugs, chemicals and domestic electrical appliances). The essential nature of such services is analysis by experts who use the results of the testing to reach a professional conclusion, such as whether goods meet specified standards;

(d) writing scientific reports;

(e) production of customised computer software (but not digitally downloaded software) as well as the services of adapting packages. However, some 'off-the-shelf' software packages are treated as supplies of goods;

---

224 See n 217.
225 HMRC Notice 741 *Place of Supply of Services*, May 2008, para 13.3.

(f)   software maintenance involving upgrades, advice and resolution of any problems. However, a contract for simply maintaining computer hardware relates to work on goods;

(g)   the provision of intellectual engineering advice or design. This includes overseeing the resultant physical work, provided that any supervision is merely to ensure that the design or other advice is properly implemented;

(h)   data processing is the application of programmed instructions on existing data which results in the production of required information. Services which simply include an element of data processing or re-formatting without changing meaning or content, however, are excluded;

(i)   supply of knowledge of any type and in any form, for example provision of on-line information. The delivery or transmission of another person's information, however, is excluded.

In practice, these categories will cover most services that are supplied in R&D agreements.

Schedule 5, paragraph 4

'Acceptance of any obligation to refrain from pursuing or exercising, in whole or in part, any business activity, or any such rights as are referred to in paragraph 1 above.'

This category is aimed at 'agreements not to pursue or undertake any business activity and refraining from exercising, or relinquishing' intellectual property rights and includes, for example, 'agreement by the owner of a trademark to refrain from using it'.

Schedule 5, paragraph 6

'The supply of staff'

This category is defined as 'the placing of personnel under the control and guidance of another party as if they become employees of that party' and therefore specifically excludes a contract for services. For example, 'the supply by a freelance or other person of a specific service or services under a contract for services' is excluded. From 1 April 2009, however, employment and recruitment agencies are required to charge VAT on supplies of temporary staff, except for special exemptions (such as providing care to patients in their own homes), and this has added to the net cost of some R&D projects carried out by charities, HEIs and other exempt bodies . For this category, the place of supply will depend on the nature of the services provided.

Schedule 5, paragraph 7A

Telecommunications services
These specifically include access to the Internet and worldwide web (but not supplies of information delivered through the internet), and the provision of e-mail addresses.

Schedule 5, paragraph 7C

Electronically supplied services
Electronically supplied services include website supply, web-hosting and distance maintenance of programmes and equipment; the supply and updating of software; and the supply of images, text and database information. Further guidance is given in HMRC Notice No 741 but, in practice, the category covers most internet information businesses.

Schedule 5, paragraph 8

> 'The services rendered by one person to another in procuring for the other any of the services mentioned in paragraphs 1 to 7C above.'

This paragraph, aimed at intermediaries, specifically includes 'patent, copyright and similar agents'. It presumably includes some commercial agents, but specifically excludes introduction agents.

Who is accountable for VAT – the supplier or the customer?

Once the place of supply of services has been identified, the supplier will know whether VAT is chargeable and in which country it is chargeable. To recap, if the place of supply is outside the EU, the supply is outside the scope of the VAT system; if the place of supply is in an EU member state, VAT will be chargeable in that member state. For most intellectual property transactions, the place of supply is the EU member state in which the business customer belongs.

Where the place of supply is an EU member state in which the customer belongs, the next question is whether it is the supplier or the customer who has to account for the VAT to that member state's relevant tax authority. This is determined by applying the relevant registration rules. If it is the supplier, he or she will have to register (or appoint a VAT registration agent) in that member state. If it is the customer (as will normally be the case where he or she is in business), he or she will have to account for VAT through the reverse charge procedure, according to the rules of that EU member state.

The reverse charge rules should, in theory, be the same in all EU member states. However, there may be differences in practice. The following paragraphs summarise (with inevitable over-simplification) the rules which apply in the UK, ie in the situation where supplies are made from another EU member state to a customer who belongs in the UK.

The reverse charge rules apply to UK businesses who receive supplies in either of the above intellectual property categories[226] from suppliers who belong overseas. The rules are explained in HMRC Notices 725 and 741 but, in a nutshell, they mean that the recipient must treat the supply as one made by him or her (to himself or herself). As a result, an unregistered person in the UK who receives the services for business purposes will become registrable for VAT if the value of the (self-supplied) services takes the total value of his or her supplies above the registration threshold.

A VAT-registered recipient who applies the reverse charge can recover the VAT charged (to himself or herself) as input tax under the normal input tax recovery rules. A trader with full input tax recovery will record the transaction twice in his or her VAT records – once as the (deemed) provider of the supplies, and once as recipient of those supplies; then, in the normal way, input VAT is deducted from output VAT when calculating the amount to pay to HMRC, so the net effect is that no VAT will ultimately be payable on the transaction.

Impact of rules on intellectual property transactions

The impact of the 'place of supply' rules for intellectual property transactions is best illustrated by examples:

Example 1: A UK company which licenses a patent to a company which 'belongs' in the US. The place of supply will be the US. The supply is outside the scope and no VAT is chargeable. The supplier will, however, be able to recover any input tax incurred in making the supply under the normal rules.

Example 2: A UK company licenses a patent to a person in business who belongs in another EU member state, France. The place of supply will be France. In this example, the French customer will be liable to account for VAT under the 'reverse charge' procedure, but the UK company will still be able to recover any input tax incurred in making the supply under the normal rules.

Example 3: A French company grants a licence to a UK company. The UK licensee must account for VAT in the UK on the licence payments under the reverse charge procedure.

---

226 Ie services involving physical performance or which are intellectual in character.

It should be emphasised that in the case of supplies made to a person in another EU member state who is not acting in a business capacity, the rules are completely different. The place of supply then becomes the country where the supplier belongs. If, for example, a UK licensor belongs in the UK, VAT will be chargeable in the UK even though the licensee is based in another EU member state. It is therefore important for a negotiator or drafter of an R&D agreement licensing intellectual property to a customer in another EU country to establish whether the EU-based licensee is in business or not.

Place of supply of services – post-1 January 2010

Overview

A package of measures to modernise and simplify the EU VAT system was adopted by EU Finance Ministers in February 2008.[227] This section summarises these changes (to be phased in between 1 January 2010 and 1 January 2015) and other changes on the European Sales List ('ESL') reporting requirements, following the adoption by European Finance Ministers in December 2008 of a Directive on the frequency of ESL reporting requirements as part of an EU Anti-Tax Fraud Strategy ('ATFS').

The VAT package includes: changes to the rules on the place of supply of services for business-to-business ('B2B') and business-to-consumer ('B2C') transactions; a requirement to complete an ESL[228] for taxable supplies of services on which a reverse charge applies in the customer's member state; enhanced administrative co-operation between member states to support these changes; the introduction of a (faster) electronic VAT refund scheme; and the introduction of an optional 'One Stop Scheme' for B2B supplies of telecoms, broadcasting and electronically supplied services. The UK legislation which implements these changes[229] also adopts the change in terminology from 'EC' to 'EU' required by the Treaty of Lisbon.

The ATFS measures mean that as from 1 January 2010 the standard reporting period for all ESLs, whether goods or services, will be monthly but it may also

---

227 Council Directives 2008/8/EC ([2008] OJ L44/11) ('the First Amending Directive') and 2008/117/EC ([2008] OJ L14/7) ('the Second Amending Directive') amend Council Directive 2006/112/EC ([2006] OJ L347/1) ('the Principal VAT Directive') with effect from 1 January 2010.

228 An ESL is a declaration that lists supplies of goods and/or services by a UK VAT-registered trader to a VAT-registered trader in another EU member state. These declarations are called 'Recapitulative Statements' in EU VAT legislation.

229 See FA 2009, s 76 and Sch 36, and the VAT (Amendment) (No 5) Regulations 2009 (SI 2009/3241) which amend SI 1995/2518 ('the Principal Regulations') and Explanatory Memorandum. See also HMRC guidance note *Cross-border VAT changes 2010*, and *VAT: Place of Supply of Services*, Consultation Response Document, 22 April 2009.

be quarterly (or, in certain circumstances the same period as the taxpayer's return[230]). Businesses making intra-EU supplies of goods and services can choose whether to report all their supplies monthly or report goods monthly and services quarterly. There are stricter time limits for submitting ESLs to HMRC. ESLs must be submitted within 14 days (for paper returns) and 21 days (for electronic returns) of the end of the relevant quarter, and there are new penalties for delay (and misdeclaration).

The new 'basic rule' (including supplies within VATA 1994, Schedule 5)

From 1 January 2010 the new 'basic rule' for the supply of services for B2B supplies is that the place of supply is where the customer is established, not where the supplier is established. The new basic rule applies to services within VATA 1994, Sch 5 (see 'Services involving physical performance' above) and electronically supplied services by non-EU suppliers to EU business customers.

For B2C supplies of services the basic rule will continue to be that the place of supply is where the supplier is established. From 1 January 2015, however, the place of supply of intra-EU B2B supplies of telecoms, electronically supplied services and broadcasting will be where the customer usually resides.

In order to ensure that the reverse charge is properly accounted for by the recipient, the suppliers of such services throughout the EU will be required to provide information[231] relating to their supplies and identify their business customers on an ESL.

Exceptions to the new 'basic rule'

There are exceptions to the new basic rule, for which ESLs will not be required. These are: exempt supplies (ie exempt according to the rules in the customer's member state); supplies of 'where performed' services (see section J under 'Services supplied where received' above), ie 'services and ancillary services relating to cultural, artistic, sporting, scientific, educational entertainment or similar activities, such as fairs and exhibitions';[232] supplies where the recipient is not VAT registered; and B2C supplies.

---

230 The circumstances are that supplies do not include a new means of transport, the return period is longer than a quarter, the taxpayer's annual turnover does not exceed £145,000 and the annual value of cross-border supplies does not exceed £11,000.

231 The customer's country code and VAT registration number, the total value of supplies in sterling and Code 3 in the Indicator Code Box if it is a supply of services.

232 These will, however, come within the new 'basic rule' as from 1 January 2011 (see HMRC guidance note *Cross-border VAT changes 2010*).

Drafting issues

A technology agreement should make it clear whether any payments under it are inclusive or exclusive of VAT. It is emphasised that, in the absence of any provision to the contrary, a payment will be deemed to be *inclusive* of any VAT chargeable. Thus, where VAT is chargeable, failure to state whether a sum includes VAT may result in HMRC deciding that a payment included VAT and that the supplier must pay the VAT element to them.

Normally, the provider of a service chargeable to VAT must issue a VAT invoice. Sometimes royalties are paid by a licensee under a licence agreement without an invoice being issued by the licensor. It is possible to apply to HMRC to be permitted to 'self-bill';[233] in such cases, it may be desirable to include in the licence agreement wording along the following lines:

> 'When sending royalties under this agreement to the Licensor, the Licensee shall also send the Licensor an appropriate VAT invoice for the amount paid'.

Finally, technology agreements made after 1 January 2010 (and, in some cases, 1 January 2011) may need to be reviewed in the light of the changes (in section J under 'Place of supply of services – post-1 January 2010' above) to ensure that the correct amount of VAT is charged and accounted for and to avoid compliance problems.

K: STAMP DUTY

Introduction

Historically, stamp duty was essentially a tax on *documents*, not transactions. Under the Stamp Act 1891 (a heavily amended statute, but one which nevertheless sets out the framework for the tax), stamp duty is payable on a range of documents. Before 20 March 2000, some transactions involving intellectual property (which excluded know-how unless it was part of a goodwill package) were taxable as a 'conveyance on sale', but stamp duty on such transactions was abolished by the Finance Act 2000 as part of a package of measures to boost innovation and R&D.[234] Furthermore, stamp duty on transfers of goodwill was abolished as from 23 April 2002.[235] As a result, the scope of stamp duty in technology agreements is now very limited. The

---

233   Value Added Tax Regulations 1995 (SI 1985/2518), reg 13(3).
234   FA 2000, s 129. Unregistered designs are not specifically covered by s 129(2)(a) although they are arguably covered by the wide terms of s 129(2)(c) which is drafted as a 'sweep-up' measure.
235   FA 2002, s 116.

following commentary is primarily a guide to documents executed *before* 20 March 2000 (especially those which were stampable but never stamped).[236]

There were basically two types of duty relevant to intellectual property transactions: *ad valorem* duty, which in most relevant cases was chargeable at the rate of 1 to 4 per cent of the contract price; and *fixed* duty which was generally 50 pence (increased to £5 as from 1 October 1999).

The Finance Act 2003 radically reformed stamp duty on land transactions by making land transactions subject to Stamp Duty Land Tax ('SDLT') whether or not there is an instrument effecting the transaction and, if there is, whether or not it is executed in the UK and whether or not any party to the transaction is present or resident in the UK.[237] Prior to the 2003 reforms stamp duty was charged on the document (or, to use the language of the Stamp Act 1891, the 'instrument'[238]), rather than the underlying transaction, and oral agreements do not attract stamp duty. As assignments of intellectual property generally had (and still have) to be in writing, it was not possible to avoid paying duty by making an oral agreement, but there were some devices to avoid the duty (eg executing the agreement overseas, which explains the drafting of some agreements executed before 20 March 2000).[239]

Consequences of failing to stamp agreements under which duty is payable

It is important to check that technology agreements which (1) grant a right to occupy or any interest in land, or (2) if executed before 20 March 2000 contain options to acquire intellectual property rights, have been presented to the Stamp Office and that any duty has been paid. Failure to stamp a document can have the following consequences:

- Civil fines of up to £300[240] may be payable for administrative offences such as failure to provide information or allow inspection of documents or stamp a document within 30 days of adjudication.

---

236 See Anderson, *Technology – The Law of Exploitation and Transfer* (Butterworths, 1996), section 10.4 for a detailed commentary on stamp duty in relation to intellectual property transactions before 20 March 2000.

237 FA 2003, s 42. This was purportedly to prepare for a new era of e-conveyancing (see HMRC's press release REV 55/03, 16 April 2003) but the changes effectively 'killed' many stamp duty avoidance schemes long targeted by HMRC.

238 An 'instrument' includes 'every written document' (Stamp Act 1891, s 122(1)).

239 FA 1999 extended interest and penalties for late stamping to documents executed abroad but brought into the UK at a later date.

240 FA 1999 introduced an entirely new penalty regime to crack down on tax avoidance, late payment and fraud (for which more serious penalties apply). See Stamp Act 1891, ss 12A(2), 16, 18.

- If a document attracts stamp duty, the liability arises when the document is 'executed'.[241] It must then be presented to the Stamp Office for stamping within 30 days. Late stamping is possible on payment of interest[242] and a penalty to the Stamp Office. The penalty is generally 100 per cent of the amount of the outstanding duty payable (subject to a maximum of £300 if the delay is less than 1 year, but not otherwise), but the Stamp Office have discretion to reduce the penalty if there are 'mitigating circumstances'.[243]

- An unstamped document on which duty should have been paid is inadmissible as evidence in civil proceedings. Upon the production of such a document in court, the court is required to take notice of the fact that duty has not been paid. Duty may be paid to the court together with interest and penalties, but if this is not done, the document cannot be admitted in evidence in civil proceedings.[244] In practice, before the 1999 changes to the penalty regime, courts accepted an undertaking of a party's solicitor to have the document stamped. Their attitude, however, may change following the changes.

Ad valorem rates of duty

For residential property transactions SDLT is payable on transactions above £125,000 (£175,000 before 31 December 2009). The normal rate of ad valorem SDLT is 1 per cent on the entire consideration where the consideration exceeds £125,000 but not £250,000; 3 per cent where it exceeds £250,000 but not £500,000; and 4 per cent where it exceeds £500,000. Duty is rounded up to the nearest £5.

For non-residential or mixed-use property transactions, ad valorem SDLT is not payable if the consideration is £150,000 or less and annual rent[245] is under £1,000, but is payable at 1 per cent if the consideration is £150,000 or less and annual rent is £1,000 or more. SDLT is payable at 1 per cent if the consideration exceeds £150,000 but not £250,000; 3 per cent where it exceeds £250,000 but not £500,000; and 4 per cent where it exceeds £500,000. For new residential leases SDLT is not payable unless the consideration exceeds £125,000, but is then payable at 1 per cent on the excess.

---

241 Ie when it is signed unless it is a deed, in which case it is executed when delivered (or, if delivered subject to conditions, when those conditions are fulfilled) (Stamp Act 1891, s 122(1), (1A)).
242 The current interest rate (from 29 September 2009) is 3 per cent.
243 Stamp Act 1891, ss 15A, 15B. See also HMRC *Stamp Taxes Manual* at www.hmrc.gov.uk/so/manual and HMRC guidance notes *Penalties and appeals – late payment of Stamp Duty*.
244 Stamp Act 1891, s 14.
245 Annual rent is the highest annual rent known to be payable in any year of the lease.

Stamp duty and VAT

Stamp duty is chargeable on the VAT-inclusive consideration. The interaction of the two taxes was tested in *Glenrothes Development Corporation v IRC*,[246] where it was held that where both taxes are chargeable stamp duty is chargeable on the VAT-inclusive price. The practical application of this point in technology agreements, however, is now limited to agreements for the sale of land and buildings and businesses which include intellectual property. In the absence of an apportionment for any intellectual property rights comprised in the agreement, stamp duty will be chargeable on the total VAT-inclusive consideration.[247]

Procedure for payment

If stamp duty is payable, the agreement must be presented to the Stamp Office, either personally or by post. The procedure for personal stamping is relatively quick; details of how to present a document for stamping, and further information, are now available from any Stamp Office.

Drafting issues

If a technology agreement grants a right to occupy or an interest in land or, alternatively, if an agreement contains intellectual property rights or R&D which includes intellectual property rights, the consideration should be apportioned. In transactions involving goodwill before 23 April 2002 the parties should apportion between it and other property (as goodwill was subject to stamp duty before that date). It is preferable if the parties state in the agreement how any financial consideration is apportioned between different elements, both for stamp duty purposes and for tax and accounting purposes generally. Any apportionment should be justifiable, as HMRC can challenge the apportionment if it appears to have been designed to avoid payment of tax. A special form ('Stamps 22') should be completed to apportion the consideration before adjudication.

Certification

Ad valorem stamp duty is not payable where the consideration does not exceed the minimum threshold. Where it is payable, it is payable at the rate determined by the threshold or band for the total consideration (eg a dwelling for £500,000 attracts SDLT at 3 per cent, ie a liability of

---

246 [1994] STC 74.
247 FA 2003, Sch 4, para 2.

£15,000). The conveyance should include a certificate in appropriate form that the consideration does not exceed the relevant threshold (in the above example, £500,000).² This is why some technology agreements executed before 20 March 2000 contain a certificate, usually in the form of an extra clause in the assignment or licence. The usual form of certification reads as follows:

> 'It is hereby certified that this transaction does not form part of a larger transaction or series of transactions in respect of which the amount or value, or aggregate amount or value, of the consideration exceeds the sum of £60,000'.

If the amount of the consideration does not exceed the relevant threshold, but no certificate is given, ad valorem duty is payable at the rate of 4 per cent. It is important to include a certificate of value to ensure that the rate of duty is limited by the ad valorem scale, and not otherwise liable to a higher rate as part of a series of transactions the value of which is or may be greater.

L: ENTERPRISE INVESTMENT SCHEME

Introduction

One way in which technology companies can attract investment for R&D projects etc is through the Enterprise Investment Scheme (EIS). EIS helps unlisted companies raise equity finance from investors not previously connected with them by offering tax breaks to encourage individuals to invest in small higher risk companies.

Changes to EIS were announced in the 2009 Pre-Budget Report (see section L under 'Interaction with Venture Capital Trusts' below), but the current rules can be summarised as follows. EIS gives investors (including non-residents) both income tax and CGT breaks for subscribing for eligible shares in qualifying companies.[248] Since introduction, however, it has been repeatedly amended to prevent general tax avoidance (especially where investors are connected with the company), and the complexity of the current legislation has restricted use of the scheme.[249]

---

248 The qualifying conditions for claiming the relief are contained in ITA 2007, ss 156–257, and the mechanism for calculating the relief is set out in ITA 2007, ss 23, 26(1)(a), 27(5).

249 The complexity of the rules is underlined by the fact that the HMRC guidance note *Enterprise Investment Scheme* provides no more than 'an overview for companies and potential investors' and comes with a caveat: 'It does not cover all the detailed rules, so companies and investors should not proceed solely on the basis of the information in it, and should consider seeking professional advice'.

Income tax incentives of EIS

The main income tax incentive of EIS is relief against income tax at the 'EIS rate' (currently 20 per cent) for qualifying subscriptions of at least £500 in any tax year. Furthermore, up to 50 per cent of any eligible shares issued before 6 October in any tax year may (by election) be treated as issued in the preceding tax year (up to a limit of £50,000 of shares).[250] Since 2007 there has been no limit on the value of the issue but the total value of the tax relief for any individual investor in any tax year is £100,000.[251] Thus, a £10,000 subscription of EIS shares will attract an up-front income tax relief of £2,000 and a £500,000 subscription will attract an up-front (maximum) income tax relief of £100,000. The investor must, however, hold the shares for at least 3 years before disposal to avoid any of the relief being withdrawn. Further income tax relief ('loss relief') is available if the shares are sold at a loss. An investor may be entitled to deduct the loss (less any income tax relief attributable to the shares in question) against income in the tax year of disposal and carry back any unrelieved losses to the preceding tax year.

CGT incentives

The main CGT incentive of EIS is that, provided the shares are held for the relevant period[252] there is no CGT liability on disposal.[253]

If, however, a chargeable gain does arise, deferment or 'roll-over' relief is available. This allows the investor to reinvest a gain (in EIS shares or other qualifying assets) and defer payment of CGT until the next disposal.[254] It also allows investors (including trustees of certain trusts) to reinvest chargeable gains arising on the disposal of other assets into EIS shares. If the shares are disposed of at a loss, then, as an alternative to claiming loss relief (see 'Income tax incentives of EIS' above this paragraph), investors can set the loss (less income tax relief attributable to the shares) against other chargeable gains.

Operation of tax reliefs

The income tax relief reduces the investor's tax liability on total income for the year in which the shares are subscribed. In certain circumstances, an

---

250 ITA 2007, s 158.
251 ITA 2007, s 158(2)(b), FA 2008, s 31(1) and ITA 2007, EN Annex, Change 37. Husband and wife have separate limits.
252 Three years for shares issued after 5 April 2000 (ITA 2007, ss 159, 256).
253 TCGA 1992, ss 150, 150A.
254 TCGA 1992, s 150C, Sch 5B.

investor can make a claim to carry back part of the subscription to a preceding year so as to relieve income from that year.[255] No claim for relief is allowed unless the company has carried on the trade or R&D activity throughout the relevant period wholly or mainly in the UK.[256]

To qualify for exemption from CGT on disposal, the shares must be held for the relevant period (currently three years), but partial relief is available where there is a disposal within this period. If the shares are disposed of at a loss, then loss relief will be available (at the marginal rate of income tax for the year in which it arises or the preceding year) but it will be reduced by the relief for income tax already given.[257] A capital loss on the disposal of EIS shares can also be offset against income for that year.

Any CGT payable on a disposal of EIS company shares can be deferred by reinvesting the gain in other EIS company shares as well as other qualifying assets.[258] Furthermore, chargeable gains can be deferred by reinvesting gains into EIS schemes.

No income tax or CGT relief is available, however, unless the EIS shares were subscribed and issued for bona fide commercial purposes and not as part of any tax-avoidance arrangement.[259]

Qualifying company

EIS is available to both trading companies and holding companies with trading subsidiaries and includes non-resident companies, provided that they meet certain conditions and use the funds raised for qualifying business activities.[260]

In a nutshell, the basic qualifying conditions are that a company must be unquoted, carry on a qualifying trade in the UK, have fewer than 50 full-time employees (or part-time equivalents) at the time the EIS shares are issued and the total value raised under EIS and similar schemes (Venture Capital Trusts and Corporate Venture Schemes) must not exceed £2m in any tax year.

---

255 Up to half the subscription or £50,000 (whichever is the less) can be treated in this way (ITA 2007, s 158).
256 ITA 2007, ss 159, 179.
257 Eg if a taxpayer invests £10,000 in eligible shares in March 2005, claims income tax relief of £2,000, and sells the shares for £7,500 in April 2009, then the actual loss of £2,500 is reduced by the amount of income tax relief claimed (ie £2,000) leaving an allowable loss of £500. See ITA 2007, s 150A.
258 TCGA 1992, s 150C and Sch 5B.
259 ITA 2007, s 165. There are other anti-avoidance provisions which should be considered before setting up an EIS as these will apply throughout the life of the scheme.
260 ITA 2007, ss 180–200.

The issuing company or a 90 per cent subsidiary company must carry on the qualifying activity throughout the qualifying period.[261] HMRC now interpret this rule narrowly, but have issued a Technical Note[262] explaining their revised interpretation and have announced a consultation exercise with a view to making the rules work better for small businesses.

Qualifying shares

Qualifying subscriptions are restricted to new ordinary shares. Throughout the period of three years from the date of issue, the shares must not carry any preferential rights to dividends or to the company's assets on a winding up. Furthermore, they must not at any time during the three-year period carry any right of redemption.

Qualifying activity – R&D

These activities include R&D provided that it is intended to lead to a qualifying trade carried on by the company or any subsidiary wholly or mainly in the UK *and* carried out immediately after the shares are issued, if not already being carried out.[263] Companies in the business of providing R&D services can also qualify for EIS. Detailed guidance on the conditions is provided by HMRC in IR 137.

Connections between EIS company and investor

To be eligible for income tax relief investors must not, as a rule, be connected (broadly, 'connected' in this context means that the investor was an employee or director or controlled 30 per cent or more of the company's voting shares) with any company in which they invest for the 2-year period before the issue of EIS shares. A paid directorship is a connection for this purpose. There is, however, an exception for 'business angels'.

Interaction with Venture Capital Trusts

An EIS company is unquoted and can therefore be the subject of an investment by a venture capital trust (VCT). VCTs are companies approved by HMRC and listed on the London Stock Exchange. There are several tax advantages

---

261 ITA 2007, s 183.
262 HMRC Technical Note *Enterprise Investment Scheme (EIS) and Partnerships*, 9 December 2009.
263 For the definition of 'R&D' see ICTA 1988, s 837A(2) and section B under 'Statutory definition of R&D' above.

of investing in a VCT. First, investors are entitled to income tax relief (at the current rate of 30 per cent) on the amount subscribed for in shares in the VCT, subject to a maximum subscription of £200,000 in any year. The relief broadly operates as it does in EIS. Secondly, a dividend by such a company is exempt from income tax. For CGT purposes, there is no chargeable gain (or allowable loss) on a disposal of VCT shares. In addition, for VCT shares issued before 6 April 2004 CGT on capital gains which would otherwise be payable can be deferred by re-investment into VCTs.

The VCT rules, which are similar to EIS rules, include numerous further requirements (including strict time limits) which must be satisfied by the VCT and the investor respectively to secure the tax reliefs. Nevertheless, for an individual investor, a VCT merits consideration as a vehicle for funding relatively large-scale R&D activity.[264] Corporate investors may also consider the allied Corporate Venture Scheme, to obtain corporation tax reliefs on cash subscriptions for shares in small high-risk trading companies and gains on a subsequent sale by re-investing sale proceeds in other qualifying shares (but any commentary on the scheme is beyond the scope of this title).

Changes to the qualifying conditions for both the EIS and VCTs were announced in the 2009 Pre-Budget Report to comply with EU State Aid requirements. In a nutshell, the proposed changes are to: restrict the schemes to companies not in difficulty, change the requirement of trading 'wholly or mainly' within the UK to allow companies with UK permanent establishments to qualify, make companies trade shares on an EU-regulated market instead of an official UK list, redefine 'small enterprise' to target the schemes to smaller enterprises and change the equity requirements for VCTs.

M: 'SPIN-OUT' COMPANIES

Introduction

A 'spin-out' company is a company started by academics or researchers (or the universities or research organisations they work for) to exploit intellectual property ('IP') developed by the academics or researchers during research projects for their employer. There are various start-up models but, typically, researchers will subscribe for shares in the spin-out company at a nominal value and the university will license or assign IP with commercial potential to the company. At a later date the company may get grants or private venture capital to fund further development. Eventually, if after various development and funding stages it proves to be commercially viable, the investors will look for an exit strategy to sell their shares.

---

264 See HMRC guidance note *Venture Capital Trusts (VCTs)* and their Technical Note *Venture Capital Schemes*, 9 December 2009; also HMRC *Venture Capital Schemes Manual* at VCM10000–17320, VCM60000 et seq for further information.

Income tax problems

The basic principle enshrined in the UK income tax rules[265] is that an employment-related award of shares or options to acquire shares by the employer is a taxable event, and income tax, and in some cases (where the shares are 'readily convertible assets'[266]) NICs, are chargeable and subject to PAYE at the time of the award. There are a number of special share option schemes with tax breaks (such as Enterprise Management Incentives) which allow small start-up companies to attract and retain the skilled staff they need to grow (although consideration of these is beyond the scope of this title). However, granting shares to employees involved in spin-out companies (as part of the employer's IP sharing policy) can create unforeseen income tax and NIC liabilities.

First, the grant of shares at a nominal value is likely to be a taxable event if the company has any value. Secondly, even where shares are granted at a time when the company is a 'shell' and has no assets, a subsequent transfer of IP into the company which adds value to the shares is itself likely to be a taxable event. Thirdly, the injection of funds into the company by the employer can also be a taxable event. Finally, if at any time after the shares are issued, any rights or restrictions attached to them are respectively increased or removed, this can also be a taxable event. Any detailed consideration of these complex rules (which are replete with anti-avoidance provisions and are amended on an almost annual basis) is beyond the scope of this book. This section therefore focuses on two important exemptions within which, in practice, any spin-out company will try to stay to save substantial amounts of tax and tax compliance costs.

Statutory exemption

The statutory exemption was introduced by the Finance Act 2005, with effect from 4 December 2004. It prevents an income tax or NIC charge arising on researchers (on the increase in value of shares of a spin-out company) following a transfer of certain IP from the research institution into the company; and where the researchers acquire shares after any IP transfer, the value of the IP will be ignored in determining whether shares have been acquired at less than their market value. The exemption applies when four conditions are satisfied:

- there must be an agreement to transfer IP from one or more research institutions to a spin-out company;

- the researcher must acquire shares in the spin-out company either before the IP transfer agreement is made or within 183 days thereafter;

---

265 The rules are mainly set out in ITEPA 2003, Pt 7.
266 See n 270 below.

- the right or opportunity to acquire the shares must have been available because of the researcher's employment with the spin-out company or one of the research institutions; and

- the researcher must be involved in research in relation to the IP in the IP transfer agreement.

The exemption applies only where the IP is transferred into a spin-out company from the researcher's employer. It does not affect the position of the research institution itself except that there will be no employer's NIC liability on the transfer. Nor does it affect the position where the research institution injects funds or other assets into the spin-out company or changes rights or restrictions attaching to the shares – these continue to be taxable events.

UNICO 'safe harbour'

Before the statutory exemption the only way to avoid the income tax problems was to come within the 'safe harbour' agreed between the University Companies Association (now PraxisUnico) and the Inland Revenue on 31 March 2004. This 'safe harbour', which remains an alternative to the statutory exemption, allows researchers to acquire convertible preference shares (with no right to receive dividends or more than the amount paid up on a return of capital, but with 'tag-along' and 'drag-along' rights in the event of a takeover) in a spin-out company at a nominal value without any income tax or NIC charge.[267] Other investors can also transfer IP or other assets into the company (thereby increasing its value) without any other income tax charge.[268] On conversion of the preference shares to ordinary shares or receipt of sums for the preference shares (eg prior to a takeover), however, a charge to income tax may arise under the 'convertible securities' or 'restricted securities' rules.[269] Furthermore, NIC charges will arise if the shares are 'readily convertible assets'.[270]

Under the 'safe harbour' provisions the rights attaching to the convertible preference shares must be set out in the Articles of Association of the spin-out company, and there is a requirement to notify HMRC of any awards of shares by 6 July after the end of the relevant tax year. The provisions are designed to create certainty in the income tax and NIC treatment of awards of shares in spin-out companies, but the structure is inflexible, the rules are difficult to explain simply and there are still income tax and NIC uncertainties. For all these reasons the statutory exemption is likely to be more attractive.

---

267 See ITEPA 2003, Pt 7, Ch 4A.
268 ITEPA 2003, s 437.
269 In Pt 7 of ITEPA 2003.
270 They will be 'readily convertible assets' if the company becomes listed and also, for unlisted companies, if there are arrangements to buy and sell shares even if they are not contractually binding agreements (this can create real uncertainty at a later date).

CGT liabilities

If the statutory exemption applies, so that no income tax or NIC charge arises in respect of a transfer of IP into a spin-out company, and the company fails, there is no income tax, NIC or CGT charge at any time in respect of the IP. If, however, the company is a success and the shares are eventually sold by the researchers, any gain is chargeable to CGT (see section D under 'Individuals' above) and the base cost of the shares will be low (reflecting the fact that there was no income tax charge when the IP was transferred into the company).

If the 'safe harbour' applies, there will be no CGT charge on sale or conversion (or sale and simultaneous conversion) of the convertible preference shares because the gain will be subject to income tax under the relevant rules in ITEPA 2003 (see section M under 'UNICO "safe harbour"' above).

Drafting issues

As with most tax breaks, 'the devil is in the detail' and it is advisable for anyone setting up a spin-out company to seek specialist tax advice from the outset to ensure that the exemption applies and will continue to apply throughout the company's 'life cycle' and avoid potentially substantial amounts of income tax, NIC and tax-compliance costs.

Index

References are to page numbers